# The 508th Connection

# The 508th Connection

Zig Boroughs

Copyright © 2013 by Zig Boroughs.

| | | |
|---|---|---|
| Library of Congress Control Number: | | 2012916347 |
| ISBN: | Hardcover | 978-1-4797-1186-4 |
| | Softcover | 978-1-4797-1185-7 |
| | Ebook | 978-1-4797-1187-1 |

All rights reserved. No part of this book may be reproduced or transmitted in any form or by any means, electronic or mechanical, including photocopying, recording, or by any information storage and retrieval system, without permission in writing from the copyright owner.

This book was printed in the United States of America.

Rev. date: 04/03/2013

To order additional copies of this book, contact:
Xlibris Corporation
1-888-795-4274
www.Xlibris.com
Orders@Xlibris.com
121823

# Contents

Preface .................................................................................. xi
Acknowledgments ............................................................. xiii

1. There Is Something about a Paratrooper ........................... 1
2. D-Day Confusion Somewhat Organized .......................... 54
3. D-Day Confusion of Isolated Paratroopers and Small Groups .......... 87
4. Scattered Elements of 508th Come Together ................. 183
5. The 508th Returned to England .................................... 218
6. Holland, Operation Market Garden .............................. 229
7. Camp Sissonne ............................................................. 317
8. The Deep Freeze .......................................................... 324
9. Return to France .......................................................... 416
10. Prisoners of War .......................................................... 432
11. Honor Guard ............................................................... 467
12. Postscript ..................................................................... 479

Index ................................................................................ 507

Dedicated to the memory of over six hundred 508th paratroopers who died and to the over two hundred who went missing in the service of their country in World War II.

Dutch commemorative monument to the 508th.

Israeli citizen Edith Jakobs Samuel with the author. The 508th rescued her family.

Belgians decorate graves of the 82nd Airborne. Right: Emile Lacroix, who helped the author as guide, interpreter, photographer, artist, and researcher.

The three squad leaders of H Company 508th Airborne Regiment divided this dollar bill in Nottingham, England, on June 5, 1944. They repieced it at their PIR reunion in Portland, Oregon, on September 1, 1983.

Ralph Busson's          Bill Farmer's          Dan Furlong's

Bill Farmer was killed in the Invasion of Normandy. These existing two pieces were returned to Normandy, France, in September 1998 by Dan Furlong.

Author at the American Military Cemetery in Belgium.

# Preface

When I arrived home after my army discharge in 1945, the challenges of adult civilian life excited me tremendously. I anticipated with a passion living as a husband and father, no longer separated by the Atlantic Ocean and a dangerous war from my wife and child. I eagerly plunged into active civilian employment, impatient to establish a career of peaceful service to humanity. Although the experiences and feelings of World War II affected my attitudes and ideals, my energies were so devoted to other interests that the memories of the war years were pushed into an inactive part of my brain. For many years I thought very little about the 508th Parachute Infantry Regiment, and I lost contact with all but one of my paratrooper buddies.

Then at 11:00 PM, Christmas Eve, 1983, a memory of Christmas Eve, 1944, forced its way to the surface. My wife and I were visiting with our daughter, Gini, and her family. We were waiting for our grandchildren to go to bed so that Santa Claus could prepare for Christmas morning. Noticing that it was 11:00 PM, I announced, "Let me tell you what I was doing at this hour thirty-nine years ago!"

I told the story "Burial and Birth," which you may read on page 346 of this volume. When I finished the story, Gini told me, "Dad, you should write this story and send it to all our family members."

Once I wrote one story, the dam burst and a floodgate of stories awoke in my memory, which resulted in the book *A Private's Eye View of World War II*. Many details had faded with time, and I needed to check with my paratrooper buddies to get my stories straight. Senator Strom Thurman's staff helped me locate Jim Allardyce, secretary of the 508th Parachute Infantry Association. Allardyce provided a roster of the association membership with their addresses. This enabled me to verify or correct my stories.

After publishing *A Private's Eye View of World War II*, other veterans of the 508th began to tell me their stories. Some suggested that I write another book and tell their experiences, which resulted in *The Devil's Tale*.

The connections I have made in the 508th Association, and among the friends of the 508th, have prompted me to write *The 508th Connections*. The *Connections* are much more than sources for writing a book. They are friends whom I treasure. They are closer than friends. We are family.

# ACKNOWLEDGMENTS

Besides the personal memories of events related to the 508th Parachute Infantry Regiment during World War II, I have collected information from others for twenty years. The most important source of information has come from other 508th veterans. Since I have been associated with the 508th Parachute Infantry Association, I have met hundreds of fellow veterans of the regiment and have listened to their stories. Through the association, I have also met friends of the 508th from England, France, Belgium, Holland, Germany, and Israel. These friends have also given me valuable information. I have chosen the title *The 508th Connections* to give credit to all those who have so generously helped as friends and as sources of information. The individual 508th connections are listed as follows:

Abraham, Robert, Captain/Colonel
Adams, Robert (Editor)
Albano, Ralph
Allardyce, James
Allen, William
Angress, Tom (German)
Archambault, Roland E. (Medic)
Arthur, Merrel
Backus, Alexis (Belgian)
Barrett, Margaret, Lieutenant (Army nurse)
Beach, Gerald
Beard, William T,
Beaudin, Briand, Lieutenant/ Captain (Surgeon)
Beaver, Neal, Lieutenant

Beddingfield, Gary (English author)
Beets, Melvin
Bell, William
Belliveau, Theodore, Sergeant
Beno, Thomas S.
Bettien, LaRue (Wife of Richard Owen)
Blackmon, L. W., Doctor
Bladen, Bill
Blue, James, Private, Corporal, Sergeant
Boccafogli, Edward, Sergeant
Bollag, Marcel, Sergeant
Bonvillain, Joe
Boroughs, John Wales (Navy)

Bos, Jan (Dutch historian policeman)
Brand, George
Brannen, Malcolm, Lieutenant/Colonel
Bre, Gillis (French)
Bressler, Joe
Brewer, Bill (Bro. Forest Brewer)
Brickley, John E.
Brister, Jane, Colonel (WAC)
Broderick, Bob, Sergeant
Broderick, Tom
Brokaw, Tom (Journalist/Author)
Brooks, Howard, Sergeant
Brown, James O. (J. O), Sergeant
Bullard, Joe E., Sergeant
Burns, Dwayne T. (Artist)
Burrows, Lewis
Busson, Ralph, First Sergeant
Byers, Wilbur
Call, William J., Sergeant/Lieutenant
Canard, Curtis
Carlson, Earl Lee
Canyon, Harold O. a.k.a Kulju, Harold O.
Chatoian, Edward
Chestnut, Joe
Chisolm, Bob, Sergeant/Colonel
Christiansen, Clarence
Clark, William E., First Sergeant
Combs, Rex, Lieutenant
Dean, William D.
De Carvalho, John P.
Delury, John
Demciak, Paul
De Vroomen, Jack (Dutch/American)
Diller, Helen (Sister of Ralph Nicholson)
Dreisbach, Orin

Elder, J. Lyn, Captain (Chaplain)
Ellsworth, Scott
Falgione, Adrian (Son of Eugene Falgione)
Falgione, Eugene
Falgione, Wilma (Mrs. Eugene Falgione)
Favela, Joseph L.
Ferey, Thiery (French)
Ferey, Genevieve Leroux (French)
Fish, Arthur
Flamand, Cecil a.k.a. Madame Cecil Flamand Gancel (French)
Fowler, James, Lieutenant
Frigo, Madge, Mrs. (Wife of Lionel Frigo, Lieutenant)
Fuller, Angelina Spera (Sister of Louis Spera)
Garcia, Ralph
Gerkin, Harold, Sergeant
Giegold, William
Gillot, Louis (French)
Gillies, Alan (English)
Gintjee, Tom (Artist)
Gladstone, Fred
Goudy, William
Graham, Chester, Captain
Greco, Benny
Gurwell, George A., Lieutenant
Gustafson, Julia Lamm (Niece of George Lamm)
Guzzetti, Louis E.
Haddy, Frank
Hambiecker, George and Yvette (Belgian)
Hamm, Joe
Hand, Broughton
Hardie, John (Doc), Doctor, Sergeant
Hardwick, Donald, Lieutenant

Harley, Rupple, Captain (Air Force)
Hasley, Lucien (French)
Henderson, Ernest (Brother of Roy Henderson)
Hernandez, Frank
Hess, Alfred
Hill, O. B., Sergeant
Hodge, John
Holman, John, Lieutenant (Eighty-second Division Headquarters Company)
Holroyd, Tom, Reverend (Translator of French)
Hood, J. B.
Hook, Kenneth
Horn, C. H., Ten Doctor (Dutch)
Horne, Doris (Wife of Kelso Horne)
Horne, Kelso, Lieutenant
Howe, William W., Sergeant
Hudec, Harry
Hummel, Ray S., Sergeant
Hunt, Richard
Hutto, James C., Sergeant
Infanger, Frederick J.
Jahnigen, Herman, First Sergeant/ Lieutenant
Jakeway, Donald (Author), Sergeant
Jakobs, Bert (Jew hidden from Germans by the Dutch)
Jakobs, Edith Samuel (Israeli, hidden from Germans by the Dutch)
Jamar, Walthere (Belgian)
Janssen, Annie (Dutch lady who hid the Jewish Jakobs family)
Jones, Homer H., Lieutenant
Jones, Thurman Davis
Kalkreuth, William T., Sergeant
Karres, Peter
Kass, Stanley
Kennedy, Harry a.k.a. Hans Kahn
Kersh, John, Sergeant
Kingstone, Rosemary (English, daughter of Clyde K. Moore, Jr.)
Kingstone, Steve (English grandson of Clyde K. Moore, Jr.)
Kissane, Joseph, Sergeant
Klein, James C., Captain (Surgeon)
Klein, John C.
Kurz, James Q., Sergeant
Lacroix, Emile (Belgian)
Lamberson, Tim Lamoille (Nephew of William Lamoille Lamberson)
Lamm, George D., Lieutenant
Lamoureux, Francis M.
Leegsma, Argardus (Gas) (Dutch)
LeGrand, Leon (French)
Lobos, Joseph L.
Lord, William G, II, Sergeant/ Lieutenant (Author)
Luczaj, Edwin A., Sergeant
Mackey, Milton E.
Mahan, Francis, Lt.
Mason, Leon a.k.a. Leon Israel
McCleod, Donald J.
McClure, Bill
McDuffie, Mary S. (Wife of James H. McDuffie, Lt.)
McGuire, Virgil
McLean, Henry
Mendez, Louis, Colonel
Mendez, Jeannie (Wife of Louis Mendez)
Merritt, Kenneth (Rock), Sergeant
Michetti, Marino
Miles, George, Lieutenant/Captain
Milkovics, Lewis (Author)
Miller, Phillip C.

Mills, Okey
Mills, Robert (Bob)
Montgomery, Edward L. (Medic)
Montgomery, George E., Captain (Surgeon)
Morettini, Joe
Morgan, Worster, Sergeant/ Lieutenant
Moss, Amoss
Mrozinsky, Anthony J.
Murray, Grady
Nation, Bill (Nephew of Capt. William H. Nation)
Nichols, Barry (Historian)
Nichols, Mickey a.k.a. Niklauski, Michael
Nienart, Benjamin
Nordwall, Stanley
O'Brien, John (Captain of Air Force, grandson of Lawrence Snovak)
O'Conner, Robert W. (Bob), Sergeant
Owen, Richard (Dick)
Palmer, Kate Salley (Cartoonist author)
Patchell, Albert J.
Peek, James O.
Pelini, Guido
Phillips, Robert (Bob)
Pike, Dave (English author)
Pitts, Jill (Mrs. Jill Pitts Knappenberger, Red Cross)
Plunkett, Woodrow C., Lieutenant
Porter, Carl H.
Powell, Charles A.
Rankin, James E.
Ray, Bobby (Marine)
Reardon, Richard
Ricci, Joseph
Richardson, Fayette O.

Risnes, Marvin L., Sergeant
Rizzuto, James
Roll, Harry
Romero, Angel
Ross, Carlos W.
Sacharoff, Leonard
Sakowski, Frank
Sanchez, Arthur
Schlegel, Jack W.
Schlemmer, D. Zane, Sergeant
Schlesinger, Katherine (Wife of Nolan Schlesinger, Lieutenant)
Schmelick, Steve
Scruggs, Rick J. (Medic)
Sellers, Herbert S., Sergeant
Shanley, Thomas J. B., Colonel
Shenkle, George
Shirley, Joseph A., Lieutenant
Shultz, John
Simmons, John L.
Skipper, Jack F.
Smith, Clyde
Smith, Frank, First Sergeant
Smith, James W., First Sergeant
Sopka, Alexander (Al)
Spera, Angelo (Brother of Louis Spera)
Staples, Lois Humphrey (Wife of Frank Staples)
Staples, Frank
Stedman, Richard E.
Still, Wilford A.
Stoeckert, George, Lieutenant
Strong, Charles
Studelska, Norbert (Norb)
Sweet, Johnny, Doctor
Thomas, David E., Major (Surgeon)
Thomas, Ralph, First Sergeant
Traband, William (Bill), Sergeant
Trahin, Jean H., Lieutenant

Tumlin, William R. (Bill)
Uchrin, Steve P.
Van de Hoever, Erik (Dutch historian, author)
Vantrease, Glen, Sergeant
Wakefield, Walter L., Lieutenant
Walczak, Stanley
Warneche, Adolph F. (Bud), Sergeant/Lieutenant
Watson, Joseph E., Corporal
Wauters, Arnaud (Belgian)
Weiner, Ruben (Eighty-Second Division, photographer)
Wenzel, Edward F.
White, Robert B., Sergeant
Wilde, Russell C., Captain
Williams, Joan (Mrs. McAlister, English)
Wills, John H., Sergeant
Wilt, Warren
Windom, William (Bill)
Winkin, Gabrielle (Wife of Bill Howe, Belgian)
Wodowski, Edward J. (Woody)
Wolfe, Conrad G.
Wynne, James T.
Yablonski, Anthony J. (Tony)
Yates, Charles A., Lieutenant
Zuccala, Rinaldo R. (Zeke, Medic)
Zuelke, Warren H.

# CHAPTER 1

# There Is Something about a Paratrooper

## Old Soldiers

The few remaining Confederate veterans of Pickens County were slowly gathering on Mrs. Queen Jo Mauldin's front porch for their annual June 3 reunion. The Civil War had been over for seventy-one years on this particular June 3, 1936. A soldier who was twenty-one when Lee surrendered at Appomattox Court House, April 9, 1865, would have been ninety-two in 1936. The old soldiers were feeble and bent with age, but a small handful of veterans were meeting once again to review in retrospect the experiences they had shared in that terrible war.

Mrs. Queen Jo Mauldin, widow of Judge Mauldin, who himself had fought for the Confederacy, was the president of the UDC (United Daughters of the Confederacy). Ms. Queen Jo, as she was affectionately called around Pickens, was dedicated to preserving the memory of the noble Confederacy and honoring those brave men who fought so valiantly to preserve the Southern way of life. It was an annual tradition for the veterans to meet at Ms. Queen Jo's house on June 3, Memorial Day in the South.

The veterans had become so feeble that the Boy Scouts were asked to help the old soldiers on this June 3, and I was one of those scouts. I listened to their stories, how they nearly starved to death, surviving for months on dried peas and corn bread. One old amputee told of how they sawed off his leg like a dead tree limb and threw it over on the pile of other dead limbs.

"I was just a youngun, sixteen years old when the war ended," one of the younger veterans said. "Never done no fightin', just got to Virginia in time to walk all the way back home. It took me three months to git back, shoes worn out, nearly barefoot, clothes just rags, and belly stickin' to my backbone."

As I listened to those tales, I wondered at the times that were past and gone forever. Nothing in the future would compare with the experiences of these old soldiers, their vivid memories of emotion-packed events still fresh in their minds after seventy-one years.

In 1936, already the seeds of a new war had taken root in Europe, and as I grew into manhood, events in Germany were taking shape to usher in World War II. I would soon be caught up in that terrible global conflict. Now it is my turn to be an old soldier and tell my stories of the emotion-packed events of my generation.

## Hans Kahn

The year 1938 was a good year for me. One of my biggest thrills was playing on the Pickens Blue Flame football team. As pulling guard, I was a regular starter. I loved to block and I loved to tackle—I even managed to block a few punts from my position in the middle of the "Big Blue Line." Then along came basketball season, and I made the basketball team. Boy! Did I feel great about myself, my school, and the lovely little town of Pickens! I agreed with the slogan that was printed every week on the front page of the *Pickens Sentinel*: "Pickens, the Gem of the Foothills, the Crown Jewel of South Carolina." I felt the world was wonderful, and Pickens, South Carolina, was the best place in this wide world. I only have happy memories of that year—the year I was fifteen years old.

The year 1938 was a bad year for Hans Kahn who lived 5,000 miles from Pickens, South Carolina. Hans was kicked out of his high school in Mannheim, Germany, because he was a Jew. Just before his fourteenth birthday, Hans and his family experienced the horrors of the "Crystal night." On the nights of November 9 and 10, 1938, gangs of Nazi hoodlums ransacked the Jewish section of Mannheim, destroying and looting and cluttering the streets with so much broken glass that the event was dubbed the Crystal night. Then the family was forced out of their apartment and was forced to move into crowded quarters with another family. For Hans Kahn, most of the memories of his fourteenth year were cruel and bitter.

Herr Kahn, Hans's father, had managed to set up his business in Switzerland and did not return to Germany after the Crystal night. He wanted to get his family out of Germany but was only able to obtain one

American visa for a single member of the family. The family decided that their young Hans should use that visa. In December 1939, Hans's mother rode on the train to the Swiss border with him, where he met his father, but before the train crossed into Switzerland, he watched as his mother was forcibly removed from the train by agents of the gestapo. That was the last time Hans ever saw his mother because she, his three younger brothers, and his grandmother all perished in Hitler's concentration camps.

Hans's father had arranged for an Italian family to meet them at the Italian border of Switzerland. The Italians took Hans to the coast, where he boarded a ship, the *SS Sarturnia*, bound for the United States. They also negotiated with another Italian family in New York City to sponsor young Hans upon his arrival in America.

On the way to America, the *Sarturnia* made a stop at the Azores, where a party of French Marines boarded it from a submarine searching for German spies. The French believed that some passengers, who were listed as German Jews, were actually German spies, posing as Jews. Some of the Jews onboard, including Hans, were rounded up and interrogated. Hans was passed over because he was a small lad, had just turned fifteen, and was still wearing short pants. Suspects were removed and taken to the French submarine. Hans remembered seeing a woman pleading for her husband who was being dragged away.

When the ship docked in New York, Hans did not immediately find the Italian family who was supposed to meet him, so he started walking and looking at the New York scenery. After an hour or so, a policeman picked him up. (His sponsors had notified the police that their charge was missing.) The cop spoke to Hans in German and asked if he was hungry. When Hans confirmed that he indeed was hungry, the cop took him to a restaurant and bought him a meal. Hans said, "I could not believe that a policeman would buy a young stray Jew-boy a meal. My concept of police in Germany was anything but hospitable."

At a very young age, Hans enlisted in the US Army and volunteered for the paratroopers. He became a member of the 508th Parachute Infantry, assigned to Regimental Headquarters Company and

Hans Kahn a.k.a. Harry Kennedy.
Photo copied from the *Devil's Digest*, circa 1945.

the S-2 (intelligence) section. To protect Hans from the Nazi fanatics just in case he ended up as a prisoner of the Germans, the army had Hans change his name. They issued him new dog tags with the good-old Irish American name of Harry Kennedy.

## War and Rumors of War

During my senior year at Pickens High School, Ms. Ruth McKinney taught us English. Ms. McKinney tried to prepare us for the expected rigors of college by requiring us to write a term paper. It was the spring of 1940, and Hitler was constantly in the news. Hitler became the subject of my senior term paper. Most of my information came from *Life* magazines. The reporters and photographers of *Life* had followed the development of Nazi Germany with sensational stories and pictures portraying throngs of Nazi supporters, who were listening to the harangues of Adolph Hitler while punctuating his remarks with cheers of "Heil, Hitler!" We saw scenes of the mighty German Luftwaffe raining terror and destruction from the skies over helpless Poland and the powerful panzer blitzkrieg running roughshod over the ill-prepared and inferior-equipped Polish Army.

In writing the term paper, I learned how Hitler's duplicity in diplomatic affairs and skillful propaganda won him much of his early territorial gains, and as his war machine became more powerful, he quickly overran Germany's weaker neighbors of Poland, Denmark, and Norway with bold initiatives and lightning speed.

His earlier annexations were accomplished by shrewd international intrigue. The Saar coalfields were annexed by plebiscite in 1935. Then plebiscites were used to convince the nations that Austria wanted to become part of Germany. Then Hitler selected the Sudetan section of Czechoslovakia for a plebiscite. The Sudetan was heavily populated with people of German origin and, according to Hitler, should be a part of the German fatherland. This set the stage for the famous Munich conference with Prime Minister Neville Chamberlain of England, who virtually gave in to all of Hitler's demands on Czechoslovakia.

My term paper ended with a summary of Hitler's diplomatic and military conquests up to the end of April 1940 and with this question: "Where would Hitler and his monstrous war machine strike next?" That question was quickly answered. Over the next few months the German army rolled over Holland, Belgium, and France and drove the British back across the English Channel at Dunkirk.

In the good old United States, we were happy to be separated from the blood and destruction by the wide Atlantic. We were concerned with our own lives and interests. It was time for me to enter college. My mother won the first round for choice of colleges. She said, "I want Zig to have one year at Columbia Bible College and get a good foundation in the scriptures before being exposed to the learned unbelievers of a secular college or university."

In September of 1940, I enrolled at Columbia Bible College. During that school year, I saw many soldiers on the streets of Columbia from nearby Fort Jackson. President Roosevelt was already helping the British with the Lend Lease Program and covertly building up our armed strength while pledging to keep us out of war.

My cousin John Wales Boroughs, who had enlisted in the navy, came to visit our family during his furlough, which was also during my spring vacation. John Wales told us about his duty flying over the Atlantic looking for German submarines. He said, "We are calling ourselves 'engaged in practice exercises,' but we are, in fact, actually dropping depth bombs on German subs."

After John Wales's visit, my dad announced, "I was an enlisted man in the last war. If we have another war, I would like for Zig to be an officer." Dad won the second round for college selection, and I was off to the Citadel in September 1941.

Then came Pearl Harbor, December 7, 1941, and FDR's famous address in which he declared, "I hate war! My wife, Eleanor, hates war! My son James hates war!" Then he spoke of the "dastardly" attack of the Japanese on Pearl Harbor, after which he declared our country in a state of war with the Axis powers.

## The Citadel

The Citadel called itself "the West Point of the South." Although a cadet could prepare for civilian vocations at the Citadel, the most urgent concern was to prepare young men for military leadership and responsibilities. The military emphasis dominated every phase of life at the Citadel.

Everything was completely regimented. Both faculty and students wore uniforms at all times. Our days and nights were scheduled around bugle calls. All of our clothing had to be folded and placed in the presses according to military regulations. Our bunks were stored every morning after reveille and reassembled each evening just before taps.

Upperclassmen were entrusted with the duty of whipping the freshmen into shape. For every mess call, the cadet companies would "fall in," which means to assemble on the quadrangle in military formation. Cadet officers and noncommissioned officers would inspect each freshman at each formation for military posture, shoeshine, shirt tuck, and other special Citadel rituals for freshmen. Those who did not pass the inspections were given demerits. Daily room inspections were another source of demerits. For every ten demerits received, the cadet would have to spend one hour of free time on Saturday walking the quadrangle with his rifle in military step.

The big inspections came just before and during the Friday afternoon parade and on Saturday mornings. Companies competed in the inspections. Cadet officers won commendations for best barrack inspection, parade inspection, marching in review, etc. There was constant pressure to shape everyone into the Citadel mold and to weed out those recalcitrant cadets who did not conform.

After about two months at the Citadel, it became obvious to me that I was marked by the cadet officers as a nonconformist who should be eliminated for the good of the corps, but I was determined that no amount of intimidation would send me packing. I did not like the Citadel, but I did not want the stigma of being a weakling who could not take the military discipline. I guess they had their methods of making a man out of you whether you liked their method or not.

In the barracks, the freshmen always had to walk in a brace and cut square corners even when going from the room to the latrine. The brace was an exaggerated military posture with special emphasis on neck-back and chin-in. We also had to be in proper uniform in barracks at all times, including going to take a shower. Bathrobes and slippers had to be worn when leaving for the shower room.

During the early spring of my freshman year, a meeting was held in the chapel with a number of invited visitors as guests. It was decided that the freshmen would remain in the barracks for this meeting to make room for the invited guests. Several of us decided this was a good time to disregard the rules and relax a little. We stripped to our underwear and ran around on the gallery, whooped and hollered, and generally acted like young colts that were cut loose from their hobbles.

What we failed to realize was that although all the upperclassmen were required to march to the chapel, the guardroom was fully staffed with the officer and sergeant of the guard on duty as was always the case. The officer of the guard sent the sergeant of the guard to investigate the noise on the gallery. Two of us were caught in the act of running on the gallery out of uniform and disregarding the rules of walking in a military brace and cutting square corners. We were duly reported to First Sergeant Manley for disciplinary action.

Left: Cadet Boroughs in parade dress uniform on the Citadel barracks gallery

Right: Cadet Boroughs off campus in white dress uniform
Photos furnished by Zig Boroughs.

The punishment prescribed by our cadet first sergeant was to stand in his room in a brace every afternoon from four o'clock until our shirts were wet with sweat or until supper mess call, whichever occurred first. This lasted for the final six weeks of our freshman year. I did not fully appreciate the cool breezes from the Ashley River during those weeks because the breeze often retarded the shirt-wetting process. Sergeant Manley also practiced the art of shouting and verbal abuse at our expense during those weeks.

An annual Citadel tradition was celebrating General Summerall's birthday by marching the corps of cadets to the general's home. (General Summerall was the president of the Citadel.) Reveille was earlier on his birthday so we could perform the celebration before breakfast. Both years I was a cadet, we marched to his home before breakfast and sang "Happy Birthday." Both years the general responded the same way. He came out the front door in full dress uniform with all his battle ribbons in place and said to us, "Young gentleman, this is indeed a schurprise." General Summerall always pronounced words that began with an *s* with a *sch* sound.

When President Roosevelt declared war, December 8, 1941, I was already eighteen years old and would soon be subject to the draft. The army sent their agents to the Citadel to sign up all freshmen and sophomores for the Enlisted Reserve Corps, so I signed up in order to avoid the draft. This allowed me to finish my second year at the Citadel and complete three years of college.

During my last month at the Citadel, army paratroopers made a parade jump landing on the Citadel parade field. I thought that jumping out of airplanes would be much more exciting than marching in close order drill. When I was inducted into the army in June of 1943, I volunteered for the paratroopers.

Citadel cadets on parade. Copied from *1942 THE SPHINX*. Used by permission of the Citadel.

## "This is the Army..."

When I entered the army, a popular song of the era emphasized the changes from civilian to military life:

> This is the Army, Mr. Jones,
> No private rooms or telephones.
> You've had your breakfast in bed before,
> But you won't have it there anymore.

I remember the instructions to prepare for induction: "Don't take anything with you. The army will furnish everything you need." I obeyed—no extra clothes, not even toilet articles. That was a mistake. It was several days before I was issued a uniform, and in the 100-degree heat at Fort Jackson, the clothes I wore soon became saturated with body sweat and odor, which was embarrassing when the girls came over from Columbia to see the soldier boys.

Maybe it was because my last name starts with a *B* and duty rosters are usually made up in alphabetical order that even before getting my uniform, I was placed on kitchen police (KP). I was roused at about 5:00 AM to get to the mess hall. It was about a 14-hour day of mopping, washing tons of pots and pans, and peeling potatoes. The cooks saw to it that we put in our day from 5:00 AM to about 7:00 PM. It didn't take me long to learn to hate KP.

Fort Jackson was just the induction center where we were given mental and physical examinations, had the swearing-in ceremony, and awaited orders sending us to another camp for basic training. I remember taking the IQ exam at Fort Jackson in an extremely warm building. The physical exam was very brief. The standard joke about the physical was one doctor would look down your throat, and at the same time, another doctor would look up your rectum. If the two doctors could not see each other's eyeballs, then you passed.

After about two weeks at Fort Jackson, our orders were cut for basic training. I was lucky enough to get sent to Camp Croft, near Spartanburg, South Carolina, for basic. Very few soldiers had basic training in their home states. The training at Camp Croft allowed me to continue a very important social relationship, namely the courtship with Mary Dougherty, a senior at Columbia College.

One thing they loved to do at Camp Croft was to "police the grounds," which means pick up trash. As the sergeant used to say, "We got to police up this here company yard and pick up everything that ain't red hot or nailed down." We had to take any cigarette butt found, empty the tobacco from the paper, and then roll the paper up into a very tiny ball.

Then there were inspections. The original idea for barrack cleanliness and order, I am sure, related to efficiency in management and maintenance of good health among the troops. Inspections, however, developed over time to be a competitive exercise among officers in command to display the effectiveness of their discipline over their troops. Praise and honor for good inspections, or severe reproof if deficiencies were reported, completely overshadowed the original purposes of regular inspections.

After basic training, I was sent to NCO school to prepare to be a noncommissioned officer and become a part of the Camp Croft training cadre. (I had already volunteered for the paratroopers, which took priority over training cadre, so that deal never materialized.) Most of our NCO training related to passing inspections. The beds had to be made so tightly that a quarter tossed on the blanket would bounce. We were even instructed to prepare a special footlocker just for inspections, in which a full set of equipment issued to soldiers could be displayed, with every garment neatly folded according to army regulations. Any clothing or equipment normally used every day had to be hidden away from the inspector's searching eye.

My basic training was interrupted when I broke my right arm. Upon arriving at the base hospital holding my arm and obviously in pain, a medical officer at the front desk gave me the order. "Open your mouth!"

I replied, "I have a broken arm. Why do I have to open my mouth?"

"Don't give me a smart answer, soldier," growled the officer, "Open your mouth!"

Then I remembered what the sergeant had taught us: "There's a right way, a wrong way, and the army way. Don't ever worry about doing it any way but the army way." I obediently opened my mouth the army way and had my teeth examined before anyone would look at my broken arm.

The broken arm kept me out of basic training for six weeks, and I did not return to the original unit but was transferred to a new company and started basic over again from the beginning. Those who started basic with me in June ended up fighting in North Africa. My broken arm kept me stateside an extra three months. It gave my courtship with Mary a chance to mature, and we were married on Christmas Day, 1943.

Mary stayed with me during her Christmas vacation from Columbia College. We rented a room in the home of a deputy sheriff of Spartanburg County. I was allowed to leave the base at night while attending the NCO school during the day. In mid-January, Mary returned to finish her senior year at Columbia College and I was sent to Fort Benning, Georgia, for paratrooper training.

We had great esprit de corps in the paratroopers, an all-volunteer group. We were reminded when we joined that weaklings and cowards would be eliminated by the rigors of training. Those of us who survived the training believed we were tough, that the paratroopers were the best fighting men in the world. We were proud, confident, and determined to prove our manhood.

Following jump training I was invited to enroll in a specialist school. I chose demolitions. One of the demolition instructors was Ralph Albano, who later was assigned to the 508th and was in my platoon. He remembered making me do fifty push-ups for needing a shave while I was in demolition school. We trained on the banks of the Chattahoochee River, digging into the sides of the bank and planting our explosives and calling out "Fire in the hole" as a warning for an expected detonation. "Fire in the hole" had a risque connotation to paratroopers, and a number of jokes developed around that expression.

The worst duty I ever had in the army was at Fort Benning, Alabama. (Fort Benning straddles the Chattahoochee River, which divides Georgia and Alabama, so there is a Fort Benning, Georgia, and a Fort Benning, Alabama.) For several days, I drew the duty for guarding prisoners. The prisoners were GIs who were in the guardhouse for various offenses, such as going AWOL (absent without leave), disorderly conduct, etc.

The army made sure these men put in their eight hours of hard labor every day, digging drainage ditches about five miles from the guardhouse. We guards had to

Bill Clark at Fort Benning Parachute School, ready for a training jump. Football helmets were standard equipment for jump-school training. Photo furnished by Bill Clark.

march the prisoners to the workplace in the morning, back at noon, back to the workplace after lunch, and back to the guardhouse again in the evening. That was four trips of five miles each added to the eight hours that the men had to dig the ditches—a very long day. All that time, we were not allowed to sit down. We were told that these were dangerous men who could easily overpower a careless guard and take his weapon. We were also strictly forbidden to talk to the prisoners or fraternize with them in any way. Furthermore, the officer of the guard rode around in a jeep, watching over the work and making sure we carried out his orders.

The commander of the prison was absolutely the most sadistic human being I ever witnessed. Everything he said to the guards or the prisoners was in terms of threats—threats of court martial for the guards who became slack on duty. According to him, at the least provocation, he could very easily put us in the guardhouse as prisoners and we would spend the rest of the war at hard labor in the Alabama swamps. It was a glad day when I got off that detail.

Since I never advanced in rank beyond PFC (private first class) when in garrison, I frequently had to pull details for menial tasks, such as cleaning latrines, guard duty, and KP. One day, while pulling KP, I promised myself if I ever get out of the army alive, I would never wash another pot or pan again as long as I live!

To show you how points of view differ, I have often said, "That was the biggest lie I ever told," whereas my wife says, "You have done your best to keep that promise."

Our overseas assignments were delayed after paratrooper and demolition training due to spinal meningitis quarantine, and probably kept me out of the Normandy invasion. My chances of surviving World War II were enhanced by a broken arm and quarantine. Finally, orders came through for shipment to Fort Meade, Maryland, to be processed for overseas assignment.

## He Wanted to Do Something for His Country

About the time I finished Pickens High School, Clarence Christiansen—called Clay by his family—took off with his older brother from Muskegon, Michigan, toward the West. The older Christiansen brother, Earle, had an arrested case of tuberculosis, and his physician advised him to spend some time in a milder climate. The two brothers pooled their resources to get enough money to strike out across the country together.

Clay and Earle ran out of money in Denver. There they found jobs in a factory making footlockers for the army. The two young men had a great time in Denver. They loved the friendly people, enjoyed their work, and had lots of fun in their spare time. Clay said, "I thought we had the greatest country on earth, and we were lucky to be Americans."

"Then on that Sunday afternoon, December 7, 1941, we heard the news about Pearl Harbor," said Clay, "and it made me mad that those Japanese would do that to us. I loved my country and wanted to do my patriotic duty."

Clay wanted the toughest challenge that he could find, something like the submarines or the paratroopers. Soon he found a recruiter and signed up for the paratroopers. At that time, Clay was too young to join without his father's consent.

He sent the papers off to his dad, and his dad wrote back, "Anything but the paratroopers—I wouldn't dare sign papers to get you into that outfit."

The next day Clay drove back to Muskegon. He talked to his dad about how he felt and persuaded him that joining the paratroopers was the right thing for him to do for his country. He went back to the Denver recruiter with his dad's signed permission.

Chris, as Christiansen was called in the paratroopers, had to take two physicals—one for the regular army and another tougher physical for the paratroopers. Chris was sent to Camp Blanding, Florida, where the 508th Parachute Infantry Regiment was being organized for basic training. The first thing they did with the new recruits was try to talk them out of being paratroopers. They used a psychologist whose special duty was to persuade the volunteers to choose some other type of military service.

Chris listened to the doctor of psychology explain how grueling the training would be, and how the chances of coming back alive from combat were only about 50-50. At the end, the psychologist said, "The choice is yours. If you are not absolutely sure you want to become a paratrooper, please say so now. We invite you to select another branch of service."

Many of the volunteers chose to back out, but Chris was determined to make it in the paratroopers. Even among those who refused to back out, many did not persevere through the basic training of the 508th. Only about half of those who started the training made it through basic and jump school.

After the men of the regiment earned their paratrooper wings, Col. Roy E. Lindquist, commanding officer of the 508th, made a speech. He told the men that he was proud of all of them, that they had proved themselves to be tough and brave and strong. Lindquist continued, "Your country is going to call on you to jump behind enemy lines, and many of you will be killed. You are going home on furlough now. This may be the last time for you to be at home alive. While you are there, think about your responsibilities to your home and family. If you think it is more important to stay alive and meet those responsibilities, you will have another chance to transfer into a safer type of military service when you return from your furlough."

Some of the men, especially those with wives and children, transferred after their furlough. Finally Colonel Lindquist believed he had a group of committed soldiers—men who could stand the strain, men who would fight under the most adverse conditions and be winners. Chris recalled, "I felt so proud to be serving my country and extra proud to be wearing the wings of the 508th Parachute Infantry."

Paratrooper wings

# Zip from Zig
## A Letter to Mother, March 11, 1944

Dear Mother,

Now I can tell you what jumping from an airplane is really like. Yesterday and today we made two jumps each morning. Every day up until Thursday was too windy or raining, so in order to get our jumps in this week, we would jump, come back, get into another chute, and jump again immediately. It is very fatiguing jumping in such rapid succession and then repacking our chutes.

The hardest thing about a parachute jump is leaving the plane. Each plane has two jumpmasters. One gives the command, "Go!" The assistant jumpmaster assists the jumpers leaving the plane. He hangs by a bar in the top of the plane and boots out anyone who hesitates. Incidentally, I never have needed any assistance. In our platoon, two men refused to jump after their second jump and one man sprained his knee. They are the only three who have fallen out of my platoon since the beginning.

The most exciting part of the jump is the time between the exit and the opening of the chute. We fall about 150 feet before it opens, and then it opens with a tremendous shock. On my third and fourth jump, I managed to keep my eyes open during that time, and I noticed that I was headed toward the ground headfirst. Then when the chute opened, it jerked my feet down and back up over my head in front of me. After the opening shock, there isn't anything to the jump. All you have to do is to avoid collisions with other chutists in the air and guide to a suitable landing place. On my second jump, I was coming down into a swamp and slipped away from it. On my fourth jump, I landed in a peanut field with a bunch of hogs in it. The hogs were unconcerned. They didn't even stop rooting as we were dropping among them.

Our next jump is scheduled for Monday night. It will be a tactical jump followed by a twenty-mile forced march. At a designated spot on the march, we will be dropped hot supper from an airplane. That will be the last jump for the parachute school.

Since we began jumping, the barracks certainly have been a chatterbox. Every fellow has to relate every detail about each of his jumps to every other member of the barracks. Then there are the discussions about the guys we observed and worlds of talk about injuries and malfunctions. If a jumper has a very slight malfunction and finds it advisable to pull his reserve, within six hours the story has developed to until the jumper's main chute failed to open completely. In our class of five hundred with four jumps each, we have had only five injuries. That is five out of two thousand jumps. None of the injuries were serious—only sprains, no broken bones.

That about covers the jumping.

Love,
Zig

Cartoon by Kate Salley Palmer

## The Rise and Demise of an NCO

Phillip "Chick" C. Miller admits, "Mom had to stretch the truth a little for me to enlist in the US Army."

Chick Miller grew up on a Tennessee farm; he matured early and looked older than his tender years. He couldn't wait to take on a man's world. Chick entered the army at fourteen and earned his paratrooper wings at sixteen. Miller completed parachute jump school just in time to be sent to Camp Blanding, Florida, as the 508th was organizing.

The sixteen-year-old Miller was already an experienced soldier, well trained in army skills. Chick was selected to serve on the training cadre for the raw recruits of the 508th. In a few short weeks, Pvt. Phillip Miller was Sgt. Phillip Miller.

The training cadre put the volunteers of the 508th through a grueling program. Fifty percent of those who entered the program at Camp Blanding washed out. After a day of hard training, the recruits were forced to march double time, and those who fell by the wayside during their evening runs were automatically transferred to other army organizations. Mental attitude was just as important as physical stamina. Col. Roy E. Lindquist, 508th's CO (commanding officer), and Col. Louis Mendez, CO of the Third Battalion, wanted men with an enthusiasm for the airborne way. Sergeant Miller was one of Colonel Mendez's trainers who inspired the airborne attitude and pushed the Third Battalion recruits to higher levels of physical endurance.

By the time the 508th had finished basic training at Camp Blanding and parachute school at Fort Benning, Georgia, and had been shipped to Camp MacKall, North Carolina, Chick Miller had reached the ripe old age of seventeen. He was beginning to feel his oats as a hotshot sergeant in the Airborne, especially when off-duty in the North Carolina towns of Southern Pines and Rockingham. He felt he had to uphold the reputation of the paratroopers as the hottest lovers and toughest fighters in the whole world.

When it came to off-duty behavior, Colonel Mendez's concept of an Airborne fighting man did not match Miller's, and Mendez had to call Miller on the carpet. Mendez loved his men as a father loves his children, and it wasn't easy for him to dish out the punishment. Miller remembers, "Colonel Mendez had tears in his eyes and I had tears in my eyes when he handed me a razor blade, asked for my sergeant stripes, and reduced me to private."

Miller, however, continued his aspiration to prove his manhood off-duty to the people of North Carolina. One morning after a bloody fight in a bar, he failed to show for reveille. At 0900 hours, when Lt. Mike Bodak came to find him, he was still in his bunk, bloody and bruised.

Bodak had promotion orders in his hands, which he immediately ripped up. Bodak announced, "Phillip C. Miller, at 0830 hours, orders were cut promoting you to corporal. At 0900 hours, the orders are being rescinded. You probably have the distinction of the shortest tenure as a corporal in the whole US Army."

Miller remained in the military until retirement. He ascended the NCO ladder, the warrant officer ladder, was commissioned as an officer, and retired with the grade of major.

Drawing by Emile Lacroix

## Privates on a Private Flight

The Tennessee Maneuvers are remembered by 508th Red Devils as a time of rain, mud, extended marches, and other tests of endurance. However, five demolitionists from Regimental Headquarters Company finagled a little fun on the side.

One of the demolitionists, Pvt. J. B. Hood, had been a civilian pilot and flew for Delta Airlines after the war. When J. B. learned that a friend Lt. Joe Bracknell was an air force pilot of a C-47 scheduled to drop troopers on their night problem. J. B. announced, "I'm going to look up an old buddy in the air force."

When J. B. returned to the demo platoon, he had an exciting announcement. "I've arranged a flight to Chattanooga for a steak supper. My buddy will take five of us if we can get passes."

Ed Luczaj, Wilber Byers, and two others went with J. B. Hood to see First Sergeant Cooper for the passes.

"No way!" said Cooper.

Hood assured his buddies, "Let's not give up yet. Let's try Master Sergeant Johnson."

Johnson, who didn't know that Cooper had already denied the passes, let Hood and his buddies go, but their troubles were not over. When they arrived at the plane, Capt. Alton Bell of the 508th was there, and he declared, "You men can't board this plane."

"But, sir, we have official passes signed by Master Sergeant Johnson."

"No matter, this plane is flying a group of officers tonight."

At that point, Private Hood's pilot friend overheard them and entered the fray. "This plane is not leaving the ground unless these five friends of mine are on board, and I don't want any other passengers! I'm the commander of this C-47, and that is final!"

Captain Bell replied, "Just kidding, just kidding!"

The five enlisted men got a charge out of seeing the air force lieutenant pull his rank on a 508th captain. They climbed on board and flew to Chattanooga, and guess who occupied the copilot's seat and shared in the pilot's chores? None other than Pvt. J. B. Hood!

After a good dinner at a fine restaurant, the group returned to the Chattanooga Airport. J. B. Hood remembered, "Almost everyone, including our pilot Joe Bracknell, had a few beers. When we had cleared the Chattanooga airspace, Joe said, 'Fly us home, J. B.' and he dropped off to sleep."

Meanwhile, Wilber "Moto" Byers, one of the dinner companions, went to sleep before the plane was off the ground. When Moto awoke and J. B Hood was flying the plane, he decided to step outside to take a leak. As Moto reached the open door, his hat blew off toward the rear of the plane. He walked back, picked up his hat, and started toward the door again. Just as Byers put one foot on the edge of the door, one of his buddies grabbed him and asked, "Where in the hell do you think you are going?"

"Just going out to take a leak," replied Moto.

His friend said, "It's a good thing I caught you. We are ten thousand feet above the ground!"

When Wilber Byers heard this story, he remarked, "If I had known J. B. was flying the plane, I would have gone ahead and jumped."

C-47 airplane.
Drawing by Dwayne T. Burns.
Permission to use by Dwayne T. Burns.

## Mules

Bob Phillips was a young man from South Georgia. He grew up on a farm near Waycross where his father raised cotton and tobacco. Like most farm boys in the days before World War II, Bob spent a lot of time plowing his father's fields with mules. As soon as Bob became of age, he looked up an army recruiter. When the recruiter asked for an area of special interest, Bob answered, "The most important thing is to get away from hardtail mules. I am sick and tired of looking at the south end of a hardtail. Can you find me an area of military service completely free of mules?"

"Well," the recruiter pondered. "How about chemical warfare? I cannot foresee any use of mules in chemical warfare. You will probably be loading chemicals on airplanes."

Off Phillips went to basic training in chemical warfare. After basic, Bob was sent to Panama to become a member of the First Separate Chemical Company at Camp Corazal, Canal Zone. Armed with .45 caliber pistols and 4.2 chemical mortars, the company patrolled the Pacific coast of the isthmus of Panama for Japanese ships, submarines, and airborne troops who might attempt an attack in that vital area of US shipping and defense. The jungle underbrush was dense and roads were sparse, and the best way to transport mortars and ammunition was by mules. So Bob was given the personal responsibility to care for one mule, a big ornery animal that was prone to run away at a sudden loud noise.

Bob's sergeant believed that the welfare of the mules came first. Whenever the men went on a march and had a chance to take a break, the mules had to be watered, fed, and rested before the men. Because of frequent inspections, the men had to spend a lot of time keeping up the appearance of the mules. That meant brushing, washing, and cleaning the mules and the harnesses. They even had to "cup" the mules.

Bob describes cupping by saying, "You had to lift the mule's tail and clean his dock with a cloth—a practice that only the army could have invented to raise the dignity of the mule and demean the enlisted man who had to perform the duty."

One day, Bob had a roll of telephone wire for laying a line by the post exchange on his mule when a lady came by wearing a big hat. A sudden burst of wind blew off the lady's hat, causing her to scream. That set the mule running, stringing wire everywhere and dragging Bob after him.

Bob was able to subdue the runaway mule, and his actions so impressed his sergeant that he was promoted to private first class and was given a horse to ride. That would not have been so bad, but now he had two animals to cup.

In order to get away from those "cussed mules," Phillips volunteered for the paratroopers. The company commander did not want to let Phillips go, but volunteering for the paratroopers was a must-honor request.

Bob finished his jump training in time to join the 508th in Ireland. He was a member of the bazooka platoon of Regimental Headquarters Company and participated in all of the campaigns of the regiment.

Bob and Jean Phillips
at 1990 Regimental Headquarter Company Reunion.
Photo by Zig Boroughs.

## A Marine in the Town Pump

A sign over a door in one of the paratrooper training camps read, "The toughest fighting men in the world walk through this door." Our training was designed to build mental alertness and physical toughness. Among us were "true believers" who felt they had to promote and maintain that fighting image.

Members of the Marine Corps also boasted of their toughness and fighting ability. Robert Ray of Greenwood, South Carolina, was a marine in World War II. One weekend while he was stationed at New River marine base in North Carolina, he decided to take a bus and visit his aunt who lived in Gastonia, North Carolina. Bobby had to change buses in Fayetteville and wait for about an hour to make his connection, so he went exploring, looking for a cold beer. Not too far from the bus station, Bobby found a watering hole called the Town Pump.

As soon as he walked into the joint, he saw it was a hangout for paratroopers from Fort Bragg. Knowing that paratroopers thought they were the toughest fighting men in the whole world, Bobby was afraid his marine uniform would act like a red flag to a bull in front of those paratroopers.

Bobby decided he would play it cautiously. He got his beer at the bar and found an inconspicuous table back at the edge of the crowd where he would not be noticed. There happened to be a sergeant sitting at the table who had a kind face and seemed to be a little older and less threatening than the boisterous crowd near the bar. Bobby sat down and struck up a friendly conversation with the sergeant. He learned that the sergeant was from the Eighty-second Airborne Division, as were most of the others patrons of the Town Pump.

Eighty-second Airborne Division shoulder patch. AA symbolizes "all-American."

Soon a fight broke out near the bar, and the sergeant turned to his marine companion and said, "Son, the best thing for you to do is to get under this table and stay there until this fight is over."

Bobby Ray said, "I was just one little old marine among all those paratroopers, and I did exactly what that sergeant told me to do."

## Little Bugzy and Big Stoop

Bugs found a home in the 508th Parachute Infantry. As far as we know, Bugs never had another permanent home, and if he had any family connections, no one ever wrote to him while he was in the army. He grew up, or rather halfway grew up (for he was the smallest trooper in the company), either in Chicago or Detroit, or maybe both. Bugzy learned his survival skills—before he reached the paratroopers—on city streets and railroad yards. One thing for sure, Bugs could take care of Bugs. He often bragged about being a hobo and seeing America from freight trains. Worldly wise and street-smart, Bugs found the paratroopers a soft life compared to what he had experienced. I had to check the official records to find out that Bugzy's real name was Stanley Andrew Cehrobec, for he was never called anything but Bugs or Bugzy.

The Big Stoop, Harry Hudec, was still growing when he joined the paratroopers. He ended up being six feet, six inches tall. About the time I entered the Citadel, Harry, who was right out of high school, went to work for the CEI (Cleveland Electrical Illumination) company. Then came Pearl Harbor and the draft.

Bugs and the Big Stoop.
Photo furnished by Zig Boroughs.

Harry didn't want to be drafted into the army. He first tried the marines. The marines turned him down due to his height. The navy uniforms didn't look good to Harry. Then he came across a recruiter for the paratroopers. The uniform looked sharp, the boots were snazzy, and they would be training in Camp Blanding, Florida. "Florida for the winter, that's for me," thought Harry.

Harry volunteered for the paratroopers and left for sunny Florida. The piney woods section of the Florida panhandle was a long way in style and distance from Miami Beach. Nevertheless, Harry enjoyed the tough training and the devil-may-care spirit of the troopers. The Big Stoop became a favorite of the men and officers of Regimental Headquarters Company of the 508th Parachute Infantry, and the feeling was mutual, for no one loved his fellow soldiers more than Harry "Big Stoop" Hudec.

The 508th completed basic training at Camp Blanding. Then the regiment moved to Fort Benning, Georgia, for parachute training and after jump school to Camp Mackall, North Carolina. It was in Camp Mackall that Captain Abraham, commanding officer (CO) of Regimental Headquarters Company, entrusted the Big Stoop with a very important military mission, making him corporal in charge of fireworks for the Fourth of July officers' party. Harry had already proven himself as a soldier with imagination and energy. As the assigned leader with several men and a weapons carrier, Big Stoop organized his patrol and made his plans, which included some private celebrations for his crew of enlisted men.

For the officers' party fireworks, they loaded their weapons carrier with enough explosive materials to blow up half of Rockingham, North Carolina. By luck, some other group was also planning a party and it just happened that they were unloading a huge supply of beer. Harry's patrol volunteered to help unload the beer truck and in the process loaded up their weapons carrier with a supply of the golden liquid for themselves.

What Fourth of July celebration would be complete without watermelons? Since the farmers around Camp Mackall had learned to keep a sharp eye out for paratroopers on patrol, shrewd strategy and careful planning were necessary for Operation Watermelon Patch. Harry had already located a field with many watermelons shining on the vines. The patrol parked their weapons carrier in a spot secure from detection and sent out scouts to reconnoiter the area. Sure enough, the scouts observed a farmer cruising about his watermelons in his pickup with a shotgun mounted in the rear window.

After the farmer parked his pickup, they crawled on their bellies, selected what they thought were choice ripe melons—even thumped them—and, still on their bellies, rolled the melons to the ditch at the side of the road. Then the weapons carrier drove by for a quick loading and a speedy getaway.

A successful military operation! Not quite! Harry and his crew enjoyed the beer, but the fireworks for the officers' party were a complete fizzle because of a torrential downpour. And the watermelons? When they cut those bastards open, the color was from green to pale pink—not a ripe one in the bunch. The watermelon disaster could have been avoided if Hudec had selected a Carolina farm boy for the operation. He didn't know that watermelons don't ripen in North Carolina until late July or early August.

Get that pre-war chow at the big party! Fried chicken, roast corn on the cob, and all the trimmings for the gourmets and all the chow hounds. Chow call is early, so don't come late and miss the grub.

Meet your husband and/or your date at camp, and see "The Facts of Life!" See the hula dancer! What a torso! Don't miss the other novelties too numerous to mention; all obtained at great cost for this one exclusive showing. Don't forget, the brawl starts at 1800 hour

FIREWORKS for your after dark entertainment will be provided by that bon suivant, raconteur and demolitionist — Lt. T.N.T. Abraham. Pin wheels, sky rockets, bombs, blasts and bedlam are guaranteed!

Come early, stay late and leave your dignity at home

### SINGLE OFFICERS!!

Let our Good Housekeeping approved matchmaker, Lt. Deeds, line you up with a partner from among North Carolina's finest. Fust come is fust served, men!

## OFFICERS CLUB POOL

## JULY 3, 1943

### 1800 HOUR

(Original flyer for party furnished by Harry Hudec)

## 1943-Style GI Weddings

In spite of the war, or maybe because of it, many couples did not wait until after the war to get married. The United States did not provide timeouts for weddings in GI schedules, but many couples managed to tie the knot regardless of the difficulties.

## Kelso Horne, I Company, and Doris Garner, June 3, 1943

Left: Kelso Horne, copied from *Life*, August 14, 1944, p. 11. Above: Hand enlarged to show wedding ring. Permission to use requested from *Time* Incorporated.

Lt. Kelso Horne and Doris Garner had planned to get married. Kelso had a short pass to go from Camp Mackall, North Carolina, to Dublin, Georgia. Kelso said, "I came home with the intention of getting married because I thought the time was getting short."

About two weeks earlier, Doris was riding with a friend when they had a head-on collision with an asphalt truck. When Kelso arrived in Dublin, he found his fiancée in bed, all banged up from the accident. The determined paratrooper lifted Doris out of bed and "toted her to the car."

The couple picked up a friend to act as a witness and started looking for a preacher. The preacher of the First Baptist Church was not at home, so Doris said, "We might as well go back home."

Kelso responded, "Not yet!"

On the next try, they found the pastor of the Jefferson Street Baptist Church, Earl Stirwalt, at home. He agreed to perform the ceremony in the car. The preacher sat in the front seat with the witness. Kelso and Doris sat on the back seat while they said their vows. By 8:00 PM they were married.

That night after the wedding, Kelso took his bride back home, got his uncle to take him to Savannah, and took the train back to Camp Mackall. The newlyweds were not able to spend their first night together until the following weekend. Two weeks later, Kelso moved his bride to Fayetteville, North Carolina, and later to Southern Pines, North Carolina, where they lived until the 508th left for their overseas deployment on December 20, 1943. Doris Horne summed up their marriage eloquently when she said, "The wedding may have lacked pomp and ceremony, but it was big on love and commitment, and it lasted fifty-seven and one-half years."

### Frank Staples, D Company, and Lois Humphrey, November 9, 1943

Lois Humphrey was a friend of Frank Staples's sisters. Lois felt she had to do her patriotic duty and write to Frank. Their correspondence blossomed into love. Before the 508th left Camp Mackall, the paratroopers were given furloughs for their last visit home before departing for the European Theater of Operations. Frank's furlough began on about November 5 and lasted until about November 16 (rough estimate fifty-eight years later).

Just prior to Frank's furlough, Lois—who was teaching school in La Farge, Wisconsin—went to their teachers' convention in Milwaukee with two other teachers who had boyfriends in the service. Her teacher-friends encouraged her to take advantage of Frank's furlough and get married. They even helped her pick out her wedding dress. Lois said, "We had been engaged for six months, and it was not difficult to talk Frank into getting married."

Frank traveled by train to Chicago. He had been two days without any water for washing on a troop train. Lois went to the Chicago Union Station to meet Frank, but he was so covered with train soot, she hardly recognized him. Together they rode a train to Duluth, Minnesota, and then a bus to Grand Marias, Minnesota.

Lois had everything planned. Her brother, an ordained minister, would perform the ceremony in the home of another brother, who lived in Duluth. Tuesday, November 9, was the day of the ceremony. They had arrived in Grand Marais on Sunday. (Grand Marais is almost in the northeastern corner of Minnesota on Lake Superior.) Monday they went to get the marriage license. The very accommodating Clerk of Court predated the license to avoid the waiting period of ten days and did not charge for the license. That same day, Monday, November 8, a severe snowstorm hit the area, and the busses did not run to Duluth.

Frank's dad and brother, who were working away from home in the Forest Service, could not make the trip due to the storm. The busses did run on Tuesday to Duluth. Family members of both the bride and the groom from Grand Marais rode the bus with the happy pair. One of Lois's friends, who lived in Duluth, went by taxi to the ceremony, bringing a wedding cake with her. The taxi skidded on the ice, and the cake bounced around inside the taxi.

The couple had about five days together after their stormy wedding before Frank had to return to Camp Mackall and Lois to her teaching job in La Farge. A short month and a half later, Frank boarded the USAT James Parker with the rest of the 508th. What was ahead for Frank or his bride?

Lois answered, "Fifty-eight years—and holding."

A popular song in World War II had one line that spoke volumes to soldier husbands far from home: "You'll be so nice to come home to." When things were quiet on the front lines and we had time in our foxholes to think, we were often comforted by the melody and words of our song and the thoughts of loving wives waiting for us to come home.

On June 25, 1944, Frank wrote to Lois from France about D-Day. A portion of that letter read, "It was very lonesome, darling, for the first two or three hours before I ran into some of our own boys. You were with me, though, smiling through it all. I had your picture taped on my rifle stock with scotch-tape so that whenever I fired, you practically looked right down the barrel too."

Frank Staples in Normandy. The white spot on Frank's rifle stock is Lois's picture. Picture furnished by Lois Staples.

## Joys of Travel

"Join the army and see the world!" There is some truth in that slogan. Most soldiers get to see some parts of the world that they might not have seen otherwise. At Fort Meade, Maryland, we were given passes to Washington, D.C., and I had my first opportunity to visit the nation's capital.

Soldiers of World War II had the unique experience of being admired and appreciated. My pass to D. C. was for about six hours, but those six hours were crammed with special experiences. It was a thrill to walk up all the stairs of the Washington Monument, look out over the city, and show off my physical conditioning as a paratrooper to the crowd of people who had to take the elevator and expressed fear of heights.

While visiting the National Gallery of Art, a civilian approached me and offered me a ticket to a dinner, which was to be served in the building. What a feast we shared! The banquet hall was filled with service people—soldiers, sailors, marines, air force men as well as some WACS and WAVES. All the guests were men and women from the armed forces, favored by some unknown benefactor.

At the conclusion of the meal, we were given tickets to various movies in town; we could take our pick of the theaters. I went back to Fort Meade that night feeling great about our country and proud to be a member of the armed services, and especially proud to wear the wings of a paratrooper.

From Fort Meade, it was on to Camp Shanks, New York. There we were able to get short passes into New York City. Three things I remember from that pass: Times Square, a ferry ride across the Hudson River, and the movie *Going My Way*. Bing Crosby played a priest and sang a lot of sweet sentimental songs that made me cry.

Also at Camp Shanks, I ran into an old friend from my days at the Citadel. We had both been members of the Baptist Student Union and often went to church together at the Citadel Square Baptist Church in downtown Charleston. He was an upperclassman and I was a freshman, and I felt privileged to share the friendship of a cadet of higher rank and status.

In June of 1943, all the able-bodied cadets at the Citadel entered the army. The two upper classes went to Officers Candidate School (OCS), and the two lower classes were inducted directly into the army as privates. My Citadel friend had gone to OCS and had been commissioned as an officer, and I, of course, was a private.

Camp Shanks had a tremendous mess hall with a rope down the middle, one side for the officers and the other for enlisted men. I looked across the rope during chow one day and saw my former friend on the officers' side. I jumped the rope to go over and speak to him and see if we could get together for a visit. To my disappointment, he acted very much like an officer who feared a reprimand for fraternizing with enlisted personnel. My friend had been better trained by the army than I had been.

It was May 29, 1944, when we left Camp Shanks and loaded on to the luxury liner *Queen Elizabeth* in New York harbor. Thousands of soldiers of all classifications boarded. It proved to be a luxury liner for the paratroopers aboard. We didn't have to pull any military duty while crossing the wide Atlantic—just enjoy the ride. Our reputation that no one could give us a command except officers who wore the paratrooper wings had gone before us.

One of my cousins had married a man who served as a commanding officer of transport ships. He told me after the war that the paratroopers were the most despicable troops he ever commanded. As part of his official duty, he had to order the troops in transport to perform such menial tasks as KP, cleaning latrines, guard duty, etc., but paratroopers refused to take orders from nonjumpers. They were also determined to prove that they were the toughest fighting men in the world and would start a fight at the drop of a hat, and woe to the MP who tried to break up the fight—that MP would soon be smelling medical aid.

The commanding officer selected nonparatroopers among the replacement troops on board the *Queen Elizabeth* to take care of the dirty details. He also made sure the billets of the paratroopers and the WACS were as far removed from each other as possible. The troopers knew that some WACS were aboard, and finding the WACS became a major military objective. I don't know if any succeeded in finding them, but I was aware that scouting parties were searching for WACS day and night.

Due to the ever-present German submarine threat, the *Queen Elizabeth* did not take a direct route to England; rather she zigzagged her way across the ocean. I stood on deck many times and observed the sharp turns the ship was making in the dark greenish-gray waters of the North Atlantic. Several times we heard the call "Now hear this!" and practiced "Abandon ship!" drills, putting on life jackets and moving to assigned stations for possible evacuation by life boats. The *Queen* was not torpedoed and made it safely over. We arrived off the shores of bonnie Scotland on the fifth of June.

## Those Black Irish Nights

About the time I arrived at Fort Benning, Georgia, for Parachute School, the 508th Parachute Infantry Regiment arrived at Cromore on the western coast of Northern Ireland, far north and close to the Arctic Circle so that the winter days were very short and the nights very long. Wartime blackouts were enforced, and the sky was most often overcast, so neither the moon, nor stars, nor lights invented by man were available to help the paratroopers see when they had a night on the town. I have heard of troopers leaving a pub on a dark night and walking right into the Atlantic Ocean.

Johnny Sweet told me that the Irish poteen further weakened their night vision.

"Poteen?" I queried, "Never heard of it."

"Poteen is homebrewed Irish whiskey made from potatoes," explained Johnny. "And poteen is potent!"

One dark night in Ireland, Johnny Sweet and some of his buddies went to town. First they got happy on poteen. Then they went to a roller rink and played Crack the Whip on roller skates. Johnny was unlucky enough to be on the end of the whip repeatedly and got popped against the wall or was sent sprawling on the floor many times. He said, "I was already dizzy from the poteen, and after bouncing my head against the wall several times, I damn well couldn't see straight."

Johnny Sweet.
Photo by Zig Boroughs.

"Walking back to camp that night, it was really dark," explained Sweet. "We couldn't see a damn thing, but we could hear voices—sounded like women."

To make a long story short, Johnny and another trooper walked fast enough to catch up with the female voices, which were giggling and talking up ahead of them. One thing led to another, and soon the two paratroopers had the two women connected to the voices in behind a building and were working up to some serious lovemaking. Suddenly, Sweet heard the other trooper let out a bloodcurdling scream, and Sweet followed his buddy running down the street.

When the troopers finally slowed to a walk, Sweet said to his buddy, "What in the hell happened to you?"

The buddy responded, "When I kissed that damn broad, I found out she didn't have a tooth in her head."

Such were the hazards of those dark Irish nights!

Johnny was a professional dancer until frozen feet in the Battle of the Bulge ended that career and introduced him to podiatry, his postwar profession.

## Irish Lasses

On their first night in camp at Cromore, Northern Ireland, three Red Devils from Headquarters Third Battalion—Donald Mitchel, Phillip Miller, and Jim Rawley—did not bother about passes but climbed the wall. It was so dark they could not see how many fingers they had on one hand. After they had stumbled on to a road, they stopped, and one of them lit a cigarette. The lighted cigarette alerted someone inside a nearby house. A door cracked a little, and a feminine voice from within asked, "Hey, Yanks, would you care for a spot of tea and some crumpets?"

No red-blooded American could turn down tea and crumpets, especially when the voice of the yet-unseen person portended female comforts beyond food and drink. The three paratroopers accepted the invitation, entered the house, and found a young mother with two teenage daughters. Mitchel, Miller, and Rawley enjoyed the tea and crumpets so much that it was hard for them to make reveille the next morning. Yet the thought of First Sergeant Orval Shaver assigning them to extra KP was enough to prompt their belated return to quarters.

According to Phillip Miller, the climb over the wall to see Mama and her girls was repeated every night that the three privates were not on duty. They never once used a pass or the front gate but always the wall. KP became less of a burden and more of a means of smuggling food to their women. A quick toss of a package of bacon through a window to waiting hands and another toss over the fence into the snow for temporary refrigeration were the first two links in the food chain of their three Irish lasses.

The lasses responded to the generous favors of their Yanks by washing and ironing their clothes, polishing their boots, and doing whatever they could to please their benefactors. It was a sad day for the Irish lasses and their Yankee friends when the 508th were shipped out of Ireland to merry England.

## Dry Run: Somewhat Wet

The 508th Parachute Infantry had settled into Wollaton Park in Nottingham, England, during the first week of April, having left the base camp in Ireland where they had trained during the early months of 1944. The regiment was attached to the Eighty-second Airborne Division and participated in tactical training with the division.

During this time I was being prepared for overseas shipment, the regiment practiced night jumps with military problems and tactical operations. As D-Day at Normandy approached, several dry runs were made in which the troops practiced for the real thing. Sergeant Gerkin of Regimental Headquarters Company recalled one such dry run.

The regiment moved to the airport. Sand tables were set up to help the troops get a mental picture of the terrain where they would land. Each small group was assigned its own particular mission to accomplish. Live ammunition was issued and weapons made ready for combat. Finally everything was in readiness, and the troopers boarded the planes loaded down with equipment and weapons. For all they knew, this was the beginning of the invasion of the European continent.

Months of preparation and training had prepared the paratroopers for the final moment of truth: the actual night jump into hostile territory. They were ready and waiting and almost impatient to prove themselves on the battlefield. This could be it.

They flew for several hours in the darkness, tense but eager and waiting. Then the red light went on. Lieutenant Johnson gave the command, "Stand up and hook up!" Nineteen men rose to their feet and hooked their parachute to the static line, a steel cable that ran the length of the C-47. Lieutenant Johnson leaned out of the door and watched the land below to try to get his bearings. Sergeant Gerkin was second, and Private Bartholomew was third. Finally the red light went off, but the green jump light failed to light up. Lieutenant Johnson said, "The green light must be malfunctioning. Let's go!" Lieutenant Johnson led the way, followed by Gerkin and Bartholomew.

Then the crew chief yelled, "Stop! This is a dry run! The green light was not turned on!" The rest of Lieutenant Johnson's demolition section remained in the plane and returned to the airport with the regiment.

Meantime, down on the ground Lieutenant Johnson was able to assemble only two men in his stick. (*Stick* means the jumpers from one airplane. There were nineteen men in Johnson's stick.) First he had to find out where he was. They were in a field. A farmhouse was nearby. Johnson said to his men, "You stay here. I will go over to that farmhouse and see if I can get some clues of our whereabouts."

Lieutenant Johnson, with his rifle ready to use, went to the farmhouse, circled the house, peeped in the windows, listened for voices. He came back and announced, "We're in England! This must have been a dry run. We can't do anything tonight. Might as well get some sleep."

The three paratroopers rolled up their parachutes and packed them in their backpacks then found themselves a nice, warm haystack to curl up in for the rest of the night.

At morning light, with their weapons, ammo, and parachutes, the combat-ready troopers moved to a highway and flagged down an army truck. The truck was headed for London. Lieutenant Johnson thought, "We can find an airport in London and fly back to our base."

The 508th command, by this time, was frantic over their missing men. An all-points bulletin describing three paratroopers in full battle gear was issued to the military network of emergency services. Search planes were combing the area trying to locate them, and ground forces were ordered to be on the lookout.

It so happened that the GI truck approached London just about the time the pubs were opening. Lieutenant Johnson and his men agreed that they might as well sample the London beer before going on to the airport. Johnson, Gerkin, and Bartholomew were all fond of English brew, so they lingered long with their glasses until the proprietor announced, "We will be closing in ten minutes."

Johnson and Bartholomew proceeded to load their gear and weapons, put on their helmets and went outside to catch a bus to the airport. Sergeant Gerkin, however, could not forget what his mother had taught him, "Never leave anything on your plate or in your glass! Think of the starving children in China!"

Since Gerk had about three fingers of beer left in his glass, he stayed to obey his mother and finished his drink. When he did go outside, Johnson and Bart were already on the bus, and it was pulling off. Gerk ran as fast as he could and was able to catch on to the back of the bus, but the bus did not stop, and he was barely able to hang on. "Stop the bus!" yelled the sergeant, but to no avail. Then the parachute, which he had folded up in his backpack, opened and billowed out behind the moving bus. The driver felt the added drag, observed the parachute in his rearview mirror, and stopped the bus.

Never before in the history of London buses had had a parachute ever stopped a bus, but then this was the first visit to London by the Red Devils from the 508th Parachute Infantry.

Cartoon by Kate Salley Palmer

## Baseball in Nottingham

On May 28, 1944, the 508th Regiment moved to airports, readying for the D-Day invasion somewhere across the English Channel. But it had previously been arranged by city officials and the Airborne Command that on May 28, the 508th Red Devils and the 505th Panthers would do an exhibition baseball game at the Notts County football ground at Meadow Lane fairgrounds.

The Red Devils's starting nine, plus one. Standing (L-R): Gene Maternowski, Walter Lupton, Joe Bonvillain, Frank Labuda, and Bud Warnecke. Seated (L-R): Lefty Brewer, Ralph Busson, Robert Brown, Lemuel Parrish, and Rene Croteau. Photo from *Airborne in Nottingham* by David J. Pike, used by permission of David J. Pike.

Other players for the Red Devils, not shown above, were the following: Elmer Mertz, D. L. Peskin, L. Hoynowski, W. Maloney, P. Pavlick, H. L. Reisenleiter, H. McLean, W. Sauer, W. Dagon, Okey Mills, J. Judefind, G. A. Shenkle, M. Blethen, K. Hook, J. M. T. Barry, J. Lakey, and T. D. MacBlane.

Neither team had uniforms or shoes with cleats. They wore their paratrooper boots and parts of their fatigue uniforms.

Okey Mills, one of the Red Devil pitchers, explained that it was a rush job to gather the baseball players from the several airfields and interrupt the preparations for the biggest Airborne operation in history for the Sunday afternoon game. Fliers had been printed and distributed throughout the Nottingham area. A large crowd of British spectators, especially young women, gathered to view America's favorite sport. It was strictly a British audience because the American soldiers were on alert. Only the players, coaches, and officials were there, transported under guard to prevent the participants from extending their time with the fans, so the usual American boisterous cheering customary to American audiences was missing.

The *Nottingham Guardian* described the British audience in their newspaper, May 29, 1944: "The frequent and prolonged clapping over what appeared to be a bit of clever play was almost riotous enthusiasm as compared with that shown at the average cricket match in England."

To the left is Lefty Brewer, in normal baseball uniform, taken when Lefty played for the Fort Benning Baseball team. Lefty pitched three years for minor league professional teams in Florida and North Carolina and was called up to play for the Washington Senators in the winter of 1940. Before he could report for spring training to the Senators, he was drafted into the US Army.

Corporal Forrest "Lefty" W. Brewer was transferred from the 507th Parachute Infantry at Fort Benning on October 21, 1942, to Camp Blanding as a member of the training cadre to organize and train the new 508th Parachute Infantry Regiment. He was one of the B Company Cadre who helped shape B Company into a tough-fighting unit. (The photo to the left was furnished by Bill Brewer, brother of Lefty, and used by permission of Bill Brewer.)

The Red Devils shut out the 505th Panthers 18 to 0. Each of the pitchers—Brewer, Okey Mills, and one other (unknown)—pitched three scoreless innings.

Ralph Busson, sitting next to Lefty Brewer in the team picture on page 35, played baseball and football for the 508th. Busson, who served in all the campaigns of the 508th, failed his physical when he first tried to join the army. His problem was discovered in high school, when at the beginning of Ralph's senior year, athletes were required to pass a physical to play football. The examining physician had discovered Ralph Busson had a hernia and he would not be allowed to play.

Immediately, Ralph left school and went home to the family farm and told his dad he had quit school because he would not be allowed to play football. His dad made a deal with Ralph. He said, "I am willing to sign a paper taking responsibility for any injuries that you might incur playing football, if you will finish your senior year and graduate from high school."

A deal was made, and Ralph went back to school.

As soon as Ralph finished high school, he joined the army, but again he failed the physical. Ralph figured out that the doctors detected the hernia by placing two fingers under his scrotum and asking him to cough. The cough caused certain muscles to tense up and reveal the hernia. Ralph practiced coughing until he was able to make the sound of a cough without using the hernia-revealing muscles. He tried joining again, and this time, the hernia was not discovered.

When Busson earned enough points for his honorable discharge from the army, he forgot to do his fake cough, and the doctor told him he would have to postpone his discharge until his hernia was corrected.

If Ralph Busson had not developed his special "taking-the-physical" cough, what would have happened? For one thing, he would have been 4-F, the classification that exempted men from military service. Also, H Company would not have enjoyed all those wonderful annual pig roasts on the Busson farm.

To illustrate the 508th's connections with Nottingham, a clipping from a recent Nottingham paper of an article about the famous baseball game written by Gary Beddingfield was sent to the author by Angelo M. Leone. Leone was mail chief for the regiment. Along with fellow postal workers Norman Deere, David Kuony, and Tom Gallagher, Angelo Leone was responsible for the wonderful experiences of "mail call" for the 508th paratroopers. Below is a selection from his letter that accompanied the clipping:

> Mrs. Carl Olson, a native of Nottingham, mailed the enclosed newspaper sheet to me. She married an Air Force Sergeant and now resides in Lakeland, Florida. From

time-to-time, she receives mail from her Nottingham friends, and subsequently forwards them to me. I made her acquaintance when I attended the movies at the Hippodrome Theater where she worked as an usherette.

I remember the game well, as I was an umpire on base for the game. We sure had a good team. It is sad so many were lost in the Normandy jump. I am impressed that the people of Nottingham have not forgotten our stay there. We must have been a trial, but they realized the sacrifices and work done by our boys.

For fifty years after, Joe Bonvillain, who hit two home runs in the Nottingham baseball game, left the 508th and had not seen or heard from any of his paratrooper friends. Then in the summer of 1994, Bonvillain, at his home in Aldelanto, California, was watching television Channel KPLA about the 1944 Normandy invasion. There on the television screen, he saw and heard Col. Louis Mendez speaking about World War II.

Bonvillain was so excited, he went straight to the phone and called the TV channel and told them that he used to be Colonel Mendez's jeep driver and that the colonel always called him Red Eye. The local station then contacted NBC headquarters in New York. NBC gave Bonvillain Mendez's home phone number in Falls Church, Virginia. When Bonvillain called the Mendez home, the colonel was not at home, but Mrs. Mendez told him that for years her husband, Lou, had been hunting for Red Eye. Col. Louis Mendez returned Joseph "Red Eye" Bonvillain's call later that day. From Virginia to California the two war buddies enjoyed a telephone reunion after nearly fifty years of no contact. That was truly a multimedia 508th connection.

Adolph "Bud" Warneche, who played second base for the Red Devils, has preserved a letter sent to his hometown newspaper in Breese, Illinois, from Freder Gray. Mr. Gray, chairman of the Anglo-American committee in Nottingham, wrote to the hometown newspapers of every player who played on both teams, expressing the appreciation of the citizens of Nottingham for the presence of the American boys in their city and the pleasure of watching them play baseball. One sentence from Gray's letter illustrates the relationship of the 508th with the people of Nottingham:

"Nottingham is very proud indeed to welcome your fine boys, but also to assure you of the intense hopes that the bonds of friendship in these days may be symbolic of the days to come."

Those "bonds of friendship" are still strong.

Six members of the 508th baseball team that played in Nottingham on May 28, 1944, were killed in action: Forrest "Lefty" Brewer, Rene A. Croteau, John J. Judefind, Joe Lakey, William F. Maloney, and Elmer Mertz.

## Thou Shalt Not Kill the King's Deer

Security was a great concern to the Allied Command. Troop placements were supposed to be top secret, but here we were in Nottingham, England, an area rich in legends of Robin Hood, and we wanted to share that with our families. Letters home were censored so that all references to our location would be blacked out. We tried to give hints in not-so-subtle ways, such as referring to the King's deer and to the forest as a safe place to escape the clutches of the scheming sheriff, but Mary, my wife, said my letters were still heavily censored.

My surprise about England was the amount of daylight we experienced in the month of June. Call to quarters was at 2300 hours (11:00 PM), and it was still daylight outside. I had not realized how far north England is compared to the southern part of the United States. The next surprise was how cold it could be sleeping in tents in the month of June. The first night in Wollaton Park, I emptied all of the contents of my duffel bag on the cot for covers to keep warm.

One interesting feature of the camp at Wollaton Park was the "ablutions," a name for a place to wash up. We had showers in a tent, but the troughs for shaving and washing face and hands were outside, and we would make our ablutions at these outside facilities. And then there were the "honey buckets"—tall thirty-gallon containers that fit under the toilet holes for human excretion. About twice a week, a crew of men would come by and exchange empty buckets for the full ones. We were told that the men on the honey-bucket crew had refused to serve in the British military for reasons of conscience.

Enterprising ladies around Wollaton Park learned how to make a few honest bucks (pounds) "working for the Yankee dollar" by washing and ironing clothes for the troopers. One lady would send her ten-year-old son, Alan Gillis, as her pickup and delivery boy. Alan was a frequent visitor to the tents of the Demolition Platoon of Regimental Headquarters

Company. While taking care of his mother's laundry business, he won our affection and Alan Gillies became our adopted little brother.

Our adopted little brother, Alan Gillies, is an active associate member of the 508th PIR Association. He emphasizes the 508th in the Nottingham area every year on Remembrance Day, November 11. He is also active in locating American fathers who, while stationed in and around Nottingham, sired children who never knew their biological fathers. Many of these children, now over fifty years old, have longed to learn about their father's side of the family. Alan Gillies has painstakingly examined records and has been successful in helping a dozen or more meet their GI fathers.

Grady Murray of Headquarters first carried his laundry to the home of Mrs. Tidwell in Nottingham. He said that he always gave fruit to the family, which the troops received and was unavailable to the British. Doris Tidwell, a teenage daughter in the family, wrote to Grady's stepmother in South Carolina. The letter was postmarked "10 Dec." She hoped to get Grady's address because "he has gone off to France." She also said that she hoped to come to America after the war and visit Grover, South Carolina.

Grady confirmed that the relationship between them was very casual. He visited with the family when exchanging dirty laundry for clean laundry and talked to them about his home in Grover, South Carolina. Doris had enough information to address the letter as seen below:

Grover is a small town where everyone knows each other, and Mrs. Murray, Grady Murray's stepmother, received the letter.

Wollaton Park was an estate of several hundred acres with Wollaton Hall dominating the highest point within the estate. The hall itself was a massive and ornate structure. We soldiers called it the castle, but it is more properly called a stately home.

It was not a fortification for defensive purposes as a castle would be but an elaborate home, headquarters of a family of noble rank where royalty would often be entertained and from which the family's wealth would be managed.

For several centuries, Wollaton Hall had been the home of a series of Lord Willoughbys. One was a famous botanist, Lord Francis Willoughby. Another had been the King's appointed governor of Barbados, an important island colony in the West Indies for England during her early colonial activities in the Americas. By the time we arrived at Wollaton Park, the estate had been placed in trust and preserved as an historical monument with Wollaton Hall housing a museum of natural history.

The tents of the 508th were located to the rear of the hall behind the barns and other domestic-type buildings. The park contained many huge trees not crowded together but each with its own space and territory. Toward the front of Wollaton Hall was a grove of lovely deodar cedars native to India. There was also a well-kept golf course used by the British and some of the officers of the 508th. Many people from the surrounding area used Wollaton Park for recreation and relaxation.

The University of Nottingham campus adjoined the park, and on one weekend I met some of the students visiting the park with their books to prepare for their final exams of the school term. I tried to talk to the college girls on equal terms, but they explained to me that British colleges were so superior to American colleges that we were not in the same league.

Wollaton Hall. Photo furnished by Dave Pike.

I remember my twenty-first birthday in Wollaton Park. The regiment was still fighting in Normandy; just a few of us green replacements were in camp. My birthday fell on a Sunday. Someone had planned a social affair (Sunday afternoon tea). The social at the Hall was a mild little party where soft drinks and cookies (squash and biscuits) were served. The English identified me at the tea as a Southerner. "I detect a Southern accent. Are you from Georgia?" someone asked.

*Gone With the Wind* was playing at the "cinema" in Nottingham at the time, so one with a Southern accent would naturally be associated with Georgia. Did I live in a house like "Tara," Scarlet O'Hara's Georgia mansion?

"No, but my cousin, Ben Kellar, lives on a plantation," I boasted, "in a Southern mansion with huge columns in front. He rents rooms to Yankees who come down in the fall and winter to hunt on his plantation."

"I say Yank, it is interesting to know that all Yanks aren't Yankees," observed my English companion. "Some Yanks are Southerners, and others are damn Yankees."

I felt that I was a liberal Southerner who had conquered most of my prejudices and could say with pride, "Many of my best friends are Yankees."

One of the guests at the tea was a young woman in British army uniform, a member of the ATS (like the WACS of the US Army) whose name was Ruth. Ruth had a hankering for Chesterfield cigarettes and wondered if I could get her some from our PX. (I let Ruth know that I was married and had a strong determination to avoid any romantic relationships with other women, but I did agree to meet her the next weekend with a carton of Chesterfields.)

Right after arriving at Wollaton, I bought a bicycle from a young boy. It was a used bicycle, functional and rather cheap. The bike gave me a great opportunity to explore the area and learn more about the community. I think I had the bike about one week when the police came to the camp and confiscated it as stolen property. So much for seeing England on a bicycle.

I searched for a Baptist Church in Nottingham and finally found one. Baptists are very much in the minority in England compared to Dixie. The church reminded me of the huge Citadel Square Baptist Church in Charleston, South Carolina. The Baptist Church in Nottingham was much too large for the tiny congregation that was seated in the first few rows of the mammoth auditorium. The service was so strange to me; I would never have recognized it as Baptist without its name.

A young man in the church invited me to his home after services to share a meal with his family. I remember the small flat where he lived, the coal grate in the living room, and the embarrassed wife who felt unprepared for a dinner guest. The food rations in England at that time were quite restrictive, and any extra mouth to feed amounted to a family sacrifice. In fact, about all a soldier could buy to eat while out of the camp were fish and chips wrapped in old newspapers.

The British food rations remind me of Roy Nash of the demolition platoon who came back from town one night imitating a waitress who responded to his request for cocoa. "I say, Yank! Even the King can't have cocoa!"

One Sunday afternoon at a park on the Trent River, I met a young Englishman who explained to me that because of a physical disability he was not in military service but served in the Home Guards. His Home Guard duties consisted of night watch for enemy aircraft. In his civilian role, he worked as a chemist (British equivalent of a pharmacist) at a local apothecary (drugstore). The gentleman invited me to come to his bachelor flat for tea. My conversation with the gentleman was a pleasant interlude, but I had to be almost rude to get away.

Wollaton Park was enclosed with a high brick wall. Normal access in and out was through a gate with a guardhouse attached, but men of the 508th decided to climb a low place in the wall that led directly toward the town of Beeston, where there were several pubs frequented by the troopers.

Wollaton Park Guard Duty.

Pub hopping was not one of my pastimes while in England, so I do not have a repertoire of stories associated with the drinking places. I attended the Methodist Church in Beeston a number of times and only once looked in at a pub for about an hour. There was a great deal of singing along with the "bitters" (bitters is an English beerlike brew.) One of the popular pub songs was "Roll Me Over in the Clover." The refrain went something like this:

Cartoon by Tom Gintjee.
Furnished by Dave Pike.

Roll me over in the clover,
Roll me over, lay me down, and do it again.

Wollaton Park enclosed a small herd of deer referred to by the troopers as the "King's deer." It was rumored that certain cooks in the regiment could be enticed into preparing late-night venison suppers if the deer were supplied. The rumors must have been true because the game warden of the park, as well as the regimental officers, posted warnings about killing the deer. We translated these warnings into our own words to add a Robin Hood flavor: "Thou shalt not kill the King's deer!"

## "Cricketiers Arms" by Leon Israel Mason
Used by permission of the author

When the 508th arrived in England, tents and honey buckets were waiting patiently in Wollaton Park, a park famous for Wollaton Hall and a beautiful botanical garden. But this is the story of a pub that was located just outside the park in the small town of Beeston. Perhaps it was the seven-foot wall that said, "No entrance!" Perhaps it was just the urge for excitement that made several members of our demolition platoon jump the wall the very first night of their arrival. Our colonel used to say unofficially, "Any man in this outfit that can't jump the wall and get back in without getting caught, doesn't belong."

The fellows came in the next morning with quite a story about a pub called Cricketiers Arms. Soon we were issued legal passes, but we still delighted in going over the fence instead of taking the long way around.

The pub, at first glance, was much like any other pub in England. There was the crowd of middle-aged and old men and women who came to sip their brew and pass an evening. Perhaps they had an occasional tune on a piano. But when the demolition platoon took over, the pub was different. At first the people didn't pay any attention to the noisy Yanks with too much money. They just tolerated them.

But the "Yankee Spirit" was contagious. The platoon took a table near the piano, and there they spent all their free evenings. They bought their beer by the pitcher, and in the spirit of comradeship they filled up, time and time again, every glass in the house. They shared their cigarettes and swapped jokes with the civilians. The boys would bring in about a pound's worth of fish and chips every night and feed the gang.

It was good, clean fun, and no one was hurt.

The civilians began to learn the names of the boys, and they invited the gang to their homes.

And the songs they used to sing! Margie just barged in one night. She was a thin blonde who was a trifle oversexed after she had had two beers. And, boy, could she play the piano! Her rasping voice kept the boys roaring with laughter as she sang:

> There were big balls, small balls,
> Balls as big as your eyeballs.
> Give them a twist around your waist,
> And throw them over your head.
>
> There stands a lovely row of coconuts.
> There stands a lovely row of balls.
> There stands my wife,
> The target for tonight,
> Singing, 'Roll your balls,
> A penny or roll your balls.'

From that she would lapse into this:

> This is number one and the fun has just begun
> Roll me over, lay me down and do it again.
> Roll me over, in the clover,
> Roll me over, lay me down and do it again.

ATS and WLA girls started drifting in and before long the boys all had girls. After the pub closed, there was a strange mixture of English and American lovemaking outside and inside of Wollaton Park.

It was all fun and a swell outlet for pent-up emotions. It was normal. Hell, the boys didn't figure on living much longer!

One night they all got sentimental. They took out their demolition knives and carved their names on the table at which they had so much fun.

Then one day the boys didn't come. The people wondered. They didn't come for a week. Then came the headlines: "Airborne Troops Spearhead Invasion of Normandy!"

The English people prayed for these boys along with their prayers for their own sons. Months went by. The pub didn't seem the same.

One night nineteen of the original fifty-one barged into Cricketiers with German helmets, rifles, trophies, and confident smiles. That night was a happy reunion, and the civilians wouldn't let the boys pay for a drink.

George, the happy fat owner of Cricketiers, showed them the room he had built in the back just for them—their table, a new piano, and all the friends they wanted in there, which was about everyone in the pub.

There were sad stories to tell. There were stories of heroics and stories of amusing incidents. Some girls cried hysterically when they heard the names of several boys who were not ever coming back to Cricketiers. Wreathes were carved around their names on the table.

Again, months passed. New replacements took the places of those who did not come back from Normandy. But the spirit of the missing men was still there. It was as though they had never left. Even our officers came down to drink and sing with us.

Then there was the Holland jump, and the boys never did go back to England.

Nancy, the wife of the owner of Cricketiers Arms, was planning to crate up the table and send it to Chuck Connors. Chuck Connors, one of the members of the demolition platoon, hoped to open the "Whistling 88" in Brooklyn when the war was over. He would serve fish and chips, and there would always be the table reserved for any of the gang from the demolition platoon who happened to drop in.

Yank at a Nottingham Pub. Cartoon by Tom Gintjee. Furnished by Dave Pike.

## "I Found the Most Gorgeous Girl in Nottingham"

"I was not a boozer and didn't enjoy the pubs, but I did like to dance. I found a big dance hall in Nottingham called Paliase De Dance. A lot of land army girls frequented the hall, and they only served soft drinks. That suited me just fine," declares John Simmons, E Company.

One night at the Paliase De Dance, a beautiful young lady, Iris Blankley, dazzled John Simmons. He managed a few dances with Iris and toward the end of the evening asked to walk her home. After that they became regular partners at the Paliase.

Sometime later, John decided to call on Iris at her home in the Bullwell section of Nottingham. When John arrived, her father, Mr. Blankley, a burly coal miner, announced to Simmons that Iris was not at home.

The next time John met Iris at the Paliase, Iris quoted her father as saying, "A Yank came calling for you, and I told him, 'Don't come back again!'"

A true 508th Red Devil, John accepted the challenge and soon became a regular visitor in the Blankley home, which was five miles from the 508th encampment at Wollaton Park. John got in the habit of staying to the very last minute, so he had to double time back to Wollaton to make bed check. "I have to thank Lieutenant Mathias for all the running forced on E Company during training," John remarks. "The five miles back to camp was a piece of cake."

One night Iris said to John, "Why don't you ride my bicycle and you can stay a little longer."

John tried it, but after a short distance, the bike had a flat tire. This time he had to double time while pushing the bike.

Then came Normandy. John was wounded on July 5 and was hospitalized in Plymouth, England. John and Iris had not become all that serious with each other, but when John was released from the hospital in August and returned to Wollaton Park, their courtship became intense.

Again, John and Iris were separated with the airborne invasion of Holland. This time they did not see each other for almost a year. Corresponding on almost a daily basis, the separation only deepened their feelings for each other.

In July 1945, when the 508th was in Frankfurt, Germany, Simmons arranged a furlough to Nottingham, and it was during this furlough that John proposed to Iris, and she accepted.

The paperwork for soldiers to marry outside the United States was horrendous in those days. Simmons started the arrangements when he returned to Frankfurt. He had enough points to be sent home and discharged from service, but he wanted to secure his bride first. Sergeant

Simmons postponed rotation home until he was the last of the original E Company men to leave Germany.

The wedding was set for Christmas Eve in St. Mary's Anglican Church in Bullwell. Simmons finally had the papers he needed from the US Army. He mailed one set and saved the other to carry with him to Nottingham.

Earlier John had sent money to his sister to buy engagement and wedding rings. His sister mailed the rings in a tin aspirin box through regular GI mail. John arrived in England with his extra set of papers and small aspirin box.

When the Blankley family met him at the train, Mr. Blankley said, "You can't get married, the papers have not yet arrived!"

"I have an extra set right here," John replied.

During the wedding rehearsal, the priest asked, "What will we do about rings?"

John reached for his aspirin box.

After the wedding and brief honeymoon in Bullwell, it was back to Germany, and soon John returned to the States and was discharged. On Easter Sunday, 1945, in New York, John Simmons met a boat filled with war brides, including his own lovely Mrs. Iris Simmons.

Even then, John had to wait because the army went through a lengthy process for each bride and did so in alphabetical order. Iris's name was no longer Blankley but further down the alphabet to *S* for "Simmons." John waited in the cold New York rain, dressed in his new summer-weight Palm Beach suit until he was thoroughly chilled and soaking wet before he felt the warm embrace of his loving wife.

Papa Blankley may have seemed cool to John at first, but later he and Mrs. Blankley immigrated to America and made their home with their daughter and son-in-law, John Simmons.

## There Is Something about a Paratrooper

I remember soldiers in basic training that did everything they could to get out of the army. When I arrived at Fort Benning, Georgia, I also found soldiers who did everything they could to stay in the paratroopers. Paratrooper training was designed to weed out the weak, but I soon learned that the desire to stay the course was the most important trait for being a paratrooper.

Wilbur Byers of Regimental Headquarters Company, a demolition specialist, had polio as a youngster, which left him with one arm smaller and weaker that the other. The training cadre delighted in giving Wilbur extra push-ups to test his endurance. Wilbur did every push-up required.

Our chief surgeon, Dave Thomas, told of a soldier who was determined to remain in the paratroopers. Just before the Normandy invasion, a young rifleman from A Company was sent to have his eyes examined. His sergeant thought that every rifleman needed to shoot straight, and this rifleman's vision was suspected of being flawed.

The medical technician put the trooper in a dark room, shined a light on the testing chart, and asked him to read the chart. There was no response. He asked again, and there was no response. Finally they tested his hearing and learned that the soldier was stone deaf.

Dr. Thomas called the trooper in for an interview and found that the trooper was such a good lip reader that he had managed to get through basic training and paratrooper training and was ready and willing to go into combat with his beloved 508th Parachute Infantry Regiment without being able to hear.

"I am sorry," said the doctor. "You do not meet the standard requirement for a military service. You should be classified as 4-F and return to civilian life."

"Surely there is some job in this outfit that I am capable of doing," answered the deaf trooper.

Dr. Thomas was so impressed with the zeal and enthusiasm that the young man had for his regiment and for serving his country that he called Captain Dowling of Service Company and asked him to find a slot for the deaf paratrooper. Captain Dowling was equally impressed and made him a cook's helper.

## Oversexed, Overpaid Killers?

A story circulated, which may not be true, about an airborne battalion commander (not from the 508th) and a WAC battalion commander. The airborne colonel said to the WAC colonel, "Why don't we arrange a dance for our paratroopers and invite your WACS as guests?"

The WAC colonel replied, "I wouldn't let my girls dance with that bunch of oversexed, overpaid killers from the Eighty-second Airborne."

Not to be outdone, the airborne officer retorted, "On second thought, I don't want my troopers to dance with your underpaid whores."

For the record and this is true: Colonel Mendez introduced a WAC officer at one of the 508th reunions, Lt. Col. Jane Brister. Colonel Brister spoke of the splendid relationship she had experienced between the 508th regiment and her command of WACS. She said something like this: "At the many social functions which our women troops shared with the 508th paratroopers, I was always impressed with two things about the troopers—how sharp they looked and their gentlemanly behavior."

The 508th did have a reputation of being both violent and obsessed with sex, but some 508th men had little stomach for killing or for the careless sexual encounters associated with their reputation.

One paratrooper, who wishes to remain anonymous, told of an experience in England:

The young Texan and his buddy were standing on a street corner in Nottingham when two pretty young ladies came up to them and said, "If you want a good time, come with us."

They were led to a large attractive house where they were greeted by the madame. Each trooper signed the register, paid four pounds, and followed his girl into a bedroom. The Texan said that his young woman had the face of an angel. They both undressed and got into bed, but as they began the sexual act, the trooper remembered what his mother had taught him: "Treat every older woman as your mother and every younger woman as your sister."

Then he heard another voice, even louder, the voice of an old country preacher: "All drunkards, adulterers, and fornicators shall have their place in the lake of fire."

He couldn't stand it any longer. He rolled out of bed, crawled over to the fireplace, and threw up into the coal grate.

Violence and killing, a part of war, also did not come easy for many brave paratroopers. Stanley Kass of Regimental Headquarters Company tells this story:

Stanley Kass, at one of the 508th reunions. Photo by Zig Boroughs.

While still in Nottingham, Kass had received a big long roll of salami in a package from his dad. Stanley thought to himself, "This is just what I need for the combat jump. I can survive on this salami for many days if I am isolated and cut off from a food supply."

Kass packed the salami in his musette bag and kept it under his head as a pillow when he slept. He must have slept soundly on the night of June 4 because when he awoke, he discovered that half of his salami was gone. Three of his buddies (Steve Uchrine, Al Hillman, and Cumer Green) were not very sleepy that night, and when Kass had rolled over, they took the opportunity to appropriate part of the salami for a midnight snack.

The next morning the three troopers teased Kass and laughed about eating his salami. Kass, however, didn't take the prank as a joke, but swore, "I'll piss on your graves for this—just you wait and see!"

"Not that I believe in hexes, but I wish I hadn't said that," Kass recalled. "Because after the Normandy jump, Hillman and Green were listed as KIA (killed in action) and Uchrine as MIA (missing in action). It was years before I learned that Uchrine had been a POW (prisoner of war) and had survived the Nazi prison camps."

On D-Day Kass landed in a cow pasture in Normandy and couldn't find anyone but the cows. A farmhouse was close by, so he thought he would investigate. As Stanley approached the corner of the house, he saw a bayonet blade ease out from behind the corner. When more of the bayonet was visible, he realized it was longer than a GI blade. As soon as the human figure came around the corner, Stanley unloaded the clip from his carbine into the German soldier. The body crumpled before him, quivered, and then was still. Stanley took a deep breath and suddenly became violently ill. He turned to the side to avoid vomiting on the enemy he had just killed.

"That was the first of seven Germans I killed," says Kass as tears welled up in the corners of his eyes. "Some people enjoyed the killing, but I really didn't have the stomach for it."

## A Little Late for D-Day

I was aboard a battleship between the Firth of Clyde near Glasgow, Scotland, and Liverpool, England, when the British captain announced over the public address system that airborne divisions had parachuted into Normandy. D-Day had arrived.

The *Queen Elizabeth* had transported us from New York to Glasgow where thousands of soldiers, destined to become replacements for the Normandy casualties, debarked to smaller vessels for distribution to various military depots. Our little ship had only recently been pressed into service to transport men. The whole storage area was divided into small pens equipped with watering and feed troughs for animals. Distinctive barnyard odors still lingered on board. Groups of soldiers were assigned to pens with identifying numbers. We dumped our gear in the pens and went on deck to keep up with the news on the "wireless" for the rest of the night.

When we arrived in England, we got off the boat at Liverpool. After that, we were shipped to a camp with no name, at a location kept secret from us, and we were restricted to the camp. The Allied command was very secretive about troop movements at that time. We were instructed not to mention place names in our letters home. All our letters were read and censored to prevent any information leaking to the enemy.

Our camp was surrounded by a brick wall about ten feet tall and was patrolled by MPs marching around the wall. One evening, a group of about five of us found a place where the wall was broken down about a foot at the top. We watched the movements of the MPs and timed them to pick the right moment to escape without getting caught.

I was the lookout and waved the other four over the wall. I was the last to jump. One of my feet landed on a brick that had fallen from the wall, and I turned my ankle. I couldn't follow my buddies as they ran across the field and out of sight. The MPs came by and picked me up writhing in pain at the foot of the wall. I was caught AWOL (absent without leave) at the wall.

The MPs did not report me AWOL, but they loaded me in a jeep and took me to a hospital where my ankle was examined and pronounced sprained but not broken. They kept me in the hospital for several days, long enough for all my buddies to be shipped out, and I never saw them again.

One of those old buddies from whom I was separated was Ralph "Slim" Blohm. I met Slim the first day at jump school. Slim was about six feet three, which was unusual for a paratrooper. When we joined the paratroopers, the height limit was six feet. I asked Slim how he managed to bypass that rule. "I slumped," he said, "when they measured me."

Slim was as young and naive as any paratrooper I ever knew. I think he joined the service at the earliest date legally possible, and maybe even earlier. He had not started shaving and had only two or three chin whiskers that were beginning to show at inspections. The sergeants would get right in his face and holler, "Trooper, when did you last shave?" The standard answer was, "Yesterday, sir!" One sergeant told Slim, "The way these three chin whiskers grow so fast, you are gonna have to start shaving every day."

My bunk and Slim's bunk were always close together. We must have been placed in alphabetical order by our last names. It seems that in our little group of buddies, all our last names started with a *B*. Slim and I were always close together in formation. I remember the eight-mile run during which Slim got sick and vomited on my fatigues as he ran directly behind me. The sergeants seemed to pick on Slim, trying to make him fall out, but he was determined to make it. He took everything dished out and was proud to be manly enough to take the rigors of the paratroopers.

Eventually I became one of the replacements for the 508th. We replacements were waiting in Nottingham at the base camp when the remnants of the regiment were brought back to England from Normandy. The veterans of Normandy were a close-knit unit, having shared their earlier training together and finally sharing the perils of the D-Day invasion, but many of their buddies (killed, wounded, or missing in action) did not return to Nottingham.

At first, I was assigned to a supply section and was very busy helping distribute equipment to the returning veterans and replacements. The troops were being equipped for battle readiness again. Soon I was transferred to headquarters company and the demolition platoon because I had been trained as a demolitionist at Fort Benning.

We replacements heard the stories of D-Day, like the one Bugs (Andrew Cehrobak) used to tell. As Bugs went around the corner of a building, he met the point of a German bayonet that pierced through his clothing but not his flesh. Bugs, who was carrying a Thompson submachine gun, emptied the whole clip of twenty rounds into the body of the German. Bugs would tell the story and complain that he couldn't even get a Purple Heart with no blood to show. We replacements stood in awe of Normandy veterans, and we were anxious to prove ourselves equal to their performance. Everything after Normandy, however, was a piece of cake according to the veterans, so our mettle was never thoroughly tested.

# CHAPTER 2

# D-Day Confusion Somewhat Organized

**Pathfinders**
Airborne paratroopers landed inland about seven hours before the seaborne troops hit the beaches of Normandy. Pathfinders jumped about an hour before the other paratroops exited their planes. Their job was to set up lights and communication systems to enable the pilots of the C-47s to drop their paratroopers on their designated drop zone (DZ).

Pathfinder team for First Battalion. Reclining: unknown. Seated: Private First Class N. Trevino, unknown, unknown, Private First Class C. Gamez, unknown, Private First Class P. Denciak (medic), Private First Class D. Krause. Kneeling: Private First Class W. Stutler, Private First Class J. Barkley, unknown, Private First Class J. Weinerth, unknown, Private. A. Cannon. Standing: Gilliam (aircrew), Wilger (copilot), unknown, Corporal. R Smith, Herro (navigator), unknown (aircrew), Miles (pilot), Lieutenant R. Weaver. In door: Unknown (aircrew). Photo furnished by James Allardyce.

A team of pathfinders had trained for each of the three battalions of the 508th. Lieutenant Robert "Bob" J. Weaver, commander of the 508th First Battalion pathfinder team, described their training in the "war room" of the Eighty-second and 101st Airborne divisions. His memoirs are briefly summarized as follows:

Weaver remembered the war room as a large room with only one door. Guards kept watch at the door at all times, allowing only a few authorized trainers and trainees to enter. Maps of all descriptions covered the walls. Carefully prepared sand tables provided three-dimensional models of Normandy's terrain.

Pathfinder team for Second Battalion. Seated: Lieutenant Perez (aircrew), Lieutenant Vohs (aircrew), Lieutenant E. Hamilton, Lieutenant Gaudio (pilot), Lieutenant L. Polette, unknown (aircrew), and unknown (aircrew). Kneeling: Sergeant Katsanis (504th), Private H. Jessup, Private H. Seale, Corporal E. King, Private F. Infanger, Private First Class M. Daly, Private J. Perdue, and Private First Class C. Jones. Standing: Private S. Messenbrink, Private R. Andreas, Private J. Gerard, Private First Class B. Moss, Private N. Willis, Private N. Forkapa (504th), unknown (504th), and unknown (504th). In door: Lieutenant Murphy (504th). Photo furnished by James Allardyce.

The teams were given an overview of the big picture of the total operation. Then each team studied in depth the area for its battalion DZ. This continued for days until the pathfinders could mentally visualize the road networks, hedgerows, enemy position, and other details of the terrain.

Francis Lamoureux, a pathfinder for the Third Battalion, said that the crews of the C-47s that transported each team trained along with the troopers. The pathfinder pilots and their crews were proven to be superior in experience and skill.

Each battalion team of airmen and paratroopers trained separately. They specifically studied the Normandy terrain in their section of the DZ. All three planes were to drop their paratroopers on or near Hill 30 at the same time. But since the spread of the C-47s' formation was that of a *V*, it meant that the teams would be spaced a short distance from each other upon landing. If all went well, three sets of lights would be visible in the vicinity of Hill 30 for the pilot that followed. However, in the event that one or two of the pathfinder planes were shot down, they hoped that at least one would be able to drop their team of paratroopers, who in turn would be able set up their lights and operate radios to guide the other planes to the DZ.

Some pathfinders carried communication radios called Eurekas. Their job was to direct the flight path of the planes toward the DZ. As the planes neared the DZ, their pilots would spot the blue lights on the ground. Then the pilots would turn on the green lights over the exit doors, signaling the paratroopers to jump.

The moment of truth had arrived. The pathfinders were trained, in their planes with all their equipment, flying over France, and ready to jump. Although the three 508th pathfinder planes received fire from antiaircraft weapons, according to Lt. Bob Weaver, his pilot managed to get his C-47 over the right place at a proper altitude and speed for safe parachuting. The green light flashed on. At the command "Go!" only one thing was on the pathfinders' minds—get out of the plane and on the ground and perform their assigned tasks.

Once the paratroopers began to exit the planes, the German gunners concentrated their fire on the descending paratroopers. It didn't take Weaver long to hit the ground. The next job was getting out his parachute harness before Germans on the ground discovered him. Weaver felt that it took him much too long to get out of his chute, get his pistol in hand, and be ready for action.

Some of Weaver's men were separated from him by a road covered with German machine gun fire. He was able to use only part of his team and only a few lights, not enough to show the *T* configuration. He tested the lights, cut them off, and waited until the sounds of the approaching airplanes were loud enough to be close. Then he turned on the lights to signal the planes to drop their paratroopers. Several planes flew over without dropping their troops. Finally, one plane flew over and dropped the first man right on top of him. About six planes dropped troops close but to the north in the area of the active German machine guns. Bob Weaver wrote, "That section was full of flares, and we thought a word but dropped our heads and prayed a quick prayer."

Weaver's pathfinders left their lights on thirty minutes longer than required and then moved to set up defensive positions. About three hundred troopers made their way to Hill 30 by June 7.

Third Battalion pathfinders: (1) Lt. Gene Williams, (2) PFC Warren Jeffers, (3) T/5 Francis Lamoureux, (4) PFC Charles Rogers, (5) Pvt. Hal Murdock, 504th, (6) Pvt. Eric Scott, (7) Cpl. Charles Calvert, (8) Pvt. Cicero Parchman, (9) Sgt. Robert Bardeaux, (10) Lt. Edvard Czepinsky, (11) PFC John Sternesky, (12) Pvt. Henry Pawlings, (13) Pvt. John Baldassar, (14) Pvt. John Rigapoulos, (15) PFC Arnolds Martin, (16) PFC Fayette Richardson, (17) PFC Walter Harrelson, and (18) Pvt. Ralph Nicholson. Aircrew: (19) Cpl. Delbert Hoffman, (20) SSgt. Harold Barr, (21) Lt. Charles Gunn, (22) Lt. Lionel Wood, (23) Cpl. Joe Comacho, and (24) Pvt. Roscoe Walker. Photo furnished by James Allardyce.

## Pathfinder Private First Class Paul Demciak

Paul Demciak, a B Company medic, was a member of Lt. Bob Weaver's team of pathfinders. Demciak said, "I was on the ground about one hour trying to find my group. No luck."

Demciak did find a mixture of 101st and 82nd troopers, all strangers to him. Over the next day he applied his medical skills and patched up a number of wounded paratroopers, including himself. He was hit in the back by a German grenade at about 2:30 PM and by another grenade in the left thigh at about 6:20 PM on June 6. Then about a half an hour later, he was captured with about fifteen other wounded Americans.

On June 7, Demciak was loaded on a truck with American and English POWs (prisoners of war). Paul was hit in his right shoulder with a .50-caliber slug from an American P-47 airplane that was firing on the German trucks. Eventually, Paul Demciak was taken to a German hospital in Rennes, where German doctors removed the shrapnel from his back and cleaned out the wound in his shoulder. Then he was moved to a POW camp near Rennes.

As American troops advanced toward Rennes, the Germans evacuated the POW camp. The Nazis loaded the POWs into boxcars, seventy to a car with one five-gallon bucket per car for toilet facilities. American P-47s strafed the train, and Demciak's right arm was hit and the bone was crushed.

Paul said, "I was a POW for three months and lost sixty pounds."

While a POW, maggots got into one of his wounds. He had learned as a medic that maggots were helpful in eating out rotting flesh, so he let them do their good work and saved his arm from gangrene and amputation.

Demciak said, "Around the sixth of September '44, French underground and English military intelligence, with the aid of American OSS, helped me escaped from Toulouse, France, to Naples, Italy."

It took Paul Demciak a year and a half in American army hospitals before he was completely healed from his wounds, including a bone graft for his right arm.

## D-Day Confusion

The Allied invasion of Normandy, France, June 6, 1944, was the most massive military assault in modern history. According to the Allies' plans, about six hours before the land troops were to hit the beaches, paratroopers were to descend eight to ten miles inland during the dead of night. Airborne troops were to prevent the enemy from reinforcing their coastal divisions. The Eighty-second Airborne was assigned an area to the rear of

Utah Beach near Ste. Mere Eglise. Specifically, the 508th was responsible for an area north of the Douve River and the task of destroying the Douve River bridges at Etienville and Beuzeville la Bastille.

The 508th DZ was between the Merderet and the Douve rivers. However, Allied intelligence did not know that the Douve and the Merderet were flooded. In the aerial photographs, the marshes looked like the other fields of the Normandy countryside. Many paratroopers and much equipment were lost in the floodwaters on D-Day.

In order to allow the paratroopers to land close together and assemble easily, the C-47s planned to fly in a tight formation, low and slowly over the DZ. However, as they approached the DZ, a thick cloud enveloped the airplanes, causing them to scatter blindly. Also the heavy antiaircraft fire discouraged the pilots from flying at the desired altitude and speed. As a result, the 508th Red Devils were scattered from the beach to forty miles inland and mixed among troops of other organizations. It was six days before the regiment was able to assemble together as a functioning unit. Those first days in Normandy are among the most vivid in the memories of the 508th troopers.

A clipping from the *Devil's Digest*, a regimental newspaper published several times on an irregular basis, records the landing of 1SG Leonard Funk of C Company and illustrates how far the troops were scattered. Funk is the most highly decorated soldier in the Eighty-second Airborne Division. The article describing Funk's appearance stated the following:

> Small, five feet four inches in height; compact, 140 pounds; his appearance is anything but that of the swaggering trooper so often detailed in fact and fiction. Among the men of his company he is more frequently referred to as 'Napoleon.'

In Normandy he landed nearly forty miles inland but successfully waged a ten-day campaign of terror and destruction before breaking through to rejoin the regiment. Funk's leadership was such that no one in his small unit was lost.

Leonard Funk added a few details of his account:

> Not knowing where we were, I took French-speaking Sgt. Andrew Loewi to a nearby house to ask directions. After we came to the first road sign, we realized we had been misled. I told Sergeant Loewi at the second French house, "Tell them, 'If you give us wrong information, we will come back after you!'"

This time the Normans showed us correctly where we were on our map. We made it with about thirty-five men to the US Ninetieth Infantry Division. Those troops didn't know anything about any paratroopers. I demanded to talk to their commanding officer. They phoned their CO, and he sent a truck to take us to the 508th.

Roy Henderson, who was with Funk's group, wrote to his wife on June 21, 1944. Below is an excerpt from his letter:

> We hid out in ditches during the day and traveled at night. The third day we ran out of food, but on the fourth day we happened to find an old Frenchman, who gave us a little bread and milk. A Nazi captain stumbled on our position and we had to shoot him. After a few encounters and I might say darn close, we ran across our own forces at 5 o'clock one morning, ten days after D-Day. We were so glad to see a doughboy; we almost kissed him on the spot.

Another example of how troops were mixed in their parachute landings was cited by Orin Dreisbach, who trained with I Company of the 508th. Orin broke his collarbone in a training jump just before the Red Devils shipped out of Camp Mackall.

When sufficiently healed and sent overseas, Dreisbach was assigned to the 507th regiment and jumped with the 507th on D-Day. To Orin Dreisbach's surprise, his first contacts in Normandy were some of his old buddies from I Company of the 508th, namely his old platoon sergeant, Sgt. Jack Skipper, and James "Mouse" Cochenour. Dreisbach reported, "I was a happy paratrooper when I saw those familiar troops."

Jack Skipper, who is six inches shorter and fifty pounds lighter than Orin Dreisbach, announced to a group of Red Devils at a reunion, "I had to whip Orin's butt once a week to make a soldier out of him."

Bill Dean of B Company explains the D-Day confusion. "Many of the actions and battles were fought by groups of troopers who not only did not know each other and had never trained together and, furthermore, did not know the officers leading them!"

The following stories describe the 508th Red Devils' first few days in Normandy as they struggled alone or in groups of various sizes. The largest group assembled on Hill 30 and eventually grew to over three hundred paratroopers. This chapter describes the most organized of these confused groups.

# 508th Area of Operations in Normandy

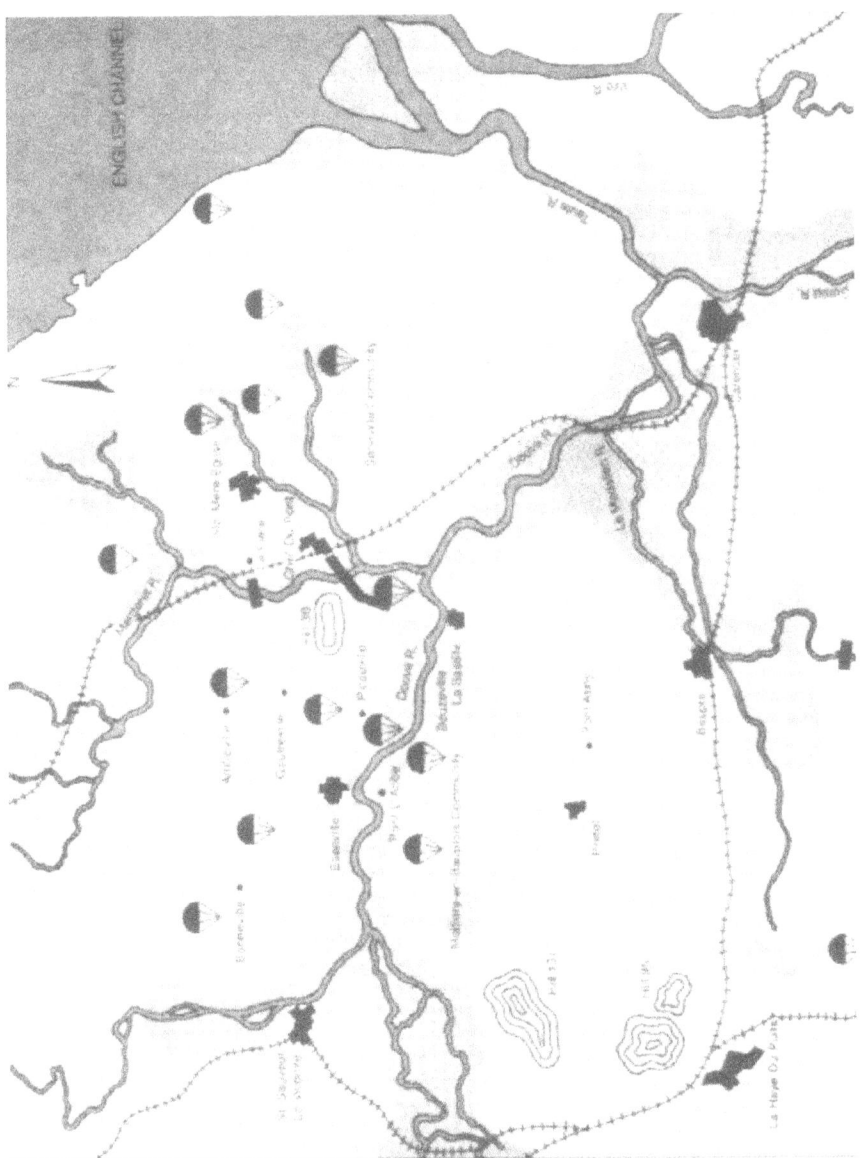

Map by Derek Lawson

## La Fiere Manoir

Life for the Leroux family, who lived in La Fiere Manoir, changed abruptly on June 6, 1944. Monsieur Leroux had worked hard the day before the paratroopers invaded Normandy and slept soundly all night. Madame Leroux heard the noise of C-47 airplanes overhead and the sounds of the German antiaircraft guns firing during the night but remained in bed. At daylight, Madame Leroux saw a paratrooper drop by parachute just outside her bedroom window. The paratrooper quickly moved away. The Germans came about five or six o'clock in the morning. They searched all the building and barns for American paratroopers. (Source: Thiery Ferey, Leroux's grandson's letter on February 26, 2002.)

Dr. John "Doc" Hardie, who was Sgt. John Hardie, C Company mortar man at the time, stumbled across the La Fiere Manoir at about 3:00 AM on D-Day but did not know where he was. Years later, Jim Blue showed Hardie a picture of La Fiere Manoir, which he recognized immediately as the farmhouse with an attached silolike structure he had seen so early on June 6, 1944. In Doc's words, "He showed me a picture which sent a chill down my spine, for it was the scene fixed in my mind on that early D-Day morning."

Doc Hardie continued his account:

> I approached that farm, barn, and silo, coming at it down a slightly sloping farm field toward a gate in the hedgerow adjacent to the silo. Strey (John Strey, a member of Hardie's mortar squad) and I went into the farmyard through that gate. It was all quiet there, but there was almost continuous gunfire going on in all directions, none of which was aimed at us. We moved through the yard to a second gate leading out to a road, which we had paralleled in our route of approach along the hedgerow. We pulled back into the yard, and I went up and knocked on the door of the farmhouse. (Was I naively stupid or what?) Nothing happened.

Not being able to arouse the occupants of the house, Hardie and Strey moved away from La Fiere Manoir and sometime later met a French girl who guided them away from "les bouches" (Germans) and led them to a collection of about thirty paratroopers from different units.

Jim Blue, A Company, had landed in the floodwaters of the Merderet. Blue pulled himself out of the marsh and assembled with a small group on the high ground of the railroad track near La Fiere. Traveling along the tracks, the group picked up several troopers with one officer, Lieutenant Hager from C Company. Lieutenant Hager designated Private First Class Blue to be his assistant. Soon they met and joined a small number of 507th paratroopers commanded by Capt. Ben Schwartzwalder (a postwar football coach at Syracuse University). The combined group of 507th and 508th men approached the La Fiere Manoir.

Schwartzwalder requested Lieutenant Hager's squad to lay down a base of covering fire so that he could deploy his 507th men to the west, behind the barns, and prepare to assault the manoir from that direction. Hager placed his squad behind a high mound with a commanding view of the tower side of the manoir. German sharpshooters were firing from the tower windows. Jim Blue recalls the heavy fire that the 508th squad concentrated on the windows of the house and tower. This was the first known action of 508th troopers in the battle for La Fiere Manoir.

Bill Howard of B Company in Hager's squad had a grenade launcher attached to his M-1 rifle. Jim Blue recalled that Howard fired a grenade into one of the manoir windows. After the grenade exploded inside the house, the Germans hung a white flag out a window.

An officer suggested to Jim Blue that he should approach the manoir and receive the surrender flag from the Germans. Blue argued that it would be wiser to let the Germans come out and bring the flag to them. As it turned out, the Germans, with weapons ready to fire, waited for the paratroopers to move.

Soon after Hager's squad began firing at the manoir, Lt. Homer Jones of B Company joined in the fight. Captain Taylor, CO (commanding officer) of B Company, assembled forty-two men southwest of Ste. Mere Eglise. Due to a severe foot injury sustained in his jump, Taylor checked into an aid station operated by the 505th at Ste. Mere Eglise. Captain Taylor then turned his command over to Lt. Homer Jones. Jones led the company westward on the road toward Etienville and en route met Colonel Lindquist, 508th Regimental CO.

Germans occupied La Fiere Manoir and its outbuildings and prevented the First Battalion of the 505th, north of La Fiere, from securing the Merderet River crossing. Colonel Lindquist had received orders from General Ridgway to send his forces to eliminate the Germans in La Fiere Manoir. Lindquist ordered Jones to take his troops, composed of men from B Company and A Company of the 508th and a few strays from other units, and attack La Fiere Manoir. Jones's group was the second force that arrived to assault the manoir.

Also destined for La Fiere was Lt. George Lamm of A Company who landed among a group of Norman milk cows near the 505th DZ. In Lamm's words, "The cows led me almost mystically to the 505th pathfinder team."

Pathfinder Lt. Mike Chester then guided Lamm to the Eighty-second Division CP (command post), where he met General Ridgway. Ridgway shook hands with Lamm and said, "I've been waiting for you. I have thirty odd 508th troopers, and I want you to take them to La Fiere and report to Colonel Lindquist there. Then help him clear and secure the bridge and causeway."

Ridgway smiled and placed his hand on Lamm's shoulder with the encouraging send-off, "Good hunting, Lieutenant."

Lamm, eager to carry out the direct orders from the highest-ranking officer of the airborne invasion force, gathered his "thirty odd" 508th men and set out for La Fiere. On the way, a paratrooper from a 507th Rifle Company challenged Lamm's group. They were waiting for a 505th unit to clear the area so they could cross the causeway. Soon Lamm's platoon came across a group of ambushed 505th troopers. A number of their dead and wounded were being attended by medics in a small gully. The 505th reported enemy strong points near the manoir and the bridge. Nearing the manoir, Lamm's men were challenged by scouts from Lieutenant Jones's main force as Jones was organizing his attack to clear the area. Here Lamm joined forces with Jones.

Trooper James Q. Kurz of B Company, who advanced to La Fiere with Lieutenant Jones, was impressed by the German marksmanship. Pvt. Bennett Green, who was next to Kurz, was hit in the head and died immediately. The German sharpshooters in the manoir had the advantage of thick stone walls, which easily protected them from the small arms fire of the paratroopers. It seemed to Kurz that the Germans were safe in their fortress and could pick off the paratroopers one by one.

Homer Jones and others described the attack as it developed, which is summarized from several sources:

In a covered position, Jones issued the attack orders to his platoon leaders, Lt. George Lamm and Lt. Kelso Horne of I Company. A small reserve group was left on the high ground where Lieutenant Hager and Jim Blue were.

Horne's platoon was on the left and was to attack to the west to include those buildings in a cluster around the manoir. Lamm was to move on the right through an orchard of small trees, which provided very little cover.

With radioman Bill Dean, point scout John McGuire, and Lieutenant Lamm, Jones led the advance toward the manoir. (Jim Blue remembers seeing the white flag still flying from a second-story window as the point advanced.) When they were about sixty yards away, the Jerries opened fire on the group, killing McGuire with a bullet between the eyes. The other three hit the ground in a vain effort to take cover behind the small apple trees.

Jones lobbed a white phosphorus grenade in front of his group. Under the dense cloud of smoke from the grenade, Lamm, Dean, and Jones returned to the cover of high ground.

Jim Kurz (left) with Yves Poisson, new owner of La Faire Manoir.
Photo furnished by Jim Kurz.

View of La Fiere Manoir from Blue's attack position.
Photo furnished by Jim Blue.

Mickey Nichols remembered, "I was behind one of those little trees firing at the Krauts. Lieutenant Jones sent me back for something. I was gone about two minutes. When I returned, McGuire was lying under the tree I had just left. He was shot between the eyes."

Jones found a sunken road leading to the five buildings in the manoir area. Lamm credits the squad of Lt. Ernie Hager and Jim Blue for keeping heavy fire on the windows and doors of the manoir, effectively suppressing enemy fire, thus allowing the others to advance.

As Jones tossed a fragmentation grenade in the window of a door to an outbuilding, the Germans simultaneously fired a machine gun through the solid part of the door, grazing Jones's knee. (Jones said that he was running very close to the building, so it was easy for him to toss the grenade though the door's window.) Then Jones found a cellar door to the manoir, entered it, and started firing upward through the floor.

Lieutenant Lamm and others had advanced to a fence line. Lamm describes the action at this point:

Lt. Lee Frigo. Photograph copied from 1943 A Company photo

Lt. Ernie Hager joined us and knelt beside me. Hager raised his head to fire, and an enemy bullet hit dead center over the Looie bar on his helmet. Luckily, the round circled his head under his helmet and only tore off some of his ear.

I met up with Lt. Lee Frigo at the same fence. He was interested in finding A Company. However, we broke off talking as the firing increased, and we heard screaming in French from the manoir. Frigo, with a good ear for French, stood up and started replying. He yelled requesting a ceasefire and continued to converse with the French inside. All participants, inside and out, were apparently concerned for the family's safety. So as Frigo expounded in French, there was no indication of the enemy declaring hostages or moving to stop their exit. The quiet continued until the parents and three children were under cover.

One of the children evacuated, who is now Madame Genevieve Leroux Farey, wrote in French, reporting her memories of D-Day. The letter was dated Jan. 1, 2002. Below is a summary of an English translation about the Leroux exit from the manoir during the battle:

On June 6, 1944, I was twelve years old. I lived with my parents, my brother, and my sister in our rented house of La Fiere, in the county of Ste. Mere Eglise.

We (Genevieve and her sister) went to the kitchen, and in a moment two wounded German soldiers entered. One seriously wounded soldier lay down on our chaise lounge. The other was bleeding but less gravely wounded and was helping his comrade.

Later we gathered in a bedroom. The Americans outside fired through the windows. The sounds of the shooting and the bullets ricocheting about the room frightened us little girls. A German soldier said, "You are afraid because you have not seen war like I have."

As the firing increased, we decided to go to the cellar where it would be safer. An American paratrooper shouted in French, "Stay where you are!"

We opened the door, and the paratrooper came and led us (the mother, father, and three children) to the cow barn.

The noise of the battle began again with renewed fury, and Genevieve Leroux was frightened out of her wits. The French-speaking paratrooper told her to hold her nose and open her mouth and the noise would not be as hard on her ears.

Someone outside the manoir yelled to Lieutenant Jones that Colonel Lindquist wanted to talk to him. Jones left the cellar and ran to a barn where the colonel was to get orders and then returned to the Manoir cellar. His orders were brief: "Get the Germans out of that building!"

Jones describes the firing through the floor as a "blind duel." The troopers would shoot up through the floor, and the Germans would fire back down. The paratroopers watched the holes getting close to them and then would jump to another spot to avoid the next volley.

Then-first sergeant Ralph Thomas, E Company, joined Jones in the cellar. Below is a summary of the events that brought Thomas to La Fiere Manoir:

Ralph Thomas landed on the northwest bank of the Mederet River. He rolled up his stick and led them toward some firing he could hear in the distance. Others from the regiment and three strays from the 101st Division joined his group. He arrived at an Eighty-second Division outpost and was questioned by an officer, who asked how many men he had, and Thomas was surprised to learn, after counting, that there were over forty. Many had joined at the rear of the group, unknown to him before the count.

The division officer directed Thomas to take his men and report to Colonel Lindquist at the 508th Regimental CP. Colonel Lindquist added men from his headquarters group to the force led by 1SG Ralph Thomas and moved all of them up the railroad track. After walking a short distant up the track, Lindquist had Thomas deploy the men in a field and wait for his instructions. The colonel then went forward toward the manoir house. Thomas said, "We were in a field joining the La Fiere farm in the direction of Ste. Mere Eglise, which put us behind and north of the outbuildings and behind a low hill making up the manoir property."

1SG Ralph Thomas, who had been waiting for orders from Colonel Lindquist, explained his part in the La Faire fighting:

> After a while, about an hour, a runner came back looking for me. All during this time there was no firing.
>
> The runner took me to Colonel Lindquist, who was in the cow barn directly to the rear of the house—the manoir.
>
> Colonel Lindquist then asked me if I could get in the house by the basement door. I said, "Yes."
>
> Lindquist said, "Fine. There are two lieutenants there, and they have rifles only and can't do anything. With your tommy gun, you can get the Germans out."
>
> I then asked the colonel, "How many Germans are in the house?"
>
> The colonel replied, "Ten or twelve at the most."
>
> I ran into the house via the cellar door. The two officers were standing against the wall that formed the front of the house. One of them told me to give him my gun, but I refused, telling him that Lindquist asked me to go in and get the Germans out.
>
> I fired through the floor at the Germans as they ran back and forth across the house. When needed, I went back to the barn four or five times for more ammunition, and each time the Germans fired at me between the manoir and the barn. Colonel Lindquist collected ammo for me from other soldiers for each trip I made to the manoir.
>
> When the Germans waved the white flag, they pitched out a dead German through the front window. I remember him bouncing when he hit the ground.

Then the Germans walked out the front door and down the steps. The first six or so Germans were not hurt. The next one was nude. He had taken off his uniform. One round had castrated him and left him in a terrible condition. As he walked by me, he broke ranks and gave me a big hug. Colonel Lindquist and I stood and watched them come toward us. All the rest, as they went by me, reached out and touched me. Colonel Lindquist said, "Thomas, they must love you."

We both laughed.

Madame Genevieve Feray, the twelve-year-old Leroux child at the time, recalled that the German soldier who was wounded in the testicles later was seen wearing her father's clothes.

Lt. Kelso Horne of I Company related his memoirs about La Fiere to Perry Knight in *Conversations with Kelso* (Perry Knight has given permission to use his material). Soon after landing between the Merderet River and the railroad track, Kelso Horne met up with General Ridgway and General Gavin. The generals sent Horne along with George Lamm to find Colonel Lindquist and assist him at the La Fiere Manoir. In Lamm's account, they joined Jones's force as Jones was about to attack the manoir.

Lieutenant Horne was sent with his platoon around the west side of the manoir. Kelso Horne explained that he saw Colonel Lindquist on a high bank above a sunken road near the manoir. He then reported to Lindquist for further orders. Kelso said that he and a sergeant were ordered to get in the downstairs part of the house (the cellar) and clean it out. Perry Knight recorded the following description of Horne and the sergeant:

> And while the rest of the men were firing at the upstairs window from behind the embankment, this sergeant and I went into the house and he ran through the first floor shooting his Thompson submachine gun up through the ceiling. Then the Germans started hollering "Kamarad, kamarad!" and hanging sheets or pillowcases out of the windows.

Lieutenant Jones remembered a sergeant entering the basement with his tommy gun, using his weapon very aggressively. Jones never learned the sergeant's name. He never saw the sergeant before or after that day, but he gave the sergeant credit for adding considerable firepower to their efforts in the basement. Jones reported that the sergeant kicked down the door to a locked room, threw in a grenade, and then entered. They discovered that the battle had "liberated Calvados" from large casks. The golden liquid spewed freely from fresh bullet holes.

Someone shouted from outside that the Germans had surrendered. They had hung a tattered white sheet out of a window. On the main floor, the GIs found eight dead and seventeen who had surrendered. Jones remembered that among the wounded, "The one that was hit in the testicles had a real sheepish expression."

Lamm recalled the scene that met his eyes as he entered the second floor:

> The room seemed full of bleeding and moaning soldiers, some on benches and tables. Some were pulling off trousers to attend to wounds. Several were on the floor with heads covered by blankets. Those not engaged in assisting a buddy held their weapons at the ready, watching us. Troopers from B Company herded those apart and took their arms.
>
> An NCO (noncommissioned officer) found an attic or hidden room. I followed, and suddenly there was loud shouting and a muffled roar. When I arrived, a bloody encounter was in progress. Apparently the ceasefire and surrender order had not been passed on or had been ignored. Troopers prodded POWs along with bayonets and pulled several Germans out of hiding places.

Bob Broderick from F Company was at La Fiere. He reported that after the surrender an officer saw his sergeant stripes and asked him to get some men to remove the dead and wounded Germans from the manoir so the French family could move back in. Broderick saw a couple of privates whom he knew and passed the order on to them. Broderick saw first one German body tossed out of the window and then the second. One of the privates sent to remove the bodies stuck his head out of the window and smiled at Broderick as if to say, "How am I doing, Sergeant?"

The officer who gave the order in the first place saw the bodies flung out of the window and ordered Broderick to have his men remove the bodies in a more dignified manner.

After the surrender, Thomas was told that the family that lived in the house wanted to meet him. Thomas remembered, "I met the Lerouxes on the front steps—the parents, two daughters, and a son. They thanked me in French and I thanked them in English. They were very shaken and frightened."

Ralph Thomas returned to Normandy and met the Leroux family again. Monsieur Leroux had died. Thomas keeps in touch with the family and talks often with Mrs. Leroux by phone.

After the war, Madge and Lee Frigo visited Normandy and met the Leroux family. The family expressed tremendous gratitude to the Frigos and called them "liberators." (It was Madge Frigo who urged the author to interview those who fought at La Fiere and write about the battle to honor her late husband.)

James Blue, from the high mound behind the manoir, observed men from the waiting 505th unit break through a hedgerow from the east as the battle ended.

Elements from three regiments of the Eighty-second Division participated in uncoordinated attacks on the La Fiere Manoir complex: the 505th, the 507th, and the 508th. Several reports of the battle have been published from different points of view. This account is compiled from the testimonies of paratroopers of the 508th, who shared their experiences with the author.

## Grandma in the Wheelbarrow

In addition to the Leroux family, Jim Blue remembered seeing a man pushing a wheelbarrow with an old woman riding in it. They were on the grounds of La Fiere Manoir. Blue said the woman reminded him of a

North Carolina granny. At the time, the Germans had already surrendered and Lt. Lee Frigo was talking to the couple.

Madame Cecil Flamand Gancel wrote a letter to James Blue in 1997. She had read *June 6 at Dawn* by Davis Howarth. Howarth quoted James Blue as having seen a woman being pushed in a wheelbarrow at La Fiere who reminded him of a grandmother from North Carolina.

Writing in French, Madame Gancel wanted to thank James Blue and the other paratroopers who helped rescue her family. She included an article describing the experiences of the family on the night of June 5, 1944, and the following days. The article had been published in a French newspaper. The Reverend Tom Holroyd of Pickens, South Carolina, has translated the article into English. Some of the events are described in the following abridged translation:

> Madame Gancel, Cecile Flamand, my name as a young girl, lived near the stud horse farm near Ste. Mere Eglise. I was going to celebrate my eleventh birthday on June 13. What a birthday!
> 
> The Germans who lived among the grooms had commandeered the horse farm. Therefore our family lived with a constant inconvenient heavy military presence.
> 
> In the small Flamand House, we had welcomed our grandmother Alix from Carquebut, who had come after having surgery. [Jean Flamand reported that his grandmother's leg had been operated on.] That made 5 of us in the house. We family looked more and more for liberation.
> 
> The bombardment of the coastal defenses that had taken place every night seemed to indicate that something was going to happen. (Each night I was terrified.) The evening of June 5 gave me an upset stomach.
> 
> We were all assembled near the fireplace close to each other. Grandmother was sleeping in the same room.
> 
> Suddenly the alarm sounded.
> 
> It was the noise of airplanes flying low, becoming deafening.
> 
> My father opened the door to see what was happening, looking into the air, dumbfounded.
> 
> "What's happening?" asked Mama.
> 
> He did not answer. Mama went out to take a look and cried, "It is the invasion. The Tommies have arrived."
> 
> My brother Jean and I remained silent during the spectacle of the hundreds of airplanes, giant bursts in the luminous night sky. The parachutes! We saw them jump from the airplanes. Incredible!

# The 508th Connection

The Germans fired upon the men suspended in their parachutes.

Mama made us go back in the house. We watched from a small window, and each in his turn watched the field as the soldiers removed their parachutes and crawled away toward the hedges.

Suddenly, a violent blow struck our door. It opens under the impact. The man did not have the helmet we expected.

"American," he said. "This is the invasion. Come help. My colonel is wounded." But this was impossible.

Suddenly, a loud noise, a violent blast made the house tremble, the ceiling exploded, and the rubble fell over us. No one was wounded. The ceiling of the small house was on the ground.

We went out of the house to lock ourselves in the wine cellar where the grooms had found shelter. My father carried my grandmother there.

In the stable the horses were neighing and kicking against the walls. "The stable is burning!"

My father hastened to leave. Outside the bullets whistled. The kicks and neighing of the horses stopped.

The incendiary ammunition fell everywhere. The door of our refuge opened and a paratrooper made a sign to come out.

What to do with Grandmother Alix? Papa put her in a wheelbarrow. Mama put a pillow behind her head. We took bags and suitcases and left single file, in all 32 people. The last in line held a white cloth.

Grandmere Alix de Carquebut.
Photo furnished by
Madame Gancel.

In the ditches, the Americans, with faces blackened, showed us the way by gestures. The ground was mined. It was necessary to look where we stepped. Because of strenuous conditions, and the fact that the ground was marked by hoof prints, it was hard for poor Grandmother in her wheelbarrow.

On the paths, it was also necessary to avoid the bodies on the ground, the bodies of a German above all. I saw the eye glazed and a gaping chest wound of the dead. This image still remains with me,

After a night on the straw in an unoccupied house in the village of Coquerie, the Flamand family continued to flee. The objective was Grandmother Alix's house at Carquebut. When we arrived, the people were surprised to see us covered in coal dust and hay. We were surprised to see the calm that prevailed at Carquebut. We had escaped the hell of battle.

Life got organized at Grandmother's house. She had found her bed again.

Cecile Flamand Gancel and Jean Flamand in front of the home, which they fled from on D-Day. Photo provided by Madame Cecile Flamand Gancel.

## Another Grandmother in a Wheelbarrow

When the Flamand family compared their route to Carquebut with the place where Jim Blue saw the "granny in the wheelbarrow," they realized that their travels had not crossed paths with Jim Blue on June 6, 1944. That led them to look for another person who traveled via wheelbarrow on D-Day. They discovered the story of Grandmere Cuquemelle.

According to Gillis Bre of Paris, France, Madame Cuquemelle lived close to La Fiere Manoir. German artillery fire from across the Mederet River set Madame Cuquemelle's house on fire. American paratroopers rescued her from the flames and, because she was unable to walk, moved her away from the burning building in a wheelbarrow. Julien Cuquemelle soon came to the aid of his *grandmere* and rolled her to the railroad-track embankment.

After the American paratroopers secured the La Fiere Manoir, Colonel Lindquist ordered 1SG Ralph Thomas to have his men dig in behind the railroad embankment. While Thomas was placing his men, he remembered the following encounter:

> A man pushing a wheelbarrow, with an elderly woman riding in the wheelbarrow, came up to me and asked what to do and where to go. I showed him the opposite bank of the railroad and told him to dig in and turn right or left and make a large room. I gave him a shovel.
>
> After placing the men in a defensive position, I went back to check on his digging. He had done a good job. He had a chair and was sitting in the doorway to his cave. The cave was shaped liked the drawing below:

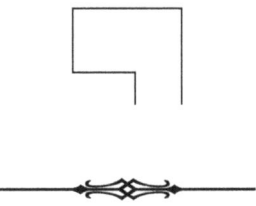

Gillis Bre reported that because the shelling and fighting continued at La Fiere, Julein Cuquemelle soon moved his *grandmere* Cuquemelle about four miles from La Fiere, where there was no fighting.

## Swimming the Merderet

As it turned out, 13 was a lucky number for Jim Kurz of B Company, considering numbers 11, 12, and 14 in his stick each had broken a leg on their D-Day landings.

Kurz jumped in the same stick with Lt. Homer Jones, who was number 1 and jumpmaster. When the green jump light went on, the lieutenant yelled to his men, "We are over water!" After a brief delay, he led his stick out of the plane. Kurz gives Jones credit for saving his men from landing in the river and swamp by that short delay.

Kurz said he hit the trees as soon as his chute opened. The plane was flying very close to the ground as the last few men jumped. When Jim Kurz cut himself free from his chute, he fell two feet into a bunch of stickers, a safe although prickly landing.

The first man Kurz found was Pvt. Arthur Wolfe, who had a broken leg. Jim promised Wolfe to locate a medic and get back to him. Kurz then joined Lieutenant Jones and the others assembled against a hedgerow. On returning with a medic to Wolfe, Jim discovered Cpl. William Theis and one other trooper, both with broken legs. "I am sure the tree saved me from suffering the same fate," declared Jim Kurz.

The three men with broken legs were helped to a nearby hedgerow and placed in a ditch where they waited for evacuation at a later time. Jones then led the remaining able-bodied squad members to link up with their company.

By daylight on June 6, about seventy paratroopers had assembled in a group that included Jim Kurz and Bill Dean. They participated in the attack on La Fiere Manoir, with the surrender of the manoir taking place about 1430 hours.

At La Fiere Manoir, Bill Dean was beside lead scout McGuire as McGuire dropped dead with a bullet in his brain. Following the battle, Dean consumed a hasty, distasteful K ration in the presence of seven or eight dead Germans.

After the La Fiere victory, Lieutenant Jones, temporary commander of B Company, and the other aggregation of troops with him prepared to lead his forces across the flooded Merderet to join the rest of the 508th. As the point scout, Jim Kurz waded through the swamp to the river. He waded until the river was deeper than his height of six feet, two inches. From out in the river, Jim saw a bridge to his right, which Lieutenant Jones elected to use. The troopers crossed the Merderet Bridge and causeway safely without encountering enemy fire.

After advancing about six hundred yards, the Red Devils spread out and were preparing to dig in behind a hedgerow when tanks, rifles, mortars, and machine guns suddenly hit them all at once.

The paratroopers were armed only with small weapons. They were not dug in, only protected by the hedgerow in front of them. When the tanks came around the hedgerow and started firing from their flank and blocked a return across the bridge, Lieutenant Jones yelled, "Every man for himself!"

"We were sitting ducks on a pond! Each of us had to make an instant decision," reports Bill Dean. "When the tank machine guns opened fire, Lefty Brewer and I broke for the water. An instant later Brewer, my old Camp Blanding platoon sergeant, lay face down in the water—dead."

This is how Dean describes his retreat across the Merderet:

> I swam the river porpoise style (under and up, under and up), during which I lost all of my gear. I emerged on the other side breathless and found I still had a ten-foot bank to get over. It would be difficult to forget that experience because it was not like being fired upon in a group. In this case they had me isolated, and every slug of lead I heard was aimed at me. When I finally rolled over and behind the lip of the bank, I lay there with water running out of my boots and leg pockets and my chest heaving until my breathing calmed down to near normal.

When Jones shouted, "Every man for himself!" Jim Kurz and a 506th trooper headed for the marsh and found a ditch leading into the river. As they crawled down the ditch, the combined fire from enemy tanks, mortars, and small arms whizzed over their heads into the marsh ahead of them. Rather than continue on toward the river through the area of concentrated fire, the 506th trooper decided to surrender. He fixed something white to his rifle and stood up with his hands raised. The Germans didn't honor the white flag. The surrendering trooper only made a better target for the Nazi marksmen, and the trooper was killed instantly.

Kurz continued down the ditch to the river where about ten men were gathered, mostly from 508th B Company. Jeff Alfonso was in this group. Jeff said, "The river is too deep and swift."

But Kurz replied, "I'm going to swim across."

Kurz started swimming with helmet and rifle, which he soon abandoned in order to keep his head above water. Almost to the other side, he turned back to aid another who was following and about to go under. Kurz, John Taylor, and a third man made the return to the eastside of the Merderet. The three of them improvised with a rope from parachute lines, throwing one end of the rope to the west side so the other seven men could cross holding the rope.

Safely across the Merderet, Kurz and his party joined a mortar squad from the 505th. By this time it was about 1900 hours—still D-Day. After dark, the mortar squad moved to a new position, with Kurz carrying the mortar tube. He then rolled up in an abandoned parachute and went to sleep ending his first day of combat as a member of a 505th mortar squad.

Meanwhile Bill Dean had recovered from his swim and headed north, thinking he was the only one from his group on the east side of the river. He stumbled upon a makeshift aid station, where medics were attending to about twenty wounded paratroopers. Dean refitted himself with weapons and other gear discarded by the wounded. Then he went back to the La Fiere Bridge, where he safely crossed to the west side during the night and finally the next morning found Colonel Shanley's group on Hill 30.

Left: Bill Dean, Frankfurt Germany, 1945.
Right: Bill Dean, 1999. Photo by Dan Lewis.
Photos provided by Bill Dean.

## Hill 30

The planned drop zone of the 508th was between the Merderet and Douve rivers. However, the sudden cloud cover and the intense antiaircraft fire caused the C-47s to deviate from their formations. The

508th paratroopers landed over a wide area, many in the floodwaters of the Merderet and the Douve and others even farther from their planned DZ. Colonel Lindquist, the 508th CO, missed the DZ and landed west of the Merderet. By radio contact Lindquist ordered Maj. Tom Shanley, Headquarters Second Battalion, and Maj. Shields Warren, Headquarters First Battalion, and other officers west of the Merderet to gather together on Hill 30 directly across the river from the regimental CP at Chef du Pont. This story tells how the paratroopers fought their way to Hill 30 and how they survived for five days until relief arrived.

Chet Graham was called Apple Cheeks because of his rosy complexion. Capt. Chester Graham, Headquarters Second, landed in an apple tree near Hill 30, fairly close to an enemy antiaircraft gun crew. Chet said, "I could hear them talk and smell their cigars but was careful not to disturb them."

During the night, Graham was able to link up with a few troopers. At the first light, Chet was trying unsuccessfully to locate his position on his maps when a young lad come out of a house and said, "Bonjour, monsieur!"

Chet replied, "Bonjour, mon jeune fil. S'il vous plait, j'ai ici, ici, ou ici?" He pointed to places on his map.

"Non, monsieur. Vous etes ici." The lad pointed to their exact location.

This enabled Captain Graham to orient himself and find correct coordinates on his map.

Some time later, a runner came with a message that Maj. Shields Warren and his men were pinned down in a creek nearby. Graham took about six men and attacked the opposing force of Germans from a different direction. The Germans turned their fire on Graham and his men, thus allowing Warren to move away from the creek and make a detour by a safer route.

Graham withdrew from the superior German group, but mortar fire followed him up the road. Surveying the landscape, Graham concluded that the church steeple in nearby Amfreville was the observation point for the German mortar crew.

With the help of an SCR radio, Graham heard talking and perceived it was friendly forces, so he requested supporting fire. He was instructed to give the coordinates and correct fire after each round. After two rounds with Graham's corrections, the third round knocked the top off the steeple, and the German mortar fire ceased.

When Graham reported "Mission accomplished," he asked, "Whom am I talking to?"

"The US battleship *Nevada*," was the reply. "We were firing 14-inch guns."

Louis Guzzetti, D Company, was one of the troopers whose parachute dropped somewhere between the Douve and the Merderet. As Louis landed in the darkness, he could hear the chatter of German machine guns and see the tracers streaking in the night sky toward the C-47s and descending paratroopers. His first move, after getting free from his chute, was away from the threatening machine gun.

Soon Guzzetti found Froelich of D Company. The two worked their way through hedgerows looking for friendly troops while avoiding the enemy. They heard the screams of a badly wounded paratrooper. When they found him, he asked to be shot and put out of his misery. Guzzetti shot the trooper with morphine, providing temporary rather than permanent relief.

A glider crashed in a field near Guzzetti and Froelich. Immediately, German machine guns riddled the glider with devastating fire. The screams of the trapped glider men could be heard above the noise of the machine guns.

The two lone troopers found a sergeant with five men. Then they linked up with Maj. Shields Warren with about twenty men. Warren assigned Guzzetti as a runner and sent him to search for others. Guzzetti located Colonel Shanley with about 150 men. Colonel Shanley then led the combined groups to Hill 30.

Bill McClure of D Company told his story:

As soon as my chute opened, I hit a tree and broke a rib and was about knocked out. I rolled into a ditch, and my chute settled on a stump. A German machine gunner shot the stump to bits. I guess it looked like the chute came down on top of me.

It was a very bright night when the moon shone through the clouds, but every time the moon went behind a cloud, I would inch backward. It took me about an hour to get out of that field. Later I wiped out the machine gun nest with my rifle and a Gammon grenade. I got away with only a hole in my canteen.

Bill McClure, Frank Staples in the rear. Photo by Frank Staples.

Billy McClure linked up with a group under the command of Lt. Norman MacVicar, E Company. MacVicar's men joined Shanley on Hill 30 after dark on D+1. By this time, the Shanley group had accumulated several hundred men and had set up defensive positions all around the hill. McClure describes an event that stuck in his memory:

> One day, when the Germans shelled us with airbursts, Paul Webb next to me was hit in the face, and I was hit in the hand and under the arm. The shrapnel went into the side of Paul's face and came out of his mouth. It took a lot of his teeth and part of his lips. His mutilated gums made him look like his brains were hanging off his chin. He could hear and understand me but could not talk.
> A trench was dug in the center of the encircled hill for the wounded. I started carrying Webb to the trench, about 150 yards away and behind a fence. We had to hit the ground several times during airbursts. When we got to the fence, I needed help getting Webb over. An officer had his foxhole nearby. I asked him to help, but he wouldn't get out of his hole. I laid my wounded buddy down, unslung my rifle from my shoulder, pointed it at the officer, and said, "I will count to three, if you don't get out of that hole and help, you'll get a bullet right between the eyes." The officer was out at the count of one.

Harold Kulju (a.k.a. Harold Canyon) of Headquarters Second Battalion described his early hours in Normandy:

> I was number 6 in my stick. As I approached the door, the top of the fuselage disappeared and the plane began its death spiral. It took every bit of my strength to get out of the door. I hit the ground about thirty feet from a German bunker already destroyed by a Gammon grenade. I paused for a moment, fully expecting the point of a German bayonet. When nothing happened, I cut myself out of the parachute harness with my trench knife.
> With carbine in one hand and trench knife in the other, I ran to the nearest hedgerow and dove over. Almost immediately two Germans came toward me from the other side of the hedgerow. As they approached, I unscrewed the cap from a Gammon grenade. When the Germans reached me they ducked down. One

rose up, stuck his rifle in my face, and fired. At the same time, I raised my arm and flung the Gammon. I was knocked out.

When I came to, my face was in the ditch and my mouth was open, drooling blood and saliva into the ditch. I could taste the gunpowder and feel the powder burns. I could not move. I was sure I was dead. I wondered how long it would take for my senses to fade. Would I be able to feel the dirt on my face when they bury me? Would I feel the maggots eating away at my body?

I could hear the two Germans moaning and groaning. Then all was quiet, my ears began ringing, and I could move.

Kulju tells of escaping both friendly and enemy fire:

> Two other troopers approached, and while we were talking together, we heard someone else coming. I yelled the challenge "Flash!" and heard the reply "Thunder!" Then a ball of fire! A bullet hit my helmet. I rolled over, and another bullet went through my pants and hip pocket; so much for so-called friendly fire. I began swearing, which was more reliable than a password, since only Americans can swear like Americans.
>
> About daylight, five of us armed with carbines lined up on a road bank. A truck came along with two Jerries on the front seat. One of us threw a Gammon grenade, which hit the windshield dead center. The Germans jumped out and ran up the road away from us. We fired, pointing without aiming, and they got away.
>
> The Jerries, who narrowly escaped our fire, must have warned their CO that at least a battalion of paratroopers were waiting for them down the road, thus causing them to maneuver in behind us for a large-scale attack. We vacated the area. The Germans continued firing long after we were gone.

Kulju's group later came upon Colonel Shanley, who at that time had about thirty men with him. It was reported that some troopers were trapped on an island. A German machine gun covered the opening between the two groups. Kulju borrowed binoculars and located the gun. He then moved around to the side so the German machine gunner would not hit the GIs when returning fire.

"When I fired at the gunner," Kulju reports, "he spotted me right away and clipped the grass one inch above the hedgerow bank. I used up two magazines before putting him out of business. Then the other group joined us, and we moved toward Hill 30 together."

Kulju continues, "We lost a few men on the way to Hill 30, men so exhausted they couldn't continue. Another trooper and I stayed with the crowd until they left us, and then we dropped exhausted. We awoke the next morning within a hundred yards of the perimeter defense."

Kulju was a radio operator without a radio. He was sent on patrol to look for equipment bundles. The patrol found nothing useful. Finally someone repaired a damaged radio and gave it to Kulju. He describes his efforts with the radio:

> I contacted a guy with two men holding a bridge. He informed me he had contact with the regiment. Colonel Shanley instructed me to send them the coordinates for artillery support in the event the message could be relayed to division artillery. The guy on the bridge said he would try. I soon lost contact with him and never found out if the message got through.

Arthur Sanchez, F Company, recalls an incident on Hill 30:

> About fifteen of us were posted on a roadblock, and we heard a German tank approaching. As the tank turned the corner, we recognized Lt. Francis Bolger sitting on top of the turret, so we held our fire. Bolger had found the tank, and he and his men were able to start it and get it working. "All I need now," declared Bolger, "is white stars to cover the black German crosses."
>
> We scrounged some lime in a barn and salt in the farmhouse and mixed it with water to make some whitewash. We applied our mixture with a rag, and when it dried, we had an American tank with white stars. Bolger and his crew then left to hunt some Kraut tanks. He blew up two then disappeared over a hill, and we didn't see him again.

Bill Dean, who managed to get back across the Merderet River and join the Hill 30 troops on D-Day night, participated in a daring attack led by Lt. Woodrow Millsaps of B Company. The Germans had surrounded Hill 30 and were constantly attacking from all directions. The paratroopers needed supplies very badly—ammunition, food, and medical supplies. The Germans were in a position at the foot of the hill, blocking access to the causeway from Chef du Pont. If the German force blocking the causeway were eliminated, a convoy of supplies was promised. Dean describes the action:

> Lieutenant Millsaps volunteered to lead an attack to eradicate the Germans blocking the causeway. He found only seven or eight from his own B Company of which I was one. Millsaps started down the hill with the eight of us and the fifteen strangers he picked up and his second-in-command Lt. Lloyd Polette. It was near midnight.
>
> After proceeding slowly to the base, the road branched to the right and the left with an orchard in between. As we advanced down the left branch, a machine gun opened up, and flares erupted and made day out of night.
>
> We switched to the right side of the orchard and formed a half circle behind a three-foot-high embankment. More machine guns fired at us, and more tracers and flares illuminated the area.
>
> The brilliant light made it difficult for Millsaps and Polette to prod us into action. Then things started happening. I truly believe we were in a state of hypnosis. We were like robots, ignoring the phosphorus and concussion grenades falling around us, killing everything that moved until the last German along the road was dead along with many farm animals caught up in the frenzy.
>
> Lieutenant Millsaps and Sergeant Klinefelter then crossed the causeway to Chef du Pont. Polette was left in command at the farm site.
>
> As dawn neared, Major Shanley withdrew Polette and the rest of us to Hill 30. Shanley decided it was too dangerous for a convoy to travel the causeway. Instead Shanley sent a patrol to wade through the river and to return with blood plasma, the most urgent need on the hill.

Left: Capt. Woodrow Millsaps.
Copied from B Company photo, 1945.
Right: Lt. Lloyd Polette.
Copied from B
Company photo, 1943.

Other troopers relate brief memories about Hill 30:

Frank Haddy, D Company: "Bryant Nelson and I were sent to look for water. We found a big wine barrel and never drank water on Hill 30 after that."

Lou Guzzetti: "I helped carry Bryant Nelson, who was shot through the chest, to the aid station in a long trench. I asked Captain Montgomery, medical detachment, about his chances. 'About 50 percent,' he said. On D+7, Doc Montgomery reported that not one of his wounded had died."

Frank Haddy: "I got a pot of soup from a farmhouse and carried it to Captain Montgomery for the wounded."

Captain George Montgomery said this:

> I set up a hospital in a ditch about 100 yards long by a hedgerow. I treated the injured who needed Mayo Clinic level of care with what I had in my pockets and what I could scrounge. It was my first experience of using a steel helmet as a cooking pot, wash basin, stool, head protector, and bedpan.

Leonard Sacharoff, Headquarters Third: "They sent me to buy eggs because I could speak French. The Norman farmers wouldn't sell me anything, but some streetwise kid with a tommy gun, talking like a Chicago gangster, came back with two hundred eggs."

Francis Lamoureux, G Co.: "On D+4 I was down to nineteen rounds of ammo and feared we would soon be wiped out, so I proceeded to write what I thought was my farewell letter to Hildegarde." (Francis and Hildegarde married after the war.)

Harold Kulju said this:

> On the fifth day, I heard we would either have to attack and wipe out the Germans surrounding us, or it would be every man for himself. Then I heard the most screeching, frightening sounds of my life. It was our division artillery right on target, catching the German artillerymen loading their guns. The same day, the beach forces arrived.

Lou Guzzetti said this:

> I remember when an armored unit from the Ninetieth Division came through Hill 30. They unloaded an ambulance full of food. Lieutenant MacVicar ordered the distribution of

one loaf of bread and a milk can full of stew for every seven men. That stew was the best!

When the paratroopers who had landed east of the Merderet crossed over and joined those on Hill 30, they had a joyous reunion as organized with their regular units.

Jim Kurz described the scene crossing the Merderet: "The first 200 yards, dead soldiers of the 325th Gliders were lying head to foot on both sides of the causeway. Then the next 600 yards there were dead Germans the same way—about 150 dead GIs and about 450 dead Germans."

The Red Devils on Hill 30 held out for five days with limited ammunition, food, medical supplies, and heavy weapons. They fought off tanks, suffered heavy artillery shelling and constant infantry attacks without giving up. They kept many German troops busy who might have otherwise crossed the Merderet to counterattack the Allied beach landings.

Chet "Apple Cheeks" Graham on a trip back to Normandy found the orchard and the tree where he landed on D-Day. The owner came to apprehend the trespasser on his property. After learning that Chet was with the 508th on D-Day, he embraced his "liberator" and they became great friends. When the fateful apple tree was damaged by a storm, the owner, Monsieur Marion Georoes, cut the tree down and sent a section of the trunk to Chet for a souvenir.

In 1998, Chet met Maurice Guillemelle, the lad who helped Graham find his location on his map. He had grown old and was in bed following a stroke. Each remembered and repeated their parts of the dialogue, "Ici, ici, ou ici?" "Non, Monsieur. Vous etes ici."

Chet Graham, copied from 1943 company picture

# CHAPTER 3

## D-Day Confusion of Isolated Paratroopers and Small Groups

### Abraham and Israel

Captain Abraham and PFC Leon "Gismo" Israel of Regimental Headquarters Company, linked by names and ethnic origin to the Biblical Abraham and Israel, flew in the same stick on the night of June 5/6—the eve of D-Day.

Left: Capt. Robert Abraham.
Right: PFC Leon Israel.
Copied from 1943 Company picture.

Leon Israel described his feelings on that historic night. The moon reminded him of a stage spotlight and the paratroopers as restless actors ready and waiting for the command performance. "This is what we have practiced and trained for," Leon mused, "but this is no theatrical act, this is the real thing."

Israel reflected on the general's pep talk to the troops, how he emphasized the importance of the Normandy invasion as if history hung in the balance. In the general's words, "If we fail, all this tremendous effort would be wasted. For us and our generation, we would never know peace."

As they flew over the English Channel, they could see the water below, and the signal light from a sub gave them assurance they were on course. Red and green lights of neighboring planes in the *V* formation also added confidence.

The sea reflected the moonlight, but as they flew over France, the land below looked like a dark blur. Then came the command, "Stand up and hook up!" The plane began to toss and dive. Something that sounded like hail was hitting the plane. As the plane dipped into an air pocket, the troopers' feet left the floor and their heads hit the ceiling.

Captain Abraham explained that just before they reached the drop zone, the planes entered a cloud, which made visibility impossible. The planes began to spread out to keep from hitting each other. Then the clouds opened up again, and they learned that they had overshot the drop zone.

The contingency plan, in case the drop zone was missed the first time, was to circle back inland to the right, but the plane was damaged by flack so that it could only turn to the left toward the Normandy beach where most of the enemy antiaircraft guns were concentrated. When they had to jump, the pilot was flying very low and too fast for good jumping conditions. Abe said, "My feet were in the trees almost as soon as the chute opened, and the opening shock was so strong it split the pants of my jumpsuit."

Most of the men from their plane landed near Mountebourg, not far from Cherbourg. Two men in the stick actually landed in Cherbourg. They were captured and held prisoners until the city was liberated.

Gismo remembered seeing a neighbor plane streaking to the earth in a flaming mass just before he jumped. Then in Gismo's words, "I went out of the doorway to hell." After the opening shock came the screaming tracer bullets close to Gismo's head.

Upon landing, Leon said to himself, "Be calm, kid, you have to get out of this chute before the wind takes you for a ride." After some struggle with the chute, he freed himself, and seeing the blue light of the equipment bundle, he started crawling across the moonlit field toward the light.

Suddenly, without warning, someone shouted, "Flash!"

It was the password, but Gismo couldn't remember the countersign, so he whispered, "Don't shoot! It's me, Izzy!"

The answer came back, "Whew—thank God! Come help me out of this mess." It was Reuben Weiner, the divisional photographer who was all tangled up in his photographic equipment.

Gismo freed Weiner from his entanglement, and the two of them crawled toward the blue light. As the two men neared the light, they could see several figures huddled against a wall. Crawling up a little closer, they called out "Flash!" and received the countersign much to their relief.

Fourteen men from the stick assembled together. They needed to move out but did not know where to go. They found a road running north and south, and the fourteen paratroopers started moving cautiously in the northern direction along the road. A six-foot barbed-wire fence bordered the right of the road and beyond the fence a chateau, which, unknown to the paratroopers, was a German stronghold. The chateau may have been full of Germans, but the German guns and vehicles along the road were unmanned.

As the troopers advanced up the unfamiliar road, their senses were straining to detect signs of danger. Israel became aware of a foul odor. It was the stench of death. Then he encountered his first view of death, not German soldiers, but French civilian—two women, three men, and a child sprawled out grotesquely by the side of the road. They were probably victims of the American bombardments.

Israel's naturally sensitive nature revolted at the scene. "My mind went into a protective stupor," Israel explained, as he described his mechanism of surviving and coping with the realities of war.

Upon reaching a crossroad, the squad stopped to consider their choice of march. They decided to wait until daylight. As they waited, a cart with two French farmers approached. The troopers lay unseen in the ditch beside the road as the cart drove by, not knowing if the travelers were friend or foe.

Captain Abraham sent out scouts at daybreak to find out where they were. Meanwhile, the rest stayed low in the ditch for protection against the shells dropping in from US naval ships.

Soon a gun duel developed between the Allied ships at sea and the German 88s on land. The shells were passing both ways over their heads when Israel had an urgent call of nature. He did not want to leave the safety of the ditch, so after begging the captain's pardon, Gismo lowered his pants right where he was. Captain Abe laughed and said, "Damn regular bowel movements."

And so we conclude the saga of the evening and the morning of the first day in the land of Normandy for Abraham and Israel, the captain and the private. Two more days and many narrow escapes later, the fourteen men were able to make their way to the main body of the regiment.

Leon Israel, Heddernheim, Germany, 1945. In 1946 Leon changed his name to Leon Mason. Photo by Zig Boroughs.

## Cemetery Landing

Bill Still. Copied from 1943 Company photo.

Bill Still of the Communications Platoon, Regimental Headquarters Company did not have a soft landing on the night of June 5/6. There was a lot of confusion in the plane the last few minutes before the jump. When they bailed out, the plane was going straight down.

Bill landed in a cemetery. The wind pulled him along so that he knocked down or broke off several tombstones before he was able to collapse his chute. The landing was as rough and bruising to Bill as it was for the cemetery. Although he was badly banged up, Bill said that he was so scared, he didn't think about his injuries at first. His main concern was to find some other troopers and join the company and regiment.

Soon he found Frank Sakowski and Stanley Rompala, two men who jumped in his stick. It made him feel better to have two men he knew to share his fate. They looked for other men from the stick. Over in a nearby field were some lumps that looked like parachutes. The three men crawled over to the lumps that turned out to be cows rather than parachutes. After that unsuccessful effort, they decided to sleep a couple of hours until daylight.

When they woke up, Bill said he began to notice the pain from his battering against the tombstones. They started out to look for friendly troops and ran into some guys from the 505th that they tried to join. They were told by the 505th men to hunt for their own unit.

On one occasion, the three paratroopers were walking beside a hedgerow. They heard a group of men approaching them from the other side of the hedgerow. The helmets of the other group were all they could see over the top of the hedgerow. Bill swears the soldiers on the other side were wearing German helmets, cut down over the ears at the side in the German style. The three American paratroopers looked across the hedge at the German squad, and the Germans looked across at them. The Germans kept going their way on one side of the hedge, and the three American troopers kept moving in the opposite direction on their side, neither group spoiling for a fight.

Bill's leg began to hurt and swell. He used the morphine shot from his first aid pack to kill the pain and kept on walking. When the shot wore off, Rompala gave Bill the morphine from his pack. The next day they met up with Sgt. Jim Smylie, the radio chief, who directed Bill to the aid station that was set up in a schoolhouse.

A German military medical unit was being utilized by the 508th, and Bill was examined and treated by German medics. The battering against the tombstones had fractured his leg and some ribs. Bill said the Germans were dedicated in their tasks of treating his injuries even though he was their enemy. Many of the medical-supply bundles of the 508th were not recovered after the jump, and the use of the overrun German medical unit was very valuable to our troops. Bill had nothing but praise for the German medics and the German doctor who set his broken leg.

After three days of waiting in the cellar of the aid station, Bill Still was evacuated to Utah Beach where he was put on a landing craft and transferred to a hospital ship in the English Channel.

At the 1994 50th D-Day anniversary celebration in Ste. Mere Eglise, Bill Still shouted to me from the rear of a bus as I entered the door, "I have found the place I landed on D-Day. Come with me and I will show you."

The bus was parked beside a cemetery. Bill took me inside the cemetery wall and showed me the tombstones, some of which had been broken and patched. The wall, the tombstones, the surrounding landmarks that Bill had seen on that fateful moonlight night fifty years ago were fixed in his memory. He was positive this was the exact spot of his parachute landing.

## "Had to Call Someone Today"

It was the evening of June 6, 1984. The family was sitting down to the evening meal when the phone rang. Someone wanted to speak to me. It was Fred Knight from Travelers Rest, South Carolina. I had not met Fred although we both served in Headquarters Company of the 508th Parachute Infantry Regiment. Fred had been in the Communication Platoon, and I had been in the Demolition Platoon.

At the company reunion, Harry Hudec had a Nazi swastika, which he had saved from World War II, in the hospitality room. A number of men had signed their names to the banner. When I saw the swastika, his name jumped right out at me: "Fred Knight, Slater, South Carolina." I looked him up on the association roster and found his present address and phone number.

Soon after returning from the reunion, I called Fred. He was not at home, so I left a message with his son. I didn't hear from him until the D-Day fortieth anniversary date, when he said, "I had to call somebody today."

Fred Knight. Copied from 1943 Company picture.

Finger pointing to name and address of Fred Knight on flag. Photo by Zig Boroughs.

The television networks had featured the D-Day invasion of Normandy, showing World War II films of the actual events that occurred on D-Day and the festivities and ceremonies that were happening on the fortieth anniversary. Fred had been watching television all day and wanted to talk to someone who had experienced D-Day as a paratrooper. He was a little disappointed when he learned that I was a D-Day replacement rather than an actual participant, but later I looked him up and heard his story. It went like this:

> I was the number 2 man in the stick, and Steve Schmelick was number 3. Our plane was really catching the antiaircraft fire when we jumped. The sky was ablaze with tracer bullets and night flares when we were going down and after we hit the ground. I pulled my jump knife and started hacking away at my parachute harness to get out as fast as I could. You know we

kept our knives strapped to our legs, and we kept them sharp. I've got a scar on my thigh today where I cut myself getting out of that harness.

As soon as I got out of my chute, I crawled over to help Steve. He was using his knife to cut away his harness, and dammed if he didn't turn his knife on me thinking I was an enemy. He recognized me just in time. Talk about confusion—you felt like saving your own skin and asking questions later. About five of us got together in the field where I landed, and about that time it was getting light. We jumped at 0210, and you know the nights don't last long there in June.

When we could see in the daylight, we moved over toward a road, and there came General Gavin marching down the road, right out in front, leading a group of paratroopers. There were troopers from many different companies, battalions, and regiments. Gavin was just gathering together anyone that had survived the jump. I stayed with Gavin about three days. I don't think I closed my eyes to sleep those first few days and nights.

Gavin led us to a high railroad track, the highest place in the whole area. That was a good place to be. We could control the area from the high ground. Gavin would send out patrols in different directions to contact the enemy. I went on one patrol, and that is the first time I ever dove into a pile of shit. We were behind this hedgerow, and the Germans spotted us and directed their machine gun fire into the hedge, and that's when I hit the drainage ditch that was full of shit. I was a stinking mess for days after that.

Another funny thing happened when the German planes strafed our position. I hit the ground so hard and must have hit my knee on something because it hurt like hell. I just knew I was hit, and I just lay there about half an hour before getting up the nerve to look at the damage. It was just a bruise.

## Prayerful Thoughts

Clarence Christiansen of Regimental Headquarters Company usually went out with other members of the Demolition Platoon to Beeston in the evening, but the night before the 508th left for the airport and the Normandy jump, Chris stayed in Wollaton Park for a quiet evening. He stopped by Louis Laurelli's tent and found him writing a letter to his wife. Chris and Lou had trained together and been in the same platoon for two years but were not close friends. Chris didn't even know Laurelli was married, but that night Chris and Lou shared their thoughts. Lou told Chris that he wanted to get that last letter off to his wife just in case he didn't make it back.

That talk with Lou put Chris in a very serious mood. He began to think, "Maybe I won't come back alive!" His mind went back to Muskegon, Michigan, his boyhood home—to his mother and father, brothers, and sisters. That night he prayed for his family and for the soldiers he had trained with and for their families, knowing that many would not return to home and loved ones.

This prayerful mood continued with Chris to the airport and the preparations for boarding. Like the other demolitionists, Chris, along with Mathew Bellucci, was added to a stick of paratroopers from a line company. Flying over the English Channel, Chris continued to meditate about home and family and to pray.

As the plane approached the French coast, the command "Stand up and hook up" interrupted the somber thoughts. Nineteen paratroopers scrambled to their feet and hooked their parachutes to the static line. As they waited, Chris could feel the cold sweat in the palm of his hands and the nausea rise from the pit of his stomach.

Soon they flew into the fireworks. The Fourth of July was coming a month early as the exploding ack-ack and tracer bullets lit up the June sky. Then the plane was hit. This was no celebration for the Yanks' arrival but rather a rude reception from the Nazi army of occupation. The pilot was having a hard time controlling the plane, and the paratroopers were struggling to stand up and keep their balance. The jump command was yelled: "Get the hell out while you can!" Chris uttered one last prayer as he left the plane, "God be with us."

Chris splashed down into a swamp and quickly removed his parachute and looked around. Someone was moving in his direction. Chris had his rifle ready with his finger on the trigger, ready to shoot, when Bellucci gave the password. It took a long time for Bellucci and Christiansen to get out of the swamp. It wasn't deep where they landed, but as they waded toward shore, it was soon up to their chins. They tried another direction and were soon up to their necks again. They had to try several different directions before they could wade out without going in over their heads.

Chris felt lucky to get out of that swamp alive and to survive Normandy. Chris did get hit on July 3, two days before the 508th pulled out of Normandy but was safely evacuated to a hospital.

Cpl. Louis J. Laurelli did not come back at all.

Chris Christiansen. Photo furnished by Chris Christiansen.

## What Happened to the War?

Steve Uchrin. Copied from 1943 Company photo.

Steve Uchrin and Al Hillman, two demolitionists from Regimental Headquarters Company, were added to the end of a stick of one of the line companies for the Normandy jump. The demolitionists were trained to work as a team. At the last minute, the High Command decided to split them up for Normandy. The way they were thinking, if the demolitionists were all in two or three planes, all might be wiped out and none would be available. If they were split up among many planes, the chances for some to survive and be available were much greater.

Steve and Al felt very much alone in their plane. They didn't know any of the other guys, and they had no time to get acquainted. Anyhow, their faces were all blackened, and even if they had gotten to know them, they would not have been able to recognize anyone.

The troopers had hooked up and ready to jump. The plane started catching a lot of flak, and Al Hillman got hit. Steve tried to get Al to unhook and try to make it back with the plane, but Al refused. Al said, "I have come this far as a paratrooper, I want to be airborne all the way. Help me and push me out of the door."

Steve pushed Hillman out and then jumped himself. After his chute opened, Steve looked down and couldn't see anything but shimmering silver water below. Just before landing in the flood, Steve pulled off his helmet and threw it away—one less weight to pull him under. The wind caught Steve's chute like a sail and dragged him across the water away from the rest of the men in his stick. When he got on dry ground, he couldn't find anyone—not an American, not a Frenchman, not even a German. Steve was so far away from the rest of the troops, he couldn't even hear any firing.

Steve wondered, "What happened to the war? Was the invasion called off? Did just a few of us jump and the others turn back?"

For two days, Steve Uchrin wandered around in a dazed condition. He ate all his K-rations he had jumped with. He was hungry and thirsty. Then he heard his first shot, which came from behind him. At the same time he felt the sting of a bullet in his elbow. Steve turned around and saw five German soldiers with their weapons pointing at him.

The Jerries took Steve's belt and cut his bootlaces to keep him from running, if the chance came. Then a young German soldier started searching through the many pockets of Steve's jumpsuit. He found a bar of C-2 plastic explosive that he probably thought was candy. Anyhow, he bit down on it and then spit it out in disgust. Next the Kraut found a bundle of demolition caps, which he threw on the ground, causing them to explode all over the young German, peppering his body with copper fragments. This made the young German soldier so angry that he acted as if he wanted to kill Steve, but an older German sergeant stepped in and took over.

Eventually Steve was loaded on a truck with some other American prisoners. Soon American planes strafed the German convoy. Steve and the other American prisoners as well as their German captors ran from the trucks. Steve thought about trying to escape, but another POW persuaded him against it. After the strafing, they returned to the trucks, which proceeded on to Chartres, France, where they were quartered in horse barns. Their next stop was POW Stalag 12-A then to Stalag B-4 and finally to Dresden, Germany. It was not too bad in Dresden—that is, until the bombing started.

Near the end of the war, Allied planes bombed the city day and night until the whole city was an inferno. The German guards deserted the camp and left the POWs to fend for themselves. Steve said, "I took off and kept going until I ran into the Russian army."

Steve became a friend of an English-speaking Russian officer, who once worked in New York as a bellhop at the hotel New Yorker. The Russian from Manhattan invited Steve to stay on until they met the American army, but he had to live as they did—off the land. They took what they wanted from the civilians. That was how they managed to eat. When the gap was closed between the American and Russian armies, the POWs were turned over to the Americans.

The Russians had collected a mixed group of POWs from different countries, and it took the American army a long time to sort them all through the proper channels. Most of the POWs were home soon after V-E Day, which was on May 8, 1945, but it was July before Steve Uchrin reached his native New York City.

Al Hillman. Copied from 1943 Company pictures.

A footnote to this story: Pvt. Albert E. Hillman is listed on the Honor Roll of the 508th Parachute Infantry Regiment of those killed in action.

## Surrender or Hide

Maj. Shields Warren, Headquarters First, organized about two hundred men under his command on D-Day near Picauville. Warren received orders from Regimental Headquarters to proceed to Hill 30 and link up with Colonel Shanley's group.

Joe Bressler of Headquarters First was in Warren's group but had fractured his ankle on the jump. They used Bressler's rifle as a splint for his fractured ankle. Before leaving for Hill 30, Warren spoke to the injured and wounded. "We do not have the facilities to take you with us. You will either have to surrender to the Germans or hide until friendly troops come along."

Oscar Prasse, buddy of Bressler in the same platoon, attempted to carry Bressler and stay with the group, but they were cut off in a firefight. Oscar carried Joe about a quarter of a mile toward a house alongside a major road, which they had spotted as a possible hideaway. They spent the first night in a field near the house. During that first night, Prasse shot a German traveling on a motorbike. He hid the bike and the body and took the German's weapon, a Schmeisser, so that both men would be armed.

The LeGrand house. Photo furnished by Joe Bressler.

The next day Bressler and Prasse occupied the third floor of the house where they had a good view of the road from both directions.

The house, which Prasse and Bressler moved into, was the home of the LeGrand family. When the LeGrands learned that the airborne invasion had begun, they hastily left for the nearby village of La Vienville, away from the concentration of Germans that were in the Picauville area.

Leon LeGrand, circa 1943.
Photo furnished by Joe Bressler.

During the first day in the LeGrand house, Prasse saw a German on a bicycle and took a shot at him but missed, and he got away. Then another German cyclist approached. Prasse used the German Schmeisser and knocked him off his bike. The Jerry, recognizing the distinctive sound of the German weapon, jumped up and yelled, "Ich bin Deutsch, dumm! Nicht schiessen!" ("I'm German, stupid! Don't shoot!"), but Prasse finished him off.

In a few days, Leon LeGrand, a son of the family, went back to their home for supplies to take to La Vienville. When Leon opened the door, in front of him stood an American paratrooper, Oscar Prasse, bareheaded and barefooted. Prasse led his visitor to the third floor and introduced Leon to another American paratrooper, Joe Bressler, with an injured ankle. Young Leon found glasses and opened a bottle of cider, and soon they were clicking their glasses, drinking and smoking American cigarettes—the first time Leon had ever smoked an American cigarette. Leon's visit was short, and he never saw the paratroopers again. But he did remember them well. He described Oscar as having blond hair and Joe as having black hair.

For five days, Joe and Oscar ate food they found in the house and slept in the beds of the absent host family. On the sixth day, troops from the Ninetieth Division arrived. Oscar carried Joe to the roadside and left to look for units of the 508th. Before leaving the house, Joe Bressler placed a 100-franc bill, with his name on the note, under a vase.

This was victory money, especially printed for the US troops to use in France. Bressler's name was written in an open circle. The supply sergeant for the company had sorted the victory money for his men in separate stacks, with each man's name on the top bill of his stack. Bressler received two hundred francs, thus the "200" written under Bressler's name. (See photo of note below. Photo furnished by Lucien Hasley.)

When the LeGrand family returned to their home on June 12, 1944, Madame LeGrand found the 100-franc bill under the vase where Joe Bressler left it.

Soon an ambulance came and evacuated Bressler to Omaha Beach then across the English Channel to the town of Melvin Wells.

As Joe Bressler began to recover, he became restless in the hospital. He wheeled himself down the hill to visit the town. When he decided to return to the hospital, he didn't have the strength to roll the wheelchair up the hill. "I know what I will do," Joe said to himself, "I'll just go back to Nottingham."

Bressler bought a train ticket and on July 30 reported back to Headquarters First, Wollaton Park, in Nottingham.

"This ain't no hospital," Bressler was told. "This is a training camp. How many deep knee bends can you do on that bad leg?"

Bressler was not sent back to a hospital. He was put on light duty and recovered sufficiently for Operation Market Garden, the airborne invasion of Holland.

## The Buddy Connection and the French Connection

At a reunion of 508th veterans in Fort Bragg, North Carolina, Joe Bressler, asked his buddies, "Has anyone heard from Oscar Prasse since the war? The last time I saw him was in the Battle of the Bulge, just before he was evacuated with frozen feet. Right after the war, I had the Red Cross to do a search for me, and they came up empty."

Bressler and Prasse were both members of the Mortar Platoon, of which Lt. George Stoeckert had been the commanding officer. George promised he would try to locate Prasse, and within weeks, he succeeded in finding Prasse's sister, who reported that Oscar was in the Medicenter Nursing Home in Virginia Beach, Virginia.

Jim Wynne, who lives in Virginia Beach, had also been a close friend of Oscar Prasse. When Jim heard the news, he immediately went to visit his old friend and also informed Joe Bressler of Oscar's address. Joe talked to Oscar several times on the phone, but Oscar died before Joe got to see him.

## Lucien Hasley and his monument to D-Day

Lucien Hasley, who as a young boy on D-Day witnessed paratroopers landing around his family's home, carved a monument to the event on one side of his house. He created a panoramic view of planes overhead and paratroopers descending earthward. He has engraved the names of many of the troopers who landed in the area on his memorial wall. The author visited with Lucien Hasley in 1994 and gave him a copy of *The Devil's Tale*.

Lucien read the story about Joe Bressler and Oscar Prasse in *The Devil's Tale*. Hasley, in turn, located the house where the two troopers hid for several days and met the owner, Leon LeGrand. LeGrand showed Hasley the 100-franc note with Bressler's name on it, thus proving that it was the same house. His friend Tom Porcella, a 508th veteran, gave Bressler's address to Lucien. That made it possible for Leon LeGrand and Joe Bressler to correspond with each other.

Many friendships have developed over the years because 508th veterans continue to piece together their experiences with those of their fellow Red Devils and with the civilians in the countries our regiment passed through. Each had a part in finding parts of the jigsaw puzzle that makes up the big picture. Lucien Hasley has contributed unselfishly in helping to make the picture more complete. *Merci beaucoup*, Lucien Hasley, from the Red Devils of the 508th Parachute Infantry Regiment.

Lucien Hasley and the monument on the side of his house.
Photo furnished by Lucien Hasley.

## The Fate of One Stick in A Company

Clyde Smith of A Company listed eighteen men from his stick who parachuted unto Normandy. They were Lt. Henry LeFebvre, Sgt. James Myers, Cpl. Kenneth Hook, T/5 Lester Green, and the following privates and privates first class: James Stassola, Robert Benthin, Vincent Dushensky, Clyde Smith, Johnny Roberts, Charles Sciandra, Robert Savage, Raymond Perry, Edward Focht, Robert Union, Robert White, Richard Hunt, Roland Hicks, and Dale Albertson. Five survivors tell the story of what happened to their stick.

These eighteen men were a part of A Company's Third Platoon, judged in the Tennessee maneuvers as the best rifle platoon in the 508th Regiment. In training for D-Day, they always covered a bridge at night while engineers placed their charges and simulated blowing the bridge. Just before D-Day, the real bridge to be blown was identified as the one over the Douve River at Pont l'Abbe near Etienville.

LeFebvre's stick. Front row, kneeling: James Stassalo, Roland Hicks, Clyde Smith, Johnny Roberts, Ramond Perry, and Charles Sclandra. Leaning over: Robert Benthin, Kenneth Hook, and Robert Union. Standing: Robert White, Robert Savage, Edward Focth, James Myers, Dale Albertson, Lester Green, Richard Hunt, and Vincint Duschensky. Photo by Henry LeFebvre, June 5, 1944, provided by LeFebvre.

The night of June 5, Lt. Henry LeFebvre and his stick of paratroopers climbed aboard a C-47 bound for Normandy and the bridge at Pont l'Abbe. When they hit the coast of Normandy, a sea of tracers greeted them. LeFebvre recalled the scene:

> As I looked down from four hundred feet above the ground, all I could see were tracer bullets headed straight for me. We were getting a number of bullets through the wing and fuselage. They made sounds like a bass drum, and they made flashes of green light as they passed through the fuselage. Fortunately no one was hit.

Shrapnel from antiaircraft guns exploded all around the plane as LeFebvre stood in the door waiting for the green light. Just before the jump, a large piece of shrapnel came up through the bottom of the plane and on through the roof, just missing the lieutenant.

Hank LeFebvre led his stick out the door as the green light went on. He landed in the middle of a small field surrounded by hedgerows. LeFebvre described the Normandy hedgerow country:

> Each of the fields in this area of Normandy was not more than fifty yards square and were outlined on all four sides by hedgerows. A hedgerow consisted of a berm of earth about three feet thick and about three feet high. On top of the berm were thick bushes growing to a height of six to ten feet. In addition, each berm had drainage ditches about two feet deep on both sides. What we found were thousands of little fields, each an island unto itself. Men could be fighting and dying in one field, and people could be taking a break in the next.

As soon as LeFebvre hit the ground, he heard a German shouting at his troops giving urgent commands in an excited voice. Hurriedly the lieutenant cut away his parachute harness. While trying to get out of his chute, a cow nearby with a bell around her neck kept looking at him, shaking her head and ringing her bell.

The lieutenant freed himself of his harness and slithered ten yards toward the opposite corner from the Germans. Then he heard a pistol pop, which he recognized to be a flare pistol. In a few seconds the whole area was flooded with light from a parachute flare, and the German fired a hail of bullets into LeFebvre's parachute and equipment left behind. Hank LeFebvre hugged the ground and was thankful that he had blackened his hands and face before takeoff.

When the flare faded, the Jerries stopped firing and Hank continued to crawl toward the corner of the field away from the Jerries. There he ran into a pathfinder. They almost shot each other before they could identity friend or foe. The two paratroopers proceeded along the hedgerow into the next field. LeFebvre described what happened then:

> We heard the sound of German voices coming toward us. We ducked down into a drainage ditch along the hedgerow and waited for them to pass. Unfortunately for us, they stopped just on the other side of the hedgerow. I heard the unmistakable sound of a machine gun being set up, the snap of the trails being

extended, and the sound of the bolt going back and forth as the belt was fed through. It appeared that we were in the middle of a German platoon. We could hear them talking quite clearly just on the other side of the berm of earth.

What to do? There was no way to throw a grenade through that hedgerow. We had to whisper very quietly. I thought that we could sneak out of our position, but when we tried to move, the dry brambles and weeds would crackle loudly and we could hear, "Vas is los?" We would freeze.

I recalled from our briefing that the troops landing on the Normandy coast would relieve us by D+1, so I figured we would just stay put until the Germans were forced to move. But the seaborne invasion didn't make it to us as planned.

My pathfinder friend almost got his hand stepped on by a German who was apparently going to a platoon outpost on our side of the berm. My friend's hand was on the edge of the ditch in which we were hiding, and suddenly two legs went by us.

Our days and nights were spent huddled together. I was sure our forces would drive out the Germans momentarily. So we waited. We lived on a little water and D-ration chocolate bars. It was three nights before we finally heard the Germans packing up to leave.

Making sure they were gone, we left our hiding place and proceeded down the hedgerow until we came to a road. After checking my compass for an easterly direction, we started out and shortly ran into our own forces. It was a tense confrontation as everyone was jumpy. I parted company with my pathfinder friend and never saw him again.

I found only five men from my platoon: Albertson, Benthin, Hicks, Hunt, and White. From then on, the Third Platoon of five men and one officer was the point for A Company. I am so proud of these men who were exposed to the first fire of every engagement. They were always there—brave, courageous, and bold. They did an outstanding job, and all six of us returned to England in one piece.

Clyde Smith's D-Day jump landed him right next to a hedgerow. Before he was able to free himself from the chute harness, he saw the tops of two helmets on the other side of the hedge and almost called to ask for help. As he hesitated, Smith recognized that the voices were speaking German. That made him decide to free his rifle first, and just as he did, a

German came though an opening in the hedge a few yards away. Clyde Smith fired and saw the Jerry drop to a sitting position and then back on his back. Quickly Smith cut off his parachute and ran in the opposite direction.

Soon Smith linked up with Johnny Roberts from his stick and another trooper, Kevin Cregan. Every direction the three troopers turned, they ran into Germans. They got close to James Myers and Kenneth Hooks, but they were pinned down and could not get together.

On June 8, two days after D-Day, Smith came across wires that appeared to be telephone connections between German units. He moved down the line cutting the wire in several places to make repairs more difficult for the enemy. The wire led him toward a German gun emplacement, and his movement soon drew their fire. Smith hugged the ground in tall grass as the bullets zinged above his head. The firing stopped. As he laid there thinking about his next move, he suddenly felt a shock and pain in the small of his back. A Jerry had sneaked up behind him and struck him with his rifle butt. Clyde Smith was quickly overpowered and taken prisoner.

Later Johnny Roberts was captured. Roberts and Smith were POWs together in Dresden, Germany, for many months.

Other men from LeFebvre's stick—Edward Focht, James Stassola, and Robert Union—were killed, and James Perry was wounded on D-Day. Lester Green and Charles Sciandra were captured. Vincent Dushensky and Robert Savage were missing.

"I landed on the roof of a two-story house and was immediately jerked off by the wind in my chute into a hedgerow," recalled Cpl. Kenneth Hook, another member of LeFebvre's stick.

Hook cut himself out of his chute and the entanglements of the hedgerow, and after moving a short distance, he heard a call for help. It was Sgt. James Myers, about ten yards into the water. Hook waded into the mud and water, which was about four feet deep. He assisted Myers in freeing himself from his chute and helped him to dry land.

"Every move we made, we encountered Germans," Hook explained, "in twos, threes, and squads. Everywhere we went we were shot at."

About daybreak two Jerries rose up from their dugout and shouted at Myers and Hook as they approached. The pair of paratroopers "eliminated" four Germans in that dugout, and then "All hell broke loose!" They advanced in a new direction.

After evading Germans all day without finding any other paratroopers, Hook and Myers ran into a group of 101st men. One A Company man,

Corporal Fontana, was with them. Kenneth Hook described the action that followed:

> We were in an orchard near a small group of houses. No one seemed to know our location. Fontana, Myers, and I went to one of the houses and found a French family. Fontana tried to learn our location from the Frenchman but with no luck. As we were leaving the house, the Frenchman fired on us. That Frenchman was eliminated, after which we went back into the house and went upstairs.
>
> Three small tanks came up the road and stopped at the house, one directly under an upstairs window where Fontana was. Fontana proceeded to drop a Gammon antitank grenade down the hatch of the lead tank while the Germans were looking at him. Cross off that tank! The other two left in a hurry.
>
> We then returned to the 101st group in the orchard. They had no officers or noncoms. Sergeant Myers was trying to organize the group but was interrupted by 88s zeroing in on the orchard. We moved out to the next field.
>
> Across the road from the field, Myers and I discovered a pillbox, which pinned us down with their fire. When two Germans came down the road between the pillbox and us, the firing stopped. That's when we threw two Gammon grenades into the pillbox and took off. No more firing from there.
>
> The river was nearby, so we waded along the bank for a short while to get out of the area. We reached another field with a farmhouse. Looking through the hedgerow, we saw numerous Germans moving about. We picked off two when they were looking in our direction. The results were surprising. Anthony Cianfrani of A Company yelled to us, "Take a powder!" He was their prisoner and was told to ask us to surrender. The Germans didn't understand him.
>
> We were behind a stone wall alongside a road. A grenade came over beside us. Myers picked it up and threw it back. Nothing happened. Another came over, but it was out of reach. We lay as flat as possible. "Pop!"—it was a dud. About the same time, Germans poured through a gate in front of us and over the wall, firing their burp guns at us as we got up. Myers was hit badly, and I took one in the thigh. This put both of us down.

They took us prisoners there. I carried Myers about a mile where we joined a group of captured troopers. Myers died soon after arriving. I was to spend the next ten months as a POW.

Another trooper from LeFebvre's stick, Richard Hunt, landed in a field of grain about three feet high. Hunt snapped his cricket but heard no response. (Toy crickets were given to the paratroopers to help with identification.) He looked around for his next move and saw a medium-sized tree not too far away and decided the tree was a good assembly point. Cautiously he crawled through the tall grain, circling so as not to give away his true direction. From behind the tree Hunt looked back to his starting point and saw a Kraut on top of his discarded parachute. He also saw two men struggling to free an orange equipment parachute from a tree. He couldn't tell if the two men were friends or foes until the Kraut, on top of Hunt's chute, shot at them. Hunt described his thoughts and actions that followed:

> How am I going to get that Kraut without giving away my position? The sound of my carbine will draw fire toward me. Having already heard some armor firing their cannons and having gotten a Gammon grenade prepared in case one of those tanks came along, I decided to throw the grenade. That's how I took care of the Kraut sitting on top on my chute.
>
> After the grenade exploded, I ran about 150 feet to the hedgerow where the guys had been pulling on the orange parachute. I dove over the hedge and upon standing up found three M-1 rifles stuck up my nose. The men thought maybe I was the one who had been shooting at them. Captain Adams and Dale Albertson of A Company, Frank Circelli of Headquarters First, Cpl. James Green, and Lt. Ray Murray from Headquarters Third were in the group joined by Hunt. [Circelli, Green, and Murray are cited in Lord's history of the *508th Parachute Infantry*, p. 45.]

Bob White, also of LeFebvre's stick, explained what happened to him on D-Day:

> After my chute opened, I looked up and saw a blown panel. I pulled the reserve and fed it out in front me to make sure it would open. It caught just before I hit the ground.

The white chute on top of the tall grain in the moonlight really drew the fire from Jerry. (Main chutes were camouflaged and reserved chutes were white.) I crawled out from under that white chute in a hurry. The Krauts were still firing at it after I was long gone.

The first trooper I met was A. B. Cannon of A Company who had jumped with the pathfinders. Cannon asked, "Where in the hell have you all been?"

We moved from field to field, and by daylight, the two of us had picked up eight men. A little later we joined with Captain Adams and his group. In an attempt to get to Hill 30, we moved out with Hunt and me at the point. I reached a road and stepped into it to find two trucks loaded with Germans bearing down on me. They pulled over, unloaded, and started firing.

Since we were outnumbered, the order was given to pull back. They spotted me with just my backpack showing above the tall grass. Machine gun bullets ripped through my pack. I said, "I'll get rid of that sucker." I unhooked my rifle belt and turned on my side to slip the harness over my shoulder, and a bullet went through the sleeve of my jump jacket, just under the American flag. I crawled away, flat on my belly and fast as a snake.

We withdrew to a nearby field and set up an all-around defense. It was D+4 before we could get to Hill 30 and assemble with the regiment. Of the eighteen men who jumped in our stick, only six made it back to England.

Bob White. Note holes in sleeve. Photo by Henry LeFebvre.

## That Donkey Almost Took Me to the Barn!

"I could see the white horse running around inside the hedgerow as I dropped, but I didn't see the black donkey," James "Buck" Hutto of I Company said about his jump into Normandy.

On one corner of the square area enclosed by a hedgerow was a farmhouse with an attached shed. Germans in the house and the shed were shooting machine guns and .20 mm canons at the C-47s dropping the paratroopers.

"I landed in the middle of a hedged enclosure," Buck said. "And the firing from that house and shed frightened the white horse and the black donkey, perhaps even more than it did me. Those animals were running like crazy round and round inside the hedgerow."

Buck Hutto recalled this:

At first I was too scared to move. I just lay there as still and quiet as I could. As long as the Jerries were firing from the corner of the lot, the horse and the donkey kept up their full speed gallop, round and round. I didn't even try to get out of my harness. My chute fluttered in the wind and stretched out the suspension lines to their full length away from me.

With a lull in the shooting, the donkey and horse stopped running. Then the donkey decided he was going back to his shed. He headed straight toward me and passed between the fluttering parachute and me, got himself entangled in the suspension lines, and started dragging me toward the shed.

I grabbed the suspension lines with my left hand and my trench knife, which was strapped to my leg, with my right hand and started hacking away at those lines. The donkey was making a beeline toward that shed full of Germans, pulling me behind him. When I cut the last line, I was only about fifty feet from the shed, and the donkey was all wrapped up in my parachute.

Carefully I got out of my harness and pack, keeping only my grenades, weapons, and ammunition, and crawled toward the opposite corner of the field away from the house and shed. I made it to the hedgerow and stopped, feeling a little relief but not much.

Then I could hear something around the corner of the hedge to my left but couldn't see anything. I recognized the sound of a machine gun as the gunner pulled back the feed lever. Could that be friend or foe? Most likely foe! I wouldn't snap that little old cricket they gave us for identification lest the enemy find me. So I waited quietly. Every once in a while I would hear a sound from the machine gunner around the corner.

Looking out of the hedge to my front, I saw an orchard. Over to the right a patrol quietly moved forward toward my position, one at a time. I could see the outline of the helmets—definitely German with that curve down over their ears. I debated in my mind about shooting at the Krauts but decided it would give away my position and they would get me in the end, so I lay quietly. The lead man in the patrol came within twelve feet of me. He stopped and signaled to those behind him, turned to the right, and moved away through the orchard.

As dawn began to break and I could see better, I noticed that the machine gunner around the corner was gone. It was time to move. I decided to go to my right toward the spot where the German patrol entered the orchard. On the other side of the orchard was a road. I looked up the road and saw a paratrooper walking toward me. Was I glad to see him! But he was so nervous that he almost shot me before I could identify myself.

Hutto and the other paratrooper moved on and in a short time collected about fifteen others. Then they united with a group of about eighty. Hutto thought that they were on the opposite side of the river from Chef Du Pont. After joining the larger group, he was assigned to a roadblock near a causeway where there had been a fierce fight. The causeway was littered with the bodies of US paratroopers and German soldiers.

## Slow Takeoff but Fast Landing

The .81 mm Mortar Platoon of Headquarters Third loaded onto three C-47s and was ready to fly to Normandy. Planes all around them rolled down the runway and took their places in line for takeoff. It was then announced, "One of the planes in the three-plane formation has engine failure. You have to unload and get on another."

Changing planes also meant changing the equipment bundles packed in the pods beneath the fuselage. The 250-pound parapacks had to be tripped and dragged by the troopers two hundred feet across the runway between planes that were taxiing by and loaded on the replacement C-47. To add to the problems, one of the bundles burst open and had to be repacked.

By the time the new C-47 was packed and the troops boarded, the rest of the vast armada of aircraft had flown the airport. The three-plane formation carrying the Third Battalion Mortar Platoon took off by itself. (Normally the C-47s flew in a nine-plane formation, three sets of three planes each. Each set of three planes formed an inverted *V*, and the three sets together formed a larger inverted *V*.)

Lt. Neal Beaver, platoon CO, describes the flight:

> I stood in the door all the way with Lt. Bill Garry. We saw the submarine light, made the left turn, and then observed that we passed by Guernsey and Jersey islands too far south.
>
> Over Normandy I could see the silver ribbons of the Merderet and the Douve rivers very plainly and also watched as much fire arose from the flack train at St. Sauveur Le Vicomte. I had no intercom to the pilot and recall saying to the crew chief, "Tell him to turn left—turn left!"
>
> He finally turned after going over the entire peninsula. We crossed a beautiful wide white moonlit beach and flew out over the channel for a few hundred yards. Then a steep left turn, several bursts of machine gun fire down to about 350 to 400 feet with wide-open engines, the green light went on. We were about ten miles inland at Sebeville.
>
> I was hit in the jaw by a spent tracer just as I jumped. Bill Garry was nicked by the same burst. (I still have the bullet. The aid-station medics dug it out of my chin three days later at Chef du Pont.)
>
> When we left Sebeville on D-Day morning, we had to leave seven men behind, with Sgt. Okey Mills in charge of the injured. All sustained broken ankles or wrenched knees from the jump. It's a miracle someone wasn't killed since we jumped so low.

Okey Mills was the last in his stick to jump. As he exited the door of the plane, the pilot accelerated his engines for a speedy getaway, which in turn jerked Okey's static line with such force, he was temporarily knocked unconscious. Before hitting the ground, Mills came to and discovered he was oscillating wildly. Actually, he was almost parallel with the chute as he landed, and his body was slapped against the earth on the downward cycle of the oscillation, with his right hip and back absorbing the impact. The landing so severely injured Mills that he was unable to walk.

Several men in the stick assembled around Mills. Some attempted to help him, but he told them, "You men will have to go without me. I am unable to get up and walk."

The men left Okey Mills lying in a ditch and disappeared from his view behind a house. Mills related what happened next:

> A German must have been waiting until the rest of the troopers were out of sight because at that time, about fifteen shots were fired at me and hit all around me in the ditch. I was waiting for another shot when I heard a horse running. Since I was lying facedown in the ditch, I couldn't see the German, but I figured he emptied his magazine and jumped on the horse to get away quickly.
>
> I started crawling toward the house nearby. As I came closer, I saw a German standing to the right of the house. He fired several shots at me, one hitting the dirt under my armpit and another right in front of my helmet. Then a squad of paratroopers appeared from somewhere and wiped out that German.
>
> Seven of us injured were gathered in the house, including a medic, Wally Polton, whose ankles were crushed. Wally crawled around on his knees and gave first aid to all the others. Medic Wally Polton deserves a lot of credit.

Five of the injured were evacuated the first day, and on the second day, Mills and Polton were taken to Omaha Beach and then by boat to Southampton, England.

## Sights and Sounds in the Night

Like many paratroopers who jumped into Normandy on D-Day, Jim Rankin and Jim Price, two men from Regimental Headquarters Company, did not know where they were. When they found each other, it was some comfort, but where was the rest of the regiment? And what can two men do against the whole German army?

With weapons at ready, troopers Rankin and Price cautiously moved in a direction they hoped would lead them to friendly troops. Then faintly ahead of them a shadowy image halted their progress.

While squinting for a glimmer of night-light, Rankin whispered to Price, "I think I can make out the barrels of a double-mounted machine gun."

"Cover me, Price, and I will crawl up closer and knock it out with a grenade," Rankin continued in hushed tones.

Carefully and quietly Rankin inched his way on his belly toward the menacing gun outlined against the night sky. When within a few feet, he pulled the pin on the grenade and took aim. As he raised himself to his knees for a better throwing position, he was able to see the lower part of the gun mount. Then he realized he was about to attack a wheelbarrow turned upside down.

Rankin and Price remained isolated from friendly troops until D+6. Rankin remembered the first English words he heard, which were music to his ears: "Get that son of a bitch!"

The words came from a GI with the troops pushing inland from the D-Day beach landing. He was referring to a German sniper in a tree, not far from where Rankin and Price were hunkered down in a hedgerow.

John Simmons, E Company, landed on a hard Normandy road in the early dark hours of June 6. About the time Simmons slipped out of his parachute harness, he heard *clop-clop* sounds coming down the road in his direction. Quickly he scrambled behind the hedgerow bordering the road.

John remembered being taught in training that one could recognize German soldiers by the sounds of their hobnailed boots. John prepared himself for a squad of Jerries marching at double time. Lying prone with his M-1 rifle poised for action, he waited for the first enemy to come in his sights. The approaching figure reflected a bit of moonlight.

Simmons recalls, "I relaxed my trigger finger just in time. I almost shot a white horse."

## A Small Package of Tremendous Courage

"The reserve chute on top of my musette bag probably saved me from being buried over my head in the muck," observed Bill Bell, as he recounted his jump into Normandy.

"As it was, two of my most important weapons were immobilized. I had slung my rifle with the barrel down. The barrel was deep in the mud, and I couldn't get to my jump knife strapped to my right leg."

Bell felt helpless until he remembered the extra knife. Fortunately some trooper had left his knife on a cot in the hangar. As the troopers were leaving to load on the planes, Bell saw it, and stuck the extra knife behind his belt buckle. The first thing he did was cut loose his rifle. He had covered the end of the barrel with a land mine spacer and four condoms, keeping out the mud. His M-1 was operational.

About the time Bell recovered the use of his rifle, he heard someone approaching. Training films emphasized the difference in the noises made by German soldiers and American soldiers. His reaction was, "That sounds like a Kraut!"

Bill parted the tall marsh grass, released the safety on his M-1, and called out the password, "Flash!"

The shadowy figure stopped. After a moment of silence he heard the countersign, "Thunder!"

"Who in the hell are you?" demanded Private Bell.

"Sergeant Hayes?"

"Hell, yes, and don't tell me I'm stuck here by myself with Pvt. William Bell!"

Just a week before the jump, Hayes and Bell clashed while on guard duty in Wollaton Park in Nottingham, England. Bell was at his post walking the fence line. An English girl asked Bill to take a message to a trooper in a tent. Bell went to deliver the message. Hayes, who was sergeant of the guard, caught Bell away from his post.

Naturally, Sergeant Hayes gave Bell a good reaming out and in the process called him a "son of a bitch!"

Bell saw red, loaded a round in the chamber, and stuck his rifle under Hayes's chin and said, "Don't ever call me that again!"

In the darkness of the night of June 5/6, Hayes and Bell were alone with each other. No other friendly troops could be found. They had landed between Picauville and Château Hout. In one direction they observed German tanks cranking up for action. In another direction, using binoculars, they observed a column of Jerries moving along a nearby road.

"Look through the windows of that house," said Hayes, handing the glasses to Bell.

"Wow! With that much gold braid, it must be some high-ranking brass!" (Bell believed this was the same officer, Major General Falley, killed a few hours later by Lt. Malcolm D. Brannen.)

The sergeant and the private decided to try to slip through the enemy to friendly territory. While moving cautiously along a hedgerow, they were surprised by the sudden appearance of Germans coming through a break in the hedge. Bell and Hayes hit the ditch, and when they looked up, the pistol of a German officer and the rifles of five Jerry soldiers were leveled at them.

When the Germans searched Bell and found a whole gross of condoms, they burst out laughing, and Bell didn't have to know German to guess what the Jerries were saying.

One may think that the war was over for Bell and Hayes, but the dangers and hardships that POWs suffered often exceeded those of combat soldiers. Air raids by Allied planes killed and wounded many POWs. The sick and the wounded often had limited medical attention. Worst of all, the crowded unsanitary conditions and limited food and water made life almost unbearable.

Bell and Hayes were separated when Allied planes strafed the convoy of trucks loaded with POWs. The guards and prisoners piled out of the trucks and ran for cover. In reloading, the two paratroopers ended up in different trucks and were never together again.

For Bell, the thirty-five-day train trip from Normandy to Germany was excruciating. The prisoners were loaded sixty to a boxcar, called forty and eights, built to carry forty men or eight horses. One honey bucket was placed in each of the straw-littered cars for toilet purposes. Each prisoner was given one loaf of bread and a small ration of water.

The prison train—consisting of an engine, three cars, and a caboose—seemed to zigzag all over the country. The train was sidetracked, waiting without moving, much of the time. About twenty-five days passed without more food or water. The honey buckets were full and splashing over.

The train stopped. Squinting through cracks they had chiseled out with belt buckles in the side of the car, the prisoners saw an open field and a town several kilometers away. The guards had gotten out of their car and were stretching their legs on the grounds.

With an eye at the peephole, one POW announced, "Here comes a line of loaded carts and a bunch of people! It almost seems as if they were expecting us."

"Look at that little lady leading the way! Say, she has on a Red Cross uniform," observed another.

"I would say she is about four feet, eight inches tall and weighs about eighty pounds, but look at the guards moving out of her way. The little lady is bringing her crew right up to this train. How about that!"

The woman marched up to the officer in charge and demanded, "You must let the prisoners out of the cars, let us bathe them, clean their cars, and give the men food and drink." (French and German were translated into English by POWs who knew the languages.)

The German officer replied, "Go away and tend to your own business."

But the Red Cross worker was persistent. "You cannot treat these prisoners like mere animals. They are human beings, and we demand that we be allowed to take care of some basic human needs."

The officer pointed his pistol at our heroine and said, "I could shoot you!"

"If you do," she replied, "the whole world will know about it. You will be responsible for your deeds."

The officer, frustrated and enraged, walked a few steps away then returned to the Red Cross leader and announced, "We will allow you to serve the prisoners, but you must make it plain in your report that I requested this service from the International Red Cross."

The small band of dedicated workers spent almost the whole day bathing the prisoners, washing their clothes, cleaning out their cars, and emptying the honey buckets.

"It was really embarrassing," Bell said. "Those women undressed us completely and started washing our naked bodies with soap and water. They boiled and washed our clothes and gave them back to us wet, but they soon dried off in the heat of the boxcars."

The prisoners ate hot barley soup, with little bits of meat, and long loaves of French bread. Each car was supplied with soup and bread for the rest of the trip.

When the prison train pulled away, the prisoners were refreshed and filled with admiration for the courage and kindness of the little Red Cross nurse and her brave companions.

Later, the POWs were talking about the incident, and one of them said, "Any of you guys ever heard of Florence Nightingale?"

With that summary statement, a hush fell over the men as if they were silently offering prayers of thanksgiving.

## What Happened to My Battalion?

"The first four days in Normandy were the most frustrating in my life. I had been trained to command a cohesive Battalion, and all I had was a combat patrol," Col. Louis G. Mendez recalled.

Colonel Mendez, CO of the Third Battalion, described his first minutes in Normandy:

> I heard the password "Flash!" and I couldn't remember the countersign "Thunder!" but I recognized Richard Fritter's voice, so I responded, "Is that you, Fritter?" The voice answered, "Yes, sir, Colonel."

Mendez assembled eight or ten men initially, but according to John Delury of the Mendez group, "The number fluctuated daily. The Germans would kill three or four of us, and we would pick us about the same number of strays."

Among those Colonel Mendez remembered that were with him early were Lt. John Daly, Lt. John Quaid, Lt. Arthur R. Stevens, Communication T/4 Desmond A. Matthews, Sgt. Jess Alley, Richard

Fritter, Glenn Fateley, Dan Koziel, John Delury, and several from the 507th.

John Delury, H Company, told of meeting Glenn "Red" Fateley of I Company the night of the jump:

> We were bordering a hedgerow in the dark when Fately came up to me and said, "You made me the happiest fellow in the world." I was his first contact. A few days later, he would be by my side dying of machine gun bullets in his stomach.

In his memoirs, *D-Day Plus 40 Odd Years Normandy Thoughts*, John described many narrow escapes, such as this one quoted with permission from John Delury:

> We were trying to cross a road one day, so I went up first and was lying inside the hedgerow on my side of the road when two German soldiers walked by chatting and smoking cigarettes. I literally could have reached out and grabbed their boots. I crawled back into the field and met Lieutenant Quaid.
>
> We were both in a kneeling position when a German tank came up the road opposite an opening that afforded it access to the field. I could have sworn they saw us. We lay flat on the ground and waited for the tank to turn into the field. I could feel my heart pounding against the ground and terror swept through me. (There is something about a tank that puts the fear of God into an infantryman.) But the tank continued straight on down the road.

John Delury was lead scout much of the time as the small group scrambled to avoid being wiped out by the Jerries while they searched to link up with a larger force of the 508th. As point man, Delury led a charmed life. When others were at the point, they didn't last long. Delury give Lieutenant Quaid credit for preserving his life many times because Quaid was right up there with him or close behind.

Delury wrote this tribute to Lt. John Quaid:

> In my opinion, John Quaid was the caliber of man that was typical of the parachute officer: handsome, intelligent, physically above average, with an esprit and elan unparalleled in our military.

I remember being pinned down behind a farmhouse ahead of the rest of the group. Machine guns were raking the road and the house. Quaid crawled up to me and told me to return with him through an irrigation ditch. Moments later a tank with a company of men came around the house. I would have still been there were it not for Lieutenant Quaid.

When we regrouped, I asked him if he wanted me to take the point with him. He said that he would take some troopers with him who had not yet been on the point.

He looked tired and reflective. Maybe he had a feeling the end was near. The Krauts were waiting behind an innocent-looking hedgerow. They killed the entire point with the first volley of their machine gun.

I have often thought of our fine company officers with their dress uniforms and snappy leather jackets with our regimental logo emblazoned on the front. They were virtually all killed.

On one occasion Colonel Mendez listened to mortar fire and, hoping it could be Lieutenant Beaver's mortar platoon from Headquarters Third, sent Delury and another trooper to find out the identity of the mortar unit. Delury and his partner came dangerously close to exposing themselves and getting into a firefight. To their good fortune, two German soldiers came up the road pushing wheelbarrows filled with mortar shells. The two scouts were able to bring back an eyewitness report that the mortar crew was a German unit. Mendez and his group had to continue in isolation from friendly forces.

On D-Day plus three, about 2:30 PM, Jim Wynne of Headquarters First was one of seven who joined Colonel Mendez's group. The names he remembered were Lt. Arthur Stevens, Carlton R. Johnson, James B. Howard, Wilbur C. Wright, and William F. Chandler, Jr. Most of these were from Headquarters First Company. Although Mendez was CO of the Third Battalion, Wynne was glad to be with Mendez. Mendez had the respect and confidence not only of the men of his own battalion but also all those who had seen him lead in training.

Wynne remembers his experience with Major Mendez (promoted to colonel later, according to Wynne):

> I was told to get a detail and gather all the canteens and fill them at a stream that we could see in the next field about five hundred feet away. I chose two men to help carry the canteens, and just before we started through the hedgerow into the next

field, one of the men spotted a company of Krauts in the woods about five hundred feet away. Talk about luck—we would have been right out into the open with no protection.

Major Mendez immediately organized a defensive position with me all the way up the field to his right. It was not long before about a company of Krauts came out of the woods. As they came across the field toward us, James B. Howard, who was next to Major Mendez, shot a German with a Red Cross armband charging with a rifle. Howard knocked the German down with his little carbine, but he got up and continued to advance. Howard asked Major Mendez, "What do I do now?" Mendez replied, "Shoot the SOB again!" Which he did.

By this time Mendez decided it was best for us to abandon the field for a better place because they were too many for us. I was still up to their right, guarding the right flank and rear. I heard the firing, but I did not see the action. James Howard called for me to come on, they were pulling out.

We left in a spread formation into a field to our rear. The field was full of weeds and stubble about twenty-four inches high. We came under intense fire, so I hit the ground. I could hear the bullets hitting the weeds and stubble. I thought the bullets were as thick as fleas on a dog's back. A tank was spraying the field and the road next to the field with machine gun fire.

I heard Major Mendez holler, "Everyone to the left!" Mendez was standing in a gate directing his men across the road. One man was hit in the fleshy part of his thigh. Mendez started toward the wounded man. The wounded man hollered for Mendez to stay back, and he made it across the road on his own. I had not yet crossed the road. It was the inspiration of Major Mendez that gave me the power to move.

All of us got across the road. We stopped to dress the thigh wound of the injured man, gave him a full canteen of water, but we had to leave him. It was a hard thing to do.

While others were taking care of the wounded man, Major Mendez and his officers were studying maps to see how to get to Hill 30. They set their course, and after traveling all night across fields and roads, even laying low once while a groups of Krauts passed by, we got to Hill 30 just about sunrise.

Delury aptly explains the feeling of relief. "When we finally entered our lines, we joined a battalion of paratroopers surrounded by a German division. But to us, after being on our own for four days and nights, we felt as secure as a baby in its mother's arms."

Col. Louis G. Mendez. Permission to use photo given by Mrs. Louis (Jeannie) Mendez.

# Five Days on the Run
Abridged from Lt. Col. Malcolm D. Brannen's personal papers, with permission from Colonel Brannen.

Lt. Malcolm Brannen. Photo furnished by Dave Pike.

Lt. Malcolm Brannen of Headquarters Third wrote this:

> I just couldn't get myself free of the parachute. Every other minute someone would run by me on the ground, and it was impossible for me to identify him. I had to quit struggling to free myself. I thought I might drop from the frying pan into the fire.

Brannen, who had landed in an apple tree and was suspended above the earth by only a foot, finally cut himself loose from his harness and found four other paratroopers in the ditch close by—two from the Second Battalion 508th and two from the 307th Engineers.

Their first task was to escape the machine gun spitting death about one hundred yards away. They wanted to go northwest, the direction they expected to find their units, but because of that machine gun and other machine guns in their way, they kept moving northeast.

The five paratroopers soon found some wires running beside a main north-south road. Brannen said, "I cut them in several places and took several yards of the wire and hid it. Anyway we figured we disrupted their communications for a while."

Continuing on, the troopers came across two tents and two motorcycles. They figured it was a German CP. They punctured the motorcycle tires and moved on.

Across another field and another road, they found Lt. Harold Richards and Sergeant Hall, both of A Company, 508th. By this time the group had grown to twelve, with two officers. After a conference they decided to ask directions at a nearby farmhouse. Brannen said he pounded on the door, and a very excited Frenchman rushed out of the house. At every window, heads appeared, with several "wild-eyed kiddos" staring from the upstairs at the strange American uniforms. From the French family's guidebooks and maps, Brannen learned they were about midway between Picauville and Etienville.

While at the farmhouse, a car came up the road. Brannen went to the road, held up his hands, and yelled, "Stop!" The driver increased his speed. Brannen jumped out of the way, and all the paratroopers fired at the car as it passed. The car crashed into a stone wall.

Brannen noticed the driver, a German corporal, trying to get in the cellar of the house. Brannen shot and wounded the corporal in the shoulder. Meanwhile, a German officer crawled toward a Luger pistol in the middle of the road. Brannen described the scene. "At the same time the officer was crawling, he was looking at me and saying in English, 'Don't kill! Don't kill!' I thought, 'If he gets to that Luger, it's either him or me.' So I shot him in the forehead. The blood spurted just like a fountain and then gradually died down to nothing."

The dead officer was identified from documents in his briefcase and from his hatband as Lt. Gen. Wilhelm Falley, commanding officer of the Ninety-first German Infantry Division. A major riding in the car was also killed, and the wounded corporal was captured.

"The sooner we can get away from here, the better," Brannen and his men decided, and set off toward Etienville, the town which the 508th Second Battalion had planned to attack.

They came upon a small settlement where Brannen's rear guard picked off a German just as he was aiming to shoot. The shot aroused others. Brannen and a corporal were standing next to each other beside a hedgerow when the corporal said, "Who shot me?"

At the same time, two more shots rang out. Brannen described the corporal:

> I saw a stream of blood actually gush from his mouth and saw him fall straight down, arms outstretched and his heels wide apart pointing to the skies. That was the first American I had actually seen killed, a paratrooper from our own 508th.

Other shots were fired, and the band of troopers ran around the house and barn and back down the road from whence they came. The firing stopped, but they could hear the voices following. At a crossroads they met a young Frenchman who directed them toward Etienville. Here they decided to lighten their load. They hid their extra gear and were off running again. Finding a small wooded area, they stopped for a short rest but were aroused when they spotted a group of German soldiers in an open field near the woods lined up for noonday chow.

When the paratroopers tried to move away from that area, the Germans detected their movement. Brannen described what happened next:

> Some of the Germans from the chowline headed for our position. We moved as quickly as we could and got into a ditch, covered ourselves, and stayed as quiet as possible. The Germans came into the woods, running and jumping ditches. They hunted systematically, taking routes a few yards apart, going to one edge of the woods and then doubling back. When they got to the ditch we were in, they had to get a running start to jump the ditch. We were lucky they looked at the ground where they were to land and not into the ditch. They actually jumped right over me. After about half an hour, the searchers returned to the area where the chowline had formed.
>
> We then crawled away from the hunted area through ditches, over mud, rocks, fallen trees, and thick underbrush. In a few minutes we came to a nice grove of trees—well cleared, quiet, and cool. I called a halt. We were tired, hungry, and thirsty and needed a break. We set up a defense with guard points. All this time we had our German prisoner, General

Falley's chauffeur. I didn't trust him. I tried to catnap, but my eyes wouldn't leave the prisoner.

Voices! Shots! Right near us, on the trail by which we entered the grove. We began to move out through a ditch. When the voices got very close and the bullets were snapping over our heads, we would lay still, hardly daring to breathe. The moment the voices got a bit faint, we would move on again. Finally we got away from the voices and took another short rest, only to hear voices again in about ten minutes.

The chase continued, and at one point Lieutenant Brannen and his scout Quigg (from the 505th PIR) took one route around a field, and the rest of the group went with Lieutenant Richards around the other way. The two groups were to meet at a road they could see ahead. Brannen and Quigg made it to the designated place. They hid in the opening of a hedgerow, covered themselves, and waited for Richards's group. Then there was about five minutes of shooting in the area where Richards's group should have been, and then silence.

Brannen and Quigg discussed their situation. Were their friends killed or captured? "We are on our own. We will wait until dark and then head northwest."

When darkness fell, they had to turn southeast to avoid a German 88 crew and after some progress found another hiding place. During the night they could hear coughing on the other side of their hedgerow. At daylight they investigated and found Pvt. Russell Nosera, 507th PIR (Parachute Infantry Regiment). Now they were three. The three hid all day and waited for darkness in order to travel again.

Brannen recalls that day. "We watched all day long from our hiding place, hardly daring to breathe or move as horse-drawn vehicles loaded with shells traveled past us toward their gun positions."

Darkness came at midnight, and the troopers started to search for friendly American forces. By daylight it had been twenty-four hours since they had eaten or drunk anything, so they decided to approach a small village to find water and directions. As Brannen stepped into a manure shed, Quigg pointed out German soldiers setting up a machine gun nearby. Brannen and Quigg were not seen from their position, but when Nosera moved into the shed, the Germans noticed the movement and pointed toward the shed. Brannen, Quigg, and Nosera decided to run for it.

Brannen led the way. As he ran from one machine gun, he ran directly into another machine gun. Without breaking his stride, he spun around like a football running back and headed in another direction. Bullets whistled by him, and one hit his trenching tool hooked to his pistol belt. Brannen described the rest of his escape:

> I ran into an orchard then cut a ninety-degree angle to the left and crossed a forty-yard field in nothing flat, dove into a ditch, and started crawling. After about ten yards, I stopped and crawled back to where I hit the ditch and camouflaged my trail. Once in a spot where I thought I could rest and hide, I covered myself with dead briars. I lay there thanking God that I was small and had made it to safety.
> 
> In just a short time, I heard voices—excited, high-pitched, nervous voices, German and American. The German voices were half-English. They were saying, "Come oudt! Come oudt! Hans oop!"
> 
> Then I heard one of my companions say, "No! No! I don't want to die."
> 
> Then *brrrrrrr! Brrrrrrr!* A machine pistol.
> 
> I knew what had happened. Like a pack of hounds, the voices came into the orchard where I was hiding. I prayed—asked forgiveness, asked blessing for my folks and my dearest friends (human and canine). Yes, I prayed and really felt like I had seen the last of life on this earth.
> 
> They came for two hours and more. They shot in every nook and corner, in every house on the border of the orchard. They shot that high-velocity machine pistol. *Brrrrrrrrrr!* Then one German walked through the briars five feet from me. I think my heart stopped beating.
> 
> More Germans came shooting over my body. I could feel the breeze from the bullets. Some of the bullets buried in the bank behind me, and dirt kicked up by the bullets fell on me. I counted twelve times that they walked past me, shooting at every step. I waited for the thirteenth time. It never came. They went away.
> 
> I entered my hideout at about 0800 hrs, Thursday. I knew I had to stay there until darkness. All afternoon our artillery fell around me, and then the P-47s and P-51s did a beautiful job of bombing, but I was right in the middle of it all. Then the German artillery and mortars would go off. It was a very poor place to be. I waited for dark, praying for it to come soon.
> 
> Then the Germans started moving in the field around me. They brought 88s, mortars, machine guns, and rifles. By dark

the field was alive with Germans and their firepower. I couldn't move. I just lay there. My binoculars were cutting into my chest. My carbine had numbed my right hand. I was hungry, I was thirsty. I had no food or water.

Daylight came, and then the fire landing around me was ours, not German, which meant that the Jerries were pulling back and the Allies pushing forward. I waited for what I thought was an eternity, and then I heard voices. I couldn't make out if they were American or German. Then I heard someone say, "Hear that gun, that's for yar."

Then I heard a German machine pistol. *Brrrrrrrr!* And the voice said, "That gun's agin yar."

No German ever said, "That gun's agin yar."

Then I yelled, "Hey, American! Hey, soldier!"

In a moment, two privates came over to Brannen and he saw the Ninetieth Division insignia. He added this:

> They pushed through the briars and bushes and picked me up and gave me a drink of water. I started to move, and my legs were like rubber. The soldiers helped me, and I soon got on my way under my own control.
>
> Then I went to the manure shed to see what happened there. I found an M-1 rifle, which was all the evidence that Americans had been there.

Brannen located a CP of the Eighty-second Airborne a few hundred yards from his last hiding place. From there he reported to Col. Louis G. Mendez, CO of Third Battalion, 508th PIR.

1st Lt. Malcolm D. Brannen ended his story by saying, "I thanked God for his guidance and comfort."

## The Bugler

Adapted from Carl H. Porter's *Men at War "Chow Call"* with permission from Carl Porter.

Every paratrooper had to learn how to pack a parachute to qualify as a paratrooper, and one of the qualifying jumps was made with a chute packed by the jumper himself. The Airborne Command considered the Rigger School, where troops were trained to pack parachutes, as one of the most important training operations in the Parachute School. Only those paratroopers who demonstrated packing skills and dependable responsible personal traits were chosen as riggers because the life of the paratrooper depended on a well-packed parachute.

The riggers had to put their life on the line and make parachute jumps like the other troopers. Some riggers stayed behind in England packing and maintaining parachutes for supply drops and other uses. However, Cpl. Carl Porter was one of the 508th Service Company riggers that made the Normandy night drop like any other parachute infantryman. Carl described his first night in Normandy:

> Two commands I remember from our pre-D-Day briefing were "Take no prisoners until we hook up with our land forces" and "You are not to load your weapon until you are on the ground."
>
> Fortunately, I was not tested on the first, and even more fortunately, I believed the second saved my life.
>
> The drop was low and fast, and I was more concerned with the tracers piercing the chute above my head than I was in checking oscillation and where the chute and I were headed. Crashing through the branches of a large hedgerow tree and winding up dangling among the lower branches reminded me that it is always a good idea to check landing positions!
>
> By the time I had extricated myself from harness and branches, three German soldiers (who had probably been responsible for the tracers through my canopy) materialized. I made a partial turn toward their shadowy figures, and the realization that I held an unloaded rifle electrified my brain. I dropped the M-1 as if it were a white-hot poker and responded to a harsh "Hande hoch."
>
> One of the Germans motioned me into the clearing that was encircled by hedgerows, and as the moon brightened their figures, I saw that one held a rifle and the other two machine pistols. It's a pretty sure bet that if my rifle had been loaded and put to use, I wouldn't be here to write this today.

Porter was searched by his captors and stripped of all weapons, ammo, and personal possessions and then marched to a barnyard where there were about a dozen other paratroopers and glidermen that were captured earlier. Porter wrote, "They took one boot from each of us, so we couldn't run off, and left us with two guards for the rest of the night."

The next morning, the POWs were given the boots that the Germans took away the night before. (Porter marveled at the Germans' efficiency in keeping track so that they returned the correct boot to everyone.) Then the POWs were forced to march with fingers laced behind their heads for a mile or two.

Porter proclaimed, "Marching for a long distance in that posture becomes excruciating."

They arrived at a formidable new prison at the end of their march, which Porter described:

> Our new home was within a stonewalled courtyard, and we were imprisoned in a room about 20 by 25 feet. The stone walls were about 2 and 1/2 feet thick, with two small windows about a head high from the floor. I believe we numbered seventeen; thirteen were paratroopers and four were glidermen. The property was an old estate, which had been turned into a German headquarters, and in which we were held prisoners.

As the US Fourth Division advanced inland from the beaches, the German forces protecting the German headquarters put up a fierce resistance. The American attackers poured rifle and mortar fire against the stone structure housing the POWs. Carl Porter described his action and that of TSgt. Henry "Hank" P. Schillinger and Cpl. Robert "Bob" Watts under American attack:

> Rifle fire, mortar shrapnel, and chips of stone had been ricocheting around our prison cell longer than I care to remember. We had hugged the floor originally, and Bob had even tried to shield Hank at one point, when a particularly hard volley peppered the room. But as time wore on and the firing remained high, we relaxed a little in the sure knowledge (we thought) that the thick stone walls would provide adequate protection and that the material coming through the small windows could hurt but probably not kill.
> 
> At this point a wild-eyed German rifleman rushed into the room and began threatening us with his bayoneted rifle. I recall vividly the look in his eyes and the hateful expression on his face as he jabbed the bayonet toward me and asked, "Russkie?"
> 
> "Nein, nein!" I replied.
> 
> "Englich?" he then shouted.
> 
> I responded again with "Nein, nein!" and very slowly turned my right shoulder and pointed to the American flag and said, "American!"

His face broke into a wide grin as he exclaimed, "Americanish! Americanish!"

He then leaned his rifle against the wall so he could embrace me. Then as I looked over his shoulder while in that bear hug, I saw Hank Schillinger grab the rifle and, with Bob Watts on his heels, head out the door of our prison room into the general headquarters.

It took me a minute to get unhitched from the now super-friendly German. By the time I barged into the next room to help Hank, Bob, and the others, about twelve German soldiers were trying to get rid of their weapons as they surrendered.

I chose a P-35 pistol and a BAR-type automatic rifle from the stack of gunnery that was in the middle of the floor. Hank, Bob, and I and others, whom I can't remember, headed into the room just off the courtyard. Germans were surrendering faster than we could take their weapons. We herded many into the inner rooms with "potato mashers" still sticking out of their belts. (*Potato masher* is the American name for German hand grenades.)

Then we started trying to get the Fourth Division's attention to let them know that we were in control. At this point, one of the glider men saw a battle-scarred bugle hanging on the wall. He took it down and blew an American message to the infantry who were still pouring it on.

The way the sounds came out, it's hard to say whether he was blowing Chow Call, Taps, or Reveille. Whatever it was, the men of the Fourth Division heard it and the firing did indeed slacken and die. And what a glorious sound, that lack of sound was.

Several of us congratulated the man who blew the bugle and told him how glad we were that he knew how to blow one. He replied, "Hell, I never blew one of the dammed things before in my life, but I had to do something!"

After all the prisoners were corralled in the courtyard and the Fourth Division was organizing them for a march to the beach, a fellow in suntans walked over and identified himself as a reporter from *Time* magazine. The reporter spoke to Hank Schillinger, who was obviously in charge, and asked, "How many paratroopers do you have with you?"

Hank answered, "Thirteen," not mentioning the glidermen with them.

Then the reporter asked, "How many Germans did you guys take as prisoners?"

Hank shot him a quick look that said, "Who had time to count, you dumb bastard?" Then his face broke into that cherubic grin of his and he said with quiet authority, "Two hundred and ten."

One final note: a small mishap got me medivacuated by air out of France to a hospital in England, where I shared a ward with forty or fifty others. Rod McLennan was in the bed next to mine, and we shared war stories.

One day in early July, Rod shouted, "Porter, here it is right here in *Time* magazine!" It took me awhile to learn what *it* was, but to emphasize his point, he read the article aloud.

"That was us, all right," I said.

To which a voice across the aisle added, "You lucky son of a bitch! My colonel was fed up with blasting away at that stone fortress and had just told me to call the beach on the field phone and have the Navy lob some shells up there and blow that place off the face of the earth. I was just ringing up when we heard that damned bugle!'

And that, as Paul Harvey would say, is the rest of the story!

Service Company riggers who jumped in Normandy.
Photo provided by Carl Porter.

Front (L-R): T/S Hank Schillinger (POW), Jimmy Hall (KIA), Carl Porter (POW), Tommy Cross (KIA), Earl Cornwall, and Frank Dasch (POW). Back (L-R): Warrant Officer Roy Barger (POW), T/S John Kersh (POW), Cecil Neal (POW), T. K. Detwiler (POW), Al Pratle, Pony DuPont (MIA), Elmer Martell

(POW), Don Hanson, Howard "Randy" Ranabauer (KIA), Larry Snovak (KIA), Harry Gerheim, Bob Watts (POW), and Master Sergeant L. Keating (POW). Absent from picture: Pat Farrel (MIA). (POW: prisoner of war. MIA: missing in action. KIA: killed in action.)

## How the French Saved Two Paratroopers

This story began with an inquiry by Capt. John O'Brien of the US Air Force. O'Brien's grandfather T/5 Lawrence "Larry" J Snovak was killed in Normandy. O'Brien contacted the 508th Association, asking for information about his grandfather's service in the 508th Parachute Infantry Regiment. John Kersh and Larry Snovak were both riggers in Service Company. Kersh wrote a report telling what he knew about Snovak and the circumstance surrounding his death and added a great deal about his personal adventures in Normandy.

## Larry Snovak

Kersh's memories of Snovak are the following:

> The first time I remember Larry Snovak was in Camp Mackall, when we played on the rigger football team. I remember he was always an excellent hard worker. I knew he was married and had lived in Pittsburgh, Pennsylvania.
>
> When we were on the English airfield at about 9:00 PM on June 5, 1944, waiting for our mission to begin, he told me he had been hoping for a letter from his wife as she was expecting to have a baby any day. I found a jeep with a driver and got the driver to take us to the mailroom to see if there was any mail. Larry had a letter. He opened it and let out a yell, "By golly, it's a boy, and he's going to grow up and play football for the Pittsburgh Steelers!" He was so happy.

Larry Snovak and John Kersh boarded the same C-47 for their D-Day jump in Normandy. (In the photograph of riggers who jumped in Normandy, page 131, Kersh is in second from the left on the back row, and Snovak is the fourth from the right on the back row.)

When the C-47 carrying Kersh and Snovak arrived over the Normandy, it received heavy antiaircraft fire. The red light came on for the troopers to stand up and hook their parachute static lines to the cable in the top of the plane. The troopers had hooked up and were ready to jump when the red light went off, but the green light signal to exit the plane did not come on. The crew chief reported from the pilot that the lights had been shot out. The plane crew rigged up a buzzer to give the jump signal. The pilot circled back over the channel and made another pass over Normandy to complete the jump mission.

For whatever reason, the pilot gave the jump signal about seven miles from the designated drop zone. John Kersh described what happened when he hit the ground:

> We dropped on a German Division Headquarters. I remember that everywhere I went all I heard were Germans. There was a lot of machine gun fire. I had a carbine, a .45-caliber pistol, and six grenades. Before long, I had used up all my grenades. By then it was nearing daybreak, so I crawled up in a thick hedgerow and was going to hide out, if I could, during the day. About 10:00 I saw two German patrols coming toward me, one on each side of the hedgerow. When they got close, I stepped out and surrendered.

The Germans took Kersh to their headquarters, where he was detained about an hour, and then he and Marcel Bollag of the Eighty-second Airborne Division Intelligence Section and attached to the 508th were loaded on a truck. In the truck were three seriously wounded riggers who jumped with Kersh—Larry Snovak, Jimmy Hall, and Howard Ranabauer. (All three are listed as KIA in the photo on page 131.) Kersh and Bollag were unloaded at a prison compound, and Kersh assumed that the three wounded men were taken to a hospital where they died of their wounds. Kersh, seeing their condition while riding in the truck, didn't think they could survive. In Marcel Bollag's testimony, he overheard a German guard say that one of the severely wounded POWs was dying upstairs.

## John Kersh and Marcel Bollag

Kersh and Bollag did not know each other before the jump, and John Kersh said it was several days after their Normandy landing before they got to know each other. Their stories, however, fit together as having shared common experiences. They flew in different airplanes, but the two C-47s sustained similar damage to their signal lights over the exit door. Bollag wrote the following about his flight:

> We flew straight through the peninsula and soon hit the East Coast. The pilot turned around and headed inland again. Flak came up very heavy and knocked out our jump light. The pilot then ordered us to jump by telephone.

Marcel described many of his experiences of D-Day. Here are some selected excerpts:

> I landed two hundred feet away from a house, which I found out later to be a German command post. I hit an electric wire with my arm, which did not hurt badly. I then came down on the road. I felt a little relieved.
> I came to a corner of a field, and the machine gun bullets began flying too close for comfort. I reached for one of my hand grenades and threw it over the bush into the machine gun nest. The gun kept silent from then on.
> I was lying on the ground with my carbine ready. I fired three shots then a stoppage. I was still pulling my bolt back when two Germans were in front of me, pulling me out of the ditch.
> I posed as though I was wounded, and they believed it. In fact, they let me put my arm on their shoulder as I pointed to them that my knee was hurt. Anyhow, we got on the road and came to the house, which was actually a German command post.

Marcel Bollag's described his interrogation by the Germans—how they took all his personal belongings but neglected to take his watch and ring and then later gave back their pay books. Then they were taken to Valognes a few kilometers to the north.

During that afternoon, Allied airplanes bombed the village of Valognes. The Germans shot down one plane, but the pilot bailed out. He was soon brought in to join the other prisoners of war.

John Kersh described his first few days as a prisoner of war:

> We spent June 6 night in the prison camp (at Valogne). This camp was surrounded by barbed wire and German guards with machine guns. The next day (June 7), we were marched to the edge of Cherbourg and put in prison barracks. We stayed there until the morning of June 10. Then they marched about one hundred of us heading south. That was before the peninsula was cut off. The only other paratroopers that I knew in that group were Sgt. Marcel Bollag. It was Bollag's first jump. He was attached to the Intelligence Section because he was fluent in both German and French. He was raised in Switzerland and came to the United States in 1939.

In Bollag's memoirs about June 7, he spoke of being served *knaekebrot*, a hard-pressed biscuit, for breakfast. "In order to eat it, you must shake the bugs out first. The noon meal consisted of *knaekebrot* again with a small cup of coffee." Bollag described the afternoon of June 7 through June 11:

> About 1:00 PM, the Germans called out all prisoners from the 101st Airborne to get up and leave. I stayed on until 3:00 PM when all Eighty-second men were told to get up. We formed a column of fours and were counted at least ten times. Then we took off and marched through Valognes. Our column arrived late in the afternoon at our destination, a prison camp at Tourlaville, right outside Cherbourg.
>
> June 9, Friday: The officers had packed up their bags, put plenty of bread and food in those little horse-drawn carts, and were ready to leave. We were allowed to eat in the mess hall. The meal itself was not different from the usual, but we could get two helpings.
>
> Suddenly at 3:00 PM we had to line up in front of the barracks. Every prisoner was given one third of a loaf of bread with a little butter, and we were told that this ration had to hold for three meals. Then we were marched away from the prison camp through Tourlaville into Cherbourg. We marched through Cherbourg singing and whistling "The Yanks Are Coming." We were loaded into cattle cars about forty to forty-five men each. My friend John, a rigger from the 508th, sat next to me with a long face. About one hour later, the train stopped at Bricquebec and everybody had to get off.
>
> We marched about two kilometers, and then we passed a long convoy (of trucks), which had stopped and was filled with American paratroopers. Our group of prisoners was marched to a side path and stopped. I could hear a German sergeant tell a corporal that the last half of us would be loaded into those trucks. When I heard it, I immediately started moving toward the front of the column together with my friend. I managed to get away from a ride.
>
> We marched about three more kilometers and then stopped at a big farm, which had been transformed into a prisoners' cage. There the Germans made the distinction of officers, NCOs, and enlisted men. We (NCOs) went into a barn.

John Kersh wrote about the events of the next day:

On June 11, we started out marching again. The sun was almost down when a P-47 (American) flew over us. I could see the smoke shooting from the front of his wings, so I jumped in a ditch beside the road. We were strafed, and he turned and started back. There was a ditch that ran crossways to the road, so I got in there. The P-47 made several more passes until his ammo ran out and he left. All the German guards had been riding bicycles, and all but three had been killed. I don't know how many Americans were killed, but the road was covered with the dead and badly wounded. A priest and some of the other people came out and helped as much as they could (with the dead and wounded).

Bollag's memoirs mentioned that the afternoon was spent burying their dead comrades. After so many prisoners and German guards were killed or wounded, both the American and the Germans were glad to rest during the day and march at night. They started the next night at a fast clip. According to Bollag, they passed through La Haye du Puits and Lessay. Both cities had been badly bombed by our air force. About 2:00 AM, the Germans guards were exhausted, and although the paratrooper prisoners were trying to act like they could keep going, they were glad to stop and spent the rest of the night in a farmer's barn.

When Marcel Bollag awoke the next morning and left the barn, he saw the German guards were eating, but no food was provided for the POWs. Marcel had made friends with a young blond German guard. He found his blond friend and asked permission to go to the farmer's house and beg some bread. His Nazi friend granted permission, provided Bollag brought some cider back to him.

While at the house getting his bread and the cider for the German, Bollag talked to a Frenchman who agreed to hide him and provide food for him if he managed to escape. Bollag returned with cider for the German guard. Then he found John Kersh and told him about the Frenchman's offer. They agreed and formulated their escape plan. Bollag passed the message to the Frenchman, a blacksmith named Albert Ourselin.

Marcel and John got permission to cross the road to a potato field and dig some potatoes for their food. It was easy for them to move into the fields beyond the potato patch without being noticed by the Germans, and they kept going for about two miles, crossing many hedgerows. They waited there overnight and returned to the farm the next day. The Germans had already left with the other POWs. They met Albert at a prearranged time and place, and Albert took them to his home.

Albert's household consisted of his wife; their fifteen-year-old daughter, Simone; Fernand and Louis, ages six and seven; the baby, Claude; and two husky boys, Jean and Albert, who helped in the blacksmith shop and lived in the home with the Ourselin family. Because of the night bombing, the whole family slept in a trench at night. They got busy and dug an extra trench for Marcel and John and added plenty of straw and blankets.

Since Germans frequently passed by, Albert brought civilian clothes for Marcel and John. He had fake photos made and French ID cards, with their own fingerprints and new names. Marcel remembers that his French name was Jules, and everyone in the family, including Baby Claude, started called him Jules. John Kersh, who could not speak French, had his ID card identifying him as a deaf and dumb Frenchman.

The family was very happy to be host to the two Americans, and so was the whole village nearby. Many of the neighbors shared food with Albert's family to help feed their guests. Marcel said, "Albert never had so much to eat before we came."

One day, Albert came home from collecting food and supplies and told them that two other paratroopers were hiding out with a family about one kilometer away. A surprise visitor named Julien came to Albert's house and told them that a neighbor of his had taken in a P-47 pilot, who had bailed out of his damaged plane before it crashed. Later the pilot came to visit with them.

Another P-47 pilot bailed out, but the Germans were there as soon as he hit the ground and killed him on the spot. Marcel said, "We buried him and took his dog tags."

As the fighting grew closer to their village, many French refugees passed by. The Germans in the battle zones would clear the people from their homes, search the houses, take what they wanted, and advise the people to seek a safer place. Some were carrying as little as a chicken underarm. Others had horse-drawn carts filled with their belongings.

On the night of June 25, a company of Germans moved into Albert's backyard. His wife hurriedly packed food and clean shirts for John and Marcel and sent them toward the next farm, where Alphonse met them and took them about four kilometers to his house on a small farm away from the village.

Alphonse told them he was going to hide them in a barn and keep their hiding place a secret from everyone except Albert. They had to stay in the barn unless Alphonse came and took them to his house. Sometimes food was brought to them in the barn, and sometimes, they were invited to the house for a meal. As time went by, they stayed more and more in the house during the day.

Once a German soldier came to the house and said he needed to use their kitchen to cook for his troops, about fifty men. American airplanes had destroyed his field kitchen. The German cook asked Marcel about his hands. He said, "Your hands don't look like a farmer's hands."

Marcel explained that he was a refugee from Cherbourg and that he had worked in an office in Cherbourg, but before that, he had worked on a farm. The German relaxed, drank cider with them, and showed pictures of his family. They all shared in the big meal, which the German cooked for his soldiers.

The situation was getting scary. Both John and Marcel were on edge. John stayed in the trench where they hid out, and Marcel carried food to him. The next day the German cook came back to use the kitchen. He asked Marcel, "Can you fly a plane?"

Marcel replied, "Hell, I don't like planes—never been in one."

Marcel decided right then to take off. He decided to go to Julien's house. He told Alphonse's wife where he was going. Then Marcel got John out of his trench, and they left walking down the road. That was July 8.

They walked to Julien's house, acting like normal Frenchmen, and arrived without interference from the Germans. Marcel and John built an elaborate underground hiding place: a deep trench covered with wood bundled to look like a woodpile. Inside they had blankets, pillows, food, and a radio.

On the morning of July 13, Julien rushed in to say the Germans had ordered everyone out of the village by 4:00 PM. Albert had buried John and Marcel's military clothes in his yard. Camille, Julien's younger brother, hurried to Albert's place and retrieved their buried outfits. Albert and his family had already left.

John and Marcel said their farewells to Julien's family and pushed a two-wheeled cart in front of them, like any other French refugees, for twenty kilometers to their next hideout. Their hostess was Madame Poirier. Her husband was in a prison camp in Northern France. He had been caught by the Germans picking up British parachute bundles containing guns and ammunitions.

Madame Poirier's place was luxurious. They had their first bath. They enjoyed fine foods. They had books to read, radios to listen to, a wonderful bedroom with water, toilet articles, etc. The house was home to two adult daughters of Madame Poirier, their children, and her adult son.

It was apparent that the opposing armies would soon be fighting very close to them. The Americans had already reached the Atlantic Ocean on the other side of Lessay Bay, not far from Madame Poirier's house. The French advised Marcel and John that the time was right for them to get behind the American lines.

The two paratroopers had been sheltered by Albert from June 13 until June 25. They stayed with Alphonse from June 25 until July 8. They were guests of Julien from July 8 until July 13. From July 13 until July 17 Madame Poirier was their hostess.

John Kersh wrote in his report:

> On July 17, at about midnight, we went to the coast and waded in the ocean. The moon was dark, but a French marine who had served in World War I led us behind the American lines. We went ashore and waited until daylight and then started walking toward La Haye du Puits.

It wasn't long before an American jeep came along. Bollag and Kersh flagged it down. They were taken to a command post and interrogated. That afternoon they met General Bradley and other high brass. The fast pace slowed down as the two had to go through GI processing. Finally verbal orders from a sympathetic colonel to a C-47 pilot put them at the head of the line. They bumped high-ranking officers with written orders for the next plane to England. On July 22, Bollag and Kersh arrived in England at their separate bases—Bollag to Wollaton Park in Nottingham and Kersh to his rigger base at Oakham.

Sgt. Marcel Bollag was attached to the 508th PIR just before the Normandy operation. He returned to the Eighty-second Division about a week after arriving at Wollaton Park from France. The only person Bollag remembered from the 508th is John Kersh.

Marcel Bollag and his wife, Anita, visited France several times and found some of the good French people who risked their lives and property to protect him and his fellow soldier John Kersh. Below is a photo of Marcel and Anita with members of the Ourselin family.

Albert Ourselin is seated center. His wife, Pauline, is directly behind Albert. Their daughter, Simone, and her husband, Roger Carpentier, are standing on the left. Marcel and Anita Bollag are standing on the right. Photo provided by Marcel Bollag.

## Five Days in "Hell's Half Acre"

Sgt. O. B. Hill, Headquarters First, heard the word "Flash!" from behind a hedgerow. He remembered "Flash!" was the challenge word of friendly paratroopers, but what was the response? His mind would not yield that important information. Finally, in disgust, Hill said, "Oh, shit!"

"Get in here, Sarge," replied Cpl. Bill Brown from his hiding place in the thick hedge. The corporal had recognized his sergeant's voice.

O. B. Hill had dropped into the floodwaters of the Douve. When he saw he was landing in water, he thought he would drown from the weight of the equipment pulling him under. Luckily, the water was only waist deep, but his careful plan to have plenty of smokes was foiled. Before the jump, he had removed his gas mask from its bag and filled the container with cigarettes. All his cigs were drowned in the Douve.

Safely out of the water, Hill started moving toward what he thought might be Chef du Pont. Up ahead he heard some noise. He lay perfectly still and observed about twenty Germans moving up a ditch. When the Jerries were gone, Hill continued and soon was challenged by Bill Brown.

Hill and Brown moved on toward their objective of Chef du Pont and by 0900 hours had collected a group of about fifty paratroopers from a variety of units, but most were Red Devils of the 508th. There were no officers in the group. Their heaviest weapon was the M-1 rifle. SSgt. Ray Hummel was the ranking noncom, and Sgt. O. B. Hill was second in command. They assembled near the village of Beuzeville behind a row of houses, close to where the Merderet River enters the Douve.

Jim McMahon, Headquarters First, was with Hummel and Hill. He also had landed in the Douve floodwaters. "I realize how fortunate I was to have my feet on solid mud," McMahon remarks. "Some troopers in deeper water were pulled under by the weight of their equipment and drowned."

McMahon describes his experiences before joining the group:

> I was in the water about fifteen minutes before getting out of my chute. During this time, I observed a group of Jerries on the opposite bank firing at the still-inflated chutes that were blowing across the water, dragging troopers in their harnesses.
>
> A chute with a dead trooper blew to within ten feet of me. This drew machine-pistol fire in my direction. Luckily the Jerries trained their guns on the half-inflated chute and ignored my head sticking out of the water a few feet away. When I had a chance, I made a fast exit to a clump of small trees and bushes on the bank.
>
> As I made my way through the trees looking for a friendly face, I was challenged by an American voice. He didn't know the password, but we worked it out after a few dumb questions, such as "Who is your company commander?" I didn't recognize his CO's name, and he didn't know mine because he was from the 101st Division.

McMahon and his friend smoked a cigarette and then moved along the bank of the river in the direction of rifle-fire they could hear in the distance. Soon they came to a freshly dug circular pit about two feet deep and about eighteen feet in circumference. Clearly the pit was prepared for some kind of gun emplacement, but no Jerries seemed to be around. McMahon recalls their entrance and exit from the pit:

My friend from the 101st and I climbed into the pit. From our position we observed a small group of Jerries patrolling the opposite bank. Feeling comparatively safe, we decided to fire a few rounds at them. This was a mistake because seconds later, we drew rifle fire from our rear out of the woods. We could hear a truck starting up and many German voices shouting commands. When a hand grenade exploded right outside the pit, we left as if we were rockets.

A good distance from the pit we were challenged again by an American voice, and this was when we joined the group led by Hummel and Hill near Beuzeville.

Hummel and Hill decided to enter a nearby house and see what they could see from an upstairs window. Having shot the lock off of the house, the three troopers—Hummel, Hill, and Jim McMahon—climbed the stairs to the second floor. (Mel Beets also remembered being with O. B. in the house.) They heard the sound of tanks and from their upstairs window saw three Renaults stop in the street. The center tank came to a halt directly below the window where Hummel and Hill were watching. The hatch raised, and a tanker stood up. Hill passed a Gammon grenade to Hummel, who dropped it into the open turret.

When the Gammon exploded, the troopers ran down the stairs and out into the field behind the house, but an elderly bedridden Frenchwoman had already outrun them down the stairs. The two remaining tanks fired their weapons at suspected targets, but they failed to hit the house the paratroopers had used.

After the tank exploded, the group moved through the fields toward Chef du Pont. They drew German machine gun fire every time they approached a road or tried to move through the water. The fields proved to be the safest route. Advancing about eight hedgerows, they came upon the road to Chef du Pont and could see the causeway across the Merderet River. The road was heavily defended by German troops, and a two-story house on the corner next to the road was filled with Germans. O. B. Hill describes the action that followed:

> We got into a firefight with the Germans in the house. After a short time we recognized an American voice (Sgt. Joseph Gagnon) shouting at us. The Jerries had several of our men as prisoners. The prisoners shouted for us to back off or they would be shot. This ended the firefight, but soon the Germans were firing at us from another direction. We thought

that we would be able to escape this corner under the cover of darkness, but every exit was well defended by the Germans. We were fired at every time we made a move.

By this time we had lost twelve men from our group and several were injured. George De Carvalho was hit by a German rifle-grenade, which was a dud and failed to explode, but the impact broke George's ankle. (George said, "It was a live grenade, and I have the scars to show for it.") C. P. Reynolds was hit in the head by a bullet. Without medics we did the best we could. We filled the wounds with sulfa powder and gave morphine.

The Germans had us completely surrounded. We decided not to surrender but to stay and do what we could to keep the enemy busy. The Jerries set up a mortar with a two-man crew across from where Ray Hummel and I were dug in. Every time the mortar men made an appearance, Ray and I would shoot them. These would be dragged off, and two others would take their places with the same results. This process was repeated a number of times before they moved the mortar.

In the middle of the third night, we heard someone approaching from the direction of Beuzeville. Out of the darkness came the voice of an elderly Frenchman. He brought us wine, cheese, and bread. He risked his life going through the Germans to bring us gifts. The Frenchman verified that the Germans had us surrounded in large numbers.

One day it rained. Everyone had been issued a gas cape, a large plastic bag to crawl into in the event of a gas attack. Troopers were using the gas cape to keep the rain off. McMahon didn't have a cape, so he crawled over to O. B. Hill's foxhole to see if he could talk him out of his plastic.

Jim McMahon explains:

> We were talking, and suddenly O. B.'s eyes almost popped out. He saw a Jerry appear over the stone wall bordering our field. The Jerry let loose a burst from a machine pistol. I said to myself, "This is the end for us!"
>
> The bullets kicked up dirt between my legs and under my armpits. It was a miracle we were not hit! O. B. dug his elbows into my shoulder blades to prop up his rifle and returned the fire.
>
> I quickly returned to my foxhole and forgot about the plastic gas cape.

—

On the fifth day, the paratroopers were still surrounded in the small field. They were almost out of ammunition. They wondered if they could hold out another day, and then they heard someone yell, "Bring up that damn bazooka!"

It was a sergeant from the Ninetieth Division. Hill recalled:

> We all jumped up shouting and waving. We made ourselves such a target that the sergeant almost had a heart attack. Friendly faces made us so happy, we forgot about the danger.

Sergeant Hummel and his "pack of strays" are given credit for harassing the German defenders of the bridge across the Douve and the causeway across the Merderet. The Germans had to reduce travel over those important crossings, so supplies and troops moved only at night.

O. B. Hill returned to Normandy several times and located some of the Norman people who remembered the five days when American paratroopers occupied the field, which the troopers named Hell's Half Acre. He met the Cortell family who lived in the corner house where a big firefight took place. O. B. had thrown a grenade into their barnyard where some Germans were milling about. After O. B. had released the grenade and before it landed, Madame Cortell walked into the yard.

After the war, when they met and talked through an interpreter, O. B., who had feared that his grenade had injured Madame Cortell, asked was she hurt. "No," she replied. "But I was so frightened, I had to change my skivvies."

The Frigoult family was another family contacted by O. B. Hill. It was at the Frigoult house that Hill smashed the lock to gain entrance on the night of June 5/6, 1944.

In 1944, Marie-Louise Frigoult was a twenty-two-year-old single lady planning for her marriage. She appropriated an abandoned white reserve parachute and made a beautiful gown with the material, which she wore for her wedding a year later.

On June 4, 1997, O. H. Hill presented Madame Marie-Louise Frigoult a new lock for her home and Madame Frigoult gave O. B. Hill her wedding dress. Hill has donated the dress to be placed among the 508th memorabilia in the Camp Blanding Museum, near Starke, Florida, where the 508th was organized as a regiment in 1942.

O. B. Hill and Madam Frigoult exchanged gifts. Photo furnished by O. B. Hill.

## "I Was with O.B. Hill," Mel Beets

Melvin "Mel" Beets, Headquarters First, was with O. B. Hill and Ray Hummel in "Hell's Half Acre." Mel said that he was with O. B. and Ray when they went into the French house and dropped the Gammon grenade out of the second-story window and blew up the German tank. He also remembered losing the race to a bedridden Frenchwoman.

Mel reported how he was separated from O. B. and his group:

> O. B. wanted someone to investigate another house, from which we had received fire. There was some question about who was in the house. It could even be Americans firing at Americans. They hoped that they could join forces with those in the house if they were Americans. It would give them a better chance for surviving. Like a fool, I volunteered to go take a look.

At the time Mel Beets started on his mission, the street was quiet, so Mel walked down the street toward the house. Bullets began to fly around Mel about halfway to the house. Mel dove into some tall grass and crawled through the grass until the firing ceased.

Then Mel heard the noise of tanks and, looking up above the grass, saw three tanks headed across the field toward him. Mel jumped up and

145

ran toward some nearby trees for better cover. Again the bullets whizzed by him; one bullet creased his knee—only a surface wound. Mel fell forward. He thought he had tripped over a fence rather than having a bullet hit him. He tried to get up, but his knee gave way on the first try. He tried again and was able to stand, and as he stood, he was suddenly face-to-face with about eight Germans.

Mel threw up his hands. The Germans responded by knocking him down and working him over with their rifle butts and their boots until he was unconscious. He came to inside a German tank. Eventually the tank delivered Mel to a holding area with other captured American prisoners.

In the meantime, back at Hell's Half Acre, O. B. Hill's group renewed firing at a house on the corner—the Cotell family home. A familiar voice called from the Cotell home, telling the troopers that the Germans threatened to kill him if they continued to assault the house. O. B. Hill was sure it was the voice of his close friend Freddie Gagnon of Headquarters First, so they held their fire.

At the holding area, a German officer interrogated Mel Beets. Mel gave his name, rank and, serial number. Then the officer put his pistol against Mel's head and said, "You had better tell the truth."

Beets replied, "I was in the regular infantry. They yanked me out my unit, put a parachute on me, put me on a plane, and kicked me out. I don't know anything else." That ended the interrogation.

Mel Beets and the other POWs were loaded on trucks. When the trucks moved out on the road, American planes strafed the convoy. During the strafing, Mel exited his truck and ran to a small out building, where he found his friend Sgt. Joseph "Freddie" Gagnon of Headquarters First bleeding profusely from a head wound. This was the same Freddie Gagnon who called out from the Cortell house.

Just before D-Day, Mel had received a package from his wife that included some handkerchiefs. Mel used all his new handkerchiefs to stop Gagnon's bleeding.

About twenty minutes later, the planes returned and strafed the convoy until all the trucks were burning. The Germans rounded up the POWs and marched them all night to the infamous Starvation Hill. Most of the POWs captured in Normandy passed through Starvation Hill.

Eventually Mel Beets was transported, over a period of time and by various means, to Chalons-sur-Marne, a city on the Marne River about eighty miles east of Paris. In the process of being moved from the third story to the second story of an old French barracks, Mel Beets moved slower than his captors expected him to move. A guard pushed Mel, causing him to fall down the stairs and to break his ankle.

The Germans took Mel Beets to a German hospital, which housed mostly amputees, which made Mel think they planned to cut off his leg. Fortunately the German doctors only made a cast for his broken ankle. Then they moved him to the second floor of the hospital, a section for the Americans only, where captured American doctors treated them.

Mel observed that as the POWs in the hospital were well enough, they were sent away, so Mel tried to hide the progress of his recovery. Secretly at night, he exercised his bad leg and gained strength.

During air raids, the hospital staff moved the patients to the basement. After one Allied aid raid, Mel Beets returned from the basement then looked out the window and observed that the guards were no longer at the gate. He retrieved his Red Cross parcel from its hiding place and went over the wall surrounding the military compound.

As he dropped to the ground, almost before he could straighten up, a small Frenchman carrying an automatic weapon stuck the barrel of his weapon in Mel's stomach. At the time Mel was wearing a GI olive drab shirt and trousers and socks without boots.

Mel threw his hands up and yelled, "American! American!"

Then the Frenchman gave Mel a big hug. He was a Free-French underground soldier.

Mel asked, "Where are the Americans?"

The Frenchman pointed down the street and agreed to take Mel to the American forces.

By this time, the streets were full of fleeing German vehicles. The Frenchman would go ahead and scout out the next street, and when there was a break in the traffic, he would wave Mel to come on. They continued this for about four blocks to the edge of the city. From there they walked down a dirt road into the country

Mel saw an American helmet duck for cover. Mel hollered at the American. He stood up, and Mel saw that he was a first-aid medic. They continued walking until they ran into the infantry that was leading the tanks.

Mel told the tank commander about the hospital. He then boarded a tank and directed their way back to the hospital. They found the Germans gone, the gates opened, and the POWs that were able to walk were celebrating in the street.

Next trip for Mel was by jeep to a well-equipped field hospital. His ankle was x-rayed, and he was given a thorough physical. He had reinjured his ankle when he dropped over the hospital compound wall and was suffering from malnutrition. From the field hospital, Mel Beets was transported by train to the coast and by hospital ship to England.

While still a patient in an English hospital, Mel witnessed the flight of hundreds of C-47s on their way to the airborne invasion of Holland. Although he missed the Holland operation, Mel Beets was well and ready for the Battle of the Bulge.

## South of the Douve

Thurman Davis Jones, a nineteen-year-old son of a Texas sharecropper, boarded a C-47 named Buzzard's Bait the night of June 5, 1944. As the paratroopers from A Company climbed through the plane door, Jones thought, "The air force plans to feed us to the buzzards." Jones remembered the names of five other A Company men who had boarded the Buzzard Bait: First Sergeant Bill Clark (leader and jumpmaster), Rod Roderiques, Robert Asher, Eugene Seawright, and Bruce Baker.

Jones felt sick at his stomach and broke out in a cold sweat. He grabbed the hook-up cable and stumbled to the door of the plane. The fresh air at the door and comforting words from Sergeant Clark made Jones feel better. He returned to his seat and soon dropped off to sleep.

"I awoke to the bouncing and bucking of the plane as the antiaircraft guns were trying to blow us out of the sky. I was glad when the call came to stand up and hook up," Jones recalled.

Jones had a hard landing, which knocked the breath out of him, but after getting out of his parachute and taking stock, he saw that he was in a wheat field surrounded by hedgerows. He soon found two other members of his stick—Rod Roderiques and Robert Asher. Before daylight, the three troopers found a large farmhouse. Several trucks and cars were parked at the house, and a Nazi swastika was waving in the pale moonlight. Jones, Roderiques, and Asher discussed blowing the place up but had no demolition equipment. Having learned that survival was the best part of valor, they decided to leave the Nazis undisturbed.

After daylight Jones, Asher, and Roderiques came across three more troopers. Now there were six. They soon spotted Germans soldiers leading nine loaded pack mules. The troopers hid in ambush to surprise the mule train, but before they were close, some tanks rumbled in behind the mules. Again the troopers decided on survival and moved deeper into the woods.

Toward evening of the first day, the six wandering troopers came across a group led by Sergeant Brewer of A Company. After Jones and his group joined Brewer, they hid in hedgerows for the rest of a cold, rainy night.

Early the next morning, a glider pilot and a glider soldier from the 101st Division struggled out of the swamp and joined the Brewer group. Their glider had landed deep in the floodwater of the Douve River. The pilot was a warrant officer, who outranked Sergeant Brewer. Brewer tried to turn over the command to the pilot, but the pilot refused since his only training had been as a glider pilot.

With their maps and the help of a friendly Frenchman, Brewer learned they were on the south side of the Douve River, about eight miles and a flooded river from their drop zone. The next two or three days, the band of about twenty wandered up and down the Douve, trying to stay away from Germans and trying to find a place they might safely cross the river to join the regiment.

On D+4 Jones and Sergeant Brewer's group met a Frenchman dressed in a brown business suit. (Lucien Hasley from Picauville identified the Frenchman as Monsieur Jean Fontaine.) The Frenchman led them to a large house, where other paratroopers had assembled.

First Sergeant Bill Clark, jumpmaster of the Buzzard's Bait, tried to roll up his stick of paratroopers immediately after landing. He moved in the direction his men should have landed, but after covering about two hundred yards without finding anyone, he hunkered down inside a hedgerow and waited for daylight.

At dawn Clark started toward the sound of small-arms fire. After two hours the firing did not seem any closer. He had found no one and was very lonely. He crawled in a depression inside a hedgerow and lit up one of those Lucky Strikes that were generously given to soldiers. Halfway through his smoke, Clark heard a voice and saw a German soldier running toward him, his rifle pointed in his direction and shouting, "Raust!" which means "Come on out!" Clark responded by killing the German and leaving in a hurry. He reasoned that other Germans were not far behind.

Clark continued on the move very cautiously until about noon, when he stopped inside a hedgerow to listen for more firing to guide his

First Sergeant Bill Clark. Photo provided by Bill Clark.

movements. Suddenly two GIs came through the hedges; one was a 508-er from C Company, the other was an Airborne engineer. The three together felt a boost of moral. They talked over their situation and decided to move northward.

After moving through a few more hedgerows, the trio found a little road. They flagged down a Frenchwoman and her son who were walking toward their house nearby. The son spoke English and informed them that farther down the road were some other lost paratroopers. Proceeding down the road they found Seawright and Baker from Clark's stick and another C Company man.

Now Clark and his men numbered six. They retraced their steps to the house to inquire more about their situation from the English-speaking French boy. He told them that they were about five miles south of the Douve River. He warned them not to go west because Germans were massing troops there. So Clark's group started north toward the Douve River.

In about an hour, a German patrol spotted Clark's band of six and opened fire, which resulted in a two-hour firefight. All the Germans were killed, except one very scared young kid, who surrendered. Clark lost one of the C Company men and the engineer, both killed in the skirmish. Now they were four paratroopers and one German prisoner. Eventually Clark found the large farmhouse where other small groups had collected.

The destiny of another planeload of troopers was closely linked to the destiny of the men in the Buzzard's Bait. First Battalion brass decided that a bridge near Picauville needed to be blown. Four demolitionists from Regimental Headquarters Company—Carlos Ross, Cumer Green, Henry Stutika, and Al Jacksich—were assigned to a rifle squad in C Company to destroy the bridge. Lt. Bruce Bell was number one and jumpmaster, Ross was second, followed by Green, Stutika, Jacksich, and the other C Company men in the stick.

Ross describes his jump:

> My legs were drawn up as far into my belly as I could get them because of the tracers coming my way. If I had hit the ground in that position, I would probably have broken every bone in my body. Luckily I made the only tree landing of my career. I still managed to hit the ground hard enough to sprain my left knee. The tree then jerked me back into the air about

two feet. After cutting myself down and assembling my gear, Lieutenant Bell and I got together.

Ross and Lieutenant Bell were hiding in a hedgerow when they heard a clicking noise. Bell sent Ross to investigate the source of the noise. Ross had not gone far when Germans fired into the hedgerow where Bell was hiding. Ross immediately returned to the spot and found the lieutenant dead. The death of Lieutenant Bell was very unnerving for young Carlos Ross who, fifty years later, broke down weeping, when relating that incident.

After Lieutenant Bell was killed, Carlos Ross was alone for two days, but on D+2, he found seven men from the 307th Engineer Battalion. Later that same day, they met a patrol of paratroopers who led them to the farmhouse with other GIs. Carlos remembers that among the group at the farmhouse were two C Company lieutenants, Lt. Leon E. Lavender and Lt. Joe Lewellen (Lewellen's thumb had been shot off). In the group were three prisoners—a captured sergeant and two middle-aged German soldiers.

Broughton Hand from C Company jumped from the same plane as Carlos Ross. Hand also landed south of the Douve. Hand was a demolitionist and was loaded down with materials to blow a bridge. After landing, Hand moved northeast, the direction his plane had been traveling, and soon linked up with three other C Company men—Bob Harper, Cornelius Connaghan, and Bob Nobles. Nobles said that Lt. Bruce Bell was jumpmaster of his plane, which means that Carlos Ross jumped from the same plane.

They continued moving northeast. About daylight, the four troopers came upon a bivouac of Germans that started popping out of foxholes. The paratroopers attempted to withdraw without being seen, but a sentry walking guard spotted Hand and fired at him. Hand returned fire with his Thompson submachine gun and in his words, "I cut loose and picked him up and laid him down."

Hand and his squad doubled back and ran back in the direction from which they came for about two miles until they found cover in a ditch in a patch of woods. They remained hidden there until dark.

While in the woods, Nobles noticed blood on Hand. The bullet from the German sentry grazed Hand's thumb, skidded on his Thompson, and passed through his clothes on his side, just breaking the skin without penetrating his body. Nobles used materials from his first aid kit to bandage Hand's side. Hand's injury was minor, and his tommy gun was still operational.

After dark, they awakened an elderly French couple in their home. Bob Nobles, who spoke French, learned that they were near the Douve River. Hand and his squad found a bridge over the Douve. They hid and watched German troop movements over the bridge during the day. They waited for the cover of darkness to set their explosives.

Meanwhile, an American glider pilot saw them and explained how difficult it would be for them to get to the main part of the bridge beyond the long causeway through the floodwater. They thought they could wade or swim to the bridge, so they hid with the glider pilot until after dark. The glider pilot was right. They could not get to the bridge and keep their fuses and primer cord dry. However, they mined the approaches to the bridge and moved on.

Soon they spotted and joined a group of about twenty troopers, including other C Company men: Sgt. Bramwell Phillips, Lt. Leon Lavender, Lt. Joe Lewellen, two British sergeants, and others. Lieutenant Lavender was in command. They planned to go to a large farmhouse, rest up for the night, and try to get a boat to cross the river the next day.

By this time the troopers had eaten most of the K rations they jumped with. Lieutenant Lavender authorized butchering a cow, which the troopers tried to cook. The lieutenant wrote a note to the French owner: "IOU one cow, US government, Lieutenant Lavender."

Hand told Lavender that Bob Nobles had asked the elderly French couple for food when they were trying to learn their location. The couple promised them food if they came back after they had time to milk their cow and gather eggs.

Hand took the three paratroopers who assembled with him and revisited the French family. Noble went inside to bargain, and the other three hid outside behind a stone wall. Soon a German soldier walked by as if he was taking a Sunday stroll. Just as the German came next to him, Hand stepped in front with his tommy gun and captured the soldier. Two more German soldiers approached alone, and Hand captured those two the same way. Hand's squad returned to the large farmhouse with three prisoners and some groceries.

Information from Jones, Clark, Ross, and Hand indicated that the combined forces included 508th paratroopers from A and C companies, Carlos Ross from Regimental Headquarters Company, engineers from the 307th Airborne, a 101st Airborne glider pilot, a glider trooper, and two Russian civilians.

Then there were the two Russians in civilian clothes. These were former Russian POWs who had deserted from a German work camp and had linked up with the American paratroopers. They asked for weapons and were given a .45 army pistol with five rounds of ammo by Richard Dugan of A Company. The Russians went on a patrol and returned with only three rounds in the pistol. They said they had killed two Germans with the missing rounds, and they brought back a German sergeant as their prisoner. One of the Russians took the sergeant's boots. The sergeant was relieved to be guarded by less-abusive Americans.

The next day, June 11 (D-Day + 5), the combined force under the command of Lieutenant Lavender moved several miles to another large farmhouse. The new location was only five hundred yards from the Douve River, hopefully a beachhead for crossing.

Carlos Ross described the situation at the farm complex:

> Between the house and the river, the grass was only six inches tall and offered no cover for the troopers during daylight hours. German soldiers were in the woods about three hundred yards away. They made their presence known by shooting at P-47 fighter planes circling above. Monsieur Fontaine took the two Russians with him to find boats. He planned to help the paratroopers cross the river in boats at night.
>
> Lieutenant Lavender was in command. Lieutenant Lewellen, who had lost his thumb and a lot of blood and was running a high fever, remained at the first house. [George Lamm confirmed that Lewellen was later found by US troops, but most of his hand was lost from gangrene.] Lavender and First Sergeant Clark placed some men in the barn, some in the house, and others along a hedgerow that was an extension of the house and barn, and finally the last group was about two hundred yards to the rear toward the river. They also maintained an outpost in front of the house on the road to the village.

Jones recalled going on a patrol with Richard Dugan into the village. The people were staying inside but would give the *V* sign from their doors and windows so Dugan and Jones knew that the Germans were close by. At the far side of the village they found another large house and saw a tall dark-haired girl in the yard carrying a basket of eggs. Dugan, who could speak French, approached her, and she invited the troopers in. (Lucien Hasley identified the girl as Mademoiselle Louise Bourde.)

The girl's mother had a pot of stew hanging over the open fireplace. A roast was cooking but was still very rare. The woman cut off pieces of the half-cooked roast and added them to the stew. This she served with bread and cider. Dugan and Jones drank two pitchers of cider while they ate. They left the house carrying a generous quantity of bread for their buddies.

Dugan talked to a French lad who told him that three Germans regularly patrolled the village and would be along soon. The troopers waited in hiding a short time but became impatient and returned to the outpost near their stronghold. While they were sharing the bread with others, the three-man German patrol appeared around the curve. One trooper shot at the patrol with his tommy gun through the fence palings. The frightened Jerries dropped their weapons and ran back around the corner.

Germans on the left then opened fire and charged toward the outpost through a wheat field. The troopers behind a hedgerow, a short distance back, fired on the charging Jerries. The Germans stopped and took cover in the tall grain and started calling out. Dugan, who could speak German as well as French, reported the Jerries wanted to surrender. Jones called back to the guys behind the hedgerow to hold their fire. Then Dugan stepped out from behind a tree, called, and motioned to the Germans to come in. Instead of coming in with hands up, they fired at Dugan, hitting him in the left arm and at the same time splattering the tree with bullets.

Dugan was helped back toward the house but left his tommy gun with Jones. When the next charge came, Jones let the Jerries have it with Dugan's tommy gun. Again the Jerries halted and took cover in the tall grain—then a long silence. Jones moved from behind the tree to a ditch where he had better protection and improved observation of the enemy.

The stew and cider were beginning to make Jones drowsy, and he dropped off to sleep in the ditch. He was awakened by a noise and looked up and saw a giant German walking in the road toward him. Jones was lying face down in the ditch with his rifle in his left hand. He quickly lifted his rifle toward the German and fired two rounds, missing both times. The German fired twice and missed also. By this time, Jones had time to get the rifle to his shoulder and take aim, hitting the Jerry with his next shot.

The German was mortally wounded and kept yelling and kicking until he died. Jones wanted to get away from the dying enemy, so he moved back toward a barn and got behind a mound of dirt. When some bullets started kicking up the dirt on the mound in front of him, Jones asked Harvey Knapp of A Company to climb to the loft and see if he could spot where the bullets were coming from.

By the time Knapp got to the loft, a large armored half-track pulled around the corner, fired its cannon at the barn, and blew the top off. Knapp came tumbling down covered with dust. Three machine guns, with a large steel plate to protect the gunners, were mounted on the half-track. When the three machine guns opened up, Jones took off to the nearest hedgerow and caught up with nine troopers trying to escape toward the river. By this time, hundreds of Germans were advancing from their flank and the half-track was pouring lead toward them.

As the advancing Germans were closing in, hollering and screaming, Mac McLemore of A Company said, "Listen to those Jerries scream. Everyone of those SOBs must be second lieutenants."

One of the ten troopers stuck his head through the next hedgerow. A bullet penetrated his helmet and made a three-inch scalp wound. He called out, "Don't come this way. I am hit."

Carlos Ross remembered that the battle started about 1530 hours and lasted until about 2200 hours (3:30 to 10:00 PM). This is how he describes the end:

> About 10:00 PM, still daylight, they brought up an armored piece with an 88 mounted on it. They threw five rounds into the house and then five rounds into the barn. Lieutenant Lavender put the white flag out of a window in the barn, but they shot it off. The German sergeant, who had been our prisoner, ran out of the barn in all that firing and stopped them. We wondered if we were about to be shot. Dugan translated the German commander's words: "We are not Russians. We are not going to shoot you."

Soon after the troopers in the house and barn surrendered, the Germans closed in behind Jones and the nine men with him. They also surrendered.

Local Frenchman Lucien Hasley, in cooperation with Thurman Jones, identified the area south of the Douve, where Lieutenant Lavender's forces made their final stand. The Bourde home, where Jones and Dugan were fed, and the house and barn, where the surrender took place, were added to the map below.

The paratroopers who had landed south of the Douve had not taken off their boots or washed the black smut off their faces since boarding the C-47s in England the night of June 5. With almost no sleep and very little food and limited ammunition, they held out for six days against overwhelming odds.

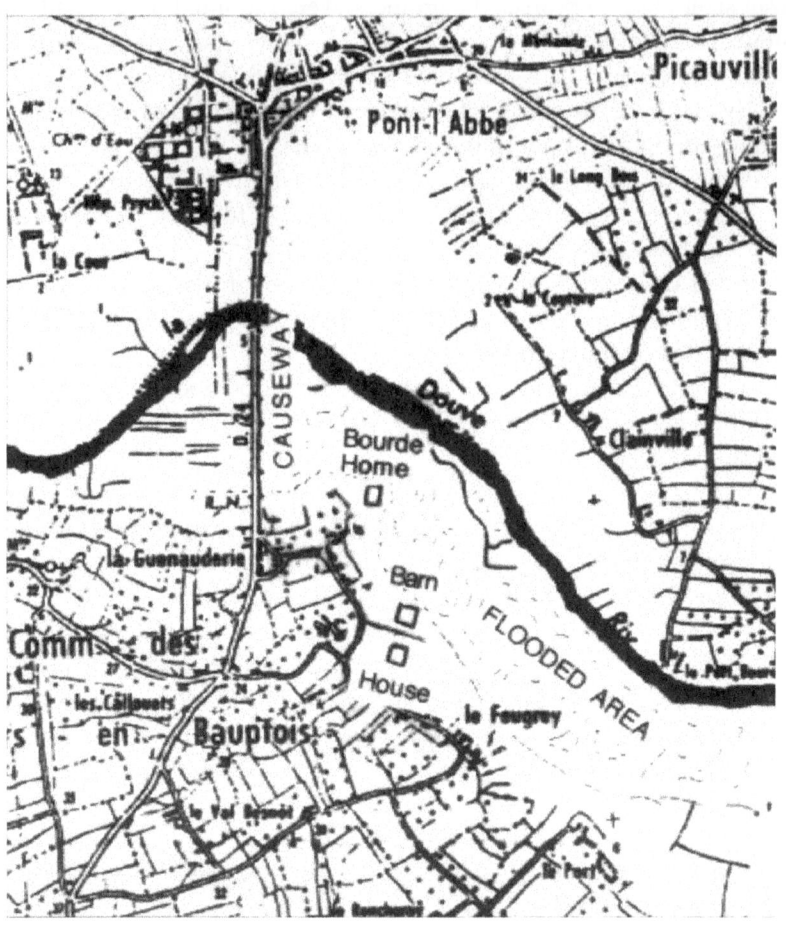

Map of Douve River section. Furnished by T. D. Jones.

## Wings and Swastikas

Some of the paratroopers from Headquarters Third Light Machine Gun Platoon were dozing when a line of tracer bullets cut through the length of the fuselage of their C-47 and caused the men sitting on either side to pull their feet in closer. No one was hit, but it got their attention, so everyone was fully alert for the next surprise, a direct hit on the left engine. The flame from the burning engine streamed past the open jump door. Immediately Lt. John Evans yelled, "Stand up and hook up!"

It didn't take any urging for the paratroopers to obey that order as the plane struggled to remain airborne. No sooner were they in place than a third hit took off part of the right wing. The plane pitched nose down and rolled to the right. Lieutenant Evans yelled, "Go!" and led the way. That was the last time anyone ever saw or heard of him.

Phillip "Chick" Miller recalled the following:

> As the plane nosed downward, we had to struggle uphill to get to the door. The crew chief pulled and tugged to help us along and out, and to his credit, all the paratroopers exited the plane. Seconds afterward, the C-47 crashed, taking its crew chief and the rest of the crew to their death.
>
> When I landed, I could hear Germans shouting orders and running along a nearby road. In looking for other members of my stick, I saw Alexander Tepsic. When I approached Tepsic, he lunged at me with a fixed bayonet. I parried the bayonet to the left and grabbed Alex, who was addled by a lick on the head having fallen twenty feet from the tree in which he landed.

The C-47 that Cpl. Jack Schlegel was assigned to was taken off line at the last minute for some reason. The paratroopers from that airplane were distributed among other C-47s. Schlegel was loaded at the end of the stick in the same plane as Chick Miller. It made the plane so crowded that Schlegel was seated next to the C-47's crew space.

Schlegel recalled his exit from the plane and its subsequent crash:

> I was the twenty-second man and last to leave the plane. I saw it go up in a ball of fire after I bailed out. I remember how the plane was going down, and I moved as fast as I could to get out. I sat next to the radioman for the C-47 on the flight. His name was Ward. He and I talked about the Bronx in New York, where we both grew up. He lived on Marion Avenue, and after the war, I looked up his mother and visited her in her home on Marion Avenue.

Jack Schlegel dropped in an open field among some cows. Schlegel shed his parachute and quickly found two or three others of the 508th. Chick Miller remembered that Jack asked him to help read a map. They used a flashlight under a raincoat to study the map, but the troopers could not get their bearings.

Shortly after that, Miller and others were separated from Schlegel and the men with him. Schlegel saw a farmhouse with a faint light inside. The group with Schlegel decided to seek information from the local Normans. Schlegel banged on the door until a frightened elderly woman timidly opened it just enough to peep at the paratroopers outside.

"Je suis Americain," Schlegel announced in school French, which was effective enough to calm the fears of the startled Normans. The paratroopers were invited inside.

Using sign language, French, German, and Americanese, the troopers learned that they were near Picauville and their hostesses were Madame Le Comte and her daughter. The Germans had taken Monsieur Le Comte as a forced laborer to Germany. The Le Comte ladies served bread and wine to the paratroopers as they sat around the dining table and planned their route. As a parting gesture, Jack Schlegel gave his paratrooper wings to Madame Le Comte as a remembrance.

Schlegel's men started on their journey to find other members of their company. About daylight, Schlegel's group came upon a bullet-riddled German staff car rammed up against a stone wall and two dead Germans in the road. One of the dead was Gen. Wilhelm Falley, CO of the 91st German Infantry Division, who had been killed earlier by Lt. Malcolm Brannen. (See "Five Days on the Run, page 140" for Brannen's story.)

In examining the car, Jack Schlegel found a package that contained a large swastika banner, the command flag of General Falley that normally flew over his headquarters.

Approaching footsteps were heard. The troopers hid behind a stone wall and waited. The footsteps were those of another wandering group of about fifteen paratroopers—members of Headquarters Third Machine Gun Platoon under the command of Lt. Michael Bodak. William Allen was in Bodak's group.

Bill Allen recalled that during those early hours, he and three others were in an orchard and drew fire from two sides. Lieutenant Bodak signaled for them to withdraw. They were able to slip out unobserved, leaving the Krauts on both sides shooting across the orchard at each other.

At one point Bodak's group came upon a large three-story brick mansion. They could see Germans milling about the building. Many wires were leading into it. Bodak judged them to be telephone connections to a German command post. He asked Allen to cut the wires. Allen spent about forty-five minutes up trees cutting wires and hiding the ends so they could not be easily found and repaired.

Chick Miller and Alex Tepsic were the point men leading Bodak's group when they intersected Capt. Hal Creary, H Company, and Lt. Joseph Shankey, Headquarters Third, with about one hundred men. But the two groups did not remain together for long. Miller remembered looking at maps with Captain Creary and identifying their position and discussing where to go from there. The Germans were all around. Small groups were cut off and then sometimes reunited. Jack Schlegel and a few men with him were split from Bodak.

Chick Miller remembered an incident involving Alex Tepsic, a tough steelworker from Pittsburgh.

According to Miller, a group of three German machine guns on a hill was giving them trouble. Lieutenant Bodak sent a five-man patrol composed of Third Battalion sergeant major John T. Little, First Sergeant Orval Shaver, Alex Tepsic, and two others to flank the machine guns. Tepsic was the only one who came back. In hand-to-hand action, Tepsic hit one German over the head with the butt of his M-1 rifle, breaking the rifle stock. Then Tepsic finished off the machine gun crew with a German rifle and bayonet. He returned to his group carrying a German machine gun (MG-34) and a German bolt action rifle with a fixed bayonet.

Sometime during the morning, Bodak's group and Schlegel's group came together again. Jack Schlegel told of running into machine gun crossfire. Schlegel and about eight others made a break through a hedgerow.

Miller remembered that they were totally surrounded when one of the paratroopers translated the words of the German commanding officer: "You have three minutes to surrender or we will sweep the ditch from both ends, and there will be no chance of anyone surviving."

Lieutenant Bodak then gave the order to surrender.

But Schlegel's group had already slipped through the hedgerow and fled toward a barn. As they entered the barn door, three Jerries were trying to get out the same door. The paratroopers grabbed the Germans and pulled them back inside as prisoners.

While the prisoners were guarded in a small room, Schlegel slipped away alone to another part of the barn. He pulled up a loose board in the floor, stuffed his package with Falley's command flag under the floor, replaced the loose plank, and covered it with straw.

With their German prisoners as insurance, the troopers left the barn safely. After travelling a few hundred yards, they came face to face with a German tank, which fired its big gun. A shell exploded just behind the group, wounding some. One of the German prisoners, although bleeding from his wounds, jumped up and waved ceasefire gestures to the tank commander. The insurance paid off. The tank commander decided to take prisoners rather than to finish off the Americans.

After capture, Schlegel and the others walked several miles to a chateau where there were about 250 prisoners—American, British, and Canadians. The next day they were loaded on twenty new unmarked German trucks with canvas covers. The trucks moved out on a main highway toward St. Lo. About noon, Allied planes strafed the convoy of POWs. Schlegel estimated the damage:

> Approximately thirty or forty of our men were killed (many from the 508th). Over eighty were wounded. All of us pitched in to help with the dead and wounded. I remember moving three from my own company with the dead and placing Lieutenant Bodak with the wounded. He was hit with three .50 caliber shells in the spine and never walked again but survived the war.

In one truck of the convoy, according to Chick Miller, were twenty officers. Fourteen of these were killed. Among them were Captain Creary and Lieutenant Shankey, who had earlier separated from the Bodak group but ended up as prisoners.

Among the survivors was Colonel Millet, CO of the 507th Parachute Infantry Regiment and ranking officer of the POWs. The Germans had Colonel Millet organize the survivors and march them on their way.

On D+4 the men arrived at an old monastery that they named Starvation Hill. Many of the 508th men who were POWs in Normandy remember the monastery where they stayed for four days without food. Miller says the Krauts were driving the monks out of the monastery as the POWs were entering.

Schlegel's family had moved to the United States from Germany when he was seven years old. Since Jack could speak German, he was selected to interpret for the Germans. The Germans told him that Schlegel was a good German name. One of the older guards at one stalag told Jack that he had gone to school with Martin Schlegel. It was Jack's grandfather. The guard sent his grandfather a letter telling him that Jack was a POW and doing well. Jack was able to visit his grandfather when the 508th was stationed in Frankfurt after VE-Day (Victory in Europe).

Jack Schlegel made his first escape the day of the strafing, which was the first of three unsuccessful attempts.

On another attempt, Schlegel and three British POWs escaped and joined up with the Free French. They were later caught in a railroad sabotage attempt. The escapees were badly beaten and treated in the hospital at Rennes. Jack was treated for his injuries, inflicted by his German captors and interrogators, by Dr. Enzinger. When he was well enough, Jack became Dr. Enzinger's interpreter with British and American patients.

Dr. Enzinger told Schlegel that Patton's tanks were near. He explained that the wounded patients would be left behind, but those POWs who were caught in the sabotage attempts (Schlegel and the British POWs with him) would be sent on to another stalag for trial and punishment. The good doctor helped Schlegel escape by giving him a pass to the hospital annex vegetable garden. Jack waited for the guards to change before going to the annex. When he arrived, Jack showed his pass, and no questions were asked. Just after dark he slipped out of the compound.

Copy of Schlegel's pass from Dr. Enzinger. Provided by Jack Schlegel.

Jack Schlegel looked up the Free French fighters again and participated in a raid on the German Gestapo headquarters in Rennes. The Gestapo team was preparing to pull out ahead of Patton's troops. In the raid, they killed the CO of the Gestapo headquarters.

Two days later, Corporal Schlegel walked out of town and met a lead tank of Gen. George Patton's advanced patrol. Then he was taken to meet the general himself.

General Patton had a drink of Johnny Walker Black Label with Schlegel and sent him on his way toward Utah Beach in a jeep driven by Major F. J. Cibulka. On the way the major stopped by the barn where General Falley's flag was hidden. Jack found the prized souvenir just where he had left it.

```
                                        Hq 4th Armd Div
                                        4 August 1944

TO:  A.C. of S., G-2, Headquarters VIII Corps.

CPL JACK W. SCHLAGEL, 1290855, 508th Parachute Inf, 82 Air-
borne Division, escaped from the Germans at RENNES 04 Aug
1944, was brought to Headquarters 4th Armored Division
G-2 Section at 1500 4 August 1944 and was sent back to
VIII Corps Headquarters at 1530 hours.

                                        F. Q. CIBULKA
                                        Major G.S.C.
                                        Asst A.C. of S., G-2
```

Copy of Schlegel's pass from General Patton's command.
Provided by Jack Schlegel.

Gen. Wilhelm Falley's Headquarters flag. Jack Schlegel, top right.
Photo furnished by Jack Schlegel.

In 1969 Schlegel visited Normandy with the C-47 Club and donated the flag to the Ste. Mere Eglise Museum. During the trip, Dr. Pierre Honriet, host to the American veterans, helped Schlegel find the Le Comte farm where he had landed on D-Day. Jack described the occasion:

> After the usual refreshments, Madame Le Comte's daughter introduced us to her invalid mother. With all of us around her bed, she pointed to her bedroom dresser. Her daughter opened the drawer and took out a little box. Inside were my jump wings with JWS scratched on the back. Then I knew this was the place I had landed on June 6, 1944.

## Schlegel's German Connections

The 508th moved to Frankfurt, Germany, in June of 1945. That gave Jack Schlegel a chance to search for Dr. Enzinger who helped him escape from the German hospital. He was able to find the good doctor and meet his family. Dr Enzinger has since passed away, but Jack continues to keep in touch with the Enzinger family.

In the course of the war, Jack came across the body of a German officer. Jack recovered the officer's papers on the body, including the address of his wife. In 1945 Jack contacted the widow of the German officer and returned her husband's official papers. These documents helped her get her widow's pension from the German government. Her two children, Johand and Ursula, call him Uncle Jack to this day.

## Letters Home

"When we were in Nottingham," Bill Still of Regimental Headquarters Company declared, "my letters were censored so severely, all that was left was 'Dear Mom' and 'Love, Bill.' Everything else was cut out."

Still had grown up in Bayport, Long Island, New York, and had a classmate and close friend Fred Jones. Fred Jones's mother, thinking Still might be sent to England, wrote to him in Ireland sending the address of her sister in Nottingham, England.

By chance, the 508th was transferred to Nottingham. Still looked up the address given by Mrs. Jones and made friends with the two families through this introduction. Both mothers of the Nottingham families wrote to Still's mother giving her many facts, which were censored from Bill's correspondence.

In a letter dated March 30, 1944, Mrs. Evelyn E. Macdonald of 176 Kerrick Road, North Apperly, Nottingham, wrote that Bill was stationed near Nottingham, had visited their home, and was in excellent health and good spirits.

Mrs. Esme Gamble of 502 Nuthall Road, Nottingham, wrote Bill's mom on May 28, 1944. Mrs. Gamble told all about the Gamble family, including the daughters Sheila, aged nineteen; Della Patricia, seventeen; and Teresa, ten. Bill and his friend Harry Osgood visited the home primarily because of the older daughters, Sheila and Della. Mrs. Gamble wrote of the youngest, "Teresa makes love to them occasionally and asks them to carry her up to bed."

Later Bill probably had to explain in a letter. "Mom, remember Teresa is only ten years old and goes to bed early. After she puts on her night clothes, she comes downstairs and asks me to tuck her in and give her a good night kiss—a harmless brotherly act."

SSgt. John H. Wills of Regimental Headquarters Company wrote his wife, dateline "France, June 10, 1944."

"We've been having very nice weather here and the country is quite similar to Ireland and England..."

On June 15, Wills wrote, "I'm here in this beautiful chateau, which isn't as beautiful as the pictures would have you believe. Tell everyone I'm doing fine, and eating plenty and getting my exercise regularly..."

How can a trooper write about the weather, the countryside, healthy food, and exercise when so much was happening in Normandy? Later Sergeant Wills explained to his wife, "We can only write of things fourteen days later."

After fourteen days, John Wills wrote what he experienced on D-Day:

> We had jumped in an area flooded by the Jerries, and I was in marshy water up to my neck, struggling to get out of my chute, which the water had tightened up so I couldn't unfasten it. I was helpless and felt any minute I would be jumped on by a Jerry and his pals. I swore a thousand swears for not having that quick-release harness. After struggling until I was fagged out, I finally managed to get my knife out and cut the harness off. All my equipment was soaked until it was twice as heavy as it ordinarily would be, and this made it a fight to make my way to dry land.
>
> After a while, I found a couple of the fellows, and we began looking for the rest of the guys so we could get organized, and this is when I saw Tullberry, who had jumped in the same area and was looking for the rest of the 507th. We saw each other

several times after that in the ensuing days of either ferreting out the Bosche or keeping out of his way.

It was only a few hours after dragging myself out of that damned marsh that I aimed at my first German and saw him sailing from his motorcycle as a machine gun opened fire on him.

Wills wrote—date line, France, June 27, 1944—concerning the helpless terror he experienced landing in the marsh:

> Honey, I want you to have Harry get me an automatic pistol as soon as possible, preferably a .45 so I can get GI ammo. At any rate, I want one good sidearm of some kind before our next operation. Have Harry do it as soon as possible, and don't hesitate to give him enough money. I don't want to go through that feeling of helplessness while trying to get a rifle untangled from my maze of equipment.

Lt. Joseph A. Shirley, C Company, sent a letter to his mother in Augusta, Georgia, from a German hospital in Cherbourg, France, in a most unusual way. In the hospital with Lieutenant Shirley was a glider pilot of German extraction, who spoke German freely. He had gained the confidence and friendship of his captors, and he had recovered enough to participate with the German medics in off-duty entertainment. Together they enjoyed the French wines and the company of the French ladies.

Shirley and the glider pilot were in a German naval hospital with many German wounded and a few wounded American POWs. Two problems confronted the Cherbourg hospital: lack of medical supplies and Allied attacks by sea and air. Bombs and shells had landed close enough to shatter the glass in the hospital windows.

Cherbourg was cut off from the main German army, and US troops were nearing the city. It became evident that the Cherbourg Naval Hospital would be liberated soon. The glider pilot persuaded his German friends to allow him to go through the German and American lines on a mission. He promised to bring back medical supplies to the hospital and give the hospital's map coordinates to the Allied command, requesting that the hospital be spared future attacks. The glider pilot also offered to take a letter from Lieutenant Shirley through the lines. The pilot succeeded in his mission, and Shirley's letter to his mother arrived several weeks later in Augusta, Georgia.

Shirley was in the lead plane in a three-plane V formation over Normandy. When the formation hit the cloud cover, the pilot took the plane below the clouds. Only the lead plane could make that maneuver without fear of hitting planes to the left or right. As a result of the pilot's maneuver, Lieutenant Shirley, standing in the door as jumpmaster, could see the ground. He observed the swollen Douve River and the town of Gueutteville. When the green light went on, Shirley led his stick out the door, followed by Sgt. James H. Ellifrit, who was killed almost immediately.

A group of about thirty paratroopers assembled in the immediate area where Joe Shirley landed. Col. Thomas Shanley, the ranking officer, was in charge. The colonel was about to send out scouts to learn their position by looking for road signs. Lieutenant Shirley had studied the maps thoroughly before the jump and had observed their location from the air, and he told Colonel Shanley, "I know exactly where we are!"

The West Point colonel disregarded the cocky opinion from the Clemson University ROTC (Reserve Officers Training Corps) officer and sent his scouts out anyway.

Later, paratroopers in Colonel Shanley's group were wounded in a firefight with German troops. The paratroopers were almost surrounded. Orders by radio from the regimental CP commanded Colonel Shanley to break through and join the Hill 30 group not far away. This meant the wounded would have to be left.

Shirley wrote his mother, "I was preparing to move out while covering the withdrawal of the others when I got a bullet through the left shoulder, which spun me around and sat me down in my foxhole. Thus I joined the wounded and was taken prisoner by the Jerries."

A battalion surgeon, Dr. Axelrod, dressed Joe Shirley's wound before leaving with the others.

In his letter from the German hospital, Joe wrote his mother, Callie Shirley: "The German doctors are the best, having had five years' experience in this kind of work, and they do everything they can for us."

After his combat experiences, Shirley recorded dates of significant events. Here are some selected quotes from his record:

5 Jun: Takeoff for Normandy, 1130 hrs, 313 TC Group
6: Landed Gueutteville, France, 0220 hrs, Wounded 1230, captured, taken to German hospital near Orglandes
7: Moved to Valognes
17: Moved to Naval Hospital, Cherbourg
27: Liberated by 9th Div.

28: Visited C Co position . . . visited the point where I landed and was wounded
28 Jul: Discharged from Hospital
29: Returned to 508th at Nottingham

Lt. Paul E. Lehman of Headquarters Third and Lt. Briand N. Beaudin, surgeon for Third Battalion, jumped together in Normandy. They were in the Orglandes German hospital with Lt. Joe Shirley before Shirley was evacuated. Lieutenant Lehman wrote to his mother on June 28, 1944, about his capture and near death. The letter was published in a government magazine that summer and was sent to Lieutenant Beaudin's mother by a relative who happened to read it. Dr. Beaudin has the copy among his souvenirs. A condensed version of Lehman's letter is quoted below:

Dearest Mom,
On D-Day about 0430 hours I was involved in a freak accident and was wounded by one of my own men.
We came across a group of five men from another battalion standing up in a close group talking. Immediately I went to them and strongly ordered them to scatter out into a patrol formation, so as to have some security, and to move out at once toward their objective. No sooner had I finished my order than firing burst out nearby and we all ducked for the ground. My chin came down on one of their bayonets that entered my throat between the chin and the windpipe. What a surprise!
The blood gushed out as if a spigot had been turned on and Lt. Beaudin could not stop the flow because of the type and location of the wound. Luckily he was with me, as he is the battalion surgeon and jumped number two in the stick I jumpmastered. A facial artery directly off the carotid had been severed and each time I swallowed, it moved the artery and thus prevented the formation of a clot. Finally Beaudin searched a nearby field at daybreak and found a medical supply bundle from which he gave me a plasma transfusion.
By then I was terribly weak from loss of blood. The plasma probably saved my life. Later in the morning he secured enough help to have me carried by litter to a stone barn and house combined, which was occupied by two elderly French women.

Several hours after that, the building was suddenly showered with bullets, and Doc put his helmet with red crosses painted on both sides on a pole in the doorway. A German patrol of about 20 men moved in. They searched us and then knocked on the door of the next room. When the French women didn't answer quickly enough to suit them, they threw a potato-masher grenade through the window and probably killed them instantly. I figured they'd put one in my room next, but they didn't. Instead we were put out in front of them, with the Doc and one of his medical aid men carrying my litter, and we were taken to their company aid station.

Shortly afterwards we were evacuated by truck several miles away [to Orglandes] where we were placed in a frame barracks.

Every day additional wounded were brought to our building, and when I was strong enough to get up and move about, I interviewed each one for information about our troops. The Doc supervised all the medical attention that was possible with the limited facilities at hand. Through his efforts a few of the most critical cases were operated on by German surgeons. They were overwhelmed with cases and worked to the point of exhaustion day and night. One (German surgeon) operated on me, tied off the severed artery and sewed up the wound.

When some of my strength had been regained, I took over the administration of our barracks: the serving of the meals, cleaning up the building, sterilization of water, carrying some of the wounded outside during the hours of daylight, salvaging equipment and collecting personal effects of those who died, etc.

From day-to-day, some of our wounded were evacuated to another German hospital to the north. After D-Day plus six, the artillery of our own forces, moving in from the beaches, fired on the road just to the rear of the hospital. It was a most trying ordeal as the shell whistled overhead or crashed nearby.

The night before our forces captured the surrounding territory; we had 108 men there. All the next morning we could see American troops passing on a road not far away. With recapture in sight, Dr. Beaudin and I took over the hospital. The pistols of the two remaining German doctors were handed over to us, as well as the keys to various supply rooms. Early in the afternoon after considerable skirmishing and firing, our troops surrounded the hospital. Their men passed out cigarettes and rations to us, and it was really some happy occasion.

The following day, the most serious were evacuated first, then the doctor, myself, a number of aid men and the lightly wounded got transportation back to our units. I received the most touching welcome by both men and officers. Stories had circulated of how I bled to death or had died any number of ways according to the imagination of the teller. Everywhere I went, men got up to shake my hand and express their happiness at my being alive.

I really looked like someone returned from the grave. I had not shaved for 12 days and my head was bandaged.

The Colonel then assigned me to Bn. S-2 [Battalion Intelligence]. After we went into a combat mission—that of attacking and occupying a certain village [Pretot]—our S-1 [1st Lt. Adjt, Gene Williams] was killed. A few days later we opened a telegram of his to learn that his wife had given birth to twin boys. It sure was a pitiful case, which affected all of us on the staff very deeply. Since then, I have been handling both his job and mine.

One thing is certain, Mom; the difference of life and death in combat is almost 100 percent luck. I am trusting in your love to watch over me and bring me luck. If anything should happen, you have my order to keep your chin up.

Bye-bye for now, Mom. Will write again soon.

Lieutenant Lehman was killed in action in July 4 on Hill 95.

Dr. Beaudin described an event of June 9 or 10, 1944:

A shell exploded just in front of the German field hospital. It killed one of their doctors. I was about forty to fifty feet from him, but the western corner of the building shielded me. It is that doctor's cap that I was wearing in the photo [next page]. The next day I was approached by a field-grade German officer. He thrust a US field telephone in my hands and ordered me to contact proper authorities to stop them from shelling the hospital compound. I told him I would not (could not, anyway). I pointed out that the battery of large-caliber German guns near the northeast corner of the hospital was inciting counter-battery fire, and I strongly suggested that they should be moved. A few hours later, I detected frenzied activity there, and the next morning, there was no trace of the German guns.

Liberated hospital POWs. Left to right: medics; Sgt. Robert B. Utley; Cpl. Frank Kwansik; Pvt. Frank Ruppe; patient Sgt. Grlando C. Peters; Lt. Briand Beaudin (doctor), wearing German officer's cap; Lt. Paul E. Lehman, patient with bandage on neck. All of the soldiers are holding German pistols. Photo furnished by Briand Beaudin.

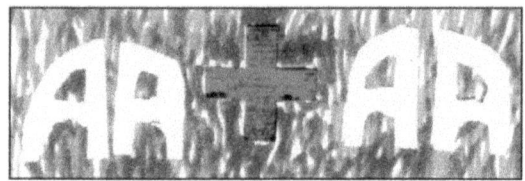

### Display on Hospital Grounds

Dr. Beaudin explained how he and his medics alerted the US airplanes of their presence in the hospital. They made a display on the hospital grounds by making a Red Cross out of bricks to indicate a medical facility. Then they cut up sheets and made white AAs and placed them on each side of the brick cross. (AA is the symbol of the Eighty-second Airborne Division, which all division troops wear on the shoulders of their uniforms)

A P-47 US airplane flew over and dipped his wings in recognition. Four years later in his home town of Warwick, Rhode Island, Dr. Beaudin met the pilot of the P-47, Leo Charbouneau, who remembered seeing his display. Charbouneau was a practicing attorney and became Dr. Beaudin's lawyer.

## Beef Steak and Whiskey

> Beefsteak when I'm hungry,
> Whiskey when I'm dry,
> Greenback when I'm hard up,
> And heaven when I die.
> (From "Boil Them Cabbage Down")

"I got a steak dinner on D-Day," declared Steve Schmelick of Regimental Headquarters Company. "And whiskey—all the whiskey you could drink."

After the jump and the company assembled, Steve and another trooper were sent out to lay telephone lines to connect the various units of the regiment. On the very first day of their landing, they ran a line through a French village and stopped off in a cafe to see if they could get something to eat. The troopers had been given French money called victory money before the jump. Steve and his buddy decided to use some of their victory money for a good restaurant meal. Sure enough, they were served a real steak dinner, but the French insisted, "Non! Non!" when offered the victory currency. The French might have feared the return of the Germans, and they didn't want to be caught with American-made victory money, or perhaps they were showing their gratitude to their potential liberators.

Later on, Steve laid a phone line by a building formerly used by the Germans as a motor pool. It was well stocked with whiskey. Also in the building was a German motorcycle with a sidecar. Steve and his buddies filled empty gasoline cans with the whiskey and loaded the cans into the sidecar. Steve was asked, "Do you know how to drive that thing?"

"Hell, no!" he replied. "But let's give it a try!"

That was the day when Steve learned to ride a motorcycle.

"And then there was the whiskey from the chateau," explained Steve.

Frank Sakowski of Regimental Headquarters Company and Steve did a little off-duty exploring, which turned into a profitable business. (These details came from Frank.) They found a tremendous cask of calvados in the cellar of a chateau. This time they used five-gallon water cans, obtained from the medics, to bottle their booze. Then they turned around and sold the calvados to the medics. Finally they left the chateau with their personal supply, a five-gallon can in each hand.

Steve explained, "That's when I nearly got killed, getting the calvados back to the CP, by our own troops, who were shooting at us."

To Steve, Normandy was a little dangerous, but beefsteak and whiskey—you couldn't beat that for good living.

## The Barn

Everyone called Harry Hudec of Regimental Headquarters Company "Big Stoop." Big Stoop was the largest trooper in the company. You would never know he grew up around Cleveland, Ohio, from his Texas size and swagger. Basically Harry has always been a gentle giant, talking big and tough but softhearted to the core.

Harry was among those paratroopers who landed near Hill 30 in Normandy. Hill 30 was a small knoll with flooded swampland to the north, east, and south. Many of those who gathered together on Hill 30 had landed in the water. Much of their equipment was lost in the swamp or to the German troops who surrounded them. They were virtually isolated with little ammunition, heavy weapons, or medical supplies.

On D-Day Harry received a grenade wound just below his left knee. He then found shelter in a French farmer's barn. The farmer's house and the barn, which was attached to the house, were built of stone. There was a metal gate to the front of the house, and in the kitchen was a large fireplace used for cooking.

The farmer took care of Harry and other wounded paratroopers for a few days, but one day, the farmer came running to the barn all agitated, talking rapidly in French and, using gestures, made it known to Harry that he had to leave. It seemed to the Frenchman that the Germans were about to take over the area again, and he didn't want the Krauts to find him harboring Americans.

Harry had already made himself a crutch and with difficulty was able to get around some in spite of his wounded leg. The Frenchman motioned Harry in a direction toward Hill 30, so Harry hobbled along on his crutch and eventually joined his fellow paratroopers on the hill.

The Germans had launched a fierce counterattack trying to drive the Yanks from the high ground. Harry was placed by the medics in a ditch with other wounded GIs. The artillery and mortar shells were dropping all around.

Finally Colonel Lindquist, with a contingent of 508th paratroopers along with help from the Fourth Infantry Division, broke through and relieved the Hill 30 group. An estimated 250 paratroopers, a mixed group from the Eighty-second and 101st division but mostly men from the 508th, had held their ground for almost a week against heavy odds.

Harry and the other wounded were then evacuated to the beach via trucks and jeeps. Harry described his ride: "On the road to Ste. Mere Eglise, it was an awful sight. The ditches along the roadside were littered with dead, both GIs and the enemy."

"The beach was truly a sight to behold," Harry declared. "No one—nowhere—ever saw so damn many ships, barrage balloons, landing craft, tanks, and soldiers scurrying like ants bringing in supplies. What an elated feeling to see so much coming ashore!"

Harry was then loaded into a landing craft (LCT) at the beach and moved out to sea to a larger craft (LST) and on to England and a GI hospital.

"As it turned out, my wound was a lucky one," explained Harry. "I wasn't hospitalized for over a month, and the wound helped get me out of that stinking mess alive."

Forty-nine years later Harry Hudec visited Normandy and returned to the house that served as the aid station for wounded American paratroopers. The new residents of the house knew Madame Dorey Gilberte Caponnet, who was a seventeen-year-old girl living in the house at the time Hudec was being treated for his wounds in 1944. Madame Caponnet lived only a short distance and came over to meet Hudec. To his surprise, Madame Caponnet recognized Hudec and remembered that he was wounded in one leg. People who know Hudec are not surprised he was remembered, for Harry Hudec is unforgettable and hasn't changed much over the years.

House left, barn right, Harry Hudec, center aid station for wounded paratroopers in barn, 1944. Photo furnished by Harry Hudec, taken in 1993.

## Doc Thomas's First Nine Days in Normandy

Maj. David E. Thomas, 508th Medical Corps, could see echelon after echelon of C-47s from his plane as the fleet flew over the Channel Islands of Jersey, Guernsey, and Alderney. They were on their way to the biggest airborne operation in history. Then the massive flock of planes hit the pea-soup cloudbank over Normandy. Upon emerging from the clouds, Thomas could see no other plane in the sky. The doctor thought, "It looks as if our plane load will have to take on the whole damned German army, but what the hell, we are paratroopers!"

Having eyeballed the landscape before the jump, Major Thomas figured he had landed near the Merderet River. Thomas related the following:

> After shedding my chute, I could make out a large white object, which I approached circumspectly to discover a dairy cow unconcernedly chewing her cud. She didn't know big events were going on and could not care less! Shortly thereafter I ran into none other than Col. Bill Ekman, our former executive officer who was tapped to command the 505th after Colo. Jimmy Gavin picked up a star. We could see one of his battalions descending on Ste. Mere Eglise, and Bill suggested I come along with him. I demurred, wanting to contact the 508th, so we parted. That was my first mistake!

Major Thomas failed to find anyone from his stick, but by dawn he had collected a group of eight or nine strays. Keeping the river on their right, they set out toward Chef du Pont. They crossed the Merderet on the railroad bridge north of La Fiere and joined a group of about fifty troopers from assorted units commanded by a redheaded major. It was here that Dr. Thomas began his Normandy medical practice.

The Germans had the small group almost surrounded, except on the side adjoining the flooded plain of the Merderet. Thomas described his situation:

> Before being contained, this group must have been kicking some butt because they had a large contingent of German prisoners. Our troops manned the ditches alongside the hedgerows, and the prisoners were in the center of the enclave with no more protection from incoming fire than the apple trees in the field. The prisoners were furnished entrenching tools and, having ample stimuli, made maximum use thereof.

I was the only medic in the group. I had plenty to do but nothing much to do it with, except the contents of my medical aid kit. Only the severely wounded were relieved of duty, and they were collected in a small farm building with a thatched roof. Even this meager shelter was lost when the roof was ignited by tracer bullets.

My most vivid memory of this time was excising the leg of a trooper. A large shell fragment had severed his leg at the knee, and the only connection was the patellar tendon. I told him that having no other option, he would have to bite the bullet, which he did. I severed the tendon, and he never even whimpered. He was a man.

The redheaded major made radio contact with a larger group of paratroopers. After dark he organized a march to join the group. Major Thomas rigged litters from doors and blankets tied between poles for all the nonwalking wounded. The doctor assigned six prisoners to a litter as carriers and an armed paratrooper per litter as an enforcer. They moved out in a column about midnight. They merged with a group of about three hundred paratroopers commanded by Col. Zip Millett, CO of the 507th Parachute Infantry Regiment.

Although Colonel Millett's group was much larger, the tactical situation was not good. The Germans had them surrounded and were inflicting casualties, which kept Doc Thomas busy. He felt rather helpless because medical supplies were limited. The best he could do was to give first aid and make the wounded as comfortable as possible. The good doctor recalled one poignant memory of this particular interlude:

> A paratrooper brought in a wounded German prisoner, who had just killed the trooper's buddy before surrendering. The prisoner was obstreperous, noisy, and demanded attention when we had many other wounded with greater priority. After repeated remonstrances, the prisoner continued to be abrasive, and eventually, the paratrooper said, "F— it!" thrusted his bayonet through the prisoner, lifted him over his shoulder, carried him to a nearby ditch, and dumped him.

On the night of the third day, Dr. Thomas received orders to move again. This time it was impossible to carry the many litter cases. Thomas left two wounded medics to look after the other wounded with instructions to surrender to the Germans.

The men had gone for three days and nights with little sleep, and the column could not hold together. The column would stop then some would fall asleep, and thus the column became severely fragmented. One sleepy trooper dropped a Gammon grenade while marching. The grenade blew off his left leg and left arm. Thomas ticketed the soldier KIA, and the column moved on.

At dawn Thomas found himself with about thirty men in a ditch next to a hedgerow on the banks of the flooded Merderet across from La Fiere Manoir. The doctor described his fourth day in Normandy:

> This was the start of my personal longest day! The Germans again had us surrounded. Any trooper who tried to exit via the water attracted the Jerries' rifle and machine gun fire, and seeing the poor odds of that ploy, I elected to dig in deeper. While sweating at this unprofessional chore and wearing a helmet emblazoned with red crosses, a bullet just missed me and plowed into the bank by my hole.
>
> I could see where the round had marked a small tree trunk. I shot a back azimuth, which revealed that the round had to come from a nearby tree. After much staring, I could make out a pair of jackboots. Obviously the boots were attached to the dude who had no respect for the Red Cross.
>
> After unsuccessfully attempting to point out my discovery to a couple of riflemen, I borrowed a carbine and let a couple of rounds go. Many days later I returned to the site and found a dead fat German, much fatter by bloat. I guess, for a medic, I was a pretty good shot. I tell this because the statute of limitations applies, and Geneva can't get me now!
>
> As the day wore on, other hairy things happened. I was lying in a ditch with a couple of dead troopers when I saw a German approaching along the ditch from the Merderet. I lay down with the dead, sprawled out, and behaved to the best of my ability like a corpse (a role I had never practiced) and breathed as shallowly as possible. The hostile stopped opposite me, hooked a toe under my ankle, flexed my foreleg on my knee, and let go. I relaxed my foreleg and let it fall by gravity. I guess that satisfied him because he moved on. That was the longest moment of my longest day!
>
> Later that day, I was lying in a ditch and noticed at about fifty yards, four of the other guys were lolling around, taking a break from their martial chores. At this time I happened to be

cradling an M-1, probably more for company than anything else. I thought, "I could kill everyone of those bastards with ease." But it occurred to me that I would sure as hell give away my position, which I elected not to do. It's this kind of stuff of which live heroes are made. Besides, no one was there to write me up for a medal!

By dusk all of the original group who remained in the area were Roy Perkins, a staff sergeant medic from the 507th, and me. We decided to hit the middle of the road and take off toward the Douve River and see what in the hell would happen. This worked fine until we got into the village of Amfreville, which was apparently a strong point for the other guys.

We tried to get out of Amfreville by crawling across a field until we hit a rope, which alerted a machine gunner, who responded with grazing fire. We tried other stratagems, all of which led to trouble, so we decided to leave town the way we had arrived, walking down the middle of the road as if we belonged there.

This time we were challenged by a sentry, who had listened during Nazi basic, and so challenged us from the shade of a tree where we couldn't see him. That ended the caper. Roy and I were in the bag.

As prisoners, Roy and I were split up. Roy was sent to Cherbourg, and some twenty-odd days later and many pounds lighter, he escaped and finished the war with the 507th. I was sent to a *kampfgruppe* (battle group) headquarters.

Shortly after my arrival at the *kampfgruppe*, the commander arrived in an open-top Volkswagen. He stood up in the car, gave the Nazi salute, and bellowed, "Heil Hitler!"

The assembled retinue returned the salute and in upper decibels of sound shouted, "Seig Heil!"

I was put to work as *kampfgruppe* surgeon, accompanied by a guard with Schmeisser machine pistol to make sure my fealty to the Third Reich remained steadfast. The medical staff consisted of a captured airborne doctor and an exceedingly jumpy *feldweber* (field sergeant) left over from the Africa Corps who had lived long enough to spend his entire purse of courage.

Major Thomas treated the German wounded and a few American wounded who were captured from the Ninetieth Division. Thomas tried to get information from the GIs, but they were wary of the doctor's true identity. Food was scarce, so the major took the hard tack from the bodies of the dead for his own sustenance.

After three days, the *kampfgruppe* headquarters retreated to a chateau where Major Thomas had some interesting experiences, which he describes in the following:

> There was an old Frenchman, a retainee of the chateau, no doubt, who on seeing me threw his arms around me, babbled on about "Bon Americain" while the Germans were saying, "Schwein" (swine). He presented me with a big mug of milk in which eight dead flies were floating on the surface. Not wanting to embarrass the octogenarian, I drank the milk through my teeth and strained out the flies.
> 
> The Germans were making defensive arrangements. My guard with the Schmeisser was digging a trench, covering it with boughs cut from the hedgerows and putting the spoils back thereon—a foxhole masterpiece. It was getting dusk, and no one was paying attention to me, so I strolled through a gate into a pasture, wandered a few steps along a hedgerow and, to be polite, relieved myself standing up. Still having attracted no attention, I slowly sauntered along the hedgerow until I reached the corner, dove into the ditch beside the hedgerow, and started crawling away.

Dr. Thomas had crawled some distance, and a group of German soldiers on bicycles stopped for a break at the very spot next to his ditch. Thomas lay very still until the troops departed and darkness came. Guided by the stars, the good doctor was able to move in the direction of friendly troops. At first dawn Major Thomas sought out a place to hide for the day.

The hiding place, in a ditch beside a hedgerow, proved to be in the line of fire between the Ninetieth Infantry Division and the enemy forces. As Thomas explains, "Periodically machine gun fire would walk down the bank behind me, and Schmeisser fire would be returned from each end of the hedgerow. At this point I learned about nervous polyuria."

When night arrived, Thomas crept out of his ditch toward a trench with GI litter about. He found a rifle and C rations, but no soldiers. After dining on the rations, he waited for a corporal in charge to come. When none appeared, the major decided to move on.

His first contact with the US forces was from a sentry who demanded the password. Thomas explained that he had been out of contact for a while and didn't know the password and requested to be taken to the commanding officer of his unit. He was led to the CP of the Ninetieth Infantry Division and then transferred to Ridgway's CP of the Eighty-second Airborne Division.

While at General Ridgway's headquarters waiting for transportation to the 508th, incoming artillery influenced Major Thomas to dive into the closest ditch. Upon looking around, he observed the general leaning against a tree as if nothing was threatening. Thomas thought, "He's making more money than I am. If he wants to show off, that's his privilege."

The concluding remarks of Maj. David Thomas about his first nine days in Normandy are "For this I went to medical school? I should have taken a degree in Library Science!"

## Scout for Two Colonels

Virgil "Mickey" McGuire of Regimental Headquarters Company made his Normandy jump in the stick of Col. Harry Harrison, the executive officer for the 508th. McGuire's position was in the middle of the stick, and he had the duty of releasing the equipment bundle before making his jump. Colonel Harrison instructed Mickey to count to three before releasing the equipment bundle and then count to three again before jumping himself. This made his jump about five or six seconds after the trooper in front of him. If the plane were travelling 150 miles per hour, that would have spaced Mickey about five hundred feet from the equipment bundle and one thousand feet from the trooper who jumped ahead of him. Usually troopers follow each other as fast as they can get out of the door, which groups them tightly together on the ground. So McGuire wondered about the instructions but carried out the orders.

Virgil McGuire at a 508th reunion. Photo by Zig Boroughs.

When they landed, the last half of the stick could not find the equipment bundle or the troopers in the front half of the stick. Colonel Harrison gathered about eight from his plane and a few others who were separated from their regular units. Harrison decided to send out four scouts in four directions: north, south, east, and west. Each scout would move straight toward his assigned direction for fifteen minutes, make a right turn, and go straight for another fifteen minutes, repeat the procedure until he had traveled in a square and returned to the starting point within an hour. McGuire was selected as one of the scouts.

McGuire managed to return to the starting point at the end of the hour. There he met one of the other scouts, who had also returned to the starting point, but no one else was there. Harrison left the area before the scouts had time to return.

About two days later, McGuire saw Colonel Harrison again, and the colonel explained that they had to leave before the scouts returned. The colonel's behavior worried McGuire. He felt that Harrison was "not mentally combat ready." Evidently the higher command had a similar feeling about Colonel Harrison, for he was transferred to a different unit and replaced by Col. Mark Alexander from the 505th PIR.

Colonel Alexander also used McGuire as a scout, but he was just the opposite of Harrison. Alexander went with McGuire in front of the lines to look for the enemy. McGuire recalls entering the back of a farmhouse, looking through the front windows, and seeing a column of German soldiers moving along a road only fifty yards in front of the house. The colonel stayed until he counted the number of soldiers in the column after which they slipped out the back door and returned to their lines.

McGuire was with Alexander on a scouting mission when the colonel was severely wounded, a wound from which he did not fully recover. Virgil "Mickey" McGuire paid this tribute to Col. Mark Alexander:

Col. Mark Alexander, photo copied from *The Devils Have Landed* by Lewis Milkovics. Permission to use stated on copyright page.

He was absolutely fearless and didn't realize that senior officers could get killed. He went on reconnaissance patrols far in front of our lines. He packed a lot of living and almost died in the eleven days he was with the 508th.

## Dick Owen Found Love

The night sky over Normandy was illuminated with tracer bullets and exploding flak as Dick Owen stepped to the door of the C-47. Dick remembered thinking as he jumped, "What in the world am I doing here?"

Pvt. Richard "Dick" B. Owen, H Company, had eagerly yearned to be a combat paratrooper. Unlike his father and brother who waited to be drafted, Dick Owen volunteered in November 1942. When the army recruiter asked Dick for his choice, he knew exactly what he wanted—the paratroopers.

While on leave from Camp Mackall, Owen read in the *Kansas City Star* about the airborne invasion of Sicily, July 9, 1943, and complained, "Here we are still in the States. If we don't ship over soon, the war will be over before I get a chance to fight for my country."

Finally Owen had his chance to fight.

Upon hitting the ground, Owen got out of his chute and checked his equipment and found he had lost his trenching shovel. His first thought was, "Lieutenant Wilde will chew me out for losing my shovel."

Someone was approaching. Owen called out the password, "Flash!"

It was Lew Zieber. Lew and Dick were two of five troopers from H Company who, before D-Day, had torn a dollar bill into five pieces, and each one took a piece into combat. They planned to put the dollar back together if they all survived the campaign. Sgt. Curtis Sides, Bob Furtaw, and Bill Kursawski carried the other three pieces. The pieces of the dollar bill were never put back together. Sides and Kursawski were KIA (killed in action).

A few troopers from Owen's plane assembled together on the ground. During the darkness of early morning of June 6, it was hard for the troopers to stay together, and when dawn came, Dick found that he and one other H Company man were alone. In their search to link up with others, they saw a building with antennae and other communication equipment about. The other trooper said, "With all that equipment around, that must be the headquarters for the whole Eighty-second Airborne Division."

When the two Red Devils presented themselves, an officer said, "We are the 101st Airborne Division. The Eighty-second is about five miles to the south with a division of Germans in between. You can take your choice—stay with us, or go hunt your own unit."

The German division in between made it easy for the two loners to stay with the 101st. They were assigned to a company and were immediately put out on the flank point as scouts in an attack. Under enemy fire, Dick Owen became separated and again found himself alone.

On June 9, Don Jakeway, another 508th man from H Company, found Owen in a barn. Owen and Jakeway then attached themselves to one of the 101st Division units nearby.

As on the previous occasion, the two strays from the Eighty-second were put on flank point. Right off, Dick Owen was hit in the head. Jakeway thought Dick had been killed, but just in case he might survive, Jakeway pulled Dick Owen behind a stone wall where medics were treating the wounded.

Eight days later, Dick Owen awoke in an English hospital; he had been in a coma. He remembered thinking after he was hit, "Dying isn't so bad after all. I don't feel any pain. I am no longer scared or hungry or tired."

Another thing Owen remembered was how cold the scissors were against his skin when the medic cut away his clothing to dress his wounds. All the rest was a complete blank.

After a short stay in England, Dick was sent to Springfield, Missouri, where a tantalum plate was put in his skull. With sufficient recovery, he was sent to Fort Benning, Georgia, for reassignment.

At Fort Benning the only assignments given Dick were the duties of firing a furnace or KP. When Dick was sent to the hospital for a physical, to his surprise, it was discovered he had tuberculosis. As the army had no facilities for long-term patients, Owen was discharged to a VA (Veteran's Affairs) hospital in Waukesha, Wisconsin. Later he was transferred to the VA Excelsior Springs Lung Hospital, Excelsior Springs, Missouri, closer to his home. It was an eighteen-month rest cure.

Part of the treatment was under the medical rehabilitation service. The plan consisted of occupational therapy, manual arts therapy, and educational therapy. La Rue Bettien was one of the educational therapists as a teacher of business subjects. Dick enrolled in La Rue's typing course. When Dick was discharged from the hospital, he went straight to a telephone and asked La Rue for a date. Four years later, after Dick graduated from the University of Missouri, it was wedding bells for La Rue and Dick.

Dick Owen thinks it was worth a hole in the head and a diseased lung to find the love of his life.

# Chapter 4

# Scattered Elements of 508th Come Together

## Beachhead across the Douve River

By June 11, D+5, thanks to the US Ninetieth Division, various groups of Red Devils, which had fought in isolation the first five days, began to assemble on Hill 30 with the rest of the 508th. The Ninetieth Division had penetrated from the beach landings, crossed the Merderet, and mopped up the German forces, which had kept small groups of Red Devils pinned down. Troopers who had been separated from their units since D-Day were able to organize into companies and battalions with their own men and officers.

The first objective for the 508th as a unified regiment was to cross the Douve River and establish a beachhead on the south side. F Company led the way. Four young Normans—identified by Lucien Hasley as Paul Manger, Gustave Depierrepont, Paul Bitouze, and Lucien Laurence—transported F Company across the river in flat-bottom boats. The crossing began in the darkness one minute after midnight, June 13.

Dick and La Rue, still lovers fifty-two years after their wedding. Photo by Zig Boroughs taken at the 508th reunion, August 2003.

183

Bill Giegold remembered the boats had metal bottoms with board sides and paddles made from boards. Richard Kulwicki was right behind Giegold as they rowed in a kneeling position. The Germans on the other side probably had machine guns in place; therefore, a quiet crossing to prevent detection was essential. Orders were passed on in whispers.

Giegold recalled, "It was a most eerie feeling. We couldn't see a thing or hear anything on the other side. It was like paddling into the jaws of hell."

About twenty feet from the south shore of the Douve, the men left the boats and ran for the shore. Upon hitting the ground, Giegold checked his watch. It took only eighteen minutes to cross the river, about a quarter of a mile in width.

Company Commander Lieutenant Goodale led his troops toward the town of Beuzeville La Bastille. Beyond the first hedgerow was a rise in the land, and Giegold could see a tank on the high point. The tank fired a round, and immediately Lieutenant Polette went into action. Polette took grenades and a bazooka, circled around and located two Jerry tanks. Edward Chatoian recalled, "Polette knocked out one tank by dropping a Gammon grenade down a vent. He destroyed the other with a bazooka rocket. Then the company moved to the edge of town."

Chatoian, radio operator, described what he remembered:

> We lined up in assault formation behind a fence. We were supposed to attack after the artillery softened up the enemy for fifteen minutes. I kept looking at my watch—no artillery, and 0115 was getting close. I radioed, "Where are the firecrackers?"
> There was no response.
> Goodale said, "We will go without the firecrackers."
> Exactly at 0115, Goodale ordered, "Run, yell, and fire!"
> It was a long run across an open field—several hundred yards. I saw one trooper stop, take out his canteen, and take a long drink (probably calvados), and start running again. (He denies he did it, but I saw him.) We took the town and didn't lose a man. It was the surprise that did it. We were better off without the artillery.

Arthur Sanchez confirmed that the artillery was silent, but the charge scared the Germans so they fled, leaving their weapons behind.

Sanchez recalled carrying a case of bandoleers packed with M-1 ammo in the river crossing. When he passed out the bandoleers, they discovered all the bullets were tracers. Goodale decided to use the tracers on the charge, spacing the men with the all-tracer bullets—one on the right, one in the center, and one on the left. Sanchez says, "I fired the tracers on the right flank. William Rogers fired tracers in the center and someone else on the left."

Giegold remembered that the bridge crossing at the edge of town was under water, and he could hear the engineers on the other side putting together a pontoon bridge. By daylight, the pontoon bridge had been completed and the rest of the regiment had crossed the river. The Red Devils did not stop but headed toward their next objective, the town of Baupte.

The official *Record of Participation of 508th Parachute Infantry in Normandy Operations* (secret document, now declassified) noted for June 13, 1944:

> Lieutenant Goodale called by SCR (radio) for artillery fire to be laid on Beuzeville to disorganize enemy resistance holding the town and covering the causeway north of the town. This artillery fire concentration was laid down at 0100 and lasted for fifteen minutes. When the artillery was lifted, Company F wiped out the German defensive position in the town after destroying two German tanks in the dark. Then the regiment crossed the causeway in columns by battalions.

Officially, the town was taken with the aid of artillery. Unofficially, the men who charged the enemy know better.

## The Battle for Baupte and Norman Par Excellence

Louis Gillot went to bed on the evening of June 5, 1944, in his rural home near Chef du Pont to be awakened during the night by the crash of a glider loaded with 101st Airborne Division troops. The glider landed in a small stream, a branch of the Merderet.

The twenty-year-old Norman youth rushed to the scene of the accident and found wounded men who needed medical attention. He hitched his horse and wagon and, carrying his new rifle provided by the troopers, transported the wounded to the nearby Carquebut hospital.

Shortly afterward, Gillot met Lt. Rex Combs, A Company, who recruited Gillot for the 508th. Like all Red Devils, Gillot volunteered, but unlike stateside recruits, basic training was not required. Louis recalls his induction. "I received the uniform, a few notions, the armaments, and I am a true American. Voila l'Americain!"

Harold Canyon a.k.a. Harold Kulju of Headquarters Second and Louis Gillot became close friends during the Normandy campaign. Louis wrote Harold, speaking to him as, "*Coul you*—a name I could not forget. You were my best friend. You took life with a smile."

Kulju and Gillot were together in the battle for Baupte on June 13. Early in the morning, the Second Battalion was moving toward Baupte in a column of twos when someone yelled, "Tanks!"

Harold Kulju described the scene:

> I raced for shelter to my left. As I went up the bank, I saw Amos Moss, Headquarters Second, running head on toward the lead tank with a Gammon grenade in his upraised right hand. Moss threw the grenade, which exploded on the tank track. Then I saw Moss go down.

Amos Moss told his version of the road to Baupte:

> I was the third man from the point. Sgt. Herb Sellers, Headquarters Second, was ahead of me, and someone else was at the point. We heard the tanks coming, and over the hedgerow we went. When I got in the field, Charles Wilkins was getting ready to fire his bazooka. I was carrying a Gammon grenade. I moved to my left to get clear of the bazooka back flash. The lead tank rolled to a stop right in front of us. All I could see was the upper part of the turret. I threw the grenade and ducked. There was a loud explosion. The bazooka and the Gammon exploded about the same time.
> 
> I was struck with a small piece of steel under my right eye. Blood sprayed from my nostrils, and my right eye was swollen shut in seconds. The medics put a bandage on my eye, and I walked back down the road where I found a truck and was evacuated.

The bazooka man, Charles Wilkins, E Company, explained that the lead tank arrived at a sharp curve in the road. Moss had turned the corner behind the hedgerow and was on the left side of the tank when he threw the Gammon grenade. Wilkins himself was behind the hedgerow at the corner and directly in front of the approaching tank. Chuck Wilkins explained what happened from his point of view:

I hit the tank head on, and Amos hit it from the side. The tank was knocked out of commission, and as the crew came out, they were quickly eliminated.

A strange thing happened after the fighting was over. One of our guys was standing on top of the tank and just keeled over. He was dead, and not a mark on him.

Eddie Wenzel, E Company, described his experience with the tanks:

I was the point for the Second Battalion. My back was hurting from landing on my spine on D-Day. I saw some horses in the field and decided I would become a cowboy. I went over the hedge to catch a horse. Then Sellers hollered, "Tanks!"

I ran down the field and jumped up the top of the hedge and shot the first tank on its top with my trusty rifle grenade launcher. Then the second tank came down to shove the first one out of the road, and I shot that one in the behind.

The hole on that tank barrel looked as big as the Hudson River tunnel. I got my guts shot out by the second tank.

Sgt. Herb Sellers summarized the attack on the lead tank. Sellers explains that Battalion S-2 was responsible for leading the battalion approach march toward Baupte, and he and Amos Moss were there for that purpose (S-2 is the code for intelligence.) An E Company scout led the way. Sellers was about seventy-five yards behind the E Company lead scout, and Amos Moss about seventy-five yards behind Sellers. All were proceeding up the narrow sunken road. On either side of the road and over the hedgerows, flanker scouts moved forward in pace with the front point. Contacts by hand signals were maintained with the different lead elements at all times.

The scouts saw the tanks in time to halt the battalion, which was then deployed on either side of the road behind the hedgerows. As Sellers explained, "The tanks did not detect us, but we were ready for them."

Sellers continued his recollections:

When the two lead tanks reached us, they were buttoned up for combat. At least three Gammon grenades, a bazooka rocket, and a rifle grenade were launched at the same time. Some of our people were firing M-1s and tommy guns also. It was a staccato of noise loud enough to hurt your ears at fifty yards. I had to scream at the top of my voice for ceasefire because every time

I raised my head, a volley from the other side of the road came my way.

I needed a prisoner to find out what to expect at Baupte. As soon as the firing stopped, I was on top of the lead tank to get the occupants out. I had the first man out when someone shot him. Then as soon as I got the second man to the top of the hatch, someone shot him.

As the battalion approached Baupte, Colonel Shanley sent a small reconnaissance patrol forward to gather information. Harold Kulju reports that Louis Gillot was a part of that patrol. It was hit hard, and only Louis and one other man returned. They reported that they were fired on by Americans. This caused considerable confusion since no other American units were supposed to be in the area. Colonel Shanley made the accurate assessment that the Germans were using US equipment gathered from parapacks.

Sellers recalled receiving fire from mobile .20mm cannons. The column was halted, and again the battalion took cover in ditches behind hedgerows. Sellers returned to the command post to give his assessment to Capt. Chet Graham and Captain Hetland. Colonel Shanley came forward while the two captains were discussing their next move. Shanley made the decision.

Shanley took Sergeant Sellers with him to find Lieutenant Albright on the right flank. Albright was assigned to form a patrol from the First Platoon of E Company and knock out the .20mm guns. Sellers reported that Albright's patrol neutralized the guns but in the firefight lost several men, including machine gunner Clifton Ducote. Albright and several others were wounded.

When the Second Battalion arrived at the town of Baupte, Colonel Shanley dispersed his troops for battle. Radioman Harold Kulju described the attack:

> Shanley ordered the companies to form a line for assault. He asked me to radio for artillery fire on the hedgerow to our front. The artillery radioed back, "We are not ready yet."
>
> The colonel looked at his watch, and muttered, "It is too late to call off the charge." He had me to radio another set of coordinates for artillery fire about one hundred yards beyond our first objective thirty minutes later.
>
> Shanley then ordered, "Fix bayonets!"

After a short pause, Shanley vaulted over the hedgerow and yelled, "Let's go!"

I was right behind him with a bayonet fixed to a Garand rifle and with a radio strapped to my back.

Louis Gillot wrote Kulju about the charge. "You rushed forward sniping at the enemy and shouting 'Diablo!' at the same time. I think the Germans, only to hear you shout like that, were in terror."

Harold Kulju's description continued:

> As we ran, I saw a man to my right carrying an .81mm mortar tube. I almost broke out laughing, thinking of the things he could do to a German with that tube. The guy on my left got hit in the chest with a .20mm antiaircraft shell, driving him about fifteen feet away. I saw Louis Gillot further to my left and heard him shout, "Kulju! Kulju!"
>
> Gillot pointed to my right. As I turned, I saw a German machine gunner preparing to open up on me; I dove to the ground as he fired. A bullet, which had to pass within a half inch of my neck, took the antenna off my radio.
>
> The man with the mortar tube also heard Gillot. Looking back, I saw his crew busily assembling the mortar to fire on the machine gun. His crew got the Kraut gun with its first round. Those Second Battalion mortar men were good. Lieutenant Trahin trained his men well. [Trahin said, "Not so. The sergeant had them already trained when I came to the platoon."]
>
> I got up and joined Shanley at the hedgerow just as a sniper hit a man beside him. A machine gunner let the German sniper have a whole belt of ammunition. As the sniper fell, his foot caught, and he dangled in the treetop, hanging by one foot.
>
> About this time Louis Gillot heard a noise in the hedgerow behind him. He turned ready to fire, but the German in the hedgerow already had his hands up. At that time, Shanley sent Louis back with the prisoner.
>
> As we started for the next hedgerow, our artillery opened up, catching the Germans retreating in the open.
>
> We got into Baupte and had the Jerries surrounded in their supply dump. A couple of tanks were still active, and I was asked to radio for heavy stuff to punch them out. Without the antenna, I could not transmit. The tanks finally closed up and left. We knocked out, or captured, seventeen tanks that day.

Sgt. Herb Sellers, as a member of Battalion S-2, was assigned as guide scout for D Company in the assault on Baupte. The firing was heavy to the right and to the left of him, but there was none to his front. Sellers moved rather quickly and proceeded to a railroad embankment to the rear of the town, where he encountered twin mobile .20mm guns, which were busy firing into the town. Sellers had the help of a second lieutenant and a private, and together they knocked off a couple of the gunners, and to their surprise, about thirty Jerries who had been lying unobserved in defilade came out with their hands in the air, calling, "Kamrade!"

When Sellers organized the prisoners to march in column of twos, some Jerries hiding in a nearby building fired on the three paratroopers. The trio hit the ground and started firing into the German prisoners. The Jerries then held their fire, and the troopers got the prisoners up and off again. About seven did not get up, and Sellers says, "I didn't take time to see if they were hit or playing possum."

As they continued advancing, Sellers heard tanks cranking up and moving in their direction. They had no Gammon grenades or other defense against tanks, so Sellers had the prisoners lie down in the road between them and the approaching tanks. The three GIs took cover behind a hedgerow. When the German tankers saw their own soldiers blocking the way, they backed up and drove off in another direction.

None of the prisoners wanted to move again. Communicating with them was a problem. Then a small bespectacled prisoner said he could speak English and would help translate. The English-speaking German agreed to lead the way into the town. Just as they rounded a corner, a 508th bazooka man at a roadblock saw the lead prisoner and fired point blank. Sellers said, "I was right behind the small German. He exploded, and his flesh and blood got all over me."

From that point Sellers took the remaining prisoners to Battalion CP and turned them over to Colonel Shanley.

Bill Giegold of F Company recalled Baupte. Giegold and Kulwicki were charging across an open field toward a German gun emplacement. Giegold's belt broke, and he almost lost his pants in the charge. Fortunately those who approached the gun position from another direction had already shot the two gunners.

Lieutenant Polette continued to lead the F Company assault, with Sergeant Seale, Giegold, and Kulwicki following. Polette had passed one German without seeing him. The German jumped up, fired, and killed Kulwicki. Kulwicki fell against Giegold as he went down. Sergeant Seale, in turn, killed the Kraut who shot Kulwicki.

The Red Devils disabled a car that was about to cross a bridge. Giegold and Joe Harrold went to see if they could find some food in the car. They propped their rifles against the vehicle and started to search. As they looked over the top of the car, they saw four Germans hiding behind it. The Germans immediately put up their hands and surrendered to the two GIs who did not have their weapons in hand.

Stanley Nordwall, Headquarters Second, remembered that during the battle for Baupte, several from the communication section of Headquarters Second were pinned down by enemy fire. The bullets were cutting the leaves from the branches just over their heads as they lay flat on the ground. Lt. Ray Sanders thought he would kid Erving "Gabe" Gulbrandson and yelled, "Gabe, stick your head up and see where the fire is coming from!"

Gabe hunkered down even lower against the ground.

Sanders yelled again, "Gabe, I told you to stick your head up and find out where the fire is coming from!"

This time Gabe answered, "Fuck you, sir!"

The lieutenant, having received the kind of reaction he expected from Gabe, retorted, "*Sir* is what I wanted hear. Carry on."

Baupte yielded considerable loot for the Red Devils. Troopers found the payroll for a whole German battalion. Thinking the money had no value, the Red Devils used the French bills for toilet paper and lighting fires. When leaving Normandy, those who kept the francs exchanged them for British pounds.

Nordwall reports that his buddy Gabe confiscated a supply of liquor at Baupte and set up bar in his foxhole, serving all troopers—that is, until he passed out from serving himself.

The battle for Baupte appeared to be over and the troops were relaxing, but not all of them were taking it easy. Charles Wilkins observed a counterattack developing and was awarded a Silver Star for his quick response. The Citation states the following:

> Charles B. Wilkins, 39319537, Private, 508th Parachute Infantry, for gallantry in action on 13 June about 1/2 mile from Baupte, France. When the enemy counterattacked to recover a motor pool which had been captured by Company E four hours earlier, Private Wilkins, a rifleman, on his own initiative and without orders, organized a group of leaderless men and led them with aggressiveness and courage through heavy fire from a light tank accompanying the German infantry and forced them to withdraw. His prompt action prevented the enemy from

recapturing the motor pool and reflects great credit on himself and his organization.

Louis Gillot served with the 508th during June and July of 1944 and developed a strong friendship with Harold Kulju. But when the 508th left France, they lost contact with each other. Not until 1989, after forty-five years, Gillot was located and the friendship renewed. The two wartime buddies have exchanged letters and plan to visit each other.

## Heaven in the Midst of Hell

Ed "Bogey" Boccafogli of B Company hung his steak on a nail protruding from the side of the barn. The steak had been cut from a freshly KIA-ed cow. That was temporary storage while he scrounged some firewood to cook the tantalizing cut of beef, but before he could even start a fire, Lieutenant Millsaps ordered the troops to move out. It was D+9, June 15.

Bogey slipped his arms in the harness supporting his rifle belt with extra ammo, canteen, and trenching tool. In preparation for the next action, Bogey had carefully reloaded his ammo pouches and hung a grenade on one strap of the harness and his first aid pack on the other strap. As he fastened his belt, he noticed that he had reversed the position of grenade and first aid pack. Normally, he carried the grenade on his left harness strap. It was handier to reach to the left to grasp the grenade for throwing with the right hand. Bogey thought to himself, "What the hell, it's still easy to reach, no problem. Let's go!"

Bogey gave one hungry look over his shoulder at the juicy steak and hurriedly assembled with his squad. B Company was to clear the town of Pont Auny, which was near Baupte. Lieutenant Millsaps ordered Boccafogli and Frank Hernandez to be lead point scouts. At first, the advance was easy; a few of the enemy soldiers on the outposts surrendered, saying, "Me Polski, not German." These were rounded up and taken back to the rear, but as they moved closer in to the village, Bogey had an eerie unsettling feeling.

Bogey remembered the following:

> There was not a sound coming from the village. No one could be seen; not a dog or a cat was stirring. That's always a sign that something is waiting to happen.
> 
> Then I heard a shrill scream, maybe a woman or child or man with a high-pitched voice. I stopped and gave the hand signal for the company to halt.

Lieutenant Millsaps came running to see what was up. Bogey told him about the scream. Millsaps decided to move Boccafogli and Hernandez to the right flank point and brought up two others for the front point. After the changes, the company moved again.

"Then all hell broke loose! A whole battalion of Jerries was waiting for us in Pont Auny. We were just one company and down to less than half strength," explained Bogey.

The two new point men who replaced Bogey and Hernandez were killed instantly. Bogey and Hernandez hit the ground and crawled toward the main unit from their position on the right flank. They got behind a small bank, and Bogey pulled the tall grass aside to see over, aimed his rifle, and fired. Then a burst of automatic fire exploded close, showering him with dirt.

Again, Bogey moved closer toward the main group, crouched behind the bank, and fired. Another shower of dirt covered him as the enemy machine gunner noted his fire. Bogey continued to move along the bank closer to his buddies, stopped, and fired. This time, the German machine gunner nailed him.

"It was like a violin string breaking—*boiong*!" Bogey explained. "Then I was out. When I first came to, I was lying on my back. I opened my eyes and could see something like a cloud. I thought I was in heaven. It was so peaceful and quiet."

Heaven didn't last long for Bogey. He soon recognized the cloud as leaves moving in the breeze above. Then he could hear the noise of the firing, which still raged about him. He said to himself, "I'm not dead, I am alive, but I must have been hit."

Bogey didn't feel pain, so he started moving his hands about his body searching for a wound. First he felt his face. His face was OK. Then he rubbed his hands over his chest and then his shoulder, and there he felt the blood. He turned his head and saw the blood spurting out in gushes from his left shoulder. Suddenly Bogey felt cold as shock started to set in.

About that time Hernandez came over to Bogey and said, "Say, you got a little scratch, no big deal. Here, let me fix it." Hernandez took a big blue German handkerchief and squelched the bleeding, and his cheery talk revived Bogey's spirits and pulled him out of shock.

Bogey's rifle stock had been shattered when he was hit and was useless, but he still had his Luger pistol he had taken from a German. Although wounded, Bogey rejoined in the fighting, firing his Luger. He remembered being alongside Paul Atwood at that time, whose machine gun was so hot, it squealed as the rounds sped out the barrel.

It was evident that the Germans in Pont Auny were too strong for the small force of paratroopers in B Company, so about 1600 hours, they withdrew and took care of their wounded. Bogey was loaded on an old captured German truck and sent back to an Omaha Beach hospital.

In reflecting over the events of the day, Bogey mused:

> I could have been dead twice: number one, if Hernandez and I had not been moved from front point to the flank. Number two, if I had not accidentally hooked my grenade up on the right strap of the harness instead of the left because the bullet which hit my left shoulder ripped through the first aid pack attached to the left strap. If a grenade had been in that spot, it would have exploded and ripped me apart.

Boccafogli summarized his feelings of semiconsciousness: "My taste of heaven was brief, but it was good while it lasted."

## A Night Reconnaissance Patrol
by Harry J. Kennedy
Used by permission of Harry Kennedy

Captain John A. Breen, in charge of the 508th Regimental Intelligence Section (S-2), called for Corporal Fred W. Robbins and me to go on a night reconnaissance patrol behind the Germans lines. Seven other men were added to our patrol for protection in case we ran into trouble.

We studied aerial photographs and maps for a couple of hours, planning our routes. On the way to the outpost, our departure point, we stopped by a forward Command Post for the most recent information on enemy movements. A small change in the enemy's positions could mean the difference between success and defeat or even the difference between life or death for the members of the patrol.

Before it was fully dark, we were waiting at the outpost. June nights in Normandy are short. Darkness only lasts about four hours. At about midnight, we left and moved slowly toward the lines of the enemy. A half-moon assisted us in finding our way, but it also provided light for the enemy to see us. There was no firing. It was so quiet; it was hard to believe a war was going on.

After passing two hedgerows, we knew we were in the German lines. An uncertain feeling came over us. Every hedgerow, bush or tree might be hiding a German machine gun. From past experience, we knew that the enemy had a good chance of detecting us long before we discovered his whereabouts. It was so quiet; an alert enemy could probably hear our movements. We needed the rustling of the trees or small arms or artillery fire to mask the noise of our movements. One scout walked in front of me. Since German was my native speech, I kept myself ready to talk back to any German challenge. We proceeded through another five fields. It took us about two hours to move through seven small fields. Suddenly our scout noticed a German standing behind a small pushcart. However, the German had not seen us. Since we wanted information and needed to avoid a fight, we moved back one field and outflanked the soldier with the pushcart.

Having seen one German, we knew there must be others about; our Tommy guns were ready for immediate action. We passed more fields and hedgerows. All of a sudden, we heard someone speak in perfect English, "Where are you going, fellows?"

The speaker then turned and spoke in German to comrades behind him.

Our patrol immediately withdrew into another field. We were very tense and keenly alert. After a few seconds we outflanked that German also. By this time we were getting jumpy and our imaginations were playing tricks on us. Every tree looked like a German soldier. We moved slower than ever. Five steps in a crouched position took thirty minutes.

We were in a corner where two hedgerows joined. The scout was ahead of me and the men behind me were in a crouch, and then the silvery moon came out from behind a cloud clearly outlining all of us. We were perfect targets. A German hollered one word. I didn't understand the word, but recognized it as German. The challenger was only a few feet away, and he could see us all. A wrong move might cause him to open fire on us.

Although my heart was beating so hard, I could hear it, I answered automatically and authoritatively in German; "Yes. What is the matter? Everything is all right!"

The next second, my mind was racing. So many things crossed my mind at the same time. Did all the members of the patrol know that I could speak German? If not, I might become a target of our own men inadvertently. I spotted two light machine guns, which could have murdered all of us. A minute seemed like an hour. The German soldier just looked at us, and then he turned and walked away.

Immediately we withdrew, and returned by our same route, very rapidly, almost running. We hurried because dawn was beginning to show. We had to get back to our lines before it got much lighter. Luckily we made it back without encountering anymore Germans.

Later, a member of the patrol thanked me for thinking so quickly, and maybe saving lives. That "Thank you!" meant more to me than the highest award on earth.

## The Private and the General

PFC Harry Kennedy had an interesting experience with Gen. James Gavin. As a member of the S-2 section, his chief duty was to go on night patrols into enemy territory and bring back information to the regimental command.

One night in Normandy, Harry had been on a patrol and had gotten filthy dirty and soaking wet, so in returning to the bivouac area, he stripped off his clothes to the skin, wrapped up in a blanket, and went to sleep. A messenger awoke Harry and told him the colonel wanted an immediate report from the patrol. Harry wrapped his blanket around him and, wearing no other clothes, reported to the colonel. He received a rebuke for being out of uniform, but his report was welcomed.

It so happened that General Gavin was also at the CP. The general interrupted Harry's report and said, "Say, Kennedy, have you had any coffee yet?"

When Harry answered, "No, sir," General Gavin pumped up the gas field stove, made the coffee himself, and served Harry a cup of coffee from his own canteen cup.

Cartoon by Kate Salley Palmer

## Red Devils Remember Pretot

The next major battle for the 508th, after Baupte and Port Auny, was Pretot. Pretot was a town south of the Douve River and west of Baupte. The capture of the town and the subsequent withdrawal under traumatic circumstances created lasting memories for the Red Devils.

Most of the conversations, listed below, were recorded in the G Company CP in 1988 during the 508th reunion at Portland, Oregon. Some of the quotes were gathered at other times and places and inserted here as if they were a part of the total discussion. (For those not familiar with 508th reunions, each company sets up a CP [command post] or hospitality room, where former members of the company visit together when not attending a planned program for the whole regiment.)

"Pretot—that's when the 88s and the mortars broke up the G Company CP. I was lucky, but Lt. James McDuffie, Lt. Woody Plunkett, Sergeant Henning, Glen Majers, and Ralph Campagna all got hit. It was June 20," Francis Lamoureux, G Company radio operator, recalled.

"We chased the Germans out of Pretot easily," added Woody Plunkett, who was G Company commanding officer. "I remember a young private. He was right behind me and said, 'Lieutenant, I'm hit!' I turned around to see, and he fell back against me. I laid him down gently against the wall of the building and kept going after the Krauts."

Sergeant Risnes recalled, "I remember coming to a house, and I started to go around by the right side but changed my mind and went around the left side. That was a good move. When I got behind that house, I saw a German machine gun pointing down the right side. The Jerry swung his machine gun around in my direction, but I shot him before he could aim at me."

Fayette O. Richardson remembered the wisdom and bravery of his friend William Medford at Pretot. Medford and Richardson led the charge for H Company on a hillside occupied by a German mortar squad. Medford, acting on the assumption that the Germans were intimidated by the assault, jumped up on the hedgerow and, in full view of the Jerries, demanded that they surrender. The Germans responded by turning their weapons over to the paratroopers.

Richardson quoted Medford's comment about his action: "There's a time to be cautious and there's a time to be bold. That was a time to be bold."

Lieutenant Plunkett reminisced, "After we took the town, two platoons dug in on line, with one platoon in reserve, and I set up the CP [company command post]."

Francis Lamoureux added, "At first the CP was in a building. A big shell hit the building, and it collapsed around us. Then we moved to an open field and were digging foxholes when one of those screaming meanies exploded on us."

"I knew we were too bunched up," Plunkett admitted. "I did send John Hargrave, one of the runners, over to the right, away from the rest of us. All the rest of us were hit. Wasn't that you, John?"

"Yeah, that was me," answered Hargrave. "As a good private, I did what I was told, and it saved me that day."

Lamoureux describes the horrors of the scene:

> Sgt. Lloyd "Preacher" Henning's face was all mangled. One eye was hanging out of its socket. He handed his pistol to me and begged me to shoot him.
>
> Majers was hit on the right buttock. The shrapnel went through a shaving brush in his pocket. It was the oddest thing the way those bristles spread around the shrapnel hole—in rays like flower petals around a central floret. Majers was still alive at this time. His wound was not that severe.
>
> The CP was moved a third time to a ravine. The Jerries must have watched our every move because the mortars hit the ravine also. Almost everyone in the G Company CP was hit sooner or later—Lieutenant Plunkett (company commander), Lieutenant McDuffie, Sergeant Henning, Ralph Campagna, and Glen Majers. I was stunned by the explosions but escaped injury.

Out on the front line, the men in the rifle platoons were catching American artillery, which was falling short. Sergeant Risnes went to the CP to send a message to the artillery that his men were receiving friendly fire. "When I got to the CP, I found all the wounded there hit by our own artillery," Risnes remarks.

"That was a German 88 that hit me," Plunkett replies.

Risnes continued:

> On the line we were catching American shells. I can tell the difference in the sequence of firing. The Americans fired in a cluster about the same time. The Germans fired one at a time in sequence. We were being hit by friendly fire.
>
> Sgt. Frank Sirovica arrived at the CP about the same time I did—on the same mission to stop the friendly fire from hitting his platoon. Sirovica and I moved the wounded into a ditch for cover

and sent for the medics. Then we went looking for the battalion CP and found Colonel Mendez. Mendez was unable to correct the artillery fire on our lines, so we were instructed to pull back.

Lamoureux commented, "After the medics carried the wounded to their aid station, the Jerries hit the aid station also, and that's when Majers was killed."

Lt. Briand Beaudin, Third Battalion surgeon, recalled Pretot:

> While I was taking care of casualties in a deep culvert by the side of a wide dirt road, General Gavin, with his rifle slung over his shoulder, strolled by my aid station and later returned without drawing fire. When I went into the road myself, I became the target of a sniper and immediately hit the dirt.
>
> Capt. Alton Bell soon came down the road without being challenged and, upon hearing my reason for crouching in the culvert, said I was imagining things. I tossed Bell my helmet with the Red Cross on it and suggested he put it on. This he did and immediately came under fire. That convinced him. Later several German prisoners told us they had special orders to try to kill American medical personnel in order to demoralize our troops. That was why the Red Cross emblem was singled out.

Concerning the aid station, the following is quoted from the late James H. McDuffie's memoirs, supplied by his widow, Mrs. Mary S. McDuffie:

> One of the troopers announced that they had received orders to withdraw and leave all the wounded behind. About that time a mortar shell exploded only a few feet behind me. I looked back and saw a young trooper had been hit in the head. It had gone through his helmet and he appeared dead. I had a burning sensation in my right heel and realized I had been hit again. The medics gave me another shot of morphine and dressed my heel. The right leg was now in real bad shape, and I felt very helpless. Plunkett was a ghastly color, and I felt he was dying.
>
> A sergeant left me a bottle of wine and said goodbye. He covered me with a German overcoat. Before they left, I gave my .45 pistol to Lieutenant Moss, and another took my carbine. We were told we had a better chance of living if we had no weapons. They pulled off my white undershirt and hung it up as a flag of surrender. Then they left.

There was nothing to do but wait. I prayed. I quoted John 3:16, "For God so loved the world that he gave . . ." and Psalm 23 was especially comforting, "The Lord is my shepherd: I shall not want." I had a vision of a strange white light, and the whole world grew silent. I felt the presence of the Lord. I promised God that if I were spared, I would do something worthwhile. I passed out—loss of blood and sleep, plus the sedative.

When I came to, some of our men were there. Plunkett was very weak and the man behind me was dead. The men whispered that Colonel Mendez had sent them to get us. There was Marvin Risnes and two others from G Company. We were hauled back to the rear aid station.

The Colonel came over and grabbed my hand. It was my turn to weep, and I shed a few tears over seeing him. He told me that Lieutenant Gene Williams, who had been on one of the pathfinder teams, was killed. We later found out that his pretty wife had given birth to twin boys on the same day.

"It felt so good when I went to my first reunion in Fayetteville," Lamoureux remarked, "and saw the survivors from the G Company CP of June 20, 1944. All were there—Plunkett, McDuffie, Henning, and my good buddy Ralph Campagna. Lloyd Henning, whose face had been so mangled, looked marvelous."

## AWOL from the Hospital to the Front Lines

Two of the men from the demolition platoon of Regimental Headquarters Company went AWOL from the field hospital in Normandy. One of these was Ed Luczaj (pronounced *Lou-chi*). Luczaj jumped into a hotbed of Germans who were shooting at the paratroopers as they descended and after they landed. He was lying on his side unhooking his parachute when a tracer bullet zinged through his side leg pocket that contained a white phosphorus grenade. He felt a burning sting against his thigh and knew he had to get rid of that grenade fast. Quickly Ed pulled out his jump knife and ripped open the pocket, grabbed the grenade, and gave it a heave. It exploded in a fiery ball upon impact.

Luczaj got rid of the grenade in time to save his life, but both of his hands were badly burned. In fact, all of his fingernails were burned off. Luczaj then found Harold Mann, who jumped next to him in the stick. Harold carried a copper sulfate medical packet designed especially for burns. He applied the copper sulfate to the wounds that relieved the pain.

Then Ed pulled out the gloves he jumped with and put those on to protect his hands from dirt and grime.

After doctoring Ed's hands, Harold and Ed sought out other troopers. They heard someone, whose parachute caught in a tree, calling for help. Ed stood guard at the foot of the tree while Harold climbed up the tree and got the wounded trooper out of his chute and lowered him to the ground. He was shot up badly, and they could only bandage his wounds. They wrapped him in his chute and told him they would send medics as soon as they found some.

Ed and Harold jumped in an isolated spot where very few paratroopers landed. Finally a group of about fifty gathered together into a fighting unit to defend themselves and harass the enemy. It was several days before they met up with any medics. Once they went back to check on the wounded trooper that they had rescued from the tree only to find out that the Germans had bayoneted him to death.

About D-Day plus 3 the troops that stormed the Normandy beaches broke through and relieved the small band of paratroopers. Medics then treated Luczaj's burned hands, and the doctor sent him to the field hospital on the beach for more adequate treatment. With a good night's rest and about three good meals, Luczaj decided he was wasting his time hanging around the hospital, so he hitchhiked back to the front and joined up with the platoon. After a few days at the front, the bandages became soiled, so Luczaj went to the aid station for a change. The same doctor that treated him the first time was there again. Remembering that he had sent Luczaj to the hospital once before, the doctor said, "This time I am sending you to the hospital to stay!" The ambulance that carried Ed back to the beach drove right up on to a landing craft, which moved out into the sea where the wounded were loaded on to a ship bound for England.

To the left:
Edwin Lucjaz.

To the right:
Wilbur Byers.

Photos provided by Zig Boroughs.

Wilbur "Moto" Byers was the other demolitionist who preferred fighting duty to hospital life. A grenade fragment nicked Moto in the hand between the thumb and the first finger. Moto used his field bandage that all soldiers carried into combat to treat his wound and went on about his business. The wound, though slight, became infected and was causing Byers some pain. Howard Brooks, a close buddy of Byers, urged him to go to the medics and have it treated, but Moto refused.

Once when the section was preparing to go out on a mission, Brooks said to Lieutenant Hardwick, "I don't want Byers to know that I told you this, but I wish you would check Wilbur's hand. I don't think he is in any shape to go out on a combat mission."

Hardwick then made an inspection of his men and their weapons and discovered that Wilbur had a nasty-looking hand—swollen and infected—and ordered him to go to the aid station. The medics sent Wilbur to the field hospital on the beach. In a couple of days his hand was better. Wilbur didn't wait for the medics to discharge him but went AWOL from the hospital and back to the front. His hand healed without any further medical treatment.

## An Experience Etched in Memory
By John Delury, H Company
Permission to use by John Delury

We were in Normandy 33 days and a lot happened during that time that I cannot recall, but things that scared the hell out of us, or were unique in themselves have stood the test of time in the memory bank. Such it was on a sunny Sunday morning. A Catholic Chaplain was giving out Holy Communion to soldiers kneeling in the grass and a sergeant was acting as his altar boy. The unique part was—kneeling with the Americans were captured German soldiers in their field green uniforms receiving communion also. Somehow the Krauts detected the assemblage and threw some fast 88s at us.

The sacrosanct scene soon transformed itself into one of iconoclastic chaos. It was every man for himself. Everyone went ass over teakettle for the closest ditch: Germans, Americans, altar boy, priest and chalice. We were so starved for any deviation from our morbid surroundings we actually found it humorous. It was seeing all the authority of heaven and earth standing for a brief moment on its collective head.

Chaplain Kenny celebrating Mass on January 6, 1945, during the Belgium campaign. Photo provided by Emile Lacroix.

## The Church Robbers

One of the troopers from Regimental Headquarters Company collected a bag full of gold ornaments that he took from Normandy churches. Matthew Bellucci of Regimental Headquarters Company, who was a good Catholic, forced the church robber to turn his loot over to the Catholic chaplain, Father Kenney. Father Kenney, in turn, returned the sacred ornaments to the bishop who served the Catholic diocese in Normandy.

Another church robber came close to meeting his maker when caught in the act by Leon Israel of Regimental Headquarters Company. When the 508th advanced across the

Matthew Bellucci. Photo provided by Zig Boroughs.

Cotentin peninsular, they were preceded by massive attacks from the air to soften up the German resistance. It also devastated the French villages. Such was the case at St. Sauveur Le Vicomte. Israel was disturbed over the "needless destruction" of civilian property. The church was bombed to shambles by our bombers. The nun's quarters, the children's school, and the monastery were all in ruins. Yet Israel, who was a practicing Jew, felt inclined to worship in the wreckage of the Roman Catholic Church at St. Sauveur Le Vicomte.

"I walked into the church and felt close to God," Israel wrote in his diary. "I wanted to tell God that I really didn't want to kill those four Germans. It was kill or be killed."

A shaft of sunlight came through a hole in the roof on a statue of Jesus that had not been destroyed by the bombs. Leon began to pray, and then he realized the presence of someone else in the building. Thinking it might be a German, he slowly and cautiously turned and, at the same time, drew his pistol. To his surprise, he saw one of his buddies climbing a statue of a saint and removing a gold locket from her neck. Nevertheless, Leon took careful aim with his .45. "I wanted to kill him more than I wanted to kill the Germans," Leon recalled, "but I couldn't pull the trigger." Leon Israel replaced his pistol and ran sobbing from the church.

## Hill 131, July 3

A brief sentence in the *History of the 508th Parachute Infantry* by William G. Lord II reads, "Reconnaissance patrols, notably three made by Corporal Ellis and Private First Class Kennedy of the regimental S-2 Section, procured information of the enemy on Hill 131."

Harry Kennedy described some of the details in connection with those patrols:

> I remember those night patrols on Hill 131. We went through the American and German line at the same place for three nights. The first night we lay quietly in front of the German line until we heard movement. A German soldier left his foxhole and walked back a few yards and took a leak. We saw him come back to his hole. He said something in German to a soldier in the foxhole next to him a few yards over. Knowing where two foxholes were helped us slip between them.
> 
> After getting through the frontline foxholes, we spotted other German soldiers toward the rear. We stayed out of their way. We found a Frenchman who told us about the location of

troops and tanks and approximate numbers. Then we slipped back through the lines.

On the second night, we went through the German line at the same place and found a French civilian who gave us more information. On the way back, we captured a German soldier and brought him back through the lines for interrogation.

In capturing prisoners, I would slip up behind them and say quietly in German, "Don't move! Be quiet! We are American paratroopers and have you surrounded." (The word *paratroopers* aroused their fear.) I would reach around and unbuckle his rifle belt and take his weapons. Then we had to get him back through both lines.

The third night it was a little scarier. Since we had taken a prisoner the night before, surely they would be on the lookout this time. Luckily, we made it through both ways and brought back additional up-to-date information on the enemy's strength and positions.

Many 508th men remember July 3 and Hill 131. The whole regiment (what was left of it) was involved in taking that hill.

Sgt. Marvin Risnes, G Company, remembered that before reaching the line of departure, a mortar shell burst nearby. Risnes hit the dirt, and when he got up, his pants were wet—shrapnel had punctured his canteen.

Two men from Risnes's squad, Forest Duncan and Theodore Gienger, were wounded on the attack before they reached the first hedgerow.

"We took prisoners galore," Risnes reports. "Just threw their arms away and sent the Krauts toward the rear."

Others told Risnes that some of the later prisoners, finding arms en route, picked them up and started fighting again.

John Delury, H Company, described the scene as he saw it on July 3:

> We started getting in position very early in the morning before daybreak. It was raining all morning—a very light foggy type rain. I found myself in a ravine, with the fields we were to attack above our heads. We were on the down side of a slope with trees and mixed vegetation. We crawled up to the top of the slope just below the fields. Machine gun fire cut the leaves on the hedges above us, sending green confetti wafting down on our heads. German mortar fire was steady all morning.

The picture that confronted this group of wet, tired, hungry paratroopers was that when the attack order was given, a lot of us would be cut down immediately.

Delury remembered how he took comfort in the fact that the whole platoon would be advancing together and would share the dangers equally. At the last minute, however, orders were given that first scout John Delury and second scout Fayette O. Richardson would lead the way. Delury said, "I felt I was standing up before a German firing squad, but over I went with my Thompson blasting."

According to Delury, H Company men lost two men KIA attacking Hill 131 on July 3—Ed Polasky and Gene Shipley.

Harold O. I. Kulju (now Harold O. Canyon) was a radio operator for Headquarters Second. Kulju described his experience on July 3:

> The Second Battalion was assigned three TDs (tank destroyers) for the attack on Hill 131, and I was the radio liaison between them and the battalion. Each TD normally had one gunner, one radio operator, the TD driver, and the tank commander. I was put in a TD with the normal crew plus the commander of the three TDs. I can assure you that for an infantryman whose total training had been to be quiet and not bunch up, this assignment wasn't my cup of tea. Six of us cooped up in that noisy can. That was no way to fight a war.
>
> We reached a point where the 508th troops bypassed a small pocket of Germans, and the Jerries opened up on us with their machine guns. At that point I was not too uncomfortable, hearing the bullets ricocheting off the tank destroyer.
>
> The TD radioman sent a message on his radio. The Germans picked up on the AM radio transmission, and almost immediately an artillery shell landed alongside us. A piece of shrapnel hit the commander. He thought he had earned the Purple Heart, but the shrapnel hadn't penetrated.
>
> Since it had been raining, most of the paratroopers had no smokable cigarettes on reaching the objective, so we shared our dry ones with them. We moved to the top of Hill 131, and each TD took a position where German tanks were most likely to attack. At that point my service as an armored soldier ended.

Sgt. Teddy Belliveau of Regimental Headquarters Company remembered Hill 131, July 3. He was part of a group attacking a German roadblock. The paratroopers circled in behind the roadblock and opened fire from a hedgerow. The Jerries responded with their machine guns and later with mortars. Belliveau was kneeling on his right knee when a mortar shell hit a nearby tree. Shrapnel from the shell caught Belliveau in his left thigh. At the time of his injury, Colonel Lindquist was within a few feet of Belliveau, but the colonel was not hurt.

Belliveau recalled that so many injured in the field hospital that those whose lives were not in immediate danger had to wait while the doctors treated the more seriously wounded.

Lt. Briand Beaudin, Third Battalion surgeon, recalls July 3, 1944:

> Word came that casualties were mounting and medics were needed right away. I was directed to the area where casualties were supposedly waiting. Soon I found myself under direct fire from my right and my left. Thinking I would be hit any second in this untenable position, I slowly turned and in a low crawl proceeded, pulling myself back as fast as I could. I thought my butt would be perforated repeatedly before I reached safety.
>
> When I came to an opening in a stone wall, I sprang through it and immediately collided with Lt. Lee Frigo of A Company. He was looking for medical help but didn't expect to be hurled to the ground before getting it. Frigo had a head wound with blood dripping all over his face like the Sherwin-Williams paint commercial "We cover the earth!"
>
> Actually, all he had was a superficial wound, which parted his hair in the center for about two inches. Pressure and a tight bandage took care of him.

By 1600 hours Hill 131 was secured. At 2000 hours the regiment moved to the base of Hill 95 and prepared for the next day's battle on the Fourth of July.

## Hill 95, July 4 and 5

In "Fourth of July Fireworks" by Fred Gladstone of I Company, Gladstone wrote, "We had heard that Hill 95 was 'the key to Paris and out ticket back to England.' All we had to do was to take it."

Lt. Briand Beaudin, Headquarters Third surgeon, remembered July 4:

I lost a very good friend that day—Lt. Paul Lehman. He was wounded and disabled by shrapnel. Colonel Mendez put Lehman across his shoulders and was moving him to relative safety. Lehman was shot dead while still on Mendez's back.

Pete Karres of I Company continued the story:

> I saw that happen. The same sniper killed our First Sergeant Raymond Conrad and Edwin De Beer. I think he got Conrad and De Beer with one bullet.
> Mendez said to me, "Pete, get that sniper!" I started after him, but when two bullets kicked up the dirt between my legs, I decided he would get me first, so I gave up on that Kraut.

During the night of July 3, Fred Gladstone had been on a two-man outpost to the front of I Company. When Sgt. Jack Elliot called Galdstone and his partner from the outpost back to the main line the morning of July 4, they were fired on from the flank as they crossed a field of grain. A German machine gun positioned on a ridge had a clear field of fire through which they had passed. Gladstone and four others were immediately ordered to form a point of attack across the same field. Gladstone tried to persuade Lieutenant Daly to zigzag behind hedgerows, which would conceal the advancing Red Devils from the view of the enemy gun emplacement. Daly responded, "Get moving!"

Gladstone describes that experience:

> We quickly got into the grain and slid along on our stomachs. The German machine gun kept raking the area from side to side, cutting the grain over our heads. Our radio operator, Cpl. George Petros, decided to run for it. He was hit as soon as he went past me. I can still remember the sickening sound of bullets hitting his body.
> I was about thirty feet from the safety of a hedgerow, and as I braced myself to make a run for it—*wham!* A bullet made a huge hole in my entrenching tool and then tore through my thigh. It felt like a red-hot poker was thrust through me.
> By this time, all five of us had been hit, and George Petros was dead. I couldn't move and was bleeding badly but managed to get a compress bandage over one of the holes in my thigh. One of my buddies, Rene Croteau, crawled out to me and asked if he could help. I wanted a cigarette. Rene didn't smoke but got

one out of my pocket and helped me light it. The enemy spotted the smoke. The bullets started again, and one smashed into my elbow.

Since none of the point men made it to the first hedgerow, Company I decided to zigzag around the grain field in behind hedgerows to avoid the fire of the German machine gun. Two I Company men, Sgt. Jack Elliot and PFC Andy Downer, removed Gladstone from the field. In Gladstone's words, "In a midst of a hail of bullets, they picked me up and hurled me over the hedgerow."

Hill 95 and the ridge it dominated was the objective of the whole Eighty-second Airborne Division. Three parachute regiments (508th, 507th, and 505th) and the 325th Glider Regiment all participated as well as the division artillery units. Unfortunately, a lack of coordination between the units caused delays and changes of plans. As a result, artillery timing was unsynchronized with infantry advances, and there were many unnecessary casualties.

John Delury recalled H Company's advance behind the artillery:

> As we were running, we watched the hill where the Germans were being pounded by artillery and smoke. We were on a kind of high. We were in the midst of battle, watching it almost as spectators because no one was shooting at us. When the whole battalion was strung out across the open field, the artillery ceased, the smoke lifted, and it suddenly turned into a Kraut turkey shoot.

Fayette O. Richardson, H Company, described the results: "Machine gun fire cut us down like a scythe cutting grass. In a few minutes thirty of our company's eighty men lay dead or wounded."

Richardson lost his good friend Bill Medford that day. "There were no officers or noncoms that far forward. Medford took charge. He stood up shouting to the company on our flank, but a moment later, a bullet cut him down."

Pete Karres was point man for his platoon of I Company. Karres remembered the following:

> Lt. Robert Mitchell, platoon CO, was right behind me to my right. That's the kind of man he was, an upfront leader. The field we crossed in the attack was covered with ferns about knee high. I remember the sound of the ferns rubbing against

our legs. When they opened up on us, the ferns weren't much protection.

Karres said to his platoon leader, "See that opening in the hedgerow? I think Jerry has a machine gun there. I'm going to find out."

As Karres approached the gap and rolled over a hedgerow, a bullet knocked off the metal adjustment tab from his helmet chinstrap. Jerry did have a gun emplacement there.

I Company had advanced with few casualties at first but was suddenly hit with all the force of the German firepower. Many of the leading officers and NCOs were wounded or killed. I Company's CO, Lt. John J. Daly, was among the KIA. Chuck Strong of I Company said, "In our section we ended up with a couple of privates first class in charge."

Strong and his buddy Guido Pelini zigzagged out of the ferns up to the next hedgerow. They moved through to the other side of the hedges and suddenly heard a noise in the bushes behind them. It was Col. Louis Mendez, Third Battalion CO, arriving to take charge.

Mendez's arrival reminded Strong of the officer's shower in Nottingham. Strong recalls, "Guido and I sneaked in, and we were all lathered up when Lou Mendez came in to bathe. No one wore bars in the shower, and Mendez couldn't tell a private from a lieutenant."

Harold Kulju, radio operator for Headquarters Second, wrote of Hill 95:

> We had to cross an open area about seventy-five feet to a hedgerow corner. The Germans were zeroed in on the open area with machine guns, rifles, and mortars. I moved as fast as I could and dove over the hedgerow, skimming the top. I felt a machine gun bullet on each cheek as I went over, and that was through two pairs of pants. At the top of the hill, a piece of spent shrapnel hit my leg and left a red welt.

Kulju spotted a New Testament with a metal cover on Hill 95. It had a bullet hole right through the center. Some soldiers carried that type of Bible over their hearts for protection. Kulju thought, "Whoever owned that New Testament found everlasting peace, and the German who shot him wore a belt buckle inscribed 'God is with us.' Probably a case of a Baptist killing a Baptist."

When the paratroopers gained the top of the hill and set up the MLR (main line of resistance), Kulju moved down the ridge in front of the MLR to a place with a good view as an OP (observation post) for the Mortar Platoon. Kulju saw some Germans moving along a hedgerow and called for each of the six mortars to fire four rounds on the area. When the twenty-four shells landed, a whole herd of cows ran off in different directions. "I'm still apologizing to the French owners of those cows," Kulju explains, "and they send me a Christmas card every year."

Kulju saw enemy mortar flashes from another area and radioed for fire on the new position. After many rounds, four Germans appeared carrying a stretcher and a white flag. Kulju had one of them in the sights of his 1903 bolt action rifle when a lieutenant behind him yelled, "Don't shoot, we want them as prisoners!"

"I did not fire," Kulju recalled, "and I stood up to let the Germans know which direction to take. A bad mistake—the first round missed, and I wasn't up for the encore!"

The crew was carrying a mortar in the stretcher, but they were taken as prisoners to Regimental Headquarters and questioned. The German prisoners explained that the American mortar attack on their position had wiped out most of their group and had prevented a counterattack from developing.

One of the casualties of July 4 was Rene Croteau of I Company. Croteau was of French extraction and fluent in the French language. He had become very close to a young French lad who attached himself to I Company. The youth was about fifteen years old and had gradually accumulated a complete paratrooper uniform. Since his feet were smaller than most troopers were, boots to fit were hard to find. When Lt. Gene Williams, Headquarters Third, was killed at Pretot, the lad inherited the lieutenant's boots.

Charles Strong remembered Croteau as Punchy Croteau, a short guy, solidly built and a good baseball player (see photo on page 35). "Punchy was a nice guy, not one of the rowdies," recalled Strong.

Strong described an event on July 4:

> About ten or fifteen of us from I Company were really catching it. Most of us were in or around a small barn. We decided to make a break toward a bridge. A burp gun got right on me. I zigzagged down the road until I saw an open hole and dived in. I said, "Wow, Punchy! Didn't know you were here!"
>
> Croteau didn't answer. He was sitting face up in the bottom of the hole, not blown up or mutilated, but he was dead. I left the hole fast and ran to the bridge.

The French lad who had become so fond of Rene Croteau heard that his buddy had been wounded. He went looking for Croteau and hoped to carry him to the rear. Some of the I Company men reported that "Frenchy" braved heavy enemy fire seeking to rescue his buddy, but both of them lost their lives on July 4, 1944, on Hill 95.

F Company reached the crest of Hill 95 on the left flank. Art Sanchez remembered that word came to them that I Company on their left was badly shelled and that "Frenchy" was killed. D Company on their right had also suffered heavy casualties from the shelling.

General Gavin was in the F Company area and ordered F Company to charge down the hill across an open field to knock out a battery of 88s. About half way to the battery, the 88s turned their guns on the advancing paratroopers. Sanchez describes the results:

> F Company was hit hard. Jack Sprinkle, next to me, was wounded. I took off my helmet and belt and laid my rifle down and carried Jack back out of the shelling. I made five more trips carrying the wounded. General Gavin said, "No more," but I went back to get my rifle, belt, and helmet. When I returned, General Gavin asked for my name and wrote it in his little notebook.
>
> That night I took a couple of Gammon grenades and sneaked down to the 88-gun position. At about 150 feet away, I threw the first grenade, which set the ammo on fire. I threw the second grenade, and the ammo started to explode. Then I ran back up the hill. We watched for about two hours. It was a good show of fireworks for the Fourth of July.

Many of the defenders of Hill 95 were Mongolians. They had been Russian conscripts and had either deserted to the Germans or were taken prisoners. They hated the Russians enough to volunteer to fight for Germany. Sergeant Risnes, G Company, described them as fierce fighters. "They were hard to capture," Risnes said. "We found one Mongolian stunned by a shell concussion. When he came to his senses and learned he was our prisoner, it took three paratroopers to subdue him."

Medics carried Fred Gladstone, wounded in the initial assault, to a roadside. Gladstone recalled, "Colonel Mendez came hurrying along the road. When he saw me, he dropped down on one knee long enough to speak a few words of encouragement and pray a short prayer."

Gladstone was picked up by an ambulance and driven to French home used as an aid station. (In 1984 Gladstone visited Normandy and found the former aid station. He also met Mademoiselle Frederique Sanson, whose family had shared their home with the wounded GIs. Mademoiselle Sanson has since visited Gladstone's home in Darien, Georgia.)

Third Battalion aid station, July 4, 1944. Photo copied from *History of the 508 Parachute Infantry* by William G. Lord II. Permission to use granted by William G. Lord II.

Shelling from both sides continued through July 5. The following incident occurred on July 5: John Simmons, an E Company radioman, thinking that a lull in the fighting would allow him time to relieve himself, told First Sergeant Frank Smith, "I'm going down the hill a short distance and take a crap."

After leaving Smith, an 88 shell exploded near Simmons, and a piece of shrapnel hit him in the face, breaking his jaw and knocking out some teeth. Eventually Simmons was hospitalized in Plymouth, England. By the time he was well enough to return to duty, the regiment was also back in England. When John Simmons returned to Wollaton Park, Nottingham, and walked into E Company Street, he was greeted by First Sergeant Frank Smith with these words, "Hello, John! That was the longest crap anyone ever took."

## "Maybe You Can Win!"

Before the Normandy invasion, Harry Kennedy of Regimental Headquarters Company was sent to a special school in London to develop skill in giving military commands in German after the usual style of German officers and noncoms. Harry credits the training received in that school as one reason he survived the war.

At the school, the American soldiers practiced acting like German soldiers and looking like German soldiers. Both armies had caps with a bill that looked similar, especially at night. The S-2 (Intelligence Section) soldiers never wore helmets on patrol but always wore their wool knit caps. There were really two reasons not to wear helmets. The first reason was they made a lot of noise. If metal struck the helmet, it would ring like a bell. The other reason was they were so different from the German helmets. The helmet was one of the identifying features looked for by both armies to tell friend from enemy.

If a patrol accidentally stumbled upon a foxhole occupied by a German soldier about half asleep, Harry would act like a German noncom and give him an order, something like the German equivalent of "Stay alert, soldier!" Then the patrol would move on undetected as Americans.

Once in Normandy, Harry was put in charge of marching a large group of German prisoners to the beach to be evacuated across the English Channel. Harry used his training in German army commands to order the prisoners to quickly form a column of two's with noncoms in front, privates in the middle, and officers to the rear. The prisoners responded with disciplined precision. He was able to march them off rapidly toward the beach barking his orders in German with studied authority.

While marching to the beach, one of the German officers told Harry, "The German army will soon drive you Americans right back into the sea. You will suffer tremendous loses of men and equipment, which will break the backs of the Allied armies and lead to a quick German victory." The German officer acted as if he were convinced of this ultimate truth.

When the column of prisoners approached the beach, they saw the enormous amount of equipment stockpiled. They witnessed the tremendous flow of armament and supplies being transported toward the front and the mass of ships backed up in the English Channel as far as the eye could see. When the German officer saw all of this, he changed his mind. He said to Harry, "If the Allies have this much backup support for their armies, I think they might win the war after all."

## Report to the CP

"Hey, Jim!" Jafet Alfonso called. "You are supposed to report to the CP on the double!"

Jim Kurz knew what to expect. He had just had a fight with a lieutenant. "I guess they plan to court martial me," Jim said, as he headed toward the CP.

The 508th was at La Haye Du Puits, preparing to leave Normandy for England. Trucks had just pulled out carrying most of the troopers' personal gear. The paratroopers would soon leave for Utah Beach and then on to merry England.

Jim had overslept the morning of July 12, 1944, which was what caused the problem. Alfonso shook him awake at 0700, saying, "Wake up, Jim, we were supposed to have our gear on the trucks by now."

Hurriedly Kurz wiped the sleep out of his eyes and lugged his pack and equipment over toward the waiting trucks. He was intercepted by a lieutenant, who promptly did his duty as an officer and a gentleman and said, "Kurz, you missed the 0700 deadline, so you cannot put your equipment on the truck." While he was dressing Jim down, the trucks pulled away.

"If you hadn't stopped me, I could have made it to the trucks before they left," Jim said.

"Well, you will just have to carry all your equipment on the march to the beach," ordered the lieutenant.

Jim was getting angry. "Hell, this rifle doesn't work good anyhow. I'm not taking it," he announced, and heaved his M-1 over a hedgerow.

"This is a direct order. Go get that rifle!"

"I am not going after the rifle, and furthermore, I will go through the rest of my equipment and throw away everything else I don't want," replied Jim.

Now the lieutenant was angry as this buck private tested his authority.

Kurz already resented the officer because he had fouled up in combat on July 4, and he was not about to be bullied by him now, and the young officer was not about to allow a private to disregard a direct order, so the battle was joined. The battle of words soon turned physical. Sergeant Warneche had to intervene, for Big Jim Kurz was on top of the lieutenant, choking him.

Before Kurz had cooled off, he received orders to report to Lieutenant Millsaps, CO for Company B. "First thing, Jim," Millsaps announced. "Let's get this straight. You must obey all orders from officers! Understand?"

Jim replied, "I understand, but—"

"The second thing," Millsaps interrupted, "I like the way you performed in combat, and I am promoting you to sergeant and squad leader."

The guys in the squad were waiting to see that hang-dog look on Kurz's face as he left the CP; instead they saw a smiling trooper, ready for the march to Utah Beach.

Three buddies at Norfolk, VA reunion in 1992. L-R: Edward Boccafogli, Jim Kurz, and Frank Sakowski. Photo by Zig Boroughs.

## We Left France
### By Leon Israel Mason
Used with the permission of Leon Israel Mason

Like a slow moving tawny caterpillar our regiment, or what was left of it, wound its way to the beach. In spite of their new clothes, the men were visibly tired and uneasy. They were going back to England for a rest. Just a few weeks ago they had started the invasion of Europe. They personified glamour, glory and guts, but now they looked older than their years. They had jumped into hell and now the tired few that were left were going back.

The stench of death was still about them. The shriek of shells, the horrors of war passed through their minds in a screaming jumbled panorama. They seem to be struggling inwardly to awaken from the nightmare.

The beach scene: One could never forget it. The large ammunition dump was spasmodically vomiting in the sunlight. The black funneled cloud arose above it like a mad genie. Barrage balloons, silver sentinels nodding in the sunlight, seemed to hold up the oil-covered sand. One could scarcely see the water due to the scurrying activity of the ants that made up the quartermaster's trucks and men. Tents and slit trenches, camouflage guns, mesh roads, craters and destruction seem to extend into eternity. Yet some order was developing out of the chaos of D-Day.

Then we saw the sea. One gasped with amazement at the sight of so many ships—ships of every type and description—ships that crawled over the land and ships that crawled back into the water. Yes, there was even a graveyard for the ships that were hit by the 88s—by some 88s we didn't find and destroy. The vastness of the ocean seemed small compared to the thousands of ships that stretched over the horizon; ships that were bringing in men and supplies so that some day the war would be over and the troops could go home.

We came to a halt and rested on a concrete embankment still blinking at the consumption of visible energy exerted by the many ants.

Some blue ants (sailors) were playing a game of ball on the damp sands of the low tide. It seemed a long time ago since we played such a game, but for awhile we put the war out of our minds, and yelled and howled with delight.

The LSTs were unloading tanks by the hundreds, reminding one of the turtles coming from under the flippers of the mother turtle.

Slowly the night came and with it the dread fear of the dark unknown. Slowly the tide started surging in. Our boat sloshed in the sand. Searchlight beacons started their nightly vigil. Then they came—German bombers dropped their flares. Our ack-acks threw rivets of flaming lead up to greet them. In the distance the still rumbling ammunition dump illuminated the scene in an unreal glow. We crouched and shivered and prayed—to be killed now after coming through so much! Then the regiment moved aboard ship. The heavy clang of the anchor pealed like bells of freedom as it came out of the dark bloody sea.

The regiment was leaving France—to heal the wounds and prepare to fight again.

# CHAPTER 5

# The 508th Returned to England

## Back to Nottingham

The battered remnants of the 508th returned from Normandy to Wollaton Park on July 15, 1944. The paratroopers had arrived the first time in Nottingham and settled in Wollaton Park on March 11. They departed on May 28 to airfields in preparations for their D-Day airborne invasion of Normandy. During that short period of two and a half months at Wollaton Park, a mutual affection was established between the paratroopers and neighboring citizens in Nottingham and Beeston, especially among the young women.

When the regiment returned from combat, many anxious British women visited Wollaton Park to learn the fate of troopers with whom they had fallen in love. Ralph Thomas, first sergeant for E Company, remembered one visitor:

> A lady came to the E Company CP with a guide from Regimental Headquarters. The lady asked about Clyde K. Moore Jr. I had to tell her that he had been killed during our last days in Normandy.
>
> As I recalled, she had two small children with her, and she was very nervous and upset. My report upset her even more. When I asked why she wanted the information on Moore, she answered, "I am carrying his child."
>
> She also told me that the father of her two children was dead.
>
> I explained to her that because Moore was dead and they were not married that there was no way the US Army could

do anything for her. I suggested she contact the American Red Cross or the British government for help.

At the suggestion of the Regiment, I wrote a letter to the lady as to Clyde Moore being killed.

Let me say that this lady and her story bothered me from the very beginning, and I carried it with me right down until today. I worried about her and the three children through the years. What happened to her? Did she make it?

In the fullness of time, Moore's daughter, Rosemary, was born. From the beginning, Rosemary's mother taught her to remember "Daddy Clyde" in her evening prayers. She always felt an emptiness that half of her was missing.

When her mother sent Rosemary a clipping from a Nottingham paper of the impending visit of the 508th for the fiftieth anniversary of D-Day, hoping to learn that her father was not really dead after all, she began to make inquiries. Rosemary learned through AWON (American War Orphan's Network) that her father's body was returned to America and buried in the USA. With this information and the help of members of the 508th Association, she was able to meet members of her father's family and visit his grave in Macon, Georgia.

Gravestone of Clyde K. Moore Jr.
Photo provided by Rosemary Kingstone.

From the Moore family in Macon, Rosemary learned that her "Daddy Clyde" was the oldest child in their family. He was named for his father and called Junior by family members. His mother died when he was eleven, and he joined the army when he was sixteen. Moore's family described him as a big, quiet, modest young man who looked older than his years. He was only twenty when he was killed.

Rosemary's son, Steve, found a newspaper article about Clyde Moore in a Macon library with his picture and the account of his service in the Pacific, having fought the Japanese on the Island of New Guinea. On returning to the United States, Junior volunteered for the paratroopers and was first assigned to the 550th Parachute Infantry, and later transferred to the 508th while the Regiment was in Nottingham. Another factor, which Rosemary says she likes, "I learned I have my father's eyes."

In 1998 at the 508th Reunion in Nashville, Tennessee, Rosemary met Ralph Thomas. He was the first sergeant who reported to her mother that Clyde K. Moore Jr. had been killed in action. She mailed Thomas a copy of the letter, which Ralph sent to her mother in 1944. Ralph wrote, "It was touching to see the letter in my own handwriting from so long ago."

Among the surviving members of the 508th whom Rosemary has contacted, no one can recall knowing Clyde Moore in a personal way, but someone did remember his military actions in 1944. Clyde Moore earned the Bronze Star for heroic and meritorious service in connection with military operations. His award is listed in the *History of the 508th Parachute Infantry* by William G. Lord, II, Washington Infantry Journal Press, 1948.

Rosemary Kingstone.
Photo by Zig Boroughs.

Clyde K. Moore Jr.
Provided by
Rosemary Kingstone.

What has it meant for Rosemary to find out more about her father and to meet members of his family? She answered that question below:

Finding out more about my father has brought mixed emotions. It is wonderful to have a photograph of him, to be a US passport-bearing citizen, to have met my uncles and cousins, and to be a part of the family of the 508th PIR Association. I wonder what he would have been like if he had lived, and I hope that he would have been as young at heart and full of life as the people I have been lucky enough to meet at the 508th Association reunions.

My heart aches knowing that he had a poor and difficult childhood and that he enlisted at sixteen as a way of escaping a similar future. I am proud of him for his obvious bravery and strength and for volunteering again and again, knowing that he might lose his life. Despite having been successful in finding out more than I hoped for, I still have the sense of loss and void that can never be filled.

I will visit my uncles and the 508th reunions as often as I can, and I would like to spend more time in the Macon Library trying to find out more.

Rosemary's Uncle Eddie Moore and her son, Steve.
Photo Provided by Rosemary Kingstone.

## "Friendly" Land Mine Explosion?

Angelina "Angie" Spera Fuller had always referred to Louis "Louie" Spera as her little brother, who at seventeen eagerly left the family farm near Madera, California, in 1941. By September 1943, he had grown from five feet, six inches to six feet, two inches, and he was wearing the boots and wings of a paratrooper.

To the left: Angelina's "little brother" Louis Spera proudly posed in his uniform as a raw recruit.

To the right: Angelina's "big brother" Louis Spera posed two years later—eight inches taller, stronger, and battle ready.

Photos supplied by Angelina Spera Fuller.

While on furlough, Louie couldn't get enough of the farm, which two years earlier he couldn't wait to leave. Having outgrown his old workclothes, he wore his army fatigues and helped his dad flip their Thompson seedless green grapes, which were drying between the rows of vines and changing into raisins. Louie's father, Luigi, also made homemade wine for family and friends and was able to pass on his winemaking skills to the next generation of Speras.

When Louie's furlough ended and he walked to the depot for his return to army duty, Angie observed how many heads turned to watch her brother. She wrote the following:

They could not help noticing the tall young soldier with broad shoulders, long legs, and tapered hips in fresh khaki uniform with razor-sharp pressed trousers, tucked in highly polished paratrooper boots, walking with pride and long strides, his head high and his shoulders back.

That was the last time the family saw their beloved Louie. He parachuted into France on D-Day and survived the Normandy campaign without a scratch and wrote his parents a V-mail letter from Normandy (page 228). It said about as much as any of us was allowed to write while in combat. Then later came the sad news that he lost his life in an accident on September 2, 1944, by a "friendly land mine explosion." (When people are killed in war from our own ordinance, controlled by our own troops, it is referred to as friendly fire or, in this case, a friendly land mine.)

Jan Bos of Holland, shared his research entitled "Tragedy at Fulbeck: September 2, 1944." The following are excerpts from Lt. Francis L. Mahan's report of the accident, which came from Bos's papers:

> I sent a detail out to drop our equipment bundles under the wings of our assigned aircraft, to be loaded in the bomb racks later on in the day. It appears that what happens was that they set a land mine bundle off the truck onto the ground very carefully as they had been taught and, for some unknown reason, toppled another bundle off the truck on top of the land mine bundle. Of course the land mine bundle blew up, killing three soldiers and destroying three aircraft and a truck. The soldiers' names were Staff Sergeant Robert W. Shearer (Co I Supply Sergeant), Private First Class William R. Mitchell and Private Louis N. Spera.
>
> I had to go to the morgue on the air base to identity the bodies. There was not much left of them.

C-47 damaged by the explosion, which killed Spera. Photo supplied by Jan Bos.

Charles Strong, I Company, was on a detail to pack land mine bundles in Nottingham. Later the regiment was transported to the airport for a planned paratrooper drop into Belgium. Strong and his buddy Louis Spera were reading the airport duty roster. They saw that Spera had KP and Strong was assigned to work on the truck distributing land mine bundles. Spera suggested they arrange to swap duties. The exchange was approved. When the fatal accident occurred, Louis Spera was on the truck and Charles Strong was working in the kitchen. The Belgian mission was later canceled. (This was summarized from Bos's research and letters from Strong.)

D Company men wrap land mines for parapacks before Holland jump. Two in photo are John Starchvich and Warren Albrecht. Photo by Frank Staples.

Charles Strong wrote that he came to the 508th in March 1944 as a replacement. His company, having trained together since 1942, was a close-knit group, and Charles felt somewhat of an outsider. However, he was able to make friends with two Italian boys in I Company, Guido Pelini and Louis Spera. Although Irish himself, Charles explained, "They were about the only two 'spaghetti benders,' and I hooked up with them because all my pals' parents in Gary, Indiana, made 'dago red,' so we related." Charles went on to say, "Looie decided to make some dago red, and he got the nickname the Grape Stomper."

Bill Chapman from San Jose, California, another one of Louie's I Company buddies, told Louie's sister, Angie, "We used to tease Louie, telling him his socks were purple from stomping grapes."

Another friend of Louie's, Bob Chisolm, wrote, "Louie and I were pretty good friends and often went on pass together. He was a real head turner, as far as the ladies were concerned. Many of us referred to him as the Gentle Giant due to his size, temperament, and wonderful disposition."

Chisolm went on to explain that there was a limit to Louie's gentleness. "There were three or four guys in I Company that everyone went out of their way to avoid an altercation with. One was Louie. He was easy going, slow to lose his temper, but when he did, he was a one-man tornado."

Chisolm continued, "I was not surprised to learn that he volunteered to trade jobs on the day that he was killed. Louie was much more comfortable doing physical labor than doing KP. It was a real shock and a great loss to our company when he was killed."

Lt. Kelso Horne is among those who shared with Angelina Spera Fuller memories of her brother. Horne told her of being in the same foxhole with Louie during the Normandy campaign when a shell from a German antiaircraft flack gun exploded in a tree above their heads. The shrapnel shattered the stock of Louie's rifle, but both Louie and Horne escaped injury.

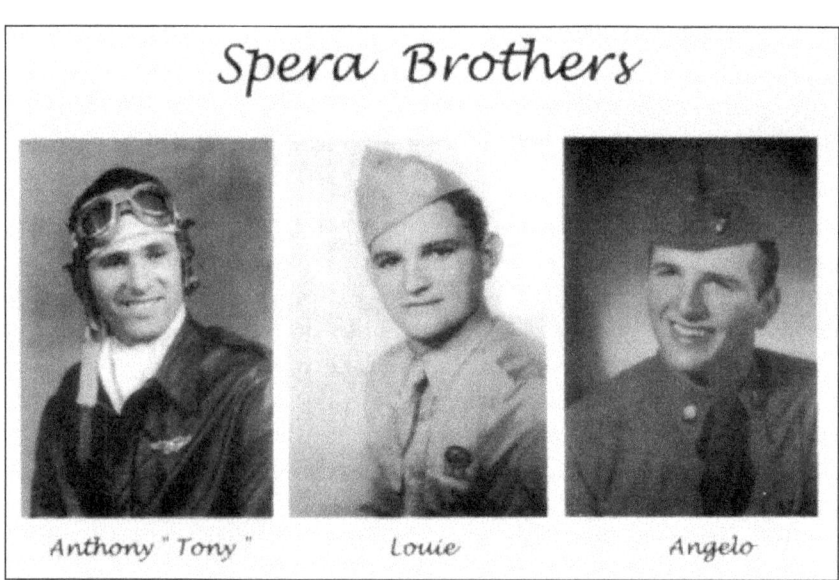

Photo supplied by Angelina Spera Fuller.

The Spera family lost two sons in World War II: Louis, the 508th paratrooper, and Anthony, a turret gunner in a bomber, whose plane was shot down over Berlin. A third son, Angelo, turned down a football scholarship to the University of Saint Mary and, following his brother Louis's example, joined the paratroopers.

When Angelo phoned home to say his unit would be going to Korea, his sister, Angie, sent a telegram to President Harry Truman. She explained that her family had already lost two sons, and that her grieving mother died shortly afterward with a broken heart. Now the father was grieving that he might lose a third son.

President Truman interceded and had Angelo discharged before his unit, the 511th Airborne Infantry Regiment, was sent to Korea.

Angelo was quoted as saying, "I was kind of disappointed, but after it was all over, I was glad. When my outfit went to Korea, they got wiped out" (Robert Adams, "Madera's Own 'Private Ryan,' Angelo Spera," *Madera Tribune* [May 26, 1997]).

Angelo Spera carried on the family tradition of making dago red wine. Angelo and two friends won the Blue Ribbon for the best homemade wine at the 1995 Napa Town and Country Fair, Napa, California.

Label furnished by Angelo Spera.

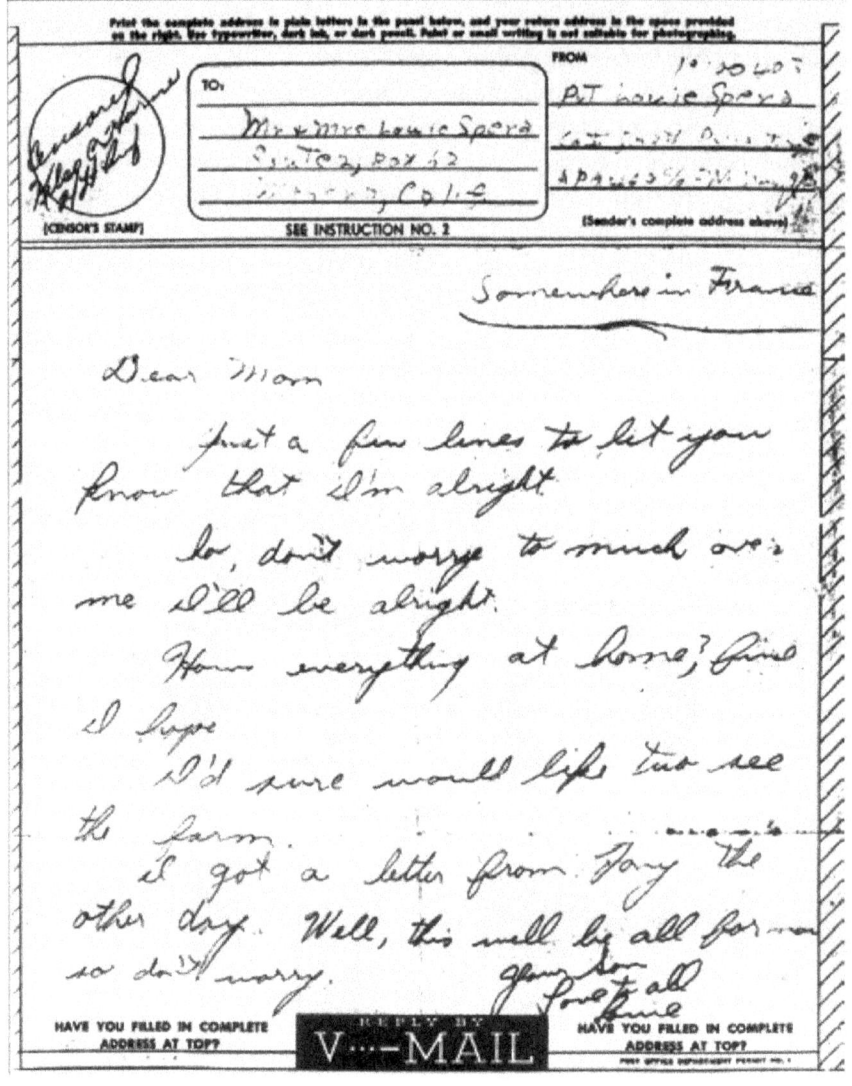

V-mail letter from Louis Spera to his mom.
Copy of letter supplied by Angelina Fuller.
Note that Kelso Horne censored the letter.

# Chapter 6

# Holland, Operation Market Garden

**Operational Plan**
During the first week of September 1944, Allied troops moved through Belgium to the southern border of Holland. Field Marshall Sir Bernard Law Montgomery and his staff planned a bold thrust with airborne troops to capture a main highway that led from the southern border of Holland to the city of Arnhem, the site of the famous "Bridge Too Far" over the lower Rhine. The plan was named Operation Market Garden.

Operation Market Garden would differ from the Normandy airborne invasion of France in several ways. Normandy was a night jump, which made the assembly of troops into organized units difficult. In Holland, the paratroopers would jump in daylight. The daylight drop was helpful for the airborne troops but more dangerous for the air force, which preferred flying under cover of darkness. The early capture of key bridges and protection of the highway corridor against German counterattacks were vital to the success of the British armor. If a major bridge were blown, the British armor would be halted until engineers could make repairs.

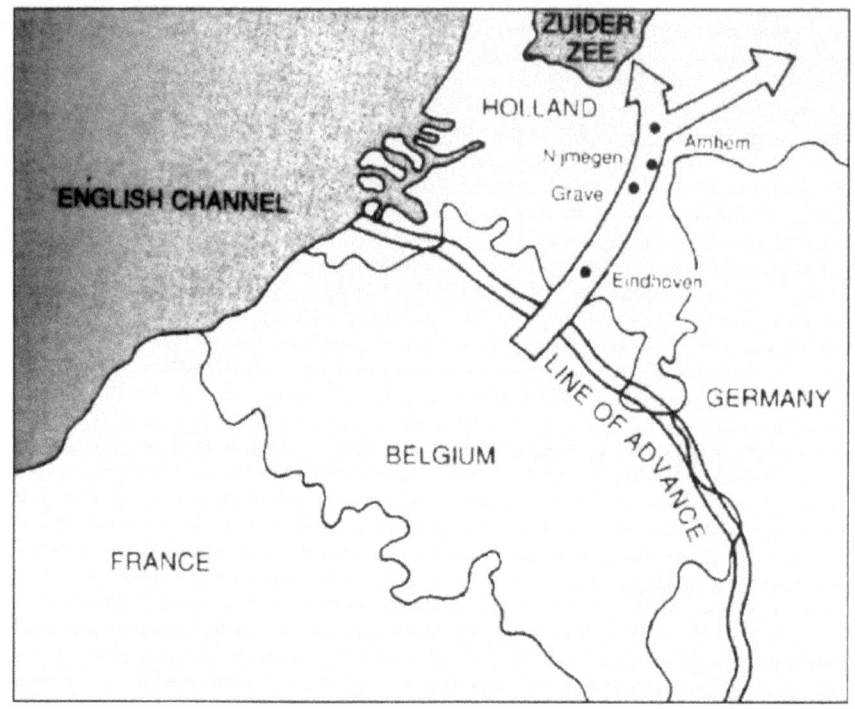

Map by Derek Lawson

Three airborne divisions—British First, the US Eighty-second, and the US 101st—would be dropped along the sixty-four-mile corridor to secure the highway and the bridges over the main waterways along the route. British armored troops would then push up the highway to Arnhem. One group would turn left to the Zuider Zee, thus cutting off an entire German army in western Holland. Another force would turn right into the heartland of Germany toward Brunswick and Hanover and on to Berlin.

The northernmost part was given to the British First at Arnhem. The 101st was assigned the southern section near Einhoven. The Eighty-second had the central area including the cities of Grave and Nijmegen.

As a part of the Eighty-second, the 508th would drop east of Nijmegen, seize the high ground facing the German border, and then secure the Highway Bridge across the Waal River north of Nijmegen. The following stories illustrate the role of the 508th Parachute Infantry Regiment in Operation Market Garden.

Drawing by Dwayne T. Burns, May 25, 1998.
Paratroopers ready to board C-47.
Drawing provided by Dwayne T. Burns.

## Before the Jump

Regimental Headquarters Company of the 508th boarded planes at Fulbeck, England, for the jump in Holland on September 17, 1944. Fulbeck is east of Nottingham and south of Lincoln. The Lincoln Cathedral was called the Lighthouse Cathedral because its towering spires were a landmark for military aircraft returning to the many RAF airfields nearby.

The airport had a massive hangar in which the various units met together for briefing. We learned that our section of the demolition platoon was assigned to blow down trees across the highway leading south out of Nijmegen for our first task. The fallen trees were to serve as a roadblock to deter enemy vehicles from escaping. The equipment bundle with the explosive materials was to be dropped in the middle of the stick. Both ends of the stick would initially assemble around the equipment bundle where we would divide the materials among ourselves for packing to our assignment.

General Eisenhower himself was there, and he explained the mission to the whole assembly of troops at our airport. I learned later that many airports were used for this mission and only a part of the 508th was at Fulbeck. Ike must have traveled from airfield to airfield to address the troops. Having had that brief experience with General Eisenhower, I can understand the slogan that later became a political rallying cry: "I like Ike!"

We had some time on our hands, which was used by various groups for different purposes. Some gambled, winning and losing large sums of money. Others attended to their weapons, cleaning and oiling and preparing them for use. The jump was to occur on Sunday, so the chaplains held services on Saturday night before the jump. I remember one thing about Chaplain Elder's sermon. His words were more of warning than of comfort. He had seen foxhole religion in Normandy and heard the commitments made by men in imminent fear of death. After returning with the troops to England, he had concluded that the men who made promises to God in the foxholes ignored their promises when safely across the English Channel. He told us that God was not interested in soon-to-be-forgotten promises made on the eve of battle or in the heat of battle, but God wanted lifetime commitments that persevered to the end.

I also dropped by the RAF canteen on the base and discovered the British men and women in uniform along with our troops raising their glasses and singing their ribald songs, such as

> This is number one, and the fun has just begun.
> This is number two, and his hand is on my shoe.
> This is number three, and his hand is on my knee.

I cannot remember the other lines, but it seems to me that the hand progressed in the direction of that part of the female anatomy most fascinating to soldiers and sailors. By the time they reached number seven, they had arrived—where else but heaven! Had Chaplain Elder visited the canteen, he might have found another illustration of the shallowness of foxhole religion.

The next morning, we loaded into the C-47s so burdened with equipment on our bodies that the scooped-out seats in the metal benches along the sides of the plane were not wide enough for a single man. I found myself straddling one of the humps instead of resting in the part that was shaped to fit our bottoms.

We spent two or three hours travelling in the plane, first over the British countryside then the English Channel and finally over the flooded lowlands of Holland. We were surprised to see so much flooded territory.

Later we learned that the Germans had flooded the lowlands to prevent an invasion through that area.

We were nearing the drop zone. We had already stood up and hooked up and made our prejump inspections when the antiaircraft guns began to pepper our plane. The crew chief told Lieutenant Hardwick, "We may not make it to the drop zone, better jump while you can."

Hardwick looked out and saw an open field ahead, gave the jump command, and led the way. Little clouds of ack-ack smoke greeted us as we stepped to the door of the plane to jump into the unknown.

## Sunny Side Up

I stepped out of the C-47 behind Johnny Danko and counted 1000, 2000, 3000. Just before I could say 4000, I felt the sharp jerk of the parachute as it snapped open above me. Then I looked down and saw my feet touching a small puff of ack-ack smoke. My body slid right on through the little cloud toward the ground. Then I realized we were being fired at from a nearby house. As soon as I hit the ground, I pulled out my jump knife and hacked off the parachute harness. I unslung my rifle and prepared to fire at the house, but Bob Lane was in my line of fire. He was kneeling on one knee with his rifle to his shoulder, firing away, so I decided to look for Johnny Danko. Johnny was the BAR man, and I was his assistant. I found Johnny, and we moved to the equipment bundle, which was dropped in the middle of the stick.

Several of the troopers nearest to the house continued to cover the house with rifle fire while the rest collected our demolition supplies from the equipment bundle. Lieutenant Hardwick then led us to the cover of a wooded area to get our bearings and plan our action. Nineteen of us assembled there in the woods. The Ripper (our nickname for Hardwick) asked if anyone was hurt. "Little Car" Austin said, "Check out Boroughs, I saw a burst of flak explode right under his feet, and look at the blood on his face and jacket." I had cut my finger slightly when slicing my way out of the parachute harness but was surprised to find I was a bloody mess from the small self-inflicted wound.

Lieutenant Hardwick was a trusted leader with a keen sense of direction. He briefly located our position on his field map and led us forth to join the rest of our regiment.

Within minutes we encountered fire from a railroad embankment at the edge of the woods. One truckload of enemy roared away at full speed close by my position. I could see individual men clearly, but for some reason, I failed to squeeze the trigger.

We could see rifle fire coming from a building across the track. A trooper fired a rifle grenade into the building. After the smoke cleared, a white flag was hung out of a window. We held our fire. Then twenty or thirty men, with hands raised, filed out. The fight was over. None of our men had been injured in the skirmish.

As we moved down the embankment, bodies of dead and wounded enemy soldiers lay in our path. One of our paratroopers pulled out his pistol to finish off a wounded German. The German reached up and caught the barrel of the pistol with one hand and pleaded, "Nein! Nein!" The words fell on deaf ears. The wounded man was blasted into eternity. This was my first view of dead people other than carefully prepared bodies laid out in neat caskets at funerals. I can still envision those ashen faces and eyes fixed in a frightful stare, but we had no time for morbid emotions that day. Survival demanded that we push on and shove those kinds of thoughts into the subconscious.

We followed a dirt road leading east from the railroad through open farmland. It was hot, and our equipment was heavy. We soon loaded all the demolition equipment on the backs of the prisoners. That made the march easier for us and harder for the prisoners to escape. Brooks, who could speak some Pennsylvanian German, found out that most of the prisoners were Czechs and Poles who had been drafted into the German army.

Soon we approached a Dutch farmhouse on the side of the dusty road. A curious couple came from the house to look at the strange creatures marching by. The woman was very attractive, and one of our lusty troopers hollered to his buddies, "I sure would like to take that broad to bed!"

The woman heard the remark and responded with a broad smile. As we passed close by, another trooper asked the woman, "Do you speak English?"

"Yes," she replied. "I understand English very well."

After several hours of uneventful marching, we linked up with other paratroopers, members of the 505th Parachute Regiment. The prisoners were taken off our hands, and Lieutenant Hardwick led us toward Nijmegen.

Our mission was to find the main highway leading south out of the city and set up two roadblocks. One roadblock was to block the escape of German forces from the city. The other at the southern edge of the city was to prevent the Germans from sending in reinforcements. It was getting dark when we found the highway. Trees lined the road with deep ditches on each side. Charges of C-2 (plastic explosive material) were placed on four trees, two on each side of the road. The trees fell perfectly as planned for the first roadblock. Some of us were left to guard that roadblock while others moved south to prepare the next one. Lieutenant Hardwick recalled, "We had a hell of a time getting the trees down for the second roadblock."

That first night in Nijmegen was spooky, dark as pitch. You couldn't see your hand in front of your face, but the sounds were ominous. We could hear the sounds of footsteps on the other side of the fallen trees. In my imagination, black-booted German soldiers were stomping around just on the other side of the fallen trees. We lay silently on our side unseen and undetected.

During the middle of the night, we heard a train steam up. The first demolition section had the assignment of blowing the main railroad track out of the city. As the train started moving, we could hear it getting faster and faster. Finally when it seemed to have reached a full head of steam, we heard the explosion. We thought to ourselves, "The first section must have accomplished its mission."

The next morning the Dutch came out of their houses to see what caused the noise during the night. They were overjoyed when they found American paratroopers. A man speaking in English asked, "What can I do to help?" Since we jumped with only K rations, we asked for food. The man went back into his house and, in short order, came out with eggs—sunny side up.

Don Hardwick supplied information for Hardwick's activities.

## They Landed in Germany

A plane with a stick of A Company troopers, with Lieutenant Rex Combs as the CO and jumpmaster, took flack that caused its right engine to smoke. While the pilot struggled to keep airborne, another hit knocked off the tip of the left wing. Combs, who was standing in the door, was hit in one leg from the same blast and staggered back from the door. Some of his men caught him and pulled him back and said, "Pappy, you have to be there to lead us out of here."

The plane was too close to the ground to make a safe jump. Combs could see troopers coming from planes above them. The parachutes of two troopers were struck by the leading edge of the left wing, which caused the pilot to turn the plane on its side, pull away from the parachutes, and gain altitude. By this time, they were over the town of Wyler, Germany. When the plane reached a safe jumping altitude, the pilot turned on the green light, and Combs led his stick out of the plane.

As Rex Combs descended, he saw a German with a Schmeisser machine pistol shooting at him and running toward his landing place. Combs tried to get his Thompson submachine gun ready to fire back, but he was on the ground before he had time to fire. Fortunately he was able to unfasten his parachute harness quickly, and immediately, he rolled away from his landing area. He then raised his head a little above the hay crop in the field and spotted the German moving in the direction of his abandoned parachute. With a quick burst of his Thompson, he eliminated that threat.

Lt. Rex Combs
Photo furnished by Jim Blue.

Combs began to gather his stick together, and another German started running toward them, waving his arms vigorously, yelling about something, which they could not understand, and approaching them without any sign of fear. Combs ordered the men to hold their fire. The German had a metal can hanging by his side, and as he got closer, he raised the lid of the can and took out some old crusty-looking bread. Combs then understood that the man was hungry and wanted food. By this time, Combs was feeling very sore from the shrapnel in his leg, so he used the hungry German as a crutch and kept going.

Moving into Wyler, the small group of paratroopers found a chaotic situation—Germans running and vehicles with flack crews and weapons scurrying about. The paratroopers fired at the German soldiers and their trucks and began to take prisoners. They came upon a building with a considerable number of Germans inside. A man, who was stripped to the waist, ran from that building toward the troopers. Combs said, "I knew he was an American officer by his pink slacks."

He was badly burned on his upper body and face, but he was very happy to see the American paratroopers. Combs had his men tend to the man's burns and bandaged them with strips of parachute cloth. The man was, as Combs had deduced from his pink slacks, an American air force officer.

They soon picked up troopers from another stick, who reported that Lt. Nolan Schlesinger had been killed. Combs told them, "Go pick up the body, and have the German prisoners carry the body. We are not going to leave him."

Combs recalls seeing Schlesinger's body. He could even see his brains exposed. Combs thought Schlesinger was dead. As they passed by a barn, Combs spotted a ladder, which he confiscated and used as a litter for Schlesinger's body. They had the German prisoners drape their coats over the ladder and tie "the body" on the ladder for carrying.

Woody Wodowski was in Schlesinger's stick. Their plane was also damaged by enemy ground fire, and the pilot had to regain position for satisfactory parachute jumping. The plane was over Germany before they could jump. After landing, Schlesinger led his men toward the DZ in Holland. They received fire from German soldiers who were guards of a work crew in a factory. The German guards were no match for the American paratroopers, but Schlesinger was killed—so they thought.

Combs's group, combined with Schlesinger's men, moved out from Wyler toward Groesbeck. They advanced with the prisoners in front of them, and when Germans attacked them, the paratroopers shifted positions to place their prisoners between themselves and the enemy as human shields. The first time the prisoners were fired on, they hit the ground. Then Combs had his men to fix bayonets and ordered his men to urge the prisoners up and moving with the points of their bayonets, which proved to be an effective strategy.

After crossing into Holland, the paratroopers came upon a glider. A couple of glider men were struggling to raise the nose of the glider. "We helped them get the nose of the glider up and their jeep out." Combs recalled that the burned air force officer boarded the jeep and was taken to an aid station by the glider troops.

The paratroopers continued moving and checked some houses in Den Heuvel, where they rescued two wounded troopers. The wounded troopers were prisoners of four German soldiers. The two older Germans had wanted to kill their prisoners, but the two younger ones had talked them out of it, lest they suffer the same, if captured. Combs's group increased by six in Den Heuvel, two paratroopers, and their four German guards, who were treated with mercy. One of the wounded paratroopers rescued was Sgt. Anthony Cianfrani, who was wounded and captured and rescued in Normandy as well as in Holland.

From Den Heuvel, the troopers moved to Voxhil. There they saw one man with a big two-wheel horse-drawn cart picking up bundles of equipment that had been dropped by parachute on the DZ. The troopers used this cart to move Nolan Schlesinger to an aid station on Voxhil. (Mrs. Schlesinger wrote, "I recall Nolan telling of the two-wheel horse-drawn cart when he was in such misery from his injuries.")

Combs said that his leg was hurting badly from the shrapnel, and he was having difficulty walking. As they moved toward Berg en Dal, his scouts located a house in the woods, occupied by a Dutch family named Vissar. The Vissars fed the troops milk, cheese, and bread. At this point, Combs had his leg bandaged.

Not far from the Vissar home toward Berg en Dal, they came to Headquarters Third CP. Combs turned over his twenty-three prisoners and checked into the aid station, where his leg was bandaged again.

Combs was proud of his men and their accomplishment on September 17, 1944. He was able to assemble eighteen men from his stick, pick up a few more from other planes, rescue several wounded, and knock out four antitank weapons near the DZ. This was accomplished without loosing a man. All this time, Lieutenant Combs was suffering from shrapnel in one leg, which he received before he left the airplane.

Mrs. Katherine Schlesinger, widow of Lt. Nolan Schlesinger, wrote that Nolan had a metal plate put in his head, which remained until his death in 1984. He was in a Veterans' Hospital after discharge until September 1948. Nolan and Katherine married on November 11, 1948, and were happily married for thirty-five years. Their marriage was blessed with two children, one girl and one boy.

She described her husband as having a great personality and loved to be with people. Although his left side was paralyzed (hand, arm, and leg), Nolan's speech was fine. He was a great leader, even commanded the American Legion Post 26 of Mesa, Arizona, in 1974. He worked as an outside salesman for Strauch Stationery and loved to drive his car.

Sources: Mrs. Katherine Schlesinger, Edward (Woody) Wodowski, and audiotape by Rex Combs supplied by Jim Blue.

## Crab Orchard Reunion

Many veterans went through their whole military experience without meeting anyone from their hometown. Okey Mills, Headquarters Third, from Crab Orchard, West Virginia, happened to be on the battlefield with three other hometown soldiers on September 17 and 18, 1944.

Okey landed just inside Holland near Wyler, Germany, among a group of imperial German marines. Every one of those marines was over six feet tall, a minimum requirement to qualify for that organization, according to Mills. Okey was on one side of a narrow road, and the marines were in foxholes on the other side.

Mills described a tower about three stories high where the Germans had mounted an automatic weapon. With a field of fire from the tower, the Germans could have wiped out the fifteen men with Mills and then swept part of the battalion assembly area with devastating results. Lt. Robert Mitchell, I Company, was with Mills. Mitchell directed a machine gunner from Headquarters Third to neutralize the Nazi weapon in the tower.

Mills declared, "It was a blessed relief to see those tracer bullets blasting that tower and knocking out the German gun. I want everyone to know that Lieutenant Mitchell saved our lives and many more."

After knocking out the tower, Mitchell sent the machine gunner back to Third Battalion Headquarters Company but stayed on to direct the firefight in progress. The Krauts shot Sgt. Wilford Mack with a machine pistol. Two bullets went through his lungs and then another grazed his lips and the tip of his nose as he fell backward.

A truck loaded with more German marines drove up and stopped right in front of Mills. Okey sprayed the truck and the driver with his tommy gun. "I never saw a truck unload so fast, the way those Krauts piled out of that truck," Mills recalled. "The driver gunned it out of there at top speed but crashed a little ways down the road."

Mills describes the subsequent action:

> Lieutenant Mitchell was shot though the groin. The bullet went through a phosphorus smoke grenade attached to his rifle belt, which set Mitchell's clothes on fire. Someone behind me asked me to pass my canteen to put out the fire. I turned to hand my canteen over, and when I turned back to face the

road, one of those marines, every bit six feet and nine inches tall, was standing up and looking up and down the road. I was close enough to spit on him. My tommy gun jammed this time, but someone behind me shot at him, nipping him a little. Talking about fast—that giant ran with Olympic speed. As other bullets zipped by him, the marine threw his rifle in the air and raised his hands to surrender.

Since my Thompson had jammed, I took over Lieutenant Mitchell's tommy gun and altogether fired about sixteen magazines of ammo in the firefight. Toward the end, two Germans at a time would jump up and fire in our direction, and two others would run back toward the rear. That was repeated several times as they tried to withdraw.

However, some paratroopers from the 505th approached from the flank and circled in behind the German marines. Then those big tall Krauts came out of their foxholes with hands up. They laid down their weapons, took off their steel helmets, and put on their bib caps. The paratroopers really looked short among those tall Germans. Every one of them was head and shoulders above their captors.

I didn't know it at the time but later learned that one of the 505th paratroopers rounding up the marines was Big John Richards who grew up right near my hometown in West Virginia.

After the shooting stopped, the Dutch people came out of their homes. They hugged us and thanked us, and a Dutch nurse and a doctor came forward to take care of the wounded. The Dutch carried Lieutenant Mitchell and Sergeant Mack and Cpl. James A. Loder, who had broken a leg on the jump, into a house already set up as an aid station. I told the wounded, "You are in good hands, I'm going on to join the company."

Lieutenant Mitchell replied, "Yes, Mills, you have a job to do."

It tore me up when I learned Mitchell died from his wounds.

Okey Mills told of meeting other friends from Crab Orchard, West Virginia:

I left the aid station and walked up the road toward the assembly area, and on the way, I met my hometown cousin Orley E. Mills, who was a medic in the 505th.

Then the next day when the gliders came in, I ran into a soldier from the 319th Field Artillery of the Eighty-second

Airborne Division, also from my hometown—Monk Kidd. I don't know his first name. We called him Monk. That made four of us from around Crab Orchard, West Virginia, who ended up in a small corner of Hollandon September 17 and 18, 1944, fifty miles behind German lines.

## Full-Course Dinner and Cold Beer
Excerpts from a letter to Jan Bos of Holland
Written by H Company Trooper Henry McLean

The landing of our entire battalion was letter-perfect, due to the fine flying of the C-47 pilots.

Upon assembling, I was told by Lieutenant DeWeese to report to Headquarters. I left the group with 12-15 men to go into the town of Berg en Dal. I was told that the bazooka men with me would set up roadblocks on the International Highway to Berg en Dal.

While the bazooka men were busily setting up their position, I walked over to the Hotel de Groot and went inside. In the dining room, I discovered that the German officers had been ready to sit down and eat their Sunday dinner when the parachute drop surprised them. They had fled across the flats leaving their dinners untouched. The tables, row upon row of them, were a pretty sight with white linens, silverware and goblets. A lovely picture window overlooked the valley. Hunger and the sight of food overcame me, so I ate, not one, but two plates full of the delicious dinners.

Someone from our group came in and said, "Let's go up and look at the rooms."

On the top floor, I stood at a window with binoculars looking across the flats toward Arnhem, not thinking about the sun reflecting on the glass lenses. A shot entered the window and whistled by me. Retreat at that moment seemed the wise move.

Back in the village-square, I noticed a small cafe across the street. I decided to investigate the cafe to see if anything was going on there. Much to my amazement, several people were sitting around talking, apparently oblivious to what was happening. A young girl at the bar asked me, "Beer?"

Never one to refuse the hand of friendship holding a beer, I accepted. To my surprise, the beer was COLD. To most people that would not be momentous, but I had had only warm beer for two years. I will never forget how good that COLD beer tasted.

A pool table caught my eye, and I was trying a few shots while enjoying my drink, when an officer of my company, Lieutenant Garry, who was called "The Big Teddy Bear," walked into the cafe. He raised hell with me for not carrying out my orders, which he said, was to return immediately to the unit.

By now the Second Platoon on the hillside to the right flank of the town was coming under fire. Lieutenant Garry told me to assemble as many men as possible to give support to the Second Platoon. The attack was repulsed with few losses. We bedded down that night in a garden behind the cafe. At daylight we were surprised to find a young German soldier sleeping in the garden with us! While we were interrogating him, a low flying German observation plane flew over us, about 50 feet above our heads. The pilot's face was clearly visible to us. He took us so completely by surprise, we just stared at him and he at us, and he flew on by.

That day we came under fire from a long-range German field gun, which killed six men in Lieutenant Garry's unit. The artillery made me seek refuge in a large section of pipe lying at the intersection of the main street of the town.

That night we were invited to one of the houses in Berg en Dal and we were entertained by a young girl playing the accordion. Safe and secure in the basement of the house, we enjoyed ourselves listening and singing. It was a few pleasant and precious hours away from war.

Our orders the next day were to secure the International Highway in Beek. S-2 informed us that Beek was still not secured, and we were to clean out the enemy troops. To our amazement, some German parachutists had been deployed at the outer edges of Beek. A firefight ensued with losses on both sides. We fell back to regroup, and were told to retake Beek with another attack. This time we succeeded in driving the enemy out of the low ground. Beek was now secure and our group moved away from the town.

In 1982, Henry McLean visited Berg en Dal. McLean looked for the small cafe. It was still there, looking much the same as when he first saw it on September 17, 1944.

Concerning Lt. William J. Garry mentioned in Henry McLean's letter, his good friend Lt. Neal Beaver reported this:

> Long-range heavy German artillery landed in front of Hotel de Groot in Berg en Dal. It took all the meat from the back of one of Bill Garry's legs from the buttocks to the knee. Doc Klein amputated the leg in Nijmegen Hospital. After the operation, Garry seemed to be fine. He was talking and having a cigarette at 11:00 PM. He died before morning.

## Free at Last

The 508th logo is a barbed-tailed, two-horned red devil wearing paratrooper boots, carrying a tommy gun, and swinging from a parachute. Some of the people in Holland, however, when they saw us drifting down from the sky on September 17, 1944, called us angels from heaven.

Sgt. J. O. Brown tells of landing in the town of Groesbeek. After the Germans were cleared out of the town, J. O. experienced a very unexpected welcome. A black man came out of one of the buildings and told J. O., "I'm from Birmingham, Alabama." Then he proceeded to give J. O. the longest, strongest hugging of his life. "I thought my eyeballs would pop out of my head, he squeezed me so hard!" explained the sergeant.

What was an Alabama black doing in German-occupied Holland during World War II? It seemed that he had been in Holland for eleven years, having joined the merchant marines as a young man, and eventually Holland became the chief base of operations for his trade as a seaman. When Hitler took over the country, the German conquerors found this American black and immediately put him in a forced labor camp. The Red Devils from the 508th had liberated him. "Thank God! Free at last!"

From left to right: man from Alabama E. S. Hubbard Jr., unidentified, Sgt. J. O. Brown. Photo furnished by J. O. Brown.

J. O Brown at one of the 508th reunions. Photo by Zig Boroughs.

## Togetherness

Before the Holland jump, Colonel Mendez was quoted as saying to members of the air force, "Put us down in Holland or put us down in hell, but put us down together!"

The colonel was reacting to the way his battalion was widely scattered in the drop on Normandy. Colonel Mendez himself was able to assemble a group of only ten men on D-Day in Normandy, and they were isolated from friendly forces for three days before contacting the group on Hill 30.

Among those in the Third Battalion lead plane with Colonel Mendez for the Holland mission were Captain Wilde, Pvt. Joe Kissane, and Sgt. Francis Lamoureux. Captain Wilde was number one, and Colonel Mendez was number two in the stick, which was characteristic of Mendez's style of command—up front leading rather than back in the rear pushing.

Col. Frank Krebs was the pilot, Maj. Howard Cannon was the copilot, and Sgt. Frank Broga was the crew chief of the C-47, which transported Mendez and his paratroopers on September 17, 1944. Although the planes delivering the paratroopers had to fly through heavy flak—as evidenced by a flak wound to the head of Francis Lamoureux during the flight—for the most part, the air force delivered the Airborne right on target. Colonel Mendez was able to assemble his battalion with few casualties and move quickly toward his first objective.

As it turned out, the crew of the C-47, which dropped Colonel Mendez and his men so expertly, also parachuted into Holland on September 17. The plane was disabled by enemy fire on the return trip toward England about 100 kilometers from Nijmegen, and the crew parachuted into a potato field. The crew—Krebs, Cannon, and Broga—learned firsthand how it was to descend slowly by parachute into hostile territory while under fire.

When the C-47 piloted by Krebs and Cannon failed to return to base, it was assumed by Allied Intelligence people that the paratroopers on the plane were also lost. Mrs. Mendez, who was living in New Jersey with her parents, heard through the "army officers' wives grapevine communication network" that her husband, Col. Louis Mendez, was lost in a plane crash over Holland on September 17. Fortunately, Mrs. Mendez's anxiety was momentary because she had just received a letter from her husband dated after September 17. Nevertheless, there was a period of terror in which she imagined herself a widow with three small children to rear without their father.

Upon landing in the potato field, the three airmen quickly shed their chutes and took cover in a ditch under some brush to avoid a German search patrol that soon arrived. The airmen lay on their backs with pistols cocked while they listened to the Germans yelling and jabbing their bayonets into piles of straw.

After the German patrol gave up their search, a friendly Dutch farmer came to their hiding place and, by pointing to Major Cannon's watch, made the airmen understand that they were to remain in that place until nine o'clock that night. The farmer returned at the appointed time. Thus began forty-two days of adventures with the Dutch underground in which the American airmen learned to appreciate the indomitable spirit of the people of Holland.

Patriots of the Dutch underground continually risked their lives to protect the US airmen. Aided by informers, the Nazis made frequent arrests among the resistance forces, and those caught aiding the Allies were subject to execution. Nevertheless, the Dutch underground succeeded in concealing the airmen, taking care of their physical and medical needs, and finally escorting them to freedom.

The airmen were hidden in such places as homes, farm buildings, and a department store. The store was closed to the public but in service to the German occupational government. When the Germans barged in, the fliers escaped notice by crawling through an underground tunnel to a home across the street or by climbing through a trap door into the ceiling.

When the numbers of British and American airmen grew too large for safe concealment in the department store, they were divided into groups of twos, provided with disguises and identification papers, and their final escapes were carefully planned. Colonel Krebs and Major Cannon were paired off for the fifteen-mile journey through roadblocks, German patrols, and no-man's land. Krebs, who could speak German, was the designated spokesman. Cannon, who knew very little German, tied a cloth around his neck pretending to have a sore throat and unable to speak. Krebs was dressed as a farmer and carried a hoe. Cannon was supposed to be the farmer's hired man and carried an armful of twigs for firewood.

The two flight officers walked from their hiding place down the street to a bridge where two boys were eating apples. Cannon pulled an apple from his pocket and took a bite. The boys recognized the signal and walked ahead; the officers followed behind. Every two or three miles the young guides were changed. They sometimes followed ditches and climbed through barbed wire barricades to avoid the Nazis. At the end of a long day, they arrived at a farm owned by a widow. Their hostess pulled a few pieces of wood from a brush pile that concealed the bottom of an old silo, which she had prepared for their hiding place.

About an hour later, a German battery of 88s moved into the farmyard. For three days Krebs and Cannon could hear the German officers shouting commands. The shells were whizzing over their heads from both sides. The 88s pulled out in the middle of the fourth night. The next morning the Americans ventured forth from their hiding place to find that the widow's house had been hit, her barn destroyed, and two sheep killed. Then they heard a patrol moving up and were about to dash for their shelter when they joyfully recognized GI slang.

After returning to their outfit in England, the grateful airmen did not forget the brave and generous Dutch people who protected them for forty-two days behind enemy lines. They loaded a C-47 with a jeep, trailer, and a mountain of supplies contributed by men of their squadron. Just before Christmas Krebs and Cannon flew back to the area, which by this time was under Allied control. Using the jeep and trailer, the pilots were able to retrace their steps and distribute food, clothing, candy, cigarettes, and other supplies to the good Dutch people as tokens of their appreciation.

Footnote: The story of the C-47 crew was summarized from "Escape to Freedom" by Senator Howard W. Cannon (D-Nev.) as told to Theodore Irwin, *Family Weekly*, March 26, 1961.

## Nijmegen Bridge

"Stand up and hook up!"

The paratroopers quickly responded to the command. They were more than ready for the green light and the jump command. Cpl. James Blue, A Company, saw the holes appear in the C-47 from the upcoming flak. Blue looked around and saw two men go down, hit by the exploding shrapnel. The injured were unhooked and moved aside. It was a relief when the green light flashed on and the troopers could exit the plane.

James Blue headed right toward the roof of a small house and had to pull hard on his risers to slip over the house and into the yard.

An orange cloth appeared on a haystack, indicating the company assembly area. Soon A Company was assembled with the exception of two planeloads, which landed beyond the DZ (drop zone) into Germany. Lt. Rex Combs successfully collected the paratroopers from those two C-47s and later in the day assembled them with the rest of the company.

The First Battalion had little trouble occupying their original objective, an area southeast of Nijmegen called De Ploeg. Leaving C Company at De Ploeg, A and B companies began marching toward the Nijmegen Bridge. A battalion S-2 patrol led the way and reached the Nijmegen Bridge during the daylight hours. Trooper Joe Atkins, Headquarters First, told that story:

> I was called on to take the point going into Nijmegen. As we entered the city, a crowd of people gathered around us, and we had to push our way through. Three of us in the lead became separated from the other troopers behind us by the crowds of

Dutch people. We three continued to make our way into the city until we came to the bridge.

At the bridge, only a few German soldiers were standing around a small artillery weapon. I had a Thompson sub and a .45 pistol. The other two were armed with M1 rifles. They covered me as I jumped up and yelled, "Hände hock!" ("Hands up!")

The Germans were so surprised; the six or seven defenders of the bridge gave up without resisting. We held the prisoners at the entrance to the bridge for about and hour. It began to get dark, and none of our other troops showed up. We decided to pull back away from the bridge, knowing we could not hold off a German attack. The German prisoners asked to come with us, but we refused, having no way to guard them. As we were leaving, we could hear heavy equipment approaching the bridge.

As A and B companies advanced into the city, Dutch civilians served the marching paratroopers cookies and sandwiches. A member of the Dutch underground worked with the lead scout of A Company's First Platoon BAR man Walter Dikcon. The BAR (browning automatic rifle) is next to the light machine gun in firepower. It can be operated by one person while advancing. The Dutchman would ride his bicycle forward a block, ride back to Dikcon, and give the all-clear signal.

Near the junction of the Groesbeek and Mook roads, the Dutchman cycled back to Dikcon and announced that the Jerries had mounted a machine gun at the next intersection. Corporal Blue remembered that, at that point, an officer from battalion headquarters joined the point and walked down the middle of the street. Others hugged the sides of the road. When the German machine gun opened up, the first burst hit the lieutenant from headquarters in the leg. Dikcon returned fire with his BAR. In a few minutes, Walter Dikcon ran back and reported the German machine gun crew was knocked out.

With the exchange of fire, Col. Shields Warren, First Battalion CO; Capt. Jock Adams, A Company CO; and Lieutenant Foley, First Platoon CO, all came running to the point. Colonel Warren exhorted, "Good work, men! Keep the ball rolling!"

As night set in, it became very dark.

Pvt. Walter Dikcon led the First Platoon toward the Keizer Karelplein traffic circle. Hostile machine gun fire from the square killed Dikcon outright. Captain Adams then led the Second Platoon through the First Platoon to attack the square.

Meantime, the paratroopers could hear motors warming up. Lieutenant Foley ordered two bazooka teams forward. When the bazooka men were in place, a German half-track came alongside loaded with soldiers. (According to George Lamm, the soldiers were members of the Tenth SS Division Reconnaissance Company) The paratroopers fired their rockets and disabled the half-track. The German troops jumped off the vehicle and ran in all directions.

Blue remembered the fleeing Germans:

> We were ordered not to fire in close combat but to use knives and bayonets. Ray Johnson and I were between two houses with a picket fence to our front. An SS Captain jumped the fence and tried to make his get away between the houses. I said to Johnson, "Get him with your bayonet!" As the captain came between us, Johnson gave a long thrust, completely missed, and his M-1 was dislodged from his hands. I was armed with a tommy gun and trench knife. I had my knife out to get this German. He reached a tall wooded fence and was trying to scale the fence. I chose to use the tommy gun and let him have a short burst of three rounds. Lieutenant Foley shouted, "Who in the hell's using the tommy gun?"
> 
> I answered, "It's me."
> 
> He knew who it was, and that closed the chapter.
> 
> I reported to platoon sergeant Van Enwyck that there was a lot of movement to our front. Van Enwyck told me to take two men and feel out the situation. I took Ray Johnson and McMillan across the square. We were standing by a large foxhole dug by the Germans when we heard the cocking action of a German machine gun. McMillan dived for the foxhole, and I followed close behind. I looked up and saw Johnson falling toward the hole with tracer bullets striking him. Johnson fell on me. He was mortally wounded. Within two hours, two of my basic training comrades had been killed, Dikcon and Johnson.
> 
> The Germans spotted us and started throwing grenades at our hole. I pushed Johnson's body aside, reached for a phosphorus grenade, pulled the pin, and threw it at the machine gun position. The grenade lit up the area. I could hear the Germans breaking down their MG. I called back for our machine guns to open up. They fired a few bursts, after which we returned to our position on the traffic circle.

George Lamm reported on first fire at the traffic circle; he heard the sounds of sporadic firing, calls of "Medic!", Krauts issuing orders, hobnailed boots on the double, and antiaircraft (AA) rounds hitting to the rear of the command group. Then Lieutenant Lamm became aware that one of his men, George Lapso, was wounded and the CO of the Third Platoon, Lt. Boyd Alexander, was dead in the street.

David Amorin of First Platoon remembered seeing a Dutch boy, who assisted in guiding the company, cut down with the first burst of machine gun fire.

George Lamm recalled the action as A Company's Second Platoon took the lead:

> Captain Adams ordered the Second Platoon to pass through the First and Third platoons to clear and occupy an area adjacent to Company B about the center of the circle, and to be prepared to assemble at a rallying point on order. This move was ticklish business. Friendly and enemy soldiers were mixed, and there was no definite line. However, the darkness, which contributed to the confusion, also assisted us in reorganizing. Instructions were passed along to units: "Fire only on orders or eyeball-to-eyeball defense! Use trench knife or bayonet when possible!"
>
> Sergeant Clements had the major portion of the Second Platoon under control and organized with task equipment. Sergeant Gushue, Sergeant Henderson, and myself (Lamm) made a recon of sorts to the curb of the circle. Peering up to the skyline, we made out the outline of a tall AA weapon in the park center. We decided to guide on it. We advanced with Gushue's unit elbow-to-elbow, without fire, and occupied the area. Others followed in column belt-to-belt buckle. (It was so dark, contact was maintained by touch.) As we moved out, there was a pause in the firing and a hush over the area, except for the calls from the lost and the wounded.
>
> Rifleman LeBoeuf slipped into a Kraut foxhole, still occupied, and used his trench knife on the unlucky German. Sergeant Henderson's men checked out the foxholes we passed over and collected a couple of AA gun crews, who were rather on the elderly side. Rifleman Stork took the POWs to the rear and returned promptly.
>
> As the platoon advanced beyond the AA guns into the center of the circle, BAR man Ed Wodowski and James Benton

were wounded. Both, along with George Lapso, were picked up later by brave Dutch volunteers and medical people. They hid the wounded paratroopers from the Germans and treated their wounds.

The Second Platoon was pulled from the circle to form the preplanned combat patrol with the mission of destroying the bridge demolition controls. A Company CO Capt. Jock Adams and Lt. George Lamm, Platoon CO, were the officers in charge. Two teams with demolitions and Thermit devices and two other teams with attack weapons received their orders as planned. Corporal Dobbs and rifleman Hampf were assigned as scouts for the point. Hampf understood and spoke Dutch, Flemish, and German. A Dutch partisan guided the patrol toward their general destiny.

The patrol checked in with the Dutch underground. George Lamm is not sure but thinks the partisan leader was a college professor. The lieutenant is more precise about the leader's daughter. He remembers her as a "blonde knockout." The Dutch Resistance agreed that their organization would scout and assist the paratrooper's movements but would not openly join the fighting at the bridge, for this would destroy their underground security. The Nazi overlords had recently executed some partisans accused of acts against the German state.

Division S-2 had passed the word that demolition controls for blowing the Nijmegen Highway Bridge were located in the Belvedere Tower, which overlooks the bridge from the south (the tower is a part of the Charles the Great Fort that stills remains in Nijmegen). It was very important for the completion of Operation Market Garden that the bridge be preserved so the British tanks could cross the Waal River and continue their drive toward Arnhem. Captain Adams's patrol, guided by a Dutchman, approached the Belvedere.

Sgt. Charles Gushue.
Photo provided by James Blue.

Gushue charged one machine gun, throwing grenades as he ran, and then bayoneted four German soldiers on the gun crew. Lieutenant Lamm recalled that the victims of Sergeant Gushue's bayonet went down with bloodcurdling screams, not silently as depicted in the movies. Sergeant

Gushue was awarded the Distinguished Service Cross (DSC) for his action with the patrol.

Germans opened up on the patrol with automatic fire as they neared the tower.

Sgt. Alvin Henderson received a posthumous DSC for his exploits that night. Henderson was credited with killing two Germans in hand-to-hand fighting and bayoneting four others. He personally destroyed four machine gun positions and assisted in the capture of six prisoners. Henderson's body was found slumped over a knocked-out enemy machine gun, which had defended the Belvedere.

Henderson had returned to the 508th about a week prior to the Holland operation. George Lamm described the sergeant's resourceful actions in Normandy:

> During the Normandy invasion, Henderson, operating with small groups lost from their parent units, used the knife to silence sentries in order to infiltrate through a Kraut unit. He was finally captured and, while being taken to the rear, overpowered his guard and escaped. Thence Henderson made his way to the English Channel, stole a boat, crossed the channel, bummed a ride to Nottingham, and reported to Captain Adams for duty.

Before the jump, Lieutenant Lamm's platoon had prepared to attack the demolition control tower, the Belvedere. Sergeant Clements and Sergeant Gushue had organized and trained demolition assault teams. The men were supplied with C-2 (plastic explosive), primers, and detonators, also white phosphorus and Thermit weapons.

Having penetrated the outside defenses of the Belvedere, the demolition teams went to work with their explosives and Thermit grenades, destroying the equipment inside and starting a fire. Some of the Krauts came out of the building in flames. The partisan guide, who had led the paratroopers to the tower, was believed killed at that time. He was never seen again by the troopers.

In the meantime, back at the railroad station not far from the Keizer Karelplein Circle, additional Tenth SS troops unloaded. These reinforcements set up roadblocks, which prevented the Adams patrol from rejoining their comrades at the circle. Also by early morning, A Company and B Company were ordered to return to the drop zone to clear the area for the glider troops, which were to arrive later in the day. By daylight, the Adams patrol was left isolated from the battalion and hemmed in by well-defended Jerry roadblocks.

Shortly after sunup, with enemy right across the street, the patrol entered a building. Lieutenant Lamm took a German prisoner while he covered for the platoon to enter the door. It was some sort of a two-story barn with a watering trough downstairs. This site became their base of operations and hideout until the evening of September 20.

Thanks to the good Dutch people, the wounded Americans were quickly removed from the battle scenes and into the safety of homes. The following are excerpts from "Declaration of a Report" by Dr. C. H. ten Horn, St. Annastraat 20, Nijmegen:

> Monday, September 18, 1944, early in the morning I was asked by Father Habets to give help to an American military doctor. Immediately I went.
>
> At the house on Groesbeekseweg 2, was an American Red Cross flag hanging. Opposite this house in the yard of De Vereeniging were American paratroopers in combat positions.
>
> In the street five or six German soldiers lay dead. In the front yard of Groesbeekseweg 8, were four captured SS men guarded by two American soldiers.
>
> The hall of the house on Groesbeekseweg 2 was stocked full of ammunition, as was the living room.
>
> The American doctor said he had to go on and asked me to take over the treatment of the wounded soldiers in the house.
>
> Right away the Airborne doctor showed me three very heavily wounded men, of whom two were in direct danger of loss of life, due to the loss of blood.
>
> I decided to transport these three immediately to the St. Canisius Hospital. The transportation was done very quickly by bicycle-stretchers of the Red Cross. The rest of the wounded stayed for the time being with some nurses.
>
> I went to the hospital to alert the blood transfusion service. Already in the emergency room, the three heavily wounded received one or more transfusions. After that I operated on them—one a leg amputation.
>
> Immediately thereafter I returned to the house on the Groesbeekseweg 2; it was about 10:30 A.M. I noticed that the

American flag on the house was gone. The American soldiers in the yard of De Vereeniging were not there anymore either. It appeared fighting was going on in the neighborhood.

The house on Groesbeekseweg 2 got several hits. However, my task was to take care of the wounded soldiers who were left behind. During the morning we transported several more wounded to Canisius Hospital. In the afternoon the unrest increased. It was observed that at the Keizer Karelplein on the west side SS patrols were seen. The firing increased.

Despite the ongoing fighting, we were still able to transport seven more wounded paratroopers to the hospital. These soldiers were rolled in blankets in such a way that they resembled civilians.

By 4 o'clock in the afternoon, the situation became critical. Into the yard of De Vereeniging at the start of St. Annastraat—also in my own front yard—but especially in de van Trieststraat, heavily armed SS troops had penetrated. None dared to be in the streets anymore.

We had hidden the two remaining paratroopers in bed upstairs, and although they were lightly wounded, we applied heavy head bandages, and they were made to look like civilians. We locked the front door firmly. Then we waited.

About half past five the SS departed the immediate environment. Through the front yard we were then able to transport the remaining two paratroopers by bicycle-stretchers. We were fired at while moving the wounded from Keizer Karelplein to the Groesbeekseweg. Fortunately nobody was hit.

With great thanksgiving I would like to report that we were not only able to transport the 17 wounded paratroopers, but all have recovered from their wounds.

Signed: Dr. C. ten Horn

Joe Atkins, Headquarters First, who led the daylight patrol to the Nijmegen Bridge, after leaving the bridge, was separated from his group in the darkness and was lost. He came across the house where Dr. ten Horn was treating the wounded paratroopers. Atkins helped the Dutch doctor load some of the wounded on the stretchers for movement to the hospital. When a shell hit the house, Atkins left and found his way back to First Battalion Headquarters.

Captain Adams and his men stayed inside during the day and went on patrols at night dressed down to their long johns and wool-knit caps, bandoleers, and weapons. The first night, Lamm and Gushue and others found an underground area, perhaps several cellars connected, and discovered a Catholic priest with many small children. They shared apples, turnips, and bread with the paratroopers. In turn, the troopers gave their D ration chocolates to the children.

The next day, the Krauts worked all day to build roadblocks at junctions using barbed wire and booby traps. That night they sent out fire raisers to burn the buildings, and they created a firestorm. The Dutch underground wet down the roof of the paratroopers' hideaway, preventing the fire from destroying their place of refuge.

The troopers also returned to the underground children's home on the second night and enjoyed canned meat and biscuits.

Before dawn, the Germans had slipped away, and Montgomery's tankers arrived in Nijmegen later that day, September 19. Contact with the British by Captain Adams's patrol was made on September 20, after which the patrol hurried to join the rest of A Company on Devil's Hill.

The British tanks used the Nijmegen Bridge to cross the Waal River. The heroic action of Captain Adams's patrol is believed to have wrecked the bridge's demolition control mechanisms prepared by the Germans and thus saved the bridge from destruction.

Belvedere Tower with Nijmegen Bridge in background.
Photo furnished by James Blue.

## Kamerad

Jim Allardyce of B Company remembered September 17-18 vividly. A and B companies were sent into Nijmegen from De Ploeg on the evening of the 17. They wanted to travel light, so they stashed their packs in a forest before moving into Nijmegen.

As B Company moved toward the city, about twilight, their route led them within sight of a German troop barracks, where they could see soldiers loading into trucks. Jim Allardyce remembered watching the Jerries load and drive off while he and his company lay silently hidden until the area was cleared.

The darkness became intense as they moved into Nijmegen proper. An SS guard post was knocked out by the point of the column in front of "Nebo," a monastery where the SS were quartered. At this point, Allardyce could hear the sounds of tanks moving in a nearby street.

In the pitch darkness, a jeeplike vehicle drove up between the two lines of the advancing column, which clung to the edges of the street. The two occupants of the vehicle finally realized that they were in the midst of troops and said something that sounded like, "Who ist dere?"

Everyone was stunned at first. Could it be friendly Dutch underground helpers or German officers? The indecision gave the driver time to turn around and start racing back from whence he came before the paratroopers started firing. Was it friend or foe? The question is still unanswered.

Jim Allardyce was with the group, which reached the traffic circle just a short distance from the bridge over the Waal River. That was when Jim got a real taste of combat. He was in the midst of a wild-west shootout in total blackness. A German SS reconnaissance unit was sent to find the Americans who had dropped from the sky and were invading the city. The two units clashed at the traffic circle. In the darkness, the Yanks and the Jerries were intermingled. Jim could hear the voices of Americans and Germans coming from the same area but could see nothing.

Allardyce was ammunition bearer and assistant to machine gunner Bill Askren. The two were set up in a forward position with their machine gun facing the traffic circle. Allardyce described what happened:

> Suddenly out of the darkness came a rush of people at us. Askren said, "Shall I start shooting?"
> Was it the SS or some of our own troops? In a microsecond my mind registered "No hobnailed boots!" So I answered, "Hold it."
> It proved to be our own people who had been lying in the darkness with the Germans, side-by-side.

The main defensive position of B Company was at a concert hall at the traffic circle. When morning came, they saw the results of the night fighting. In the streets around the concert hall were damaged German trucks and the bodies of German SS troops killed during the darkness.

Captain Millsaps sent Jim Allardyce and Bobby Mills to look for food in the German trucks. Mills grabbed a body under a tailgate to pull it out of the way so he could get into the back of the vehicle. To the surprise of Mills and Allardyce, the body sat up and pleaded, "Kamerad!"

The only food they found were a few ripe tomatoes, which they playfully threw to the other troopers. It was easier to raise the dead that morning than to find enough food for the hungry paratroopers.

Three B Company veterans at 1999 508th Reunion, L-R: Jim Allardyce, Ed Boccafogli, and Tony Yablonski. Photo by Zig Boroughs.

## Thank-You Note

Early in the evening of September 17, a four-man patrol set out from the G Company assembly area to reconnoiter deep into Nijmegen toward the Waal River Bridge. Angel Romero, Merle Beach, George McGraph, and a Third Battalion S-2 man advanced about two miles forward and found no German troops.

The patrol questioned civilians who spoke English, but they were very nervous and uncooperative. "They wouldn't even tell us the way to the bridge or how far we were from the river," Romero remembered.

In contrast to the reaction the night before, Romero describes how the Dutch responded the next morning:

A couple of civilians walked toward us. They were not aware we were there. They carried lunch and were going about their Monday-morning business. They were dumbfounded to see us and more so when one of the paratroopers told them in English that they couldn't go through and they should go home and stay there. They stood for a few minutes without saying a word.

Suddenly one of them said, "Americans," and came and kissed the flag on our uniforms. He let out a loud yell, threw his lunch in the air, and ran back to some nearby houses. In a few minutes people were all over everywhere, some in their nightclothes. When the company moved toward the bridge, the crowds lined the streets and cheered as if the troops were on parade. The crowds thinned as the troopers drew nearer the bridge until there were no spectators at all. Then all of a sudden, the Germans opened fire.

Francis Lamoureux surrounded by Dutch civilians.
Photo furnished by Francis Lamoureux.

"I ducked into a doorway to avoid the bullets, and that's when I met the Dutchman, Argardus 'Gas' Leegsma," Romero recalls. "Gas had detailed maps of gun emplacements and knew exactly where the Germans placed their 88s to defend the bridge. Gas insisted that we should not continue on the route we were going."

Romero took Gas Leegsma to his platoon sergeant, Sergeant Sirovica. Sirovica and Lieutenant Covey were directing the attack.

Sergeant Vantrease was leading the point squad composed of Romero, McGrath, Beno, Metar, Carter, Calcagno, Beach, and others. The platoon was stopped dead about a block from the bridge. Captain Wilde caught up with the lead element at that point and began personally directing the attack.

Gas Leegsma guided the lead squad away from the direct fire of the 88s and away from the machine guns mounted on rooftops. He led them through the backyards of houses. It meant scaling high steel-link security fences, but that was easier than facing the pointblank fire of the 88s. When they arrived at the street next to the river, Captain Wilde came up close to their position and yelled, "Get that joker across the street!"

Vantrease's squad crossed the road and started down the river embankment. Romero describes what happened next:

> It didn't take us long to realize we were greatly outnumbered and the shape of the terrain left us sitting ducks. The Germans had all kinds of guns on the opposite bank and were having a field day firing pointblank at us. We were ordered out of there because it was certain death if we stayed. Vantrease had gone a little farther down the embankment from me. When we were ordered out, he was hit as he turned to leave. He said it was shrapnel. I thought it was a direct hit from a .40mm. He flew about ten feet, and it was obvious he was seriously wounded.
>
> After he and I got out, Beno, Metar, McGrath, and a medic carried Vantrease a good distance. Some of the residents came to offer help. He was given first aid. One of the residents told us to carry him to a basement where he was hidden a few days until he was evacuated.
>
> The fighting within two blocks of the bridge was fierce. I don't think there was a house in the area that wasn't hit by artillery, rifle, and machinegun fire. We would go to one side of the bridge and then the other, and it was the same heavy fireworks. The Germans were everywhere, and we still held our own.
>
> During the afternoon we were ordered back to clear one of the glider landing zones. Our squad was the closest to the bridge and thus the last to leave. We had gone about a half a mile when complete exhaustion hit me. I sat to one side of the street, and in a moment Gas Leegsma was again at my side. He said I could rest later, but for now we had to move out or chance the Germans catching up with us. He offered his hand and helped me get up. He walked with me awhile until he was sure I could make it.
>
> Leegsma calls me his liberator because I was the first American he met. I have the highest respect and esteem for him. This man was super in what he did for G Company with his maps and diagrams and guiding us around Nijmegen. He stayed with us throughout the Netherlands and most of the Battle of

the Bulge. His ability to speak so many languages still amazes me. In my opinion, he did more for the Netherlands than the boy who plugged the dike to keep the country from flooding.

G Company fitted Leegsma with a 508th uniform, which was not easy to do because of his size, six feet, five inches tall. His feet were so large, G Company was never able to find boots to fit.

Captain Wilde remembered Gas Leesgma "as a helluva fighting man with the highest capacity for food in the European Theater."

A few months before he died in 1988, Glen W. Vantrease of Clearwater, Florida, wrote to his old paratrooper friend Angel Romero in El Paso, Texas, the following letter:

> Every September 17, I am reminded of our flight to Holland: the flooded lowlands, the P38s buzzing around to protect us, the low altitude drop and the quick assembly.
>
> A day later, G Company was the 508th point to advance to the Waal River and our squad was the company point. We went through the back yards of homes with those seven-foot cyclone fences. As we neared the road parallel to the river, an outpost raised his head and McGrath shot him. We crossed the road and started diagonally down the long riverbank when all hell broke loose. The Germans were shelling us with 88s from the opposite bank. A piece of metal hit me in the back like a sledgehammer and sent me flying several feet.
>
> The squad beat a hasty retreat under severe fire. You hesitated and called back to me, but I was temporarily stunned. You came back alone, half slung me over your shoulder and took off. After we were in a safe position, several others helped to carry me into a house where the Dutch hid me.
>
> Many times, but every late September, I think of my wife, our four children, and our successful and happy life. Then each time I thank you for that time of bravery when you risked your life and saved mine.

## Bridge Number 10

During the early predawn hours of September 18, the Eighty-second Division asked the 508th Red Devils to carry out an unexpected mission. The Germans had destroyed most of the bridges across the Maas-Waal Canal. Lieutenant Polette was sent with a platoon to save the Honinghutjes bridges across the canal, a railroad bridge and a highway bridge side by side. US military referred to the set of bridges as Bridge Number 10.

Bill Giegold of F Company tells of an incident on the way to the bridges. As the platoon was skirting the edge of Nijmegen, their progress was halted by a machine gun dug in at an intersection. The Krauts had a periscope sight, which allowed them to fire their machine gun without sticking their heads out of their foxhole. Clarence Berry from Tennessee, the Volunteer State, volunteered to take on the German machine gun crew.

Berry crawled across the street and into the hole with the Germans. The other Red Devils waited for something to happen. After a few minutes, Platoon Sergeant Glenn Bell called for the bazooka team to fire a phosphorous shell into a pile of dirt next to the machine gun foxhole. The fire and smoke scattered from the impact, some going into the foxhole, and four men hurriedly jumped out of the hole, Clarence Berry and the three Germans.

According to Bill Giegold, Berry, in his slow Tennessee drawl, was trying to talk the Germans into surrendering. Giegold says, "It was hard enough for me to understand Clarence Berry's accent, how could you expect the Germans to understand him?"

Before the platoon left the intersection where they had encountered the machine gun, a Dutch woman came out of her house and made motions toward Bill Giegold and to her mouth to indicate food. Giegold, who had not eaten in a day and a half, accepted the gestured invitation. He was led to a table covered with a lace tablecloth and set with fine china and silverware. Giegold quickly ate a bowl of chicken noodle soup and returned to his unit. Other troopers were also invited to share the Dutch lady's chicken noodle soup.

Polette and his platoon continued on to the bridges. The bridges were defended by well-dug-in German troops with mortars and machine guns. The concentration of German firepower inflicted heavy casualties among the attacking paratroopers. Polette called Second Battalion Headquarters to send mortars to support his force.

Sgt. Zane Schlemmer, Headquarters Second Mortar Platoon, loaded his mortar equipment on two cows found in the drop zone area. The cows were cooperative and functioned nicely as beasts of burden. Schlemmer could have said, "Have cows, will travel!" Zane Schlemmer became known as the Groesbeek Cowboy. (Years later, a German artist designed and produced a T-shirt as a gift for Schlemmer. The T-shirt emphasizes the theme "Groesbeek Cowboy.")

When Schlemmer's group came across the first Dutch people, they seemed disappointed to see foot soldiers leading cows. They asked, "Where are the tanks?"

The tanks were to come along later. Meanwhile, the bridges needed protection against German demolition crews. Schlemmer's mortar group traveled to a small farmhouse near Bridge Number 10, where they set up their mortars to support Polette's platoon.

Mortar crews arched their shells high into the air, which allowed the shells to drop on top of their targets. The mortars were usually operated behind a hill or embankment. This made it necessary to use map coordinates and a forward observer to give instructions on targets and on adjusting the fire. Those who fired the mortars seldom had the opportunity of seeing their targets. But the land was so flat at Bridge Number 10 that Schlemmer and his crew could see the tops of the bridges and the explosions of their shells.

As the firefight between Polette's men and the German defenders raged, small groups of enemy were observed preparing demolitions on both the highway and the rail bridges. The Red Devils then poured on the firepower and drove the demolitionists away. This occurred several times, but the Germans finally succeeded in detonating their charges.

A declassified and formerly secret US Army report "57 Days in Holland and Germany with the 508th Parachute Infantry", page 7, states the following:

> At 1030 hours the enemy blew the charges, destroying the railroad-bridge and damaging the highway-bridge. At 1100 hours a section of 81mm mortars arrived and immediately went into action against the enemy around the bridge. The intensity and accuracy of this fire caused the enemy to withdraw, leaving the highway-bridge only slightly damaged . . . . Lieutenant Polette's force remained in position defending the bridge until recalled by the battalion commander at 1730 hours. By this time a company of the 504th Parachute Infantry had arrived at the bridge and was able to take over responsibility for its defense.

After the heavy fighting and during the mopping-up processes around the bridges, Schlemmer borrowed a horse and cart from a farmer and obtained a white sheet from his wife. Schlemmer then painted a Red Cross on the white sheet and hung it on a long pole. Then with their Red Cross flag held high, and without drawing enemy fire, they used the horse cart to pick up the dead and wounded.

Zane Schlemmer noticed planes bombing in the direction of Nijmegen. In order to prevent Allied planes from destroying Bridge Number 10, he climbed one of the bridge towers and tied an orange identification panel to it. While on the tower, Schlemmer spotted the 504th men attacking from the other side.

Lt. Lloyd Polette was awarded the Distinguished Service Cross for his leadership and personal courage at Bridge Number 10.

Several times after the war, Zane Schlemmer visited Holland and with the aid of a Dutch historian located the family, which loaned him the horse and cart and gave him the white sheet. The historian reported to Schlemmer that the woman had only one sheet at that time but had given it willingly when she learned of its purpose. Schlemmer arranged a meeting and short ceremony with the Dutch family. In 1977, after thirty-three years, Zane Schlemmer presented the Dutch lady a replacement sheet brought from America.

Old Honinghutjes Bridges (Bridge Number 10) being replaced by new bridges. Photo furnished by Zane Schlemmer.

## Guess Who Stopped for Tea

Getting back to our roadblock at the edge of Nijmegen, half of our section guarded the roadblock inside the city. The rest of us guarded the roadblock outside the city against an attack from the south. There we were, all by ourselves. Lieutenant Hardwick came and went, dividing his time between the two roadblocks. Over on the right, which was to the west, was the farmhouse—the house from which the Dutchman brought us the eggs for our first breakfast in Holland. To the left was a section of low trees,

trees about as tall as a man's head as if the timber and been cut and a new stand was growing up again. The growth of trees was very thick and scary because we could hear shouts of human voices in those bushes but couldn't see anyone. It sounded like a crazy person out there.

About D-Day plus two, Jack Warren showed up at our roadblock. Jack had jumped with our stick but did not assemble with us. I am not sure what had happened to Jack. We had considered him missing in action, but there he was, alive and well and somewhat of a mystery.

The scariest part was the thought of German tanks. Johnny Danko had a BAR (Browning automatic rifle); the rest of us were armed only with M-1 rifles. Here we were, less than ten men to defend Nijmegen from a German tank attack. About the third day we heard the roar of engines. As the noise increased, so did our anxiety. How could we defend ourselves with rifles and a BAR against enemy tanks? Finally the lead tank appeared in view, and the Ripper (Lieutenant Hardwick) jumped up on the trees forming the barricade and using his binoculars identified the tanks as British. What a relief that was!

The tanks stopped at our roadblock and waited. According to Brooks, the British stopped for tea. Sure enough, that was the first thing they did—got out their brewing equipment—and soon each British soldier was enjoying a nice cup of tea.

The sitting tanks invited air attacks from the Germans, and we got a taste of strafing as the low-flying planes came in over our position spraying the roadway with machine gun fire. We hit the ditches and watched the bullets splatter around us, but no one was hit. It was almost like the movies, watching the exciting action while sitting safely in the theater seats.

About this time during the war, the Germans tried out a new kind of plane—jet propelled. The German jets were showing their superior performance over Nijmegen.

We expected the tanks to move on through Nijmegen and on to Arnhem. It seems in retrospect that the British stayed at our roadblock for days. Lieutenant Hardwick had told us that the bridge across the Waal had been secured on both sides. Troops from the 504th Parachute Regiment made an assault landing across the Waal in canvas boats, driving the Germans away from the north approach to the bridge. The 508th had attacked from the south on D-Day evening and saved the bridge from being blown up. The bridge was cleared of the enemy, and a bridgehead was established on the north side of the river.

We asked the tankers why they didn't move. They replied, "Our supply lines to the south have been cut. We must wait until we are sure the breaches are repaired."

In the meantime the British First Airborne Division was surrounded and being destroyed just a few miles to the north. We said to ourselves, "Too bad, old Blood and Guts Patton wasn't here with his tanks. He would have the Germans reeling back toward Berlin."

Speaking of tea, several of us paratroopers approached a group of Montgomery's troops who were sipping their afternoon tea. One Brit was wearing a coveted German pistol. A paratrooper asked him, "What would you sell your pistol for?"

"I say, Yank," replied the Tommie. "I wouldn't sell this pistol for all the tea in China!"

Members of the Demolition Platoon, Regimental Headquarters Company. Standing: Sgt. Ed Luczaj, Pvt. Zig Boroughs, and Sgt. Harold Gerkin. Seated: Lt. Don Hardwick, Lt. Charles Yates. Luczaj, Boroughs, and Hardwick were at the roadblocks. Photo furnished by Zig Boroughs.

## "They Even Took My Dog Tags"

The Germans overran D Company's Second Platoon, which was defending a roadblock. Two members of the platoon, Louis Guzzetti and Pvt. Albert Anderson, decided they would make a run for it rather than surrender. Lou Guzzetti said, "We were shot at but were running so fast the bullets couldn't catch up with us."

The Jerries moved the wounded into a Dutch home. The other paratroopers were taken prisoners of war and marched to Germany. Pvt.

James Rizzuto was one of the POWs, and Sergeant Joe Bullard was one of the wounded who were left behind.

Joe Bullard recalled, "The Germans stripped us down to our shorts. They even took our dog tags. Then they used our uniforms to wear on patrols."

Joe and another wounded GI were placed in a bed together. Joe said, "A Dutch woman gave us a quart jar of canned meat. It was the only food we had before we were found by our troops."

Two days after the platoon was captured, the 508th counterattacked, first sending in mortars to prepare for the assault. Joe Bullard remembered the shells hitting the roof of the house and the slate shingles falling down through the ceiling onto his bed. He and the other wounded soldier got under the bed to avoid the falling debris.

Bullard describes what happened to him after friendly forces occupied the house and evacuated the wounded:

For a time I lapsed in and out of consciousness. When I became more alert, I realized I was hearing voices in another language. All the other wounded were speaking German, but the medics were speaking English. Without my dog tags and uniform, the medics assumed that I was a German and placed me in a tent full of wounded Germans. I soon convinced the medics of my true identity, and then they moved me to a hospital with Americans.

Sgt. Joe Bullard.
Photo copied from 1943 Company pictures.

When James Rizzuto and Joseph Bullard attended the 508th reunion in Charleston, South Carolina, in 1987, they saw each other for the first time since Rizzuto marched off as a POW, leaving his seriously injured sergeant at the roadblock on September 18, 1944. That was a special reunion forty-three years later.

Jim Rizzuto was responsible for locating another 508er who was captured at the roadblock with him—Benjamin Nienart. Rizzuto told Nienart about the 508th Association and our reunions. Nienart told about his experiences as a POW.

It so happened a small sliver of metal from a German shells hit Ben Nienart in one of his eyes. Since his injury did not prevent him from walking, he was taken prisoner with the others. One of the German army doctors took a special interest in Nienart's eye injury and sent him to a civilian German doctor, who removed the metal fragment from his eye. When he returned to the prison camp, the army doctor made sure Nienart had special treatment so the eye would heal properly. He did not have to suffer the usual rigors as others in the stalag.

Lt. Temple Tutwiler commanded the platoon at the roadblock. According to Joe Chestnut, a friend of the Tutwiler family, a rifle bullet through his midsection wounded Lt. Temple W. Tutwiler early on the morning of June 6 in Normandy. He was operated on and evacuated later that night. He recovered in time to make the jump into Holland on September 17 but was captured on the morning of September 18. Tutwiler's short combat experiences resulted in a lengthy hospital stay and an even longer stint as a prisoner of war.

Lt. Temple W. Tutwiler
Photo provided by Joe Chestnut.

The German offensive that resulted in the capture of the D Company platoon pushed forward into the 508th drop zone (DZ), which was also the planned landing zone (LZ) for the glider troops that expected to land later that same day.

## The Gliders Arrived

C Company had remained near the DZ on high grown while A and B companies of the First Battalion were fighting in Nijmegen. With Tutwiler's platoon captured and the rest of D Company almost surrounded, A and B companies were ordered to return to help C Company clear the LZ for the glider landing. The gliders were on their way with the 325th

Glider Infantry Regiment, 319th Glider Field Artillery, artillery pieces and ammunition, Jeeps, and other vital supplies.

By noon B Company and C Company were in place at the edge of the woods above the LZ. A Company was ready to follow 400 yards behind. First Sergeant Leonard Funk was point lead for C Company, followed closely by his able assistant Sgt. John "Doc" Hardee. They were met by heavy German fire from small arms and .20mm guns on the LZ. C Company's charge was so rapid that they overran the German positions and had silenced the last of sixteen .20mm canons just as the first glider was landing. The attack began at 1230 hours. The LZ was cleared for the glider landings by 1400 hours.

Sgt. Jim Kurz led the charge for B Company along with BAR man Chester Stanley and machine gunner Tony Mrozinsky. Kurz notice a line of foxhole that indicated that they were approaching the enemy from the flank. Kurz positioned Mrozinsky so he could fire straight up the line of foxholes. Kurz and Stanley moved to the left, and as they approached a foxhole, Morzinsky would hold his fire and Stanley would cover as Kurz moved to the foxhole and fired his pistol into the hole. Mrozinsky then would resume firing down the line of foxhole as Kurz, and Stanley advanced to the next one. This process was repeated until the line of German foxholes was neutralized.

Bob Mill, B Company, recalled events after the main battle:

> Ernest Chase and I remembered being fired on in the beginning of the attack from a small bush patch. We went back to the area and flushed out six or seven Germans. When we found they had souvenirs from our paratroopers, they were afraid and begged us not to shoot them.
>
> A little later First Sergeant Leonard Funk came riding on the hood of a jeep up a lane through a cabbage patch, double-timing ten or twelve Germans ahead of the jeep. Suddenly, a well-hidden group of German jumped up from among the cabbages. Some were shooting, and some were holding their hands up to surrender. I heard the bullets from Funk's tommy gun ping on helmets. That lasted a few seconds, and then he had more prisoners.

When Funk was asked about the event, he said, "I appropriated the first jeep and driver unloaded from the gliders. I thought I was motorized with a chauffeur, but an officer from Regimental Headquarters took the jeep."

Funk received the Distinguished Service Cross, and Kurz received the Silver Star for their part in clearing the LZ.

## Red Devils on Devil's Hill

Lieutenant Foley announced orders that A Company would be taking high ground, across the border inside Germany called Devil's Hill. German paratroopers were dug in on the ridge, which was about two hundred yards long, from fifty to seventy-five feet wide and about three hundred feet above sea level. The high ground provided the Germans an important observation and firing position, allowing them to control a large surrounding area.

Earlier in the day, September 19, a G Company platoon functioning as a combat patrol started up Devil's Hill and was repulsed by sharp-shooting German paratroopers. An additional squad, including Angel Romero, was added to the platoon for a second assault on the hill. Again the superior numbers and firepower of the Nazis repulsed the Red Devils.

"The hill will be taken at all cost," commanded Foley.

Besides the men from G and A companies, a group which was assigned to set up a roadblock on the International Highway connecting Holland and Germany got involved in the third attack. Four demolitionists—Joe Favela, Joe Ricci, Colinos "Killer" Morgan, and Ray O'Connell—from Regimental Headquarters Company were sent to pick up some men from the DZ area and with them were to prepare and man the roadblock. Alex Garcia of C Company, a longtime friend of Joe Favela from his home barrio in Phoenix, was one of the men added to the detail.

Third Demolition section, Regimental Headquarters Company. Standing (left to right): Colinos "Killer" Morgan, Joe Ricci, Donald "Danny" Sloan, George Fredrick, and Millard "Snuffy" Shull. Kneeling (left to right): Larry O'Connor, Lyle Smith, and Joe Favela. Favela, Ricci and Morgan fought on Devil's Hill. Photo provided by Joe Favela.

As the detail started out, they were strafed by Nazi planes and took cover in the ditches and trees along the roadside. In the confusion, they became a part of the group moving toward Devil's Hill where they spent five days, never reaching their assigned destination.

Bill Giegold and Sgt. Jim Caruso, both from F Company, were assigned to haul ammunition to battalion supply near Devil's Hill. Sergeant Caruso hunted up ammo equipment bundles on the drop zone that had not yet been opened while Giegold borrowed two horses and a wagon from a Dutch farmer Piet Langveldt. Giegold remembered the strafing from the German plane that almost hit Caruso while he was opening an equipment bundle.

After a severe kicking from a young horse unused to the harness, Bill Giegold hitched up an older mare with the young horse to Langveldt's wagon. Giegold and Caruso loaded the wagon with ammunition and headed for Devil's Hill area. They went through the town of Beek en route. On the edge of Beek they saw a tavern and decided it was time for a drink. Entering the front door they saw seven beer mugs on the table, some empty, others with varying amounts of beer still in them. The barman looked toward the beer mugs and said, "Deutsch!" Evidently the Germans saw the paratroopers entering and left by the back door.

After a quick cool one, Giegold and Caruso continued on and delivered the ammo near Devil's Hill. Giegold turned the two horses loose to let them get home the best way they could. Later Bill saw Piet Langveldt and learned that the older mare made it back, but the young horse was killed about one hundred meters from home.

The earlier G Company patrols had approached Devil's Hill from the west. However, Foley, guided by a Dutch civilian, moved his assault group across the Wyler-Beek road and into the woods at the southern side of the hill. Foley then sighted an enemy force approaching from the direction of Wyler and dropped off a part of the first platoon to protect his flank. Cpl. James Blue was a member of the holding force. Blue's group dug in along the Wyler-Beek road in the woods with a good field of fire. The Germans held up. Meanwhile, an old German farmer continued to work around his barn with horse and wagon while Germans and Americans prepared for battle.

Angel Romero and his squad from G Company led the way as point for the third attack as they advanced toward the hill, but when they approached the base of the hill, Romero's squad was relieved and sent back to about the middle of the column. The Jerries attacked the left flank. Eight men led by "Take Charge" Sergeant Piper reacted quickly and ran up a trail after the attackers and started a firefight. The eight men included Angel Romero, Russell Ludemann, Refugio Muniz, a lieutenant observer from the artillery, Sergeant Piper, and others. Piper's group thought things were going their way until they discovered that the Jerries had gotten in behind them and cut them off from the main force. Angel describes what happened next:

> The firefight took us up the hill, and we were driven down the other side and cornered in a small ravine. With no place to run for cover and what seemed about ten to one in firepower, Piper asked if we should make a break for it or surrender. Russell Ludemann spoke fluent German and talked to the Jerries about two minutes. We were getting complacent when the Germans opened fire. Piper had a Thompson and immediately returned their fire. Someone said, "Let's try to get out, we're done for, anyway!"
>
> I was in back and closest to the best exit in the ravine. I ran out toward the top of the hill. I used to run pretty good, and on that day, I would have beaten any of today's runners, steroids or no.

The ruckus created by this group fighting on the backside of the hill probably diverted the attention of the Jerries dug in on the ridge line, allowing the remainder of the Red Devil's attacking force to quietly approach unopposed until they were in striking range.

In the meantime, the Foley force advanced through the wooded area at the base of the hill and went into a skirmish line. Foley observed a road, like a logging road, off to the left and sent a scout to investigate. The scout was killed by a machine gun. A second scout was sent up the same road and was also killed. Then a bazooka team was wiped out by the machine gun. Sergeant Jahnigen was then sent to set up a machine gun on top of a mound a spur off Devil's Hill, which was higher than the enemy's outpost machine gun. Jahnigen's team silenced that gun, and the assault force continued.

Sgt. Bob White of A Company Third Platoon told his version of the initial assault: "We attacked on the run over the hill and down the northeast side of the hill. The Germans on that side of the hill had their backs to us. The ones we did not kill ran down the hill to the woods."

John Brickley, A Company, described the assault from his position:

> The sergeant told us to yell like Indians and charge up the hill. We did. I ran between First Sergeant Taylor and a replacement. Halfway to the top, a burst was fired into us. Taylor and the new man went down. I thought it best to hit the ground myself. I turned to the man on my left to see how he was. He couldn't answer. He was bleeding from the mouth.
> 
> Sergeant Taylor said, "Brick, take my sub-Thompson and move up if you can. I'm hit in the shoulder."
> 
> I reached the top of the hill with the others, and the Krauts moved back from their guns and took off down the other slope.
> 
> After we dug in, I reached for a K ration in my bulging jump pockets. There were bullet holes in each pocket. How's that for the luck of the Irish?
> 
> The next morning Sergeant White volunteered to try to contact Battalion Headquarters. He was out of sight five minutes when we heard his sub-Thompson. Taylor and I ran toward the shooting and found White, who announced, "I just killed seven Germans."
> 
> Sure enough, in the nearest clearing was a German patrol. They were apparently taking a break when White surprised them.
> 
> We realized we were cut off. Headquarters confirmed this by radio.

Joe Favela, demolitionist from Regimental Headquarters Company, recalled the charge up Devil's Hill:

> When we hit the hill, everyone opened fire. The Germans jumped out of their foxholes, and we kept after them. They hit the level field, running toward the dike and toward a farmhouse to hide. One German regrouped his machine gun crew and opened fire at the hill, aiming about three or four feet above ground. The lieutenant that was giving commands was hit as well as others that were standing.

The Foley force awaited the counterattack. When the counterattack came, the Red Devils drove the enemy back down the hill and held on through the first night.

Favela remembered a trooper next to him with a BAR, who shouted, "They are crawling!" Everyone started firing, and the BAR man hit a Jerry about ten feet from his foxhole. Favela remembered hearing the wounded German near the BAR trooper's foxhole, moaning throughout the night. When dawn came, the BAR man checked on the wounded German and had our medics pick him up.

John Shultz, a nineteen-year-old private, recalled the first day and night and the next morning on Devil's Hill:

> I remember the fighting was quite fierce at times, but the part that made the greatest impression on me was the action after we were dug in. The soil was quite sandy, so the digging went well, but the sand was to haunt us later as it was constantly getting into the working parts of our weapons. During the first night on the hill, we were on edge with every rustle in the underbrush. We knew we had to conserve our ammunition, but intermittent fire went on all night as no one was about to take the risk of the enemy using the cover of darkness to regain the high ground.
>
> With morning came, noises of motorized equipment at the base of the hill and voices shouting as in preparation for an assault. Then came the mortar fire on our position. We were sure this was the cover for the charge to follow. One of the shells hit close by and sprayed our foxhole with sand. On my next attempt to fire my rifle, I found it to be jammed. This appeared to be the end for me. I was suddenly useless to help defend our position. I was sure this was it. My one last and only shot would be my hand grenade, which I jerked from my harness and stood ready for the exact moment. If I went, at least one Kraut was going with me! I pulled the pin and removed the tape from the handle; I crouched in my hole, awaiting that moment when I could "see the whites of their eyes." Well, they never got that close. There I was, stuck holding a grenade with only the pressure of my hand to keep it from exploding. After things quieted down, I salvaged the tape and use the safety pin from my ammunition bandoleer to replace the pin.

The next morning, Jerry decided to concentrate on the holding force protecting the flank along Wyler-Beek road, using duplicity. Cpl. James Blue describes that action:

> Two German soldiers came forward with arms raised as if to surrender. At a distance of about fifty yards, we could see that one of them had something on his back. Shortly he fell forward, and the second soldier attempted to fire the machine gun attached to his comrade's back. We had our sights set on them; they were riddled with gunfire.
>
> Later in the morning we received the order to join the Foley forces. As we moved from the position, a barrage of mortar fire came in. We were in luck to have moved just in time. We left on the double and were fired on by a machine gun. A bullet struck the heel of Don Johnson's boot, partially removing it. Foley greeted us as we arrived on the hill, and we were given a section of the hill to defend.

Corporal Blue describes a potential personal catastrophe during his first night on Devil's Hill, the Foley group's second night, which demonstrated Blue's clear thinking under stress:

> At dusk I thought it a good time to give my sub-Thompson a cleaning. Standing in my foxhole, I began to disassemble it. The driving rod, which is compressed by a spring, slipped by my thumb and flew away. This is the first time in combat that I panicked. I went crazy, feeling in the foxhole and around the outside. I knew my life, and the life of others, depended on that weapon.
>
> I got myself together and formed a search plan. My plan was to start around the foxhole patting the ground one hand span, second time around another hand span, and so on. When I was one arm's length out, I felt the driving rod. I reassembled the weapon in the darkness and was a pleased soldier under those circumstances.

During the second night, enemy patrols probed for a weak spot. Again the Red Devils kept the enemy at a distance from their holes. When a few shots were fired after dark, Foley ordered, "Go easy on the ammo, we are running low."

At daybreak a BAR opened up full blast. Foley shouted, "Who in the hell is wasting ammo?"

Sgt. Joe Boone answered from the east side of the ridge, "If you think we've wasted ammo, come take a look!" Boone had knocked off the lead element of an attack force.

On the night of September 20, the British relieved the A Company Platoon under Capt. Jock Adams and Lt. George Lamm that had been isolated near the Nijmegen Bridge. George Lamm remembered that their group was then ordered to join the other A Company men on Devil's Hill. Captain Adams came along although he was suffering from two wounds.

They approached the hill after dark and decided to bivouac in the woods until daylight. While in their hidden position, they observed a German patrol pass close by. Soon they heard firing. A Red Devil outpost killed four Jerries from that patrol. Lamm and his group then followed in the same route, making themselves known to the outpost and entering into the defensive perimeter.

Ralph Garcia remembered Private Weeks on Devil's Hill:

> One night Antonio Alverez called to me, "Garcia, someone is down the ridge hollering."
>
> As assistant squad leader, I alerted the men on the line I would go check on the hollering. I cautiously worked my way down to where I recognized Private Weeks's voice. Then I called out, "Come on up, Weeks!"
>
> Weeks suffered from somnambulism (sleepwalking), and while asleep, he walked out of his foxhole toward the German lines. When he awoke and realized he was lost, he called out for help. Subsequently Weeks was assigned to noncombat duty for lack of medication for his illness.

During a lull on the third day, Corporal Blue and Sergeant Van Enwyck were ordered to organize a detail and bury the eleven men of A and G companies killed in action. G Company losses included Lt. Kenneth Covey and Pvt. Daniel Kuszmaul. A Company Honor Roll Lists eight men killed between September 19 and September 24: Pvt. Manuel L. Alverez, Pvt. George S. Barron, Pvt. Richard R. Davis, Pvt. Willard H. Davis, PFC Julius P. Musmeci, Sgt. V. G. Pierce, Jr., Pvt. Paul B. Singer, and Pvt. John F. Tulley. Ralph Garcia remembers that on the charge up Devil's Hill that he was running between Richard Davis and Willard Davis, and both Davises were killed, one on each side of Garcia.

After the men were laid out face up in a mass grave, the detail decided to see if they could find some covering for the faces before filling the grave with dirt. Van Enwyck made a dash with four men to a guesthouse (tavern), somewhat down the hill and away from their protective positions, to search for some covering for the dead. They made the trip without being fired on and returned with tablecloths to use as shrouds.

On the night of September 23, Foley asked for a volunteer to go back to the regiment and return with ammunition. By this time, the Germans encircled the hill. Private Bonge volunteered. Bonge said that he was not worried about getting through the Germans, but he was worried about getting back on the hill without being shot by the Red Devils.

Jim Blue promised Bonge that he would personally stand guard until he came back, and he could use the password "Blue." Bonge left for the ammo about 2200 hours. Just before daylight, Jim Blue heard the password—"Blue."

"Come on up, Bonge," Blue replied.

The ammo-carrying detail followed Bonge up to the waiting defenders of Devil's Hill, who were down to five rounds per rifle and no ammo for automatic weapons. Blue declares, "Bonge is one of the many heroes that are not on record for valor."

John Shultz recalled the soup brewed by Sergeant Mullen on Devil's Hill. Mullen used the facilities in a little cottage at the peek of the hill. He had meat from a cow killed in the crossfire and red cabbage from the cottage garden. Mullen cooked up a huge pot of cabbage beef soup laced with grease and hair.

Since German patrols and mortar fire were a continual threat, a constant alert was needed at all times, but by covering for one another, one or two at a time could leave their foxholes for a meal of Mullen soup. Dead German soldiers left unburied were used for directional signs to the cottage mess hall. According to Shultz, "To get to the cottage we went as far as the noncommissioned officer lying on his back, with his mouth wide open and left hand raised, then turned right on the path."

Tom Beno, G Company, was acting squad leader for one of the G Company squads on the hill. He had given out watches taken from German prisoners to his men on the line. The watches helped them stay awake for the allotted time at night when they were taking turns getting sleep and staying alert for counterattacks.

Tom gave one of the watches to Yerah Allsup, who said in response, "Tom, I'm going to keep this watch as long as I live."

When Allsup realized what he said and the life-threatening implications of his words, he clammed up.

The Red Devils repulsed several counterattacks, and each time, the pressure built a little higher. During the night, the troopers could hear noises at the foot of the hill, indicating that yet another attack was on its way. Allsup took off the watch and flung it down the hill and announced to the Krauts, "If you want the damn watch so bad, take it."

Tom reported, "The guys in earshot had some laughs and made some bright remarks over the incident. It was the kind of comic situation that helped us get through those trying times."

After five days on Devil's Hill, the MLR (main line of resistance) was consolidated to include the hill in the division's perimeter. A Company of the 504th regiment relieved the gallant defenders of the hill. James Blue recalled that day:

> As the Foley forces departed the hill, we glanced back for the last time at the mass grave of our comrades. We paid a high price for this hill, but we knew we had trained for this type of mission. We were all volunteers, and this was a part of a day's work for Airborne troops.

A Company men who fought on Devil's Hill.
Copies from 1943 A Company photos.

## Red Devils or Angels from Heaven

While the Red Devils were fighting on Devil's Hill, another stuggle was in progress to secure the area around the little village of Beek. Several attacks and counterattacks by the Germans took a heavy toll of killed and injured paratroopers of the 508th. Sgt. Alfred Hess of I Company told of his experience in the area of Kalorama-Beek:

> As they rounded a curve in the road a machine gun opened up on the group, killing Sgt. Maryld Price, Sgt. Stanley Stevens, and PFC Henry Wade. Sergeant Hess took cover behind a tree just in time as bullets splattered the tree. Hess said that losing three friends in a matter of seconds, gone forever, as one of the most traumatic experiences of the war for him.

Bert Jakobs was the one who called the Red Devils "angels from heaven" when he saw the paratroopers of the 508th descending from the skies as he looked through an attic window in the village of Beek. Bert was a ten-year-old Jewish boy who had been living in hiding with his family for twenty-five months to escape deportation to Hitler's death camps.

The Jakobs family was composed of the parents, Aron and Freda, and four children—Martin, Rose, Edith, and Bert. The family had lived in Oldenberg, Germany. Before World War II, about four hundred Jews lived in Oldenberg, a city with a total population of about 100,000. Mr. Jakobs was a wealthy cattle dealer and rancher, and his family enjoyed the luxury of four servants—a chauffeur, a governess, and two maids. When Hitler came into power, the comfortable life for the Jakobs family began to change.

One of Hitler's ploys in gaining political power was to exploit Germany's anti-Semitism by blaming the Jews for Germany's economic problems. Hitler coupled his anti-Jewish propaganda with promoting pride in the German race and convinced his loyal supporters that it was their patriotic duty to help eliminate the Jewish problem in Germany. With the Nazi party in control of the government, laws were passed to legalize exploitation and harassment of Jewish people.

Edith Jakobs remembered that when she was a student in an Oldenberg public school, their teacher had all the Jewish students line up on the school playground. Then he ordered the other students to pass by and spit on the faces of their Jewish classmates.

Mr. Jakobs could see that Germany was no longer safe for Jews. Aron and Freda Jakobs laid careful plans to immigrate to Holland. Both of their parents were formerly from Holland. They had relatives living in Holland, and the family could speak Dutch. Holland was the logical place for them to relocate.

Aron sold his property at a fraction of its value. He transported the sale value in gold to Holland using a clever scheme. Freda Jakobs would leave Germany to visit relatives in Holland wearing a dress with gold buttons covered in cloth. She would return from Holland in the same dress, with ordinary buttons. By Freda's many visits to see relatives, Mr. Jakobs accumulated enough capital to start a cattle business in Nijmegan and thus support his family.

The Jakobses found temporary respite from Hitler's persecution, but their peaceful existence in friendly Holland was short-lived.

Jakob family. Standing L-R: Edith, Rose, Bert, and Martin, Seated L-R: Freda and Aron, circa 1939. Photo Provided by Edith Jakobs Samuel.

Before Germany occupied Holland, Aron Jakobs moved his family from Nijmegen to Den Bosch, in southern Holland behind the "water line." The Dutch had flooded certain sections on the border to prevent the Nazis from invading their country, but the Nazis used their airborne troops to skip over the water barrier. The German paratroopers were disguised in uniforms of Dutch soldiers and policemen.

After the Germans occupied the Netherlands, it wasn't long before Hitler's policies toward the Jews were applied in Holland with the same systematic vigor as in Germany. Members of the Jakobs family had to wear a yellow six-pointed Star of David sewn to their clothing at all times. The children were not allowed to go to public schools. None of the family members could legally enter a public park, ride a train, or travel from one city to another. The Germans were beginning to deport the fathers, heads of Jewish families, supposedly to work in war plants. The Germans took Aron's car, but he continued his business traveling by bicycle from cattle market to cattle market.

Both native Dutch and Jews feared the *razzia*. *Razzia* is a Dutch term for the midnight roundups by German soldiers of people needed as workers in Germany. The Germans would cordon off a section of a city, search every house, and take away anyone they thought would be useful. Many fathers of families and able-bodied young men and boys were summarily snatched away from their homes without warning in the middle of the night.

If the Dutch people were apprehended for protecting the Jews against the designs of the German conquerors, they themselves could be deported or executed for their kindness. Yet a brave Dutch family prepared a haven for the Jakobs family in the attic of their home in the little village of Beek at the address Nieuwe Holleweg 382.

Because of the *razzia*, Rose and her twin brother, Martin, had already found a place of refuge before the rest of the family went into hiding. Aron Jakobs carefully planned the move of the four remaining members of the family. They removed the yellow stars from their clothing, went to the train station, and bought their tickets to leave the city.

The family left Den Bosch in pairs. Edith and her mother, Freda, left first on one train, and Bert left with his father, Aron, a day later on another train. Freda and Edith arrived in Nijmegan, traveled to Beek, and spent the first night in the attic of their host and hostess, Aunt Annie and Uncle Gerrit. (*Aunt* and *uncle* were terms of endearment and did not signify kinship in this case.)

Bert and Aron had about two hours in Nijmegan to wait for a streetcar to Berg en Dal, so father and son spent those two hours in a public park.

Young Bert reminded his father that they as Jews could not use the park, but he discovered that without the gold stars on their clothing, no one knew the difference.

When they got off the streetcar at Berg en Dal, Bert and his dad walked about a mile to the small village of Beek. Bert recalled his father saying, "See that farmhouse to the right. We are going to stop at that house for a glass of milk."

Bert drank his milk and met the Janssen family. Then he and his dad went into the barn and climbed a ladder into the hayloft. They found a trap door hidden under the hay that led into a secret compartment, where they found Bert's mother, Freda, and sister, Edith. Aron paid the Janssen-Dreissen family the equivalent of $400 a month to stay in their hideaway.

Food was rationed for the Dutch people, and it was difficult to feed four extra mouths on the limited supplies allotted to the Janssen family. They mostly lived on potatoes, oatmeal, raw onions, and milk. The confinement and boredom for a child who could not run and play and yell to the top of his voice but had to endure long periods of silence and stillness was most traumatic to young Bert who entered the hideout at the age of eight.

After eight months, the older sister, Rose, came and joined the others—one more person to feed. However, her twin brother, Martin, remained in his original hiding place. Rose gave the family added emotional strength for the difficult times they faced.

Bert remembered his two sisters teaching him basic school subjects such as reading, writing, arithmetic, and geography. Geography was important to keep up with the progress of the war from the newspapers that they were able to read. Rose also taught Edith English while they were in hiding.

Grandfather Janssen came to the attic every day to play checkers with Bert. Bert followed his dad's instructions and always managed to lose at checkers with "Grandpa"—that was to keep the host family happy.

Bert explained that the cow barn was attached to the rear of the house, and that the Jakobs family lived over the barn. Their toilet was in the cow barn, and to get to the toilet, they had to climb down a ladder. He described the seat as a boxlike facility with one hole and a deep drop underneath. Their only facility for bathing was a bucket.

The birth of the Janssen's first son brought a sudden change for the Jakobs family. Gerrit Janssen feared that the Germans might discover that he was harboring a Jewish family. Many visitors came to see the new baby, which meant that the Jews upstairs had to remain as silent as possible for fear a visitor would get suspicious and report their suspicions to the German authorities.

Edith remembered overhearing Uncle Gerrit argue with Aunt Annie about getting rid of the Jews. Aunt Annie took the side of the Jakobs family in arguments with her husband, which helped prevent the expulsion of the Jakobses from their hiding place.

Edith's diary reported comforting and instructive words from her mother, Freda, when the family was depressed about their forced confinement and harsh conditions. Mrs. Jakobs said something like this: "We have three things to help us through these times—faith, hope, and love, and love is the most important of the three."

Those words are similar to 1 Corinthians 13:13 in the Christian Bible, which reads, "But now abideth faith, hope, love, these three: and the greatest of these is love."

Then one day, a date Bert remembers well, September 17, 1944, they heard the roar of hundreds of planes overhead. Bert remembers peeping through the tiny window in their attic hideaway and seeing the "angels from heaven" dropping by parachute from the sky. Surely this was their day of deliverance.

It was apparent that their house was in a battle zone, and everyone in the house moved to the basement. On their first night in the basement, several nearby houses were set afire by the shells of the opposing armies. Aron Jakobs decided to take Bert with him and crawl out to a haystack about fifty yards away and take a look. They got to the haystack and were seen by both the Americans and the Germans. Both sides fired at the haystack. They felt lucky that they were able to crawl back to the house without injury. Four days passed with the Jakobs and the Janssen families hovering in their basement in no-man's land.

Jory Farr wrote "Horror, Hiding, and the Holocaust" from an interview with Bert Jakobs that described the following events:

> In the early morning of the fifth day, Sept. 21, an American patrol passed near the house. Rose, who spoke English, hollered at them. Two GIs bore a stretcher with a mortally wounded soldier. After hearing their story, the GIs agreed to take all twelve of them across the American lines.

Bob Nieblas, Headquarters Third, one of the stretcher-bearers, described the events leading up to the contact with the Jakobs family, which is summarized as follows:

A new lieutenant, Lt. William E. Pulverman, was in charge of a patrol to probe into the town of Beek. Cpl. Bob Nieblas was a member of that patrol. The Germans fired at the patrol as they entered the town. Nieblas was slightly wounded. Pulverman was hit and fell in full view of the Germans riflemen. The Jerries shot him time and time again, and each time he was hit, Pulverman screamed. The Germans finally pulled back. Then Bob Neiblas and another member of the patrol carried him to the Janssen house and asked for a blanket. An old man came out with the blanket. They wrapped the blanket around the wounded lieutenant and moved him against the wall.

Then Rose Jakobs came out of a house and examined Nieblas's wound and told Nieblas that he was not badly hurt. She cleaned the blood off his face, talked to him in English, and calmed him down. Nieblas in describing himself at the time said, "I was a basket case, all nerves."

After calming down, he led the Jakobs and Janssen families out of the zone of fire to a safer area covered by the American paratroopers. Bob Nieblas then found a medic. He and the medic returned to the Janssen house and carried Pulverman to an aid station. Lieutenant Pulverman was still alive, even talked to them, but he died during that night. Nieblas tried to recall the medic's name. He believes it was Kelly. We later found T/3 Joseph Kelly in a 508th Medical Detachment roster of the 508th.

## After the Joy of Liberation

The Jakobs family, after surviving twenty-five months in the attic of Annie Dreissen Janssen's home, took refuge in the town of Berg en Dal. They occupied a vacant house across the street from a 508th aid station. Rose Jakobs, who was nineteen years old, and Edith Jakobs, age seventeen, volunteered to work in the aid station with the wounded. They fed the wounded soldiers, lit their cigarettes, and did whatever they could to be of assistance.

For almost two weeks Rose and Edith exulted in their new freedom. Once they even rode bicycles into Nijmegen to visit their old home by the Waal River. They enjoyed working in the aid station, feeling as if they were making a small contribution to those who had come from so far and had liberated them from Hitler's horrors. It was great for them to be able to come and go and breathe the fresh air and enjoy the sunshine of the world outside of their attic confinement, which had lasted so long.

Then came the fatal day of October 2. As the two sisters were crossing the street in Berg en Dal, they stopped to speak to American soldiers and inquire about the fighting at the front when a German plane flew over and dropped a fragmentation bomb among them. Edith fell to the ground and blacked out. When she came to, Edith found her sister, Rose, had a fragmentation splinter through her heart and was dead. The bomb also killed four American soldiers. Annie Janssen suffered the loss of her husband, Gerrit Janssen, and her brother, Leo Driessen, from the bomb.

Suddenly the Jakobs family plunged from the heights of joy to the depths of despair. Rose's father and mother went into shock over the death of their daughter. Perhaps it was the culminating blow, following years of suffering and deprivation from Hitler's rule of terror that finally broke the spirit of Mrs. Jakobs, for she never recovered from the shock of Rose's death. Rose had those special qualities of strength, understanding, and leadership that had contributed so much to the survival and hopes of the Jakobs family.

The body of Rose Jakobs was buried along with the bodies of American paratroopers in a temporary grave in the woods near Berg en Dal. After the war, Rose's body was reinterred in the Jewish cemetery of Nijmegen.

Mr. Jakobs desperately wanted to move his family away from the fighting front after Rose's death. Much of Nijmegen was burning out of control due to bombs and the shells of the opposing armies. Edith, who was taught to speak English by her sister, Rose, during their months of confinement, became the family spokesperson. She was able to persuade an officer of the 508th to transport them in a jeep through the burning city of Nijmegen to the relative safety of Wijchen, where they lived until after the war.

## Bert Jakobs Returned to Oldenburg

In 1985, a Christian organization in Oldenburg, Germany, the city where the Jakobs family lived until 1938, invited the Jewish survivors of the Holocaust from Oldenburg to come back for a visit. They wanted to help heal the wounds inflicted by the Nazis on the Jewish people. Bert Jakobs and his brother, Martin, attended the ceremonies

November 9, 1938, was named *Kristalnacht* because so much glass was broken as Nazi terrorists attacked Jewish homes and businesses all over Germany. In Oldenburg on that night, the Nazis burned the Jewish synagogue. At the "healing ceremony," the citizens of Oldenburg unveiled a monument they built on the grounds of the destroyed synagogue. The inscription on the monument reads, "Don't we all have one Father? Weren't we created by one God? Why do we hate each other?"

With tears in his eye, Bert Jakobs put his arms around a German veteran of World War II, who was in tears also and who confessed to Bert that they had done terrible things.

## Explanations of Israeli, Dutch, and Buddy Connections

I included a short version of this story in *A Private's Eye View of World War Two*. I had heard Bert Jakobs speak at one of our 508th reunions in Los Angeles. Later I met with Edith Jakobs in Nijmegan, Holland, while she was visiting with her brother, Martin. On that same trip I visited the Janssen home in Beek and talked with Anne Dreissen Janssen.

Jan Bos, a Nijmegen policemen, took me to the Janssen home and served as translator for me. Bert Jakobs, Edith Jakobs, and Anne Janssen were the sources for the original story.

Additional information for the story came from my 508th buddy Bob Neiblas and a Dutch translator:

Many years ago Edith Samuel-Jakobs, who lives in Israel, sent me a copy of a hand-typed booklet, which she had prepared for her family. She wrote the booklet in Dutch for her children and grandchildren for the celebration of the thirty-fifth anniversary of her marriage to Benjamin Samuel. The major part of the booklet came from Edith's diary and Rose's diary, written during their months in hiding. Until recently the book was just Dutch to me until I met Jack de Vroomen. Jack de Vroomen, a native of Holland, has a business in Greenwood, South Carolina. Jack kindly translated the booklet into English on audiotapes.

★Bert Jakobs sent me a copy of "Horror, Hiding, and the Holocaust," subtitled, "How Bert Jakobs Outlived the Third Reich" by Jory Farr from *Orange County News, Arts and Entertainment Publication*, vol. 5, No 41: June 16-22, 2000. Jody Farr graciously agreed for me to use his material.

## Did Bugs Get His Purple Heart?

Bugs (Andrew Cehrobec) of Regimental Headquarters Company was really excited. "Now I will get the Purple Heart!" he boasted. Bugs seemed to have a special angel. Bugs often told the story about how, in Normandy, a German bayonet went through his clothing without touching his flesh. It didn't draw blood, so he couldn't get a Purple Heart. Bugs also invited danger, like when we were near the supply drop zone (DZ) in Holland.

After Montgomery passed through with his tanks, our demolition section moved to a position on high ground above a valley, which had been used as a DZ for parachute bundles to supply the regiment. Our section dug in at the edge of a woods with farmland sloping down toward the valley. Some equipment had not yet been recovered from the DZ. We foraged into the DZ to recover our supplies. Germans occupying high ground on the other side of the valley could see us when we moved into the field. Machine gun fire would often kick up the dust close to us on such trips, but we always managed to get safely back to cover.

On one such trip, I ran across a German soldier sitting against a low bush. He was holding an American K ration in his hands—hands stiff with rigor mortis. He must have been looting our supplies when he was surprised and shot. (The drop zone was in German hands for a short time but was cleared out by C and B companies.) I just let the dead man hold on to his goodies. Bugs, however, laughed at my timidity, pried open the dead man's fingers, and recovered the goods.

Shortly after that incident, the Germans zeroed in on our position with 88s. As well-trained soldiers, we took cover in our foxholes, except Bugs. He lay on top of the ground, smoking a cigarette and joking while the 88s were whistling into our area. "I'm so mean," Bugs boasted. "God doesn't want me, and the devil wouldn't have me."

Bugs had lived as a hobo in civilian life. One day he said, "I'm tired of these damned K rations. I'm going to make you bastards some genuine hobo soup." He went hunting with his submachine gun and came back with some chickens and cabbages, which he cooked up in his helmet over a fire of C-2. (The C-2 was our plastic explosive that would not explode without a cap. It would make a quick hot fire and was ideal for field cooking.) We had one problem with Bugs's soup. Since he had shot the chickens with his submachine gun, the soup was full of lead.

The Purple Heart? A German plane had been shot down near us. Bugs went to investigate the ruins. A minor explosion occurred as he approached the plane, and a small fragment of metal cut his face ever so slightly, the kind of scratch that would make a kid cry for a Band-Aid. I wonder if Bugs really got his Purple Heart.

## Thorensche Molen

Argardus "Gas" Leegsma, the Dutchman who furnished maps and guided G Company into Nijmegen on September 18, had become a regular member of Sergeant Queen's squad by September 23. In less than an hour after meeting the paratroopers, Gas had picked up the carbine of a wounded trooper and joined in the firefights. He fought with G Company when they drove the Germans out of Beek and Ubbergen and on September 23 had advanced with his squad into the flat lands toward Thorensche Molen to the village of Persinghen.

Gas described the fighting:

The flat lands were stubbornly defended by German paratroopers and SS troops. We had to fight for every inch while under heavy fire from self-propelled 88s, machine guns, and small arms fire.

Sergeant Queen had assembled his men in a broad circle to pass on new orders for the next phase of the attack when a mortar shell dropped in their midst. Eight of the men were wounded, including Sergeant Queen and Gas Leegsma.

Leegsma remembered the following:

Argardus "Gas" Leegsma.
Photo furnished by Argardus Leegsma.

After getting wounded in the right foot, I was brought behind a dike with the other wounded to the forward aid station. I met the very popular and brave medic Frank Ruppe and Doc Beaudin. They were a splendid team. Under heavy fire they did their duty, saving many lives.

Thorensche Molen was a small community of a few houses, named after its most prominent landmark, the windmill Thorensche Molen (*molen* means "mill" in Dutch). The town was located on top of a dike; a canal ran alongside.

During the morning of September 23, G Company fought its way into Thorensche Molen. Sgt. Marvin Risnes and Theodore Geinger crossed a small wooden bridge over the canal to reconnoiter their left flank. Risnes directed Geinger to turn left and check out that area while Risnes moved to the right. Before he knew it, Risnes had walked into a well-dug-in platoon of Germans. Risnes described what followed:

A German threw one of those potato-masher grenades at me from his foxhole. I dove behind a shock of corn on the roadside for cover. Every time I stuck my head out from behind the shock to take a shot at the Kraut, he would throw another grenade, and I had to dive for cover again.

I decided to work my way around the stacked corn. As I eased along, I suddenly felt the barrel of a rifle on my left shoulder. By reflex action, I whipped around and shot into the corn shock. Then I ran across the road and jumped into the canal.

My shot hit a young German in the arm. He got scared, dropped his rifle, and ran also. He wasn't chasing me—just running. It so happened that he ran for the canal also. As he came over the bank, I caught him and held him under water until I could tell he wasn't putting up a fight. Then I let him up and took his grenades. He was a small lad, not over seventeen years old—a young German paratrooper.

Sergeant Sirovica and Loren Carter came to my rescue. Carter, with his BAR, got the German who had thrown the grenades at me. Sirovica sprayed the corn shock with his tommy gun and hit another German concealed there.

My prisoner and I crawled out of the canal and took cover beside the bridge. The rest of my squad crossed the bridge and attacked the Jerries dug in along the banks of the canal. We secured the area to protect the left flank of our company.

We could hear intense small arms and artillery fire in the village on the other side of the canal where the rest of the company was engaged.

In about thirty minutes, the artillery subsided. During this lull George McGrath crossed the canal to tell us the company was withdrawing and we were about to be cut off. The Germans were advancing on the other side of the dike as we withdrew on our side. While we were withdrawing, I noticed George McGrath staggering and getting weak. He had been hit, probably while on his way to warn us.

After reaching the edge of the town, we received several heavy shells—very close. One of these made a direct hit on Bob Veasey. Veasey was an air force sergeant, a close friend of my assistant squad leader, Merle Beach. Veasey had come to visit Beach in Nottingham, England, on a fourteen-day leave. He arrived the day we were notified of the Holland operation. Bob wanted to make the parachute jump and spend a few days watching and participating in combat with his paratrooper friend.

The same shell that killed Bob Veasey also wounded Cicchillo in the hand. I told Cicchillo to go to the rear for medical aid and take the wounded prisoner with him. The young German soldier was reluctant to leave. I guess he felt more secure with me.

One of the shells buried Richard Graham in his foxhole. His buddy Loren Carter went to his aid to dig him out. In his haste, Carter's trenching tool struck Graham several times. Graham uttered some choice words of displeasure for Carter's worthy efforts. Fortunately, neither the German shell nor his buddy's shovel inflicted permanent wounds to Richard Graham.

The next day, G Company again took Thorensche Molen, but the enemy artillery made holding the town untenable. Regimental command decided to abandon the position. The risk of continued high casualties in unprotected terrain was too high. G Company withdrew and established the MLR at Wercheren Lake.

Sergeant Risnes was awarded the Silver Star for his action at Thorensche Molen. The citation in part states:

> Sergeant Risnes launched a single-handed attack on the maneuvering element of the enemy. Employing his rifle and fragmentation grenades, he killed six of the enemy and caused the remainder to withdraw.

Marvin Risnes, in commenting about the citation, gave credit to his men, saying, "My whole squad assisted in this action."

Concerning air force sergeant Bob Veasey who was killed at Thorensche Molen: after his fourteen-day leave expired, Veasey was carried by his unit as AWOL and later as a deserter. It was difficult to convince the air force of his death and clear his record because his body could not be found.

Shortly after the war, those who witnessed the circumstances of his death submitted sworn statements, and his status was changed to KIA. His body was recovered years later.

Marvin Risnes said of Veasey, "He proved himself to be a very brave and capable soldier during his short tour of duty with the company."

## The Deep Sleep

Soldiering can be hard, exhausting work—like the night we laid an antitank minefield in Holland. To keep the Germans from breaking through the corridor protected by the Eighty-second, it was important that open fields through which armor could advance be well defended. The field, which we mined, had already drawn German armor. One disabled tank and other destroyed armored vehicles were still sitting in a nearby field as a grim reminder that there may be more armored forces where these had come from, poised for attack against us.

A few nights earlier, I had been on a patrol to further disable the armored vehicles so the Germans could not recover them. I remember clearly how loud the sounds were that night as we were placing our explosive charges and Thermit against the vital parts of the machines. We were between the two lines, and we did not want our presence to be known to the Germans. The accidental clanging of metal against metal sounded like a bell ringing.

Preparing the minefield was a long, tedious task. A truck loaded with the mines pulled within two hundred yards of the field, staying behind the ridgeline so it would not be spotted by the enemy. The mines were laid in a pattern recorded by Lieutenant Hardwick on the field map. Sergeant Luczaj paced off the field and marked the spots. Others dug holes for the mines. One of the most responsible jobs was to cover and camouflage the mines after taking off the safety so they would be ready to explode against the tracks of the enemy tanks. My duty was a simple one, carrying the mines from the truck to the field. I carried two twenty-pound mines in each hand, eighty pounds a trip. When working in no-man's land, you work fast in order to get out in a hurry. We were able to finish laying the minefield that night in about five hours and returned safely to our bivouac area without drawing enemy fire.

Little Car Austin and I shared a foxhole together. We took off our helmets and boots and laid them beside our foxhole and went to sleep. The next morning Little Car couldn't believe how heavily I slept. Our bivouac area had received artillery shells during the night. Four men in Regimental Headquarters Company had been killed and others wounded. Little Car's helmet had a shrapnel hole through it, and one of my boots had a piece of shrapnel wedged between the heel and the sole. (In a few days, the heel came off.) I was so tired from the night's work; I did not even wake up during the shelling.

## Voxhil

October 1 was a normal evening before all hell broke loose. Norb Studelska, a member of D Company's Third Platoon Mortar Squad, described the scene and the activity along D Company's line:

> I was dug in with the rest of the platoon beside a country road near the small village of Kamp. Flat green farmland spread over the area to our front, with the border of Germany and the Reichwald forest a little more than a mile distant. A thick hedge along our side of the road offered excellent cover. Because of the flatness of the terrain, we had an unusually good view and field of fire.
>
> My foxhole was a model of comfort. I took great pride in making my home the best on the block. It was chest deep, long enough to lie flat when I slept, and narrow at the top. To keep things neat and clean, as my mother had taught me, I completely lined the hole with the canopy of a main chute. (This was in the area of the drop zone. Parachutes were easy to find nearby.) I had a built-in shelf for my personal gear and a picture of my childhood sweetheart, Elaine Olson, whom I married after the war.
>
> As the light faded, the troopers were getting ready for their usual rounds of sleep, guard duty, or outpost duty at a farm site about one hundred yards to our front. After dark, the Kraut attack started with what appeared to be an enemy patrol action. This put us on the alert, and before long, hell seemed to engulf us.
>
> A combination of artillery bursts, Kraut flares, machine gun tracers, and mortar shelling from the enemy and our own forces created a nightmare of insane fireworks. At the time I was struck with the calm matter-of-fact soldier tasks that were taking place around me. Forms of enemy to our front were clearly visible during the many flares and shell bursts. From my vantage point, I could see the enemy alternately running and hitting the ground. Some were tossing potato-masher grenades, some were firing rifles, and others were firing burp guns. For a moment I felt guilty because I thought I hit a medic attending a downed comrade.

Bill Still was operating the regimental switchboard when the German artillery hit the 508th Regimental CP. Bill remembered that all connections were cut so that no one in the regiment could be reached by telephone from the Regimental CP. Telephone connections were repaired in about one hour. In the meantime, messages were transmitted via radios and runners.

Four men in the Regimental Communication Section were killed by the artillery: Clyde Fisher, George Hartman, Martin "Jonsey" Jones, and Richard "Red" Thomas.

Harry Hudec recalled the following:

> When the artillery hit the regimental CP area, I jumped into Johnny Danko's hole, which was the closest. It was also wide and deep. Shortly after the barrage, I heard Colonel Shanley calling, "Captain Abraham, get these men out of here!"

Abraham ordered Hudec and Danko to remove the four who were killed. Harry remembered that a can of green beans had exploded and scattered over the bodies.

The noise of fighting increased sharply in the Second Battalion area. Major Holmes, CO of Headquarters Second, tried to phone Regimental CP unsuccessfully and switched to radio communications to ascertain the situation from regiment. He sent two S-2 officers, Lieutenant Wakefield and Lieutenant LeFebvre, to check on the E Company roadblock. Wakefield remembered trying to interview two German prisoners at the roadblock, getting little information, mostly chatter and gestures. The officers returned to the battalion CO and reported that the roadblock was holding out.

Major Holmes moved his CP forward to the border of woods overlooking the open fields of Voxhil. Three or four German prisoners had been brought to the edge of the woods for interrogation by battalion S-2. Moonlight and a burning vehicle outlined the prisoners clearly. Wakefield remembers, "Just as I started out to meet them, a shell screamed in and killed every one of the prisoners instantly."

Sgt. Fred Infanger of E Company had watched demolitionists from Regimental Headquarters Company lay antitank mines in front of the MLR, and on the night of the October 1, he saw the Germans calmly picking up the mines and making a safe lane for their armored vehicles.

Infanger describes the action from his section of the front:

> That afternoon, a smoke shell landed right behind my squad of the Second Platoon, E Company. I tried to smother it with sand, but it was too late. We knew they were zeroed in on us. About ten o'clock that night, we got hit with everything but the kitchen sink.
>
> The Germans poured out of the Den Heuvel woods like Indians, whooping and hollering. I had a box of rifle grenades, and I thought, "This will be good." After firing three grenades, a shell hit my foxhole, and it caved in.
>
> When I dug myself out, I discovered my rifle had a ruptured cartridge. I used the extractor from the butt of the rifle but just couldn't remove the shell. I saw the Krauts were about fifty to seventy-five yards from us, and I started firing my .45 pistol.
>
> Upon looking around, I realized that a new officer and I were the only ones left. We both had lost our communications, he to the Company CP and I to the outpost one hundred yards to the front.
>
> I asked the officer, "What's the story?"
>
> He answered, "We had better get our asses out of here!"
>
> We then started shooting at five or six Krauts coming along the ditch where our position was.
>
> The officer said, "Let's go!"
>
> We crawled back some distance and then got up and ran like hell to the edge of the woods, where the platoon was setting up a new line.
>
> Afterward, F Company counterattacked and retook the position.
>
> I lost my hearing for a few days due to a near miss.
>
> Sgt. Dale Roudebusch's squad was at the outpost, having relieved me there the night before. He withdrew his men along the tree-lined dirt road in good order. Frank Tofoya received the Bronze Star for his action on the outpost. He put down quite a few Germans with his machine gun.

Meanwhile, over in D Company, Lieutenant Sickler's Third Platoon was dug in to the right of E Company. Frank Haddy and Luis Arellano, a bazooka team, had their foxhole beside a small tree-lined road that led down the hill toward Germany.

Arellano was cleaning his rifle when the German artillery barrage started. He turned to his partner, Frank Haddy, and asked, "What does this mean?"

Haddy replied, "I think it means that in ten minutes we will either be dead or prisoners of war."

According to Bill McClure, D Company, the lead tank turned on a spotlight, which lit up the whole line of defense. Bill says, "I raised my M-1 and fired. The lights went out immediately."

A Mark IV Panther tank rolled up the road toward D Company's line. Frank Haddy and Luis Arellano loaded their bazooka, and Haddy waited for a good view of his target. "The barrel on that tank seemed a mile long," Frank claims. "At about ten yards we let her fly. The tank exploded and lit up the area like daylight."

Bill McClure claimed that Frank Haddy stood on the road bank next to the burning tank, and while tracer bullets were flying in all directions, Frank put one foot on the tank's track, beat on his chest, and yelled like Tarzan.

Haddy retorted, "Bill McClure lies like a rug."

The bazooka team of Haddy and Arellano reloaded and prepared for the next tank, which soon approached. They fired at a greater distance, hitting and damaging the second one but not disabling it. It backed off and rattled out of sight.

Frank Haddy was awarded the Silver Star for his action that night.

Later in the night, Lieutenant Sickler gathered some of his men, including Norb Studelska, behind the farmhouse, which Sickler used as his CP. The lieutenant informed the men that Krauts had broken through and a group of them were forming behind their position.

While Sickler was talking, George Thorne, a runner from D Company CP, staggered toward Sickler and his men, with a bullet hole through his stomach. His message from the company CP was "Hold at all cost!"

D Company held their ground.

At daybreak next morning, Bill McClure and Norb Studelska were sent on a detail to pick up C Rations at the company CP in the woods some distance behind their front line foxholes. Since he had to return carrying a case of C rations, McClure decided not to take his rifle. On the way back to the line with the case of rations on his shoulder, he came up on the rear of two Jerries in a foxhole behind a haystack. The German soldiers had their backs to Bill McClure and were looking around the other side of the haystack when he came upon their foxhole. The Krauts were armed with a machine gun, a rifle, and grenades.

McClure describes his reaction:

> I stood there with my C rations on my shoulder and no gun. I decided to kick one in the head and take the other with my hands. When I dropped the C ration box, they spun around. I jumped up to their foxhole, drew my foot back to kick, and they both fell backward and raised their hands. I made them get out of the hole. Then I took their weapons.
>
> About that time, my buddy got there. Norb had a rifle with a strap slung over his neck. He almost injured himself getting his rifle over his head. Both Germans dropped to their knees and started begging us not to shoot. I guess they had been told they would be killed if captured. Anyway, we took the prisoners to be questioned for information and to carry the C rations the rest of the distance.

A Dutch family lived in a small house right on the MLR of the Second Battalion. A few days before the battle, Capt. James Klein, an obstetrician in civilian life, helped deliver a baby boy in the home. That was a rare chance for the medical officer to practice his preferred specialty.

The morning after the battle, the family that had hidden in the cellar of their house during the fighting was forced to move to a refugee center. Lt. Walter Wakefield recalls seeing the family trudge up the hill with a few of their belongings. The mother was carrying her newborn son. Wakefield found an overcoat discarded by a wounded man and gave it to the mother. The mother, in turn, handed the baby to Wakefield to hold while she put on the coat. The lieutenant declared, "Just for a moment, I held a baby on a battlefield."

On a trip to Holland in 1971, Walter Wakefield located the family whose baby was born amidst the fighting in 1944. The father reported that the baby boy had grown to be a six-foot bricklayer and was out a-courting that evening.

Bill Giegold, F Company, and Clun Keys, D Company, hauled mortar shells for D Company's mortar men during the battle for Voxhil. Giegold identified the farmhouse at the mortar position as belonging to a Dutch farmer named Piet Langveldt. Bill had gotten to know Langveldt earlier when he borrowed a wagon and horses from the farmer to haul ammo. Many years later, Bill Giegold visited Holland and found the house. Langveldt was still living there.

Giegold and Langveldt talked about the night of the big battle. Giegold's partner, Clun Keys, was in the Langveldt barn attached to the house when a shell crashed through the roof and killed a cow right next to Keys. Pieces of tile from the roof rained down on Giegold, who was outside.

Langveldt had taken his parents to a safer area and was away during the battle but returned the next day and counted twenty-five dead Germans in front of his house.

Farmingdale, Long Island, New York, and the summer of 1958: the familiar bell of the Good Humor ice cream truck rang, and neighborhood people gathered around for some cool refreshments.

The friendly vendor announced to his customers, "This is my last trip on this truck. I have just been sworn in as an American citizen, and I am starting a better job tomorrow."

Benny Greco, E Company, offered his congratulations and inquired, "What country are you from?"

The question started a conversation in which Benny Greco learned that his ice cream man was from Germany. He had served in the German army and had fought with the Panzer division, which attacked Voxhil the night of October 1, 1944. Two former soldiers, who had opposed each other in deadly combat, were talking together as friendly neighbors fourteen years later.

A paraphrasing of "Beating swords into plow shares" might be "Men shall exchange their armored tanks for ice cream trucks" or "Send Pepsi Colas and Big Macs to Russia instead of ICBMs."

## New Boots

The 508th Parachute Infantry Regiment was composed of three battalions plus Headquarters Company and Service Company. Each battalion had three infantry line companies and a headquarters company (Headquarters First, Headquarter Second, and Headquarters Third). I was in the Demolition Platoon of Regimental Headquarters Company. In a stable combat situation, the Regimental Headquarters Company was positioned somewhat to the rear of the front-line troops. In the Regimental Headquarters Company were the command staff and four specialty platoons: the Intelligence Platoon (S-2), the Communication Platoon, the Bazooka Platoon, and the Demolition Platoon.

Several members of S-2 spoke German. Their duties took them on night patrols behind the enemy lines. Often their mission included bringing back a German prisoner for interrogation.

The Communication Platoon was responsible for telephone and radio communication. The Regimental Command Post (CP) needed instant contact with all the battalion CPs. The Regimental CP was equipped with a telephone switchboard with lines to every battalion CP. The lines were often broken, and the linemen repaired lines day and night.

Airborne troops did not have antitank heavy weapons used by regular infantry against armor but utilized bazookas to defend against tanks. A bazooka is a two-man rocket launcher. It is useful for paratroopers because of its portability. The Bazooka Platoon defended the Regimental CP against tank attacks. In the photo to the left, a bazooka is propped against the tree.

Frank Staple, with rifle and bazooka.
Photo provided by Frank Staples.

When the Demolition Platoon was not on special assignments, members often shared with the bazooka platoon the duty of guarding the perimeters of the Regimental CP. On one such occasion, Rosy Akins and I manned a 50-caliber machine gun at the edge of a turnip field. (Rosy was so called because of the perpetual bloom on his cheeks.)

The turnip field brought back childhood memories of Uncle Ross O'Dell's farm. I remembered visiting Uncle Ross's turnip field and pulling up turnips and peeling and eating the raw turnips in the field. I found a bit of back-home nostalgia eating the raw turnips in Holland.

Rosy and I were standing by our machine gun watching a dogfight overhead between an American airplane and a German airplane when suddenly the German plane started pouring smoke and plunged toward the turnip patch. We were expecting a crash, but when the plane was about twenty feet from the ground—so close to us we could see the pilot's brown leather helmet and goggles over his eyes—the pilot pulled out of his dive and roared over the treetops. By the time we realized what had happened, he was safely away from our machine gun, which remained unfired.

Sergeant Luczaj told us that from his vantage point, he saw the pilot parachute out of the plane just before the plane exploded. We were only a few miles from the German border. Luczaj believed the pilot landed in German territory.

A few days after the dogfight, Supply Sergeant J. O. Brown asked a group of us, "Anyone here need a new pair of boots?"

"Yes," I replied. "I lost a heel from one of my boots."

"What size do you wear?" counted the sergeant.

"Eight 4-E," I said.

Sergeant Brown threw the boots to me and declared, "You're in luck, just your size."

I asked, "Where did you get these boots?"

Brown explained the following:

> Rosy Akins had these extra boots in his pack. You know he was killed last night on patrol. We are sending his personal effects to the next-of-kin back home, but we are distributing useful gear to those who need it among the troops.

I thought, "How horrible. I'm in luck because Rosy is dead."

Yes, I wore Rosy's boots—mournfully, a constant reminder of the horrors of war.

## Duffle Bag Detail

Chris Christiansen was wounded in Normandy. He spent most of July and August in a military hospital in England. Meanwhile, the 508th went back to Wollaton Park in Nottingham. Replacements filled the ranks of the casualties of Normandy and preparations were being made for a new airborne operation.

By early September, Chris was well enough for a brief furlough from the hospital but not well enough for active duty, so Chris took leave to visit his buddies in Nottingham. He could tell by the activities that something big was going to happen. Everything was so secretive. No one knew exactly what to expect. Yet it was clear that another combat mission was imminent for the 508th.

One evening after training, the guys were speculating about their future combat role. Chris announced, "I am feeling so good now, I think I will tell Captain Abe that I am ready to return to the unit."

Rosy Akins replied, "Chris, come with me!"

Rosy proceeded to take Chris behind one of the tents.

"Why do you want me back here?" inquired Chris.

"I want to get you here away from the other guys. They might try to stop me, and I have a job to do," declared Rosy.

Rosy continued, "You think you are so damn fit that you can go back in combat. Well, I'm going to beat the hell out of you to make sure you won't do something foolish like getting released from the hospital too soon. When I finish with you, you will be glad to see the hospital again."

"Okay, I get the message. I know you are right. If I am not in peak condition, I may be more trouble than I am worth," Chris responded.

Soon Chris was released from the hospital and sent back to Wollaton Park. Only a few men were there—those like himself, recently recovered from combat wounds, and new replacements, who soon would be filling the slots of combat casualties.

Chris was given the job of going through the duffle bags of those killed in Holland and getting the personal effects ready to be sent back home to their families. One of the first bags he had to look through was Rosy Akins's.

## Chaplain Elder Calls "Medic!"

The medics and the chaplains were grouped together in the same unit and functioned as a team in the 508th. The chaplains sometimes helped evacuate the wounded at the battalion aid stations, and they were there to add a word of comfort and prayer as the medics applied their first aid and, on

Photo of Rosy Akins's grave.
Photo by Zig Boroughs.

occasions, to administer the last rites to the dying. When the urgency of medical needs subsided and the front was relatively quiet, the medics would assist the chaplains in transporting and setting up the equipment for religious services.

Chaplain Kenney (Catholic) and Chaplain Elder (Protestant) both jumped in the same stick with Medic Ed "Monty" Montgomery, September 17, 1944 in Holland. They landed on the Dutch side of the border near the German town of Wyler. The medics and the chaplains shared the same equipment bundle dropped by parachute in the middle of the stick. They gathered the religious and medical equipment from the bundle and assembled with other troops to a secure position where they inspected their material.

Monty heard the familiar call: "Medic!"

It was Chaplain Elder. The small portable pump organ used for services by both chaplains had suffered a ruptured bellows in the parachute drop. Monty responded by applying three rolls of adhesive tape to the damaged bellows, but he was unable to save this one. The organ had breathed its last note.

Soon a battalion aid station was set up in Dutch home. Monty noticed a pump organ in the home and requested the use of it for the chaplains. He personally signed an IOU, promising to take good care of the organ and return it to its owners when it was no longer needed for the troops.

The new organ played well but was large and cumbersome, and two men were required to load and unload it when moving to a worship service site. It hung out over the edge of the jeep trailer and had to be securely tied down. Medic Monty Montgomery traveled with Chaplain Elder and his assistant, David Oldemeyer, as they led the Red Devils in worship. Oldemeyer played the organ, and Montgomery helped with the organ-moving chores.

When the 508th was preparing to move out of Holland, Monty Montgomery personally returned the borrowed organ to its Dutch owner. You would naturally expect a Red Devil to honor his word as a good Christian.

## If the Tanks Don't Get You, the Goblins Will

Lt. Briand Beaudin, Medical Detachment Headquarters Third, remembered some scary events in Holland:

> After exiting the plane, I took out and cocked my .45 pistol. As I was oscillating downward, I realized that my peashooter was no match for the antiaircraft (AA) weapons aimed in my

direction, and I put the pistol away. I landed just outside the enclosure of the then-silent AA battery, and many enemy soldiers came toward me to surrender.

After assembling, the Third Battalion walked from the drop zone to Berg en Dal, where I set up an aid station in the home of a Nijmegen banker named Van Gorp. The banker's eldest son, Gerard, a member of the Dutch Underground Resistance, loaded me on the back of his motorcycle, and we went in search of a car. We appropriated an abandoned late-model Oldsmobile, which we were able to start by crossing wires under the steering wheel.

In returning from our forward aid station in Beek where we had help from Dutch nurses, Lieutenant Schools, my assistant surgeon, was driving the Olds when he took the wrong road and sped by our advance soldiers at a roadblock. On realizing this, we climbed an embankment to turn around, and the car stalled. We had some terrifying moments trying to restart it and escape back to our own lines.

Later on, I was seated in the front seat of a jeep used to pick up wounded. We were moving slowly atop a bank above the flats when suddenly we rounded the corner of a house and found ourselves facing the menacing big gun of a German tank.

My driver came to a complete stop, put the jeep in reverse, and shot back to the protection of the house then sped away while the tank guns were exploding with fury. The expert driver was so unnerved by this experience; he was unable to drive again and was assigned less stressful work.

Then there was the time I had walked and crawled forward to assess the combat situation concerning casualties. I had to hit the dirt because of incoming shells. I found myself behind a British tank and saw two British Tommies beneath it, calmly having their afternoon tea.

I have forgotten many things, but some things stand out, such as those eerie night creatures. On the move one night, we were startled to see many people completely in white aimlessly walking about in the woods. They were not ghosts, merely terrified occupants of the nearby insane asylum.

## Guilders and Milkers

"Are you sure you are strong enough for combat?" Captain Millsaps asked Cpl. Ed "Bogey" Boccafogli.

"Positive," Bogey replied.

B Company was doing a little early morning calisthenics, and the corporal had just returned from the hospital.

The truth of the matter was, Bogey's left arm and hand had not fully regained its strength after the wound he suffered in Normandy. It was even difficult for him to hold up the end of his rifle with his left arm and hand, but nevertheless he persuaded Millsaps that he was fit to fight. Anyhow, under fire, Boccafogli found that the strength returned to that hand very rapidly. It was also true that Bogey needed all the strength he could muster at Wyler, Germany, the second day after the 508th jumped into Holland.

As the Red Devils dug in on the edge of the German border town of Wyler, Boccafogli chose a spot next to a building along the roadside for his foxhole. He used two logs, which he arranged for a bulwark, and started digging his hole where one of the logs had been. Bogey's trenching tool hit something glass. It was a two-gallon-sized jar, and it was full of money. Bogey emptied the jar into his helmet. He called some of the guys over to his foxhole and showed them the treasure and gave each of his buddies a sampling of the coins and paper bills. The rest of the bills Bogey rolled up tightly and filled one of the side pockets of his jump pants.

Boccafogli was one of a three-man patrol sent to reconnoiter the German border town of Wyler. Bogey remembers that Lt. Edward Gleim and Private Mendez were also with him as they cautiously moved around and through the town. It gave Bogey an eerie feeling because everything was so quiet—not a person could be seen, not even a dog or a cat. It reminded Bogey of Pont Auny in Normandy, where Bogey was wounded.

After reporting to Captain Millsaps, Boccafogli was ordered to set up a roadblock on the other side of Wyler. Bogey and his men moved to the eastern side of the village and positioned themselves where the land dropped off toward the swamps and on a road that led into some woods where Jerries might hide. In support of the B Company roadblock was a .57mm antitank gun from the 80th Airborne AA Battalion. The .57mm was positioned up the hill behind the B Company group with their gun trained on the road toward the woods.

Darkness came on thick and heavy. The troopers at the roadblock strained their eyes into the blackness. Hours passed, and nothing happened. Then about dawn Bogey thought he heard the faint sound of a motor coming from the woods. He fixed the grenade launcher on the end of his M-1, loaded a grenade along with a blank cartridge in the rifle chamber, and waited. The corporal knew that the grenade would not stop an armored vehicle, but it would alert the .57 antitank gun behind him for action. The motor sound was coming from a truck loaded with German soldiers. When the truck came within range, Bogey fired the grenade. It fell short, but the .57 opened up and made a direct hit. Some Jerries were killed, but others fled from the truck and escaped.

With morning light, a large German force attacked B Company. The Jerries came streaming across the Wyler Meer, a swampy marshy area, and engaged B Company in a fierce firefight. German fire was tearing the town of Wyler apart.

Boccafogli's rifle had jammed when he fired the grenade. He tried desperately to get the ruptured shell out of the chamber of his rifle. His right hand was cut and bleeding from ramming the chamber lever with the heel of his hand. He was still trying to fix his rifle as the Germans entered Wyler. Bogey was huddled against the side of a church, holding his useless rifle, when three Germans came out of the church door. They could see him. He could not hide. His heart was racing, and he stopped breathing.

Quickly Bogey slammed the butt of his rifle on the ground, jumped up on the lever with his foot, and the full weight of his body was able to spring open the chamber. This action freed the chamber of the spent shell and immediately loaded a live bullet in its place. Just as quickly, the corporal raised his weapon to firing position and dropped one of the Jerries with his first shot. The other two Germans ran for cover.

During the firefight, Boccafogli and his squad moved through a barn at the edge of town, entered the front of the barn and out the back, crossed a road, and jumped a stone wall. Soon the German troops were in the barn firing at them. Then Pvt. Herbert Ellerbusch did a brave thing. He crawled up behind the wall to an open gate with his bazooka and fired. The rocket set the barn on fire. Ellerbusch had to expose himself in the open to get in position to hit the barn; as a result, Ellerbusch was mortally wounded. Boccafogli described the scene afterward:

Six or seven of the Jerries came out of the burning barn and surrendered. The other Germans in the barn ran back toward the rear of Wyler. Milton Mackey and I went over to Ellerbusch. He was lying in the mud, making a gurgling sound. A bullet had entered the left side of his chest and out the right side, making a clean deadly wound with little external bleeding but tearing up the vital parts inside. He didn't have long to live. Anyhow, I pulled him out of the mud and up onto some potatoes stored in a bin against the barnyard wall. Then I gave him a shot of morphine from his first aid packet. The family of Herbert Ellerbusch received the Bronze Star medal in honor of the heroic action of their fallen son.

After the barn burning, Boccafogli's squad was caught in the crossfire of German 88s and the British tanks, which had lined up on the ridge in support of B Company. Because they were so vulnerable to artillery, the company was ordered to withdraw to higher ground above Wyler that was more easily defended.

The withdrawal was accomplished that night under the cover of darkness. They moved five hundred yards uphill, with wounded troopers carried on ladders and doors using German POWs as litter bearers. The darkness was interrupted when the Germans fired incendiary bullets into haystacks, setting them on fire. The burning haystacks along with Jerry's machine gun and mortar fire lit up the area like New York's Times Square.

The next day, with a lull in the fighting, Boccafogli and another trooper gathered canteens from up and down the line and went toward the rear to fill them with water. Suddenly, as Bogey was returning with several canteens, Nazi planes came swooping down and strafed the line of British tanks and headed right toward him. The corporal was in the middle of a field with no cover in sight except two cows standing close together. He dropped the canteens and hurriedly got in between the two cows, crouching under their bodies and hugging their legs together.

About a week later Edward Boccafogli again found bovine protection. Bogey and Clyde "Big Mo" Moline were in the midst of dressing out a cow that had been appropriated without receipt near the German line when one of those big German blockbusters came thundering in close by.

"Those babies make a crater big enough to bury a boxcar," explains Bogey, "so I jumped right inside that carcass, blood and guts and all."

The British troops, who had arrived in the area, had booze to sell to the American paratroopers. Boccafogli, not knowing the value of the Dutch bills he had found earlier, offered a few guilders to a Tommy in exchange for booze. The English trader knew the value of the bills and supplied Bogey with enough booze for his whole company. The corporal shared the purchase with his buddies, making sure the officers were well supplied to stay on the safe side of the brass.

Toward the end of the Holland campaign, one or two from each unit of the 508th were given leave to spend forty-eight hours in Brussels. Cpl. Edward Boccafogli was one of those selected. The troopers were lodged in "La Hotel Grande," the one with the statue of the "Le Garcon Piss" out in front.

Among the rear echelon officers and men of the British and Canadian forces in the hotel, Boccafogli felt grubby in his combat uniform, which he had been wearing for six weeks without changing. "Those chaps looked like they really knew how to enjoy a war," observes Bogey, "with tea and crumpets twice daily."

Boccafogli was able to get a hot shower and a change of clean underwear but no new outer clothes. After the luxurious hot shower, Bogey went down to the hotel lobby and found a Canadian officer changing money into Belgian francs. Bogey had a couple of pounds he had on him when he left England, so he had that changed. Then he decided, "What the hell, let's see if this paper I found in the foxhole is any good."

The Dutch guilders were oversized notes, much longer and wider than ordinary currency. When Boccafogli pulled the huge wad of money from his pocket, the officer acted as if he were thinking, "What bank did you rob?"

Bogey laid one of those large notes on the table, and the officer counted out a big stack of Belgian notes in exchange.

Then Bogey went over to the bar to see how the Belgian notes would spend. He ordered a drink, laid one of the Belgian bills on the bar, and got back a stack of smaller bills in change. He said to himself, "This must be real good money, I think I will share it."

Good-hearted Bogey passed out money to all the paratroopers he could find in Brussels then gave away some to the elderly citizens living in the hotel who seemed to be on hard times. Maybe Boccafogli could have changed the guilders into dollars and sent the money home for a nice nest egg, but he said to himself, "I may not get home alive, so I might as well share this with my buddies who share life and death with me on the battlefields."

## An Airman in Nijmegen

"I was in Nijmegen. Hey, man, that was scary, those 88s! One almost got me," exclaimed Rupple Harley.

Capt. Rupple Harley from Orangeburg and Greenwood, South Carolina, was with the Ninth Troop Carrier Command. His unit was a part of the support group for airborne troops. He had been stationed in Fulbeck, England, at an airbase where some of the 508th took off in the Holland jump.

Harley explained that almost every night, the Germans bombed their airbase at Fulbeck. It was just like clockwork. Every night, about ten o'clock, alarms would sound and everyone would head to the underground air-raid shelters.

Then they moved to Aldermaster, which was worse than Fulbeck. At Aldermaster, they were directly in line with self-propelled rocket bombs called buzz bombs, which were targeted at London. When the buzz bombs fell short, they often fell on the Aldermaster air base.

Rupple Harley's duty consisted of working with parapacks, gliders, and C-47 troop carriers. Shortly after the Holland Operation Market Garden began, Harley was sent to Nijmegen to help recover gliders for future use.

The glider operation in Holland was very successful. About 950 gliders for the Eighty-second Airborne were air lifted, and over eight hundred landed safely in the general area of the landing zone (LZ). Many of the gliders could be used again with only minor repairs.

The LZ was near the German border and the Reichswald forest. A heavy concentration of German troops concealed their presence under the forest cover. It was high ground with a commanding view of the LZ.

Harley and his men unloaded their equipment at an airstrip near Nijmegen and moved by GI trucks to the LZ. There they erected a shop-tent and set up their equipment for work. Meanwhile, the Germans fired their 88s from the Reichswald at the airmen's tent. Each round was getting closer. Capt. Rupple Harley told his men, "Get ready and pull out of here. Those shells are coming too close for us to work here."

Harley then left to prepare to move to another location. He was about fifty meters from the tent when he heard another 88 whistle close by. He hit the ground, and about the same time, he heard the explosion. After recovering from the shock, he looked toward the tent and saw that the

88 had made a direct hit. Harley hurried back to the tent to check on his three men. He could only find bits and pieces of their mangled bodies.

## Center Stage under the Lights

The footbridge was over a canal with dikes on either side. It was known that the Germans were dug in on the other side behind the ridge of the dike. The colonel decided that the bridge should be mined to prevent the Germans from crossing.

Two demolitionists, Howard Brooks and Wilber Byers of Regimental Headquarters Company, were selected to plant the antipersonnel mines on the bridge. Harry Kennedy from S-2 was sent along to gather information on the activities of the enemy on the other side of the canal. A platoon of riflemen was added for strength and firepower if needed.

The patrol moved as quietly as possible in the darkness of night to the bank of the canal; however, the Germans must have heard suspicious sounds because they fired two or three rounds across the canal. The paratroopers hugged the ground and waited to see if any more shots were to be fired.

After a few minutes of silence, Brooks and Byers crept up on the bridge and selected a place to set their mines. Kennedy moved across the bridge until he came upon some German soldiers on the opposite dike.

"I don't know how Kennedy did it," Brooks exclaimed, "but when I looked up, I saw Harry was talking in German to a couple of Krauts soldiers, as if they were old friends."

Meanwhile, Brooks and Byers hurried to get the mines set up without being detected by the enemy. Brooks said, "I could just feel myself getting caught out on that bridge between the Germans on one side and our rifle platoon of paratroopers on the other and getting shot to pieces."

Fortunately neither side started shooting at each other, but then the Germans shot a parachute flare over the bridge that slowly flooded the bridge with light. "It made me feel as if I was on center stage under the lights," explained Brooks. "I thought the next thing would be the mortars."

Brooks explained that ever since the mortar barrage in Normandy, when men on both sides of him were blown to bits, mortars had terrified him. Brooks continued his story:

> I was so nervous under the flare that I couldn't release the safety on the mines. I had to get Byers to do it. After we finished, I wanted to get the hell off the bridge, but Harry Kennedy was still talking to the German soldiers on the other side. We waited an eternity, crouching low against the bridge,

waiting for the flare to go out, waiting for the mortars to come in, and waiting for Kennedy to stop talking to the Krauts so we could leave. Harry Kennedy didn't persuade any German soldiers to surrender, but we all got safely back to the American lines.

## Stalemate

The rain and mud of late October and early November reduced the fighting in Holland to a stalemate. The troops of the 508th manned outposts and went on patrols to maintain knowledge of enemy activities and exchanged frequent artillery fire with the Germans. Otherwise, there was more time for noncombative activities.

Some time was spent in improving the foxholes to keep out rain and to make them as warm and comfortable as possible. I cannot remember being in a building from our jump date, September 17 until November 9, while in Holland. All that time we lived in the open. How did we manage? GI soldiers make foxholes. In a letter to my mother, dated October 9, 1944, I described my foxhole:

Cartoon by Kate Salley Palmer.

I am writing from my foxhole. It is a comfortable hole—about 5 feet deep, 2 feet wide, and 6 feet long. I have a wood, tobacco leaf and earth roof, a small opening and a step at the entrance, covered by my tent half. The floor is covered with six inches of straw for easy resting. I am quick to acknowledge that most of the credit for such a cozy home belongs to the one that dwelled here before me, a Canadian soldier. We are living in an orchard of apple and pear trees. The farmer had planted tobacco plants between the rows of trees. The Canadian soldier had torn up apple crates, which he placed on top of the hole, then covered the cracks with tobacco leaves, and placed dirt of top of that.

Men of Regimental Headquarters Company used their expertise to add luxury to their foxhole environment. Steve Schmelick, lineman in Communications Platoon, wired several foxholes with radio headsets connected to Axis Sally. I was lucky enough to have Axis Sally piped into my foxhole. She came on the air with her sexy voice announcing American hit songs such as Glen Miller's "In the Mood" and Bing Crosby's "I'm Dreaming of a White Christmas" and the universally popular German song "Lili Marlene."

Axis Sally told us that while we GIs were suffering in the miserable cold and mud, the American prisoners of war were enjoying good food and comfortable living quarters. She promised us a better chance to be home by Christmas if we came over to the German lines with a white flag of surrender.

Matthew Bellucci and Dick Nelson from Demolition Platoon rigged up a gasoline generator and a light bulb for their foxhole. No one was able to improvise indoor plumbing, but Bugs Cehrobak came close to it. To avoid leaving his cozy foxhole in foul weather to urinate, Bugs kept a supply of condoms. He would fill a condom and sail it out of his foxhole to land where it hit. One day, when another trooper was walking close by Cehrobak's hole, a full rubber came flying out into the branches of an apple tree. The bladder burst and spilled its contents on the unsuspecting trooper. That trooper used his repertoire of profane language to the fullest.

Germans facing the Allied lines were also struggling to make life bearable. Stanley Kass, a demolitionist, recalled a time when comfort was more important to the enemy than killing Americans. The Jerries had an artillery piece that was inflicting casualties on our forces, and the Allied artillery was unable to knock it out. This gun was well protected inside a reinforced concrete structure, and the 508th command decided that a demolition team was needed to blow up the whole structure. Stanley Kass was part of that team. Kass and the others blacked their faces and carefully approached the gun emplacement. They planted their explosives, returned over the same route and, from a safe distance, set off the charge. The bothersome gun was silenced.

A few days later, one of the S-2 troopers who had been interrogating German prisoners told Kass about the German spider hole. (A spider hole is a foxhole, which has a smaller opening and is more carefully camouflaged to blend into the natural surroundings.) The two Jerries had a very comfortable spider hole out in front of the gun emplacement. They observed the patrol coming and going. The Jerries said, "We could have killed everyone on that patrol. They walked right over us twice."

When asked why they had refrained, the Jerries responded, "We wanted a good night's sleep."

On another occasion, B Company's Sgt. Mickey Nichols (a.k.a. Mickey Niklauski) was on a four-man night patrol. Lieutenant Cross, a former sergeant with battlefield commission, and Bill Windom were with him. (Bill Windom became a Hollywood actor who plays in "Murder She Wrote.") Upon arriving at a dike, Mickey crossed the canal on a narrow makeshift board. The other members of the patrol remained on the near side.

The first thing the sergeant saw was a Jerry lying under a blanket fast asleep. Nichols placed his trench knife on the sleeper's throat with the idea of quietly taking him across the canal as a prisoner. The cold steel awakened the soldier with some bluster, which in turn alerted other German soldiers.

Fearing he would never be able to get his prisoner safely across the narrow footboard, Mickey abandoned the project and made a quick dash back to the other side. "Crossing to the dike was almost like running on water when the Germans started firing at me," Mickey remembered.

On the other side of the dike, Mickey lost a shoe in the mire amid a hail of bullets and just kept on running to a nearby barn. Mickey scrounged around in the barn looking for something to replace his lost boot. In a pile of debris, he found a pair of discarded work shoes. Mickey appropriated one of them, which he used until a new pair of boots was available.

Ed Boccafogli was on outpost in a drainage ditch along side the canal. Captain Millsaps had send Bogey with a telephone and roll of wire through the marshy flatland to listen for German activity on the other side of the canal and report by phone. He had heard Germans talking and even heard someone whistling "Lili Marlene." Then he heard shooting and reported it by phone. Millsaps asked Bogey to investigate the shooting.

Bogey left the phone with his assistant and moved toward the shooting, bending below the top of the weeds until he found Bill Windom helping the lieutenant, who was wounded. Boccafogli returned to the phone and made his report to Millsaps. Millsaps sent another trooper with a shelter half and ordered them to roll up the wire and come back in with the wounded man. They used the shelter half as a stretcher for the wounded Lieutenant Cross.

Sometimes, the 508th Red Devils were tempted to appropriate good Dutch meat on the hoof, which wandered through their area. The regimental commands issued strict orders against killing local livestock, with some exceptions allowed for animals injured from shells and were beyond recovery. Also, the owner needed to give consent and be compensated.

Harry Roll, H Company, remembered when a pig wandered into H Company area. Donald Veach aimed at the pig, but the pig kept turning his head. Impatient bystanders urged him to go ahead and shoot, but Veach replied, "I have to get the squeal with the first shot."

Veach, an expert with both rifle and slaughtering, killed the pig in the proper manner, and Ralph Busson hung it up from a tree and gutted it. Colonel Shanley came by and saw the dressed-out porker hanging from the tree and its head nearby. He asked, "Where did you get the beef?"

Colonel Shanley admitted, "My West Point training has failed me. I can't distinguish between the carcasses of beef and pork."

Ralph Busson had started something, which became a tradition on his farm in Ohio—an annual pig roast for H Company.

Virgil "Mick" McGuire of Regimental Headquarters Company became restless during the long period of stagnation when the 508th was attached to the British 231st Brigade north of the Waal River near Bemmel. McGuire, who had served Colonel Harrison and Colonel Alexander as an advanced scout in Normandy, decided to do some private scouting.

McGuire had learned that between Allied and German lines was a building, which had served as a winery. Mick and two of his buddies held a staff meeting to discuss the progress of the war and to plan strategies for the next operation. The triumvirate decided that since intelligence indicated a continued holding position for some time that supplies needed to be stockpiled for the long rainy nights and muddy days. Mick observed, "As the nights get colder, we will be needing antifreeze."

Plans were made, and just before dusk, the three arrived at the winery, having successfully slipped by the GI outposts. They selected seven bottles of the best wine and strapped it on McGuire under his jacket, fastening his belt tightly to prevent any of the bottles from falling out.

They were able to get back through the GI lines again without getting shot. The next obstacle was to get back to their foxholes at Regimental Headquarters Company without being apprehended. The command had warned the soldiers of possible court-martial and heavy fines for looting.

About a half mile from their assigned area, a British jeep, with driver and sergeant, gave the three GIs a ride in the back seat. The driver drove like wild, hitting bumps without slowing down and bouncing his riders about in their seats.

When they arrived at the turnoff place, Mick, being afraid he would break one of the bottles strapped to his body, said, "Would you guys give me a hand? I can't move."

Mickey's buddies were very solicitous, saying, "Now, you be careful, let us help you." They practically lifted McGuire out of the jeep to protect their cargo.

This brought on apologies from the English driver. "The poor chap is wounded and never said a word. If you had just told me, I would have driven more carefully."

For fear of revealing their secret, they continued the charade, partially supporting Mick as they walked away. They even managed to keep from laughing until the British were out of sight.

## College Talk

Members of the Demolition Platoon had to take turns at an outpost at the front of the regimental main line of resistance (MLR). The outpost was used as a listening and viewing observation post (OP). Until the weather was more favorable for troop movements, the Allied command had decided to hold the line in Holland that we occupied at that time. It was important, however, for our defense to be alert to enemy movements. In case the phone lines were cut, a radio operator from the Communications Platoon was always at the OP to report any German activities, which were seen or heard. Demolitionists were used as riflemen for extra security at the OP.

Radio operator Fred Knight spent a lot of time at the OP. Fred said it was very nerve-racking because it was so close to the German lines. Fred said, "If you stuck your head above the foxhole, you might by chance see one of the Germans looking at you. We knew where the Germans were, and we knew that they knew where we were—very nerve-racking."

Upon being relieved and returning to the company bivouac area, I gave directions to Little Car Austin who, with a partner, would be taking their turn at the outpost later. I had used the word *diagonally*. My instructions were, "Go the corner of the fence, and from the corner go diagonally across the pasture."

Little Car had an excellent command of profane English, but he thought diagonally meant to follow the fence line. I had been to the outpost in daylight, but Little Car's tour came after dark. Little Car and his partner went to the corner of the pasture then followed the fence until they could hear talking in the distance. They stopped and listened carefully—definitely not English, it had to be German. They retraced their steps and got directions in "plain damn English."

The next time I saw Little Car, he let me have some of his style of English—not the kind spoken in Sunday school. His final summation was, "I could understand that (expletive deleted) German I heard last night better than your (double expletive deleted) college talk!"

### "Where's the Meat?"

Lieutenant Hardwick explained the new rules to the Regimental Headquarters Demolition Platoon. "It's not a joke. Fines taken out of your pay will be strictly enforced—$50 for killing a cow, $25 for killing a chicken. Got it?"

"Yes, sir! Yes, sir!" was the obedient reply of the members of the Demolition Platoon.

When Hardwick left the group, platoon members conspired to keep the meat from being seen by an officer. The cow had shrapnel wound in her side. After all, they kill horses when they break a leg, and the wound may not heal. It will be a merciful act to put the cow out of her misery. Nevertheless, Brooks had a difficult time pulling the trigger because the cow looked at him with her big mournful eyes as if to infer, "Please don't kill me!"

Wilber "Moto" Byers was the chief butcher. Having been raised on a farm, he had experience in dressing beef and locating the best cuts for roasts and steaks. For a while, the demolitionists were living "high on the hog."

Lieutenant Hardwick (the Ripper) had the reputation of being tough about the essentials. If the men did not keep their weapons clean and battle ready, he could be rough with them. He also had the reputation of being lax about nonessential regulations. We considered him a leader whom we could depend on to help keep us alive. He did not insist on following every little regulation passed down from the military brass.

Chris Christiansen told about how the Ripper chewed him out for losing the grenade for his grenade launcher when it was needed in battle. Then, only a few minutes later, when Chris was wounded, the Ripper braved enemy fire to get to him to give assistance and comfort. We were proud to have Lieutenant Hardwick as our leader.

A few days after Hardwick passed on the orders about killing farm animals, he demanded, "Okay, guys, where is the meat?"

A chorus of replies answered, "Meat? What meat, sir? We don't have any meat!"

"Damn it, men," declared the Ripper. "I'm hungry. Where is the meat?"

## The Apple Polisher

During our last weeks in Holland, when it rained almost every day, there was very little combat action, but the military was active in a different way.

Word came through that visitors were coming to the Regimental CP: General Horrocks, CO of the British Thirtieth Corps; General Dempsey, CO of the British Second Army; along with General Gavin, CO of the Eighty-second Airborne. We had orders to spruce up and look sharp, shave our beards of several weeks' growth, etc.

One day a tremendous tent was unloaded at the CP. Members of our Demolition Platoon were called upon to put up the tent. The tent was about twenty-five feet long. Two central poles about fifteen feet high supported it. In order to erect and peg down the huge tent, our men had to struggle with the unfamiliar structure, heaving and pulling and slipping in the mud accompanied by generous quantities of profane utterances.

The tent became the officers' latrine. We enlisted men had to dig individual slit trenches for our defecation, but the officers at the Regimental CP could now take care of their toilet activities in relative luxury. Our platoon had to prepare the conveniences for the officers' latrine, digging the pits and installing the two-hole boxes over the pits. After taking part in the preparation of the officers' latrine, my normal happy disposition was rankled every time I had to lower my pants over a straddle trench in the rain and the mud.

The orchard in which our foxholes were dug was barren of fruit. I never remember eating an apple during those rainy weeks, but I did run across a first sergeant with a bucket full of apples.

Cartoon by Kate Salley Palmer.

The Apple Polisher

This sergeant was a replacement who came to the regiment after Normandy the same time I did. The army had appealed to other units in the army for volunteers for the paratroopers. Under the program, men were promised to retain their rank if they volunteered. Then they were given abbreviated jump training in England.

This policy gave us many noncommissioned officers (noncoms) without combat experience. It also prevented the promotion of men who were assigned leadership positions based on their combat experience. It was also difficult to find jobs for some of the new high-ranking enlisted men worthy of their rank. This particular first sergeant was assigned to Colonel Lindquist as a sort of manservant.

Indeed, this sergeant became a devoted servant to the colonel. He had been foraging orchards in the countryside and found a bucket full of apples. I came across him sitting under a tree rubbing an apple with a cloth. I asked, "Sergeant, what are you doing with those apples?"

The sergeant replied, "Polishing them for Colonel Lindquist." I had heard of "apple polishing" in the military but had never before witnessed a literal performance.

## Payday in Guilders

Members of my section stopped over in Nijmegen for two days before leaving Holland. We had been out in the weather, the mud, and the rain for so long that the warm dry Dutch home with flush toilet was next to heaven. I was sick with the flu. I had all those symptoms, which modern over-the-counter remedies are supposed to cure when administered by the tender hands of a loving wife. I fixed myself a warm pallet on the floor and slept those two days and nights and got rid of my malady.

During those two days and nights I was mostly asleep, but my mind kept going in and out of conscious awareness of what was going on about me. For one thing, we were paid in Dutch guilders, and immediately a rip-roaring poker game started and continued day and night until one paratrooper had almost all the earnings of his fellow gamblers.

Since the odds of surviving the war as a paratrooper were not too high, I think the same risk-taking characteristics that prompted soldiers to volunteer for the paratroopers carried over to their gambling behavior. Not all the gamblers played with reckless abandon, however; some were shrewd and calculating. One trooper told me that he had a nest egg at home of over $10,000 from gambling earnings. The first thing he would do after winning big was to send the money home, otherwise those he had cleaned out would try to borrow from him until next payday.

Another thing that aroused my slumber to a conscious state was the "accidentally on purpose" shooting that occurred. I think it was an accident, but because the front-line miseries had gotten to the stage that many a soldier would love to have a minor wound in order to get evacuated, some of his buddies claimed he shot himself in the foot on purpose. He was evacuated, but then we were all evacuated from the front two days later. I think it was an accident.

One trooper in our platoon had been evacuated to an English hospital from Holland for a few weeks because of a sinus infection. When he came back to the unit, he bragged about how much better it was to be in England in the fall compared to the summer. In the summer, the days were so long that we had to check back into camp before it got dark. In the fall, the nights were twelve to fifteen hours long compared to the four to eight hours in the summer. The point was that the English girls were much more cooperative on dark nights than they were in the light of day.

I couldn't resist teasing my friend by quoting the scripture verse, "Men love darkness rather than light because their deeds are evil."

## Why Some Nurses Wore Paratrooper Boots

The 508th Red Devils were evacuated from Holland on November 11, 1944, the anniversary of World War I Armistice Day. From the mud and rain of the flats of Bemmel, the regiment moved into comfortable French Army barracks at Camp Sissonne, France, near the city of Reims.

Some of the Red Devils, those wounded in actions, were in various hospitals in England. When the wounded from the Eighty-second Airborne Division recovered from their wounds, they were returned to their former bases in England. The 508th maintained a small service force in Wollaton Park in Nottingham. The other regiments in the division maintained their bases in other English cities.

Lt. Margaret Barrett, an army nurse, told of her experience with Eighty-second Airborne paratroopers. Barrett served in the US Army 163rd General Hospital, Nocton-Dunston Village, Lincolnshire. The nurses in England were getting their share of mud and rain, much like what the front line troops experienced in Holland. Lieutenant Barrett recalled sloshing around in her US Army GI boots, which she describes as made of leather turned inside out. Those boots leaked like a sieve and were the ugliest footwear the army could have dreamed of putting on nurses.

The 163rd General Hospital consisted of four rows of wooden buildings. When more space was needed, two or three tents were pitched to the rear of each of the wooden buildings. The tents had dirt floors. Around the tents, it was especially muddy. A pot-bellied stove in the middle of each room and in each tent heated the facilities. The nurses had to walk to the hospital, which was about a mile from their quarters in Nocton Hall. While they were on duty, the nurses' feet usually stayed wet all day, or all night, as the case may be.

One day a patient who was a sergeant from the Eighty-second Airborne Division asked Nurse Barrett, "What size boots do you wear?"

Barrett answered, "Size seven."

"I have an idea," the sergeant announced. "Most of you nurses have small feet, like between size five and size seven. We have received a shipment of paratrooper boots with lots of small sizes under eight, too small for most of our paratroopers. Let me see if I can get some of those surplus small sizes for you nurses."

After the sergeant was released from the hospital, he returned as he had promised, bringing the nurses paratrooper boots. Lieutenant Barrett said that when she wore her new boots in the hospital, Eighty-second patients would say, "Let me polish your boots like they ought to be polished."

The paratroopers not only furnished her boots; they also kept them polished parade perfect and waterproof. Those paratroopers knew how to finagle a good back rub.

# Chapter 7

# Camp Sissonne

### The Parade

We left Holland on November 11, the celebrated date of the Armistice that ended the fighting for World War I. The 508th had a brief respite from combat until we were aroused from our bunks on the evening of December 17 to be trucked into Belgium to the Battle of the Bulge. Our new home was Camp Sissonne, near Reims. We lived in old French Army barracks. Our quarters were very comfortable compared to the unsheltered battlefield conditions in Holland or the tents which were our billets in Nottingham, England.

While in Sissonne, Regimental Headquarters Company organized a football game played without pads and also played without adjusting the rules for the lack of protective equipment. I leaped high into the air and caught a pass, and while still airborne, Frank Sakowski plowed his shoulder into my ribs and bounced me against the hard ground, nose first. (Frank later played for the 508th football team, which won the military football championship in Frankfurt, Germany.)

When I gathered myself together, I tried to relieve the congested feeling developing in my nose with a vigorous blowing, which caused my right eye to close. Such an unusual phenomenon called for an investigation. Our local medics sent me to a large hospital at Reims for observation and treatment.

My case was "diag-*nosed*" as a broken nose bone, which ruptured a thin membrane between the air passage of the right nostril and the right eye. The swelling under my eye would subside until I blew my nose again, which I soon learned not to do. In a few days, I was back to normal and was sent back to Camp Sissonne.

While at Camp Sissonne, two famous celebrities came to visit the troops and raise our morale, the actress Marlene Dietrich and the New York Giants baseball player Mel Ott. That meant we had to get our dress uniforms pressed and boots shined and practice close-order drill for a parade.

In my youthful experience, I had never seen a real live movie actress or a big league baseball player, but I did get a once-in-a-lifetime opportunity. Ms. Marlene Dietrich and Mr. Mel Ott were standing on either side of Colonel Lindquist on the reviewing stand. It was just a fleeting glance, however, between the commands "Eyes right!" and "Eyes front!"

## Sewing Paratroopers

Perhaps it may seem incongruous, but when I returned from the Reims hospital to Camp Sissone, a sewing machine was set up in the middle of our squad room. One of the troopers had established a thriving sewing business. It started with the parachute material brought back from Holland.

After the British passed through Nijmegen with their tanks, we were moved to a section where supplies were dropped by parachute, and a lot of parachutes were scattered around the area. We discovered that the nylon material from the parachutes kept us warmer at night than our GI blankets. Also the material could be folded up in compressed small bundles and took up little room in our packs. So almost everyone in our company had parachute material among our gear.

I had some of my nylon made into a neat triangle with white nylon on one side and camouflage nylon on the other. It was decorated with an airborne emblem in the point of the triangle. I sent the scarf home as a Christmas present to my wife.

The nylon cords, which were attached to the harness of parachute, were used for bootlaces—white for dress up and camouflage for every day. The old narrow black ties were replaced with white nylon cravats worn underneath open-neck shirts and bloused up and out in front.

Our paratrooper tailor progressed from nylon accessories to tailored Eisenhower jackets. The regulation blouse or jacket fit tight to the waist and then had a split tail that extended over the hips, very much like a civilian suit. General Eisenhower changed his dress blouse to a short jacket, and if the general could alter his uniform, why couldn't the paratroopers? Soon the troopers were turning dress blouses into Eisenhower jackets.

One reason the guys were dressing up so much was that passes were being given to Reims and, in some cases, to Paris. Personally, I never left the camp except for my brief stay in the hospital from my football injury. Most of the talk about going to Reims and other places was about getting drunk and visiting the whorehouses. Neither of those activities appealed to me.

One of the first times the Eighty-second Airborne troops had passes to Reims, the line at one whorehouse was so long that an impatient trooper had such a burning desire that he set the whorehouse on fire. For some time after that, passes to Reims were denied. In order to satisfy the sexual cravings of the paratroopers, the Airborne command set up a brothel right outside Camp Sissonne, which was supervised by the US Army Medics.

Since the demand was greater than the supply, troopers had to wait their turn. The building that housed the establishment was described to me as having a large open room downstairs, where beer and wine were sold, and rooms for girls and their customers upstairs. The girls would parade downstairs to receive their next customer. The troopers, waiting their turns, were seated on benches around the walls of the beer parlor. One young trooper, who was slowly working his way to the front of the line, looked the girls over as they came down the stairs for their next partner. The closer he got to the front of the line, the worse the girls looked to him. Some had their heads shaved—that marked them as collaborators with the Germans. (As French patriots were liberated, they caught those women who patronized the Nazis and shaved their heads.) Finally, in disgust, the trooper gave up and decided to leave.

The army had set up a prophylactic station, and no soldier was allowed to leave the building without a "pro." As the trooper tried to leave, the medics demanded, "Come in this room and take a pro!"

"But I didn't do anything," protested the trooper.

"We've heard that before. The next time we see you, you will tell us you caught the clap from a toilet seat."

So the paratrooper was forced to take the prophylactic treatment.

Venereal diseases had a debilitating effect on the army's readiness for battle. Every time a soldier left the camp, he was a potential victim. As a precaution, whenever a soldier went to the Orderly Room for a pass, he was automatically given several condoms.

With an oversupply of condoms, troopers discovered a practical use for the surplus. Instead of stuffing the bottoms of our pant legs into the top of our boots, we tied a condom around each boot and neatly tucked the trousers legs up and under and then bloused them over.

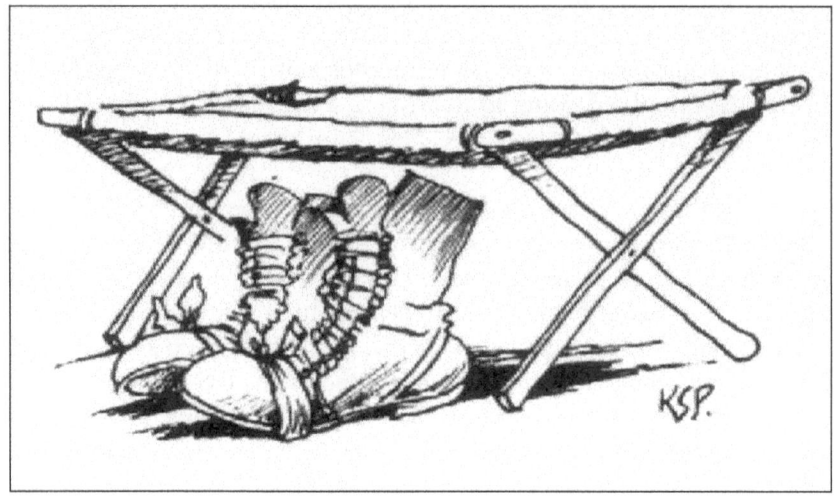

Paratrooper boots with condom for blousing pants legs.
Cartoon by Kate Salley Palmer.

## Tell it to the Chaplain

If someone made a nuisance of themselves talking about their troubles in the paratroopers they were often told, "Blow it out your barracks bag!" or in a similar tone of voice, "Go tell it to the chaplain!"

Mary wrote me that, according to her doctor's prediction, the birth of our first child would occur on or about December 10. I did not think that we were doing anything important at Camp Sissonne during the early days of December. I nursed the hope that it might be possible for me to catch a ride on a military plane to Donaldson Airfield in Greenville, South Carolina, so I could be at home for the birth of our "son." My friends advised me to forget that idea. Nevertheless, I decided to look up Chaplain Elder and tell it to him.

Chaplain James Lyn Elder.
Copied from 1943 Company picture.

Chaplain Elder's office was in one of those military 10×10 tents with a pyramid top. I found him very busy at a small table typing away. I remained silent, not to disturb his work but made sure he saw me hanging around. He looked up and saw me but continued typing. Finally he stopped and reread what he had typed before asking, "What can I do for you?"

320

After presenting my request to Chaplain Elder, he told me something like this:

> My first priority, right now, is to write letters to the families of our men who were killed in action, and I don't have time to try to help you go home for the birth of your baby, even if the request were justified. I can tell you that we are under-strength now, and we need every man we have. Who knows when the regiment will be in combat again? By the way, do you like to sing?

The chaplain did take the time to inform me of the opportunities of the week: I could join the Eighty-second Airborne Chorus, which would be presenting a program of Christmas music the next Sunday night, and also I was welcome to attend the Wednesday-night Bible study. Below is a letter that I wrote my mother on December 17, 1944, from Camp Sissonne:

> Dear Mother,
> Received a Christmas card from you yesterday while on KP. One of the boys, Bellucci by name, brought me seven letters from Mary, one from you and one from Pop while I was bending over the sink washing pots and pans. I quit work to read my mail and was ordered to recommence, but I told the cook he would have to wait, which provoked him to anger and the use of profane language.
> This has been a very busy week for me, but I was glad to have something to do besides sweating out the birth of a son. I was on KP two days—once for Bob Lane, who paid me 825 francs ($16.50 in greenbacks). I went to school on gas warfare one day. We practiced basketball every morning. The divisional chorus and regimental octet consumed five nights practicing. Then there was the Bible class on Wednesday evening and chorus performance tonight, Sunday.
> Goodnight.
>
> Love,
> Zig

I wrote the above letter and put it in the company mailbox before going to bed that night of December 17, 1944, knowing nothing of the German breakthrough of December 16 on the Belgium front. Within an hour, our sergeants were awakening the sleepers, distributing arms and equipment, and hustling us into transport trucks headed toward Belgium.

Chaplain Elder performed a much-greater service writing letters to the bereaved families of my fallen comrades than he would have in a useless effort trying to send me home for the birth of what turned out to be a lovely daughter. William C. Nation has allowed me to copy a letter Chaplain Elder wrote to his grandmother on behalf of his uncle Capt. William H. Nation, who was killed later in the Battle of the Bulge:

CHAPLAIN'S OFFICE
508th Prcht. Inf.
APO 230, New York

March 19, 1995

Mrs. E. G. Nation
Arlington, Texas

My dear Mrs. Nation,

It is part of a Chaplain's Ministry to write to the families of the men of his regiment who die in combat. In these days thousands of such letters are written. However, I shall never write such a letter with as deep feeling as I do this one. Captain Nation was your son but to me he was a close personal friend and a continuing inspiration. As his mother, you feel the deepest grief but I want to assure you that everyone who knew him feels a grief just as genuine.

Bill was killed instantly. His death was simultaneous with his injury. If he had to go, there could have been no easier way. His body is buried in one of our cemeteries. In time you will be notified of the exact location of his grave. His personal belongings will be handled in accordance with your requests.

From the manner of his life, Mrs. Nation, I know that he must have had fine Christian parents. The greatest compliment I can pay him would be to wish that every officer in the regiment had a character like his.

May God grant you strength and peace to help bear the loss of your son.

Very sincerely yours.

JAMES L. ELDER
Chaplain

Capt. William H. Nation. Letter to family and photo courtesy of Bill C. Nation.

The last time I talked with Chaplain Elder was at the 1989 508th reunion in Portland, Oregon. He had retired from Golden Gate Baptist Seminary as a professor, but he was active as a volunteer, helping families who were grieving after losing a loved one.

# CHAPTER 8

# The Deep Freeze

### Rest Cure Prescription by First Sergeant Jim Smith

Sgt. James Kurz, B Company, arrived by train in Camp Sissonne at 0430 hours the morning of December 18, 1944. Kurz, having recovered from wounds received in Holland, reported to First Sergeant James Smith and announced to Smith that the doctor had ordered two weeks of rest for him before heavy duty. Many of the Red Devils who were wounded in Normandy and Holland had recovered from their wounds enough to rejoin the regiment. A large number of these veterans, fresh out of the military hospitals, arrived at Camp Sissonne by train on that fateful December morning.

The Red Devils were aroused from their bunks during the night and told to get ready immediately to move out. The Germans had overrun the American lines on the border of Belgium and Germany. General Eisenhower had called on his best troops to stem the tide. All during the dark morning hours of December 18, the troops were getting ready and the trucks were lining up to haul them away.

When Kurz announced to First Sergeant Smith that he was slated for light duty, Smith answered, "You can rest when we get to Belgium. Right now go check out a rifle and a blanket and load up on one of those trucks with your squad."

By 0600 Jim Kurz was rolling across France toward the Belgium border. Jim remembers turning north following the sign toward Liege. Another sign at that crossing pointed east toward Bastogne. Only dim blackout lights were used on the trucks after dark, and during the night, the trucks were traveling over steep mountain roads with sharp curves. The truck behind Kurz's didn't make one curve, and he watched the tiny blackout lights go down the mountainside. Several from B Company were injured on that wayward truck. Among those injured were Philip Klinefelter, James O. Peek, and Paul Atwood.

Peek recalls his experience. "Just outside of Werbomont, the Germans started shelling us. The driver got scared, turned the wheels on the truck, and rolled it over on twenty-eight of us."

The truck behind the wrecked truck stopped; the troopers unloaded and helped remove the injured. Milton Mackey was one of those helping the injured. James Peek had been unconscious but came to while someone was pulling him from the wreckage. He heard the man say, "Here's another one, but I think he's dead."

Peek was treated for his injuries in four hospitals, located in four countries: Belgium, Luxembourg, France, and Wales. If he had been well and fit, it would have made an interesting travel itinerary.

The other trucks continued on to Werbomont, Belgium, arriving early in the morning of December 19. On December 20, B Company was moved to the main line of resistance (MLR) west of the Salm River and across the river from Vielsalm.

On December 16, the Germans had broken through the thin line of defense about twenty-five miles east and, with lightning speed, drove about seventy miles deep into Belgium, forming what was known as the Belgian Bulge. Resistance by the 106th Infantry Division and the Seventh Armored Division had slowed the German advance on the northern shoulder of the Bulge, which allowed the Eighty-second Airborne Division time to set up a defense line through which the 106th Infantry and the Seventh Armored could make an orderly withdrawal.

The Germans had the advantage of cloud cover for a week after their breakthrough, but on December 23, the sun came out and Jim Kurz witnessed a tremendous air show over his position. Over one thousand Allied planes, bombers, and their fighter protection passed overhead toward Germany. These were met by German fighters, and in the dogfight that followed, Kurz saw many planes fall to the ground and many parachutes float down over German-held territory. Then in a split second, German planes swooped in low, strafing and bombing the B Company position. Jim remembered, "It seemed as if all the bombs and bullets were headed straight for me."

Sergeant Kurz was ordered to take twelve men and relieve the roadblock at the bridge over the Salm River at Vielsalm. The Seventh Armored and 106th Infantry were withdrawing over this bridge. During training days in the States, members of the 508th and the Seventh Armored had a rivalry that often broke out into bar fights, but on this occasion, nothing but friendly banter was exchanged between the paratroopers and tank-troopers.

During the afternoon of December 24, sergeants of the four platoons in B Company were called together by Captain Millsaps. He explained the planned withdrawal to a new MLR. One platoon would be selected to stay on line as a rear guard. The sergeants drew lots, and Sergeant Boccafogli drew the longest stick, so Boccafogli's platoon had to stay to defend the line formerly manned by all of B Company. The rest of B Company pulled back about eight miles to the new MLR.

James Kurz recalls, "No one could understand why we were withdrawing."

Captain Millsaps explained, "General Gavin had his orders from General Ridgway that we were sticking out like a sore finger into the German lines and could easily be cut off from behind."

Kurz described his baggage on the eight-mile forced march that beautiful clear moonlit Christmas Eve. "I carried two extra boxes of .30-caliber machine gun ammo, a pistol, an M-1 rifle and ammo, several grenades, and I filled all the pockets of my jump suit with food."

The march was exhausting to Kurz, not many weeks out of the hospital and on First Sergeant Smith's "two-weeks-rest cure." In his account of the ordeal, Kurz lists several reasons he almost collapsed at the end of the march, such as carrying so much stuff, climbing hilly terrain, and walking through snow.

For those who were dreaming of a white Christmas, the scene Christmas morning, 1944, with the 508th in Belgium, was a dream come true. Jim Kurz described the scene. "As far as you could see were undisturbed white fields and evergreen trees draped in white. God had done a great job decorating."

Christmas Day was quiet, but by 2200 hours that night, the Jerries had caught up and attacked the B Company's outpost about four hundred yards in front of the MLR. The outpost was driven in, and a firefight continued for about three hours.

The next day, Lieutenant Gleim asked Sergeant Kurz to take twelve men on a combat patrol across an open field to the woods from which the Germans had attacked on Christmas night. His mission was to draw fire from any Germans that might still be in the woods. If any prisoners were taken, they were to be sent back immediately to battalion headquarters for interrogation. After checking the woods, Jim was to reestablish an outpost on the other side of the woods. Jim selected his foxhole buddy and BAR man, George Banks, along with Cpl. Ralph Bennett, Everett Bruce, and others for the mission. The lieutenant handed Jim a radio and said, "Let me know when you get to the woods."

Kurz, with George Banks about twenty yards to his left, led the way across the open field. Corporal Bennett was instructed to send the other men out one at a time at intervals of twenty yards. The patrol made it across the field to the woods without drawing fire. Jim Kurz describes what he found in the woods:

> We could see where our artillery had hit. There were German helmets, gas masks, packs, rifles, and Panzer Faust [antitank weapons] scattered all over, but no Germans dead or alive. Then I saw what looked like a dead German. I ran over and hit the German on the helmet with my rifle. He rolled over and got up slowly. We searched the area and couldn't find any more Jerries. I called the lieutenant and reported we had found one German and were sending the prisoner back.

The patrol then moved through the woods and set up the outpost located about three fourth of a mile in front of the MLR. Jim and his men occupied the outpost through December 27 when they returned to their lines.

The remaining time in of the "two weeks of rest" as prescribed by First Sergeant James Smith for Jim Kurz was not so strenuous. Jim Kurz and George Banks worked on their double foxhole to make it as safe and restful as possible. In spite of the subfreezing weather and deep snow, Jim and George felt quite comfortable in their foxhole when not under enemy fire.

# Area of 508th Activity from December 20, 1944 to January 20, 1945

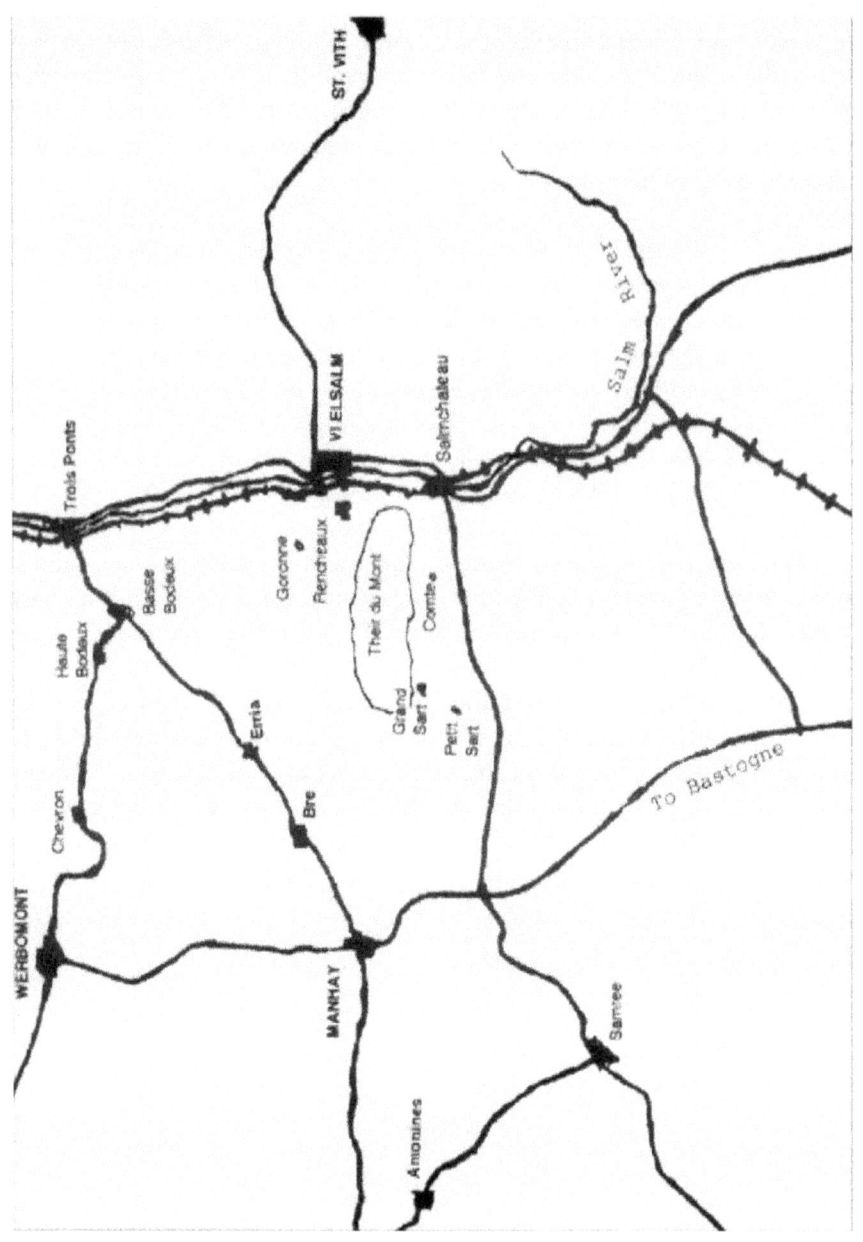

Map prepared by Zig Boroughs.

## The Saga of the Half-Track

The Red Ball Express, the trucks that transported us from Sissonne, France, stopped in a wooded area near Werbomont, Belgium, and we unloaded. Immediately we started marching into the unknown. We did not know where we were. It was a dark misty night with no lights, no smoking, and little talking—only the sounds of marching boots on the hard frozen surface of the narrow dirt road and the heavy breathing of soldiers packing their burdens. Just after dawn on the morning of December 19, Regimental Headquarters Company stopped at Goronne, a village of a few houses and barns, and we dug in around the village.

After unloading from the trucks at Werbomont, each regiment marched twenty-five kilometers to their places on the main line of resistance (MLR). The Eighty-second Division dug in from Trois Ponts to Salmchateau to near Manhay in a rough V-shaped continuous thin line. (See map on previous page.) The logistics of such a rapid transport of a whole division on such short notice, and over such a long distance, was an amazing accomplishment.

The whole division was in place by December 20. At the top level of Command and Control, the generals planned well. They knew where we were, but the average soldier did not know. We only knew that the Germans overran the Americans' MLR on the Belgium-Germany border and had penetrated deep into Belgium. It was our job to stop them.

Conrad Wolfe of D Company was wounded in Holland, hospitalized in England, and returned to Wollaton Park, Nottingham, England. Paratroopers who had been hospitalized with combat wounds and replacements from parachute schools in England and the United States at Wollaton Park were sent to Camp Sissonne, France, as replacements after the Holland campaign. When Conrad Wolfe arrived in Sissonne on December 17, 1944, orders had already been issued for the 508th to join the defensive forces in the Battle of the Bulge.

Corporal Wolfe had little time between his ride to Sissonne in a railroad boxcar and his ride to the Belgian Ardennes in a crowded cattle truck. Soon he would be traveling in an armored half-track. The D Company commanding officer Lt. Hoyt Goodale sent Wolfe to the Eighty-second Division Headquarters, where he picked up an assignment from Gen. James Gavin.

Gavin told Corporal Wolfe that Colonel Orr of the Thirrd Armored was in trouble and needed men to patrol his area. Wolfe quoted Gavin as saying, "Your CO says you are the best. I want a good job. Go get 'em!"

Wolfe and four other Red Devils were sent to meet with Gen. Maurice Rose, CO of the Third Armored Division. General Rose gave Conrad

Wolfe an armored half-track, instructed him to pick up demolitionists from the 508th Regimental Headquarters Company, and take them to Col. William R. Orr's Third Armored Task Force.

The task force was virtually surrounded in the village of Amonines. The demolitionists were to lay antitank mines in front of Orr's defensive perimeter. Wolfe and the other paratroopers were to carry out scouting patrols. Altogether, eleven paratroopers traveled in the half-track to Amonines. As they entered Amonines from the rear, the Germans were attacking from the front.

Sgt. Harold Gerkin led the demolitionists. They included Fred Taylor, Donald "Danny" Sloan, and others. Fred Taylor, upon arrival in the midst of the German attack, jumped on top of an abandoned American tank and fired a .50-caliber machine gun mounted on the tank until the German attack was repulsed. Taylor received the Bronze Star for his action, recommended by Colonel Orr.

After the demolitionists laid antitank mines

Fred Taylor. Photo provided by Zig Boroughs.

in front of Colonel Orr's MLD, the colonel sent Gerkin on a patrol with some of his demo men to locate an armored vehicle, which was firing on their positions. The patrol found the menacing vehicle. Gerkin reported the coordinates to the supporting artillery, which silenced the armored vehicle's guns. However, the enemy spotted the patrol and fired on the paratroopers. Gerkin was hit under his armpit. The wound injured a nerve in such a way that Gerkin lost the feeling in his right hand. The medics evacuated Harold Gerkin, and he was treated in an army hospital.

When released from the hospital, Gerkin was transferred to a chemical warfare outfit. It took two years before the feeling in his right hand was completely normal.

The other demolitionists returned to the Regimental Demolition Platoon in the armored half-track. Platoon members understood that Colonel Orr provided the vehicle to the demo men for their use. Conrad Wolfe and his scouts were asked to stay on with the Orr task force for additional patrols.

On Christmas Day, Colonel Orr began to evacuate Amonines, taking all his vehicles with him to join other Third Armored troops. Wolfe and his four men were dismissed to find their way back to the 508th Regiment by foot. They had to fight their way back toward their unit. Wolfe praised the alertness and fighting skills of one of his men with saving his life on at least two occasions. Wolfe cannot remember the trooper's name.

During a firefight, Wolfe and his partner became separated from the other three men who started with them. An American outpost sentinel challenged the two troopers. They were told to come on in, but they were unable to prove their identity to the satisfaction of the suspicious GIs. The soldiers took the two paratroopers to their commanding officer, suspecting them to be German infiltrators masquerading as US soldiers. They were later taken to a room full of American officers for interrogation.

Conrade Wolfe. Copied From 1943 Company picture.

With a German name like Conrad Wolfe, Wolfe had difficulty persuading the officers that he was born and raised in Ohio, trained at Camp Blanding, Fort Benning, and Camp Mackall, jumped in Normandy and Holland, and had been wounded three times in the service of his country. As his head hung down in discouraged desperation, Wolfe noticed a pair of paratrooper boots on one of the officers. With renewed hope, he looked up to the officer's face, walked over to him, and said, "I know you. You are with the 508th, Third Battalion. You are Major Mendez."

That was close enough for Mendez and the rest of those with him to change their attitude from suspicion to welcoming the two suspects—plus they were given great meals, warm clothes, and a good night's sleep before returning to the 508th.

Colonel Orr cited Conrad Wolfe for heroic action while with Orr's task force, and Wolfe received the Oak Leaf Cluster that was added to his previously awarded Bronze Star.

Demolitionist Bill Bladen remembered the half-track. Bladen was with Donald Sloan transporting mines in the half-track when Sloan tried to drive it across a half-frozen creek. The half-track stalled and froze in the middle of the creek. Sloan and Bladen had to abandon the vehicle. They waded in the creek, entered a vacant house, built a fire in a pot-bellied stove, and went to sleep. Bladen had taken his boots off to dry. He awoke to learn that the fire was out and his feet were frozen. Bladen was evacuated with frozen feet, and that was the end of the Battle of the Bulge for Bill Bladen and the end of the "half-track saga."

## With the Seventh Armored Division at St. Vith

Fred Knight of Regimental Headquarters Company told how he was wounded in action:

It was in the Bulge December 23. I was sent to the CP of the American Seventh Armored Division at St. Vith as a radio operator. Two of us, David Wheaton and I, were on top of the building radioing back to the 508th what we could find out. As it happened, the German tanks had broken through and were passing about four blocks away from our position. The Germans knew where we were and fired into the CP. Both of us were hit. We went into the basement for safety until we could get help. An officer found us in the basement and told us that everyone was clearing out of the CP and for us to get out in the street for evacuation.

Fred Knight. Photo copied from 1943 Company pictures.

Soon after getting into the street, a jeep came along with wounded. They threw me on top of the other wounded and took me to an aid station. I was transferred to an ambulance at the aid station to be taken back to a hospital. I told the ambulance driver that I was not sure all the wounded were picked up at the place where I was hit. I was thinking about Wheaton who, in fact without my knowledge, had gotten out before I did.

The ambulance driver knew that the engineers were preparing to blow a bridge as soon as all the Americans had crossed. He had to make a decision between getting out safely with those wounded that he already had and going back for others and risk the bridge getting blown before returning. Well, he made the right decision and returned to the old CP, only to find no one was there. It was nerve racking, but we made it back to the bridge in time and safely to the military hospital.

## Proper Military Courtesy, Sir!
From "How We Won the War" by Fred Gladstone
Permission to use by Fred Gladstone

Arriving in the Ardennes section of Belgium, we soon found that we had to contend with more than just a determined foe. The terrain presented a real challenge with its steep ridges, deep ravines, dense forest, winding roads and war torn villages. Then there was the snow, ice, fog and intense cold—all part of Europe's most severe winter in fifty years. But we paratroopers were a unique breed of soldiers and simply accepted all these things as a test of our courage and endurance.

Bill Sobolewski and I were members of I Company. We had some good and hilarious times together in England, and in combat, Bill and I were foxhole buddies. We kept an eye out for one another and Sobolewski, being five years older, took it upon himself to watch over me in a special way.

Bill and I had formed a reconnaissance patrol on the night of December 23. At the time the regiment was on Thier du Mont, a long ridge south of Liege that provided a blocking position against the German drive toward that city. Our mission was to determine if the enemy was approaching. I still remember Bill Sobolewski saying, sort of half seriously, "You go first. I have a wife and kids." The snow glowed in the moonlight and crunched beneath our feet as our route took us to the crest of another ridge.

Suddenly there was movement ahead of us and we instinctively dropped into the shadows of some trees. About fifty troops approached without seeing us. It was a tense moment until we recognized them as American soldiers. We sent a cautious signal, made contact and found that they were a wandering remnant of a unit which had borne the brunt of the German assault a week earlier. They were overjoyed when we revealed ourselves as members of the 82nd

Fred Gladstone, at 1993 508th reunion.
Photo by Zig Boroughs.

Airborne Division. I recall the officer in charge was so excited that he kept saying "Yes, Sir!" to me, a private.

We led them to the safety of our lines. The Germans, it turned out, were not very far behind them.

## You Will Never Be Bothered with Sinus Trouble

Al Patchell, one of the men on the rear guard covering the withdrawal of the 508th to a new MLR, was in Sgt. Don King's squad of B Company's Third Platoon. Orders were received from the Eighty-second Division that one platoon from each rifle company would remain as a rear guard to allow an orderly withdrawal of the rest of the 508th Regiment.

On Christmas Eve, the last remnants of the Seventh Armored and 106th Infantry Divisions cleared through the 508th lines. According to Lt. George Gurwell of Regimental Headquarters Company, in the final armored convoy sandwiched between two big tanks was a truck with Red Cross doughnut girls who waved cheerfully to the troops as they passed.

Jill Pitts, Helen Anderson, and Phyllis McGlocklin were the doughnut girls on that clubmobile. They named their clubmobile Cheyenne. Jill related her ordeal:

On December 16, we were sent for our assignment with the 106th Infantry Division at Vielsalm and immediately were cut off and surrounded by the enemy. My twin bother, Jack Pitts (Capt. John Joseph Pitts), was with the 590th Field Artillery Battalion, which was assigned to the 106th Infantry Division. Being twins, we were very close. Jack was born first, and Jill came tumbling after. Jack was killed December 16, the day we contacted his battalion. We were under the same enemy shelling that killed my twin brother. That really shook me up. We were constantly under shelling and gunfire, with no radio communication and little food.

Jill Pitts. Photo provided by Jill Pitts Knappenberger.

They did, however, give out dough and flour to the troops as they passed through the 508th as attested by Capt. Robert Abraham of Regimental Headquarters Company.

Don King's squad occupied the right corner of B Company's defense. Next on the B Company line was Sgt. Ed "Bogey" Boccafogli with his squad. Bogey was also platoon sergeant in charge of the whole platoon. Boccafogli had his men well dug in on the hillside with good fire control over the valley below down to the Salm River. A machine gun was placed on each flank and one in the center, with a BAR man supporting each machine gun and the riflemen spread out in between. The mortar section was up the hill behind them. The rear guard for the First Battalion was composed of a platoon from C Company to the left, the B Company platoon in the center, and a platoon from A Company to the right at the Vielsalm bridges.

Boccafogli recalled events before the main attack:

> Lt. Maurice E. Wheelock and Lt. Thomas L. Rockwell, new replacement officers, were added to our platoon during the afternoon of December 24, with Wheelock as the platoon CO and Rockwell as his assistant.
>
> After consulting with Lieutenant Rockwell, I decided to take one man with me to contact C Company. We passed word along the line that we would be leaving and we crossed the valley about 150 yards and found C Company's sergeant in charge. We informed him of our position and asked him to give covering fire with his light machine gun to our front. We then went along the edge of the woods near the river. We could hear enemy activity near the bridge and sounds of enemy armor across the river. We returned to our position and reported all of this to Lieutenant Rockwell.

Ed Boccafogli at 508th reunion. Photo by Zig Boroughs.

Boccafogli continued his defense preparations by changing the position of the bazooka team, getting additional ammo for the machine guns, and pointing out the target area for the mortar squad. In the meantime, without informing their men on the line, the two new officers Wheelock and Rockwell went in front of the platoon emplacements to investigate the enemy noises. On returning to the platoon area, the officers were fired on by Germans and while they were running toward our line were fired on by their own men, who thought the officers were a part of an enemy patrol. When the officers screamed, the paratroopers held their fire, but Lieutenant Rockwell had been hit before they discovered their mistake.

Medic Roland Archambault went to check on the wounded officer and found Rockwell dead. Archambault did not get back to the CP before the Germans attacked B Company's position in force. The Jerries started with artillery fire all along the line. Then about 2130 hours, the SS infantry came out of the valley running up the hill, shouting in German, and firing their weapons. When in good range, B Company's light machine guns cut loose on the advancing Jerries and drove them back. Archambault took refuge in a ditch to avoid the firefight.

For a brief period, the Red Devils could hear wounded Germans crying for help and Jerry noncoms shouting orders. Soon the SS attacked again. The second time, deadly fire by the paratroopers stopped the charging SS; however, the Germans were able to keep up a steady fire on B Company's position. Bullets were flying all over the hill. Suddenly Sergeant Boccafogli recognized the rip-rip-rip sound of German automatic weapons in the village of Rencheux to his rear. Somewhere along the line the Germans had broken though a seam between the thinly strung-out Red Devils.

Al Sopka described the breakthrough:

> To our right was the BAR man (Patchell and his buddy) and farther to the right the machine gunner (Robert Hart and his assistant). With Patchell and Hart both wounded, which I did not know at the time, those two positions gave way, and the Germans were getting through. Emmet Boyce and I were the only ones to see this happening. We were firing to the right when we were both hit, Boyce fatally. I was wounded in the face. After checking Boyce, I crawled to my left to Sgt. Don King, telling him that the Germans were through on our right.

About 0100 hours, Captain Delameter, officer in charge of the battalion covering force, ordered PFC John Klein to take a message to the B Company platoon to withdraw to the designated area. On the way, as Klein went around a building in Rencheux, he came face to face with three Germans. Klein, with a fixed bayonet, lowered his rifle to get the first Kraut, but before he could follow through, one German grabbed Klein's hands and the other two jumped him. Klein was taken prisoner. The message to withdraw never got through to the men on the line.

Pvt. Marino Michetti was a new replacement just assigned to the mortar crew of Sergeant Boccafogli's platoon. Michetti wasn't in the platoon long enough to learn any names. He remembered a corporal directing the mortar fire at some distance. After the mortar crew had fired all the available rounds and the noise of the battle increased, Michetti remembers taking cover in a foxhole, and suddenly from the right rear, he was fired on by Germans, "All I could see," recalled Michetti, "was the white tracers of the burp gun! I am glad the Germans were not sharp shooters!"

Michetti was rounded up with a few other prisoners in the B Company Platoon CP area and taken to a house where he and the others were interrogated. Michetti recalled being frisked by his captors, but they failed to find his trench knife concealed in his boot.

Boccafogli realized that the platoon would soon be surrounded. It was past midnight, and he had not received word to withdraw. Bogey then went up the hill to the mortar position to check on the mortar crew. All he could find was a mortar tube beside an empty foxhole. Bogey thinks he must have arrived just after Michetti was captured.

Boccafogli then returned to his men on the firing line and ordered them to assemble on Hoffman's machine gun position. Bogey went from foxhole to foxhole to gather his men together. He remembered pulling out Walter Trippe, Robert Kabot, John Payet, Raymond Wilson, James Naro, Manual Lira, Milton Mackey, Al Sopka, Vernon Ford, and finding the dead body of Emmet Boyce.

Since there was much firing to the rear and none to the left front, Bogey decided to move his men down the hill to a small pond and then contact the C Company platoon holding the left flank. When he covered the 150 yards to the C Company position, the sergeant discovered that C Company had already pulled out. Boccafogli rejoined his men waiting at the pond and proceeded to move his men to the withdrawal assembly area. Boccafogli recalls working their way back keeping near the road but over in the brush for cover. Sergeant King led the group, and Sergeant Boccafogli brought up the rear.

German soldiers surprised the medic Roland Archambault, still in the ditch and unarmed, having left his .45 at the CP when he went to attend the fallen lieutenant. After his capture, Archambault dressed the wounds of machine gunner Robert Hart and his assistant gunner who was shot in both legs. Archambault also remembers Sgt. Floyd McElfresh from the platoon CP as a POW captured that night. It was hard for Archambault to believe that Boccafogli was able to bring sixteen men out of that attack alive.

Marino Michetti recalled what happed after he was captured:

> We stayed in this area until dawn. It was Christmas morning! The Germans gave us some coffee and doughnuts.

(Could this have been from the supplies the German confiscated given to our troops by Jill Pitts from her Red Cross clubmobile Cheyenne?) Among the twenty or so prisoners was the assistant machine gunner, who was shot four or five times in both legs. Archie, the medic, suggested we make a stretcher for the crippled man. As the Germans marched us away from the battle area, I served as a stretcher-bearer, and I remember helping the wounded man urinate by turning him on the stretcher.

When Boccafogli pulled his men off the line and moved them out, Al Patchell was not with them. In a letter to Monty Montgomery many years later, Patchell describes his rescue:

> I was shot Christmas day about one o'clock in the morning. I knew I was shot pretty bad. All I could think about was trying to stop the bleeding and stay alive. I tied my scarf around my face real tight and just waited in my foxhole until someone came. In about thirty minutes a guy came to my foxhole and asked me if I were still alive and if I could walk. This guy said he was a replacement and had just come to the company a few hours ago. I didn't know him, had never seen him before. Anyhow, he got me out, and we started walking to the aid station. [Boccafogli thinks the replacement was Lieutenant Wheelock.]

The unknown replacement was able to speak German. This skill was a lifesaver for Al Patchell, whose sight was impaired by his wound. The guide led Patchell by the hand, and when they came to a place where they could hear German spoken, he would have Patchell hold on to a tree. Then he would move nearer to the Germans, all the time keeping concealed in the darkness. The guide would listen and even engage the Germans in conversation. Then he would go back to the tree, take Patchell by the hand, and lead him around the German forces. This process was repeated several times before Patchell arrived at the aid station.

Medic Monty Montgomery was selected to stay with the last ambulance to leave the regimental aid station that Christmas morning. Monty recalled, "I saw this trooper coming out of the snowstorm with a scarf over his face. It was Al Patchell. A bullet had zinged through one cheek then pierced through his nose and out the other cheek."

In dressing his wound, Monty kidded with Patchell and promised him, "You will never be bothered with sinus trouble after this."

Army doctors worked five and a half years reconstructing Patchell's face. After that, the Veterans Affairs (VA) doctors continued the plastic surgery. Altogether eighty-five operations were performed. As for sinus trouble, Montgomery was correct. Patchell never suffered with his sinuses after that.

As to Lieutenant Wheelock, Ed Boccafogli affirms that Wheelock was not seen by the men on the line after Lieutenant Rockwell was killed, not until three or four days later. However, in his after action report, Wheelock claimed credit for pulling out the B Company rear guard platoon intact and was awarded a Silver Star for his action. Lieutenant Wheelock was immediately transferred to another unit.

Jill Pitts and her clubmobile Cheyenne followed the troops until V-E Day (Victory in Europe.) She witnessed the horrors of the holocaust victims at Ordurse and Buchenwald. She even saw the lampshades made from the skin of concentration camp inmates. After the war, she married and is now Mrs. Jill Pitts Knappenberger.

## The Vielsalm Bridges

Two bridges over the Salm River at Vielsalm were the only places in the 508th area of defense where German tanks and other heavy armor could cross without new construction. These two bridges had to be blown to prevent a German armored breakthrough. They also had to be preserved as long as possible to allow units of the US Seventh Armored and the 106th and Twenty-eighth infantry divisions to cross. These troops were not overrun in disarray during the Belgian Bulge breakthrough but had fallen back in an orderly manner from St. Vith toward Vielsalm.

Lt. George Lamm of A Company was in charge of the defense and demolition of the bridges. Lamm explained the situation. "The mission to destroy the crossings and deny them to the enemy advance was primary. The additional instructions, to hold open the sites for the rear guard elements dropping back from St. Vith, was secondary."

Demolitionists set charges in readiness to blow the bridges, and Lamm placed some of his men on the far side of the river to detect and defend against the first enemy arrivals. Most of the friendly troops passed over the bridges during the daylight hours of December 23. George Lamm describes the first contact with the enemy on the moonlit evening of December 23:

An outpost fell back and warned us that a platoon was coming up the tracks from Salmchateau. Enemy scouts passed us at arm's length, halting upon sighting the bridge. Our fire caught them in column, and they never did deploy. After the first burst of fire, there was complete silence and no movement from their direction. As we moved to withdraw, we encountered a second enemy platoon approaching through Vielsalm from the direction of Proteau. These we scattered with marching fire as we moved in that direction.

Sgt. Richard Hunt and a squad of five occupied an OP (observation post) in front of the railroad track overlooking the Salm River. They were on a small section of a cliff that dropped off on three sides with the railroad to their back. They had a good view of the buildings across the river in Vielsalm, and on December 24, they began to see Germans among the buildings to their front. Hunt described some of the action from his squad:

> Bob White saw a German climbing a ladder and getting straw out of a loft. White took a shot at him and, believe it or not, nailed him good. Gabris, our BAR man, started burning ammo at every target that presented itself. To my right, Nixon and Names were dug in together facing an old two-story building. Nixon called over to me that someone with field glasses was eyeballing us from a second-story window. Not being able to see the window from where I was, I told Nixon to shoot him. In a few minutes I heard his M-1 sound off, and Nixon let out a rebel yell and declared, "I got him right between the eyes!"

Lamm and his men returned to the near side of the river and attempted to blow the bridges, but the first attempt failed. This made it necessary to counterattack and keep the enemy away while the charges were rewired. The railroad overpass was the first successful detonation. The Germans sent a tank and a half-track along the railroad near the blown overpass to harass the work on the other bridge.

Flanking elements of Lamm's platoon laid down a heavy base of fire to allow counterattacking Red Devils to recross the river. Sergeant Clements and Sergeant Boone took the bazooka and rifle grenade teams forward to engage the enemy armored vehicles. From under the old railroad pass, they were able to fire up and underneath the heavy protective armor. The enemy vehicles replied with great blasts of cannons but could not depress their muzzles low enough to hit the antitank teams. Lamm recalled the outcome of the contest:

> Blinded by a steady volume of our machine gun fire, harassed by our rockets, and sitting ducks for the night fighting rifle elements, the enemy tanks clanked off. The platoon attack drove the enemy from the railroad bed, and we continued to clear them from the buildings. Finally the road bridge was rewired and blown. We mined and booby-trapped the remains, installed outposts on the near shore, and settled in for the defense of the site.

When the first attempt to blow the bridges failed, an emergency hot line was laid to the platoon. The chief lineman remarked to George Lamm with pride, "We can patch all the way to General Ridgway, and even to Eisenhower from this point."

During the confusion of enemy buildup and fire from the far shore, a platoon runner picked up the phone and, thinking he was talking to the A Company operator warned, "You guys better get your rear-area asses in high gear cause the Krauts are on their way." That phone call stirred up a flurry of activity among the high brass.

Grady Murray, Headquarters First radio operator, relayed messages via radio to First Battalion Headquarters for Lamm. Murray remembered additional details about the demolition of the road bridge, which Lamm did not report. Murray recalled that the shelling must have cut a wire because after the first attempt to set off the explosives failed, Lamm traced the wires and found a break. Lamm pieced the connections and tried again. The second attempt failed also, which prompted a more-thorough check and tightening of all connections. The third time they pushed the charge-plunger, it blew the road-bridge.

With both bridges blown and having set up the bridges area defense, Lieutenant Lamm proceeded to establish a combination platoon CP/OP (command post and observation post) in the attic of a Rencheux house. Rencheux was located on a ridge above the Salm River across from Vielsalm. From this vantage point, Lamm, using field glasses and range finders, directed fire on the white-clad SS storm troopers and on the armored forces massing on the opposite shore. It was December 24.

Lamm described the enemy activity:

The enemy laid down smoke for concealment and lined up their tanks and half-tracks and relentlessly blasted directly into our positions as they attempted to repair the crossing sites. The Germans angrily tore the roofs off the houses searching for ops with their beloved 88s. Finally, they got around to us, and down the attic stairs we tumbled amid flying debris, radios, telephones, field glasses, and several bottles of the best champagne. We relocated the CP in the cellar, and the OP was moved to the railroad bed.

Grady Murray remembered that Lamm ordered all the stashed booze, which could not be conveniently carried, from the CP destroyed. Murray salvaged two bottles by tying a string around each and hanging them around his neck under his combat jacket. The German infantry crossing followed the heavy shelling by artillery; some came over the damaged railroad bridge and others crossed the open river. The main attack began about 2200 hours. Although the moon was bright, the smoke screen covered the river crossing.

Many years later, Bob White learned how the Jerries crossed the open river. When visiting Belgium and the Historical Museum at La Gleize, Bob met a German veteran who had crossed the Salm the night of December 24, 1944. The German told White, "We carried rocks into the stream and filled in the deeper places. Then the taller men supported the shorter men as we waded in the river."

Enemy fire intensified. Lieutenant Lamm stepped out of the CP to check on his men and was greeted by a stream of Schmeisser bullets blasting the doorframe. Turning to a dark figure behind him, Lamm asked, "Are the Germans back there, Sergeant Boone?"

The figure responded with a burst from a machine pistol, missing Lamm. Lamm's return fire was more accurate than his adversary's.

Lieutenant Lamm located Sgt. Joe Boone and Sgt. Bruno Preztos busily defending against advancing SS infantry. He ordered them to withdraw their men, moving around the village of Rencheux, which was by now occupied by the enemy.

Edward "Woody" Wodowski, BAR man, was at the railroad tracks when the Germans crossed the river. When his buddy, B. L. Hicks, was wounded, Woody carried Hicks back behind a wall. The wall was located on a high bank next to the road. By this time, the Germans were streaming up the road toward Wodowski's position. From his vantage point behind the wall, he had a good field of fire with his BAR. After using all his BAR ammo, he threw grenades at the advancing Jerries, and when he ran out of grenades, he threw rocks. Finally he received the withdrawal order.

As they marched toward the assembly area, Lamm recognized the sound of a US light machine gun. One light machine gun crew was missing, Roblette and DeMario. Lamm returned toward Rencheux, calling out for his men above the noise of battle. Out of the darkness came the two soldiers carrying their gun and two boxes of ammo.

A shell burst had buried Roblette and DeMario. They dug themselves out, fought through the Germans, and reported to Lieutenant Lamm for further duty.

By this time, the midnight hour had passed, and it was well into Christmas morning. The night became quiet. As the tired defenders of the Vielsalm bridges marched toward their new assembly area, they experienced a fleeting reality of "Peace on Earth."

Lt. George Lamm decorated with Distinguished Service Cross by Gen. James Gavin for his action in the defense of the Veilsalm Bridges. Photo furnished by Julia Lamm Gustafson.

## Two Brooklyn Boys and a Bridge
Abridged from a Story by Leon Israel (Gismo) Mason
Permission to use by Leon Israel Mason

The paratrooper stood watching in front of the Belgium farmhouse. Men and equipment in vast quantities were pouring past the house from the east. The Germans were counterattacking. Artillery was falling close—its pattern was definitely planned—it flanked the town.

In the air it was an American show. Bombers stretched as far as the eye could see. Occasionally a plane would drop out of formation, down beneath the deadly flak—screaming and twisting to a quick death.

"O.K. First Demolition Section, let's go!" commanded Lieutenant Charlie Yates.

Yates gave them the big picture. The 82nd Airborne Division was pulling back to high ground eight miles to the rear. The demolitionists were to prepare a bridge to be demolished, but not blow it until all of our troops had passed over.

At the bridge the men worked under the frozen superstructure, their legs and backs missing the stream by scant inches. Sergeant Shull fell in. He gave a convulsive shiver. Lucky a jeep came along and they bundled him in.

Finally the job was done: one and a half tons of explosives were set in place. The men were tired, yet two had to stay. The lieutenant thought for a moment, then picked two of the more experienced men, "Hey Kass and Gismo, you guys stay here, and if you see a Kraut coming over the ridge, blow the bridge and hit it back. We will try to get relief for you tomorrow."

They stood gazing intently for signs, listening for sounds of the enemy. Relief would come in 16 hours with no food and no fire. Slowly the night came, and with it the snow. The kids shivered, talked of home, but mostly they paced up and down, swinging their arms, looking and listening, pacing up and down.

"Hey Kass—I just happened to think—do you realize that we are the advanced front for the whole U. S. Army?"

"Damned if you ain't right!"

They kidded each other about it—time passed slowly, 10 hours, 11 hours, 12 hours, 13, 14, then the welcomed dawn. With the coming of the day, the snow stopped. Lieutenant Yates found them as he left them. But they looked more like snowmen than two frozen sleepy kids.

Yates reached in his pocket and gave each of them a chocolate D-ration and greeted them with, "Merry Christmas guys!"

The next night the Jerries came—the bridge went up a mile—the Jerries never did advance again—stopped by two frozen kids from Brooklyn.

Cartoon by Kate Salley Palmer

## Burial and Birth

It was the night before Christmas. In a few minutes it would be midnight and Christmas Day. Jack Warren and I were chipping away at the frozen sides of a foxhole near Goronne, Belgium. We were digging a grave for a very tall soldier. Our unit had prepared to move back after having forced a wedge into the Belgian Bulge to rescue entrapped American tanks and infantry. For three days the tanks and foot soldiers poured through the protective corridor of the Eighty-second Airborne Division. The last of the tanks had already cleared our lines when one last straggler, a tall soldier with one arm blown away, staggered into our aid station. The medics were unable to save him. In an hour or so he was dead.

We had our packs on ready to move out when the burial officer rushed up to Lieutenant Hardwick and asked for a detail to bury the one-armed man. It was 2300 hours (11:00 PM). Jack and I were given the assignment. Regimental Headquarters Company, to which we belonged, marched off. The burial detail was left to march back with the rear guard, which was exchanging small arms fire with the Germans a few hundred yards down the road.

Jack paused after cracking a large hunk of frozen mud from the side of the hole and asked, "Say, Boroughs, when was that baby of yours supposed to be born?"

"If we calculated right, sometime around the tenth of December," I replied.

"Would you guys stop the baby talk and hurry up?" urged the burial officer. "The firing is getting closer. We've got to get this man buried before the rear guard pulls out and leaves us here all alone."

About midnight we had covered the shallow grave. The firing stopped. The officer explained that the rear guard must be pulling out since their guns were silent. We tied two sticks together in a cross to mark the grave. The officer hung one of the man's dog tags on the cross and placed the other dog tag among his records. Then he knelt on one knee. I thought he might have been saying a prayer. "Listen!" whispered the officer. "Do you hear anything out there?"

"Maybe it's Santa and his eight tiny reindeer," joked Jack. "Can you read your watch? See if it is Christmas yet."

"Christmas! Santa! The Krauts could sneak up on us!" replied the officer. "Let's get the hell out of here."

We were able to link up with the rear guard and move out with them. As we marched through the night that predawn Christmas Day, Jack teased, "I bet the baby is a girl." Previously I had shown Jack a snapshot of

Mary, who was very pregnant and bragged, "This is my wife and the big boy on the way."

By daybreak Christmas morning we had reached a staging area safely away from the front. We enjoyed our first hot meal since December 17, when the Germans broke through the Belgian Bulge.

Another surprise awaited us that Christmas Day—mail call and a letter from Dad. He had just come from the hospital where he had visited Mary and little "Gene."

"Gene?" I asked myself. "Is that a name for a boy or a girl?" That question was answered a month later, January 31, when the cablegram arrived: ELIZABETH IMOGENE BOROUGHS BORN DECEMBER 7. MOTHER AND DAUGHTER FINE.

## Christmas Surprise

Most of the 508th felt somewhat ashamed of the strategic withdrawal of December 24. We had heard about the American troops being overrun by the Germans on December 16, resulting in the Belgian Bulge, a Nazi penetration deep into the previously liberated section of Belgium. We had seen hundreds of GI armored vehicles and thousands of beleaguered American troops pour through our lines. The airborne troops were sent to plug the gap and turn back the Nazi flood, and here we were being pushed back like the others. The average paratrooper understood what was happening only in a small section of the front.

Later, when we were in a rest area, General Gavin explained to us the big picture. The Eighty-second Division was stretched out in the shape of a *V* over twenty-five miles. Some riflemen on the extreme right flank were a hundred yards apart. Gavin was desperately shifting troops to protect the thinly defended right flank. When he received orders to withdraw to an almost straight MLR that was less than half the length of the *V*, he understood the advantage of the withdrawal. The shorter front had a better cover and a better field of fire. His explanation of the "strategic withdrawal" made us feel better.

Christmas morning the 508th was digging in on our new MLR. Early warning outposts were established some distance in front of the MLR. Lt. Don "the Ripper" Hardwick received orders to prepare a bridge in front of the MLR for demolition. Hardwick was the commanding officer (CO) of the Second Demolition Section, which served the needs of the Second Battalion of the regiment. I was a member of Hardwick's Second Demo section.

The bridge was a wooden bridge over a fast-moving small stream and located about seventy-five yards in front of the MLR on a main access road for a possible German attack. Instructions from Regiment were to place the explosives to destroy the bridge and leave men to detonate if enemy troops or armored vehicles appeared on the bridge. Hardwick and his men placed the explosives and ran a wire with hand detonator to the D Company area.

When Hardwick saw how the water splashed on the bridge, wetting everything down and how the icicles were forming, he wondered if the water might short out the wiring. He called Regimental Headquarters and requested to immediately destroy the bridge. The request was denied with the explanation that if no attack came from that direction, the bridge would be needed later for a counterattack.

Louis Guzzetti of D Company had his foxhole about seventy-five yards from the bridge. According to Guzzetti, a German half-track and two motorcycle escorts halted on the bridge during daylight hours. The Germans surveyed the situation and pulled back. Louis wondered why no orders were given to fire at the Germans while they were on the bridge at that time. Later he was told the bridge was supposed to blow up, but the charges failed to detonate.

After dark, Germans soldiers returned and appeared to be cutting wires. Then the half-tracks and infantry came across the bridge and turned down the D Company line. D Company men felt as if it was a hard-fought battle. The extreme cold caused so many of their weapons to jam, thus limiting their firepower. The battle also postponed the traditional Christmas dinner with all the trimmings for D Company until the next day. Lou Guzzetti recalled, "We were too busy combing the Germans out of our hair. However, we eventually did receive the turkey dinner. It was really appreciated after a steady diet of K rations."

Headquarters Second radioman Harold Kulju (a.k.a. Harold Canyon) was on the other side of a small wooden bridge on Christmas night. Headquarters Second CP was unable to contact an outpost set up for early warning of an enemy approach. A five-man patrol, including Lt. James M. Tibbetts, Kulju, a BAR man, and two riflemen, were sent to find the squad on the outpost or find out what happened to them.

The patrol departed by jeep just after sundown through the forward battalion position. After about a mile, they pulled the jeep off the road and proceeded by foot for another mile to a driveway, leading to a set of farm buildings.

Kulju recalled that about five hundred yards up the driveway was a bridge and the farm building about five hundred yards uphill beyond the bridge. Lieutenant Tibbetts left three of the men at the bridge and took Kulju with him to investigate the buildings. Kulju described their investigation:

> The lieutenant and I walked around, looking into the buildings. We saw signs that Americans had been there. We then walked behind the main building and saw a man standing in full view a short distance away. I shouted, "Are you a member of Sergeant Brogley's squad?"
> 
> Hearing no reply, I started toward him, and about twenty feet from him, I recognized his German style helmet. Immediately I dove behind a pile of manure and took aim with my .45 pistol. Then I realized that shooting would alert our presence to all the Germans in the area.
> 
> When I dove behind the manure pile, Lieutenant Tibbetts ran into a lean-to shed. Giving up the idea of shooting my way out, I joined Tibbetts in the shed. We tried to exit the back, but chicken wire covered that end, and we had no wire cutters. The only way out was the way we came in.
> 
> Since I was burdened with the radio, I suggested that the lieutenant go first because he could move faster. Tibbetts ran first, and nothing happened. Then I followed, and nothing happened.
> 
> We started back the way we came so we could warn the others of the presence of the Germans. We had to expose ourselves going down the driveway, but still nothing happened.
> 
> I radioed Headquarters Second that we had encountered Germans and the missing squad was not found. They acknowledged, and we proceeded to cross the bridge and pick up the other men. When we reached the far side of the bridge, the Germans sprang their trap and bullets were flying everywhere.
> 
> The lieutenant jumped off the road on the side near the Germans. I knew for sure that he would die. A bullet caught my overcoat shoulder seam and spun me around. I jumped off the bridge away from the Germans and started running down the creek. As long as I ran, the Germans kept shooting at me. When I realized that, I lay down in the creek at a place where reeds were growing.

I saw a half-track turn its .20mm gun on the BAR man whose weapon jammed after a few rounds, so I knew he was dead. Then the Germans fired on our other two men. I continued down the creek to a place where the stream veered across our forward line. Fearful that our own troops would shoot me, I lay down in the creek out of view. Snow was everywhere, and the creek was full of ice. Just then the Germans attacked about three hundred yards to my right. I was sure I was in trouble then, but I shouted anyway, "Can I come across the opening?"

On the second shout, I was told to come on in. After some trouble convincing the men that I was who I claimed to be, they let me through. I went back to battalion and gave my report and said the other four were killed. I was wrong. All four miraculously survived.

At the Regimental CP in Haute Bodeux, firing was heard in the distance. Then Dick Nelson, a demo man who was left to detonate the small wooden bridge, came running up the road. Breathlessly Nelson reported to the CP that the bridge didn't blow and that German tanks had crossed. All the spare men from the demolition and bazooka platoons were placed along the road leading to the bridge to save the Regimental Headquarters from being overrun. It appeared that German tanks would soon be roaring up the road, bringing death and destruction to all.

Lieutenant Hardwick told about what happened next:

> I was awakened by a phone call from Regiment Headquarters and told that the bridge didn't blow and that enemy troops had crossed with armored vehicles. I asked where the enemy was, but they did not know. Several of us fixed some blasting caps with short fuses and started across country to the bridge. We were afraid to use the road lest we would run into the attacking enemy.
>
> When we arrived at the ridge overlooking the bridge, Bugzy (Andrew Cehrobec) and I went on to the bridge. Bugzy crossed over to give me protection from the other direction. I felt around locating some primer cord, taped a cap tightly into a loop of primer, and inserted a match in the split fuse. I called to Bugzy, and when I heard him go by, I lit the match and

followed him up the hill. The bridge blew quickly, and debris fell all around us. Bugzy and I found a depression and holed up until daylight.

In William Lord's official *History of the 508th Parachute Infantry*, only a single paragraph is devoted to the Christmas Day events associated with the bridge that didn't blow, with no mention of the bridge itself. The event is described as a brief enemy penetration between A Company and D Company by two companies of German infantry and four half-tracks and that in three hours the Germans were driven back beyond the regiment's forward outposts.

Right, front of farmhouse. Below, rear of house and out. Buildings Farm identified by Emile Lacroix as Noirefontaine, the location of patrol by Kulju and Tibbetts.

Photos by Emile Lacroix and used by permission of Emile Lacroix.

## What Really Happened to PFC Curtis Canard

Upon arrival in the Ardennes, the 508th formed a defensive line, which roughly followed the western side of the Salm River. Vielsalm (meaning "village on the Salm") and Salmchateau (meaning "chateau on the Salm") were two of the towns where the 508th was on the main line of resistance (MLR). E Company was on line in a forest about two miles north of Salmchateau before the withdrawal on December 24, 1944.

Curtis Canard of E Company was part of the rear guard on December 24. Canard remembered being in a half-finished silo about two hundred yards from the bridge over the Salm. As the German infantry began crossing the river, Canard and the others shot at the Jerries and saw them either falling off the bridge, or maybe some of them jumped off.

During the battle of January 7, 1945, the 508th regained the same territory from which they had withdrawn. Between the withdrawal and the January 7 attack, outposts were established in front of their new MLR. One of the outposts established by E Company had lost contact with the E Company command post (CP). A patrol consisting of Curtis Canard, a BAR man, a machine gunner, and a radioman was sent to check on the outpost and to set up a roadblock. The company also had information of enemy tanks and infantry in the area.

The patrol did not find anyone at the E Company outpost, so they prepared a roadblock with some logs. The BAR man and the machine gunner set up behind the logs. Curtis Canard took cover in a ditch beside the road. That night, five Jerry tanks approached the roadblock. The BAR man fired at the lead tank. The tank returned fire and killed the BAR man. Then the machine gunner took off running over the hill and has not been seen since.

Canard lay unobserved in deep snow in the ditch beside the road while the five tanks and about two hundred infantrymen moved by him. Canard said, "The Germans were close enough to spit on me."

The exchange of fire between the tank and the BAR alerted our artillery, and they poured artillery on the road. Canard described what happened next. He wanted to set the record straight because the incident was reported with many errors in the *Devil's Digest*, April 9, 1945, vol. no. 1:

> When all the Germans got by my hiding place in the ditch, I ran down hill and then over a frozen lake. Suddenly I went through a spring hole in the ice. I went clear under, rifle and all. The water was cold as ice, and when I got out on the bank, my clothes and overcoat froze stiff as a board immediately.

PFC Curtis Canard.
The photo above appeared along with an
article about Canard in *The Devil's Digest*
Monday, April 9, 1945, vol. 1, no. 1.

I found a farmhouse nearby. Our artillery was hitting the eaves of the house. While in the yard near the house, I got hit in my back and my right arm by our artillery. I bled some, but the shrapnel did not penetrate my flesh, and I never reported the wounds. It did knock me down.

I tried to get in the house, but the people would not open the door. A breezeway connected the house and the barn of the farmhouse. I went into the breezeway and sat on a sack of onions against the wall of the barn and slept for a few hours.

A noise awakened me, and I got my rifle ready to use. Someone shined a flashlight in my face. I thought it might be the farmer who owned the house, so I did not shoot. It was not the farmer but a German soldier. The German grabbed my rifle and tried to take it away from me. In the struggle, I was able to place the end of the barrel under his chin and pull the trigger. I was not sure it would fire after being in the lake, but it did. The Jerry jerked his head to the side just as the bullet exploded and the bullet hit the side of his face, taking off his ear. He turned loose of the rifle, let out a terrifying scream, and started running.

The concussion from the bullet caused both of us to turn the rifle loose. I quickly picked it up and fired again as the German fled from the breezeway. It knocked him down, but he was up and running again in a second. I saw him take off around the corner of the house, and I went to the other side of the breezeway and shot him again when he came into view from that side. This time he fell and did not get up. I am not sure if he died or not. I did not check to see.

During the scuffle, I heard two other Germans talking to each other. I watched to see what they would do. They never went to check on their comrade. They seemed to disappear. I stayed awhile, searching my mind for the password for getting back into our lines. It finally came to me—"Alamo!" But I was not sure. It worked. "Alamo!" got me safely through our MLR.

## Erria

"I really hated to force that Belgian family out of their home near Erria on Christmas night," Sgt. Marvin Risnes, G Company, recalled.

"The middle-aged couple, with two kids about seven and eight years old, hitched their horses to a sleigh and loaded up a few belongings. We added some GI rations to their meager load to replace food they left behind."

It was a good thing the family moved out because an 88 shell crashed through the roof a few hours after the family drove away in their two-horse open sleigh.

The small village of Erria became a part of the MLR. The Second and Third platoons of G Company dug in along the perimeter of the village facing an open field of snow with an evergreen forest beyond the field. The First Platoon, having served as part of the rear guard for the Christmas Eve withdrawal, arrived later and was placed in reserve along a sunken road running parallel to and about one hundred yards to the rear of the MLR.

Rumors were rampant among the men of the 508th when the orders were given to withdraw on December 24—rumors of superior numbers of men, tanks, and artillery concentrated against the Eighty-second Airborne division, which was thinly spread and in danger of being cut off from the rear. The uncertainty of the situation, the withdrawal order, the extreme cold, and the fact that it was Christmas Eve made it tough on the troopers' morale, but the Red Devil spirit prevailed. As Angel Romero put it, "It was a period of 100 percent uncertainty, but I felt a sense of security by having Beno, McGrath, Lawhon, Beach, Metar, Carter, Calcagno, and others surrounding me. We weren't talking to each other much, but we were aware of what had to be done, and we were doing it."

The orders from Sergeant Sirovica were "Dig in, and dig in good! We have to stop the Germans here! We are not giving up any more ground!"

Angel Romero said, "The ground was frozen hard as stone, but one thing for sure, digging helped keep us from freezing to death."

Sergeant Risnes and three men set up an outpost 125 yards into the woods in front of the MLR. The outpost was connected by telephone to the company CP.

Risnes and BAR man Ernest Beck, during the afternoon of December 26, went to look for an F Company outpost four hundred yards to their left. Returning to their own post with Beck on the left, Beck started firing and hit the ground. In falling, he jammed his BAR and could no longer use it. Risnes saw some Germans running and fired his M-1 at the fleeing patrol.

Sergeant Risnes remembered, "A wounded German kept screaming and calling for Alfred. He got away but left his rifle, belt, and maps, which I collected and took to the CP."

On that same afternoon, in the E Company area, a squad of Germans was spotted, and a patrol was dispatched to find it. Fred Infanger, lead scout for the patrol, described the search:

> We kept trailing the Krauts until dark. We crossed a field into some woods. The lieutenant said we would go into the woods for a while and then we would head back. I was moving slow and easy when I stopped and stood still. Next to a big tree to my right front stood a Kraut about six feet from me. I thought then that I really had it. I had my rifle at port arms and took a flying leap at him. We both went down, my rifle on his neck under his chin. I wonder to this day why he did not shoot me first.
>
> When the lieutenant and the other scout heard the commotion, they came running. The lieutenant told us to take the Kraut back to battalion. I took a Mauser, with telescope attached, and a pair of night binoculars from the prisoner.
>
> As we arrived at the road into Erria, another Kraut jumped out of a ditch and ran into the barnyard of a house. I ran after him and finally caught him in the doorway of the house.
>
> We took the two prisoners to Second Battalion Headquarters for questioning. We heard that the Germans were placing these guys to infiltrate in preparation for an attack.

Incidentally, I was pretty popular with a few officers who wanted to buy my newly acquired loot.

According to Sgt. James "Buck" Hutto, I Company was in battalion reserve, with foxholes in a wooded area on top of a high ridge. Hutto remembered that his company caught more than their share of the artillery that preceded the German assault. Hutto had gone down the backside of the hill where he prepared for toilet activities, hoping to be out of range from the big guns. After disencumbering himself from some of his bulky clothing and settling in for a peaceful time over a slit trench, a shell landed just a few feet from him. Hutto dove into the snow behind a tree, which was less than a foot thick. The small tree absorbed three pieces of shrapnel from the shell, but Hutto escaped injury.

Shortly after that incident, the afternoon of December 26, Sergeant Hutto and Sgt. Andy Downer, both of I Company, were placed on two separate three-man outposts in front of the battalion MLR. Downer's was to the right of Sergeant Risnes's outpost and Hutto's outpost to the right of Downer's.

Risnes recalled what happened later that night about 2100 hrs:

> A German platoon got in the woods between our outpost and the open field. We could see shadowy figures and hear the noncoms giving orders in German. I phoned requesting mortar and machine gun fire on the area. The resulting fire against the Jerries was very effective. When some mortar shells fell dangerously close to us, I tried to call to adjust the mortar fire. The line was dead. I pulled in the line and found it was cut by the mortars about ten feet out.
>
> The CP tried to call me with no results. They pulled the line in from their end and learned the line had been cut. Captain Wilde sent Lt. James Russell and Sgt. Harry Waltman with a patrol to contact the outpost. The patrol shot their way through the Germans to our outpost and reestablished communications with the CP. Lieutenant Russell's patrol returned to the CP with a wounded German prisoner, whose soldier's book revealed that he was a member of the Ninteenth SS Panzer Grenadiers.

Sgt. Albert Hess from North Dakota and his G Company mortar team, consisting of Bill Swint, John Hodge, and Robert Lindsey, prepared mortar pits ready for firing and then occupied a house near the G Company CP. For two days the Germans shelled their area. Hess checked with outposts of Sergeant Risnes and others at different times. Hess warned his mortar men to be constantly on alert for enemy infiltrators, especially at night.

Risnes continued his memories:

> Two men from an I Company outpost came to our position and reported that a platoon size force of Germans was moving through the woods toward the open field. I immediately called the Company CP, and Captain Wilde ordered us to withdraw to the company.
>
> We secured our equipment and departed by the most direct route toward the company area. At the edge of the woods we saw two people standing about one hundred yards in front of the Third Platoon of G Company. I couldn't recognize them as Germans, so I challenged them. They answered in German as if we were one of them. We opened fire, and to our surprise, about a dozen men, lying between us and the two men, jumped up and took flight. None of them returned our fire.
>
> Yelling at the top of our voices to identify ourselves, we dashed toward the Third Platoon position. We made it to the defense line just minutes before the Germans opened fire all along the wood line for several hundred yards.
>
> The Germans charged in waves, and we kept up our fire. They were able to penetrate between F Company and the Third Platoon of G Company. Then they circled into the village and overran the Third Platoon CP and G Company CP.

Captain Wilde, G Company CO, had previously ordered Sergeant Hess to set up his crew and mortar in readiness for an attack but to withhold fire until enemy troops were close. Hess was instructed to fire flares to illuminate the enemy. At 0115 hrs (1:15 AM) two battalions of the Nineteenth SS Grenadiers attacked. Hess went to his prearranged OP (observation post), fired flares, and directed Bill Swint, his mortar gunner, who fired mortar shell after mortar shell on the attackers. Robert Lindsay and John Hodge were busy carrying ammo for Swint.

John Hodge reported an incident on one of his trips from the supply hole:

> I was returning when I saw a figure coming toward me from a corner of a building. It was so dark it was hard to identify the enemy from our own men. The German helmet and long

overcoat helped. I dropped my mortar shells and raised my rifle. The soldier said, "Me hendi ho," meaning "I surrender." There was too much going on for me to take him to the CP. I took his rifle and threw it on the ground and gestured for him to put his hands behind his head and pointed toward the CP. The German moved toward the CP, and then another German jumped up, threw down his rifle, put his hands behind his head, and moved toward the CP. I continued to our gun emplacement with my mortar shells.

Hodge described what happened later:

After what seemed like a couple of hours since the attack began, we ran out of mortar shells. By then Swint had the mortar almost in a vertical position since the Germans seemed all around us. Swint told Lindsey and me to go on back to our main line and that he would wait for Hess and come later.

Lindsey and I began our trip back toward a house at an intersection. We were running pretty fast as we approached the house, and as we came around the corner, we saw the silhouette of soldiers. We could not make out whether they were paratroopers or Jerries. I hit the ground. As I was falling, I looked toward Lindsey and saw what appeared to be sparks coming from Lindsey's chest. Something told me to play dead. When I hit the ground, my helmet fell off and rolled in front of me. My forehead was resting on my left arm that was crooked in front of me.

I could see the Germans in the doorway to the house. I saw this German take dead aim at my head and pull the trigger. The bullet struck to the left of my nose, came down, and knocked out three and half of my upper teeth, going through my lower lip, and cutting a gash in the bottom of my chin. I didn't move but waited for the next bullet to blow my brains out. I was not a professing Christian, but I recalled making peace with God, and I believe that if the second bullet had come that I would be with him today.

I was slowly freezing to death, almost afraid to breathe for fear the Germans would see the vapor from my breath. After a long time, a German came out and pulled the body of Lindsey against the house, and then he grabbed my arm to pull me over next to Lindsey. Seeing my face he jumped back as if he had seen a ghost. He grabbed my rifle and broke it against the ground and then helped me into the house.

A German officer dressed my wound and asked my name, rank, and serial number and placed me in a separate room and had one of his men give me an overcoat off one of my dead comrades.

In the meantime, over at the gap between G Company and F Company, an F Company machine gun team with Warren Zuelke as gunner, Roger Young as assistant gunner, and Joseph Amore as ammo bearer occupied the extreme right flank of their company's MLR next to G Company's position. Warren Zuelke told his experience:

> Just after midnight, the Germans, making a lot of noise, attacked in mass to our front and to the right against G Company. A portion of G Company was overrun, and we heard the Germans to our right and partially toward our rear. Rather than be surrounded, I moved my light machine gun out of our foxhole and to the rear of it. This enabled me to fire to the right as well as to the front. The Germans were in the open field and getting near our CP, still coming like crazy. Some were so close; they got into the foxhole we had just left. It was a sin, and I'm not proud of it, to have murdered as we did that night both Germans and cows. You know my ancestors were German. I might have killed some of my cousins, but we did what we had to do.
>
> While in our new position in open ground, a small German plane made a couple of passes, strafing our lines. The strafing plane hit Joseph Amore, my ammo bearer, in the back. Amore and Young were great team members. They hung in there with me during the tough fighting.

Angel Romero was in the area where the Germans broke through and recalled. "The Germans were yelling and calling the roll and cursing Roosevelt. But their yells turned into screams as our machine guns opened up on them."

Romero continued:

> Our artillery covered the area to our front with the most devastating and accurate fire I ever saw. The rifles, Thompsons, and BARs didn't stop firing until some of the SS had gone past

us. A machine gun behind us stopped firing, and I was sure the Germans got to it.

It wasn't long before a firefight developed behind us, and the Germans came running back over the top of our holes. This time we held our fire, which was a good thing because some of our guys were in close chase.

Lt. James Fowler, who commanded the First Platoon in reserve to the rear of the MLR, reported on the action of his platoon:

> Automatic fire was heard from across the Erria road, indicating a German attack on the Third Platoon. Within minutes, figures appeared in front of our line. The troopers were ordered to hold their fire, fearing the people were members of our Third Platoon withdrawing from the MLR.
>
> When many cried out that the helmets were German, the order to fire was given. By holding their fire, thinking our own men may have been in the field, the platoon allowed the aggressive SS troopers to fill the field and come within close range of our rifles and machine guns. The results were seen when daylight revealed the bodies of about sixty SS Panzer Grenadiers in front of the First Platoon's line.

When the firing became intense, Sergeant Hutto's men in the I Company outpost begged him to pull back. The sergeant wanted to remain at the outpost until ordered to move. One of the men volunteered to return to Battalion CP for instructions.

Headquarters Third Machine Gun Platoon was well placed on high ground, and their .50-caliber machine guns were sweeping the open field between the outpost and the CP. To avoid the field of fire, the volunteer had to detour around but even so found dead Germans on his route. The runner returned quickly with orders from Colonel Mendez: "Get the hell out of there."

When Colonel Mendez, CO of Third Battalion, saw that the MLR had been broken and Germans had occupied houses in the village of Erria, he called for help from E Company of the Second Battalion. Lt. Lloyd Polette, CO of E Company, and Lieutenant George Miles, E Company executive officer, reported to the Third Battalion CP for instructions. Miles recalled the meeting with Mendez and the subsequent action:

Just the day before, Polette and I had discovered on awakening that shrapnel had torn holes in our blankets without hitting us. The shrapnel had shattered a canteen, filled with good British rum, at our heads. So we were feeling cocky, if not indestructible, when we reported to Mendez. I remember we joked with Lou Mendez about pulling him out of trouble. Colonel Mendez was extremely calm as he gave us instructions indicating where the hostile fire was concentrated.

When we advanced toward the village, the place was brightly lit from a burning building, which produced a stagelike scene. We moved quite easily forward despite loud gunfire and much shouting. It was here, for the first time, I heard enemy soldiers crying out, "Me katholisch!" ("I'm Catholic!"), and being myself a Catholic, I was saddened and repelled at hearing the cry.

At one point, Polette and I and a couple of riflemen stopped at a farm building. Hesitating about whether to open doors and enter, I instinctively smashed a window and tested the interior with a burst from my Thompson submachine gun. This action, I will always remember, drew praise from the legendary Polette, and I felt as if I had won a medal.

My shots had driven one German soldier from the building, and I found myself facing this guy about twenty-five yards away. He was holding a rifle at port arms. Polette had gone off with a trooper who had been shot in the foot, and I was suddenly and shockingly alone. I motioned to the German to drop his weapon (I kept thinking of the "I'm Catholic!" shout). Just as I sprayed the ground at his legs, he raised his weapon and fired. I saw tracer bullets coming toward me, missing me. I saw him turn and run off into the darkness, and then it was all over. Shortly afterward, we reassembled, the Germans having run off or surrendered, and E Company returned to its reserve position.

I've made a point of the "Me katholisch!" plea because it represents, I think, the folly, the tragedy, and the contradictions of war, particularly as it involves ordinary men under the constraints of obedience to orders and, of course, the need to defend one's self.

Fred Infanger remembered the early part of the E Company counterattack:

I was in my foxhole trying to get some sleep when a German plane, sounding like a flying cement mixer, flew over strafing our troops. Right then, we got the word that we would counterattack. Lieutenant Polette led us in a charge down the hill into Erria, shooting Germans along the way until we reached the road into Erria.

At this point, the Jerries seemed to be very disorganized. I remember them calling to each other trying to regroup. We got to the road and heard a bunch of them in a barnyard just across the road. We threw grenades over at them. That really got them moaning and groaning.

We then crawled down the road into town. A house was on fire, and my buddy, Mark Chesnick, and I were by a shed next to the burning house. I told Mark to cover me while I crossed the road and then we could set up a machine gun and get the rest of the Krauts in the barnyard.

I started across the road and was hit in the leg with a burp gun. I was knocked flat. I got up and went back to Mark and asked, "Where is that Kraut?"

Mark spotted him up in a second floor window, plain as day, thanks to the light from the burning house, which also made me such a nice target when I tried to cross the road. As we edged along the side of the shed to shoot at him, a grenade exploded, getting both of us, which ended our participation in the counterattack. After I was wounded, someone else appropriated my Mauser and binoculars.

Medics gave immediate attention to Infanger and Chesnick. It was so cold that the wounded could not survive long before freezing to death. Most of the 508th wounded survived because of the heroic and skillful efforts of the medics. Our medics treated our own wounded first, and by the time the medics were free enough to treat the German wounded, many of them had already frozen to death.

F Company counterattacked from the left, and I Company counterattacked from the right. Sergeant Hutto described his memories of the I Company counterattack:

> We advanced toward the village following the road but off on either side. The Germans were firing a machine gun from a second-floor window. Someone fired a bazooka into the window that knocked out the machine gun. I went around the back of

the house, and there in the small paved courtyard was the body of Cpl. Brassie S. Cascio of I Company. He lay in a pool of blood, his head almost severed by a Schmeisser machine pistol. The Germans had already taken his boots.

Cascio had had a premonition that he would not survive another campaign, and before leaving Camp Sissonne, he distributed his personal belongings to friends and sent some mementos back to his mother in Chicago.

When things quieted, I found an old mattress on the side of the road. I cut the end out of the mattress, and Sergeant Elliot and I crawled into it like a sleeping bag for some warm sleeping. Then I heard some hobnailed boots walking up the road toward us. I didn't want to get out of the mattress, so when he got close, I yelled, "Halt!"

That Kraut dropped something and took off running back the other way like a scared rat. Next morning, when it was light, we found the machine gun ammo which the Kraut had dropped.

During the darkness, a wounded German kept saying, "Save us, Amerikanisch! Save us!"

I could also hear the German noncoms yelling orders as they pulled back and regrouped. We weren't about to risk getting shot helping the wounded Krauts.

After Sergeant Hess's mortar crew had exhausted all their flares and mortar shells and John Hodge and Robert Lindsey had unsuccessfully tried to get back to the rear, Hess returned to the G Company CP. The Germans were entering houses in the area and occupying positions around the perimeter. The company CP was in a house connected to a barn with a hallway. Hess entered a door to the connecting hallway. As Hess started down the hall toward the barn, an SS trooper entered through the front door, pointed his rifle at Hess, and ordered him to raise his hands and surrender. The sergeant looked over his shoulder at the German and said, "Go to hell," and at the same moment Hess turned the corner of the barn leading to the loft. He felt the heat from the German's bullet as it passed close by his elbow. The next moment one of our paratroopers came through the door from the barn and shot the German, who dropped immediately.

Sergeant Hess claimed he made it up the ladder to the loft in one leap. The men in the loft could hear the wounded German soldier moaning and groaning through the remainder of the siege.

Building to the right identified by John Hodge as G Company CP and the house next to the road where Hodge was a prisoner of the Germans. Photo by Barry Nichols. Permission to use by Barry Nichols.

During the I Company counterattack, a soldier threw a white phosphorus grenade that hit the window frame in the house where John Hodge was a prisoner. Some of the shrapnel from the grenade came through the building and hit a German, causing a painful burn. The I Company trooper was wounded on the heel by the same grenade. He was captured and put in the room with John Hodge.

When I Company men set up a machine gun and started spraying the area where Hodge was a prisoner, the Germans began leaving the building. Hodge recalled, "The last German to leave looked over at us, smiled, and gave a salute as he left."

Hodge was sent to an I Company aide station, given a morphine shot, and sent by ambulance to a field hospital. Since G Company could not account for Hodge, they listed him as missing in action. In less than three hours, John Hodge was wounded in action (WIA), became a prisoner (POW), was listed as missing in action (MIA), was liberated by friendly troops, and became a Christian.

By 0400 the town was cleared and defense lines reestablished. Sergeant Risnes reported that when the house used as G Company CP was cleared of the enemy, Lieutenant Greenwalt and Sergeant Waltman came up from the basement where they had hidden in a potato bin, and Sergeant Hess and Lieutenant James descended from the hayloft.

The 508th Connection

Marvin Risnes says, "The battle for Erria was the most aggressive German attack I experienced during the whole war. We lost a few men, but those SS troopers, Hitler's best, lost many more."

General Gavin visited Erria after the battle and personally congratulated the men of G Company.

In the G Company official log, kept by Operations Sergeant Joe Kissane, the following six men were listed as KIA from the battle: Joseph P. Bizefski, Refugio A. Muniz, Herbert L. Williams, William A. Williams, Harold H. Roberts, and Robert T. Lindsay. Thirteen G. Company men were listed as WIA and two as MIA. One of the MIAs listed was John Hodge.

The next morning, the paratroopers collected the bodies, which littered the fields in front of G Company, and moved them to a loading area. Later that night, under the cover of darkness, Sergeant Risnes took trucks to the loading area and supervised recently captured German prisoners as they filled two trucks with the bodies of their German comrades. Risnes declared, "Those prisoners were very subdued and cautious as if they were thinking, 'If we don't watch our step, we might end up on top of the heap.'"

Marvin Risnes and Warren Zuelke received medals and citations for their part in the Battle for Erria.

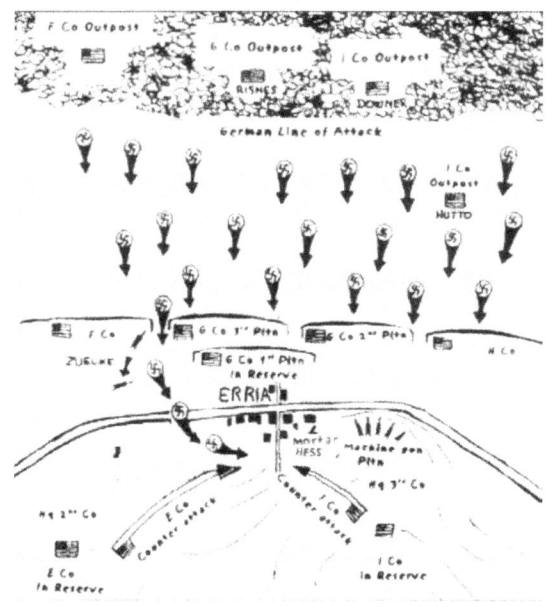

Battle for the village of Erria. Original design by Emile Lacroix in French. Final design modified and in English by Zig Boroughs. Permission to use by Emile Lacroix.

## "Their Faces Were Like Wax"

The morning after the Battle of Erria, our demolition section was called upon to lay a minefield in front of G Company. It was a foggy morning. We moved up to the front with our supplies and stopped behind the foxholes of the paratroopers defending the main line. I was surprised to see Ford, a former member of our demolition platoon, behind a mounted machine gun on the battle line. I remembered him as being in our unit while we were in Nottingham, England. At that time there were three men in the platoon whose names were the same as familiar automobiles—Ford, Nash, and Austin. For some reason Ford left our platoon and became a member another company. Once before, I had seen Ford marching by our position with his machine gun on his shoulder when his company was being deployed to a new area of the front.

We had to wait for the troops along the line to be alerted to our activities before going out in front of their guns, and while we waited, I had a chance to talk with Ford. He told me about a terrible battle that his company had fought from this position the night before.

Ford's platoon was dug in behind the bank of a narrow farm road before an open snow-covered field. The enemy had gathered a large force for a surprise attack in a wooded area beyond the open field. The Germans waited until night, a very dark night, and crept up in their white camouflage battle clothing very quietly and were undetected until about thirty yards from the American lines.

When the advancing Germans were detected and the paratroopers began shooting, the Jerries charged at full speed but were mowed down with machine gun and small arms fire. By the time our troopers could get reloaded and tend to the wounded, another wave of Germans attacked with the same reckless abandon. Again they were mowed down. Wave after wave of determined SS troopers attempted to overrun the American defensive position. Some even penetrated our lines and had to be killed in hand-to-hand fighting, but our paratroopers never gave ground but continued their murderous concentration of fire on the advancing attackers.

Finally, after several hours of continuous fighting, the attacks stopped. Our men were poised for another attack, loaded and ready and waiting and hoping for morning light. Even though the fighting was over, the tension and wide-eyed alertness mounted as expectations of additional attacks filled their thoughts.

When the firing stopped, the groaning began as the wounded Germans right out in front of the lines moaned and groaned and cried out for help during the long hours of darkness. Our own wounded and killed had been moved to the rear, and our medics were busy caring for our own and did not expose themselves between the lines to help the enemy. The groaning of the German wounded was nerve racking. Some of the wounded closest to our lines were put out of their misery by merciful pistol shots.

The groaning became less and less until it finally ceased before morning. When daylight finally dawned, Ford said that they left their foxholes to examine the carnage, and they learned why the groaning had finally faded out. All the wounded had either been put out of their misery by the pistol shots in the night or had frozen to death in the subzero weather.

Lieutenant Hardwick announced that the troops up the line had been fully notified that we were friendly demolitionists and would be laying a mine field for their protection and that they should not become trigger happy by our presence in their line of fire. Then we left Ford by his machine gun and moved out to plant the mines, stepping over the frozen lifeless bodies in our way.

Afterward George Brand described the scene, "The field was literally covered with bodies. They looked so young, and their faces were like wax."

## Not Damn—Dern

Did I ever shoot at anyone during the war? Yes, I actually squeezed off a few rounds of my BAR (Browning automatic rifle) at a man I could see. I was assigned the BAR after John Danko was transferred to another unit. Johnny had the size and strength needed for a BAR man. The BAR was the heaviest weapon in our section, and the BAR man had to carry more ammunition than others, so the frame and muscles of a football linebacker was a decided advantage. Johnny was the largest and the strongest man in our section. I had been Johnny's assistant and carried extra BAR ammo in my rifle belt along with my own M-1 ammo.

It was the day we laid the minefield at Erria. Bugs with his Thompson submachine gun and I with the BAR were posted in front of the field while others in the section were digging the holes and placing the antitank mines in position. We positioned ourselves in a gully. I set up the BAR on its bipod on the left bank of the gully and peered out through the fog to watch for the enemy. Bugs watched the approaches from the right. Then Bugs whisper-shouted to me and pointed, "Boroughs, look over here behind that bush!"

The outline of a man was clearly visible through the fog. He is clearly visible now, in my mind's eye, hunched over in a semicrouch, holding his rifle in his left hand beside his left knee. I can see the silhouette of his helmet, high in front and curved lower toward the sides in the German style. We had been shown training film depicting the differences between the style and appearances of German field soldiers and Americans. Americans were trained to carry their rifles in front of their chests, the Germans to the side. Our helmets were straight around the rim whereas the Germans' were curved.

I had a problem. Bugzy was between me and the German. I had to stand up and fire over Bugs holding up the heavy BAR with bipod dangling uselessly from the barrel. We both fired. The German backed off further behind the bushes and disappeared from our view into the fog.

Lieutenant Hardwick came quickly to check on the shooting. I was disgusted and blamed my poor shooting on the hindrance of the bipod and having to fire from an upright position to keep from hitting Bugs. Later, when we were in a group again, Brooks said, "Lieutenant Hardwick really was surprised to hear you swearing this morning, Boroughs."

"Me, swearing?" I asked. "I haven't been swearing!"

"The Ripper said, 'You should have heard Boroughs swearing at his damn bipod,'" replied Brooks, laughing.

"Not damn," I explained. "I called it a *dern* bipod."

There was some doubt that the man we shot at was a German after all. We heard later that one of our own patrols had been out that morning and had trouble getting back to our lines. It was probably a good thing we missed.

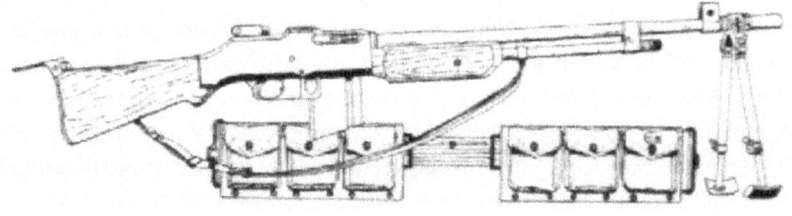

BAR (Browning automatic rifle) with ammo belt. Drawing by Emile Lacroix. Permission to use by Emile Lacroix.

## Thier du Mont, January 7, 1945

Marvin Risnes, G Company, witnessed a most unusual sight on Thier du Mont, which he relates. "Those 88s were firing point blank at our men as we advanced. I saw a machine gunner whose head was blown off by a direct hit. With his head gone, he took three or four more steps with the gun still on his shoulder before dropping in the snow."

This event was verified by Bob Phillips, I Company, who declares, "I saw that soldier lose his head and thought he never would drop."

Bill Beard, another I Company veteran, said that he had been carrying the machine gun himself until he felt like he couldn't continue any longer through the deep snow. Beard did not know the man who relieved him of the gun, but in a few minutes, he saw the unfortunate soldier's head blown away and his headless body continued several steps before falling forward in the snow.

G Company departed Thier du Mont during the Christmas Eve withdrawal. Two weeks later G Company led the Third Battalion, attacking the same position they had formerly held.

Two hills formed the ridge rising above the Salm River: a lower smaller hill—Thier dol Preux—and a higher and longer hill, Thier du Mont. The crests of the hills were covered with evergreen forest, but the saddle between the two hills was open with little cover except some slate pits.

The march toward Thier du Mont began at 0400 hrs. At 0815 G Company led the assault on Thier dol Preux. They paused briefly at Thier dol Preux to reorganize for the advance across the open approach to Thier du Mont.

Germans tanks, mortars, and machine guns from Grand Sart located just behind the saddle were covering the open area with fire. Their 88s were positioned along the fringes of the woods. G Company had to cross several hundred yards of open terrain to reach their objective.

The 88s opened up point blank on the Second Platoon. Sergeant Sirovica led the platoon into the open area along the slate pits. The First Platoon followed Sirovica's men. They had advanced about fifty yards into the treeless field when Lt. James Fowler, platoon CO, received a direct hit. The armor-piercing .88mm projectile ripped off Fowler's left leg.

Angel Romero recalls the 88s. "Our machine gunner, Kovensky, got hit trying to cross a wire fence. He flew through the air about five feet even though he weighed about 200 pounds, but he was not killed."

Medic Zeke Zuccala helped evacuate those wounded by the German 88s. "We formed a daisy chain," Zeke recalls, "And passed the wounded from man to man down the hill to the ambulances."

The men leading G Company's point, according to Angel Romero, included Staff Sergeant Sirovica, McGrath, Beno, Carter, and Captain Wilde. When the heavy stuff opened up, Captain Wilde, knowing that his men would be slaughtered if they didn't move, ordered a charge toward the ridge.

Sirovica urged his men to move full speed ahead and knock out the 88s. Warren Wilt fired his bazooka at one 88. Wilt recalled, "The rocket exploded very close to the gun—close enough for the crew to blow the breach and run."

Sergeant Risnes chased after the fleeing gun crew. He found them in foxholes about one hundred yards from their 88. The German gunners surrendered to Risnes, who sent them back toward the rear.

Bazookaman Gerald G. Jones and machine gunner William T. Kenny were each credited for destroying an 88.

Sirovica was awarded the Distinguished Service Cross for his action at Thier du Mont. The citation reads as follows:

> Staff Sergeant Frank L. Sirovica, 32044934, 508th Parachute Infantry, United States Army: For extraordinary heroism in action against the enemy on 7 January 1945, in Belgium. When his company's advance was halted by a devastating barrage from enemy high-velocity guns, small arms, and machine guns, Staff Sergeant Sirovica led his platoon in a charge across open ground toward the gun positions. As a result of his courage and action, three machine guns and three 88mm guns were neutralized. After reorganizing, the company again advanced, only to encounter direct fire from a German artillery weapon. Ignoring the intense fire, Staff Sergeant Sirovica moved forward alone toward the hostile gun position, killed two members of the crew and forced the others to surrender. Still advancing aggressively, he personally attacked four cabins, killing several Germans and capturing many others.

Joe Kissane, G Company operational sergeant, recorded the names of Elen D. Bucholz and Howard B. McDonald as KIA in the Thier du Mont attack. Kissane also listed thirty men from the company as WIA, 7 January 1945.

Angel Romero was one of those listed as wounded. He was knocked unconscious early in the attack by two banana-sized pieces of shrapnel, which hit him in the back, leaving two large welts. He came to about nightfall. The first thing he became aware of was a trooper saying, "You had better get moving before you freeze to death!"

With that urging, Romero started walking and came upon a man with a gash on his arm and another on his side. The two set out together. Romero describes their rescue:

> We were close to the base of the hill when some medics caught up with us. They were pushing and pulling a "weasel

ambulance" [a jeep with tracks]. They asked if we had seen other wounded. These medics were exhausted to the point that I thought they needed to be tended to more than we did. The bottom part of their legs was covered with ice, and they were half frozen themselves, but they let us ride while they pushed and pulled.

While I Company waited at the line of departure, Bill Sobolewski shared an apple with his buddy, Fred Gladstone. On the approach march, I Company had passed a US tank, and one of the crewmembers had given the apple to Sobolewski. Gladstone remembers that the two men talked of life and death and God and life after death as they waited in the cold. Gladstone describes the events that followed:

> Our conversation did not last long. We soon jumped off in the attack with G Company leading the way. As we moved forward in the deep snow, the sounds of battle increased and intensified. Over on my left, I noticed our supporting tanks moving across the field. Suddenly .88mm guns began picking them off with deadly accuracy. The tanks burst into flame, and all I could do was pity the poor crews.
>
> Then the Germans aimed their guns in our direction. The 88s were only a few hundred yards away, and the shells came in on a flat trajectory, slamming into the trees around us with deafening explosions. The bursting shells sent sharp and jagged slivers of steel cutting through the air.
>
> I heard Bill Sobolewski calling for help. Dashing through the snow and shrapnel, I found Bill lying on his back. The snow beneath him had already turned pink. I could not tell where all the pieces of steel had torn into his body, but I could see that one leg was badly broken and twisted. His whitened face was marked by intense pain.
>
> As soon as the 88 fire let up, our platoon sergeant, Jack Elliot, came over and told me that I Company had orders to move through G Company and I was wanted up front right away. I hated to leave Bill Sobolewski. Speaking a few words of encouragement, I covered him with my overcoat and stuck his rifle up in the snow in a way that medics could find him. Bill

Sobolewski was evacuated but later died of his wounds in an army hospital.

The First Battalion waited in the cold and snow. They watched and listened to the fierce fighting by the Third Battalion on Thier du Mont. After the Third Battalion reached their objective, orders were given for First Battalion to attack.

Jim Kurz, B Company, describes his experience:

> Things were easy until we got abreast of the Third Battalion. Then we were hit with rifle, machine guns, .20mm, and 88 fire. During this heavy fighting, Sergeant Savage was killed. I took over the squad, and we moved forward and overran the Germans. It was getting dark.
>
> We continued forward with George Banks and myself leading the way. We attacked another group of Germans, and they withdrew after a short fight. I heard a cry behind me. Jesse Womble had been hit in the stomach. I ran back and got a medic for him.
>
> We reached our objective and set up our defense in about the same spot we left on December 23. I told Banks to see to it that the squad dug in, that I was going back to make sure Jesse Womble got to the aid station.
>
> The temperature was below zero and the snow two to three feet deep. It was dark when I found Womble. Two medics were putting him on a stretcher. I told them I would make sure Womble got to the aid station, and they could hunt for other wounded. I found three others to help carry Womble. Womble weighed over two hundred pounds, and it was tough carrying him over the hills and through the deep snow.
>
> I would never have let Jesse freeze to death. [The wounded that could not be found that night died of hypothermia.] Jesse had helped me when I had sprained my ankle on the Holland jump, supporting me as we marched.
>
> The next morning we received word that Jesse Womble had died. I wrote to Jesse's mother about her son. George Banks and I had lost a truly great friend. It really hurt.
>
> Later that day General Gavin and Colonel Lindquist came by and told us what a fine job we had done.

At night after the attack, the medics set up an aid station in a log cabin, which had been used as a hunting lodge. The cabin was located on the backside of the ridge toward the German front. Zeke Zuccala and a German medic POW were taking care of about twenty wounded. One of the paratroopers, John Tomaseski, died during the night. Medic Zeke Zuccala worried about getting the remaining wounded men off the snow covered ridge before losing others. Zeke himself was wounded in the hand but continued working.

Next morning medic James Tiernan arrived with a truck. He had persuaded a driver from Service Company to take his vehicle over the hill for the wounded.

Angel Romero, who was wounded on Thier du Mont, gratefully remembers the medics with this tribute: "To this day, I always salute the men and women who wear the medical insignia."

## Memories of a Belgian Youth
By Emile Lacroix
Permission to use by Emile La Croix

Alexis Backus was 18 when the Red Devils fought over Thier du Mont ridge. Alexis worked in the quarry with his four brothers on Hill Thier dol Preux, a part of the Thier du Mont ridge. The 508th records refer to slate pits on Thier du Mont, but Alexis Backus says they mined a stone called "coticule," a rare formation used to sharpen razor blades. The stone cutters descended through a shaft about 100 feet underground to extract the stone.

December 17, the night the 508th was alerted to load on trucks and move to Belgium, Alexis planned to attend a dance in the village of Goronne. Since the US troops in the neighborhood, having heard about the German breakthrough, were in a frenzy, Backus decided to remain in his home village of Grand-Sart.

The next morning, December 18, Alexis and his brothers were not allowed to enter the mines for work and were sent back home for security reasons. The following day they began to hear gunfire, which kept getting closer and closer, and by dawn Christmas morning, German troops occupied Petit-Sart and Grand-Sart and rounded up 25 men as hostages, including Alexis Backus and his three brothers. Later 24 more men from other villages nearby were added to the hostage group. All of them were marched to Verleumont.

At dawn the hostages were taken outside and forced to move some vehicles destroyed by the US artillery during the night. It had frozen hard and everything was covered white with snow. Alexis counted 48 shells, which exploded near their place of confinement on Christmas night.

Suddenly Alexis saw a woman approaching and waving big signs. It was his mother searching for her 4 sons. In her search, she had heard reports that the hostages were all shot and other reports that they were seen marching toward Lierneux. Madame Backus was overjoyed to see all of her sons pushing those wrecked cars. She brought waffles for her sons who shared them with the others. Every day Madame Backus returned to comfort her sons and bring them food.

In early January American artillery near the hostage prison house became so fierce, the hostages were moved to a cellar. The barrage disorganized the Germans, and one soldier came to the cellar door and announced, "We are leaving."

Alexis stayed in the cellar until night and then left to return to his home. On his way, Alexis and others with him came upon German troops digging foxholes. They had also seen American troops in the distance around some of the villages they passed by. The Germans held them up, but when they said they were refugees, the Germans let Alexis' group pass on through to their homes.

Alexis recalled watching the fight for Thier du Mont:

> The 7th of January I took the risk of getting out by the door leading to the bake-house. I was in a secure place where I could see the movements of the American troops around Thier dol Preux. Those troops had been fighting fiercely since morning on Thier du Mont against well camouflaged Germans who where harassing them from everywhere.
>
> It was about 1500 hours. I saw the American troopers darting through a rain of tracer bullets running from Thier dol Preux and attacking Thier du Mont hill. They were running across the open fields and fences, then hitting the ground to avoid enemy fire.
>
> Some Germans of the elite SS troops camouflaged by a white sheet and protected by large trees were situated about 10 yards from where I was. They were firing sporadically at the

attackers. Then I saw Americans entering our house. They came out pushing before them about a dozen German prisoners.

When the snow melted, I found the head and shoulder and arm of one of the soldiers who attacked Thier du Mont. The rest of his body could not be found. This was a sad fate for a brave soldier who came from a far away continent to liberate us. After the battle many German bodies were found here and there. In May after it became hot, I found a dead German with a big cigar in his mouth. I will never forget those scenes.

L-R: Alexis Backus, Warren Wilt (508th veteran), and Belgian veteran. Photo taken at the 1995 March in the Footsteps of the Eighty-second Airborne, sponsored by the Belgian Eighty-second Airborne Jeep Club. The club erected the monument in the background, honoring the 508th at Thier du Mont. Warren Wilt shows a bazooka similar to the one used to neutralize an 88. Photo provided by Emile Lacroix, president of the Belgian Eighty-second Airborne Jeep Club.

## The Hostages

The small village of Comte was the objective of I Company, January 7. When G Company reached the top of Thier du Mont ridge, I Company moved through them toward Comte. Fred Gladstone was selected as lead scout. Gladstone recalled, "The objective was over a mile away, and the snow was so deep, I felt more like a snowplow than a scout."

Gladstone continued his account:

> As we neared Comte, I moved silently from tree to tree and was able to slip up on the lookout at a German outpost. He was startled by my sudden appearance and quickly obeyed my order to drop his weapon and to raise his hands. When the other Germans at the outpost saw this happen, they came out with their hands held high.

The rest of the company advanced, and there was a skirmish to my right, but it didn't last long. Soon we were overlooking the village where, according to the prisoners, most of the Germans were. With only about thirty able-bodied men left in the company and the short winter day about to end, Captain Dress, I Company CO, decided to dig in for the night.

Sergeant Elliot called on me again. I was to join another trooper and set up an outpost for the night between our position and the Germans. We cautiously descended the slope to a point about forty yards above the village. No sign of life could be discerned, but the Jerries were there in the darkened houses. Our bedrolls had not reached us, but we had a raincoat. Finding a slight dip in the ground, we lay down and huddled beneath the raincoat for warmth.

Toward dawn it began to snow, and as Gladstone and his partner lay under their raincoat, the soft white snow covered them like a warm blanket. Before long, the two troopers fell asleep from exhaustion.

While Gladstone and his partner slept, a five-man German patrol advanced toward their position. Their white capes and helmets blended in with the snowy landscape. When they were only about ten feet away, a shot rang out. Gladstone and his partner popped out from under their slicker. Gladstone recalled, "For a split second, we stared at five startled Germans. They, in turn, looked at us as if we were ghosts out of nowhere."

The five Germans, with their rifles ready, could have easily shot the two troopers. Instead, they turned and fled running and sliding down the slope at breakneck speed. The two troopers regained their composure, dusted the snow off their weapons, and made a lot of noise firing, but it was too late, the Germans had already reached the safety of the houses below.

Cpl. James Campbell on the I Company line above the outpost had fired the shot that awakened the troopers. Campbell had seen enemy troops at the edge of the village. Shortly afterward, as I Company prepared to assault the village, about forty Germans came out waving a white flag of surrender.

The next day, Sgt. James "Buck" Hutto, I Company, sat by the fire in one of the village houses, cleaning his tommy gun. From upstairs he could hear the sounds of women at a funeral wake, crying over the body of an old man who had just died. (The doctor said the oldster died of "combat fatigue.") At the same time Hutto heard the sounds of hammering and sawing from the basement, where some men were putting together a crude coffin.

As the sergeant contemplated the separate roles of those who occupied the three levels of the building, his thoughts were interrupted by a runner who announced, "Sergeant Elliot wants you to help get a sniper who shot one of our men. He is hiding in a house down the street."

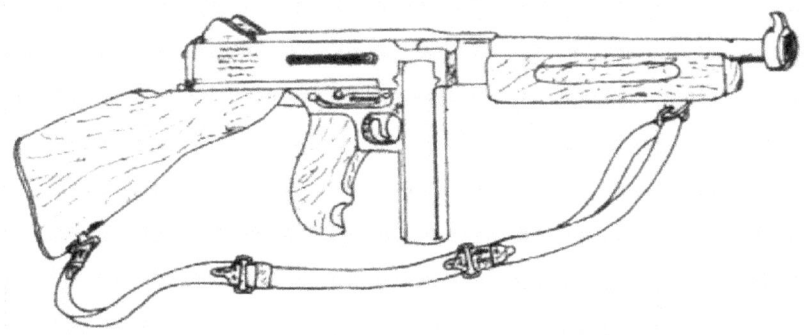

Thompson submachine gun (tommie gun).
Drawing and permission to use by Emile Lacroix.

Quickly, Hutto reassembled his weapon, shoved in a loaded magazine, and reported to his platoon sergeant. Elliot, crouching behind the corner of a building, pointed out the upstairs window from which the Jerry had fired. The two sergeants planned their strategy. Elliot told Hutto, "Buck, you sneak around the back of the house and I will approach from the front."

Buck Hutto happened to kick up an antitank Gammon grenade in the snow as he started around the house. He came back to Elliot and said, "Look what I found! Let's try blasting the Heinie out with this grenade."

Hutto threw the grenade on the roof of the house. The Gammon exploded with terrific power and destruction. The German sniper, groping through the smoke, flung open the front door and stood there with his hands raised but holding his rifle. Seeing that he was still armed, someone gave the order in German, which means, "Drop your rifle!" The sniper did not respond, and Elliot and others fired. The sniper fell headlong into the snow.

Then the Belgian family who had been held hostage emerged from the house. "One woman was so furious," Hutto declared, "She attacked the body, kicking and stomping, making sure that no life was left in the hated enemy."

The next day Bob Phillips, one of the I Company men occupying Comte, was placed on an outpost to the front of the village. He crawled on top of a small shed so he could get a good view of the area. Soon a shell hit close to the shed. Phillips was knocked unconscious and fell from the building. Much later in the day, he was revived by a medic who found him in the deep snow half frozen. Phillips was evacuated and treated in an army hospital for frozen feet.

Bob Phillips said, "I was lucky I didn't lose any toes like so many of the soldiers who suffered from frozen feet during the Battle of the Belgian Bulge."

## "Praise The Lord and Pass the Ammunition" Syndrome

After the MLR was restored to its former position before the Christmas Eve withdrawal and the Germans were driven back across the Salm River, a lull occurred for the fighting Red Devils. The medics had only minor duties such as tending to frozen feet, and dosing troopers on paregoric for the GIs. Since Chaplain Elder had caught up on writing letters to the families of the Red Devils recently killed in action, he planned worship services for the troops in the field.

David Oldemeyer was Chaplain Elder's assistant. Oldemeyer drove the jeep, played the portable pump organ, passed out hymnbooks, and gave other assistance to the chaplain as was needed. Medic Monty Montgomery usually went along with Chaplain Elder to help unload the organ from the jeep trailer and reload it after each service. Chaplains on the battlefield could not announce church for Sunday morning at 1100 hours and invite the whole regiment to meet in a central place. They operated more like old time-circuit riders that traveled to small groups of people wherever and whenever they could be found.

Chaplain Elder was on his circuit. He looked at his map and said to his driver, David Oldemeyer, "I think a mortar platoon is located just behind this knoll. Stop here and let's take a look."

They found the platoon where the map indicated. Since the platoon was not busy at the time, they were happy to have a short worship service. Oldemeyer and Montgomery unloaded the small pump organ and carried it over the knoll. They went back to the jeep and brought the hymnals. With the men spread out, not bunched up too closely, they sang some hymns. Chaplain Elder led in prayer, read scripture, and preached a short sermon.

After the worship service, Chaplain Elder lingered around the area, talking to various men, when an order came by telephone for the mortar section to fire on a designated target. In the meantime, Oldemeyer and

Montgomery had loaded the organ on the jeep trailer and were collecting the hymnals.

The sergeant in charge asked Chaplain Elder, "How would you like to throw a few rounds down the mortar tube?"

Chaplain Elder answered, "I think I would like that."

Montgomery, suspecting that Jerry knew where the shells would be coming from and would return the fire, suggested to the chaplain, "Let's get the hell out of here! Pardon the French!"

Chaplain Elder, however, felt a sudden urge to "praise the Lord and pass the ammunition." He elected to remain and fire the mortar while Oldemeyer and Montgomery waited in the jeep. The Germans didn't waste much time returning the fire. When the crew heard the incoming shells approaching, they shouted, "Take cover!"

Chaplain Elder tried to escape over the knoll, but a round came close enough to pepper his rear end with shrapnel.

Monty and David rushed to recover the chaplain and give first aid. No one else was hit. The chaplain made some remark to the effect that it served him right for trying to assume the role of a combat soldier.

Since the organ filled the trailer and the chaplain could not sit, Monty and David draped Chaplain Elder over the hood of the jeep, stomach down and wounded part up—a rather undignified posture—and thus transported him to the regimental aid station. Chaplain Elder soon recovered from his wounds and returned to his spiritual duties, completely cured of the "praise the Lord and pass the ammunition" syndrome.

Cartoon by Dick Owen, H Company, 508th Parachute Infantry.
Used by permission of Dick Owen.

## Rest

"Look at all those animal heads mounted on the wall," exclaimed the trooper in amazement. "This must have been King Leopold's hunting lodge." Actually, it was one of the three large ancestral homes owned by members of the Jamar family of Chevron: the Jamar House, the Neuville Castle, and the Chateau Rouge. The 508th Red Devils were withdrawn from the fighting front for a short rest period. They were billeted in all three houses owned by the Jamars. Erik Van der Hoever, editor of an annotated English version of the diary of Mr. Walthere Jamar, *Another Bridge Too Far, Another Longest Day, Chevron: A Belgian Village*, identified "King Leopold's hunting lodge" as the Neuville Castle.

Neuville Castle.
Photo provided by Erik Van der Hoeven.

Lt. Jack Sniederman, an MP from the Eighty-second Division, and other rear echelon officers, had been using spare rooms in the Jamar House. The officers shared their ample GI rations with the family, and Monsieur Jamar enjoyed the genteel company of the gentlemen officers. However, he found the common soldiers of the 508th crude and destructive and unwashed. Some of Jamar's impressions are quoted from his diary:

Jan 11: It is 02:00 p.m., my house has been transformed into barracks, in total disorder, bringing my girls to the point of total despair. These soldiers from the battle zone are much more the rough-and-rowdy type than those who have just left; these are like savages that take everything that they like . . . We haven't seen the new officers yet who are staying here: they need to take measures to put an end to these abuses.

These soldiers returning from the battle zones are really to be pitied. They fought in the snow and the cold and then, after long days of very heavy fighting, they were transported on trucks to Chevron, where they will rest . . . We have to excuse them for many things. One has to admit, however, that they are not looking friendly, they look like real savages, with their unkempt hair and their faces that have not seen water in several days.

Several hundred of us were billeted in the Neuville Castle. I had my bedroll in the large master room on the first floor, which was as large as a standard basketball court. At one end was a huge fireplace about fifteen feet wide. Hunting trophies were mounted all along the walls: heads of deer, caribou, buffalo, and exotic African animals. I remember a bear's skin and head with snarling teeth made into a throw rug and placed in front of the fireplace.

Some of the troopers extended their privileges to the use of fine china from the castle for their meals and dressing up in fancy tuxedos found in the closets. At one point, a caretaker came through with a notebook and wrote down all the damages done by the troops. The regimental officer escorting the caretaker was overheard explaining how lucky this place was compared to the total destruction of property elsewhere.

General Gavin visited the troops of the 508th while we were in Chevron and explained the big picture. Many of the paratroopers were confused about the actual role of the 508th and the Eighty-second Airborne Division. The heroic role of the 101st Airborne Division at Bastogne had been given prominence in the *Stars and Stripes*. It made the Red Devils of the 508th feel good to know that we also had an important part in stopping the penetration of the Germans into the Belgian Bulge and of turning the Nazis back toward their own border.

Many years later at a 508th reunion I overheard a paratrooper say to an old buddy, "This is my wife, whom I met, courted, and married in Belgium."

"In Belgium?" replied his buddy in disbelief. "How in hell did you find time to court a woman during all that fighting?"

"It was during our week of rest in Chevron," was the answer. "I needed a woman more than I needed rest. I found the right one, and we have been having fun together ever since."

## Wrong Leg

Jim Rankin of Regimental Headquarters Company S-2 section was returning from a reconnaissance patrol somewhere in Belgium. Rankin, and those with him, had walked a long way in heavy snow. They were glad to see a GI truck going their way toward the regimental CP. They waved the truck to a stop and learned that the 508th Graves registration officer was using the truck to pick up bodies for burial.

The officer offered, "If you guys don't mind sharing the space with a few stiffs, hop on the back of the truck."

"We are just glad to get a ride, even with dead men!" the troopers replied as they vaulted into the back.

The discussion of the men while riding with the dead went something like this:

"I think that the Graves officer has about the worse job in the whole regiment. I wonder how he got that assignment."

"He probably goofed leading the living, so they put him to burying the dead."

"Hey, look up ahead! Looks like a bunch of fresh troops at the crossroads."

Some Jerry, from his observation post, also must have seen the troops bunched together at the crossroads and phoned in the coordinates to his artillery crew. Several shells soon whistled over the truck and landed among the new GIs.

One of the men said, "More bodies for the Graves registration officer, and more work for the medics!"

The truck stopped, and Jim Rankin and the others helped with the wounded. After one man who had lost a leg was loaded on a truck, the injured soldier asked Rankin, "Would you please find my leg and let me take it with me?"

Jim looked around and found a severed leg and handed it to the soldier.

The soldier looked at the leg and said, "This isn't my leg!" and handed it back to Rankin.

Rankin took the leg, laid it down, and looked until he found another severed leg and presented that one to the soldier.

The soldier smiled and said, "Thanks, this one is mine."

Typical GI truck used by the Eighty-second Airborne. Drawing and permission to use by Emile Lacroix.

## Old Red

"Old Red was our private cow," declared Joe Hamm. "We took her all over Belgium, fed her, and milked her. Every time we moved, we took Old Red with us."

Joe Hamm was in the message center of Regimental Headquarters Company. Joe, John Wills, Roger Duffy, and John Teele were among those in the message-center group who took care of Old Red.

Right after Christmas, Regimental Headquarters was moved to Basse Bodeux. The people had fled or had been evacuated, leaving some of their livestock behind. The men in the Demolition Platoon enjoyed fresh milk while in Basse Bodeux. The cows were hurting. Their udders were full and their stomachs empty. It was a relief for the cows to be fed and milked. Joe Hamm doesn't remember where the message center section became attached to Old Red. It could have been Basse Bodeux.

Old Red was a good milker, and the chances of her surviving without care during that bitter winter were slim. When the message center prepared to move out, they discussed the situation. "Who is going to take care of Old Red when we leave?"

For the mutual benefit of the section and Old Red, she took her place in the column as the company marched off to its new location. They took her with them for several moves until one day when the unit was under enemy mortar fire and Old Red was killed.

But that was not the end. The group decided to have steak for supper. Milking was one thing, but Hamm was no expert with beef. Hamm admits, "I don't know where we went wrong, in the butchering or the cooking, but when we tried to eat Old Red, we all got sick."

## Deidenberg

In late January the 508th relieved parts of the Second Infantry Division and Seventh Armored Division in and near the town of Deidenberg. Deidenberg is located in Belgium about fifteen kilometers from the German border, but the area is inhabited by German people who speak German and whose sons fought for Germany in both World War I and World War II.

The troops that the 508th relieved had been staying in homes with the citizens of Deidenberg. As these troops moved out, the Red Devils moved into these same houses. Pictures of German soldiers in uniform looked down from the walls and shelves of those homes.

Often the occupying troops shared rations with the German families, who were forced to share their shelter with their enemies. Okey Mills, Headquarters Third Mortar Platoon, recalls that when he wasn't out on the OP (observation post), he would be in the house. The mother of the family would heat up the GI C rations on her stove, and the family would sit down at the same table and eat with the soldiers. One of the family's sons, a young man in his late teens, was usually at the table with Mills and the other troopers.

At that time, German artillery was extremely accurate, hitting areas of US troop concentration and firepower. Then it was discovered that a Jerry soldier, on leave visiting his grandmother, was sending firing positions via radio to the German artillery. That prompted a search of all the houses in the area. Mills came in from the mortar OP and was told that the youth who had been eating at the table with them was caught trying to bury his German furlough papers under a manure pile. He was taken as a POW (prisoner of war).

Okey's buddy said, "Look at that picture on the shelf."

Sure enough, it was the same lad in a German army uniform. The paratroopers were dumbfounded. They had eaten at the same table with the guy, saw the picture of the German soldier on the shelf, and never associated the photo with the youth.

Having discovered that the people of Deidenberg were loyal and helpful to the enemy, all the civilians were forced out of their houses and marched through the deep snow toward the German front. This was a reversal of the usual practice of the 508th. Usually civilians were sent to the rear for their protection. This time they were sent toward Germany to protect American soldiers. It was a bitter scene of mostly old people, women, and children. Many were wrapped in blankets, which they clutched tightly against their bodies. The sound of the howling wind was mixed with the wails of the Deidenberg people as they walked away from their homes.

The CP of B Company was located in one of the farmhouses near Deidenberg. A photograph of a German soldier in uniform hung on the wall. A woman gave birth in a bedroom while paratroopers were in the house.

Sergeant Boccafogli of B Company remembered setting up an outpost in front of the main line. He assigned two new replacements to the outpost. During the night, the new men ran back to Boccafogli and reported that a German patrol dressed in white had just passed the outpost. Boccafogli examined the area and saw fresh tracks in the snow where the German patrol went into the pine forest. He relieved the two men who seemed a little timorous for the job and placed Sgt. Harry Austin, also a replacement but with combat experience, in a ditch where he could see anyone coming from that direction. Boccafogli told Austin, "They will probably return this same way. Lay low, and you will see their feet under the snow-covered pine trees as they come toward you."

In about an hour, Boccafogli heard firing and went back to the outpost. Austin had killed one German soldier; two others escaped through the woods. Boccafogli searched the body and sent all papers, which might provide military information to the B Company CP. Later Captain Millsaps, B Company CO, sent a detail to bring the body of the German soldier to the CP.

The same night Jim Allardyce and Bill Windom had been on a patrol for B Company. In returning to the CP, Captain Millsaps said to them, "Look at this wallet photo we found on a German soldier we just killed. Now look at the photo on the wall!"

The photo on the wall was an enlargement of the one found on the dead German soldier.

Monument to Deidenberg soldiers and civilians killed in World War II. Photo and Permission to use by Emile Lacroix.

Red Devils, who retrace their steps of World War II, will find a monument in the town of Deidenberg with names of their people who died in the two world wars. Three names from the Muller family are listed as civilians who perished on January 20, 1945. Two other civilians, Marie and Ludwig Daubach, died on January 21, 1945. Matthias Genten, a soldier, was listed as a casualty on January 27, 1945. Records indicate that the 508th was in the Deidenberg area from January 21 through January 24, 1945.

Men of Headquarters First, 508th on tank.
Extreme right: Allen Johnson. Behind Johnson, Sgt. Maj. John Sivetz.
Photo and permission to use by Emile Lacroix.

A relative of Steve Tetak, Headquarters First Company, who was reported killed in action on January 22, 1945, requested information about the circumstances of Tetak's death.

Bill Goudy of Headquarters First, a sergeant in the mortar section, responded:

> Here is how Steve was killed: We had moved in during the night. In the morning at daybreak, we found we were on the forward slope of the hill and getting heavy artillery fire. Sgt. Glenn Somerville and myself called our squad leaders in and

told them to move the .81mm mortars to the backside of the hill. We were in a large stone barn. Steve was the last man in for instructions. A shell came through the wall between Glenn and myself. Steve was between us and got the full force of it.

Glenn Somerville lost his left arm, left eye, and the toes on his left foot. I had shrapnel in my mouth. A boy named Potym had a broken leg from stone falling on him. The back wall covered some men in foxholes. I think they were from Headquarters Second Communications.

My hospital and service records show that this was January 21, 1945, and not January 22 at Deidenberg, Belgium.

Deidenberg, January 1945. Civilains fleeing, paratroopers on tank. Photo provided by Emile Lacroix.

## Combat Fatigue

We were on the move near the Belgian-German border to a new battle area of combat. Rumors were flying that we would be attached to an armored command and we would be riding tanks into battle. We had stopped to rest at the edge of the small village of Deidenberg when the 88s started whistling in close. The 88s were among the most dreaded weapons of the German arsenal. They gave you very little time to take cover. If you could hear the whistle, the shell was probably passing over because the whistle and the shell arrived at about the same time.

It was just before entering the village when the 88s were whistling in that a trooper's nerves stretched to the breaking point. He threw down his weapon and started running across the field of snow. Lieutenant Hardwick ordered Nelson and Bellucci to catch him. They chased him, tackled him, and brought him to Hardwick, who said, "Take him on to the medics." That was the last time I saw my friend, who lost control. He was removed from the front and later discharged because of combat fatigue.

Howard Brooks explained why my friend lost control. On D-Day in Normandy, he was with Lieutenant Johnson when he was wounded. He helped the lieutenant get to an aid station in a French house. Some German soldiers came in the house and started shooting with their automatic machine pistols until there was no more sign of life among the GIs. He hit the floor. In the melee that followed, some of the dead fell on top of him. He pretended to be dead. He remained still and quiet until the Germans left. Brooks expressed the belief that the trooper's nerves had been raw ever since.

I thought that another member of our section had suffered combat fatigue in Holland. He went berserk, picked up his weapon, and started darting hither and thither, ready to take on the whole German army by himself. His behavior, however, made him more dangerous to our side than to the enemy.

Brooks and Rosy Akins were given the assignment of getting him to the medics. He was so big and strong and raving like a bull that Brooks and Rosy had more than they could handle. Rosy even tried hitting him over the head to reduce his vigor, but that didn't seem to help much.

It was explained to me later that this trooper did not suffer combat fatigue. What really happened was caused by a new distribution of alcoholic drinks to the 508th officers by the British command. In both the Holland and the Belgium campaigns the Eighty-second Airborne was under the command of the British High Command, headed by Field Marshal Montgomery. The British routinely issued rations of booze to their officers. This was extended to the American officers under the British command.

When Lieutenant Hardwick received his first ration of booze, he shared it with his enlisted men. This trooper apparently overindulged, and his aberrant behavior was due to alcohol rather than combat fatigue. He did not come back to our section but was assigned to another unit within the company.

## Fourth of July Hero, 1944

We had been marching in columns of two a good part of the day. It was January 1945, east of St. Vith, Belgium. That morning we had passed two army trucks loaded with bodies of American soldiers that were killed in December of 1944, when the Germans first broke through the Belgian Bulge. These bodies were found when the territory was regained. We were in a fir forest when we came upon the bodies of five paratroopers. It was a collection point for recent KIAs (killed in action).

Lieutenant Hardwick exclaimed the following:

> Look! There is Lieutenant Goodale! What a loss! He was such a fine man—a gentle soul but strong and brave when duty called. Remember July 4, in Normandy, when we were in the low area parallel to Hill 95, how Goodale exposed himself to enemy fire so that our machine gunners could pinpoint the German positions?

Some of the other men, veterans of Normandy, echoed Hardwick's sentiments of admiration and grief for the fallen hero as we passed the lifeless bodies of the lieutenant and the other KIAs.

Charles A. Powell Jr. of D Company wrote a letter to his family, dated May 11, 1945. That was after VE Day (Victory in Europe) and after censorship of soldier's letters was discontinued. The letter was a digest of his war experiences. Below are excerpts from his letter:

> All was quiet, and again a shot and a scream. Our barber got it in the head and our Lieutenant Goodale got it in the stomach and Scruggs our medic was working on him, but I saw the lieutenant's guts coming out and later he died.
>
> What had happened was, we were following the 505th that was attacking. They missed a German patrol of about 10. They [the German patrol] ran into us, and the fireworks started. We killed them all but two and they gave up at an outpost.

Rick Scruggs, the medic, described his action and commented on the situation. He said that they had been marching all day and had stopped for the night. They dispersed in the forest, and he was getting ready to bed down for the night.

Scruggs heard the unmistakable sound of a German machine pistol, the equivalent of our Thompson submachine gun but much faster when firing. He found the lieutenant still living with a large wound in his stomach. Scruggs poured penicillin powder in the wound and applied a bandage. The other casualty was lying on his face. Scruggs checked his pulse and found none. When he turned him over, he saw that most of his face was blown away.

In 1948 my wife was reading the *Spartanburg Herald Journal* when she stopped and asked, "Did you know a paratrooper by the name of Lt. Hoyt T. Goodale in the 508th?"

"No, I did not know Lieutenant Goodale personally," I replied, "but I remember seeing his dead body in a snow bank on the side of a narrow mountain road in Belgium."

My wife read on, "Lieutenant Goodale's body has been returned. The funeral is tomorrow. The family is receiving visitors at their home near Boiling Springs tonight."

I visited with the family that evening and shared with the grieving father the impressions that I had received of his son who had served his country so bravely.

When I visited with the Goodale family, I was a teaching-principal of a small rural school just five miles from the Goodale home. About forty-five years later, I was invited to a reunion of students from the school. While at the reunion, I asked a group seated with me at the dinner table, "Does anyone remember Hoyt Goodale?"

One of the men answered, "Yes, he was my scoutmaster—the best man I ever knew."

Left: Lt. Hoyt Goodale. Right: Lt. Norman MacVicar.
Photo furnished by George Miles.

## "I Love Paris in the Winter"

Regimental Headquarters Company had just marched past two parked trucks loaded with GI bodies. The booted feet stacked five feet high showed in rows and columns at the rear of the trucks.

Then we passed the five dead paratroopers, which included Lieutenant Goodale of "Fourth of July Hero."

"This scene is getting depressing," observed Henry Sellers. "Why can't I get one of those furloughs to Paris?"

"Yes, I think I would love Paris in the winter," Worster Morgan declared.

"By the way, Pappy, I hope you have your cards. The first time we have some time, we've got to play off the rubber," suggested Jim Rankin.

"Pappy" was Worster Morgan's nickname. He was twenty-eight years old, which to troopers under twenty-one was ancient. Pappy and his crew in the S-2 section were bridge addicts. Every chance they had, they would deal the cards for a round of bridge.

Toward dark, the column halted and Regimental Headquarters Company bivouacked in a small clearing. The men built a couple of fires. The smoke curled up above the surrounding trees. The S-2 men settled down by one of the fires and broke out the cards. Pappy spread his pack for the bridge table. Then he took off his helmet, sat on it, and pulled his wool cap down over his ears.

Fred Robbins dealt. Rankin bid one club and waited. "Come on, Pappy, your bid."

"Oh, I was just thinking of Paris in winter. Two spades."

*Whistle! Boom!* The noise of an 88.

"Hey, that one was close!"

The next shell came in without the whistle, just the boom, and Pappy Morgan was knocked off his helmet seat.

Someone hollered, "Medic! Morgan is hurt!"

"You sit on your helmet and get a head wound—smartass!" scolded the medic.

The shrapnel glanced off Morgan's head, stunned him a little, and drew some blood. Since it was a head wound, special attention was required. He was tagged for a Paris hospital.

The wound healed quickly, and Morgan had some time to see Paris in winter. On returning, Sgt. Worster Morgan was awarded a battlefield commission and moved up to second lieutenant.

Harry Kennedy saluted the new officer and asked, "Say, Pappy, how was Paris in winter?"

Morgan replied, "I didn't exactly paint the town. I only had two $2 bills. What could you do in Paris with $4?"

Kennedy replied, "Well, at least, you got out of this frozen hell for two weeks."

## The Bacon, the Water, or the Length of the Day

I'm not sure what made me sick. It could have been the bacon, or it could have been the water, or it could have been the length of the day. I will explain about the bacon first. Moto (Wilbur Byers) had worn out his boots, so he was assigned to the regimental kitchen until a new pair of boots could be found. He had just rejoined the squad with his new boots and some bacon, which he managed to smuggle out of the kitchen.

While we were sitting around eating our K rations at the end of the day, Moto pulled out his package of bacon to share. We had shoveled the snow down to the earth and built a small fire to cook the bacon. When the bacon was only half cooked, we received a burst of artillery. This was the shell that gave Wooster Morgan his "million-dollar head wound" and a trip to Paris. It could have been that the smoke from our fire alerted the enemy to our position.

Lieutenant Hardwick ordered us to put out the fire. Someone said, "The Eskimos survive the cold by eating blubber, which is raw fat. If we have to live in the snow like Eskimos, why not eat like them?" So, thinking it would help us fight off the cold, we ate the bacon half cooked.

Before daylight we were back on the march, and this is the beginning of my longest day. At midmorning, we stopped to fill our canteens from a beautiful mountain stream flowing swiftly between its banks of snow. After marching a few hours with weapons, pack, and heavy winter combat clothes, we were thirsty enough to drink heartily from the stream water. We continued our march upstream and soon came to an area that had been fought over. There was a dead body in the stream, prompting some of us to empty our canteens. It could have been the water.

It was mid-afternoon when we came to the mountain village of Holzheim. This was the town where First Sergeant Leonard Funk saved the day by preventing the escape of eighty German prisoners.

We arrived at Holzheim after the sweep of the village by C Company. Members of my platoon were assigned to escort the prisoners to a secure rear area. By this time, many more Germans had been rounded up, and there were as many as two hundred prisoners. We were warned that this group might try anything. Guarding these prisoners was not exactly a relaxing assignment. We feared that if they tried to escape, we would not have enough ammo.

Since I carried a BAR (Browning automatic rifle), I was placed at the rear of the column along with my buddy, Leon Israel Mason, with orders to shoot to kill if the prisoners acted up. Lt. Don Hardwick was in charge. Among the other guards were Chris Christiansen, Howard Brooks, Joe Ricci, Fritz Nitschke, and Andrew "Bugs" Cehrobak.

Before we moved the prisoners, one of our paratroopers from S-2 spoke to them in German. He was a small German Jew who managed to get out of Germany before Hitler got to him. He stood on something high so he could be seen, and soon he had the prisoners laughing as if they were in a comic theater. Whatever the small trooper said, it must have worked. The prisoners did not try to escape or overpower us.

Lieutenant Hardwick remembered that while we were escorting the prisoners, he heard a tommy gun firing at the head of the column. Hardwick rushed to find out the cause. He discovered a jeep, which had been stuck in the snow, being pushed by some of the German prisoners. But what was the shooting about? Bugs Cehrobak ordered the prisoners in front to push the jeep free of the snow bank. The prisoners refused, saying that they were officers. A few rounds near their feet persuaded them that their officer status did not count with Bugs, so they decided to push.

The anxiety over the prisoners and the length of the march in heavy snow without food was exhausting. It took us the rest of the day and part of the night to reach a place where there were enough troops to guard the prisoners securely.

Eventually we managed to get back to Holzheim, but our day was not over yet. I had just unfastened my rifle belt and lifted my pack to the ground when we were told to move out. With my BAR ammo and other gear, I must have been packing about eighty pounds. A buddy helped me back into my gear, and off we went.

The going at first was easy, downhill then up the other side of the mountain. It seemed we were going uphill for hours. It never happened to me before or since, and I, who thought of myself as a tough paratrooper, was terribly embarrassed. I passed out on the march. Little Car Austin was rubbing snow in my face when I came to. Little Car was left with me, and later on that morning, we caught a ride on a jeep and joined our company in another little village—Lanzerath.

It was daybreak when we entered the village. We had been on the go for twenty-four hours. But the day was not over yet. Our squad was assigned to defensive positions around the village.

After three hours, Sergeant Belliveau called us from our foxholes, one or two at a time, for some hot oatmeal. To be perfectly honest, another trooper told us where we could get the oatmeal. We did not wait for Belliveau's summons. When we arrived at the field kitchen, Sergeant

Belliveau reamed us out vigorously to the point of threatening us with a court martial for leaving our post without his orders.

Shortly after eating, the GIs hit me. (The meaning of GI is "government issue," but it was our euphemism for battlefield diarrhea.) I had a bad case of the GIs for the rest of the day while we watched for the enemy from our foxholes. I remember the slit trench near my foxhole. Soldiers were taught to dig a slit trench in the field for sanitary purposes. The worse thing was exposing my bare behind to the cold so many times.

After starting the day with twenty-four hours of marching and spending the next eight hours dividing my time between the foxhole and the slit trench, I was able to get four hours of sleep before another tour of watch. What caused the GIs? It could have been the bacon; it could have been the water; or it could have been the length of the day. One other possibility comes to mind: the reaming out from Sgt. Teddy Belliveau.

## The Berlin Connection

Werner "Tom" T. Angress, who addressed the German POWs at Holzheim, was living with his family in a suburban area of Berlin when Adolf Hitler came to power on January 30, 1933. Tom attended high school (*Realgymnasium*) as the only Jew in his class. He suffered some anti-Semitic abuse, but Tom considered himself fortunate compared to many other Jewish students in Berlin. The Angress family, who wisely foresaw the fate of German Jews, immigrated first to England in 1937 and in 1938 to Amsterdam, Holland, where Tom's father invested in a business.

Young Tom Angress managed to get approval, through the US consulate in Holland, to immigrate to a farm in Virginia, established to accommodate young Jews as a refuge from Hitler. His arrival in the United States, November 10, 1939, was on the first anniversary of the infamous Crystal Night. The farm work lasted until the spring of 1941 when the project folded, and the Jewish refugees had to seek alternative employment. Tom Angress chose to volunteer for the US Army. Eventually after training for interrogating German prisoners, Tom was assigned to the Eighty-second Airborne Division and attached to the 508th Parachute Infantry Regiment.

Although Tom was not trained as a paratrooper, he persuaded General Gavin to let him jump with the paratroopers into Normandy. He made three parachute jumps during his four and a half years in the army—Normandy, Holland, and the Marlene Dietrich parade jump at

Camp Sissonne. Gavin also allowed Tom to use an army jeep to look for his family in Amsterdam after V-E Day. He found his mother and his two younger brothers, who had been protected by the Dutch Underground. His father, however, had been arrested by the Nazis and gassed at Auschwitz.

Tom taught history for thirty-five years at the University of California at Berkeley and the State University of New York at Stony Brook. Since retiring in 1988, Werner T. Angress has lived in Berlin, Germany.

## First Sergeant Leonard Funk Saved the Day

First Sergeant Leonard A. Funk Jr. of C Company was the most highly decorated soldier in the Eighty-second Airborne Division in World War II. For his action at Holzheim, Funk was awarded the Congressional Medal of Honor. Funk's Congressional Medal of Honor citation described the sergeant's action at Holzheim in preventing the escape of eighty German prisoners:

> An enemy patrol, by means of a ruse, succeeded in capturing the guards and freeing the prisoners and had begun preparations to attack Company C from the rear when First Sergeant Funk walked around the building and into their midst. He was ordered to surrender by a German officer who pushed a machine pistol into his stomach. Although overwhelmingly outnumbered and facing almost certain death, First Sergeant Funk pretended to comply with the order, began slowly to unsling his submachine gun from his shoulder, and then, with lightning motion, brought the muzzle into line and riddled the German officer. He turned to the other Germans, firing and shouting to the other Americans to seize the enemy's weapons. In the ensuing fight, twenty-one Germans were killed, many wounded, and the remainder captured.

Merrel Arthur, a member of a mortar squad that was bringing up the rear of the C Company's attack on Holzheim, was an eyewitness to Funk's heroism. Arthur explained the way he saw the event. As he and his squad were approaching the village, Sgt. Bill Traband turned over to them about eighty prisoners. They marched the prisoners about three hundred yards away from the village and came upon Sergeant Funk with three or four men. The prisoners were ordered to sit down. Suddenly, the prisoners jumped up and yelled, "Heil Hitler!" Arthur looked toward the rear of the group and saw men approaching dressed in snow capes, yelling at the other guards. Sergeant Funk came up and asked Arthur, "What's going on down there?"

A German SS officer, accompanied by an aide and a captured American, was approaching. When he saw Funk's first sergeant stripes, he came straight to Funk. He waived his Schmeisser at Funk and jabbered in German. In the meantime, some of the German prisoners started running toward a vacant house about fifty yards away. Funk looked bewildered until the captured American explained that he had been captured and the German officer was ordering the others to surrender. Funk had his tommy gun slung over his shoulder, but in a flash, he had the gun in the German's belly and ripped off a burst. The German slowly sank to his knees. He tried to raise his gun and fire, but he lacked the strength.

Sergeant Funk then sent Merrel Arthur for help. Arthur found his buddy from the mortar squad, Corporal Askew, shot in the leg and dragged him to an aid station. Arthur then raced back to Funk, who by this time had some help. Many of the prisoners were dead, and all the others were rounded up and under control.

Lt. Joe Shirley was the executive officer for C Company during the Battle of the Bulge. I asked Shirley about the Holzheim incident. Shirley responded, "The first time I saw Leonard after the prisoners were secured, he was all shook up because he had just learned that his good friend and dependable company clerk Edmund Wild was killed."

When the monument honoring First Sergeant Funk was dedicated at Camp Blanding, Florida, Dr. John Hardie spoke in tribute to Funk. Hardie described an incident after the action in Holzheim:

> Continuing the attack thereafter, C Company moved on through Holzheim until nightfall gave a lull in the action. Soldiers wounded and dead were strewn about in the snowdrifts amid the trees, and everything was on hold. Communication Sergeant John Entler went looking for Leonard, and hearing murmurs in German off to one side, Entler approached cautiously to find Leonard comforting a severely wounded German, who shortly afterward died in Funk's arms. Funk let John know that under no circumstances was Entler to let the rest of the company know what he had seen. I learned of it only years later, when we were discussing that day over a "small one" in hand.

President Harry Truman decorated First Sergeant Leonard Funk with Congressional Medal of Honor. Picture provided by Emile Lacroix.

## Capt. William H. Nation

After securing Holzheim, the First Battalion pushed on the next day, January 31, to objectives beyond the village of Lanzerath. Sgt. Jim Kurz, B Company, reported, "We were going through country with pill boxes and dragon teeth tank traps. We were in the Siegfried Line. We took a few prisoners but had no casualties."

The enemy resistance was light, but the map reading was difficult. According to Jim Kurz, B Company arrived at their so-called assigned objective only to be thanked by Captain Adams for clearing A Company's area. Three hours later, after breaking trail through waist-deep snow, B Company occupied their assigned position on the MLR (main line of resistance).

Colonel Lindquist wanted to be closer to the frontline deployment of his troops and ordered the 508th Regimental CP moved to Lanzerath. Colonel Shanley, regimental executive officer, in consultation with Colonel Lindquist and his command staff, selected a site just behind the MLR. The coordinates for the CP were located on the map, and the advance team set out during the evening of January 31 to occupy and establish the new CP.

Capt. Robert Abraham, CO of Regimental Headquarters Company, said, "The initial establishment of the farmhouse CP was militarily sound and by the book."

However, there were some problems. They had unknowingly selected a site in front of the MLR rather than at a convenient distance to the rear. Also, it was a clear cold night with bright snow, which decreased the cover of darkness and amplified the sound. They thought they were a comfortable distance from the enemy. Captain Abraham admits, "A mild departure from light or noise discipline occurred, which alerted the crew of a Tiger tank, which was well camouflaged and probably within two hundred yards of the farmhouse."

The German tankers accurately bore-sighted their 88 cannon on the flashlights and lanterns moving about the farmhouse CP. Captain Abraham remembered that Sergeant King and Capt. William H. Nation (Regimental Adjutant and S-1) were among those in the farmhouse with him when the Tiger fired its 88. Abraham recalled three rounds whamming into the house, at which point his recollections were temporarily interrupted by a concussion.

Harry "Big Stoop" Hudec, who was with the advanced Regimental Headquarters group in the area of Lanzerath, had the unpleasant task of searching through the rubble of the destroyed farmhouse. Hudec could find no survivors, only the body of Captain Nation. Hudec and crew loaded Nation's remains on a six-by-six GI truck and transported the body to a designated place for collecting KIAs (killed in action).

Captain Abraham thinks he ended up in the barnyard of the farmhouse after the tank fired. Anyhow, he remembered being covered with barnyard debris. Abraham describes his medical treatment. "I was hauled off to a hospital, loaded up on 'blue 88s' *(pain pills)* to get some rest, cleaned up, and bandaged in various spots, given a physical by a T/5 who cared less about the task, and subsequently returned to the regiment."

## The Replacement

The GIs, which started in Lanzerath, lasted for days and weeks. The medics treated me with paregoric, which made me feel dopey, but it did not relieve the problem. My first visit to the aid station reminded me of my status as a replacement.

I had suffered with the GIs for a couple of days when I went to the aid station for a checkup. I felt that there was a chance of getting evacuated away from the front. Captain Klein, the doctor serving our unit, had established an aid station in a vacant house in Lanzerath. Three of us were waiting outside his examination room. One had a shoulder wound and was tagged for evacuation. The second soldier had lost feeling in his feet, and his toes were turning black. When he left the examining room with an evacuation tag, he shouted for joy. "Thank God for these frozen feet. These feet are taking me out of this frozen hell."

With two tagged for evacuation, I was getting hopeful. When my turn came, Doc Klein bellowed, "What's wrong with you, soldier?"

I described my bad case of GIs and told him I felt feverish and was sure that my temperature was high. Doc stuck a thermometer in my mouth and sat back to smoke a cigarette while he waited. When he read the thermometer, he muttered, "Just a couple of degrees." Then he yelled, "Soldier, did you jump in Normandy?"

I humbly relied, "No, I was a replacement immediately after Normandy."

"Just as I thought!" Klein complained. "We don't have many tough soldiers left. Go back to your foxhole and try to be a real paratrooper!"

## The Unburied Dead

Not all the dead were buried during the winter of '44-45. The frozen bodies of animals and even men—those men belonging to the army of the enemy—were left unburied until the spring thaw. One particular unburied German often disturbs my memory.

Three demolitionists—Howard Brooks, George Brand, and I—were assigned to a bridge over a railroad, near the German town of Losheim. This was an advance outpost between the American and German lines. Our troops had fought their way to this point, set up the outpost, and then pulled back to a more strategic defensive position. Our mission was to blow up the bridge if and when German tanks or other enemy vehicles approached.

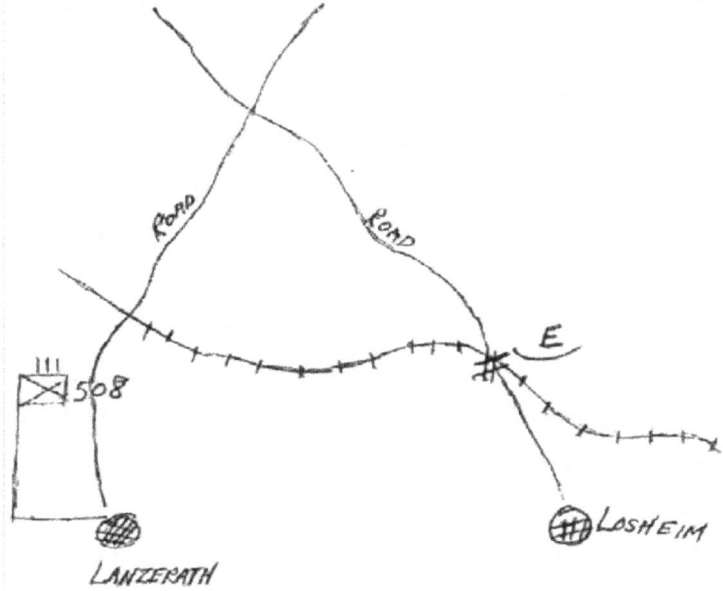

Copy of hand-drawn map given to Howard Brooks locating the bridge over railroad. Map supplied by Howard Brooks.

Quite a few frozen bodies of German soldiers lay near our position. One body was in the middle of the road between the bridge and a nearby house we were using. We had to be on watch day and night, so we took turns, the three of us—two hours at the bridge and four hours off around the clock. When we were off duty at the bridge, we would go to the house where we would eat, sleep, and try to keep warm. We kept stumbling over the body of the German soldier in the road, especially at night. After falling over the corpse one night, I decided the body needed to be moved.

The next morning I rolled it (I know now to call a dead body "it," but then I thought of it as "him."). I rolled him out of the road as one would roll a log. We had been warned in training about looting enemy dead because the Germans sometimes booby-trapped bodies. I figured, however, that this body would have already exploded if it had been booby-trapped. In spite of the risk, I took out his wallet for a look.

In the wallet were photos—a beautiful young woman, a blonde like Mary, my wife. I wondered, "Is she his sweetheart or wife?" I imagined that she was his wife and that maybe she had a wee baby, perhaps born since he had been away at the front. Like me, he could have been the father of a child he had never seen.

Then there was an older couple among his snapshots. "Could they be his parents?" I mused. I pictured them at home following the war on the radio and in the newspapers, worrying about the safety of their soldier son. They would soon receive a message from their government: WE REGRET TO INFORM YOU THAT YOUR SON _____ IS MISSING IN ACTION ON THE WESTERN FRONT. I carefully replaced the photos and the wallet on the body and silently prayed that someday the soldier's family would receive the personal effects of their fallen loved one.

## Sleeping Warmer

Near the railroad overpass where Brooks, Brand, and I were posted, Zane Schlemmer found his cold-weather sleeping partner. Zane was a sergeant in Headquarters Second 81mm Mortar Section. Zane usually served as an observer for his mortar crew. He advanced with forward elements of the Second Battalion, staying on the lookout for a suitable OP (observation post). About one-half kilometers from our bridge, Zane came across a deep railroad cut with a lot of dead Germans who had been ambushed by our troops. He also found a longhaired white German dog running around like he was disoriented. When Zane offered the dog K rations, the dog calmed down and became his friend. Zane and his buddies named him Adolph.

Adolph stayed with the mortar platoon. During the day, George Fairman and Irv Shanley fed and cared for Adolph while Schlemmer was at his OP. Zane had found a hunters' lookout tower for his OP, from which he had a good view of the forward terrain, including the dragon's teeth of the Siegfried Line. At night he came back to the Mortar Platoon area and slept with Adolph. Adolph was a good heater for cold nights.

When returning to his platoon area one evening, Zane met an irate officer in a rage. The officer had been using a slit trench. He had taken his toilet paper from his helmet, a good dry place for storing the paper, and laid it nearby, ready when needed. Adolph, in the meantime, stole the officer's precious toilet paper and ran off with it. To pay for Adolph's mischief, Zane had to resupply the officer from his own helmet.

## Sweetest Bitter Words I Ever Heard

It was the same outpost, the bridge over the railroad, that I experienced the greatest fear of the war and also the greatest sense of relief. I am not sure how long we were at the bridge. I used to think it was about three days and nights. Brooks convinced me that it was a much shorter time. I had the sense that the three of us—Brooks, Brand, and Boroughs—were all alone for a long time with no one else around but a few dead, frozen German bodies.

Brooks had been a mechanic and shipyard worker—not bad preparation for a combat soldier. We could depend on his skill with things mechanical and electrical. He selected the proper spot to place the C-2 (plastic explosive material) where it would do the most damage. He made sure that the wires were securely connected to the hand-operated generator at the lookout point. Our lookout was well protected from potential detonation of the bridge and located at a vantage for viewing the approach from the German side. Brooks was a dependable soldier.

George Brand and I had been college students before entering the army—not the best preparation for a combat soldier. Yes, I had spent two years at the Citadel, the "West Point of the South." I had learned military courtesy, saluting and saying, "Sir," to officers. I had plenty of practice polishing brass and preparing for inspections. I knew how to handle a rifle in close-order drill for Friday afternoon parades. I am sorry, but that kind of training had little transfer value for the battlefield.

Brooks, Brand, and I had been taking turns at the lookout where we were poised to activate the generator and blow up the bridge if enemy tanks approached. It was the middle of the night. Brooks was at the bridge. Brand and I were at the house in the basement, a safe place in case of artillery. I was sleeping. Brand was awake. (Only one person could sleep at a time.) Brand shook me awake and whispered, "Listen!"

We heard footsteps upstairs. At first it sounded like one person moving very cautiously. We prepared our weapons for firing. Then there were more footsteps, like a whole roomful of men, and no longer moving cautiously but stomping around as if they were knocking snow off their boots. By this time, I had little hope of survival. I just hoped to be brave enough to die fighting. This I did remember from the Citadel, the words of General Summerall: "The most important word in the English language is *duty*."

I wanted to die doing my duty. It was then that I heard those sweet, bitter words upstairs, "Goddamn son of a bitch."

They were English words, spoken by a man from the 508th Parachute Infantry, our regiment. We were safe!

Cartoon by Kate Salley Palmer

## The Human Animal

If I were to try to write a running account of all my World War II experiences, there would be many gaps of memory, but I have another memory of that night at the railroad bridge. It was about chow time.

By the time of this story, we had spent about two months on the front, most of the time out in the open weather in deep snow. The losses from killed, wounded, and frozen feet had greatly reduced our ranks. Our duties were intensified as our numbers shrank. Some of our men had suffered combat fatigue, the name for a battlefield nervous breakdown.

We were in an area of small mountains, and we had advanced a long way from our supply base. Food was scarce. If a few inches of snow can tie up transportation on modern highways, think how two feet of snow can hinder getting supplies into a mountainous area with only a few narrow roads traveled mostly by foot soldiers.

The platoon that came to relieve us at the bridge packed in a small quantity of K rations. K rations were packaged meals in small cardboard boxes. When we jumped into combat, we had carried six K rations in our gear to last for two days. Now the lieutenant in charge gave each man one K ration. Some of the K rations were breakfast boxes, which contained powdered coffee; others were for supper, which contained powdered cocoa. No one wanted the lunch ration because it contained powdered lemonade. That's what started the fight.

One of the soldiers whose ration contained lemonade wanted to swap for coffee or cocoa. No one would agree to trade, so he decided to switch packages with someone not looking. He was too slow. "Get your goddamned thieving hands off my rations, or I will blow your brains out!" shouted the soldier as he pointed his rifle in the thief's face. The thief quickly pushed the rifle barrel above his head with one hand and pulled out his jump knife with the other. Both men were soon overpowered by their fellow soldiers, after which the lieutenant took away their weapons. He told his men, "If you expect to survive, you have to act like humans, not animals."

## The Valley of the Dead

After clearing a portion of the fortified Siegfried Line on the German border, the 508th was relieved. The regiment returned to the Veilsalm-Rencheux section of Belgium, where the Red Devils enjoyed three days of rest. On February 8, the 508th was on the move again by truck to the Huertgen forest of Western Germany and beyond to the Roer Valley.

The Huertgen forest was no longer a forest but splintered spikes of trees so devastated that most of the life-supporting tops of the trees had been shattered by months of shelling. The Americans had fought through the fall and winter in this area with little to show for their efforts except wrecked vehicles, destroyed villages, and unburied mangled, grotesque long-neglected bodies both GIs and Germans.

From mid-December until early February, a hard freeze had preserved the bodies of men killed during the bitter winter conflict. A blanket of deep snow had hidden most of the dead from view, but a February thaw had set in motion the twin processes of melting the snow and decomposing the bodies.

The winter had been harsh, but the snow had been clean and white, and the air had been fresh and invigorating. With the thaw, muddy slush replaced clean snow as the dominant surface beneath the feet of the plodding foot soldiers. Their nostrils were assaulted by the putrid smell of decaying flesh. All of their senses were flooded with the full force of raw gruesome death.

Photo by Donald J. McCleod, provided by Harry Kennedy.

The Regimental Headquarters Demolition Platoon had the unpleasant duty of checking American bodies for booby-traps. They then loaded the bodies on trucks to be taken away for identification in order to notify the next-of-kin.

Fortunately I was spared the danger, the stench, and nausea of checking bodies in the Roer Valley due to an unusual assignment. When our convoy of trucks transported us from Belgium to the new area of combat in Germany, those of us in the last truck were dropped off at intersections along the way to guide trucks, which were expected to arrive later.

My post was at a fork in the road in the Huertgen Forest or, better said, in the ruins of the Huertgen Forest. I remained at that road junction for the rest of that day and the next night. By the time I arrived at Regimental Headquarters Company's new position, members of my section were busy checking the bodies. Although I was spared that detail, I was assigned to another distasteful task—preparing a latrine for Col. Lindquist and his command staff. Captain Abraham affirmed that everywhere we went in combat, Colonel Lindquist made sure that his two-holed latrine box was not far behind.

The CP was set up in the rubble of a small village. One barn had a portion of a roof left, so it was chosen for the officer's latrine. We dug through the muck of the barn floor, about a foot and a half, and hit concrete. We mounted the "two-holer" and had a good laugh about how the officers would be adding their own to the manure in the barn floor.

When the 508th moved into the Roer Valley, the troops relieved by the 508th were so happy to leave the macabre scene, they neglected to inform the Red Devils of the existing dangers. Lt. Joe Shirley of C Company recalled, "They did not tell us of the minefields facing us. If we had known, we would have sent the engineers to clear a passage through the mines before advancing."

As the First Battalion pushed off toward their objective, C Company suffered several casualties from the mines. Lieutenant Shirley was one of the wounded.

Lieutenant Shirley told Sgt. Bill Traban, "I've been hit. You must take command of the platoon."

The first thing Traband did was to check the injured. He found Cpl. Roy Henderson mortally wounded and cradled Roy's head in his arms as he breathed his last breath. Even in the midst of a battle, combat soldiers take time to aid and comfort their wounded and dying comrades.

Cpl. Roy Henderson Jr. Photo supplied by Ernest L. Henderson.

Bill Traband was very emotional as he responded to a phone call initiated by members of Henderson's family seeking information about the death of their loved one. Corporal Henderson was Sergeant Traband's trusted and dependable assistant.

Traband remembered Roy Henderson as a strong Mormon Christian from Utah, an example of moral goodness and an excellent soldier.

Sgt. John "Doc" Hardie told Roy Henderson's brother Ernie, "He was a great friend, a fine soldier, and a man of integrity."

Sgt. Jim Kurz, B Company, remembered the minefields in his company's drive toward the Roer River:

> At 0200, C Company started their attack up the valley, while A and B companies flanked the hill. We could see and hear the great amount of fire C Company was laying down.
> It was dark, but we could make out bodies of men beside the path. Then our scout hit a mine. When the Germans realized one of their mines had detonated, they fired mortars at the area where the mine exploded, wounding one of our men. Captain Millsaps told everybody to stay right where they were. He then sent for engineers to clear a path through the minefield.

Kurz told about an overambitious young officer:

> A new lieutenant, just out of West Point, asked me if I would go with him to get around the minefield. I told him the captain had ordered us to stay in place. However, this lieutenant wanted to be a hero. He got a couple of privates from another squad to go with him. In a few minutes, I heard mines go off. The lieutenant lost a foot; one private with him lost his eyesight, and the other private broke his back and one arm. This was caused because a lieutenant didn't follow orders. He had spent years in West Point and lasted only two days in combat.

The engineers arrived and worked through the minefield, laying a white tape for B Company to follow. Everyone went safely through the minefield, walking step by step on the white tape.

Radio operator Bill Dean was given a small walkie-talkie radio for the advance. Dean led the company through the minefield communicating by his walkie-talkie radio to those who followed behind to make sure the troopers kept in the cleared area. Dean was awarded a Bronze Star for his action. A portion of the award cites, "Technician Fifth Grade Dean voluntarily took the lead and with the aid of his radio relayed guiding messages back to the company."

After traversing the minefield, B Company opened fire on the enemy. This allowed C and A companies to press their attacks. By crossing the minefields at night in three different locations at the same time, the Red Devils made it through where other outfits had failed. At 0830, the First Battalion was on the objective, a hilltop overlooking the Roer River.

Having secured high ground above the Roer River, the Red Devils expected their next objective to be a river crossing. Beyond the Roer, one could see the distant spires of the Cologne Cathedral, the most prominent building in the German city of Cologne. The next few nights, reconnaissance patrols probed the opposite bank of the Roer in preparation for a crossing.

Jim Rankin and Harry Kennedy from Regimental Headquarters S-2 were on some of those reconnaissance patrols. Rankin remembered that Harry Kennedy (nee Hans Kahn) who lived the first fifteen years of his life in Germany, recognized places he had traveled to with his father.

During the last days we were in the Roer Valley, Sgt. Lawrence "Whoopee" Dunn and Stanley Kass installed antipersonnel mines in front of the First Battalion's MLR. It was decided that the battalion would make a night attack. The two demolitionists, Dunn and Kass, were sent to remove the mines before the attack. In the darkness, Sergeant Dunn accidentally set off one of the mines. His body was riddled with shrapnel. Kass gave Dunn a shot of morphine to relieve the pain, but the sergeant died a few minutes later.

Left: Lawrence Dunn. Right: Stanley Kass. Copied from 1943 Company pictures.

## A Good Scout

First Sergeant Ralph Thomas of E Company recalled that Lamberson "was a good scout and pulled that duty with dignity and bravery in Normandy."

Thomas explained, "A scout goes out in front as a unit goes into a fight."

Perhaps Lamberson was the lead man out front when he received his first combat wound. Carl Nilsen described the event:

> He was walking down a hedgerow at port arms. At a single step at an outside corner of the hedgerow, he came face to face with a German soldier. There was a scuffle. The German bayoneted him in the arm. Bill ran back the way he came, wondering every step when that German was going to shoot him. Confused when that shot never came, he turned and looked back. There was nobody there, only his rifle lying on the ground. He cautiously went back to retrieve it then peeked around the corner. There was no one in sight. He explained to us later, "That kraut ran off the other way. Hell, he was as scared as I was."

William Lamoille Lamberson. Photo provided by Tim Lamberson.

Lamberson's bayonet wound must not have been very serious. He was probably treated by the 508th medical personnel in a field hospital or aid station and returned to his unit without leaving France. This was according to Ralph Thomas:

> Lamberson received his second wound on July 5, on a patrol working its way up Hill 95. General Gavin came to me after the patrol was shot up and we were out of officers. The general told me that we had to take the hill. I told him we could take it if we received support from a tank. The general's aid ordered up a tank destroyer, and I told the commander of the tank destroyer where

to aim. He shot the heads off the Germans, who happened to be Mongolians.

The whole battalion had to take time to regroup and assign leadership responsibilities to others within their rank to take the places of their fallen comrades. Carl Nilsen described the scene after Lamberson was wounded:

> It's likely Bill was given a shot of morphine when first hit then another shot when the medics got to him. Anyhow he was flying high when he came wandering up to our positions. We were hugging the ground, trying to make ourselves as small a target as possible. We were yelling at him to get down, not only for his own safety, but by exposing himself, it would bring additional fire on us.
>
> He paid no heed but insisted on telling his story: "They bayoneted me in one arm. You think that was enough to satisfy them? Oh no! They had to shoot me in the other arm too." Not at that moment, but all of us, including Bill, had a big laugh about that episode later.

After the second wound, Bill Lamberson was evacuated to England where he spent a long convalascence. Lamberson was in the hospital until January, at which time he returned to combat duty.

In his last letter home, Lamberson complained about wading knee deep in the snow. His foxhole buddy, Carl Nilsen, wrote to Tim Lamberson, "Bill was in my squad, and we shared foxholes from early January until at least February 8, 1945."

They were in the Roer Valley area of West Germany, an area that was devastated by three months of steady fighting without any progress. American and German forces had slogged back and forth over the same territory for three months. Portions of frozen bodies of men and animals protruded through the snow that covered the earth. The Germans had planted mines in the paths of the advancing American troops, and no new territory could be gained without first clearing a path through the minefields.

Bob O'Connor said that there were three engineers with mine detectors and three E Company men in the Group. O'Conner said Floyd "Benny" Goodman, Bill Lamberson, and a new replacement he did not know, along with the three minesweepers, made up the advance patrol to clear the mines.

Joe Morettini remembered that E Company followed the minesweepers at a distance. They were told to walk down the middle of the road with the assurance that the middle was clear of mines. Joe heard machine gun fire, and he hit the ground. Joe recalled the following:

> Before I hit the ground, I saw someone's helmet fly up in the air. After hitting the ground, I saw a puff of black smoke coming from Lt. David Liebmann's shoe. I saw Pvt. George Randolph about ten feet in front of me get in a sitting position to fire back. I told Randolph to get down. Then he got hit, and I saw him keel over. [Morettini learned later that Liebmann lost a toe from a German bullet, and Randolph was hit in one leg by the enemy]
> 
> I thought I should look for better cover and ran down the road about ten feet and jumped over the side of the road. A German shot up a bush about two feet to my left and then shot about two feet to my right and then about six rounds at me. When mortar shells dropped on the road close by, I got up and ran down the road to where Capt. George Miles was.
> 
> Captain Miles asked the medic if all the wounded were evacuated. The medic said that only the dead ones were left on the road. So Captain Miles ordered E Company to withdraw to our last position.

E Company reassembled where they had dug in the night before. The next morning, the company took a different route and ending up on top of a hill overlooking the Roer River. Captain Miles reported, "There was no resistance the following day when we advanced by a different route."

The day after reaching their objective on the Roer River, First Sergeant Lionel Gagnon sent Sergeant O'Conner and Morettini back to check on those that were killed, to get their names and dog tags. O'Conner and Morettini took a jeep to the road where the bodies were and then walked the rest of the way. They found all six of the bodies lying in the snow. Bob O'Connor collected the dog tags from the three engineers, Goodman and Lamberson, but when he came to the replacement, he was startled. O'Conner recalled the event:

> The replacement was lying on his back with his arm over his eyes. When I reached down to check his dog tags, he raised his arm and spoke to me. I asked him what happened, and he told me that they were caught in the crossfire by German

machine guns and all six were shot. He grabbed me by the arm, thinking I was going to leave him. I assured him I wasn't. I asked Joe Morettini to send someone back for a stretcher. We carried him back to the aid station. Captain Montgomery told me later that he died in the hospital of exposure.

Morettini remembered that the wounded man was redheaded. He also remembered seeing Bill Lamberson's body about fifty feet up the road from the others. Lamberson was probably the lead scout for the patrol.

Later the Lamberson family received the official word that PFC William Lamoille Lamberson was killed in action on February 9, 1945 near Schmidt, Germany.

In the US Army, he was William L. Lamberson, and his paratrooper friends called him Bill. Carl Nilsen first met Bill Lamberson in October 1942 in Camp Blanding, Florida. Nilsen and Lamberson were together in the 508th, in the same company, in the same platoon and in the same squad until Lamberson's death. Carl Nilsen wrote to Tim Lamoille Lamberson, who is the nephew of William Lamoille Lamberson, and told him about their friendship.

Tim Lamberson has had a special interest in learning about his uncle. He was born on his uncle's birthday twenty-seven years later and was named Lamoille after his uncle.

Joe Morettini visited the Henri Chapelle Cemetery for American soldiers in Belgium in 1994. A Belgium couple, George and Yvette Hambieckers, asked Morettini to recommend a grave of an American soldier that they could decorate with flowers. Morettini recommended Lamberson's grave. The Hambieckers continue to decorate Lamberson's grave, and his nephew Tim Lamberson has received a Christmas card from them.

A letter from the Hambieckers told of a recent visit in June of 2002 to the Henri Chapelle Cemetery with American veteran Joe Cicchinella of the 551st Parachute Infantry. During the visit, they honored William L. Lamberson and Floyd O. Goodman of the 508th, along with fourteen veterans from the 551st and two from the 507th. They wrote that their visits to the cemetery to honor American servicemen are "normal and satisfying." It causes them to feel "strong emotions."

## The Shower

From the middle of December to the middle of February, that was two months between baths. Although I washed my hands and face and most importantly my feet and socks, not a drop of water touched my back in that long interval. A heavy coating of oily grime covered my body, which served as insulation against the cold. During the depths of winter, that was not too bad, but with the February thaw, the army decided the troops needed a good spring cleaning.

A few of us at a time from each unit were loaded on trucks and driven some distance from the front for showers. The process was repeated until the whole regiment was washed. We were ushered into a large tent with a slatted wooded floor and ordered to strip off our clothes. For the first time in two months, I took off my combat jacket and pants, my wool ODs (olive drab), and my wool long johns. I had changed socks several times. As a precaution against frozen feet, we were required to take off our socks occasionally, rub our feet and, when possible, wash them. Extra socks were part of our combat pack.

We threw our dirty clothes into huge crates to be fumigated and washed. One improvement of World War II over World War I was the control of lice. DDT was developed in time for World War II. It was used generously to keep down vermin. We did not have to fight body lice in our war.

As we stood there naked, I noticed how thin and frail we all looked. (If I could get a supply of K rations today, I might be able to market it to as a weight-losing diet.) I decided to use my fingernails to test the thickness of the grime on my body. It would be an exaggeration to say the grime was a quarter of an inch deep, but it did remind me of furrows plowed for spring planting.

We were then moved into the showers, hot and steamy, and we luxuriated for as long as we were allowed before another group came to take our place. After the bath we were given a complete set of recycled clean clothes. Then we were loaded on the open trucks and transported back to the front.

How did the bath make me feel? I felt weak and washed-out, like a wet wash rag. Without the insulation of dirt and body grease, I got chilled to the bone riding in the open truck in the brisk February air. The next day I came down with a terrible cold.

A few days after the showers on February 18, 1945, the 508th marched away from the MLR. We boarded trains in Aachen, Germany, which transported us back to our base in Camp Sissone, France. We were cleaned just in time to return to garrison duty.

## Up Front with General Gavin

Most of the officers of the 508th were respected and loved by the enlisted men under their command. The men prided themselves for their physical stamina and accepted the hard standards that their officers demanded of them. The men admired officers who demanded more of themselves than they did of their men, who demonstrated courage and leadership in battle and showed respect and appreciation of those who served under them. Gen. James M. Gavin, Commander of the 82nd Airborne Division, was such an officer. The following are a few stories about the general told by 508th paratroopers:

Autographed photo of Gen. James M. Gavin given to Emile Lacroix. Photo provided by Emile Lacroix. The picture was taken at Erria, Belgium, the morning after the 508th fought off the Ninth SS German Division.

### "Walk, Sergeant, Don't Run!"

It was one of those deadly barrages of mortar and 88mm shells bursting among his men. Bodies exploded. The friend next to him no longer looked human, more like a mangled mass of raw meat. The sights and sounds of the battle bombarded the sergeant's psyche. Although his body was untouched by the flying shrapnel, his emotions were shattered.

The sergeant did not make a conscious decision to start running, but he suddenly realized he was running as fast as his legs would carry him. The shells were no longer falling around him, but he could not stop running.

Ahead, in the middle of the narrow road, stood a tall slim figure. The sergeant slowed to avoid a collision with the man obstructing his way. As he drew closer, he recognized it was an officer. He slowed even more. The officer called, "Sergeant, why are you running?"

It was General Gavin. The sergeant came to a halt in front of the general and said, "Sir, my men are getting slaughtered, I'm going for the medics."

In a calm and fatherly voice, General Gavin spoke, "Sergeant, walk, don't run! You want to set a good example for your men."

The words and manner of General Gavin reduced the sergeant's compulsion to run away. He continued toward the rear—walking. Realizing that fear had taken control, he said to himself, "Fear will not conquer me. I must conquer my fears."

As the sergeant walked, he circled back toward the front. He took his place among his men and rallied his squad.

## A Private Talks Back

Paratroopers from the 508th were advancing down a road somewhere in Normandy. Suddenly the sound of German rifle fire and bullets whistling overhead caused most of the column to hit the dirt, except for Michael Niklauski (a.k.a. Mickey Nichols). Someone yelled at him, "Get your ass down, soldier, before you get shot."

Mickey looked around to see who gave the order and saw a paratrooper standing tall and straight, and yelled back at him, "You had better get your ass down also!"

A few minutes later, Mickey dashed across the road and came face to face with the tall slim paratrooper at whom he had yelled. It was General "Slim Jim" Gavin. Mickey snapped to attention and saluted. Gavin returned the salute, smiled, and went on about his business.

## "He Remembered My Name"

After a reconnaissance patrol during the Normandy campaign, Harry Kennedy of Regimental Headquarters Company reported to the 508th CP. General Gavin was with Colonel Lindquist and his staff. General Gavin gave Harry a cup of coffee while Harry was making his report.

Many months later during the latter part of the fighting in Belgium, Harry Kennedy felt a touch on his shoulder. Kennedy turned around and saw it was General Gavin. Gavin said, "Hi, Kennedy! How are things going for you?"

Harry declared, "It impressed me that the general made the effort to speak to me, a PFC (private first class,) and I was even more surprised that he remembered my name."

## "He Wished Us a Merry Christmas"

It was Christmas Eve, 1944, the night the 508th withdrew eight miles from their positions along the Salm River to a new MLR. Lt. Charles Yates, Regimental Headquarters Company, had just received his orders. A certain iron bridge over a tributary of the Salm had to be destroyed before the Germans attempted to cross. Yates took a truckload of explosives to the bridge for demolition. Their instructions were to wait until the rear guard crossed over. When all friendly troops had passed over, they were to blow the bridge. Sgt. Willard "Snuffy" Shull, Leon Israel Mason, and Stanley Kass were among the team of demolitionist with Lieutenant Yates for the mission.

Yates recalled an incident that gloomy Christmas Eve:

> We were working on the bridge, hip deep in the icy water, when I heard a vehicle stop overhead. I went up to investigate. General Gavin introduced himself and asked who I was and what I was doing. I identified myself and told him that we were wiring the bridge to blow it when the last of the rear guard had crossed over.
>
> Gavin remarked, "It's a tough way to spend Christmas Eve." Then Gavin said that he wanted to see how the rear guard was getting along, and he requested, "You won't blow it until I get back, will you?"
>
> I warned him that he had better return before the rear guard because we were going to blow it when the last man crossed. On returning, General Gavin made sure we knew that he had crossed the bridge. He wished us a Merry Christmas and drove away into the night.

## Chapter 9

# Return to France

### Frozen Feet Lead to Warm Romance

It was during the cold January of 1945, when the Belgian snow was deep and the temperature was below zero, that Gerald "Jerry" Beach of Regimental Headquarters Company was evacuated because of frozen feet. The medics loaded him in an open jeep and transported him all the way back to Camp Sissonne in France, about a twelve-hour journey. Beach recalled, "By the time I arrived, not only were my feet frozen, but my whole body was stiff from the cold."

Jerry Beach didn't start thawing out until the vision of a beautiful nurse with Titian hair stood over his hospital bed. The vision was not an aberration but a real human being—Lt. Virginia Lea Stiles. The tender loving care of Virginia Stiles soon raised Jerry's temperature to normal and sent warm blood flowing to the end of his toes, producing a quick recovery. The cure was too quick for Jerry, who would have enjoyed a prolonged healing process attended by lovely statuesque Virginia Stiles.

Within a week, Jerry was discharged from the hospital and sent back to Belgium. He served with the regiment through the Battle of the Bulge and on to the Roer Valley in Germany. Returning to Camp Sissonne with the regiment in late February, the first thing Jerry did upon arriving was to find his favorite nurse, Lt. Virginia Lea Stiles.

This time it was Virginia who was about to freeze. The nurses were living in old French Army barracks with very little heat and no winter clothes. Jerry found ways to light her fire: he persuaded Supply Sergeant Sherman Boyd to share some of the winter clothing designed for combat soldiers such as long wool underwear, wool sweaters, wool scarfs, and wool-knit caps. Then Jerry gave the warm woolies to Virginia.

The nurses' barracks were heated by small coal-fired stoves in each room, and each room was rationed one bucket of coal a day. Jerry finagled a whole truckload of coal and unloaded it through Virginia's window. The gifts of coal and warm woolies kindled their friendship to a glow. By the time the lilacs were blooming around Camp Sissonne, the friendship of Jerry and Virginia had blossomed into a warm romance.

The only Red Devil that I know who remembered lilacs at Camp Sissonne is Jerry Beach. Maybe that's because he strolled about the camp with Virginia Stiles when the lilacs were in bloom. Virginia and Jerry fell in love with lilacs as well as with each other and later planted lilacs around their home in Lupton, Michigan.

Jerry was in the Communication Platoon of Regimental Headquarters Company, but when in garrison, he was in the Regimental Band. The band was assigned to provide entertainment for the troops. When we got back to Camp Sissonne, all the buildings were filled with other troops, so we had to live in tents without electricity in our section of the camp. The band was able to get movies to show to the troops but had no electricity to run the movie projector.

Jerry solved the electrical problem: he called his brother Don Beach, who was with the engineers stationed on the Atlantic Coast of France. He asked Don, "Do you think you can get us a generator for our unit?"

"No problem!" Don replied. "If you can come here with a jeep and trailer, we will have a transformer ready for you when you arrive."

Jerry had an eye for pleasure as well as business. He took Virginia with him. The trip across France together was an adventure they will always remember.

Although the 508th did not stay long at Camp Sissonne, they stayed long enough for Virginia and Jerry to become engaged. Their love affair was maintained through correspondence from Chartres, France, and Frankfurt, Germany. The wedding date was set for July 25 in Paris.

Virginia was working in a Paris hospital and Jerry was a part of the 508th Honor Guard for General Eisenhower's Headquarters in Frankfurt. A furlough was arranged for the nurse and the paratrooper at the same time, a major accomplishment in itself. The couple was married by an army chaplain and again by the mayor of Paris. (The French government required a civil ceremony.) For their wedding present, the nurses, with whom Virginia worked, hired a horse and carriage for the honeymooning couple to tour Paris.

The wedding and honeymoon was too short, for both had to return to their military posts in separate countries. Finally, in January of 1946, six months later, Mr. and Mrs. Gerald Beach were able to get together as husband and wife in the good old USA.

Gerald "Jerry" Beach at the 1992 508th reunion. Photo by Zig Boroughs.

## Marlene Dietrich

After the long winter campaign in Belgium and Germany, Christmas packages awaited the men of the 508th when we arrived at Camp Sissonne. Leon Israel Mason's parents sent him canned anchovies. Leon—or "Gismo," as he was called by his friends in Regimental Headquarters Company—took the delicacy to the office where he was temporarily assigned to work on the regimental newspaper, the *Devil's Digest*. Gismo was munching on anchovies when an unexpected visitor arrived, causing quite a titillation in the office. It was the curvaceous actress Marlene Dietrich, famous for her million-dollar legs.

When Gismo was introduced to the actress, he was trying to swallow his food. "Pardon me! I was just eating some anchovies my parents sent me."

"Anchovies!" Miss Dietrich replied, "What would I give for anchovies right now?"

"How about a kiss?" snapped Gismo, always a sharp trader.

Marlene agreed to the deal and laid a big old smackeroo on Gismo for her part of the bargain.

Marlene Dietrich washing mess gear after GI chow.
Photo provided by Scott Ellsworth.

Ms. Dietrich was brought to the *Devil's Digest* office to provide maximum publicity for the 508th Parachute Infantry Regiment, Col. Roy E. Lindquist commanding. A regimental parachute exercise just happened to coincide with her visit, and she was to be the honored guest to view the exercise. The high command called it a training jump, but the men of the regiment referred to it as a parade jump for Ms. Dietrich.

Francis Lamoureux, a pathfinder for the Third Battalion, recalled having a little fun with the honored guest. Since pathfinders jump early and set up signals for the rest of the paratroopers, they were on the ground first and had Ms. Dietrich to themselves. Lamoureux remembered that Ms. Dietrich paraded some herself. She rolled up her pants legs and strutted around and said, "Take a good look, boys!"

For this particular jump, Bernard Levin, G Company, did not wear a parachute or combat gear. Instead he carried his sketchpad to make drawings of the jump. Levin boarded a C-47 with members of Regimental Headquarters Company men from the Demolition Platoon. Among those in the plane were Lt. Charles Yates, Leon Israel Mason, Stanley Kass, and Edwin Luczaj. Ed Luczaj remembered Levin studying him during the flight as an artist studies a model, looking up at him and then back to his drawing pad. After the troopers hooked up for the jump, the artist moved to the cabin to get out of the way of the jumpers. As the men shuffled toward the exit door, the plane began to falter. Lieutenant Yates, the last man in the stick, made it to the door but was hit by the tail wing. Yates's left leg was broken in five places.

The plane, which had thrown a propeller, crashed in flames a moment later, killing the crew and the trooper artist, Bernard Levin. As the plane fell, it hit and killed six paratroopers who were in the air floating to the ground. Those killed in the air were Lt/ Nick C. Emanuel, Charles "Chief" Under Baggage, Luther M. Tillery, Alfred J. Vaughn, George W. Wall, and Charles I. Clemons, all of Regimental Headquarters Company.

The tail of the plane snagged the parachute of Richard "Dick" Stedman as it descended, but Stedman survived. Stedman said, "I remember hooking up and jumping, and then I woke up in the hospital with a slight concussion. I was told that my chute caught on the tail of the plane and that I fell free just before it hit the ground."

The brother of Alfred Vaughn, who was killed by the plane, was stationed at Reims and came to witness the jump. Ed Luczaj had the sad duty of informing the brother that Alfred was one of those killed in the accident.

Meanwhile, Marlene Dietrich was nearby, crying hysterically. Lt. Worster Morgan of Regimental Headquarters Company was ordered to take charge of the actress, keep her away from the crash scene, and calm her down.

**C-47 after the crash.** Note Stedman's chute over tail.
Photo provided by Richard Stedman.

L. W. "Red" Blackmon of Headquarters Third suffered from an accident on that same jump, which was not related to the plane crash. When he landed, the impact of his rifle against the hard ground banged up under his chin and caused a temporary concussion. As Red was regaining consciousness, someone touched his elbow and asked, "What happened, buddy?"

Blackmon rubbed his jaw then looked at his hand and saw blood. Thinking he was talking to a medic, he spouted off about the SOB who ordered rifles strapped in front for a parachute jump. Then he turned and saw two stars about fourteen inches from his face and realized he was talking to Gen. James Gavin. General Gavin laughed and said, "You're all right, buddy! Let's get going!"

"And I went," declared Red Blackmon.

Postscript, July 1953

In 1953 Stanley Kass operated a liquor store near the exclusive Savoy and Madison hotels in New York City. One hot July day, Kass stepped out of the store to catch a breeze. He looked up the street and recognized Ms. Marlene Dietrich coming toward him. The former paratrooper bravely stepped in front of the unapproachable actress and spoke inquiringly, "Ms. Dietrick?"

"Yes," she answered. "And do I know you?"

"Let me say two words," Kass replied, "and then you decide—Sissonne, France."

The words aroused Ms. Dietrich's memories of the plane crash. She explained to Kass that since the parade jump was staged in her honor, she had suffered grief and guilt ever since those eleven men lost their lives.

Stanley Kass told Ms. Dietrich that it was a necessary training exercise and that her presence had nothing to do with causing the accident and that accidents happened at other times during training. The discussion seemed to ease her guilty feelings. She thanked Kass for stopping her and gave him a parting kiss.

After that encounter, Ms. Dietrick remained in New York for a week. On her daily walks, she would always stop by Kass's store for a brief visit.

Stedman's stick. Standing (L-R): Lt. Worster Morgan, Thomas Plemon, Robert Peterson, James Rankin, Mark Bradley, Fred Robbins, Alfred Vaughn (killed by falling C-47), and James Kulmer. Kneeling (L-R): Tom Angress and John McCall. Sitting (L-R): Clift Campbell, Joel Lander, Richard Stedman, and Greenwalt. Photo provided by and used by permission of Richard Stedman.

## Furlough to London

When we returned to Camp Sissonne, I was given the assignment of acting corporal for a week or two. My main duty was to get those who lived in my tent out of bed every morning for reveille and to platoon formation. When called upon by Lieutenant Yates, my duty was to sound off as the acting corporal for my tent, "All present and accounted for, sir."

Details for the day were assigned at the early morning formations. One day, Lieutenant Yates assigned me to a detail, and instead of calling me "Boroughs" as he usually did, he used my nickname.

Yates knew my nickname because of his duty censoring letters. He noticed that I always signed my letters with "Zig." When Yates called me Zig in platoon formation, everyone laughed because they had heard prostitutes in Reims asking, "Voulez-vous zig-zig

Zig Boroughs and Lt. Charlie Yates. Photo by Lewis Milkovics.

avec moi?" From that day forward, members of my platoon called me Zig. My friend Little Car Austin took great delight in telling everybody my nickname, with the added commentary, "Zig means half of a zig-zig." To set the record straight, my middle name is Zeigler, which was my mother's maiden name. My family and friends and everyone in Pickens, South Carolina, my hometown, shortened Zeigler to Zig.

At one of the reveille formations, Yates announced that I had been granted a furlough to London. When furloughs were allotted to our platoon, names were drawn by lot, and I was the lucky one for the London trip.

First we were sent to Calais on the English Channel. We stayed in Calais until we combat troops were made presentable. We got haircuts. We were given new dress uniforms. Tailors were hired to sew on the Eighty-second Airborne patches. Our records were checked to make sure we had our correct service ribbons. We were inspected to see that all were properly shaved, shined, showered and had uniforms pressed and fit for a parade. Afterward we boarded a ferry to cross the English Channel. Then we traveled by train to London.

Every night the V-bombs landed somewhere in London, but in such a large city, V-bombs landing randomly didn't seem to disturb those parts of the city not close to the explosions. We saw the scars of war, barricaded areas of rubble, and deep holes where bombs had hit, but the rest of the city was fully operational; theaters, restaurants, taxis, hotels, and prostitutes were all busy.

On one London street, I found a Baptist Church and attended an evening prayer service. One of the prayer concerns was for the children of the city who were sent to safer parts of the nation where they would be less likely to be hit by German air attacks.

I returned from furlough to find the men of Regimental Headquarters Company in shock over the parade jump in honor of Marlene Deitrich, which happened when I was away. Six men from the company had lost their lives, and Lt. Yates was no longer with us. Yates described his injury many years later at a 508th reunion. "My left leg had four breaks between the knee and the ankle, and another between the knee and the hip. After one and a half years in various hospitals, my left leg is one and a half inches shorter than the right one."

Joan Williams, who later became Mrs. Joan McAlister of Greenwood, South Carolina, was one of the children who was sent west to St. Arvens in Wales from their family home in Dover on the English Channel.

Joan was the oldest of four children in her family. Peter and Peggy were six-year-old twins. Patsy, the youngest, was four years old and was deaf. The family was notified that the children should be ready to be evacuated by five o'clock the next morning. Mrs. Williams hastily got the children ready for their trip across the country. Patsy cried all the way. The four children were assigned to four different families in St. Arvens. Patsy clung to her older sister's leg and had to be taken away by force while kicking and screaming at the top of her voice.

When Mrs. Williams learned the destination of her children, she traveled to St. Arvens and rented a tiny cottage. Then she gathered her children together and lived with them in St. Arvens until the war was over. Her husband, Sergeant Williams, was serving his country in the army and seldom had a chance to visit his family.

Having heard Joan McAlister's story forty years later, I understand why the members of the Baptist Church in London were praying for their children from whom they were separated.

## Morality Lecture

A sergeant announced, "Two things on schedule today—short-arm inspection and morality lecture."

The medics came to the company area to inspect all the men for venereal diseases (VD). Each man was ordered to "peel it back and milk it down." If the medics observed symptoms of VD from the short-arm inspection, those troops were sent to the hospital for a more thorough diagnoses and treatment.

John Holman, who was an officer attached to the Eighty-second Division Headquarters, recalled that the day after a short-arm inspection he was on duty to censor letters. He remembered a letter a paratrooper wrote to his wife, which said, "Today we had a short-arm inspection. The doctor said that my short arm was clean and healthy—but terribly homesick."

Later that afternoon all were assembled to hear the lecture from the medical officer Capt. Doc Klein. Doc started with a summary of the current problem. "We have identified many new cases of gonorrhea this week. The problem is getting serious. Since we have arrived at Camp Sissonne, we have had the highest VD rate in the regiment's history."

The Eighty-second Division Command feared that venereal diseases would reduce the number of fighting men who were battle ready for our next assignment. It seemed that everywhere the 508th was stationed, the medical officers told us that our VD rate was the highest. According to Dr. Dave Thomas, "The prostitutes flocked to the airborne to get some of that good jump pay."

Thomas reported that the only thing that limited the amount of VD in the 508th was supply-side economics. He said, "The rates varied from zero when the troops were in combat, with no available supply, to the top of the charts, when the regiment was in garrison with plenty of disease-carrying females around."

The morality lecture did not lower the VD rate among the paratroopers, so the Eighty-second Airborne Division Command decided to set up its own brothel outside Camp Sissonne. The medical detachment controlled the business. Prostitutes were carefully screened and given frequent medical examinations, and soldiers were forced to take a prophylaxis before leaving the premises.

One of my buddies decided he would sample the wares at the Eighty-second brothel. He described the downstairs as a large dimly lit room with a bar where beer and wine were sold, with tables and chairs for the men to sit around and drink. Benches lined the walls of the room where men sat waiting their turn to go upstairs. The head of the line was at the bottom of the stairs. When one of the girls was free, she would walk down the stairs and take the first soldier in line.

My buddy said that when he was at the end of the line in the dimly lit room, the girls looked enticing as they descended the stairs, but the closer he got to the head of the line, the worse they looked, so he decided to leave. When my friend tried to exit the building, medics blocked the door. They wouldn't let anyone pass without taking a prophylaxis treatment. My friend argued, "But I didn't do anything."

"We've heard that before," answered the medic. "And the next lie you will be telling is that you caught the clap from a toilet seat."

French Army barracks, Camp Sissonne.
The 508th lived in barracks after Holland. After the Ardennes and Roer Valley campaigns, tents within Camp Sissone housed the 508th.
Photo copied with permission from Lewis Milkovics's *The Devils Have Landed*.

## New Combat Mission

Our stay in Camp Sissonne was interrupted by orders to prepare for another combat jump. This time we moved to airfields. The Third Battalion moved to Dreux, east of Paris. The rest of the regiment moved to Chartres, southwest of Paris.

L-R: Col. Louis Mendez, Private Kajewski, Maj. Alton L. Bell. Photo taken at Dreux Airbase. Note the water bag supported by tripoles. The army treated the water with chemicals to make local water safe for drinking. Photo supplied by Gen. Dave Thomas.

Chartres is an ancient city about seventy-five kilometers from Paris. It is dominated by its famous gothic cathedral, which took three hundred years to build. It was under construction from the eleventh through the thirteenth centuries. I once walked into town and observed the robed priests and nuns moving about performing their duties. I was amazed at the carved statures attached to the building, especially the figures of farm animals and grotesque figures of gargoyles.

When Regimental Headquarters Company arrived at the Chartres Airbase, our first meal was with the air force men who flew the C-47s. We were pleasantly surprised when a C-47 crew chief, who recognized those of us who jumped from his plane in Holland, spoke to us. His captain had ordered us to jump before we reached the drop zone for fear the damaged plane was about to crash.

We had worried about the fate of the plane and its crew, and the crew chief had worried about the fate of his paratroopers who had jumped a long way from the drop zone in the midst of enemy fire. The chief told us how the crippled C-47 managed to limp back to England, and we reported to him that most of us survived the fighting in Holland and the Battle of the Bulge.

The 508th remained at the Dreux and Chartres airbases for several weeks. We were briefed and prepared on three different occasions for combat jumps, only to have the regular army move so fast that our objectives were taken by others before we boarded planes. We had been scheduled to jump on prison camps of Allied soldiers and on concentration camps where the Nazis imprisoned Jews and other political prisoners.

For the first night of liberty in Chartres, the 508th followed its tradition of intimidating the American MPs (military police). As usual, the MPs were unable to arrest any unruly paratroopers but rather had several members of their force so rudely treated by paratroopers that they ended up a military hospital. This behavior imposed upon the regiment the additional duty of pulling our own MP duty. I had one evening of MP duty in Chartres, wearing an armband imprinted with the letters "MP."

One of our MP duties was to keep the troops out of the brothels, which were off limits due to the high rate of VD associated with these houses. One young man from the Demolition Platoon managed to sneak around to the back of a brothel and climb a stone wall with pieces of jagged glass cemented into its structure. The glass was designed to discourage wall climbers. The paratrooper was discouraged but not restrained. In spite of cut and bleeding hands, he reached his objective and accomplished his mission. However, his wounded hands were just the beginning of his troubles. A week later, he came down with a case of the "clap."

I received one six-hour pass to Paris from Chartres. The army trucks unloaded us at the Arc de Triomphe. When on furlough earlier in London, I met a US soldier from another outfit. By coincidence, the same soldier was on pass the same time as I was. My London pal recognized me as I was getting off the truck, and we teamed up for our evening in Paris. (I am sorry that I retain no memory of the soldier's name nor the name of his army unit.)

Our first adventure was to find a café and enjoy some French cuisine. We selected a café on the Champs Elysees. My friend gave his order, and I said, "I'll take the same." I had no idea what we were ordering.

While waiting for our food, two girls came to our table and inquired in English if they could join us. We did not object, and they occupied the two vacant chairs. Soon I felt a knee rubbing against mine. I moved my leg and said, "Pardonnez moi, s'il vous plait!" After that the girls left our table for more promising game.

We finished our meal and went back on the street. Inside the café, the lights were very dim. Outside in the broad daylight, we saw the two girls who had joined our table briefly. In the bright light, they looked wretched. We were happy to have escaped their designs especially when we noticed they were counting a large roll of money.

Next we headed for the Follies Bergers, the famous theater, notable for musical extravaganzas, including bare-breasted chorus girls. One act was called "The Bird in the Gilded Cage." It featured a huge birdcage with what appeared to be a nude girl swinging from a bird perch like a trapeze performer. A male dancer, dressed like a cat, danced about the cage as if he wanted to catch the bird for dinner, but the cage was always manipulated by stage apparatus so that the bird was always just out of the cat's reach.

We had only enough time after the show to get back to our trucks at the Arc de Triomphe by departure time, and we had to walk very fast to make it. By this time, the prostitutes were out in force, dogging our every step with "Vous zig-zig?" or the more elaborate proposition, "Voulez-vous coucher avec moi?" Thankfully, I managed to avoid the clutches of the prostitutes and get back to camp in time.

On May 8, VE Day (Victory in Europe) Germany surrendered unconditionally. The 508th celebrated the end of fighting in Europe along with the French people in Dreux and Chartres. War with Japan in the Pacific was still raging, however, and airborne troops were expected to fight a different enemy on the other side of the world. What would be our next assignment?

508th troops parade in Chartres on VE-day. Photo copied from *History of the 508th Parachute Infantry*. Permission to use from the author William G. Lord II.

### Next to the Throne

Shortly after VE Day, Col. Roy E. Lindquist called the regiment together to announce the new assignment. We anticipated shipping out to the Pacific area to fight the Japanese. Instead of a new fighting role,

General Eisenhower selected the 508th as the honor guard for SHAEF (Supreme Headquarters, Allied Expeditionary Force.) The colonel was absolutely euphoric. He emphasized what a great honor this was for our regiment. He did not mention that it would give a greater recognition of the Regiment's Commanding Officer and greater potential for his promotion.

Col. Lindquist enthusiastically explained how we would shift our emphasis from a fighting unit to the pomp and ceremony, which accompanies the highest officer of the Allied forces. He tried to inspire the troops to share in his excitement, reminding us we would enjoy marching before and escorting presidents and other heads of state. He promised us that our quarters would no longer be tents but civilian apartments in Frankfurt-am-Main in Germany. He described how our dress uniforms would be beautified with white parachute scarves to replace the ugly black string neckties. He told us that he was confident that we, who had fought so gallantly in war, would perform equally as well to the different challenges of future. Finally he announced the ultimate privilege: "We will be next to the throne!"

Some of the paratroopers responded negatively to the colonel's announcement. They could take the blood and guts of the battlefield better than the spit and polish of parade exercises. When the colonel announced, "We will be next to the throne!" one disgruntled paratrooper shouted, "Flush it!"

Scott Ellsworth of E Company, who later transferred to Service Company as a truck driver, remembered the move to Frankfurt. Ellsworth was assigned to go back over the route of travel by the troops, to look for and pick up those members of the 508th who had dropped by the wayside en route and bring them to Frankfurt in his truck. According to Ellsworth, a large number of our men opted to take unauthorized furloughs in towns and cities along the way. I know of one highly decorated lieutenant with combat medals who was reduced to the rank of first sergeant. He pulled guard duty of a private as punishment for behavior unbecoming to an officer and a gentleman. Eventually he was reinstated as an officer. Such was the painful transition for a few paratroopers from combat soldiers to honor guards.

Early in June we arrived in Frankfurt-am-Main and moved into apartments in the suburban community of Heddernheim. As we unloaded our personal gear into our apartments, Polish laborers, recently liberated from German slave labor camps, were filling trucks with furniture and other properties of the former occupants of the apartment to take to garbage dumps. The former tenants were ousted by the conquering army and allowed to take only clothes and cooking utensils with them. These people moved to areas destroyed by Allied bombings and hastily erected shanties, using materials salvaged from the wreckage.

Stanley Walczak, veteran of Headquarters Second, told about his first assignment in Frankfurt. Stanley's parents were Polish immigrants to the United States. He was born in America, but his parents sent him to a Polish language school for the first few years of his education. He had learned the Polish language from his parents and his early school experience. For several weeks, Walczak served as translator for one of our officers who supervised the Polish laborers. Stanley Walczak's association with these men from Poland helped him appreciate how much the Polish people suffered under the iron rule of the Nazis.

Stanley Walczak. Photo by Zig Boroughs at a 508th reunion.

The Heddernheim apartments were located on an escarpment, with the upper level opening up on the street in front and the lower level adjoining an attractive walled-in garden with shrubs, flowers, and lawn. At a still-lower level was a vegetable garden for each apartment. Beyond the vegetable garden, a flood plain of high grass stretched out to the Main River.

In one of the vegetable gardens was a tool shed, where a family was living. The father was an older German man, perhaps fifty years old or more, with a somewhat younger Jewish wife and their teenage daughter. German people who had lived in the apartments had sheltered this family from the gestapo throughout the long regime of Adolf Hitler. A sad thing happened to this German-Jewish family. The mother and the daughter soon began to serve the new tenants of the apartments as prostitutes. They were protected by the Germans only to be corrupted by the Americans.

One of my first duties in our new quarters was KP (kitchen police.) I was assigned by the cooks to a detail of loading garbage on a truck, traveling with the truck to the local dump, and helping with the unloading. At the dump we saw the German people working the garbage, picking up scraps of food and other needed materials. I noticed that used coffee grounds was one of the prize finds of the scavengers. I was really surprised to see well-dressed people, such as men wearing business suits and neckties, working the garbage.

The kitchen was set up under a large tent in the field of high grass near the Main River. Women and children crowded around us as we ate, begging for food. Soon a fence was built around the mess area to prevent the nuisance of the beggars. However, small children persisted in pushing tin cans through the wire fence and asking for morsels of food. Finally, armed guards were posted to keep the beggars at a distance from the kitchen with orders to shoot over the heads of the beggars before they got too close. One day the guards saw the tall grass rustling and knew that some kids were crawling unseen toward the mess area, so they shot above the grass. At that moment, a German woman stood up in the tall grass and was shot dead through the head.

My early impressions of being "next to the throne" were more of pathos than of privilege.

# CHAPTER 10

# Prisoners of War

## POWs Celebrate Christmas

Bill Allen of Headquarters Third was captured in Normandy. After several stalags along the way, his final place of incarceration was in Frieberg, Germany, which is southwest of Dresden and just north of Czechoslovakia.

Allen described the stalag in Frieberg as good compared to other stalags. The food was poor, but otherwise the treatment was not bad. About the food, Allen said that they sure had a lot of rutabaga turnips, which they ate all kinds of ways: boiled, mashed, fried, and even raw.

Those in the Frieberg camp worked in several ways, all of which contributed to building prefabricated shacks for civilians who had lost their homes to Allied bombs. This was allowable by the International Red Cross, whose rules would not allow Germany to use POWs in industries primarily beneficial to the German war efforts.

Some of the prisoners worked in the woods cutting logs. Others sawed the logs into lumber, and others assembled the lumber into sections for small temporary structures for homeless civilians. Bill Allen worked in the pine forest cutting trees.

Allen described the foreman of the group as an old experienced logger, about eighty years old, who was easy to get along with. The NCO in charge of the stalag was also a nice person, a former high school English teacher. He told the POWs, "I don't want to be here any more than you do. We will get along just fine, unless you cause trouble."

The English teacher kept his word. The only person who got into trouble was Alexander Tepsic. (Tepsic is mentioned in the story "Wings and Swastikas.") Several times Tepsic tried to escape. He was always caught and severely punished. Everyone else was treated with fairness and kindness.

Christmas was a special time for the POWs in Frieberg. The Germans provided a Christmas tree for them. A special Christmas dinner, much better than their regular fare, was also served. Other POWs testified that this type of kindness was not enjoyed at other POW camps.

Although the fighting was tough and the weather was cold in Belgium, none of the 508th Red Devils on the front lines would have exchanged places with their brothers in POW stalags.

## Bitch of Buchenwald

SSgt. Bill Kalkreuth and twenty men from B Company were posted on a roadblock near Beek. Three Jerry trucks approached their position. Kalkreuth ordered his men to hold their fire until the trucks were close enough for a sure kill. After the paratroopers shot up the three trucks, two German tanks came around the curve and zeroed in on the paratroopers with their cannons and machine guns, killing three of the troopers and wounding ten. Bill Kalkreuth was one of the wounded. Kalkreuth was captured along with most of his men.

German doctors treated the wounded. Sergeant Kalkreuth had shrapnel in his right shoulder, which the German medics left in place. They kept his wound dressed and clean, but he was unable to use his right arm while he was a POW. Bill wore his arm in a sling until he was liberated in May of 1945, at which time the American doctors removed the shrapnel and his shoulder began to heal.

Kalkreuth and about forty paratroopers were sent to Buchenwald concentration camp. The dominant figure in the camp was Frau Ilse Koch, wife of Col. Karl Koch, commandant of the camp. She was famous for her hobby of collecting lampshades made of the skins from tattooed prisoners and for her insatiable appetite for sex. According to Kalkreuth, the "Bitch of Buchenwald" really ruled the camp, riding around on her jet-black stallion.

Reporting on the Nazi war crimes in Dachau, James O'Donald wrote of Frau Koch:

> At Buchenwald, evidence introduced at the trial reveals that she would ride her prized stallion down to the camp to view the incoming prisoners. Although the fact that she was looking for

tattoos for lampshades made the headlines, more often she was looking for a prospective lover. Those who struck her fancy were assigned to her house as servants. [James O'Donald, *Newsweek*, July 28, 1947]

The first day Kalkreuth and the forty paratroopers arrived at the camp, Frau Koch had them line up in the evening for her inspection. She picked out four of the most handsome and well-built troopers for a special assignment. That was the last time the Americans saw those troopers. The next night, the same thing happened. Bill said, "I started to make the evening formation unshaven, with a dirty face and as sloppy and unattractive as I could make myself look."

When it was announced that men were needed for a work camp at Rostock near the Baltic Sea, the paratroopers volunteered for the assignment. They moved out of Buchenwald in about ten days. Bill Kalkreuth as staff sergeant was the highest-ranking man among the group of POWs at his camp. He was unable to do much work with his shoulder wound requiring frequent treatment and with his arm in a sling, so he was made NCO in charge of the other men and was excused from hard labor. Among those from the 508th that he remembered with him at Rostock were two B Company men, Frank Novak and Paticio "Poncho" Mendez.

As the war neared its end and the Russian Army guns could be heard in the distance, Kalkreuth asked for an interview with the corporal in charge of the guards and this is what he said:

> The Russians are getting close, and you probably don't want to fall into their hands. We will make a deal with you. You get rid of your weapons and get out of those German uniforms. Put on some of our prison clothes, and we will all head out together toward the west to link up with the Allies.

The guards agreed to the deal and disguised themselves as American POWs like the paratroopers, and they all set out toward the west. The Russians, however, had bypassed their area and had gotten in behind the camp, and even though the prisoners marched toward the west, they ran into the Russians.

The Russians hugged them all, including the disguised German guards and said, "You are too skinny, we must feed you."

The POWs were offered raw fish and vodka. Sergeant Kalkreuth politely refused for his group, saying, "This food and drink is too strong for us after existing on black bread and soup for months. You let us see if we can find some eggs and potatoes and other things from the farm here, and then we will continue moving on toward the Allied lines."

In that way the POWs were able to leave the Russians and take their guards with them until they met the British army and freedom.

## Broughton "Hap" Hand
Abridged from *A Collection of Interviews* by Myra Hand Norman
Permission to use by Broughton Hand

After being surrounded by the Germans and holding out with small arms until the Germans moved in with armor and machine guns, Lieutenant Lavender surrendered his command to the Germans on June 12, D-Day + 6. Broughton Hand of C Company was with Lieutenant Lavender's groups and became a prisoner of war (POW). Hand said, "I was a prisoner for ten months, ten days, and ten hours. We walked and worked across France and Germany, and I ended up in Czechoslovakia."

Broughton Hand. Photo provided by Broughton Hand.

Hand was in sixteen different prison camps. The first one was in Alencon, France. When the Allies bombed the town, the POWs were used to clean up the mess. Sometimes they had to clean around an unexploded bomb in preparation for German bomb experts to destroy it.

From Alencon they traveled by boxcar southwest to Nantes. En route, American planes strafed the train. Hand remembered, "It was a terrible time. Blood everywhere—men screaming and dying and no place to hide."

The POWs were forced to march through the streets of Paris. The French, whom Hand believed were supervised by the Germans, shouted obscenities and threw all kinds of junk at the POWs. Some Frenchmen beat them over their heads with walking canes. Hand recalled, "All we could do was to give them the old finger. That's international. It speaks for itself."

Hand's stay in most of the sixteen different prison camps was so short that he doesn't retain significant memories about them. He did recall a great deal about Falkenau in Czechoslovakia. He was one of about fifty POWs who were shipped from Stalag XIII-B near Weiden, Germany, to Falkenau to work in a coal mine.

One of the POWs died of sickness or starvation. Hand, who was on the night shift, was on the burial detail. The day-shift POWs wanted to go to the funeral but were not allowed to miss work. The day-shift crew decided to strike, and the men stayed in bed the morning of the funeral. The Germans ordered the strikers up and out, but they didn't move. One of the guards, whom the POWs called Big Stiff, shot a POW in his bunk. After that, the POWs got up and went to work.

A couple of days later Hand was on the burial detail for the man that was shot to death. They buried him in a plain wooden box whereas the Germans buried the one who died in a nice coffin.

Demolitionist used explosives to break up the coal for the miners to load on rail cars. Broughton Hand told about a near-fatal accident after one of the explosions:

> One night I was working in the mine in my usual place that had been blown the day before. Everyone had been warned to listen. You go by what you hear in the coal mine: the wooden braces, the struts, the coal itself. They talk to you all the time. You get a little warning sometimes and sometimes you don't . . . That night it caved in on me, I was able to get back against my car. I was standing right by it throwing coal in it. Most of it hit the coal car. It knocked out my light, and it knocked out me.

At the end of the shift, the miners noticed that Broughton Hand was missing. His fellow POWs went back into the mine, dug him out, and carried him to their camp. The cave-in injured one of Hand's legs. After a day or two, swelling and infection was so bad that a German doctor was summoned.

The German doctor's medical supplies were limited. All he could do was cut into the infected leg, clean out the infection, and wrap it in paper. After that, the POWs had to take Hand to a nearby village to see the doctor.

The prisoners made a sleigh out of a wooden box. They wrapped Hand in a blanket and put him in the box for the sleigh ride. Hand's fellow POWs attached a rope to the sleigh and pulled him three miles to the doctor. On the second trip by sleigh, the doctor opened up the wound, cleaned it, and inserted a rubber drainage tube into the infected area then sewed up the incision. Hand commented, "The old doctor did his best. He came to see me a time or two on his motorcycle. He would work on my leg, cleaning it and then apply a new dressing."

In late February, the Germans transferred Hand to a *lager* (German for *hospital*) in Nuremberg, Germany. A German guard, a soldier too old for combat, accompanied Hand to the lager. They called the guard Long Tom. Hand described the trip:

> We rode the train fifty or sixty miles to Cheb, Germany, where we met three other POWs, who joined us from an English POW stalag. From there we walked for more than one hundred miles. At night we stayed in barns, empty houses and, at times, in German houses. Where we stayed, Long Tom did the same. We lay down all together to stay warm. I believe that Long Tom's rifle was glued to his body.

On the long march, Hand felt privileged to have a pair of Dutch wooden shoes. He had worn out his jump boots working in the coal mine. He learned that the wooden shoes were better for working in the mine, and they were better for walking in ice and snow on stony German roads.

Nuremberg, once a beautiful city, had been bombed so much that few buildings were left standing. Long Tom and the four POWs had to pick their way over broken stones and other debris from the destroyed buildings on both sides of the road. They saw the flicker of fires scattered over the city and smelled burning buildings and decomposing animals.

The POWs arrived at the lager during the night. A mixture of snow, sleet, and rain was falling. Long Tom entered the hospital and returned with the message that they would not be admitted until the morning. They waited for daylight, huddled together against the building, trying to keep warm.

Broughton Hand noticed some objects against the building wrapped in blankets. He learned that they were dead bodies. He decided to take one of the blankets. The first blanket he tried to remove was frozen stiff. The next one was limp, so he unrolled the body and wrapped the blanket around his shoulders. Hand commended, "There lies a true hero. He not only gave his life for his country, but even in death, gave up his blanket to someone who needed it more that he did."

The hospital came to life at daybreak, and Long Tom learned that since his POWs were able to walk, they would not be put in the *lager* but in small huts inside the hospital compound.

It was time for Long Tom to return to the coal-mining camp in Czechoslovakia. Hand had come to appreciate Long Tom. He shook his hand and wished him good luck and a safe journey. He gave this tribute to Long Tom:

> He not only got us to Nuremberg safely but past some angry citizens and half-wild animals in all the bombed-out cities and towns, especially the Hitler Youth Cadets, who would have liked to have gotten some of our skin.

Early in April, an American lieutenant, who needed medical help, came from Oflag 13-B (Oflag, POW camp for officers) to live in Hand's hut. He was a regular GI Joe, without officer privileges, and he developed a close friendship with Broughton Hand. Since the lieutenant was such a good Joe, the other men named him Joe.

Later that week an American Sherman tank drove over the *lager* fences into the compound. The tank commander promised to return the next day with food, water, and trucks to evacuate the POWs. The next day no one came to the *lager*, but all the German guards had disappeared. They waited without food and water for three days because a fierce battle was going on in the city.

The POWs stayed in trenches for protection. On the fourth day, as the POWs looked out from their trenches, they saw a small Catholic priest pushing a two-wheel cart. The priest brought wine and sacramental bread, two hundred wafers and two bottles of wine, which was all he had to offer. Hand said, "We got on a glorious drunk, and some of the boys got sick from too much on empty stomachs." The priest returned the next day with wafers and wine but limited the men to one bottle of wine.

Hand described his liberation:

> April 22 dawned damp and foggy, but at 10:00 AM a string of GI trucks entered our compound. Then the army took over. We lined up and waited to sign in with name, rank, serial number, and POW number. Lieutenant Joe and I got on the first truck out, and our trip back to the States began.

Broughton Hand and Lieutenant Joe continued to stick together. The GI truck took them on a four-hour ride to an American airbase in Germany. A few hours later they boarded a flight together to a hospital in Paris.

In Paris the two were admitted to the 282nd hospital and placed in beds next to each other. Hospital officials either did not notice that Hand was an enlisted man or did not enforce army segregation rules. However, the army hospital did faithfully administer penicillin injection around the clock. Hand described the treatment:

> Every three hours they'd give me a shot of penicillin. I got both my arms black and my butt black, and everywhere else they were jamming needles in me. Whether you were awake or not, it didn't make any difference, they would roll you over and pop a needle in you. By then I was down to 110 pounds, and I didn't have much flesh for them to put needles in. The lieutenant and I had a good time joking and laughing with them about that.

One day a nurse from San Antonio asked the lieutenant, "How do y'all want to go home?"

The lieutenant told the nurse that they would like to go the quickest possible way. The nurse indicated that they could fly. The lieutenant made sure that Broughton Hand would be flying with him and told her, "OK, sign him up too. We're flying back together."

Hand and Lieutenant Joe flew to New York City, where they were hospitalized agan. Hand was in a New York hospital about a week and was transferred to Brooks General Hospital at Fort Sam Houston, near San Antonio, Texas. He remained at Fort Sam Houston until his discharge from the army on October 16, 1945.

## Heil Roosevelt

A school in the suburban town of Freital, Germany, on the southern edge of Dresden housed one hundred American POWs. Clyde Smith, Johnny Roberts, Thurman Davis Jones, Robert Asher, and Harvey Knapp, A Company men of the 508th, survived that stalag. The second floor of the building served as a school for young German students. The POWs and their German guards lived on the first floor. Every day the POWs worked in the city of Dresden, replacing water pipes.

All the POWs in this stalag were privates. Since the Germans could not designate a leader from among the POWs by rank, they asked the prisoners to choose their own leader to serve as liaison between them and their German stalag commandant. They elected Jess Collins of the 505th Parachute Infantry, a spirited mountaineer from Hazard, Kentucky, with piercing eyes and bushy brows.

When addressing the Nazis, Collins would use profane and abusive language. A Bostonian named Schrach from the 101st Airborne, who was fluent in German, was the interpreter. At first Schrach would translate exactly what Collin said. The guards reacted by kicking and hitting Schrach, the translator, rather than Collins, the speaker. After getting a few bruises, Schrach learned to eliminate the insults from the translations.

Thurman Davis Jones described the morning formations:

> When all the POWs were assembled with Collins out in front, the Nazi commandant would come forward with his Hitler moustache, shiny boots, flared riding breeches, and riding crop. He would click his heels together, give the Nazi salute, and shout, "Heil Hitler!"
>
> Collins would respond by clicking his heels together, giving the Nazi salute, and shouting, "Heil Roosevelt!"
>
> One day Schrach announced to the POWs that Roosevelt had died. The next time Collins gave the salute, he shouted, "Heil Eleanor!"

Clyde Smith kept a brief two-page diary, recording main events while a prisoner. In the middle of February, Clyde wrote in his diary:

> Feb. 13, 2 big night raids on Dresden, some very close.
> Feb. 14, Another raid (day).
> Feb. 15-18, No work because of raids.

British and American planes dropped incendiary bombs on Dresden. The city had a normal population of six hundred thousand, but its ranks had swelled another four hundred thousand with refugees who had fled the advancing Russian army. Over one hundred thousand died as the city was destroyed by fire.

Clyde Smith told how the temperature changed from cold to hot:

> It was 25 below zero when the raids started. Then the city turned into a blazing inferno. The streets were so hot; people fleeing from the fires had their shoes to burn off their feet. It was estimated that in the center of the city, the temperature reached 3,000 degrees.
>
> After the raids, the POWs were used to search for the living among the dead. At the railroad station, people inside the train coaches were burned to a crisp; their clothes burned off,

flesh mostly gone, with maybe a metal belt buckle left in the lap of a charred skeleton.

Thurman Davis Jones remembered how the civilians searched for their loved ones:

> Where a wall was still standing, two lists were written of the wall—one to list the known dead and one to list the known living. The dead list was always the longest. The people would weep as they read the lists.

Many people sought protection in the basements of their houses. The fires above the basements sucked out all the oxygen, and most of the people in the cellars died of suffocation.

Clyde Smith and Johnny Roberts were assigned by their guards to search the cellars in the central part of Dresden. By this time the smell of burnt and decaying flesh made the air putrid, but that didn't spoil the appetites of Smith and Roberts when they came across a basement full of potatoes. The fireproof exterior protected the potatoes, so that the potatoes did not burn; they just baked good and tender. The two POWs gorged themselves quickly on a few baked potatoes before reporting to the German guards outside, "No survivors."

During the weeks following the

Left: Clyde Smith. Right: Johnny Roberts, 1943.
Photo copied from A Company pictures.

big fire, the Russians were getting closer to Dresden. On April 14, the POWs were marched under guard to a town named Dispoldiswalde and on the next day to Zinnewalde on the Czechoslovakian border. The prisoners remained in Zinnewalde about three weeks, until May 7, when the Russians attacked the city.

During the Russian attack on Zinnewalde, Thurman Davis Jones and Robert Asher escaped the guards. After three days walking and catching rides with refugees fleeing the Russians, Jones and Asher met the American army at Karlsbad.

Clyde Smith reported on his final day as a POW: the POWs were moved from Zinnewalde under guard across the Czech border the next morning. They turned southwest toward Komotau (now called Chomutov.)

On the way to Komotau, the POWs took the guns from their German guards. The armed POWs thought walking was too slow, especially after they saw Russian tanks in the distance and some of the Russian bullets fell near them. A charcoal-fueled bus stopped on the road. The driver cleaned out the ashes and stoked the engine with fresh charcoal. Clyde Smith and other POWs with him waited until the refueling was accomplished then they hijacked the bus and forced the driver to take them to Komotau. They arrived May 8 (VE Day).

By this time the news of VE Day had reached the local population. The next day the Russians occupied the town. A few days later Clyde Smith's group linked up with American troops and freedom.

After his liberation, Thurman Davis Jones experienced emotions of a lifetime. He explained the following:

> From a high hilltop, I could see lights from towns, villages, and farmhouses, which had been blacked out throughout the war. What a thrill!
> 
> I remembered the words of a familiar song:
> 
> When the lights go on again all over the world
> And the boys come home again all over the world.
> 
> At last those words were beginning to come true.

## Eugene "Gene" Falgione

VE Day was the beginning of the process that freed American prisoners of war (POWs). It took some time for all of the POWs to connect with American troops, and their records often took extra time to catch up with them thus delaying their return to home and freedom. Such was the case of Eugene Falgione.

Gene Falgione was captured on Christmas Eve, December 24, 1944 in Vielsalm, Belgium. Gene and five others, with machine-guns and BARs, were positioned by Lt. George Lamm at key points to defend the railroad and motor vehicle bridges over the Salm River. He was a member of Lt. George Lamm's rear guard platoon left to defend the two bridges as the main body of the regiment pulled back to a new MLD (main line of defense).

German artillery hit near Falgione. He suffered shrapnel wounds and a concussion, which left him unconscious. When he came to, the rear guard had pulled back and Germans were guarding him. His captors had stripped him of his outer clothing and boots. They marched Gene, wearing only long underwear and socks, to a building filled with other POWs awaiting interrogation.

Some had already been questioned and had been treated roughly by the interrogator. The GI nearest to Gene confided to Gene, "I'm really scared because I'm Jewish."

Gene suggested, "Pretend you converted to Christianity."

"If I knew some Christian prayers, I might try that," replied the Jewish POW.

Gene offered, "Take my rosary, and we will repeat together Our Father and Hail Mary until your turn comes to be questioned!"

The Jewish prisoner was a fast learner, and as he was led away, he counted his beads and repeated, "Our Father, which art in heaven" and immediately followed with "Hail Mary, Mother of God."

The interrogator, who was probably sympathetic toward Christians, dealt kindly toward the pious prisoner. Gene's friend successfully disguised his ethnic background, and he was not singled out for extra brutal treatment.

All of the POWs with Gene Falgione suffered terribly in the days that followed as they were marched by foot out of Belgium and through southwestern Germany into Czechoslovakia. The Germans took their outer layer of clothing, overcoats, combat jackets and pants, and their paratrooper boots. It left them with their long-john wool underwear and wool shirts and pants. Gene told about the treatment of the German population as they marched through their communities. Some threw rocks at them and screamed obscenities at them as they marched through. Gene wrapped his feet with pieces of pasteboard and rags, but he ended up with frozen feet from the exposure. After walking to Czechoslovakia, the POWs traveled by train to a German prison camp.

While on a work detail away from the prison camp, Falgione escaped and was able to join the advancing Russian army. During a battle between the Russians and the Germans, Gene saved the lives of two Russian women. These Russian women sent letters on his behalf to his family and to his future wife, Wilma, letting them know he was still alive.

The Russian and American armies met at the Elbe River, but the Russians blocked the access to the bridge when Falgione tried to cross to the American side. Not to be denied, Falgione jumped into the icy waters and swam across. The Russians fired at him in the river, but the Americans fired back at the Russians, which aided his swim to safety.

Gene could not prove his identity to the American authorities, so he borrowed some clothes and made his own way across country to a French port, where he was put on a ship to the USA.

By coincidence, on the same ship was the Jewish POW to whom he had given a rosary and taught Christian prayers. They landed in New York together. It was Gene's turn to learn about Jewish traditions. His friend took him to his home in Brooklyn, and they had a Jewish celebration. After the party, Gene found several fifty-dollar bills stuffed in his jacket pocket by guests at the party.

Gene's son Adrian Falgione wrote, "Dad suffered from frozen feet that gave him trouble all his life, and I remember, as a kid, the doctor digging shrapnel out of Dad from time to time."

Eugene Falgione was discharged from the army in October 1945 and returned to Blue Hill, Nebraska, where he found his fiancée waiting for him. They married early in 1946 and settled on a farm near the school where Wilma was teaching. Gene built a welding shop on his farm and repaired farm machinery along with his farm work. He set to work making a living and raising his family and put the war behind him. For years he never mentioned his war experiences, not even to members of his own family.

Then late in life, Gene and Wilma started attending the 508th PIR Association reunions. Gene heard other veterans tell their stories, and eventually, Gene shared his own stories with his family and war buddies. Wilma Falgione and their children were happy to learn about Eugene Falgione the paratrooper and veteran of World War II. They have also enjoyed meeting other veterans and their families. Even though Gene passed away a few years ago, Wilma still attends most of the 508th reunions with her children and grandchildren.

Photo to the left: Eugene and Wilma Falgione. Taken soon after Eugene's return home from the war in 1945. Photo supplied by Wilma Falgione.

Photo to the right: Eugene and Wilma at the Dedication of Monument to the Airborne in 1983. Photo supplied by Wilma Falgione.

## Survival
**Condensed from *Normandy, June 6, 1944, D-Day***
A Personal Account by Arthur Fish
Permission to summarize and quote portions given by Arthur Fish

"Ergebt Euch!" (Give yourself up!). I knew what that meant, and turning to my right I saw two German riflemen and an automatic rifleman on the road about 40 feet from me. By the time I could point my carbine in their direction, it would be all over. I could see my mother reading a telegram stating that I was killed in action. There wasn't much choice. I slowly raised my arms and said, "Kamerad". [Arthur "Art" Fish]

PFC Arthur Fish of F Company landed near a German machine gun nest on D-Day. He had pulled the pin from a grenade thinking he might use it but never did. Still holding the armed grenade, Fish crawled a long way through tall grass with enemy bullets cutting the grass above his body. A glider crashed in the field nearby, and the enemy guns were diverted to the glider, which gave Fish a few minutes to get farther away from the machine gun. Eventually the firing stopped with no response from the glider, and Fish fell asleep holding the grenade.

The dawn was breaking as Arthur Fish awoke, and he realized he had been clutching that grenade while asleep. If his hand had relaxed, the handle would have released the detonator and the grenade would have blown up in his hand. Finding a pair of spare bootlaces in his pocket, Fish tied the handle down and put the grenade in his left breast pocket. With the grenade secured, he set out to look for friendly troops.

Arthur Fish. Photo copied from 1943 Company pictures.

Fish described the moments following:

> Something happened that made the events of the previous night seem like a Sunday-school picnic. My left forearm had been brushing against the pocket with the grenade, causing the handle to come loose. It made a bang that sounded like a cap pistol. I recognized it immediately. I had just five seconds to get it out of my pocket and away from me before it blew up!
>
> I dropped my carbine and lunged into my pocket with the speed of a rattlesnake. I managed to get my hand around the lethal device and tried to pull it out. No luck! The opening was too small to allow me to pull my hand out as long as I held the grenade. I knew there was no other way to get the damned thing out. About two seconds had gone by. It won't be long now.

> I would soon know if all those things I had heard about the hereafter were true.
>
> One more tug, and then it happened. The top of the pocket ripped, and the grenade went flying out to my right about thirty-five feet. I had a split-second decision to make. Should I drop to the ground facing the grenade or should I turn my back to it? I turned to the left as I started to drop. BAROOM!
>
> I heard fragments zing over my head. I felt other fragments embed in my right leg and felt the warm blood streaming down my right sleeve. I had been blown up by my own grenade and would be lucky to come out of this alive.

After the accident, Fish crawled to the edge of the field, pulled himself over a five-foot hedgerow, and lowered himself into a ditch beside a dirt road. By this time the pain was unbearable. Art reached for his trench knife to cut away the first aid pouch from his belt harness. The grenade had blown the knife away, so he shot the package loose with his carbine. Finding the morphine Syrette, he was able to give himself a shot to dull the pain, but he could not relieve his growing thirst because he found his canteen punctured and dry.

Fish wondered if anyone would find him before he bled to death. Trying to attract attention, he fired ten rounds from his carbine then reloaded and fired another fifteen rounds. After a short wait, he heard someone say, "Hey, trooper! How's it going?"

Two GIs from Eighty-second Division Headquarters were there. They looked at his wounds and said, "Wait! You will need a stretcher. Just relax, and we will be back in ten minutes."

For more than an hour Fish waited impatiently for the Eighty-second troopers to return. No paratroopers were to be seen. Then he heard the guttural voices in German ordering him to surrender.

Fish's captors did not immediately attend to his wounds. After carrying him up the road to an open area, they placed him under a tree, and the leader left. Arthur Fish observed a pile of American weapons nearby about three feet high, which made him think, "Things are not going so great—at least not for the men who had those weapons."

When the leader returned with an aid man, the German medic asked, "Packet—hast du Sanitator Packet?"

"Ya, ich habe," Fish answered, and showed the first aid pouch on the rear of his belt, believing they planned to use it on him.

"Gut!" the medic answered and proceeded to remove the packet, after which his captors and the medic left with his aid packet. Art Fish tried to get in a truck nearby but found it locked. He crawled away from the truck and then fell unconscious.

Fish recalls he regained consciousness in a German aid station. "I found myself on a stretcher. The first voices I heard were those of Pvt. John Finnicum and Bob Bussell from Headquarters Second. Ernie Burton, F Company medic, was bandaging Bussell's left knee. Bussell had lost part of his kneecap and part of his thigh."

Then Dick Stanley, E Company, entered the room and spoke to Fish. "Well, I'll be damned, I think you might make it. Man, you sure look better than when I found you under those trees. You know those damned Jerries wanted to just leave you there."

While talking to his buddies in the German aid station, Fish fell into a deep sleep and woke up six days later in an ambulance, which took him to Hotel du Parc in the village of Bagnol, forty miles southwest of where he had jumped. German doctors and nurses at the hotel placed Art Fish on a large dining table and removed the remaining pieces of shrapnel in his arm, leg, and buttocks. Then he was taken to the second floor of the building.

After a brief sleep, Arthur awoke with a terrible thirst. He was among about thirty other wounded lying on the floor. He could hear some of the patients talking in German. From time to time, the doctors would take a look at one of the Germans, but Art was ignored.

Then he heard a nurse speak in French. Art called "Water, water! American! American!"

The French nurse responded immediately, fetched him a glass of water, and tenderly lifted his head and helped him drink, but he was not able to swallow the water. She then went for a French priest, who gave Art the last rites.

Occasionally the doctors and nurses would pull the death blanket over the heads of others. Everything added up to a bleak picture for Fish, but he took heart because of the friendliness of the French nurse and priest.

The next morning, the dead were removed first and then the living were moved to the third floor into rooms with luxurious beds and even sheets. Art was in the room with three Americans paratroopers from the 101st Division and 507th regiment and another soldier who survived the 29th Division beach landing. Two British Airborne medics came to the room and introduced themselves as Tom and Jerry.

When Tom found out Fish had trouble swallowing, he brought in a German doctor and nurse and said, "This will take care of your swallowing problem, Yank."

The nurse emptied a long hypodermic needle into his hip. In a few minutes he was able to retain fluids, and the next day Fish was beginning to eat a little.

On the second day, Tom explained to the Allied patients that so many German casualties were being brought to the Hotel du Parc that they would have to be moved to make room for the German wounded. Fish and his roommates were moved to the basement and occupied crude wooden bunks with burlap-covered straw mattresses—no sheets or pillows. A Frenchwoman, who worked in the hospital, stole food from the Germans, which she hid in her petticoat under her long full-skirted dress, made their stay somewhat brighter. She would walk up to an open window, lift her skirt, remove the food, and pass it through the window.

On the evening of the third day, Fish was loaded on a truck with others and transferred south to the City of Rennes, arriving about nine o'clock on the morning of June 16. With the tender loving care from French nurses Roxanne and Evette and extra food smuggled in at night by a friendly Tunisian POW who had special privileges, Arthur Fish improved rapidly. On July 7 he was judged fit enough to be released from the hospital and be moved to a POW camp in Rennes.

Arthur Fish was a survivor. He survived his wounds although left to die by both Americans and Germans. He also survived the rigors of several Nazi stalags, with rations of a bowl of soup and one slice of bread daily. Life in the Nazi stalags was as tough, if not tougher, than on the fighting front. Like the combat soldiers, the POWs found strength in each other's comradeship and good humor.

Other 508th troopers who were POWs with Fish were John Richards of I Company and three F Company men—Stanley Roth, Whitey Bauman, and John Finnicum.

## Bill Clark's Odyssey

First Sergeant William "Bill" Clark of A Company was captured by the Germans six days after landing in Normandy. Clark and other 508th men were taken to Stalag III-C on the Oder River, bordering Poland near Altdrewitz and Kurstin, Germany. Clark is one of four POWs who have described their trips from Stalag III-C through Poland and Russia to the United States. Each story is unique and deserves to be told.

On January 30, The Russian artillery could be heard at Stalag III-C. The Germans decided to evacuate the camp. They divided the POWs into three groups of about ninety men each and assigned POW sergeants to be in charge. First Sergeant Bill Clark was in charge of one group. Sgt. Leroy Coleman and Sergeant Butz were assigned to the other groups. On

January 31, the Germans started marching the POWs out of the camp. They marched out of Stalag III-C toward the east rather than toward the west and Germany. Clark wondered why the Germans were leading them away from Germany.

The POWs marched about half an hour from their prison when the Russian mistook the POWs for Hungarian troops and raked the column with small arms and mortar fire. The Germans guards fled. Five of the POWs were killed, and five others were wounded. In one sense of the word, without their guards, it was the beginning of their freedom, but on the other hand, they were not as safe as they had been in the stalag. So the POWs went back inside the protective walls of their prison.

First Sergeant Bill Clark had served as liaison between the stalag commandant and the POWs. Clark went to the commandant's office and found that the commandant had killed himself, so he armed himself with the commandant's pistol. (The Russians later took the pistol from Clark.) Clark expressed a favorable opinion of the commandant, saying that when he complained about the conditions of the POWs that the commandant listened and sometimes responded with corrective action.

First Sergeant Bill Clark. Photo supplied by Bill Clark.

The next day Clark led a group of about ten men to go with the Russians to Altdrewitz to the railhead to look for supplies. They found no useful supplies in Altdrewitz. The group decided to spend the night under a railroad shelter in Altdrewitz to avoid travelling in the dark.

Upon returning to the stalag the next day, only about forty of the POWs were still there. The others had acted on their own initiatives and left in small groups and went their several ways, most headed east toward Warsaw. The Russians then instructed Bill Clark, as the ranking POW remaining, to gather all the POWs left in the stalag and start marching them toward Warsaw. He was given the understanding that an American consulate in Warsaw would help them get back to America.

Clark estimated, fifty years after the fact, that his group left the prison camp about January 3, 1945. It was miserably cold; snow was on the ground, and the ex-POWs were ill equipped for a long march under those conditions. They stopped the first night at the German city of Landsberg.

Landsberg was a German enclave inside the Polish border, and the Russians were ruthless in their assault. The whole city was on fire. Even on the outskirts, where Clark's men were camped for the night, they could feel the heat from the raging fires within the city. In fact, Clark remarked, "This was the first time we had been warm in a month."

The group stayed in the area of Landsberg for two days trying to find transportation to Warsaw, a distance of about 400 kilometers or 250 miles. The Russians were more interested in continuing their attack on Germany than on transporting POWs, so Clark and his men started walking toward Warsaw. Two of the men developed frostbitten feet from walking in the snow with poor footwear and had to be helped along, sometimes carried on piggyback. Clark remembered that one of the men with bad feet was Sergeant Gagnon of Headquarters First of the 508th.

In about four or five days, they reached Poznan. Clark tried to get some medical aid for the men with the bad feet from the Russians but without success. The Polish people were helpful. They gave them food and some burlap, which they used to wrap the feet and shoes of the men with frozen feet. (Or trench foot. Bill Clark was not sure of the diagnosis.)

After walking about fifteen miles beyond Poznan, Sgt. Leroy Coleman flagged down a group of American Studebaker trucks transporting Russian wounded from the front. The Russian exclaimed, "Good Americaniski!" Their commander was compassionate and allowed the Americans to ride to Kunin, where there was a hospital for the wounded Russians.

The ride lifted the morale of the Americans, but they were still about two hundred kilometers from Warsaw. They spent one night and day in Kunin, where the Poles scraped together some food for them, and they started walking toward Warsaw again. Their progress was slow. Clark's chief concern was taking care of the two men with bad feet. That slowed the pace, but the other men were very helpful with their lame comrades. Clark said, "I can't blame it all on the boys with bad feet, we were all getting weaker and discouraged. Our minds were playing tricks on us."

A Russian convoy of trucks came along, and the Americans got out in the middle of the road and stopped them. At first the Russians didn't want to talk to them, but they finally found a Russian officer who spoke English. He was in charge of the convoy and reluctantly agreed to take the Americans as far as he was going. They were able to ride to within about twenty kilometers of Warsaw. Clark estimated that they walked all but about fifteen miles of the total distance from the stalag to Warsaw.

About February 20, Clark's group walked into the center of Warsaw, a wrecked city, which had been destroyed by the Germans as the Polish citizens fiercely defended their capital. The Poles, who were desperately poor and had suffered both from the Germans and the Russians, gave the Americans bread, ersatz butter, and tea. They got no food from the Russians. After seeing and experiencing so much death, destruction, and human suffering, Bill Clark wondered, "Are there any winners in war?"

They stayed the night in a warehouse. The next morning Clark went to the rail station and found a Russian official who told him that a train was making up for Odessa. They even provided stretchers to carry the two lame men to the train. Clark's groups were assigned to two flatbed cars, somewhat like pulpwood cars in America. The cars had bulkheads on each end. The men were able to find tarpaulins to fasten to the front of the cars to break the wind as they traveled.

It took them about four days to get to Odessa, the port city on the Black Sea. The winter weather had moderated, and as they moved south, the climate was naturally warmer. The men huddled against each other behind the tarp and kept fairly warm compared to the cold they experienced walking toward Warsaw.

Bill Clark revised and improved the roster he had tried to keep of the men that he brought from Stalag III-C to Odessa. Then he made a duplicate copy. When Clark learned that a British ship had docked at the port, he looked up the ship's captain, gave him a copy of his roster, and asked that his men be accepted to board the ship. The captain agreed, and they boarded the ship.

The British sailors could not have been nicer to the American former POWs: the two cripples were taken into sick bay and given the best medical treatment. All were fed good food and as much as they could eat and were given everything available on ship to make them comfortable.

The ship sailed out of the Black Sea and into the Mediterranean and then to Port Said in Egypt. Clark recalled the following:

> Help of every description was there to greet us—the US Army, the International Red Cross, the Salvation Army, you name it, and it was there. What a joy! We felt free at last. After showers, haircuts, new clothes, shoes, the works, we were beginning to look almost human. Only one thing was wrong: our clothes were about four sizes too large. We were told, "Don't worry, you will grow into them."

When they were given physical examinations, Bill Clark weighed only 128 pounds. Unlike the other ex-POWs, Clark was not enjoying his food. In fact, he regurgitated every time he ate. The doctors told Clark that his system had not yet adjusted to regular food. (After his discharge, a civilian doctor discovered that he had an intestinal parasite, which the doctor treated and cured.)

They sailed from Port Said to Naples, Italy. By this time, the men with bad feet felt like dancing. Clark commented, "Their feet smelled a lot better also."

Finally on March 30, Bill Clark boarded a ship in Naples for the good old USA. He had traveled for two months and over 4,000 miles from Stalag III-C to Naples. He was now on the last leg on his journey home. As a good first sergeant, Clark felt responsible for his troops. Now he could relax in the knowledge that he had not lost a man on the long journey. Clark gave his men credit for being good troopers, who held up under the hardships endured with courage and determination.

Map by Zig Boroughs, assisted by Bill Clark

## Ken Hook

Like Bill Clark, Bill Tumlin, and Dave Nagle, Kenneth Hook of A Company was in Stalag III-C. The four 508th paratroopers had some similar experiences in their journeys home from prison camp. Yet each lived through unique personal events peculiar to their individual histories.

They all started out together, marching away from their prison camp guarded by German soldiers. When the Russian army fired on the column of marchers, most of the POWs went back to the stalag for personal safety. The German guards, however, fled the scene.

The Germans fought fiercely trying to prevent the Russians from entering their homeland, and the Russians were just as determined to keep on driving toward Berlin. According to Ken Hook, the first night the POWs were back in camp, Russian tanks advanced from the east in a pincher movement on both sides of the stalag and almost met in front. The tanks stopped at a large trench that they could not cross.

Ken Hook remembered the first Russian tank he saw. The tank commander was a woman with the rank of major. The Russians then directed the POWs to come out of the barracks and get in the trench. From this position, Hook remembered observing the Russians firing rockets at the Germans.

The Russians withdrew, and the next morning, the Germans retook the camp briefly but left again. Then the German Air Force strafed and bombed the camp with antipersonnel bombs. Ken Hook, Sgt. Robert Brewer of A Company, and MSgt. John Haley of the 504th and the original Parachute Test Platoon were standing next to a doorway of a building. When an antipersonnel bomb exploded near them, all three dove for the doorway. Haley was the quickest and landed in the doorway first. Hook was next and landed on top of Haley, and Brewer landed on top of the other two. Brewer was hit in the back. Hook and Haley were uninjured.

John Haley and Ken Hook took Brewer to a building within the stalag compound where an American lieutenant was tending to several wounded men. The lieutenant used an instrument and tried to pull a piece of shrapnel out of Sergeant Brewer's back. He was unable to retrieve the shrapnel and asked Hook to try. Hook could not dislodge the shrapnel either.

Leaving Brewer with the other wounded, Hook and Haley went to their barracks to sleep. After midnight, someone came into the room, calling, "Hook! Hook!"

It was Brewer, who had walked to their barracks by himself through the snow stark naked. Trying to keep him warm, Hook and Haley put Brewer between them in their bed, which consisted of straw with two blankets on a dirt floor. The next morning, they returned Brewer to the building with the other wounded, hoping he would be cared for. Hook recalled that Brewer was still alive when his group left the stalag later that night.

Hook and Haley went to the office building where the POW records were kept and found it had been ransacked. Someone had found Hook's official POW photo and gave it to him.

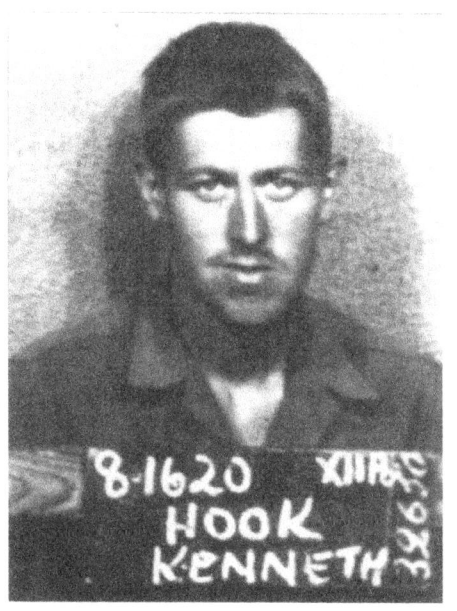

This photo of Kenneth Hook was taken in Stalag III-A. He was later in Stalag IV-B and finally in Stalag III-C. Photo provided by Kenneth Hook.

The opened safe contained all kinds of money: US, British, German, and Russian. Hook and Haley stuffed their pockets with Russian rubles, which came in handy later.

The Russians had returned to the camp by this time. That night a Russian officer took about twenty of the POWs through the forest across the Oder River into Poland. It was an all-night trip. The Russian officer then told the POWs, "You are on your own. Go toward Warsaw and Moscow or Odessa!"

At that point, Ken Hook and John Haley teamed up with three other paratroopers from the 101st Airborne: John Frank Jones, Archie Sanders, and Robert Martin. The five troopers set a fast pace and made it to Landsberg the first night, where they set up camp in a hotel. Some drunken Russians in the hotel built a fire in their room on the third floor. Soon the whole building was burning. The five American paratroopers didn't hang around after the hotel caught fire. They left Landsberg and headed east.

Hook's group stopped next at a farmhouse. A friendly Polish woman was glad to see them. She gave them a horse. Haley got on the horse and rode it a short distance, and the horse threw him. Hook then tried to ride the horse, and he was thrown. A Russian officer saw them and took the horse from the Americans. The Russian rode a little ways, and the horse threw him also. Then the officer shot the horse.

Soon the five troopers came to a Polish town and found a vacated bicycle shop. They "borrowed" five bikes from the shop and began pedaling on their way, but not for long. A group of Russians stopped them and acted very hostile as if they were arresting the five POWs. The Russians demanded identification papers. Jones happened to have a soldier's pay card with the signature of the paymaster, who was an adjutant general. Jones pretended that he was that adjutant general. The Russians then showed more respect and were less abusive. They did not arrest the troopers, but they took their bikes and let them continue their journey by foot.

The five troopers—Hook, Haley, Martin, Jones, and Sanders—later joined forces with a group of about twenty other POWs on the move. The combined group cooked pork in an open fireplace, and everyone got sick from eating the meat.

At this point, the Russians were more active in the POWs' welfare. They provided showers for the group. At the same time about twenty-five Jewish women were taking showers with only a railing between the two groups. When asked how they were affected by the sight of nude women, Hook replied, "A POW's priority list was (1) food, (2) home, (3) women. At that time in our lives, we had very little interest in women but tremendous interest in food and in getting home."

After showers, the Russians loaded them on trucks, and they rode through the rubble of Warsaw. They saw a lot of unburied German soldiers in the rubble and alongside the Warsaw streets. The trucks took them to a station where they boarded a train bound for Moscow, but the train to Moscow stopped and went back toward Warsaw then turned south toward Odessa.

Hook remembered the miles and miles of flat landscape in the Ukraine. The Russian guards enjoyed taking pot shots at the jackrabbits as they rode by. The snow was about three feet deep, so the rabbits must have been snow-shoe jackrabbits.

Once the train stopped at a farmhouse, and the farmer and his wife greeted the POWs in a friendly manner. The troopers asked for food. The only food the farmer could provide was about two dozen eggs. In exchange for the eggs, Hook handed the farmer a handful of Russian rubbles, which had been taken from the stalag safe. The farmer was overwhelmed with the amount of money he was paid. Back in the boxcar the POWs boiled the eggs on a small pot-bellied stove. It was their main source of food for the remainder of the train trip.

When they arrived in Odessa, they were still hungry. After getting off the train, they saw a peddler pushing a cart loaded with soft pretzels.

Hook offered the man a handful of Russian rubles, and the man gave him the whole load, including the cart. The peddler walked away very happy with his bargain.

While Hook and his buddies were in Odessa, they witnessed a tragic event. A sailor from an American Navy ship anchored in the harbor visited the camp and found his brother among the POWs, a 505th paratrooper. The two brothers had a joyful reunion. Then the sailor had to return to his ship. Later, the 505th paratrooper was sitting with another POW beside a wall of a bombed out building when the wall suddenly collapsed, killing the two men. Ken Hook and some of his fellow POWs had just walked away from the wall when the accident occurred.

Haley, Jones, Martin, and Sanders were still together in Odessa. They embarked on a British ship together with about twenty-four other POWs. The ship sailed straight to Naples, where Haley found his old 504th buddies in charge of the depot. There they received new clothes and money. They even had a chance to do some sightseeing in Naples.

The ex-POWs, in new uniforms and with regular army status, departed from Naples on Friday, April 13, 1945. Hook remembered the date because some of the men thought sailing on Friday the 13th was a bad omen. Onboard were about a hundred WACs (Women's Army Corps). The men didn't get excited over the WACs because all were obviously pregnant.

While on deck the first night of the voyage, Hook heard a familiar voice. It turned out to be Kenny Elsman, who joined the service with Hook. Elsman was returning home after completing his tour as a crewmember on a B-24 bomber based in Italy.

When they enlisted, they both wanted to get in the air force. Elsman was sent to the air force. Hook was sent to Camp Blanding, Florida, by mistake. Hook vowed he did not volunteer for the paratroopers, but he also declared that he has no regrets whatsoever for hooking up with the paratroopers.

The *USS Wakefield* sailed to Boston. Ken Hook had two more brief stays in military camps before his furlough home—Camp Miles Standish in Boston and Camp Atterbury in Indiana.

Ken Hook concluded his account with this statement: "I feel I am one of the lucky ones, having returned. I wouldn't take a million for the experience, and I wouldn't give a million to do it again."

## Bill Tumlin's Journey from Stalag III-C to the USA

Pvt. Bill Tumlin, like First Sergeant Bill Clark, was an inmate at Stalag III-C. Much of Tumblin's travels paralleled Clark's. However, Tumlin was never a part of Clark's group on his journey.

Bill Tumlin, C Company, 508th Parachute Infantry Regiment, was wounded on D-Day in Normandy, captured by the Germans, and shipped to Stalag III-C. Tumblin filled thirty-three pages of a small pocket notebook diary from January 31 through April 16, 1945, briefly outlining his personal experiences during those eventful two and a half months. In his first entry, Bill Tumlin was in Stalag III-C. In his last entry he was almost home, riding a train, having slept through the night in a pullman sleeper.

The following is an abridged edition of Tumblin's diary.

William R. Tumlin, copied from 1943 C Company pictures.

Jan 31-45: Germans attempted to evacuate our camp this morning at 6 AM. After a lot of stalling we moved out at 11:30. Russian spearhead cut the road ahead, cutting our column in two—tanks fired into us, thinking we were Hungarians—20 killed—200 retaken, the rest of us returned to camp.

Thirty minutes after the Jerries again tried to move us out. After threats of shelling camp, a large part of the men started out—this time in the direction of Krustin. Those of us who stayed behind began to take cover for the expected fight—it came soon enough. The Russians drove almost up to the camp with tanks and infantry—the men who had left camp began to return to the cover of the air raid shelters. Fifteen Jerry guards were trapped in the camp—at least twelve have now died for the Feuhrer. After Russian tanks passed by camp with both 37s and MGs (37-millimeter canons and machine guns) firing. This went on all night.

Feb. 1-45: This morning at 6 AM the camp got their first look at the Red Army's famous rocket guns in action. After the Feuhrer's Air force was up (They still have one.) and worried hell out of us all day. After dark we had some pretty close shells from Jerry's 88s—not much sleep.

Feb. 2-45: Fighting heavy today—Russian rockets and big guns shelling hell out of Oder River defenses and Jerry Fighters and Stokker Dive Bombers trying vainly to knock then out. Bombs are landing right outside camp—one inside. One man killed, several wounded. The night was sort of quiet.

Feb. 3-45: Today not as rough as usual. Lots of planes around, but not as close as before. U. S. Fortresses came over today—one down in flames. Four men bailed out.

Camp evacuated tonight at 4 PM. Got to Zoendorf at 3:30 AM—living in German homes—eating steaks, chops and French fries—plenty of food.

Feb. 4-45: Slight air activity this morning—lots of Russians moving up to the front—lots of U. S. trucks. Quite a few dead Jerries lying around. Night quiet—Slept well.

Feb. 5-45: Today after a fare well steak, we left with a small group for the town of Landsberg—34 miles away. Stopped off en route at Vietz for the night—slept night in baby bed.

Feb. 6-45: This morning my group of eleven men ate nine grown hens along with two pots of stew, coffee, jam etc. We pulled out about noon for Landsberg—only myself and one man (Vernon McGuire, C Company) went all the way—the rest preferring to stay on a farm and come in next morning. (Tumlin explained that those who stayed saw some rabbits in a pen and wanted to eat the rabbits before travelling on.) Road is littered with people torn to bits—some burned—men, women and children—also hundreds of dead horses. Met 2 friends of ours and slept in Jerry Colonel's apartment.

Feb. 7-45: This whole day we spent in wild goose chase for transportation—the four of us went back to the Colonel's apartment for the night—having quite a time going through the Jerry stuff.

Feb. 8-45: Left this morning on bicycles for Schwerin—there we caught a convoy to Pinne. One of the drivers got us a room—there were fifteen of us in one room—didn't sleep much.

Feb. 9-45: Got a passport to Shemituly this morning. We gave our bicycles to a Pole who was helpful to us; we got to Shemituly this afternoon by convoy and were taken to Red Cross. They fed us our best home cooked meal in nine months—there were half a dozen languages spoken at our table—everybody very friendly—after we were given a private room, food, & music—very enjoyable time.

Feb. 10-45: Still traveling by truck—pretty slow—spent night in Polish village—slept on floor.

Feb. 11-45: In Geinesin—met most all my first group there—rode off and on all night. Weather colder.

Feb. 13-45: Caught train into Prague arrived late at night—no where to sleep.

Feb. 14-45: Spent most of the day looking over Prague—only part of Warsaw not destroyed. Polish are removing two hundred bodies from a cellar of church where they were trapped during bombing raid—Germans refused request for rescue so they all died from bombs or fire. Slept night in Polish home.

Feb 15-45: Left Warsaw this morning for U. S. Camp at Rambettof, not much here, very dirty but improvement in order.

Feb. 16-45: Getting settled out here—eating two meals a day (soup and barley) sleeping on floor. Lots of refugees here.

Feb. 17-45: Getting hot showers—nothing else new,

Feb. 18-45: New men coming every day—getting BBC news.

Feb. 19-45: Pulled my first guard duty in nine months today—heard news of leaving for P. O. E. (Port of Embarkation) tonight. Probably be Odessa.

Feb. 20-45: Preparing for move.

Feb. 21-45: Everybody sweating out move—move expected tomorrow.

Feb. 22-45: Loaded rations on train today—boarded train late at night.

Feb. 23-45: Cut wood and carried water for cook car today—started moving tonight—fifty-one men in boxcar.

Feb. 28-45: Moving slowly—expect to reach Odessa tonight.

March 1-45: In Odessa this morning. Moved out to crude camp—signs of heavy fighting all through town—still eating soup and barley.

March 2-45: Walked over a large part of the city today in search of showers—left group on way back to look over the rest of town. It's mostly ruins—(News tonight) British Transports expected in about the fourth, bringing Russian prisoners retaken on western front. We should be aboard by eighth.

Explanation of Russian prisoners: The 508th took prisoners on Hill 95 in Normandy whom they called Mongolians. The paratroopers understood that they were former members of the Russian army, captured by the Germans on their Eastern front and used to fight against the Allies. Monsieur Henri Vasselin, a Frenchman whose home is in the neighborhood of Hill 95, described them as East Russian mercenary soldiers of the ROA (Russian Liberation Army, English translation.) The ROA was made up of Armenians, Turks, Georgians, and Mongolians. Their native homes were a part of the USSR, but they opposed Russian communism. They were willing to fight for the Germans against Russia and their Allies.

The Russian drove a hard bargain. They demanded that the POWs whom the Western Allies held, who were formerly in the Russian military forces, be returned in exchange for Allied POWs liberated by Russia. The ROA prisoners did not want to return to the USSR, for they believed they would be treated as traitors. In the end, Russia executed the ROA men who were exchanged.

March 3-45: Getting American chow from ships in Dock—our boats on time. Expected tonight.

March 4-45: Boats in harbor—not yet docked—may get aboard in a couple of days. Turkey and chicken dumpling for supper.

March 5-45: Waiting for boats to unload—expect to go aboard tomorrow or next day—supposed to be one stop before States.

March 6-45: Issued cigs and candy today—going aboard ship tomorrow—8 A. M.

March 8-45: Black Sea very smooth sailing—sailed through straits to Istanbul—arrived just after noon meal—expect to be here a couple of days—very beautiful city.

March 9-45: Pulled out of Istanbul about noon—very smooth sailing—always in sight of some island.

March 11-45: Passed Crete this morning—weather warmer, water little rougher—expect to get to Egypt—change boats—clocks run back one hour.

March 12-45: Landed at Port Said 10:30 A. M. Met by band and crowds of people—boat lousy with reporters. Sailed by ferry to U.S. Island camp—Ate two big meals and saw three shows one stage and two movies.

Lots of Egyptian workers—some Italians—sleeping in tents.

March 13-45: Today was busy day signing papers—getting new clothes—getting paid, etc. Sent Mom a cable.

Went to Port Said this afternoon on pass—Arabs pretty rough but enjoyed freedom.

March 16-45: Left camp this morning by ferry—boarded ship about 10 A. M.—sailed at four P. M. Lots of British and French aboard—expect to be in Naples Monday.

March 17-45: Making good time—smooth sailing—sleeping in hammocks.

March 20-45: In Naples this morning before breakfast—debarked at 9:30 A. M. Still lots of ruins here—city pretty filthy—expect to be here several days.

March 21-45: More paper signing and clothing issue today. Nothing else doing except ball games and sun bathing.

March 22-45: Getting shots and physicals today—legal papers to town this afternoon.

March 25-45: Another group of men came in today—lots of guys I knew—passes to town tonight.

March 28-45: Red Cross attempts to give a dance—only fifty women turned out, a flop but ice cream was good.

March 29-45: Officially alerted today. Everything ready for shipping tomorrow.

March 30-45: left camp little after ten—boarded Mahposh, US ship and sailed about four—eating two meals a day, have nice cabin.

April 1-45: (Easter Sunday) had eggs for breakfast and Easter Service up on deck. Passed through straits at the Rock of Gibraltar just after dark—Spain off starboard, and Morocco off port.

April 3-45: Music by Bing Crosby and Andrew Sisters today—still going strong.

April 5-45: Rough as hell today, taking water—lots of men getting sick.

April 8-45: Docked at Boston—pier 5 this afternoon—disembark in the morning.

April 9-45: Disembarked this morning at ten A. M.—took train forty miles to Camp Miles Standish—eating damn good chow—expect to be here five days.

April 10-45: Signing more papers today—sent telegram to Mom today.

April 11-45: Finished physical and payroll signing today—everything going slow.

April 12-45: Went out on pass this afternoon—heard news of President's death in town.

April 15-45: Left Miles Standish at 4:05 P. M. Riding in Pullmans—passed through Rhode Island and Conn. before bedtime. Slept good.

April 16-45: (Date but nothing else added.)

## Dave Nagle

Dave Nagle's trip from Stalag III-C to the United States began like the journeys of Clark, Tumlin, and Hook. When the Germans marched the POWs away from the stalag, Dave was among those who were fired on by the Russians. Dave Nagle remembered that the Russian tanks were traveling on the frozen Oder River when they fired on the column. The ice was thick enough to support heavy tanks.

The next day the Russians pulled back, and the Germans left the camp. There were no guards and no food in the camp. About ten POWs, including Dave Nagle, left the camp with the idea of finding a seaport on the Black Sea.

They stopped for the night at a vacant house. The POWs caught a goose, cooked and ate the goose, and slept in the house. They continued on foot until they arrived in the Polish city of Posnan, where they met some Russian soldiers. The Russian soldiers hugged them, rejoicing to see Americans. However, the Russian lieutenant in charge could not understand English. Communications failed, and the group of ex-POWs were arrested and put in prison with German POWs.

Nagle awoke the next morning very sick with a high fever. A Russian guard took Dave to a mansion being used as a hospital. Dave was sick several days. When he recovered, the Russian doctor, who spoke English, asked him to stay on and help with the other patients. Dave wanted to be with his friends from the stalag, but they had already left. So Dave agreed to help out for a while.

There were twenty-three bed patients in the hospital, a mixture of Russians and Americans. Dave made friends with Johnny Ernst, an American pilot of a B-17 Bomber that had been shot down. Ernst had lost a leg in the process.

Dave emptied bedpans, fed the patients who could not feed themselves, and did other routine chores. The Russians were good to him, gave him vodka and showed him around town. Nagle remembered that the Russians were dismantling factories and shipping the machinery back to Russia.

When it came time to move, they put the bed patients in a boxcar with a potbellied stove but no food. They sent Dave Nagle to scrounge for food, but no one would give him any. Ernst told him he had to act with more authority. He gave Dave his captain's badge, and with the badge and acting like an officer, he was able to get some food. He returned to the boxcar and cooked for the patients on the potbellied stove.

The train traveled to Lodz, Poland. There the bed patients were taken to a hotel, which had been made into a hospital. Nagle and an air force gunner, the only two ambulatory patients, were taken to a hotel, where they were given a comfortable room.

The next morning they went to the hotel lobby and found a restaurant. After a wholesome meal, they went back to their room but found it occupied by someone else. They didn't know what to do, so they returned to the lobby and tried to talk to the desk clerk. The clerk acted confused because he couldn't understand English.

Dave noticed some men in good-looking military uniforms in the lobby. They were US Air Force officers. They had overheard Dave trying to communicate with the hotel clerk. One of the officers approached Nagle and inquired about his problem, and Nagle explained the situation. The spokesman was a C-47 pilot. He told Dave and his partner, "Just keep quiet. Don't say anything to anybody, but come with us."

The C-47 pilot and his crew were touring Poland, picking up crewmembers that had been shot down in Poland. They were also trying to find the wreckage of the planes. American planes had superior bombsights. The C-47 crew was removing the bombsights from crashed American planes to be recycled in US airplanes. They also had a Russian crew onboard as required by the Russian government.

Nagle and his partner spent three days flying about Poland picking up US flight crews and bombsights. Then they flew to Poltava, a city in Russia, close to the Polish border, to an American/Russian shuttle base.

Dave explained that the purpose of the base was to bomb the enemy both ways on their round trips from Western Europe. US planes would leave their western base, drop bombs over Germany, land in Russia, load up with more bombs, and drop those on the way back to their home airfields.

Nagle enjoyed his first shower since his capture at the shuttle base. The Americans at the shuttle base interrogated him. This was the first of many interrogations on his way home.

The next move for Dave Nagle was in a C-46, which is larger than a C-47. He flew from the shuttle base in Russia all the way to Tehran, Iran, in a C-46, carrying sick patients. When they flew over the Ural Mountains, Dave could see the deep snow on the mountains, and over Iran, he saw camel caravans.

In Tehran, the first thing on the program was another interrogation by the Americans. A car took Dave to a headquarters building for questioning. A driver of another car saw Dave go inside the building and recognized him. He was Bernic Hardigan, who lived three doors from Dave in the Bronx. Bernie was waiting for Dave when he came out of the building.

After Nagle was given new clothes and money, Bernie Hardigan showed him around Tehran, including the Shaw's palace. Dave bought some silver jewelry in Teheran as gifts for his mother and his sister.

Next they flew to Cairo, Egypt. Again American officials interrogated Dave Nagle. In Egypt, Nagle had another sightseeing opportunity, and he enjoyed touring the Pyramids and the Sphinx.

From Cairo, Nagle flew in a C-60 plane to Casablanca in Morocco. The C-60s were even larger than the C-46s. They refueled in the Azores and in the Bahamas and landed in Miami, Florida.

Again another interrogation in Miami, and from Miami he traveled by train to Langdon OSS offices (OSS, the forerunner of the CIA) then to the Pentagon, with interrogations at each stop. Next on to Fort Dix, New Jersey, but when others got off at Fort Dix, Dave folded his hands, sat back in his seat, and journeyed on to Pennsylvania Station in New York City. He called his dad at his office at the *New York Daily News*. Dave's dad hurried to meet his son and hailed a taxi to take him to their home in the Bronx.

When Dave went to Fort Dix a few days later, the army ignored his tardiness in reporting and sent him for a week of R and R (rest and rehabilitation) in Atlantic City. Dave remembered that President Roosevelt died while he was in Atlantic City.

Then Dave was given an official furlough home to the Bronx, after which he had to report to Fort Benning, Georgia. There he met Joe Watson and Calvin Bennedic, who had served with him in E Company of the 508th. His old E Company buddies looked after Dave's best interest. They made sure Dave made a parachute jump at an early date so he could get back on jump status with extra jump pay. On December 6, 1945, Dave was discharged from military service.

Dave Nagle at 508th reunion, August 2003. Photo by Zig Boroughs.

# Chapter 11

# Honor Guard

## A Change of Attitude

We arrived in Frankfurt, Germany, on June 10. In chapter 9, I described the difference in Colonel Lindquist's idea of "being next to the throne" and the lack of enthusiasm among some of the troops. My early experiences as a part of the Honor Guard for Gen. Dwight D. Eisenhower's Supreme Headquarters, Allied Expeditionary Force were mostly negative.

Excerpts from letters home illustrate how my attitude changed:

> Frankfurt, Germany
> June 13, 1945
>
> I was on detail for four hours this morning. One of the officers wanted a desk out of the apartment of enlisted men, and I was on the crew assigned to transport it. Great indignation was shown by the men who lost the desk and gloating possessiveness by the officer who acquired it. Just to be mean, we locked the drawers and threw away the key. Then we helped some German prisoners clean up some rubbish. After that we had to wash the Colonel's windows. The Colonel has an orderly and two maids.

> Germany
> July 5, 1945
>
> Our guard duty comes around much too regularly—four hours on and twelve hours off for 7 days a week. It interrupts

our sleep and meals, and becomes very boring. We are posted around homes of Generals and around several officers clubs, swimming parks, etc. It lowers the morale of the boys to see the officers with so much entertainment, when we have none. Mainly the boys steal the officer's liquor and get drunk.

One of the guards from my squad beat up a lieutenant, a major and a chauffeur. The officers were having a big party and were pretty drunk, and tried to drive off in a jeep, which belonged to someone else. The guard got away with it too.

Frankfurt
July 13, 1945

I was selected to teach math in the school our regiment is setting up.

Yesterday I made my tenth parachute jump—from 1800 feet. This is the highest jump I have ever made. It is more fun to spend a lot of time in the air. I wasn't very excited and I really enjoyed the ride. Parachute jumping is nothing to be afraid of.

Frankfurt
July 24, 1945

I am very happy teaching algebra. My students are very attentive and interested.

Frankfurt
Aug. 11, 1945

Teaching is a lot of fun. It is by far the best army job I have had and I don't know another I would rather have. I remember when I thought that teaching school would be the last thing I would want to do.

On November 7, 1945, I was discharged from the army. On November 8, the superintendent of Pickens High School hired me to teach math and science, and I began my civilian teaching career the next Monday morning, November 11, 1945.

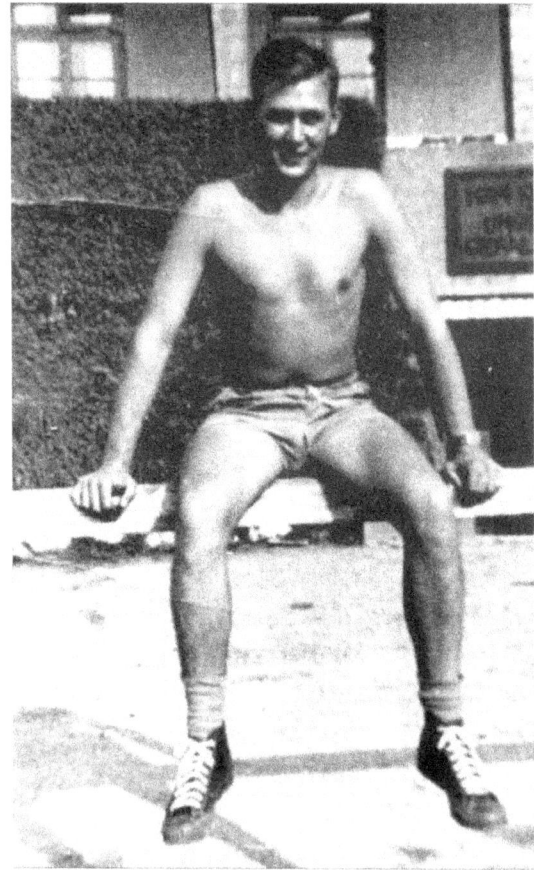

Zig Boroughs, taking a break after playing tennis in Frankfurt, one of the leisure activities enjoyed in his new assignment as a teacher. Photo provided by Zig Boroughs.

## Angel in Wooden Shoes

When we arrived in Frankfurt, the role of the 508th changed from combat soldiers to a new emphasis on looking sharp and impressing visiting dignitaries. The change was difficult for some of the combat veterans. For Bill Howe and John McLean, who had served in the Third Battalion Headquarters Company through all its combat campaigns, the adjustment was downright painful.

Howe and McLean were drinking booze and griping about the upcoming "parade jump" for figure skater-actress Sonja Henie. All during the active war in Europe, Sonja Henie could not visit her homeland. Since the hostilities of World War II had ended in Europe and Ms. Henie was at that time vacationing in her native Norway, Colonel Lindquist invited the Hollywood actress to come to Frankfurt. Furthermore, he planned for her to perform as honorary jumpmaster for a parachute jump. Officially, it was routine training, but the troopers called a staged parachute jump involving a celebrity a parade jump.

Bill Howe complained to John McLean, "It wasn't enough to get a bunch of us killed in the parade jump for Marlene Deitrich. Now the colonel has to bring Sonja Henie here for another spectacle. Wish I could skip this one."

After another swig from his bottle, a brainstorm suddenly hit Bill Howe, who proclaimed, "Listen, John, I've got it figured out. We don't have to make that jump. We will catch a plane to Brussels. From there you can take a plane to Marseilles and see your brother before he sails to the Pacific. From Brussels, I can hop a train to Goronne and visit Gabreille Winkin."

"All we have to do," Howe continued, "is to call Ed Garrity, our battalion clerk at Regimental Headquarters and ask him to type us orders for a plane to Brussels."

When they called Garrity, he explained, "I can't type orders for a plane without an order number."

"Ed, just get the number off of Sonja Henie's flight and use that number to type orders for Howe and McLean to Brussels," Howe argued.

Garrison followed Howe's instruction, and the orders went through without a hitch. Howe and McLean flew to Brussels, and Howe continued to Goronne.

Supply Sergeant Bill Howe had met Gabrielle soon after the 508th arrived and established the Third Battalion MLD on Thier du Mont Ridge. The story began on December 20, 1944. It was bitter cold on the ridge where the Third Battalion was digging in, and Howe was worrying about his men suffering frostbite.

Sergeant Howe turned to his assistant, John McLean, and ordered, "I want a place where I can send a few men at a time to get warm and have a hot cup of coffee. John, find a warm house close by and supply it with plenty of coffee, sugar, and canned milk!"

In short order, McLean returned and reported to Howe. "Bill, I found a nice warm farmhouse and took coffee and stuff from Regimental supply to the house. And one more thing, the two prettiest girls in the whole area live there."

Howe retorted, "We have a war to fight, no time for girls. Tell the troops, 'Hands off those girls.'"

McLean answered, "Sure, I'll tell the troops that, but how about you and me, Bill?"

"The same goes for you, and that's an order!" growled the sergeant.

Howe was very busy for the next twenty-four hours, hustling ammo and rations and preparing his men for the expected attack. Just before dawn on the second night, he felt he had caught up enough to visit the Winkin house for himself. There he saw the farm-fresh beauty Gabrielle Winkin. She was wearing wooden shoes and a traditional babushka over soft brown hair and was serving two women hot coffee. Beneath the warm wool winter dress and clean white apron, Bill detected the outline of a strong, healthy, enticing feminine body.

To make conversation, Bill asked Gabrielle about the two women drinking coffee. "Votre Mere? Votre Tante?" (Your mother? Your aunt?)

"Non, Allemande Juif," replied Gabrielle. (No, German Jews.)

The two Jewish women were fleeing from St. Vith. Gabrielle and her brother Maurice were active members of the Marquis (Underground Resistance to German Occupational Forces.) Their home was a temporary haven for the Jewish women seeking to escape the Nazi's attempts to exterminate Jews.

Howe's first impression of Gabrielle was of a compassionate caring person with a strong sense of patriotism.

After one canteen cup of coffee and bits of conversation consisting of gestures and a mixture of French and English, Sergeant Howe returned to his duties at battalion supply. The next day, Howe visited again; this time, he shaved while there and stayed for two cups of coffee. While Bill lingered, Gabby cooked and served Bill some delicious French fries.

The regiment withdrew on Christmas Eve to a new defense line, and the Germans moved in and occupied Goronne and the Winkin farm. This lasted until January 7, when the 508th retook Thier du Mont Ridge. The battle rolled over the Winkin farm twice. Every window in the house was broken, and every cow on the farm was killed during the fighting. However, the Winkin family rejoiced that their home and village was again liberated from German occupation.

In late January, the 508th was relieved at the front and sent to Chevron for a rest. Some of the troops had passes, but there was no place to go and nothing to do. Bill Howe told one of his buddies, "I know where we can get some good French fries."

Howe and his friend drove a jeep to the Winkin farm, and sure enough, Gabrielle cooked and served the two soldiers a large serving of French fries. Howe made two more trips to Goronne for fries while in Chevron.

Six months later, Howe made the trip to Goronne all the way from Frankfurt, Germany, which he planned as an escape from the Sonja Henie parade jump. He hurried from the village to the farm and knocked on the Winkin's front door. There was no answer. Neighbors pointed up the hill toward a hay field. The family was busy loading hay on a wagon.

The Winkin family had not wasted time getting their farm back in operation. Gabrielle and her brother Maurice had been trained by the Marquis in deactivating mines. As soon as the snow melted, Gabrielle and Maurice started pulling land mines from their fields. When the ground was ready for sowing, they planted a crop.

The Winkin family had never seen Bill dressed in anything but combat gear. Bill was wearing his dress uniform, with new Eisenhower jacket and shiny boots—a big difference from his combat appearance. The family was totally surprised to see the handsome sergeant. Immediately the family stopped work and returned home to celebrate.

Howe was completely smitten by his Gabby. (Gabby was his pet name for Gabrielle.) This is his description of her:

> Sonya Henie, with all her Hollywood glamour, is no comparison to my angel. Gabby is a real beauty—devoted to her family, warm and compassionate to strangers, a loyal and daring patriotic, hard working, talented, and intelligent. And yes, good-looking also. I could have looked the whole world over and never found my ideal woman, but here she was in an isolated little village in Belgium. Even her name is angelic—Gabrielle!

Howe arranged two more weekend passes to Goronne and began seriously courting his ideal angel. On his third trip, Bill proposed and Gabby accepted, but when he returned to Frankfurt, he received a letter from Gabby saying, "I'm sorry, I just can't leave my family and follow you to America."

The Winkin family, the village priest, and the whole village of Goronne were horrified at the idea of Gabrielle marrying an American Protestant. They turned on her with a vengeance. She gave into the pressure and wrote the letter renouncing her engagement.

The persistent sergeant was not going to let the prize slip through his hands. Off to Belgium again, and this time, he won the approval of the family and the village. Wedding plans were on again.

Howe's persistence was also tested by GI red tape. Finally all the paperwork was completed, and the bride and groom stood before the mayor of Goronne, the honorable Monsieur Rene Demarteau, for the civil ceremony.

The religious ceremony was more of a problem. The parish priest was not allowed to marry a Protestant to a Catholic, but he cooperated in a round-about way. He left town and sent a newly ordained priest to perform parish duties in his absence. The young priest, without asking any question, performed the briefest of ceremonies in the hallway of the priest's home before two witnesses.

The Winkin family had prepared a well-stocked reception to celebrate the wedding. According to Gabby, family and friends cooked ten cakes and thirty pies and prepared plenty of coffee and cocoa for the guests. The community enjoyed the reception and gave their full blessings to the bride and groom.

Wedding picture of Bill and Gabrielle Howe. Photo provided by Gabrielle Howe.

## Three-Day Pass

During the summer of 1995, while in Frankfurt, I arranged a three-day pass to make a trip to Verdun, France. My sister-in-law, Virginia, was engaged to a soldier named Andy Anderson. Andy had been an officer in an armored division and during the European fighting was killed in his tank and was buried in the military cemetery near Verdun. My mission was to visit Andy's grave.

During the three days away from Frankfurt, the first day was needed to travel by train to Verdun. On the second day, I planned to visit the grave and take pictures. The third day was needed for the return trip on the train. I purchased the round-trip train ticket and set out on my journey. Since the train was to pass through Verdun in the middle of the night, I worried about getting off at the right station. I tried to communicate my concerns to the conductor, who gave me his assurance, "Oui, oui, Je comprends."

Nevertheless, the train went right through Verdun without stopping until it arrived in Paris about daylight the next morning. The next train back to Verdun did not leave until the afternoon. It was after dark on the second day of my leave before I reached my destination.

At a café in Verdun I found some friendly GIs. They put me in a spare bunk for the night and helped me the next morning get a ride to the cemetery, which was about ten miles from town. The cemetery dates back to World War I and contains the graves of thousands of Americans who fell in the two world wars. The white crosses with an occasional Star of David marker were laid out in neat patterns, giving a sense of geometric flow of lines and curves.

Cemetery officials quickly directed me to Andy's grave. I took several pictures trying to get the inscription of Andy's name on the neat white cross. I did not know Andy, but my emotions filled with a sensation of thousands of dreams and of hopes for the future buried beneath the peaceful French countryside. I thought of the multitude of young women who lost sweethearts and lonesome wives made widows, of grieving parents mourning their fallen sons, and of children who would never see their fathers again.

It was almost noon of the third day of my pass when I left the cemetery. If I took the train, I would never make it back to my company orderly room in time. My only hope was to hitchhike. The US Army vehicles were much faster than the international railroads in 1945. The first ride took me deep into Belgium and the second ride all the way to Frankfurt. I checked in at 2300 hours, one hour before the midnight deadline.

## Adventures in Frankfurt

Leon Israel Mason and I were both chosen to teach in the Regimental School. There were only four classes: motor mechanics, chemistry, business management, and Algebra. Leon and I were both from the Demolition Platoon of Regimental Headquarters Company, and we lived in the same apartment at Heddernheim. Leon, nicknamed "Gismo," taught business management, and I taught algebra. The school was in the next building to our apartment. I had only two classes: one with eight students and the other with twelve. The classes only lasted about an hour and a half each, and we were finished before noon chow time.

Gismo. Photo by Zig Boroughs.

Gismo and I had lots of free time left over from our teaching responsibilities to enjoy leisure time. Leon had been with the regiment from its beginning and had many friends. Someone was always stopping by to visit at our apartment. On the surface Gismo was a joker, always having fun, laughing, singing, and keeping things lively and about the friendliest trooper in the regiment. Deep down, however, Leon was very serious and very troubled about the war and the conditions of the world. He and I had many discussions about moral, social, and political issues. We took advantage of the regimental library, one of the new fringe benefits, and shared our thoughts about our readings. The intellectual stimulation, which I experienced from my associations with Leon, was exhilarating.

Gismo and I often hitchhiked to the "Olympic swimming pool" for an afternoon swim. We had heard that this pool was famous for having been used in the 1936 Olympic Games. It was a long way from our apartment on the other side of Frankfurt. Besides enjoying the swimming, we sometimes had interesting adventures along the way. Once we were given a lift in a jeep driven by a British soldier. He said he was the chauffeur for Princess Margaret Rose who was an officer in the ATS (British equivalent to our WACS). He had dropped her off somewhere, and she had dismissed him for the afternoon. He was headed to a fancy noncom club and invited us to come along. As privates, we tagged along as his guests.

When I see World War II movies depicting clubs where soldiers enjoyed social activities, I think of this club in Frankfurt. Social activities in the army were highly segregated by rank. Privates had such things as the Red Cross, where we enjoyed some recreational activities such as ping pong, pool tables, and the Doughnut Dugout, but the NCO Club in Frankfurt was as elaborate as any Officers' Club depicted in movies.

Walking from the swimming pool between rides, we observed some interesting things about the German civilian life. Many times we saw people trying to salvage scraps for useful purposes, such as old women gathering fallen sticks and limbs for fuel. Once we met two girls walking from the country toward the city with suitcases. They told us they had been to the country to buy potatoes and their suitcases were full of potatoes. One former German soldier was making a home in a bombed-out section of the city, salvaging materials here and there and using his craftsmanship to create his own place.

An army truck driver picked us up one afternoon. He was headed for Mannheim, sixty miles away on the autobahn. The driver said that there was nothing to slow him down and that we would be there in less than an hour. Hitler had built a network of autobahns, four—and six-lane highways with cloverleaf intersections so he could rapidly deploy his armies toward every border of the fatherland. We arrived in less than an hour, but there was nothing to see except a completely destroyed city.

The German autobahns must have inspired General Eisenhower. When he became president of the United States, he pushed through the bill to establish the Interstate Highway System, which now crisscrosses our nation.

Then there was the famous parade jump in Frankfurt in honor of Ms. Sonja Henie. Miss Henie dressed out in paratrooper jump uniform. She was so tiny and cute. I had a front-row seat this time. She acted as jumpmaster in the very plane I was in. Of course, an officer prompted her so that the command to jump was right on the drop zone. That was more fun than passing in review. (Usually the jumpmaster leads the way and is the first one to leave the plane. This time Sonja Henie only gave the command for the others to jump. She remained in the plane.)

The 508th sports events were weekly attractions to enjoy. Boxing, baseball, and football teams were organized, and the regiment competed with teams from other military organizations. Every time one of our teams won a match, the Frankfurt issue of the *Stars and Stripes* would carry a caption something like this: "The 508th Baseball Red Devils, Col. Roy E Linguist Commanding, Wins Again," or "The 508th Boxing Team, Col. Roy E. Linguist Commanding, Wins Every Bout with the Sixth Ordnance." It wasn't long before Colonel Linguist became brigadier general.

The summer of 1945 in Frankfurt made lasting impressions on my mind: about the military, about war and peace, about world politics, about human needs and man's inhumanity to man. It also introduced me to teaching, to which I have devoted most of my working life.

## Forgotten in Frankfurt

The old outfit was not the same. After the Japanese surrendered, very few of the men and officers in the 508th wanted to remain in service. Most of us were counting our points and waiting for the magic number of 85. It would be just a matter of weeks, or even days, for Gismo and me. None of the old officers, who had commanded Headquarters Company, were around anymore. Most of the old noncoms had also been rotated back home.

Gismo and I had settled into the nonmilitary routine of teaching school—no guard duty, no KP, feeling almost like civilians. And then one of the new replacement officers came by our apartment to make an inspection, white gloves and all. He stroked one of our glass windows with a finger and examined the smudge marring his once-clean gloves. After staring at his glove for a few seconds, as if he were examining an important piece of evidence, the officer declared, "These windows have to be cleaned!"

Gismo put up a determined defense, pointing out how much time we had to devote to our teaching, preparation, grading papers, etc. The officer was unimpressed. "These windows must be washed! Conversation closed, period!" The officer then left with a commanding air as if he had just performed, as required of an officer and gentlemen, to keep up the discipline and the standards of the troops.

Being a dutiful private with a good conduct medal, I immediately found a bucket and rag and started preparing to wash the windows. Gismo, however, persuaded me that the order to wash the windows did not implicitly state *when* we should do it. It was his studied opinion that *later* was implied, so we put aside our bucket and rag for later.

Not many days after the white-glove inspection, Gismo and I received our orders for leaving the 508th and the army and joining the civilian ranks back home. The journey home began at 9:30 AM, October 9, 1945. We were sent from Frankfurt to a processing camp in France. Then we were sent to the port city of Marseilles, in Southern France.

Military duties were still imposed on the almost-civilian GIs but with less rigorous enforcement. I had to pull guard duty one time, but as it turned out, the sergeant of the guard failed to report, and I was made acting sergeant for the guard duty. My job was to wake up the men when it came their time to stand guard.

Gismo also had to pull guard once in Marseilles. He was posted outside a brothel with the orders to keep the soldiers from entering. The officer in charge told him that the women were diseased and the military felt obligated to send the men home to their wives and sweethearts clean and free from venereal diseases.

The October evenings were getting cool, even in Southern France. Soon Gismo began to pace up and down in front of the brothel to warm his blood. In the process of pacing, he happened to glance toward the entrance as one of the girls opened the door and called, "Babee, you cold?"

As a matter of fact, Babee was cold. Gismo, being an honest soldier answered, "Oui, Babee beaucoup cold!"

The girl, clothed in the mere scanties used by her profession to entice prospective customers, flung open the door and invited him. "Babee entrez!"

Gismo, who was skilled in applied military logic, said to himself, "The officer only told me to keep other soldiers out. I could do the job just as well in the warmth of the house as out here in the cold night air, maybe better."

Having satisfactorily determined that he could serve his country better from the inside than from the outside, Gismo dutifully entered the house of prostitution. He was greeted with many coquettish offers to entertain him, but Gismos gallantly refused. He told the girls, "Me arteest. My passion is art."

The girls in turn furnished the "arteest" with "papier et crayon" as well as interesting and provocative poses.

Gismo's military logic happened to be right on target this time. The officer of the guard commended Gismo for carrying out his duty with imagination and talent and thanked him profusely for the sketches of the girls, which Gismo contributed to the officer's art collection. Gismo enjoyed the process of drawing the girls but was not interested in taking the product home for June to see.

Finally we boarded a liberty ship and began the long tedious trip out of the Mediterranean and across the wide Atlantic. The little boat dipped and rose with the waves, and so did our stomachs, often sending us to the rails to feed the fish.

Gismo and I had lots of time to reflect over our days in the military and to bless the day we would finally set foot on the good old USA. We felt good about serving our country in the 508th Parachute Infantry. We felt we had done our best to do our duty to God and country, but then Gismo had to remind me, "Zig, we forgot to wash the windows in Frankfurt!"

"You are right," I replied. "I will have to throw my good conduct medal overboard."

# Chapter 12

# Postscript

## A Trip Back in Time

In 1978 Lewis Burrows visited Normandy with a group of 508th veterans, Burrows was most interested in finding the place of his D-Day landing. The language barrier hindered Burrows from getting information, but Madame Lucien Hasley came to his rescue. Madame Hasley had a cousin who had studied English. She arranged for her cousin Fabreinne to serve as Burrows's guide and interpreter and to ride with him on a bicycle tour of the area.

Burrows described his 1944 Normandy experiences:

> We jumped at 2:21 just north of the causeway that connects the town of Beuzeville La Bastille with the road leading to Chef du Pont. I was able to glide back to the road but hit a telephone pole that connected the German Headquarters with their artillery unit west of Beuzeville. I saw two others that jumped after me land further to the east. I am sure they didn't get far because firing was very heavy in that area. The Germans were shooting everything that moved in the water. I got into the water on the south side of the road as I felt it was the only safe place. The Germans, like a pack of hounds, were on the other side getting the people that were thrashing around in the water.
>
> After daylight German artillery marched by at double time, looking straight ahead, as good soldiers should, and failed to see me hiding in the marsh. Later that day two tanks were in

the crossroads area. One was blown up. The other drove by me with turrets open and the officer sitting in full view. I had no trouble keeping quiet as the tank officer could have looked me in the eye if he had glanced down at the water's edge. Since the Germans were in control of the road in either direction, I had no motivation to move at night.

On June 7 the road was fairly busy with a command car and a motorcycle traveling back and forth on the road above my head. In the afternoon two Germans came trotting by. Someone across the swamp shot at them. The Jerries flopped down off the road near me, set up a machine gun, and returned fire. I thought I was going to get hit by GIs shooting at the Germans. The Jerries soon picked up their equipment and went on toward Chef du Pont, where the fighting was intense.

Things quieted down on June 8. No shots were heard, and no Germans were on the road, so I plotted to get out of there. About eleven o'clock in the morning, a motorcycle went up the road and returned in about twenty minutes. The motorcycle kept going back and forth every twenty minutes. About the third time, I shot the rider off his motorcycle. A few minutes later artillery opened up about fifty yards from me and kept getting closer and closer. As I looked up, a shell exploded close enough for a fragment to knock out my left eye.

I came out of the water, slung my rifle, and headed for the Buezeville area. I wanted out of that spot. To my right at the edge of the water was a barn. I ran past the barn along a hedgerow and, at the first opening in the hedge, turned in.

A German soldier was waiting with a gun pointing at me. He hollered, "Handi Ho!"

Soon about ten Jerries surrounded me. One noncom kept shaking his pistol at me as if he was going to shoot me. The Germans didn't like what they found on me, caps prima cord and twenty-four pounds of C-2 explosive compound. They made me keep my hands up all afternoon and gave me a few kicks in the groin. One good thing they did was to take compress from my first aid packet and put it over my injured eye. Like I used to tell my mother when I did something wrong, I kept telling my captors "I'm a good boy!"

Later that day, they marched me to a place where they had a cutout in the bank of the road with beds and a field kitchen. A German medic fixed me up. I was questioned extensively about some house in the neighborhood. They wanted to know how many men were in the house.

When I convinced the interrogator that I knew nothing, they drove me in a command car to a chateau. At the chateau I was given bread and ersatz coffee. I promptly vomited, which did not win any friends among my new acquaintances.

Both eyes were then bandaged, and I was driven in a jeeplike vehicle for a long time. When they stopped, I was taken into a building and put in a bunk bed with a straw sack and no covers.

As I awoke in the morning, I could hear people speaking English. I asked someone to remove the bandage from my right eye. When this was done, I saw a medic and a medical officer from the 508th. Also in the bunk next to me was my squadmate and best friend, Charlie Koons.

Burrows was in the German hospital at Orglandes with many other 508th paratroopers. The hospital was liberated by American troops on June 13, and the wounded patients were transported to GI hospitals.

Getting back to Burrows's bicycle trip with Mademoiselle Fabreinne, Lucien Hasley reported on that event:

> As Fabreinne and Burrows rode bicycles toward la Bastille, Burrows began to recognize landmarks he had seen from his hideaway by the causeway. Then while riding through an area where cows were grazing, an area that had been flooded on D-Day, Burrows came to a sudden stop. He recognized his hiding place.
>
> He left his bike and ran across the dry ditch into the meadow. As he ran, he accidentally touched an electric service wire and received a shock. Then Lewis Burrows became very emotional. Seeing the place where he had hidden from the enemy brought back all the bad memories.
>
> The next day, we learned our friend Lewis Burrows had suffered a heart attack and returned to his home in America. Later we heard the good news of his recovery and improved health.

The fact that Burrows could not see the town of Beuzeville or telephone poles in 1978 that he remembered seeing in 1944 at his hiding place caused him to doubt that he had found the exact spot. In 1980 he again visited Normandy. This time a French farmer, who owned the land, explained the changes that had occurred since 1944. Trees had grown up between his hiding place and Beuzeville, concealing it from view. Also the telephones were temporary German arrangements for military purposes. Local Normans had no telephone service at that time. After the war, the farmer sold the wire and burned the poles for firewood. With these explanations, Burrows was sure he had found the exact spot of his D-Day hiding place.

Lewis Burrows. Picture supplied by James Blue.

## Tom Broderick

Tom Brokaw, in his book *The Greatest Generation*, spotlighted Tom Broderick as one who, in spite of being blind from a war wound, established a successful business and supported a large family. Broderick was instrumental in establishing the Blind Veteran Association to help other blind veterans succeed in life. Tom's life and work gave hope and support to many who knew him. Since Brokaw's widely read book was published, hundreds of readers, who never knew Tom Broderick personally, have been inspired by his example.

Reading Brokaw's book prompted me to learn more about Tom Broderick from members of the 508th and from Tom himself.

Sgt. Kenneth "Rock" Merritt recalled his impressions of Tom Broderick:

> Tom joined us in Nottingham. He was in my section of four machine gun squads, and I was the section sergeant. In

the two months that he was with us, you would never see him without a clean well-pressed uniform and highly polished boots. The day before he got shot, he had not had a chance to shave or change clothes, and I told him, "Tom, now you look like a damned paratrooper."

## Lt. George Stoeckert said this of Tom Broderick:

Although Tom's combat experience lasted only five days, in those five days, he experienced every possible facet of war with all its horrors, hardships, and heroics, and he acquitted himself courageously with distinction and honor.

Tom was a member of a machine gun squad, Headquarters First, in support of A, B, and C companies, which parachuted into Holland, south of Nijmegan, at 1330 hours on September 17, 1944. His squad participated in the attack on Nijmegen, which advanced to the bridge over the Waal River the night of September 17. The next day, his squad supported the First Battalion forces, which cleared the landing zone for the gliders. While A Company was taking Devil's Hill and B Company sustained aggressive attacks from the German town of Wyler, Tom's squad was active in their support.

On September 21, A Company held Devil's Hill and was defending a roadblock below Devil's Hill at the junction of the Nijmegen-Wyler road and a major causeway that led to the Waal River. The entire 508th area was infested with German snipers and small combat patrols. The Germans opposing the 508th were skilled marksmen. Of the seventeen men killed while taking Devil's Hill, ten died from head wounds.

About noon, the Germans launched several determined attacks against 508th positions, including a company-sized attack toward the A Company and B Company boundary. As the .81mm Mortar Platoon leader, I started forward to reinforce our mortar observers in the area. En route I stopped at the B Company forward command post to use a phone and call for an adjustment of artillery fire in front of B Company positions.

When I got closer to the fighting area, Sgt. Rock Merritt called for my help. He had a man down—Tom Broderick. I used my radio to call medics who, upon arrival, said that Tom's head wound was too serious for him to survive. After some discussion, Rock and I loaded Tom on a jeep stretcher, and he was evacuated. Rock and I were sure that Tom was dead or dying. Later that day, we captured a German SS trooper between the B Company rear and the .81mm Mortar Platoon area. He may have been the man that shot Tom. We will never know.

Rock Merritt described the situation from his point of view:

> I was next to Tom when he got shot. I believe it was September 21, and we were under attack from Wyler and Devil's Hill. Tom's squad leader hollered, "More ammo!"
> The ammo bearer threw a box of 250 rounds that hit Tom in the back. At the same moment, a German sniper hit Tom in the head. I did not realize he had been shot until we got him out of the foxhole.
> Lt. George Stoeckert called for the medics and helped me load Tom on the med-vac jeep. George and I had no hope that Tom would survive. After about two months, we received a letter from Tom's family, telling us he was just fine except that he would be blind for the rest of his life.
> Tom Broderick was a credit to the 508th Parachute Infantry Regiment as he is to our country today.

George Stoeckert summed up his opinion of Broderick: "Tom was a good soldier, he is an outstanding friend, and he has been a lifelong model of patience, determination, and courage."

In a telephone conversation with Tom, he told me about two of his close army friends, Henry Wardenski and Earl Lee Carlson. The three buddies—Tom, Henry, and Earl—started out together in basic training, joined the paratroopers together, and the three were all assigned to the 508th Parachute Infantry Regiment in Nottingham, England. Wardenski and Carlson were both married at the time, but Broderick was still single.

Tom thought of Henry Wardenski as an old man at thirty-three years old, but Henry was in good shape and took the rigors of paratrooper training in stride. His buddies asked Wardinski, "Why would a married man like you, with three sons, want to join the paratroopers?"

Wardenski explained that his family had come to America from Poland. His mother and sister returned to Poland in 1939. Germany invaded Poland that same year. Both his mother and his sister were killed by the Nazis. He joined the paratroopers to have a greater opportunity to fight the enemy that killed his mother and his sister.

Tom remembered getting a letter from his friend Henry Wardenski, written on Christmas Eve on December 24, 1944. Tom remarked, "It was a beautiful and inspiring letter. Later, I learned that Henry was killed shortly afterwards."

According to Historian Jan Bos of Holland, Henry L. Wardenski, ASN 33801683, was killed by artillery fire on December 24, 1944. Wardenski's body now rests in Gettysburg National Cemetery in Pennsylvania, plot number 3-315.

Kenneth "Rock" Merritt remembered that on December 24, 1944 one squad of the Machine Gun Platoon of Headquarters First was assigned to support A Company in defense of the two bridges at Vielsalm over the Salm River. The squad lost some men killed by German 88s when the Germans assaulted the bridges.

Edward "Woody" Wodowski was on the A Company's rear guard at the Salm River that fateful night. Woody remembered seeing the Headquarters First machine gun crew digging in and setting up their gun emplacements. He surmised that the Germans observed the location of the machine gun fire and zeroed in on their positions with their 88s. Woody personally witnessed the 88s knocking out the machine guns one by one, killing or wounding all the gun crew numbers.

Broderick and Wardenski were in the same platoon, but Broderick's friend Earl Carlson was assigned to C Company. Tom saw Earl one time in Holland before being wounded. His machine gun was dug in to support C Company as they advanced to clear the glider landing zone. Carlson was moving cautiously by Tom's foxhole, carrying his rifle at firing readiness. Tom saw his buddy and called out to him. Earl, who had neither seen Tom nor his foxhole, was startled and noticeably frightened. He was relieved to see an old friend rather than an enemy.

After the war, Tom kept in touch with his buddy Earl Carlson, who was a fire chief in Kansas City, Missouri. The 508th Association met in Kansas City for the Annual Reunion in 2000. By this time both Earl Carlson and his wife were retired and lived in a nursing home north of Kansas City. While attending the reunion, Tom and his wife visited the Carlsons at their nursing home. Earl Carlson had read Tom Brokaw's book, *The Greatest Generation*. Earl told Tom that the picture in Brokaw's book of Tom was not Tom at all but a photo of himself, Earl Carlson.

Tom and his wife, Eileen, had a good laugh about the mix-up. Of course, Tom could not see, and Eileen had picked out the pictures to send to Brokaw. She did not know Tom until several years after the war, and Earl Carlson and Tom were about the same size, and the picture was among the personal effects that Tom had sent home after jump school. Eileen had assumed it was a photo of her husband, Tom Broderick.

Eileen and Tom Broderick at Headquarters First Reunion in San Antonio in the year 2000. Photo taken by Zig Boroughs.

## A Tea Set Remembered

Lt. Herman Jahnigen of A Company was a soldier's soldier. The former first sergeant had the confidence of officers and enlisted men alike and because of his proven leadership in battle was given a battlefield commission.

During the late days of October and early November of 1944, the 508th was stuck in a static position on an island between the Waal River and the Rhine River in Holland. The stalemate required outposts, frequent patrols, exchange of artillery and mortar fire but no aggressive combat action for the paratroopers. The troopers often had time on their hands.

Lieutenant Jahnigen's platoon slept in the basement of a partially destroyed house in the village of Bemmel. One day Jahnigen, with out any pressing duties, poked around in the ruins of the house above his basement sleeping quarters. To his surprise, Jahnigen found a beautiful tea set in the rubble and put it away in his soldier's pack. After the war, the tea set found a place among the veteran's war memorabilia in his Indiana home.

In 1987 Herman Jahnigen returned to Holland hoping to return the tea set to its former owners. He had the help of Charles Derksen, a Bemmel policeman, but they were unsuccessful in finding the former owner, so Herman placed the tea set in the airborne museum at Groesbeek. The Nijmegen newspaper published the story along with pictures of Jahnigen and the tea set, hoping the rightful owner would claim it.

Two years later Jahnigen received a letter from Charles Derksen. The Dutch policemen had not given up on the case. He announced that he had found the original owner of the tea set. The story began in 1942, when Nellie Huibers was employed as a maid by the Van Horssen family in Nijmegen. The Van Horssens gave Nellie the tea set as a goodwill gesture after Nellie had helped with the planning and organization of their daughter's wedding.

Nellie took the tea set to her parents' home in Bemmel and packed it away in anticipation of her own wedding. Two years later, when the town of Bemmel became a part of the main line of resistance (MLR), civilians were evacuated and moved to Eindhoven for their own safety. Nellie had left her precious tea set behind.

When things returned to normal and the people of Bemmel moved back home, the Huibers found their house badly damaged and most of their possession missing or ruined. Nellie soon married Mr. Evers. Her husband restored Nellie's parents' home. She and her husband are still living in the same house where Jahnigen camped in the basement.

Finally the policeman met the Evers' daughter, Christa, and told her about his efforts on behalf of Herman Jahnigen. Christa had heard from her mother the story of her lost tea set and brought Derksen to her parents' home. Derksen showed a picture of the tea set to Mrs Nellie Evers, and she recognized it as her long-lost possession.

The museum returned the tea set to Mrs. Evers, who wrote to Jaknigen thanking him. Below are a few excerpts from the letter:

> Dear unknown American, Mr. Herman Jahnigen . . . For more than 40 years we have had a certain connection, a little tea set.

I admire your courage to bring this tea set back to Holland. I am very grateful. When you come to Holland again, please visit us. You are always welcome!!!

Mr. and Mrs. Evers of Bemmel, Holland, with the tea set. Photo furnished by Herman Jahnigen.

## Emile Lacroix of Belgium

The German army invaded Belgium on May 19, 1940. Thirteen days later, May 23, Emile Lacroix was born in the small Belgian coal-mining town of Maurage, near Mons. When the German army marched in, most of the villagers evacuated Maurage, but the Lacroix family remained because of the imminent birth of Emile.

It took the Nazis about a month to conquer Belgium. The small country capitulated on May 28, 1940. The German armies set up a military government to control and exploit the nation. Since Maurage was a coal-mining village, its coal was important to fuel the German factories. Consequently, Maurage had its contingent of German soldiers.

When Emile was four years old, a German officer was murdered in Maurage. The blame was laid on the Belgium civilian population. Rumors were flying that the Germans would arrest the men of the town, kill some of them, and send the others to work camps in Germany. Such acts of reprisals were common events under German martial law.

Monsieur Lacroix did not wait for the strong arm of the oppressor to reach into his home. He packed some light luggage and, with his wife and small son, slipped out of town by train in the middle of the night. They traveled to the village of Hambraine, Cortil-Wodon, near Namur and moved in with Emile's uncle.

Although Emile was only four, when his family left Maurage in June of 1944, he had memories of the village of his birthplace. He remembered the Russian prisoners who worked the coalmines: how each morning the prisoners, looking wretched and miserable, were marched to the gate of the mine by German soldiers. Then by night, after a day of grueling labor deep underground, they were escorted by their guards back to their squalid camp.

Emile remembered how the villages would try to gather a few bits of coal for themselves as the railcars departed for Germany each morning. The people would wait until the cars started leaving the railyard then they would jump on top of the cars and push coal off with their hands and feet. Before the train picked up speed, they would jump off and collect the scattered pieces of coal in sacks. Once German guards hid on the train and shot at the scavengers. No one was hit. Maybe the guards didn't want to kill the villagers but were merely carrying out orders.

Emile recalled a poignant incident, which occurred shortly after their village was liberated. His father took him to see a German soldier, who was temporarily locked up in an unused stable attached to their home. The lone soldier had been captured far behind the German lines by Belgian partisans. Emile recalled, "I felt sorry for the dejected-looking man sitting on a box, with his elbows on his knees and his head in his hands. I still wonder about him. Was he a fanatic SS killer or just a poor young man

Emile's jeep, L-R: Carolyn Lacroix, Zig Boroughs, Emile Lacroix. Photo furnished by Emile Lacroix.

obliged to follow the crazy ideas of his country's insane leader?"

"Among my most vivid souvenirs," Emile recalled, "was the day of liberation."

He described the great crowds of people lining the streets, waving Belgian, US, and British flags as the Allied troops and their vehicles passed by. Emile was especially intrigued by the tanks, trucks, and jeeps. The jeeps were his favorites.

After most of Belgium was liberated, the Germans counterattacked through the Ardennes and threatened to overrun Belgium again. The Eighty-second Airborne and the 101st Airborne were rushed to the Ardennes. The Airborne troops helped halt the advance and helped push the Nazis back into Germany.

As a boy, Emile dreamed of someday driving his own jeep. As an adult, Emile bought an old World War II jeep, which he refurbished and decorated with Eighty-second Airborne marking. Others with the same hobby joined Lacroix to form the Eighty-second Airborne All-American Jeep Club (See club decal, right) and the Belgium chapter of the C-47 Club. Often Emile dons his Eighty-second Airborne uniform and, driving his jeep, leads the Eighty-second Airborne Jeep Club in parades that celebrate historic World War II events. Not only do members of the club own jeeps but also other World War II vehicles such as trucks, ambulances, staff cars, and the amphibious vehicles called ducks.

The jeep club and the C-47 club have built monuments honoring the Eighty-second Division and each of the regiments that served with the Eighty-second in the Ardennes. Emile is the president of the two clubs and has been the prime mover in designing the monuments and in raising the money for the construction.

Emile Lacroix at the monument honoring the 508th Parachute Infantry Regiment. Photo furnished by Emile Lacroix, circa 1986.

The monument honoring the 508th is located on Their du Mont Ridge, the site where some of the fiercest fighting of the regiment happened.

Lacroix and another member of the All-American Jeep Club place flowers on graves of Eighty-second Airborne troops. Photo furnished by Emile Lacroix.

On America's Memorial Day, the clubs honor the KIA (killed in action) troops of the Eighty-second that are buried in the Neuville en Condroz US cemetery in Belgium by placing flowers on the graves of our fallen comrades.

Marchers in the Footsteps of the Eighty-second.
Photo by Arnaud Wauters.

Marchers at the monument. Standing, L-R: *James Rankin, Dan Furlong, Tom Porcella*, Philippe Jenaux, Emile Lacroix, *Jim Blue, George Lamm, Edward Wodowsky*, Jean Delfosse, and Jacqueline Bosman. Kneeling: Armand Penns, Roger Tislair, Frank Lacroix, Nicole Tislair, Serge Boton, and Alain Taburau. Photo provided by Emile Lacroix. The names of the 508th veterans are italicized.

Every winter the clubs organize a twenty-five-kilometer march called In the Footsteps of the Eighty-second Airborne. Each march honors one of the four regiments of the Eighty-second, with a ceremony during the march at the regimental monument.

Emile Lacroix has been an unselfish friend in helping veterans who return to Belgium to visit the scenes of their war experiences. He has helped us find places and people and artifacts and photos. With his help, we have gained a better understanding of our World War II experiences. He has accompanied us to places we would not have been able to find and served as an interpreter and translator when we could not understand the language.

The author, as a guest in the Lacroix home in 1986.
Back row, L-R: Frank Lacroix, Zig Boroughs, Nicole Lacroix, and Emile Lacroix.
Front row, L-R: Guy Lacroix, Sylvie Lacroix, and Carolyn Lacroix.
Photo supplied by Emile Lacroix.

## Brooks—A Sergeant?

I never knew that Brooks was a sergeant until our company reunion of May 1984. He was always just Brooks to us. We used the rank title for Sergeant Gerkin, Sergeant Belliveau, and Sergeant Luczaj but never for Brooks. I thought he might have been a corporal because he had so many responsible duties, but we never referred to him as corporal as we did for others.

Brooks explained to me that he was made sergeant in Belgium when someone else had been busted. He would not reveal the name of the busted NCO because he said, "He is a good friend of mine, and a hell of a nice guy." Howard Brooks is not the kind of person who would seek self-advancement at the expense of someone else.

The way it happened, a bridge did not blow as planned. The person in charge of the detail had to take the rap, and perhaps unjustly. Lieutenant Hardwick turned to Brooks and said, "Brooks, I am making you sergeant."

Brooks answered, "But I don't want to be sergeant, sir!"

"I'm not asking you what you want!" replied the Ripper. "I am telling you what you have to do. You are now the sergeant!"

Whether or not one knew Brooks was a sergeant, everyone knew that Brooks was a dependable team member, a knowledgeable demolitionist and very thorough with technical details.

One more thing about Howard Brooks: those of us who came into the 508th as replacements came into an organization of close-knit friendships built up over many months of shared training and combat experiences. Replacements were often considered as outsiders who never really counted. Howard Brooks, on the other hand, made the replacements feel that we were important members of the regular team.

Howard Brooks, 1945            Howard Brooks, 1984.
Photos by Zig Boroughs.

## Memories of a Leader

The name of Lt. Robert "Patrick" Mason Mathias, who died on June 6, 1944, surfaced many times in the reminisces of veterans enjoying the 1983 reunion of the 508th Parachute Infantry Regiment Association in Portland, Oregon. The E Company survivors of World War II decided to prepare a "book of remembrances" about Mathias for his family. Richard Reardon volunteered to compile the written testimonies from paratroopers who served with Mathias. The following quotations were chosen from that selection:

(From Joe Lobos)
I remember him as a carrot-topped soldier whose hair looked as if it had never been combed. He had steely blue-gray eyes, a battered nose with flaring nostrils, firmly set jaws with thin lips and a wide mouth that gave him an almost priestly look. His ears protruded like oars from a rowboat. He had an athletic build, broad chest, muscular arms and the most unforgettable hands, rather large with gnarled knuckles.

Lieutenant Mathias was a strict but fair man and officer. He was religious, not given to womanizing or to strong drink and was dedicated to his career as an officer and as a paratrooper.

(From Joseph E. Watson)

Life in the Second Platoon was anything but easy. In all the training Lieutenant Mathias always required more of his platoon than was expected of other platoons in the regiment. He led, cajoled and drove us to meet the standards. He seemed deeply hurt on the few occasions that the platoon failed to meet his expectations but he never lost his temper. I also never knew him to utter a profane word.

(From Earl Hinebaugh)

Lieutenant Robert M. Mathias was a damned good man and officer. He worked our butts off during our training, but was apt to deliver candy bars to us in the barracks later. Lieutenant Mathias was a good Christian man, who wanted the war over. He never let up.

Lt. Robert M. Mathias. Photo provided by Richard Reardon.

(From Dick Reardon)

When we reached Camp Mackall, the three of us used to dread the call, "Sergeant Reardon, Corporal Benedict, Corporal Watson."

This meant that Lieutenant Mathias wanted to spar a few rounds. Each of us would go two rounds with him. Bene and I would conspire to make Joe go first. He was the fastest. Bene, second fastest, would go next, and I, biggest and slowest, last. These matches were conducted after a full day of training, while wearing paratrooper boots in the loose shifting sands of Eastern Carolina—exhausting.

(From Louis Yourkovich)

I remember Lieutenant Mathias being in charge of the whole company marching back from the firing range. He would shout out, "E Company will now sing *When Irish Eyes Are Smiling.*" This was followed by *Margie* and *Around Her Neck She Wore a Yellow Ribbon* and *The All American Song*. Lieutenant Mathias was in his glory in charge of the whole company, setting a fast pace and singing at the top of his voice.

(From Fred Infanger)
Lieutenant Mathias knew that I was Catholic and he made it his business that I did not miss Mass on Sunday mornings. He did this by personally assisting me from my bunk on Sunday mornings with admonition, "Just because you are in the Army, away from home and your mother, is no reason to miss Mass."

(From Dick Reardon)
We were participating in a field problem in the North Carolina/South Carolina area. Our platoon was confronted with an enemy machine-gun nest ensconced in a wooded area across an open field to our immediate front. We were faced with two choices—a straight charge across an open field or a long time-consuming flanking movement to stay under cover. Due to time constraints, the flanking movement had to be discarded. Lieutenant Mathias decided to cross the open field. The platoon spread out in the approved "charge the enemy" configuration, and upon Lieutenant Mathias' command, we began our assault.

When we reached the enemy machine-gun position, we were met by a Major wearing an umpire brassard, who informed Lieutenant Mathias, "You and your platoon are retired. You have been wiped out."

Lieutenant Mathias argued the decision, maintaining that within the time restraints, he had followed the only possible course of action, that the tactics used in the field crossing and the aggressiveness of the platoon would have prevailed. The umpire did not buy the argument, and when Mathias continued to protest, the Major whipped out his notebook and demanded, "What is your name, Lieutenant?"

Without blinking an eye, Mathias replied, 'Cornelius Alexander McGillicuddy.'

The Major wrote down the information and departed. I suspect that he was much chagrined to find out the Cornelius

Alexander McGullicuddy was the long-time manager of the Philadelphia Phillies baseball team.

(From Harold Cavanaugh)

On an inter-platoon competitive hike, we were on the last mile. Things were nip and tuck. To say that every part of me was hurting would be putting it mildly. I was going on the old fashion saying, "You can always take one more step." Evidently a lad in our platoon had used up his incentive because he folded up on us. Our boss man carried him the last three quarters of a mile on his back. Golly, I had seen everything. Boy, was I glad that this man was on our side.

Any task he understood was done correctly, but best of all, it was done in the right spirit. Many a dry lecture was made tolerable by his show of enthusiasm and timely witty remarks. However, he was far from a book-soldier. The tactics of Lee and the like were skillfully varied to suit the hedgerows of England, which were similar to those of France. Every now and then he would point out something like, "Foxholes will be easy to dig in France. They have ditches alongside the hedgerows." Or "There will be more covering in France because the hedgerows are on top of four feet dirt mounds." When I got to France and saw for myself the important things that Mathias had pointed out, it was difficult to realize that he had never been to France before the jump.

To best compete against an enemy, it is wise to speak the language. Mathias adhered to this belief and followed it implicitly. He could speak German fluently. In order that we might pick up some, he drilled us using German commands and held classes where he taught useful phrases. French was another important language, so he added that to his unlimited talents.

(From Eddie Wenzel)

I was sitting in the company orderly room with my feet on the First Sergeant's desk cleaning my fingernails with my trench knife, when Lieutenant Mathias walked in.

He called out, "As you were Corporal."

I put me feet back on the desk and continued to clean my fingernails. Lieutenant Mathias went over to the Captain's desk and began paperwork. Fifteen minutes later the lieutenant recited to me the duties of CQ (Charge of Quarters.) First he called me to attention, and then he had me to do fifty pushups—because I was sitting at the First Sergeant's desk cleaning my fingernails.

After the fifty pushups, he said, "Here's my proof of what you were doing." He handed me a perfect freehand drawing of me sitting behind the desk—feet and all.

(From Joseph Watson)

My last recollection of Bob was as we shook hands and wished each other a safe flight as we prepared to take off for Normandy; one of the men who jumped from Bob's plane gave this account of Mathias' final moments:

Lieutenant Mathias was wounded by a shell burst outside the aircraft, while he was standing in the door awaiting the green light. When the green light came on, Lieutenant Mathias half-turned to face his men in the stick. You could see the blood upon his chest. He raised his right arm in a 'Follow me!' signal and jumped out of the door.

(From Joe Lobos)

Our stick landed in 'Fortress Europe' near Picauville, France, at 2:30 A. M., the morning of June 6, 1944, right in the middle of a bivouac area of three German infantry companies, a battery of artillery and four medium tanks.

In the darkness, confusion reigned. Daylight showed that many of us were wounded, killed or captured, and that some few had scrambled to safety. Lieutenant Mathias was not one that escaped. The morning found him hanging in a tree, still in his harness, dead.

(From Joseph Watson)

How prophetic were the words of Colonel Roy E. Lindquist when he remarked, "Lieutenant Mathias will either earn the Medal of Honor or be the first 508th man killed in action."

## "Does Anyone Remember My Brother?"

"Any of you G Company troopers remember Ralph Nicholson? I've got a letter from his sister," Tom Beno announced in the G Company CP at the 1987 El Paso 508th Reunion.

"That must be Nick Nicholson. I remember Nick Nicholson. He was a pathfinder and jumped in my stick in Normandy," Francis Lamoureux replied.

On February 25, 1987, Helene Diller of Nashua, Iowa, read an Eighty-second Airborne Division Association advertisement in the *Nashua Reporter*. Shirley Gossett, the National President of the Association, gave his address and asked Airborne veterans to contact him. Mrs. Diller had always wondered about her brother Ralph Nicholson, who was killed in Normandy. She said to herself, "Maybe someone in this organization remembers my brother."

Helene Diller wrote to Gossett, who passed the letter on to the executive secretary of the 508th Association, O. B. Hill, who in turn sent it to Tom Beno. Six months after she wrote the letter, Helene Diller heard by phone from Nick's paratrooper friend, Francis Lamoureux.

Ralph Nicholson grew up on an Iowa farm. His sister, Helene, describes him as a serious, hard-working, and reserved man, whose main hobby was hunting. Soon after finishing Nashua High School, Ralph joined the paratroopers with two of his close friends, Harold Roy and Alton Jacobs.

Prior to the Normandy jump, Ralph "Nick" Nicholson volunteered for the pathfinders. The pathfinders were the first paratroopers to land. Their mission was to set up radar equipment and ground lights to guide the remaining fleet of planes to the designated drop zone. Nick was one of the light men who carried halogen lights. On landing, they were to arrange the lights to form a *T* as a signal for the pilots to turn on the green-light jump command.

The Airborne troops preceded the assault on the Normandy beaches, and the pathfinders jumped in advance of the regular Airborne. The pathfinders were the first to contact the enemy, the first to draw blood in the invasion.

Fayette O. Richardson, a close friend of Nicholson wrote a column about Nick (Rich Richardson, "Recalling D-Day," *The Berkshire Eagle*, June 6, 1987, A 11). An excerpt follows:

> The day before our D-Day parachute mission into Normandy my pal Nick decided he wanted a haircut. So Nick, Sternesky and I went over to the Army barber's shop. The

barber wasn't there but his tools were. I lied and said I was good at barbering, so Nick sat down in the chair.

I started up the back of Nick's head, but I cut such deep notches that Sterno started laughing and Nick hollered, "Hey!" and felt his hair where I had been cutting and jumped up.

Then the barber came in. He had to clip Nick's hair nearly down to the skin. Sterno and I couldn't see what difference it made. We wouldn't see any girlfriends for a while and by then the hair would be grown out. But Nick was disgusted. He couldn't stop fussing. He'd feel his head and say, "Damn it Richardson, you said you knew how to cut hair!" Then he would look in the mirror, shake his head in disgust and say, "Jeez!" while Sterno and I laughed.

The next day, on the evening of June 5, we were to take off before midnight, and we started getting on our gear, and Nick started complaining about the order to carry a land mine. He fussed and moaned and said it was impossible to carry a land mine along with all the other stuff.

"What do they think I am anyway? I can't carry this thing!" We laughed. It relieved the tension. Nick finally managed to pack the land mine along with all the other junk we had to carry: a weapon, a bunch of D-rations, a knife, a canteen, first aid stuff, ammo, a fragmentation grenade, a Gammon grenade, a phosphorous grenade and so on.

An Army photographer came out to take pictures. Nick and I posed toasting each other with our tin coffee cups.

The sun had set and it was getting dark when we took off and the plane's engines sent sparks flying past the windows. My spot was near the door. Nick had gone by me to his place further down. That was the last time I saw him. After awhile there was the shining water of the English Channel below us in the moonlight.

Then we were over a dark hostile land and tensed for the jump. When we jumped, German tracer bullets streamed up at us. In the landing we were scattered and many of those who survived didn't see each other for days. It was a week later before I heard about Nick. They said a shell exploded his phosphorous grenade. They said he burned to death before he hit the ground. That was a couple of hours after we'd posed for the picture. [Used with permission of Rick Richardson.]

Photo above: Lamoureux the tallest in back row.
Photo provided by Jim Allardyce.

Left: enlargement of picture above, showing the two buddies touching canteen cups—Rick in helmet, Nick in cap. Photo provided by Jim Allardyce.

## Friendships

"Friendships formed among the 508th Red Devils meant more to me than anything," says Stanley Nordwall, Headquarters Second. "And the worst experience in the 508th was losing some of those friends to the war."

Nordwall continues, "I remember the day I signed up for the paratroopers in Rapid City, South Dakota. I went to Red Lake Indian Reservation to say good-bye to my grandmother and after that, the train ride south. Yes, I am a card-carrying member of the Chippewa Tribe."

John "Jack" B. Evert was Stan Nordwall's closest friend in the regiment. The train that took Nordwall to Camp Blanding, Florida, went by Chicago. Jack Evert boarded at Chicago, and the two traveled together. At Camp Blanding and Camp MacKall, they bunked side by side.

On furlough Stan visited the Evert home. Jack's room was filled with tennis trophies. The whole family was addicted to tennis, and a generation later Chris Evert would become an international tennis champion. Chris Evert's father was Jack's brother.

Stan and Jack were together during all of their training but were assigned to different C-47s for the D-Day Airborne invasion of Normandy. They shook hands and wished each other luck before boarding their separate planes. That was the last time Stan Nordwall saw his friend Jack Evert.

"The hardest thing I ever did," Nordwall declares with a sigh, "was to visit the families of the buddies I lost during the war."

## Farewell to a Friend, My Sergeant
by William W. Bell

Sergeant Bruno S. Prestos.
Photo furnished by William W. Bell.

Sgt. Bruno S. Preztos and William W. Bell, two 508th paratroopers from A Company, were neighbors in Toms River, New Jersey. At the time of Preztos's death, Bell wrote this poem as a tribute to his departed friend (used with permission of William W. Bell):

# The 508th Connection

I followed slowly behind him
With softly muffled tread.
With many of his comrades,
To bury our own dead.

The thoughts among us private,
Yet joined in our remorse.
For he had been our sergeant,
And often set our course.

We thought of him as forceful,
And drew our strength from him.
He gave assurance and confidence,
To know that we could win.

He was coarse and brisk,
Yet gentle too, a very special man.
And when the battle started,
He was in command.

The war was over many years,
Before we found each other.
It was he who brought me back again
To my airborne fellow brothers.

It was he who made me realize
That we were special men.
What we went through and had to do;
We'd never do again.

So short a time passed quickly by,
Till death had come to claim him.
Our families met to begin anew
With friendship strong within.

We've had our time of glory,
God willing we survived.
To take our place in family life;
Till this sad day arrived.

We knew him and we loved him.
This paratrooper brave.
And now he's made his final jump,
As we lay him in the grave.

He's not alone; he's with his men,
His Commander gone ahead.
And we who wait our final flight,
To join our gallant dead.

Will board our plane when we are called;
To fill our place in ranks.
Again to leave our loved one,
With final tears of thanks.

Then we'll be gone to join our men,
In line at heaven's gate.
And proudly pass to history—
With the men of the 508th.

# Catalog Registration

Type of Work: Text

Registration Number / Date: TXu001177623 / 2004-05-20

Title: The 508th Connection

Description: 511 pages

Copyright Claimant: Zig Boroughs

Date of Creation: 2004

Previous Registration: Prev. reg. 2002, TX 5-488-833 and 1987

Basis of Claim: New matter: additions, compilations

Names: Boroughs, Zig

# Index

## A

Abraham, Robert, xiii, 87, 89, 291, 334, 397-98
Adams, Jonathan E. "Jock," 108-9, 247, 249-51, 254, 274, 397
Adams, Robert, 227
Akins, Hugh "Rosy," 296-98, 388
Albano, Ralph M., 10
Albertson, Dale E., 102-3, 105, 108
Albrecht, Warren, 225
Albright, Barry E., 188
Alexander, Boyd A., 249
Alexander, Mark J., 180
Alfonso, Jafet "Jeff," 77, 214-15
Alix (grandmother), 72-74
Allardyce, James R., xi, xiii, 55, 57, 255-56, 385, 501
Allen, William E., xiii, 158, 432
Alley, Jess M., 117
Allsup, Yerah V., 276
Alverez, Antonio, 274
Alverez, Manuel L., 275
Amore, Joseph, 359
Amorin, David, 249
Anderson, Albert J., 264
Anderson, Andy, 473
Anderson, Helen, 334
Andreas, R., 55
Andrews Sisters, 462
Angress, Tom, 394, 422

Archambault, Roland E., 336-37
Arellano, Luis, 293
Arthur, Merrel, 395-96, 446
Asher, Robert, 148, 439, 442
Askren, Bill, 255
Atkins, Joe, 253
Atwood, Paul B., 193, 325
Austin, Harry, 385
Austin, Little Car, 289, 311-12, 393
Axelrod, David, 166
Axis Sally, 308

## B

Backus, Alexis, 373-75
Backus, Madame, 374
Baker, Bruce, 148, 150
Baldassar, John, 57
Banks, George F., 327, 372
Bardeaux, Robert, 57
Barkley, J., 55
Barr, Harold, 57
Barrett, Margaret, 315
Barron, George S., 275
Barry, J. M. T., 35
Bartholomew, E. E., 32-33
Bauman, Leroy "Whitey," 449
Beach, Don, 417
Beach, Gerald L., 416-18
Beach, Merle A., 256, 287
Beard, William T., 369

Beaudin, Briand N., 167-71
Beaver, Neal, 112, 119, 242
Beck, Ernest, 355
Beddingfield, Gary, 37
Beets, Melvin H., 142, 145-48
Bell, Alton L., 18, 199, 426
Bell, Bruce E., 150-51
Bell, Glenn, 260
Bell, William W., 115, 502
Belliveau, Theodore, 207, 393-94
Bellucci, Matthew, 94, 203, 308, 321, 388
Bennedic, Calvin K. "Bene," 465, 495
Bennett, Ralph L., 327
Beno, Thomas S., 257-58, 276, 354, 369, 498-99
Benthin, Robert, 102-3, 105
Benton, James, 249
Berry, Clarence, 260
Bettien, La Rue, 182-83
Bitch of Buchenwald. *See* Koch, Ilse
Bitouze, Paul, 183
Bizefski, Joseph P., 365
Blackmon, L. W. "Red," 421
Bladen, Bill, 331-32
Blankley, Iris, 47-48
Blankley, Mr., 47
Blankley, Mrs., 48
Blethen, M., 35
Blohm, Ralph "Sim," 52
Blue, James, 62-66, 71-72, 75, 239, 246, 250, 254, 269, 273, 275-76, 482, 492
Boccafogli, Edward, 192-94, 216, 256, 301-4, 309, 335, 337-39, 385
Bodak, Michael, 17, 158-59
Bolger, Francis, 83
Bollag, Anita, 140
Bollag, Marcel, 133-34, 136, 139-40
Bonge, Donald Wayne, 275
Bonvillain, Joe, 35, 38
Boone, Joe H., 274, 342
Boroughs, Elizabeth Imogene, 347
Boroughs, John Wales, 5
Boroughs, Mary, 347

Boroughs, Ralph "Zig," 5, 7, 14-15, 20, 50, 90, 92, 179, 183, 201, 203, 216, 220, 243, 256, 264, 321, 328, 333, 335, 365, 418, 422-23, 466, 469, 478, 486, 489, 493-94, 505
Bos, Jan, 224, 241, 284, 485
Bosman, Jacqueline, 492
Boton, Serge, 492
Bourde, Louise, 153
Boyce, Emmet L., 336
Boyd, Sherman, 416
Bracknell, Joe, 17
Bradley, Mark, 422
Brand, George, 367, 399-402
Brannen, Malcolm D., 115, 122-27, 158
Bre, Gillis, 75
Breen, John A., 194
Bressler, Joe, 98-101
Brewer, Bill, 36
Brewer, Forrest W. "Lefty," 35-36, 39, 77
Brewer, Robert R., 149, 454
Brickley, John E., 271
Brister, Jane, 49
Broderick, Bob, 70
Broderick, Eileen, 486
Broderick, Tom, 482-84, 486
Broga, Frank, 244
Brogley, Steve, 349
Brokaw, Tom, 482, 485-86
Brooks, Howard, 202, 234, 263, 306, 312, 368, 388, 393, 399-402, 493-94
Brown, Bill, 140-41
Brown, James. O., 243, 297
Brown, Robert, 35
Bruce, Everett, 327
Bucholz, Elen D., 370
Bullard, Joe E., 265
Burns, Dwayne T., 19, 231
Burrows, Lewis, 479, 481-82
Burton, Ernie, 448
Bussell, Bob, 448
Busson, Ralph J., 35-37, 310
Butz (sergeant), 449

Byers, Wilbur "Moto," 18, 48, 201-2, 306, 312, 392

## C

Calcagno, Louis, 257
Calvert, Charles, 57
Campagna, Ralph, 197-98
Campbell, Clift, 422
Campbell, James, 376
Canard, Curtis, 352-53
Cannon, A. B., 109
Cannon, Howard, 244, 246
Canyon, Harold O. *See* Kulju, Harold O.
Caponnet, Dorey Gilberte, 173
Carlson, Earl Lee, 485-86
Carpentier, Roger, 140
Carter, Loren, 257, 287-88, 354, 369
Caruso, Jim, 269
Cascio, Brassie S., 363
Cavanaugh, Harold, 497
Cehrobak, Andrew "Bugs," 22, 53, 284-85, 308, 350, 367-68, 393
Chamberlain, Neville, 4
Chandler, William F., 119
Chapman, Bill, 225
Charbouneau, Leo, 171
Chase, Ernest W., 267
Chatoian, Edward, 184
Chesnick, Mark W., 362
Chester, Mike, 63
Chestnut, Joe, 266
Chisolm, Bob, 225-26
Christiansen, Chris, 95, 297, 312, 393
Christiansen, Clarence, 12, 93
Cianfrani, Anthony, 107, 238
Cibulka, F. J., 161
Cicchillo, Robert M., 287
Cicchinella, Joe, 411
Circelli, Frank, 108
Clark, William E., 11, 149-50, 152, 449-53, 463
Clement, George W., III, 249
Clemons, Charles I., 420
Cochenour, James, 60

Coleman, Leroy, 449, 451
Collins, Jess, 439
Comacho, Joe, 57
Combs, Rex, 185, 236-39, 246
Connaghan, Cornelius, 151
Connors, Chuck, 46
Conrad, Raymond, 208
Cooper, Lester B., 18
Cornwall, Earl, 131
Cortell, Madame, 144
Covey, Kenneth A., 275
Creary, Hal E., 158
Cregan, Kevin, 106
Crosby, Bing, 462
Cross, Tommy, 131
Croteau, Rene A., 35, 39, 208, 211
Cuquemelle, Julien, 75
Cuquemelle, Madame, 75
Czepinsky, Edvard, 57

## D

Daly, John J., 117, 210
Daly, M., 55
Danko, John, 233, 263, 291, 367
Dasch, Frank, 131
Daubach, Ludwig, 386
Daubach, Marie, 386
Davis, Richard R., 275
Davis, Willard H., 275
Dean, William A., 60, 65, 76-78, 83-84, 406
De Beer, Edwin, 208
De Carvalho, George H., 143
Deere, Norman, 37
Delfosse, Jean, 492
Delury, John P., 117-19, 121, 202, 205-6, 209
DeMario, John J., 343
Demarteau, Rene, 473
Demciak, Paul, 58
Dempsey (British general), 313
Depierrepont, Gustave, 183
Derksen, Charles, 487
Detwiler, T. K., 131

de Vroomen, Jack, 284
DeWeese, Ralph E., 241
Dietrich, Marlene, 318, 394, 418-21, 423, 470
Dikcon, Walter, 247-48
Diller, Helene, 499
Dobbs, Thomas M., 250
Dougherty, Mary, 9
Dowling, James A., 49
Downer, Andy, 209, 356
Dreisbach, Orin, 60
Dress, Hellman C., 376
Driessen, Leo, 283
Ducote, Clifton S., 188
Duffy, Roger, 383
Dugan, Richard, 153-55
Duncan, Forest, 205
Dunn, Lawrence "Whoopee," 407
Du Pont (Pony), 111
Dushensky, Vincent, 102, 106

## E

Eisenhower, Dwight D., 341, 467
Ekman, William E., 174
Elder, J. Lyn, 232, 298-99, 320-23, 378-79
Ellerbusch, Herbert, 302-3
Ellifrit, James H., 166
Elliot, John T. "Jack," 208-9, 371, 377
Ellis, Robert H., 204
Ellsworth, Scott, 419, 429
Elsman, Kenny, 457
Emanuel, Nick C., 420
Entler, John, 396
Enzinger, E., 161
Ernst, Johnny, 464
Evans, John E., 156
Evers, Christa, 487
Evers, Mr., 487
Evers, Nellie, 487
Evert, Chris, 502
Evert, John B. "Jack," 502

## F

Fairman, George, 401
Falgione, Adrian, 444
Falgione, Eugene, 442-44
Falgione, Wilma, 444-45
Falley, Wilhelm, 115
Farr, Jody, 284
Farrel, Pat, 132
Fateley, Glenn A., 118
Favela, Joseph L., 268, 271-72
Feray, Genevieve Leroux. *See* Leroux, Genevieve
Ferey, Thiery, 62
Finnicum, John, 448-49
Fish, Arthur, 445-49
Fisher, Clyde E., 291
Flamand, Cecile. *See* Gancel, Cecile
Flamand, Jean, 72, 74
Flamand family, 74-75
Focth, Edward J., 102-3, 106
Foley, John P., 247
Fontaine, Jean, 149
Fontana (company man), 107
Ford (former demolition platoon member), 366-67
Ford, Vernon C., 337
Forkapa, N., 55
Fowler, James, 360, 369
Fredrick, George A., 268
Frigo, Lionel O. "Lee," 66, 71-72, 207
Frigo, Madge, 71
Frigoult, Marie-Louise, 144
Fritter, Richard E., 117
Froelich, 80
Fuller, Angelina Spera, 223, 226, 228
Funk, Leonard A., Jr., 59, 267-68, 395-96
Furlong, Dan, ix, 492
Furtaw, Robert J., 181

## G

Gabris, Thomas, 340

Gagnon, Joseph F. "Freddie," 142, 146
Gagnon, Lionel, 410
Gallagher, Tom, 37
Gamble, Della Patricia, 164
Gamble, Esme, 164
Gamble, Sheila, 164
Gamble, Teresa, 164
Gamez, C., 54
Gancel, Cecile, 72-74
Garcia, Alex, 268
Garcia, Ralph, 274-75
Garner, Doris, 25
Garrity, Edward, 470
Garry, William J., 112, 242
Gaudio (pilot), 55
Gavin, James M., 93, 174, 196, 329, 343, 347, 395, 413-15, 421
Geinger, Theodore, 286
Genten, Matthias, 386
Georoes, Marion, 86
Gerard, J., 55
Gerheim, Harry, 132
Gerkin, Harold, 32-33, 264, 330
Giegold, William, 184-85, 190-91, 260, 269, 295
Gienger, Theodore H., 205
Gilliam, 55
Gillies, Alan, 39-40
Gillot, Louis, 185-86, 188-89, 192
Gintjee, Tom, 43, 46
Gladstone, Fred, 207-9, 212-13, 333, 371, 375-76
Gleim, Edward, 301
Goodale, Hoyt T., 184, 329, 389-90
Goodman, Floyd O. "Benny," 409-11
Gossett, Shirley, 499
Goudy, William, 386
Graham, Chester E., 79, 86, 188
Graham, Richard J., 288
Greco, Benny, 295
Green, Bennett M., 64
Green, Cumer, 50, 150
Green, James, 108
Green, Lester, 103, 106
Greenwalt, 364, 422

Groesbeek Cowboy, 260
Guillemelle, Maurice, 86
Gulbrandson, Erving T., 191
Gunn, Charles, 57
Gurwell, George A., 334
Gushue, Charles S., 250, 254
Gustafson, Julia Lamm, 343
Guzzetti, Louis E., 80, 85, 264, 348

## H

Habets (priest), 252
Haddy, Frank, 85, 293
Hager, Earnest J., 63, 66
Haley, John, 454-57
Hall, Jimmy, 131, 133
Hambieckers, Yvette, 411
Hambirckers, George, 411
Hamilton, E., 55
Hamm, Joe, 383
Hand, Broughton, 151
Hardie, John "Doc," 62, 396, 406
Hardigan, Bernie, 465
Hardwick, Donald W., 202, 233, 235, 262, 264, 312, 347-48, 388, 393, 493
Hargrave, John L., 198
Harley, Rupple, 305-6
Harper, Robert, 151
Harrelson, Walter, 57
Harrison, Harry, 179-80
Harrold, Joseph, 191
Hart, Robert W., 336
Hartman, George, 291
Harvey, Paul, 131
Hasley, Lucien, 100-102, 149, 153, 183, 481
Hayes, Wendell E., 115
Henderson, Alvin H., 251
Henderson, Ernest L., 405
Henderson, Roy, 60, 405-6
Henie, Sonja, 469-70, 472, 476
Henning, Lloyd, 197
Hernandez, Frank R., 192-94
Herro, 55

Hess, Albert, 356
Hess, Alfred, 277
Hetland, Eugene C., 188
Hicks, B. L., 342
Hicks, Roland, 102-3
Hill, O. B., 499
Hillman, Albert E., 50-51, 96-97
Hinebaugh, Earl, 495
Hitler, Adolph, 4, 243, 277-78, 365, 393-94, 476
Hodge, John, 356-58, 363-65
Hoffman, Delbert, 57
Holman, John, 424
Holmes, O. E., 291
Holroyd, Tom, 72
Honriet, Pierre, 163
Hood, J. B., 17-18
Hooks, Kenneth, 35, 102-3, 106-7, 453-57, 463
Horn, C. H. ten, 252-53
Horne, Doris Garner, 25-26
Horne, Kelso, 25-26, 64, 69, 226, 228
Horrocks (British general), 313
Howard, James B., 119-20
Howard, William J., 63
Howarth, Davis, 72
Howe, William W., xvii, 469-72
Hoynowski, L., 35
Hubbard, E. S., Jr., 243
Hudec, Harry, 22-23, 92, 172-73, 291, 398
Huibers, Nellie, 487
Hummel, Ray S., 141-43, 145
Humphrey, Lois, 26
Hunt, Richard, 102-3, 108, 340
Hutto, James C. "Buck," 110-11, 356, 376-77

## I

Infanger, Frederick J., 55, 292, 355, 361-62, 496
Irwin, Theodore, 246
Israel, Leon. *See* Mason, Leon Israel

## J

Jacksich, Al, 150
Jacobs, Alton, 499
Jahnigen, Herman, 486-88
Jakeway, Donald I., 182
Jakobs, Aron, 279, 281
Jakobs, Bert, 277, 281, 283-84
Jakobs, Edith, 278, 282, 284
Jakobs, Freda, 278
Jakobs, Martin, 277
Jakobs, Rose, 277
Jamar, Walthere, 380
James (lieutenant), 364
Janssen (grandfather), 280
Janssen, Annie, 283-84
Janssen, Gerrit, 280
Jeffers, Warren, 57
Jessup, H., 55
Joe (lieutenant), 438-39
Johnson, Allen, 386
Johnson, Carlton R., 119
Johnson, Don, 273
Johnson, Ray, 248
Jones, C., 55
Jones, Fred, 163
Jones, Gerald G., 370
Jones, Homer H., 63-64, 76
Jones, John Frank, 455
Jones, Martin, 291
Jones, Thurman Davis, 148, 155, 439-42
Judefind, John J., 35, 39
Julien, 137-39

## K

Kabot, Robert E., 337
Kahn, Hans. *See* Kennedy, Harry
Kajewski (company man), 426
Kalkreuth, William T., 433-34
Karres, Peter, 208-10
Kass, Stanley, 50-51, 308, 344, 407, 415, 419, 421
Katsanis (sergeant), 55

Keating, L., 132
Kellar, Ben, 42
Kelly, Joseph, 282
Kennedy, Harry, 2-4, 194, 196, 204, 213, 306-7, 391-92, 404, 407, 414
Kenney (father), 203
Kenny, William T., 370
Kersh, John, 132-37, 139
Keys, Clun, 295
Kidd, Monk, 241
King, Donald L., 334-37, 398
King, E., 55
Kingstone, Rosemary, 219-20, 222
Kissane, Joe, 244, 370
Klein, James C., 294, 336, 399
Klinefelter, Philip, 325
Knapp, Harvey J., 154-55, 439
Knappenberger, Jill Pitts, 334, 338-39
Knight, Fred, 92, 332
Koch, Ilse, 433
Koch, Karl, 433
Koons, Charlie, 481
Kovensky, William A., 369
Koziel, Dan, 118
Krause, D., 55
Krebs, Frank, 244-45
Kulju, Harold O., 81-83, 85, 186, 188-89, 192, 206, 210-11, 348-49, 351
Kulmer, James E., 422
Kulwicki, Richard, 184, 190
Kuony, David, 37
Kursawski, William J., 181
Kurz, James Q., 64-65, 76-78, 86, 214-16, 267-68, 324-27, 372, 397, 406
Kuszmaul, Daniel, 275
Kwansik, Frank, 170

## L

Labuda, Frank, 35
Lacroix, Carolyn, 489, 493
Lacroix, Emile, viii, 17, 203, 351, 365, 368, 373, 375, 377, 383, 385-87, 397, 413, 488-93
Lacroix, Frank, 492-93
Lacroix, Guy, 493
Lacroix, Nicole, 493
Lacroix, Sylvie, 493
Lakey, Joseph L., 35, 39
Lamberson, Tim Lamoille, 408-9, 411
Lamberson, William Lamoille, 409, 411
Lamm, George D., 63-66, 69-70, 153, 248-51, 254, 274, 339-43, 443, 492
Lamoureux, Francis M., 56, 85, 197-98, 244, 257, 419, 499
Lamoureux, Hildegarde, 85
Lander, Joel R., 422
Lane, Bob, 233, 321
Langveldt, Piet, 269
Lapso, George, 249-50
Laurelli, Louis, 93-94
Laurence, Lucien, 183
Lavender, Leon E., 151
Lawhon, William T., 354
Lawson, Derek, 61, 230
LeBoeuf, John B., 249
Leegsma, Argardus "Gas," 257, 259
LeFebvre, Henry E., 102-4, 109
LeGrand, Leon, 99, 101
LeGrand, Madame, 100
Lehman, Paul E., 167, 170, 208
Leone, Angelo M., 37
Leopold, King, 380
Leroux, Berthe, 62, 71
Leroux, Genevieve, 67, 69
Leroux, Louis, 61, 71
Leroux family, 61, 71
Levin, Bernard, 419-20
Lewellen, Joe, 151-53, 438-39
Liebmann, David, 410
Lindquist, Roy E., 13, 16, 63, 68-69, 79, 172, 404, 419, 428-29, 498
Lindsay, Robert T., 356-58, 363, 365
Lira, Manual, 337
Little, John T., 159
Lobos, Joseph L., 494, 498
Loder, James A., 240
Loewi, Andrew W., 59
Long Tom, 437-38
Lord, William G., II, 204, 213, 220, 428

Lucjaz, Edwin A., 18, 200-201, 264, 297, 419-20
Ludemann, Russell, 270
Lupton, Walter, 35

## M

MacBlane, Tom D., 35
Macdonald, Evelyn E., 163
Mack, Wilford, 239
Mackey, Milton E., 303, 325, 337
MacVicar, Norman, 81, 390
Mahan, Francis L., 224
Majers, Glen W., 197-99
Maloney, William F., 35, 39
Manger, Paul, 183
Mann, Harold, 200
Margaret Rose, Princess, 475
Martell, Elmer, 131
Martin, Arnolds, 57
Martin, Robert, 455
Mason, Leon Israel, 44, 87, 90, 203-4, 216, 343, 392, 415, 418-19, 474
Maternowski, Gene, 35
Mathias, Robert Mason, 494-98
Matthews, Desmond A., 117
Mauldin, Judge, 1
Mauldin, Queen Jo, 1
McCall, John, 422
McClure, Bill, 80-81, 293-94
McDonald, Howard B., 370
McDuffie, James H., 197-200
McDuffie, Mary S., 199
McElfresh, Floyd E., 337
McGillicuddy, Cornelius Alexander, 496
McGlocklin, Phyllis, 334
McGrath, George F., 256-59, 287, 354, 369
McGuire, John, 64
McGuire, Vernon, 459
McGuire, Virgil, 76, 179-80, 310
McLean, Henry, 35, 242, 469-71
McLean, John, 469-70
McLemore, Mac, 155
McLennan, Rod, 131

McMahon, James J., 141-43
McMillan, Eugene, 248
Medford, William A., Jr., 197, 209
Mendez, Jeannie, 38, 121, 244
Mendez, Louis G., Jr., 16, 38, 117, 119-21, 127, 199, 208, 210, 244, 331, 360-61, 426
Merritt, Kenneth "Rock," 482
Mertz, Elmer, 35, 39
Messenbrink, S., 55
Metar, Joseph, 257
Michetti, Marino, 336-37
Miles (pilot), 55
Miles, George, 360, 390, 410
Milkovics, Lewis, 180, 422, 425
Mill, Bob, 267
Miller, Glen, 308
Miller, Phillip C. "Chick," 16-17, 31, 157-60
Millett, Zip, 160, 175
Mills, Bobby, 256
Mills, Okey, 112-13, 239-40, 256, 286, 384
Mills, Orley E., 240
Millsaps, Woodrow, 83-84, 193, 215, 301, 309
Mitchel, Donald, 31
Mitchell, Robert, 209, 239
Mitchell, William R., 224
Moline, Clyde "Big Mo," 303
Montgomery, Bernard Law, 229
Montgomery, Ed "Monty," 299, 338, 378
Montgomery, George E., 85, 411
Moore, Clyde K., Jr., 218-20
Moore, Eddie, 222
Morettini, Joe, 410-11
Morgan, Colinos, 268
Morgan, Worster, 391, 420, 422
Moss, Amos, 186-87
Moss, B., 55, 186
Mrozinsky, Anthony J. "Tony," 267
Mullen, John, 275
Muller family, 386
Muniz, Refugio A., 270, 365
Murdock, Hal, 57

Murphy (lieutenant), 55
Murray, Grady, 40, 341-42
Murray, Mrs., 40
Murray, Ray, 108
Musmeci, Julius P., 275
Myers, James, 102-3, 106-8

## N

Nagle, Dave, 453, 463-66
Names, Arthur A., 340
Naro, James S., 337
Nash, Roy, 43
Nation, Bill C., 323
Nation, Mrs., 322
Nation, William H., 322-23, 397-98
Neal, Cecil, 131
Nelson, Bryant, 85
Nelson, Richard H., 308, 350
Nichols, Barry, 364
Nichols, Mickey, 66, 309, 414
Nicholson, Ralph "Nick," 57, 498-99
Nieblas, Bob, 281-82
Nienart, Benjamin, 266
Nightingale, Florence, 117
Niklauski, Michael. *See* Nichols, Mickey
Nilsen, Carl, 408-9, 411
Nitschke, Fritz, 393
Nixon, Richard M., 340
Nobles, Robert, 151-52
Nordwall, Stanley, 191, 501-2
Norman, Myra Hand, 435
Nosera, Russell, 125
Novak, Frank, 434

## O

O'Brien, John, 132
O'Connell, Raymond T., 268
O'Connor, Bob, 409-10
O'Connor, Lawrence J., 268
O'Dell, Ross, 296
O'Donald, James, 433-34
Oldemeyer, David, 299, 378-79

Olson, Elaine, 290
Olson, Mrs. Carl, 37
Orr, William R., 330
Osgood, Harry L., 164
Ott, Mel, 318
Ourselin, Albert, 136, 140
Ourselin, Camille, 138
Ourselin, Claude, 137
Ourselin, Fernand, 137
Ourselin, Pauline, 140
Ourselin, Simone, 137
Owen, Richard, 181-82, 379

## P

Palmer, Kate Salley, 15, 34, 196, 307, 313, 320, 345, 402
Parchman, Cicero, 57
Parrish, Lemuel, 35
Patchell, Albert J., 334
Patton, George, 161
Pavlick, P., 35
Pawlings, Henry, 57
Payet, John E., 337
Peek, James O., 325
Pelini, Guido, 210, 225
Penns, Armand, 492
Perdue, J., 55
Perez (lieutenant), 55
Perkins, Roy, 177
Perry, James, 106
Perry, Raymond J., 102
Peskin, D. L., 35
Peters, Grlando C., 170
Peterson, Robert, 422
Petros, George, 208
Phillips, Jean, 20
Phillips, Robert, 19-20, 369, 378
Pierce, V. G., 275
Pike, Dave, 35, 41, 43, 46, 122
Piper, Robert, 270
Pitts, Jill. *See* Knappenberger, Jill Pitts
Pitts, John Joseph "Jack," 334
Plemon, Thomas, 422
Plunkett, Woodrow C., 197-200

Poirier, Madame, 138
Poirier, Monsieur, 138
Poisson, Yves, 65
Polasky, Edward, 206
Polette, Lloyd L., Jr., 55, 84, 184, 190, 260-62, 360-61
Polton, Wallace E., 113
Porcella, Tom, 492
Porter, Carl H., 127-29, 131
Powell, Charles A., 389
Prasse, Oscar S., 98-99, 101
Pratle, Al, 131
Preztos, Bruno S., 342, 502
Price, James, 113
Price, Maryld, 277
Pulverman, William E., 282

## Q

Quaid, John A., 117-19
Queen, Hugh B., 285-86
Quigg (scout), 125

## R

Ranabauer, Howard, 132-33
Randolph, George, 410
Rankin, James E., 113-14, 382-83, 407, 422, 492
Rawley, James, 31
Ray, Bobby, 21
Reardon, Richard, 494-96
Reynolds, C. P., 143
Ricci, Joe, 268, 393
Richards, Big John, 240
Richards, Harold V., 123
Richards, John W., 449
Richardson, Fayette, 197, 206, 209, 499-500
Ridgway, Matthew B., 63
Rigapoulos, John, 57
Risnes, Marvin L., 198, 200, 205, 212, 286, 288, 354-57, 365, 368, 370
Rizzuto, James, 265-66
Robbins, Fred W., 194, 391, 422

Roberts, Harold H., 106, 365, 441
Roberts, Johnny W., 102-3, 106, 439, 441
Roblette, Rum S., 343
Rockwell, Thomas, 335-36
Roderiques, John "Rod," 148
Rogers, Charles, 57
Rogers, William, 185
Roll, Harry, 310
Romero, Angel, 256-58, 268, 270, 354-55, 359, 369-70, 373
Rompala, Stanley, 90-91
Roosevelt, 465
Roosevelt, Eleanor, 5, 440
Roosevelt, Franklin D., 5, 7, 465
Rose, Maurice, 329
Ross, Carlos W., 150-53, 155
Roth, Stanley, 449
Roudebusch, Dale R., 292
Roy, Harold, 177, 499
Ruppe, Frank, 170
Russell, James, 356

## S

Sacharoff, Leonard, 85
Sakowski, Frank, 90, 171, 216, 317
Samuel, Benjamin, 284
Sanchez, Arthur, 83, 184-85, 212
Sanders, Archie, 191, 455-57
Sanders, Raymond, 191
Sanson, Frederique, 213
Savage, Robert, 102-3, 106
Schillinger, Henry "Hank", 129-31
Schlegel, Jack W., 157-63
Schlemmer, D. Zane, 260-62, 400-401
Schlesinger, Katherine, 238-39
Schlesinger, Nolan, 237-38
Schmelick, Steve, 92, 171, 308
Schools (lieutenant), 300
Schrach, 440
Schwartzwalder, Ben, 62-63
Sclandra, Charles, 102-3, 106
Scott, Eric, 57
Scruggs, Rick J., 389-90

Seale, Robert L., 55
Seawright, Eugene W., 148, 150
Sellers, Henry G., 391
Sellers, Herbert S., 186-88, 190
Shankey, Joseph I., 158
Shanley, Thomas J. B., 79, 81, 84, 166, 188-89
Shaver, Orval L., 31
Shearer, Robert W., 224
Shenkle, George A., 35
Shipley, Eugene P., 206
Shirley, Callie, 165-67, 396
Shirley, Joseph A., 165, 167, 396, 405
Shull, Millard C., 268
Shultz, John, 272, 275-76
Sickler, Robert L., 293
Sides, Curtis, 181
Siegfried Line, 397, 401, 403
Simmons, Iris, 48
Simmons, John L., Jr., 47-48, 114, 213
Singer, Paul B., 275
Sirovica, Frank L., 198, 287, 369-70
Sivetz, John, 386
Skipper, Jack F., 60
Sloan, Donald, 268, 330-32
Smith, Clyde, 102-3, 106, 439-42
Smith, Frank, 213
Smith, James W., 324
Smith, Lyle, 268
Smith, R., 55
Smylie, Jim, 91
Sniederman, Jack, 380
Snovak, Larry, 132-33
Sobolewski, William J., 333, 371
Somerville, Glenn, 386-87
Sopka, Al, 336-37
Spera, Angelo, 223-25, 227
Spera, Louis, 223-25, 228
Sprinkle, Jack L., 212
Stanley, Chester, 267
Stanley, Richard M., 448
Staples, Frank, 26-27, 80, 225, 296
Staples, Lois Humphrey, 27
Starchvich, John, 225
Stassola, James P., 102-3, 106

Stedman, Richard E., 420, 422
Sternesky, John E., 499
Stevens, Arthur R., 117, 119
Stevens, Stanley, 277
Stiles, Virginia Lee, 416-17
Still, Wilford A., 90-91, 163, 291
Stirwalt, Earl, 25
Stoeckert, George, 101, 483-84
Stork (rifleman), 249
Strey, John, 62
Strong, Charles, 210-11, 225
Studelska, Norb, 290
Stutika, Henry J., 150
Stutler, W., 55
Summerall, Charles P., 402
Sweet, Johnny, xvi, 30
Swint, Bill, 356-58

T

Taburau, Alain, 492
Taylor, Frank C., 271
Taylor, Fred, 330
Taylor, John, 77
Taylor, Royal B., 63
Teele, John, 383
Tepsic, Alexander, 157-59, 433
Tetak, Steve, 386
Theis, William M., 76
Thomas, David E., 49, 174, 179, 424, 426
Thomas, Ralph, 67-68, 71, 75, 218, 220, 408
Thorne, George, 293
Tibbetts, James M., 348-49, 351
Tidwell, Doris, 40
Tillery, Luther M., 420
Tislair, Nicole, 492
Tislair, Roger, 492
Tofoya, Frank, 292
Tomaseski, John A., 373
Traband, Bill, 395, 405-6
Trahin, Jean H., xvi, 189
Trevino, N., 54
Trippe, Walter G., 337

Truman, Harry, 227
Tullberry (trooper), 164
Tulley, John F., 275
Tumlin, Bill, 453, 458-59, 463
Tutwiler, Temple W., 266

## U

Uchrin, Steve P., 50-51, 96-97
Under Baggage, Charles, Jr., 420
Union, Robert E., 102-3, 106
Utley, Robert B., 170

## V

Van der Hoever, Erik, 380
Van Enwyck, Sherman, 248
Van Gorp, Gerard, 300
Van Horssen family, 487
Vantrease, Glen W., xvii, 258-59
Vasselin, Henri, 461
Vaughn, Alfred J., 420, 422
Veach, Donald, 310
Veasey, Bob, 287-88
Vohs (lieutenant), 55

## W

Wade, Henry, 277
Wakefield, Walter L., xvii, 291, 294
Walczak, Stanley, 430
Wales, John, 5
Walker, Roscoe, 57
Wall, George W., 420
Waltman, Harry R., 356
Ward (radioman), 157
Wardenski, Henry L., 484-85
Warneche, Adolph F., xvii, 38
Warnecke, Bud, 35
Warren, Jack, xvii, 79-80, 98, 263, 346
Warren, Shields, 79-80, 98, 247
Watson, Joseph E., 465, 495, 498
Watts, Bob, 129-30, 132
Wauters, Arnaud, xvii, 491
Weaver, Robert, 55-58

Webb, Paul E., 81
Weeks (company man), 274
Weiner, Reuben, 88
Weinerth, J., 55
Wenzel, Edward F., 187, 497
Wheaton, David, 332
Wheelock, Maurice E., 335, 339
White, Robert B., 102-3, 108-9, 271, 340, 342
Wild, Edmund, 396
Wilde, Russell C., xvii, 181, 244, 257-59, 356-57, 369
Wilger (copilot), 55
Wilkins, Charles B., 186, 191
Williams, Gene H., 57, 169, 211
Williams, Herbert L., 365
Williams, Joan, 423
Williams, William A., 365
Willis, N., 55
Willoughby, Lord Francis, 41
Wills, John H., xvii, 164-65, 383
Wilson, Raymond G., 337
Wilt, Warren, xvii, 369, 375
Windom, Bill, 309, 385
Winkin, Gabreille, 470
Winkin, Maurice, 471
Wodowsky, Edward J. "Woody," xvii, 237, 239, 342, 485, 492
Wolfe, Arthur, xvii, 76, 329-31
Wolfe, Conrad, 329-31
Wollaton Park, 39, 41-45, 47, 93, 100, 139, 213, 218, 298, 329
Womble, Jesse M., 372
Wood, Lionel, 57
Wright, Wilbur C., 119
Wynne, Jim, xvii, 101, 119

## Y

Yablonski, Tony, 256
Yates, Charles A., xvii, 264, 344, 415, 419-20, 422-23
Young, Roger, 359
Yourkovich, Louis, 495

## Z

Zieber, Lew A., 181
Zuccala, Rinaldo R. "Zeke," xvii, 369, 373
Zuelke, Warren H., xvii, 359, 365

Lightning Source UK Ltd.
Milton Keynes UK
UKHW010654100921
390324UK00008B/454/J